# Lecture Notes in Computer Science 3073

Commenced Publication in 1973
Founding and Former Series Editors:
Gerhard Goos, Juris Hartmanis, and Jan van Leeuwen

T0180123

**Springer**
*Berlin*
*Heidelberg*
*New York*
*Hong Kong*
*London*
*Milan*
*Paris*
*Tokyo*

Hsinchun Chen   Reagan Moore
Daniel D. Zeng   John Leavitt (Eds.)

# Intelligence and Security Informatics

Second Symposium on
Intelligence and Security Informatics, ISI 2004
Tucson, AZ, USA, June 10-11, 2004
Proceedings

 Springer

Volume Editors

Hsinchun Chen
University of Arizona, MIS Department
Tucson, AZ 85721, USA
E-mail: hchen@eller.arizona.edu

Reagan Moore
San Diego Supercomputer Center
9500 Gilman Drive, La Jolla, CA 92093-0505, USA
E-mail: moore@sdsc.edu

Daniel D. Zeng
University of Arizona, MIS Department
Tucson, AZ 85721, USA
E-mail: zeng@bpa.arizona.edu

John Leavitt
Tucson Police Department
270 S. Stone Avenue, Tucson, AZ 85701, USA
E-mail: John.Leavitt@tucsonaz.gov

Library of Congress Control Number: 2004106662

CR Subject Classification (1998): H.4, H.3, C.2, H.2, D.4.6, D.2, K.4.1, K.5, K.6.5, I.5

ISSN 0302-9743
ISBN 3-540-22125-5 Springer-Verlag Berlin Heidelberg New York

Springer-Verlag is a part of Springer Science+Business Media

springeronline.com

© Springer-Verlag Berlin Heidelberg 2004
Printed in Germany

Typesetting: Camera-ready by author, data conversion by Olgun Computergrafik
Printed on acid-free paper       SPIN: 11009931       06/3142       5 4 3 2 1 0

# Preface

The past two years have seen significant interest and progress made in national and homeland security research in the areas of information technologies, organizational studies, and security-related public policy. Like medical and biological research, which is facing significant information overload and yet also tremendous opportunities for new innovation, the communities of law enforcement, criminal analysis, and intelligence are facing the same challenge. As medical informatics and bioinformatics have become major fields of study, the science of *"intelligence and security informatics"* is now emerging and attracting interest from academic researchers in related fields as well as practitioners from both government agencies and industry.

Broadly defined, intelligence and security informatics is the study of the development and use of advanced information technologies and systems for national and homeland security related applications, through an integrated technological, organizational, and policy based approach. The First Symposium on Intelligence and Security Informatics (ISI 2003) was held in June 2003 in Tucson, Arizona. It provided a stimulating intellectual forum of discussions among previously disparate communities: academic researchers in information technologies, computer science, public policy, and social studies; local, state, and federal law enforcement and intelligence experts; and information technology industry consultants and practitioners.

Building on the momentum of ISI 2003, we held the Second Symposium on Intelligence and Security Informatics (ISI 2004) in June 2004 in Tucson, Arizona. ISI 2004 followed the tradition of ISI 2003 in bringing together technical and policy researchers from a variety of fields and in providing a highly interactive forum to facilitate communication and community building between government funding agencies, academia, and practitioners. From a technical perspective, we are very pleased to note that the papers accepted at ISI 2004 are of high quality and from diverse disciplines. Using ISI 2003 papers as a benchmark, there is a clear indication of tangible research progress made on many fronts both in depth and in coverage. In addition, several new research topics of significant practical relevance (e.g., trust management, information assurance, disease informatics) have emerged.

ISI 2004 was jointly hosted by the University of Arizona, the San Diego Supercomputer Center, and the Tucson Police Department. The one-and-a-half-day program included one plenary panel discussion session focusing on the perspectives and future research directions of government funding agencies, two invited panel sessions (one on terrorism research, the other on knowledge discovery and dissemination), 41 regular papers, six posters, and three panel discussion papers. In addition to the main sponsorship from the National Science Foundation, the Department of Homeland Security, and the Intelligence Technology Innovation Center, the symposium was also co-sponsored by several units within the

University of Arizona including: the Eller College of Business and Public Administration, the Management Information Systems Department, the Internet Technology, Commerce, and Design Institute, the Center for the Management of Information, the NSF COPLINK Center of Excellence, the Mark and Susan Hoffman E-Commerce Lab, the Artificial Intelligence Lab, and several other organizations including the Air Force Office of Scientific Research, the National Institute of Justice, and Silicon Graphics.

We wish to express our gratitude to all members of the symposium Program Committee and additional reviewers who provided high-quality, constructive review comments within an unreasonably short lead-time. Our special thanks go to the members of the symposium Organizing Committee, in particular, Mr. Chienting Lin, who provided significant help with managing the conference Website and compiling the proceedings, and Ms. Catherine Larson, who did a superb job in managing local arrangements. ISI 2004 was run as part of the workshop series of the Joint Conference on Digital Libraries (JCDL 2004). We wish to thank the JCDL staff for their conference support.

Our sincere gratitude goes to all of the sponsors. Last but not least, we thank Gary Strong, Art Becker, Michael Pazzani, Larry Brandt, Valerie Gregg, and Mike O'Shea for their strong and continuous support of this symposium and other related intelligence and security informatics research.

June 2004

Hsinchun Chen
Reagan Moore
Daniel Zeng
John Leavitt

# ISI 2004 Organizing Committee

*Symposium Co-chairs:*

| | |
|---|---|
| Hsinchun Chen | University of Arizona |
| Reagan Moore | San Diego Supercomputer Center |
| Daniel Zeng | University of Arizona |
| John Leavitt | Tucson Police Department |

*Organizing Committee:*

| | |
|---|---|
| Homa Atabakhsh | University of Arizona |
| Chris Demchak | University of Arizona |
| Kurt Fenstermacher | University of Arizona |
| Catherine Larson | University of Arizona |
| Chienting Lin | University of Arizona |
| Mark Patton | University of Arizona |
| Tim Petersen | Tucson Police Department |
| Mohan Tanniru | University of Arizona |
| Edna Reid | University of Arizona |
| Ajay Vinze | Arizona State University |
| Chuck Violette | Tucson Police Department |
| Feiyue Wang | University of Arizona |
| Leon Zhao | University of Arizona |

# ISI 2004 Program Committee

| | |
|---|---|
| Yigal Arens | University of Southern California |
| Art Becker | Intelligence Technology Innovation Center |
| Brian Boesch | Corporation for National Research Initiatives |
| Larry Brandt | National Science Foundation |
| Peter Brantley | California Digital Library |
| Donald Brown | University of Virginia |
| Robert Chang | Criminal Investigation Bureau, Taiwan Police |
| Sudarshan Chawathe | University of Maryland |
| Andy Chen | National Taiwan University |
| Lee-Feng Chien | Academia Sinica, Taiwan |
| Bill Chu | University of North Carolina at Charlotte |
| Christian Collberg | University of Arizona |
| Tony Fountain | San Diego Supercomputer Center |
| Ed Fox | Virginia Tech |
| Susan Gauch | University of Kansas |
| Johannes Gehrke | Cornell University |
| Joey George | Florida State University |
| Victor Goldsmith | Pace University |

| | |
|---|---|
| Valerie Gregg | National Science Foundation |
| Bob Grossman | University of Illinois at Chicago |
| Steve Griffin | National Science Foundation |
| Alan Hevner | University of South Florida |
| Robert Horton | Minnesota State Archives |
| Eduard Hovy | University of Southern California |
| Joseph Jaja | University of Maryland |
| Paul Kantor | Rutgers University |
| Erin Kenneally | San Diego Supercomputer Center |
| Judith Klavans | Columbia University |
| Don Kraft | Louisiana State University |
| Ee-peng Lim | Nanyang Technological University, Singapore |
| Clifford Neuman | University of Southern California |
| Greg Newby | University of Alaska, Fairbanks |
| Jay Nunamaker | University of Arizona |
| Mirek Riedewald | Cornell University |
| Gene Rochlin | University of California, Berkeley |
| Olivia Sheng | University of Utah |
| Elizabeth Shriberg | SRI International |
| Mike O'Shea | National Institute of Justice |
| Sal Stolfo | Columbia University |
| Gary Strong | Department of Homeland Security |
| Paul Thompson | Dartmouth College |
| Bhavani Thuraisingham | National Science Foundation |
| Andrew | Whinston University of Texas at Austin |
| Karen White | University of Arizona |
| Chris Yang | Chinese University of Hong Kong |
| Mohammed Zaki | Rensselaer Polytechnic Institute |
| Maria Zemankova | National Science Foundation |

## Invited Panelists

| | |
|---|---|
| Art Becker | Intelligence Technology Innovation Center |
| James Ellis | Memorial Institute for the Prevention of Terrorism |
| Johannes Gehrke | Cornell University |
| Valerie Gregg | National Science Foundation |
| Rohan Gunaratna | Institute for Defense & Strategic Studies, Singapore |
| Joseph Heaps | National Institute of Justice |
| Paul Kantor | Rutgers University |
| David Madigan | Rutgers University |
| Michael Pazzani | National Science Foundation |
| Edna Reid | University of Arizona |
| Michal Rosen-Zvi | University of California, Irvine |
| Marc Sageman | University of Pennsylvania |
| Joshua Sinai | Department of Homeland Security |
| Gary Strong | Department of Homeland Security |

# Additional Reviewers

| | |
|---|---|
| Richard Adderley | A E Solutions |
| Jason Bengel | University of Kansas |
| Benjamin Barán | National University of Asuncion |
| Haidong Bi | University of Arizona |
| Jinwei Cao | University of Arizona |
| Michael Chau | University of Hong Kong |
| Fang Chen | University of Arizona |
| Li-Chiou Chen | Carnegie Mellon University |
| Yufeng Chen | Zhejiang University, China |
| Wingyang Chung | University of Arizona |
| Csilla Farkas | University of South Carolina |
| Mark Ginsburg | University of Arizona |
| Mark Goldberg | Rensselaer Polytechnic Institute |
| Dale Henderson | University of Arizona |
| Zan Huang | University of Arizona |
| Yichuan Jiang | Fudan University, China |
| Naren Kodali | George Mason University |
| Ju-Sung Lee | Carnegie Mellon University |
| Jorge Levera | University of Illinois at Chicago |
| Xiangyang Li | University of Michigan at Dearborn |
| Therani Madhusudan | University of Arizona |
| Malik Magdon-Ismail | Rensselaer Polytechnic Institute |
| Jian Ma | University of Arizona |
| Kent Marett | Florida State University |
| Byron Marshall | University of Arizona |
| Dan McDonald | University of Arizona |
| William Neumann | University of Arizona |
| Joon Park | Syracuse University |
| Jialun Qin | University of Arizona |
| Benjamin Shao | Arizona State University |
| Moon Sun Shin | Chungbuk National University, Korea |
| David Skillicorn | Queens University, Canada |
| Cole Smith | University of Arizona |
| Svetlana Symonenko | Syracuse University |
| Charles Tappert | Pace University |
| William Tolone | University of North Carolina at Charlotte |
| Douglas Twitchell | University of Arizona |
| Gang Wang | University of Arizona |
| Jenq-Haur Wang | Academia Sinica, Taiwan |
| Jiannan Wang | University of Arizona |
| Robert Warren | University of Waterloo, Canada |
| Zhengyou Xia | Nanjing University of Aeronautics and Astronautics |
| Jennifer Xu | University of Arizona |

| Christopher Yang | The Chinese University of Hong Kong |
| Bülent Yener | Rensselaer Polytechnic Institute |
| Myung-Kyu Yi | Korea University |
| Wei Yue | University of Texas at Dallas |
| Xiaopeng Zhong | University of Arizona |
| Yilu Zhou | University of Arizona |

# Table of Contents

## Part I: Full Papers

### Bioterrorism and Disease Informatics

### Data Access Control, Privacy, and Trust Management

### Data Management and Mining

# Data/Text Management and Mining

# Information Assurance and Infrastructure Protection

# Part III: Extended Abstracts for Posters

# Part IV: Panel Discussion Papers

# Aligning Simulation Models of Smallpox Outbreaks

Li-Chiou Chen[1], Boris Kaminsky[1], Tiffany Tummino[2], Kathleen M. Carley[1,2], Elizabeth Casman[2], Douglas Fridsma[3], and Alex Yahja[1,2]

[1] Institute for Software Research International, School of Computer Science
[2] Department of Engineering and Public Policy
Carnegie Mellon University, Pittsburgh, Pennsylvania 15213
{lichiou,borisk,ttummino,carley,casman}@andrew.cmu.edu
[3] Center for Biomedical Informatics, School of Medicine, University of Pittsburgh
Pittsburgh, Pennsylvania 15213
fridsma@cbmi.pitt.edu

**Abstract.** We aligned two fundamentally different models of smallpox transmission after a bioterrorist attack: A location-explicit multi-agent model (BioWar) and the conventional epidemiological box model, called a SIR model for Susceptible-Infected-Recovered. The purpose of this alignment is part of a greater validation process for BioWar. From this study we were able to contribute to the overall validation of the complex agent based model, showing that, at the minimum, the epidemiological curves produced by the two models were approximately equivalent, both in overall and the time course of infection and mortality. Subtle differences on the model results revealed the impact of heterogeneous mixing in the spread of smallpox. Based on this foundation, we will be able to further investigate the policy responses against the outbreaks of contagious diseases by improving heterogeneous properties of agents, which cannot be simulated in a SIR model.

## 1 Introduction

Numerical simulation models can be used to estimate the impact of large-scale biological attacks and to design or select appropriate response strategies. The "correctness" of the model is critical since the "wrong" model may lead to "wrong" decisions, but no model is perfect and few models can ever be considered thoroughly validated. Studies [32, 33] have agreed that it is often too costly and time-consuming to determine if a model is absolutely valid. Instead, evaluations are conducted until sufficient confidence is obtained that a model is valid for its intended application. We developed a methodology to align an agent-based model of biological attack simulations (BioWar) against the classical susceptible-infected-recovered (SIR) box model as part of the validation process. Our purpose is to verify whether the agent-based model can produce results that closely resemble those of the well accepted and venerable SIR model, thus giving BioWar a sort of reflected credibility from the SIR model. This is not sufficient validation, but it is a confidence building step in the much larger task of validating BioWar.

Aligning the two types of model is challenging because of their radically different structures. We demonstrate an objective methodology for translating key parameters

H. Chen et al. (Eds.): ISI 2004, LNCS 3073, pp. 1–16, 2004.

between models, for running the models in concert to supply aligned inputs during simulations, and for evaluating the agreement between the models.

BioWar is a multi-agent simulation tool of biological attacks. It combines computational models of social networks, disease models, demographically resolved agent models, spatial models, wind dispersion models, and a diagnostic model into a single integrated system that can simulate the impact of a bioterrorist attack on any city [7]. For this paper, we restrict the alignment to the smallpox simulation in BioWar. The SIR model and its variations have been widely used to model the spread of epidemics and to study immunization strategies [1, 2, 4, 13]. The SIR model is a "population-based" aggregated representation of disease transmission that assumes homogeneous mixing of individuals. In contrast, BioWar models the complex social interactions and heterogeneity of mixing absent in most SIR models.

Model alignment, also referred to as "docking," is the comparison of two computational models to see if they can produce equivalent results. Properly done, model alignment can uncover the differences and similarities between models and reveal the relationships between the different models' parameters, structures, and assumptions. The purpose of aligning BioWar with the conventional box model is to demonstrate a general equivalence, as part of a greater validation process for BioWar. The concept of model alignment was first proposed by Axtell et al. [3]. We have used this method previously in validating BioWar's anthrax simulation [10].

This paper is organized as follows. The next section provides background information on smallpox and the two models. Section 3 explains our methodology of model alignment. Section 4 discusses our findings and compares the two models based on the simulation results. Conclusions and discussion of future work follow.

## 2   Two Models of Smallpox Transmission

Smallpox has several distinct stages, including incubation, prodrome (early-symptoms), and fulminant (late-symptoms). The initial site of viral entry is usually the mucous membranes of the upper respiratory tract. Once a person is infected, the incubation stage usually lasts for about 12 to 14 days. During this period, an infected person experiences no symptoms and is not contagious. The first symptoms of disease include fever (typically high), head and body aches, and possibly vomiting. This prodromal stage lasts about 2 to 4 days. During this time infected persons are usually too sick for normal activity, and may be contagious, although infectivity is often negligible [14].

The fulminant stage begins with the onset of rash. The rash appears first on the tongue and inside the throat or mouth, then appears on the face and limbs, usually spreading across the body within 24 hours. An infected person is most contagious within the first 7 to 10 days after the dermal rash appears. The rashes become bumps on about the 3rd day of the fulminant phase. The pox fill with liquid and acquire a distinctive shape with a depression in the middle by the 4th day of the period. Most smallpox deaths occur on the 5th or 6th day after the onset of rash [27, 23, 35]. Over a period of about 5 days after the pox fill with liquid, they become firm, sharply raised pustules; over another 5 days, these pustules crust and scab. Within about 14 days of the appearance of the rash, most of the pustules will have formed scabs. Within about

3 weeks after the onset of the rash, all of the scabs fall off, though the scab material is infectious somewhat longer.

Transmission of smallpox from an infected person to an uninfected person usually requires face-to-face personal contact, inhalation of droplets formed by coughing or sneezing, or contact with infected body fluids or contaminated objects (e.g., bedding) [8]. While infection has occurred through the spread of the virus through the air in buildings or other enclosed areas, this type of transmission has been rare. Humans are the only known reservoir of the virus, and there has been no known transmission via animals or insects.

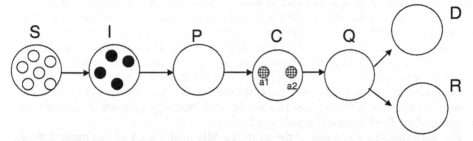

**Fig. 1a.** An illustration of the SIR model. Individuals (represented as dots) in a state have the transition probability of moving to next state

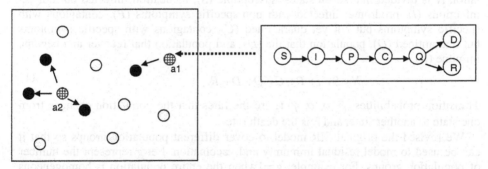

**Fig. 1b.** An illustration of the disease transmission process in BioWar. Each individual (such as a1) has its own state machine and has a different reproductive rate (e.g. a1 infects one case but a2 infects 3 cases)

Two types of models have been used to study the progression of smallpox outbreaks. They are population-level box models [6, 17, 24, 26] and individual-level agent-based models [19]. These population-level models are either variations or stochastic versions of the basic SIR model. The SIR model [1, 2] is a widely used model of the spread of a disease through a population. As noted, the SIR model describes the epidemic diffusion process by categorizing the entire population into three states – susceptible, infectious and recovered – linked by differential equations. The SIR model assumes that the population is homogenous and completely mixed. All members of a particular state are identical and have predefined transition probabilities of moving to another state in the model (Fig. 1a).

In contrast, agent-based models assume a heterogonous population with mixing only within socially defined networks (Fig. 1b). BioWar models the residents of a city (agents) as they go about their lives. When a bioattack occurs, those in the vicinity of the release may become infected, following probabilistic rules based on received dose and age of the agent. The infected agents modify their behaviors as their disease progresses and they become unable to perform their normal functions. Susceptible agents are infected if they come within a certain distance with infectious agents following probabilistic rules concerning the likelihood of infection. BioWar is not just an agent-based model, but a network model where the networks vary dynamically based on agent activity. Agents interact within and through their social network which is based on their age, race, gender, socio-economic status, and job. Consequently, which agents are likely to be infected and to infect others, depends on things like time of day, location of attack, time of year, age of the agent, and so on. Unlike many other agent-based models, BioWar is tightly coupled to demographic, school, economic, and social data as well as physiological, disease, geographic, weather, and climate data. The fine grained detail by which heterogeneity is defined, and the level of detail in agents behaviors (e.g., they don't just get infected and die, they go to the hospital, to the doctor, to the pharmacy, and so on) means that BioWar, unlike SIR models, can be used to examine response behavior far beyond mortality indicies. A detailed description of the BioWar model is published in [7].

The mathematical equations of the modified SIR model used in this paper follow. This modified SIR model allows us to simulate the residual immunity in the population and vaccination or patient-isolation response strategies. As in (1), the total population $N$ is divided into seven states: susceptible ($S$), incubation: infected but not yet infectious ($I$), prodrome: infected with non-specific symptoms ($P$), contagious with specific symptoms but not yet quarantined ($C$), contagious with specific symptoms but quarantined ($Q$), population that die ($D$), and population that recover and become immune ($R$).

$$N= S+ I+ P+ C+ Q+ D+ R. \tag{1}$$

Transition probabilities, $\beta$, $\sigma$, $\alpha$, $\gamma$, $v$, are the rates that the population changes from one state to another state, and $\lambda$ is the death rate.

We revised the original SIR model to cover different population groups so that it can be used to model residual immunity and vaccination. Let $g$ represent the number of population groups. For example, $g =1$ when the entire population is homogeneous as in our base scenario and $g = 3$ when we separate the population into three groups (no vaccination, residual immunity, vaccinated) as in our vaccination scenario. In this case, the population in each state is divided into these groups and the total population $N$ is equal to $\sum_{i=1}^{g} N_i$ . Each group has its own transition probability of reproduction $\beta$ and death rate $\lambda_i$. We assume that the disease-stage durations are the same across groups. Thus, transition probabilities, $\sigma$, $\alpha$, $\gamma$, $v$, are the same for each group. The differential equations of the SIR model are as (2) and (3).

$$\frac{dS_i}{dt} = -\beta_i S_i C, \quad \frac{dI_i}{dt} = \beta_i S_i C - \sigma I_i, \quad \frac{dP_i}{dt} = \sigma I_i - \alpha P_i, \quad \frac{dC_i}{dt} = \alpha P_i - \gamma C_i,$$

$$\frac{dQ_i}{dt} = \gamma C_i - v Q_i, \quad \frac{dD_i}{dt} = \lambda_i v Q_i, \quad \frac{dR_i}{dt} = (1-\lambda_i) v Q_i. \tag{2}$$

$$\frac{dS}{dt} = \sum_{i=1}^{g} \frac{dS_i}{dt}, \quad \frac{dI}{dt} = \sum_{i=1}^{g} \frac{dI_i}{dt}, \quad \frac{dP}{dt} = \sum_{i=1}^{g} \frac{dP_i}{dt}, \quad \frac{dC}{dt} = \sum_{i=1}^{g} \frac{dC_i}{dt},$$

$$\frac{dQ}{dt} = \sum_{i=1}^{g} \frac{dQ}{dt}, \quad \frac{dD}{dt} = \sum_{i=1}^{g} \frac{dD_i}{dt}, \quad \frac{dR}{dt} = \sum_{i=1}^{g} \frac{dR_i}{dt}.$$

(3)

## 3  Model Alignment

We first aligned the input parameters (Section 3.1) of the two models by calculating the reproductive rates from BioWar experiments (Section 3.2). We then designed scenarios to simulate smallpox outbreaks using the two models (Section 3.3), and compared population level results (Section 4). Fig. 2 illustrates our alignment methodology.

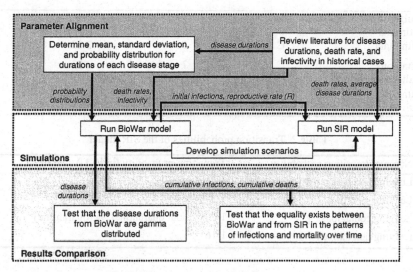

**Fig. 2.** The process of model alignment

### 3.1  Parameter Alignment

Although BioWar and SIR use are structurally very different, some of their model parameters are related. The parameter alignment process helped us to tune BioWar parameters to current epidemiology studies and to compare these parameters with those in the SIR model.

Both BioWar and SIR simulate disease progression in terms of the transition of infected individuals between disease stages, but with different stochastic framing. Bio-War utilizes probability distributions to determine the duration of each disease stage for each infected agent. Based on statistical analyses of several empirical data sets [14], we model smallpox stage durations as gamma distributed with a mean $\mu$ and a standard deviation $\sigma$ [12, 14-15, 18, 20]. Table 1 lists the values of $\mu$ and $\sigma$ for the disease stages (incubation (I), prodrome (P), and fulminant. The fulminant stage is divided into fulminant-contagious (C) stage and fulminant-quarantined (Q)). In contrast, SIR uses transition probabilities to represent the rates sectors of a population move from one state to another. To align the SIR model with BioWar, we set the transition probabilities[1] to $(\mu)^{-1}$. Table 2 shows this parameterization for the SIR model based on the mean disease-stage durations from BioWar. Although we can conduct Monte Carlo simulations of the SIR model treating $\mu$ as a random variable of gamma distribution, the stochasticity is different from that in BioWar. In BioWar the gamma distribution describes the variation among individuals and in the SIR model it describes the variation around the population sector mean.

**Table 1.** Means and standard deviations for disease-stage durations of smallpox

| | State in SIR model | Mean ($\mu$, in days) | Standard deviation ($\sigma$, in days) |
|---|---|---|---|
| incubation | I | 11.6 | 1.9 |
| prodromal | P | 2.49 | 0.88 |
| fulminant | C and Q | 16 | 2.83 |
| contagious (without quarantine) | C | 7 | 2.83 |
| contagious (with quarantine) | C | 2 | 1 |

**Table 2.** Transition probabilities of the SIR model

| Name of transition probability | Transition probability (in [0,1]) |
|---|---|
| Leaving incubation ($\sigma$) | 1/11.6 |
| Leaving prodromal ($\alpha$) | 1/2.49 |
| Leaving contagious ($\gamma$) | 1/7 (without quarantine), ½ (quarantine) |
| Leaving quarantine ($v$) | 1/16 |

The disease transmission in the two models is also different stochastically. In BioWar, at a certain probability (infectivity), an infectious individual will infect other individuals whose physical distance is less than 100 meters from the infectious individual. As a result, the disease transmission probability (the number of new infections at a certain time) is determined by social factors influencing the interactions among agents, such as infectivity, social networks and their daily activities. In contrast, in SIR the disease transmission probability is equal to a transition probability of reproduction ($\beta$) multiplied by the number of susceptible people plus the number of infec-

---

[1] In a Markov model, the transition probability from one state to another state is estimated by the inverse of the expected continuous duration of that state [21].

tious people in the population. This transition probability is constant across the entire course of a simulation but the transmission probability is not.

Although we cannot align the two models stochastically, we can align the models at the same average level of disease transmission probability by using reproductive rates and the number of initial infections. Since BioWar can simulate the interactions among agents, reproductive rates are emergent properties (outputs) from simulations. Similarly, the number of initial infections is also an emergent property since BioWar can roughly estimate it from information about the location of an attack, the released amount of smallpox viruses, and the daily activities of the agents. In contrast, the SIR model cannot simulate the interactions so that it needs to determine $\beta$ and the number of initial infections before running the simulations. We experimentally derived both from BioWar experiments.

## 3.2  Deriving Reproductive Rates from BioWar Experiments

The reproductive rate $R$ is defined as the expected number of secondary cases produced by an infectious individual in a population of $S$ susceptible individuals. The basic reproductive rate $R_0$ represents the value of $R$ in a totally susceptible population $N$. When the natural birth rate and death rate are negligible compared to the transition probabilities, the expected reproduction rate R can be approximated as $\dfrac{\beta S}{\gamma}$ and $R_0$ is approximated as $\dfrac{\beta N}{\gamma}$ [1].

Based on the above definitions by Anderson and May, we experimentally calculated $R_0$ from BioWar outputs using equation (4). In this case, we can estimate $\beta = \dfrac{\gamma R_0}{N}$. This method of deriving $R_0$ has been used in another agent based simulation [14].

$$R_0 = \frac{\text{the number of secondary cases infected by initial infections}}{\text{the number of initial infections}}. \qquad (4)$$

Alternatively, we can also derive $\beta$ from BioWar directly. The number of new infections at certain time is equivalent to $\beta SC$ in the SIR model in which $S$ represents susceptible individuals and $C$ represents contagious population. Thus, $\beta$ at time $t$ can be approximated by (5).

$$\beta(t) = \frac{\text{new infections (t)}}{\text{susceptible (t)} * \text{contagious (t)}}. \qquad (5)$$

Since BioWar is an agent based model, unlike SIR, the estimated transition probability is not a constant. In order to compare the average case in BioWar with SIR, we calculated $E(\beta)$ as the average of $\beta$ across time when it is larger than 0 ($\beta=0$ means no new infections at the time). We can then estimate $R$ as (6).

$$R = \frac{E(\beta)S}{\gamma}. \qquad (6)$$

## 3.3  Simulations

To compare the population level results from both BioWar and SIR, we simulated three smallpox attack scenarios: "base", "vaccination", and "quarantine". We started with a simplified base scenario and varied some of the parameters in other scenarios to increase the fidelity of the simulation. Table 3 lists the definitions of the three scenarios. For each scenario, we present the results as averages of 100 runs because the fluctuation of disease reproductive rates is negligible in around 100 runs.

We simulate an attack on the Washington, DC area, scaled down to 10% of its original size to speed up our simulations. The total population after scaling was about 55,900. In the base scenario we assume the attack goes undetected and no public health responses or warnings occur after the attack. We assume that infected individuals are not contagious when they are in early-symptomatic stage because infectivity in this stage is considered to be negligible relative to the infectivity of later stages [14, 15]. All individuals in the city are assumed to be completely susceptible to smallpox in the base scenario.

**Table 3.** Simulation scenarios

| Scenarios | Residual immunity (% of total population) | Fresh vaccination (% of total population) | Is infected population quarantined? |
|---|---|---|---|
| base | 0% | 0% | no |
| vaccination | 46% | 50% | no |
| quarantine | 46% | 0% | yes (on average, 2 day after the onset of rash) |

We modeled an indoor smallpox attack where a random number of agents (less than 10) are initially infected. For the second and third scenario, we categorized the population based on their immunity: residual immunity, fresh vaccination, and no vaccination. Agents with "residual immunity"[2] are assumed to have been vaccinated 30 or more years previously and their immunity against smallpox has weakened. In the US, 90% of the people born before 1972 were vaccinated, so about 50% of the contemporary population should have some level of the residual immunity [17]. In the scaled down DC population, approximately 46% (25,653 out of 55,930 people) were assigned residual immunity. Agents with "fresh vaccination" are assumed to have been vaccinated around two months before the attack. These individuals have high (but not perfect) immunity against smallpox. "No vaccination" means that the individuals had never been vaccinated. Table 4 lists the assumed probability of death following infection and infectivity for each of the three immune status categories [5, 9, 20].

Both "vaccination" and "quarantine" scenarios consider the residual immunity of the population. In addition, the "vaccination" scenario examines the effects of fresh vaccination among the population and the "quarantine" scenario examines the effects

---

[2] Here we refer to individuals who were vaccinated many years ago in contrast with fresh vaccination. However, this term is usually used to describe all individuals who have been vaccinated.

of infectious individuals being quarantined in around 2 days after the onset of rash so they will not infect other agents. In the "vaccination" scenario, agents are randomly selected for vaccination and agents who had been vaccinated before 1972 may be vaccinated again.

**Table 4.** Simulation parameters for different population categories

|  | Residual immunity | Fresh vaccination | No vaccination |
|---|---|---|---|
| Infectivity | 50% | 5% | 95% |
| Probability of death following infection | 7% | 2% | 30% |

# 4  Results and Discussion

We conducted both qualitative graph comparisons and statistical tests on the population level results. For each set of results from BioWar and SIR, we first compared them graphically and then statistically. For the disease-stage durations, we conducted parametric chi-square ($X^2$) tests to see if BioWar results are gamma distributed. To compare the rate of transmission and mortality from smallpox over time, we used non-parametric two sample hypothesis tests to compare the data generated by the two models.

## 4.1  Disease-Stage Durations

BioWar smallpox stage (incubation, prodrome, fulminant) durations are modeled as gamma distributed while SIR disease-stage durations are the average case of the gamma distributions. The average of the individual stage durations generated by BioWar should be close to the durations the infected population spends in each disease-stage in SIR. To verify this, we tested if the BioWar disease-stage durations are actually gamma distributed. The point of testing is simply to verify that BioWar is doing what it is told to do. In agent-based simulations, this should not be taken for granted.

We calculated the three disease-stage durations for 1000 infected agents in Bio-War. Graphically, Fig. 3 shows that the BioWar distribution of duration of the incubation period is similar to the gamma distribution and to literature values [15]. However, $X^2$ tests rejected the hypothesis that the incubation period is gamma distributed (p-value > 0.05), but could not reject this hypothesis for the prodrome and fulminant stages (Table 5).

**Table 5.** Goodness-of-fit test for smallpox stage durations of BioWar. ** Gamma distributed, significant at $\alpha > 0.05$

| Disease stage | $X^2$ | *Degree of freedom* | *P-value* |
|---|---|---|---|
| incubation | 17.75 | 9 | 0.04 |
| prodromal** | 8.95 | 5 | 0.11 |
| fulminant** | 19.89 | 13 | 0.10 |

The prodrome and fulminant stage durations simulated in BioWar are gamma distributed. The distribution of the incubation stage (Fig. 3) resembles the gamma distribution, but is too peaked.

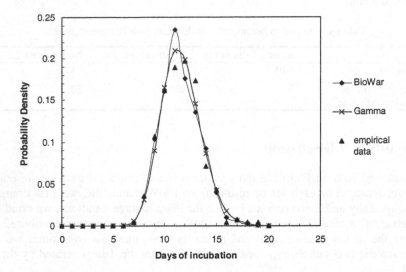

**Fig. 3.** A comparison of distribution of the incubation stage duration in BioWar with the theoretical [14] and empirical [15] data

## 4.2 Infection and Mortality

We aligned the transition probability of reproduction ($\beta$) of SIR using reproductive rate $R$ generated from BioWar, shown in Table 6. Table 7 displays BioWar and SIR estimations for the three scenarios. The difference in total mortality among infected individuals from the two models is less than 1% in all three scenarios. As illustrated in Figures 4a-4c, the progression of infection in the BioWar and SIR models are qualitatively similar. We obtained similar results from graph comparisons on over-time mortality.

We conducted nonparametric two-sample hypothesis tests to statistically compare the patterns of infection and mortality from the two models over time. Using the Peto-Peto-Prentice test [11], we tested the hypothesis that the over-time infection data from the BioWar and SIR models are statistically equivalent, in the sense that they could be generated from the same population with a unique underlying over-time pattern of infection. The Peto-Peto-Prentice test estimates expected numbers of infections at each time point using the combined output from the BioWar and SIR models, under the null hypothesis that there is no difference between the over-time patterns of infection in the two groups. The expected values are compared to the observed number of infections predicted by each model at each time point. These differences are combined into a single global statistic, which has a $X^2$ distribution with 1 degree of freedom (for the test, df = number of groups compared − 1). The same test is used to compare the mortality patterns in the BioWar and SIR models.

**Table 6.** Reproductive rates estimated from BioWar for three scenarious and three population categories

| Scenario | reproductive rate | no vaccina-tion | residual immunity | fresh vacci-nated |
|---|---|---|---|---|
| base | $R_0$ | 4.92 | N.A. | N.A. |
| | R | 3.86 | N.A. | N.A. |
| vaccination | $R_0$ | 2.13 | 1.28 | 0.44 |
| | R | 1.31 | 0.53 | 0.20 |
| quarantine | $R_0$ | 1.84 | 1.45 | N.A. |
| | R | 1.17 | 0.38 | N.A. |

**Table 7.** A comparison of BioWar and SIR average results for the three scenarios

| Scenario | Model | Initial Infections | Cumulative Infections | Cumulative Deaths | Mortality among Infections |
|---|---|---|---|---|---|
| base | SIR | 7 | 54,765 | 16,851 | 31% |
| | BioWar | 7 | 54,345 | 16,724 | 31% |
| vaccina-tion | SIR | 6 | 27,262 | 4876 | 18% |
| | BioWar | 6 | 25,766 | 4748 | 18% |
| quaran-tine | SIR | 5 | 30,119 | 7008 | 23% |
| | BioWar | 5 | 27,815 | 6597 | 24% |

The results for our three scenarios are shown in Tables 8a and 8b. A large $X^2$ (and correspondingly small p-value) indicates a statistically detectable difference between the output generated by the BioWar and SIR models. Note that the total number of infections or deaths in the BioWar and SIR output combined roughly reflects the amount of data available to the test. Even a small difference between infection or mortality curves may be detected with large amounts of data.

A statistically significant difference between over-time infection was detected in all scenarios (p-value < 0.05). The test shows that the models are in better agreement in regards to cumulative mortality, at least in the base case and vaccination scenario. For these, the test was unable to reject the hypothesis of equality for the two time series.. While the Peto-Peto-Prentice test cannot prove equivalence between the Bio-War and SIR mortality results in "base" and "vaccination" scenarios, the fact that it was unable to detect a significant difference supports our qualitative conclusion that the patterns of smallpox deaths in the two models are similar, though not identical.

**Table 8a.** Results of Peto-Peto-Prentice tests for BioWar and SIR estimates on cumulative infections. Number of infections refer to the combined infections resulting from the BioWar and the SIR model

| Scenario | $X^2$ (degree of freedom=1) | P-value | Time series of infections | Number of infections |
|---|---|---|---|---|
| base | 113.03 | <0.001 | Different | 109,096 |
| vaccination | 4.08 | 0.0434 | Different | 53,016 |
| quarantine | 233.82 | <0.001 | Different | 57,924 |

**Table 8b.** Results of Peto-Peto-Prentice tests for BioWar and SIR estimates on cumulative deaths. Number of deaths refer to the combined deaths resulting from the BioWar and the SIR model

| Scenario | $X^2$ (degree of freedom=1) | P-value | Time series of deaths | Number of deaths |
|---|---|---|---|---|
| base | 0.59 | 0.4438 | Same | 33,575 |
| vaccination | 0.6 | 0.4369 | Same | 9,624 |
| quarantine | 15.45 | 0.0001 | Different | 13,605 |

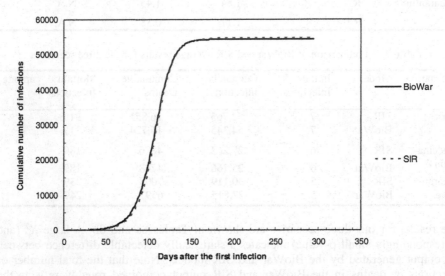

**Fig. 4a.** The comparison of BioWar and SIR in cumulative infections ("base" scenario)

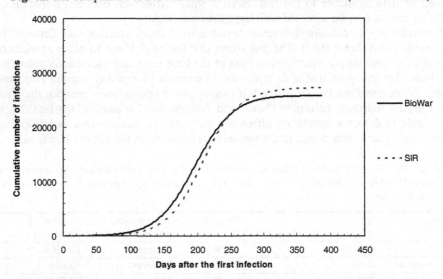

**Fig. 4b.** The comparison of BioWar and SIR in cumulative infections ("vaccination" scenario)

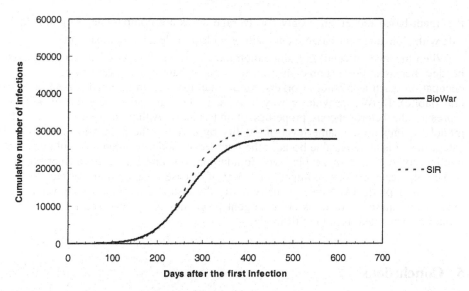

**Fig. 4c.** The comparison of BioWar and SIR in cumulative infections ("quarantine" scenario)

## 4.3 Discussion

Using smallpox attack simulations, we developed a methodology for comparing the BioWar agent-based model to the equivalent SIR model for contagious disease outbreaks. On a gross level such models should give approximately the same results, but subtle differences should exist because of the differences in mixing assumptions. This was the outcome of the docking, and serves as a partial validation of BioWar, demonstrating that it is at least able to produce fairly similar results to the accepted standard epidemiological model. The differences between BioWar and SIR were most evident in the scenarios involving vaccination and quarantine. It would be expected that the agent-based model would produce different results here, as the agent-level complexity required for such scenarios is easily accommodated by BioWar, but not by SIR.

The main benefit of validating the disease progression process separately from the disease transmission process is to clarify the sources of discrepancies in the simulations. We detected a deviation from expected incubation-duration distribution in BioWar which may have contributed to the differences found in model outputs.

Only certain aspects of the models could be compared. Because of the different ways the models account for parameter uncertainty, it is necessary to compare average results over numerous runs. We found that $R_0$ (average number of secondary cases in a totally susceptible population infected by one primary case) commonly used in SIR model, is not comparable to $R_0$ in BioWar. In BioWar, $R_0$ changes each run. $R$ (the reproduction rate over the entire simulation) is different from $R_0$ and is calculated as an average reproduction rate over all relevant time steps in a simulation. However, no distinction between $R$ and $R_0$ is made in SIR and $R$ is constant for each run and at each simulation step. This finding implies that, when comparing an agent-based model and the SIR model, modelers should align $R_0$ (or $R$) in the SIR with $R$ in the agent-based model since only the average cases are comparable. Aligning $R_0$ in SIR with $R_0$ in an agent-based model will provide a misleading comparison.

When the level of detail in a simulation increases, the number of model parameters needed increases. For example, the transmission probability may vary by age group or occupation (such as medical workers, family members of an infected person, or general public). BioWar provides a way to manage these model parameters in order to represent the heterogeneous properties of individuals. Although we can revise SIR model to simulate the same level of fidelity by dividing the population into several categories, it is not advisable because the number of model parameters would increase nonlinearly to an unmanageable level. In addition, revising SIR to have finer population categories overlooks an important aspect of disease transmission: the fact that the population reproductive rate is actually partly the result of interactions between individuals and these interactions are emergent properties of agent-based models which cannot be generated from the SIR model.

# 5  Conclusions

We developed a methodology to align a multi-agent model of weaponized biological attacks, BioWar, with the classical susceptible-infected-recovered (SIR) model. Using smallpox attack simulations, we showed that average results from BioWar are comparable to the SIR model, when the models are properly parameterized. The key parameters include the average disease-stage durations, the reproductive rate, the initial infection and the probability of death following infection.

The successful docking of the two radically different models provided a degree of confidence in the agent-based model, showing that its results are not far from those of the established SIR model. This work is our first step of the larger task on validating BioWar. Tools for finer-granularity validation of agent-based models are underway [36]. Based on this foundation, we will further investigate the policy responses against the outbreaks of contagious diseases by changing heterogeneous properties of agents (such as social networks, daily activities, and reactions to an attack), which cannot be simulated in a SIR model.

The differences in model inputs of smallpox simulations may lead to a different result [30]. It is important for policy makers to understand the differences and similarities between agent-based models and the SIR model before making decisions based on any one model. It is also important for modelers to realize what model inputs and outputs are comparable between the two models. We expect our results will help policy makers and other modelers.

# Acknowledgements

The authors would like to thank Neal Altman and Démian Nave for their support on this paper. This research was supported, in part, by DARPA for work on Scalable Biosurveillance Systems, the NSF IGERT9972762 in CASOS, the MacArthur Foundation, and by the Carnegie Mellon Center on Computational Analysis of Social and

Organizational Systems. The computations were performed on the National Science Foundation Terascale Computing System at the Pittsburgh Supercomputing Center. Any opinions, findings, conclusions or recommendations expressed in this material are those of the authors and do not necessarily reflect the views of DARPA, the National Science Foundation, the Pittsburgh Supercomputing Center, the MacArthur Foundation, or the US Government.

# References

1. Anderson, R.M. and May, R.M.: Directly transmitted infections diseases: control by vaccination. Science. Vol., 215 (1982) 1053–1060.
2. Anderson, R.M. and May, R.M.: Infectious Diseases in Humans: Oxford University Press (1992).
3. Axtell, R., Axelrod, R., Epstein, J.M., and Cohon, M.D.: Aligning simulation models: a case study and results. Computational and Mathematical Organization Theory. Vol. 1, (1996).
4. Bailey, N.J.T.: The Mathematical Theory of Infectious Diseases and Its Applications. 2nd ed. New York: Oxford University Press (1975).
5. Bartlett, J., Borio, L., and et. al: Smallpox Vaccination in 2003: Key Information for Clinicians. Clinical Infectious Diseases. Vol. 36, (2003) 883-902.
6. Bozzette, S.A., Boer, R., Bhatnagar, V., Brower, J.L., Keeler, E.B., Morton, S.C., and Stoto, M.A.: A model for a smallpox-vaccination policy. New England Journal of Medicine. Vol., 348 (2003) 416–425.
7. Carley, K., Altman, N., Kaminsky, B., Nave, D., and Yahja, A.: BioWar: A City-Scale Multi-Agent Network Model of Weaponized Biological Attacks, Technical Report (CMU-ISRI-04-101). Pittsburgh, PA: CASOS, Carnegie Mellon University (2004), http://reports-archive.adm.cs.cmu.edu/isri2004.html.
8. CDC: Smallpox fact sheet: smallpox overview. Centers for Disease Control and Prevention (2002). http://www.bt.cdc.gov/agent/smallpox/overview/disease-facts.asp.
9. CDC: Smallpox fact sheet: vaccine overview. Centers for Disease Control and Prevention (2003). http://www.bt.cdc.gov/agent/smallpox/vaccination/facts.asp.
10. Chen, L.-C., Carley, K.M., Fridsma, D., Kaminsky, B., and Yahja, A.: Model alignment of anthrax attack simulations. CASOS working paper, Carnegie Mellon University (2003).
11. Cleves, M.A., Gould, W.W., and Gutierrez, R.G.: An Introduction to Survival Analysis using Stata: Stata Press (2002).
12. Creighton, C.: A History of Epidemics in Britain. Vol. 2. Cambridge: Cambridge Univ. Press (1891).
13. Diekmann, O. and Heesterbeek, J.A.P.: Mathematical Epidemiology of Infectious Diseases: Model Building, Analysis and Interpretation. New York: John Wiley & Sons (2000).
14. Eichner, M. and Dietz, K.: Transmission potential of smallpox: Estimates based on detailed data from an outbreak. American Journal of Epidemiology. 158 (2003) 110–117.
15. Fenner, F., Henderson, D.A., Arita, I., Jezek, Z., and Ladnyi, I.D.: Smallpox and its Eradication. Geneva: WHO (1988).
16. Ferguson, N.M., Keeling, M.J., Edmunds, W.J., Gani, R., Grenfell, B.T., Anderson, R.M., and Leach, S.: Planning for smallpox outbreaks. Nature. 425 (2003) 681-685.
17. Gani, R. and Leach, S.: Transmission potential of smallpox in contemporary populations. Nature. 414 (2001) 748–751.
18. Gelfand, H.M. and Posche, J.: The recent outbreak of smallpox in Meschede, West Germany. American Journal of Epidemiology. Vol. 93, 4 (1971).

19. Halloran, M.E., Longini, I.M., Nizam, A., and Yang, Y.: Containing bioterrorist smallpox. Science. 298 (2002) 1428–1432.
20. Hammarlund, E., Lewis, M.W., Hansen, S.G., Strelow, L.I., Nelosn, J.A., Sexton, G.J., Hanifin, J.M., and Slifka, M.K.: Duration of antiviral immunity after smallpox vaccination. Nature Medicine,. Vol. 9, 9 (2003) 1131-1137.
21. Henderson, D.A., Inglesby, and et al.: Smallpox as a Biological Weapon - Medical and Public Health Management. Journal of the American Medical Association. Vol. 281, 22 (1999) 2127-2137.
22. Henderson, D.A.: Smallpox: public health threat. Encyclopedia of Life Sciences. Elsevier (2000).
23. Henderson, D.A.: Smallpox. in Encyclopedia of Microbiology (2000).
24. Kaplan, E.H., Craft, D.L., and Wein, L.M.: Emergency response to a smallpox attack: The case for mass vaccination. Proceedings of National Academy of Science USA. 99 (2002) 10935–10940.
25. Mack, T.: Smallpox in Europe, 1950-1971. Journal of Infectious Disease. 125 (1972) 161-169.
26. Meltzer, M.I., Damon, I., LeDuc, J.W., and Millar, J.D.: Modeling potential responses to smallpox as a bioterrorist weapon. Emerging Infectious Disease. 7 (2001) 959–969.
27. NDSC: Biological threat agents. National Disease Surveillance Centre (2003).
28. O'Toole, T. and Inglesby, T.V.: Facing the Biological Weapons Threat. The Lancet. Vol. 357 (Editorial), (2001).
29. Patrick, W.C.: Biological Terrorism and Aerosol Dissemination. Politics and the Life Sciences. Vol. 15, (1996) 208-210.
30. Powell, K.: Models call for vaccinations before bioterror attack. Nature. 15 Nov. (2002).
31. Rabiner, L.R.: A tutorial on hidden Markov models and selected applications in speed recognition. Proceedings of the IEEE. 2 (1989) 257-268.
32. Sargent, R.G.: Simulation Model Validation. in Simulation and Model-Based Methodologies: An Integrative View, T.I. Oren, B.P. Zeigler, and M.S. Elzas: Editors. Springer- Verlag: Heidelberg, Germany (1984) 537-555.
33. Sargent, R.G.: Verification and validation of simulation models. in Proceedings of the 2003 Winter Simulation Conference (2003).
34. Schlesinger, S., Crosbie, R.E., Gagne, R.E., Innis, G.S., Lalwani, C.S., Loch, J., Sylvester, R.J., Wright, R.D., Kheir, N., and Bartos, D.: Terminology for model credibility. Simulation. Vol. 32, 3 (1979) 103-104.
35. UPMC: Smallpox Fact Sheet. Center for Biosecurity, University of Pittsburgh Medical Center (2003). http://www.upmc-biosecurity.org/pages/agents/smallpox_facts.html.
36. Yahja, A.: WIZER: Automated Validation of Large-Scale Multi-Agent Systems. CASOS, Carnegie Mellon University (2004).

# Data Analytics for Bioterrorism Surveillance

Donald J. Berndt, Sunil Bhat, John W. Fisher, Alan R. Hevner, and James Studnicki

University of South Florida, Tampa, FL 33620, USA
{dberndt,sbhat,jfisher,ahevner}@coba.usf.edu
jstudnic@hsc.usf.edu

**Abstract.** Research on techniques for effective bioterrorism surveillance is limited by the availability of data from the few actual bioterrorism incidents and
the difficulty of designing and executing simulated bioterrorism attacks for
study. In this research, we describe a preliminary study of a naturally occurring
incident, the Florida wildfires from January to June 2001, as a reasonable fac-
simile of a bioterrorism attack. Hospital admissions data on respiratory illnesses
during that period are analyzed to uncover patterns that might be expected from
an airborne terrorism attack. The principal contribu-tions of this research are the
online analytic processing (OLAP) techniques employed to study the adverse
effects of this natural phenomenon. These techniques could provide important
capabilities for epidemiologist-in-the-loop surveillance systems, ena-bling the
rapid exploration of unusual situations and guidance for follow-up investigations. Research implications are discussed for our on-going development of effective bioterrorism surveillance systems.

## 1 Bioterrorism Surveillance Systems

The ability to identify and react effectively to a biological or chemical attack on military, government, and civilian targets is of real concern to all nations. Recent events,
such as the on-going war on terrorism and the building of a revitalized Iraqi nation,
require that reliable surveillance and alert mechanisms be implemented throughout
the world to thwart radical terrorists. However, biological and chemical weapons can
be based on a number of different agents and can take many forms of distribution,
making the detection and response to such attacks very difficult to prepare for [6].

At the University of South Florida, we have an active research program to design
and implement bioterrorism surveillance systems that use a comprehensive healthcare
data warehouse as a basis for identifying abnormal patterns of diseases related to
biological or chemical agents [2, 3]. In a previous paper [4], we analyzed several of
the technical challenges of developing an effective bioterrorism surveillance system.
Fundamentally, there are three major challenges required for such a system to be
effective:

1. It must be *multidimensional*. In other words, it must include a range of appropriate indicators and sources of information in order to monitor as many types of
   threats and health effects as possible.
2. It must accelerate the transmission of findings and data to closely approximate
   *real time surveillance* so as to provide sufficient warning.
3. It must have the capability for *pattern recognition* that will quickly identify an
   alarm or alert threshold value, raising the issue for further investigation or possible intervention.

H. Chen et al. (Eds.): ISI 2004, LNCS 3073, pp. 17–27, 2004.

Based on these objectives, in [4] we propose an architecture for an effective bioterrorism surveillance system and showcase a demonstration project that connects existing Florida surveillance systems with our healthcare data warehouse. The data warehouse provides the historical context in which to analyze unfolding events and associated real-time data feeds.

In this paper, we investigate analytic methods that support the rapid exploration of complex, multidimensional data relevant to biochemical threats. Such research is made difficult by the limited availability of data from the few actual terrorism incidents that have involved chemical or biological agents, as well as the difficulty of designing and executing simulated bioterrorism attacks for study. As an alternative, we propose the study of naturally occurring incidents to serve as reasonable facsimiles of terrorist attacks. We have selected a six-month period of wildfires that occurred in Florida from January to June 2001. We analyze hospital admissions during this time period for respiratory diseases to determine if abnormal patterns can be detected. The principal contributions of this research are the example online analytic processing (OLAP) techniques employed to study the adverse effects of this natural phenomenon. These techniques accelerate the investigative processes that characterize human-in-the-loop (or more appropriately epidemiologist-in-the-loop) efforts to understand and respond to critical events. Research implications are discussed for our on-going development of effective bioterrorism surveillance systems.

## 2   Florida Wildfires of 2001

Several years of drought conditions led to a record number of wildfires throughout the State of Florida during the first six months of 2001. The majority of these fires were caused by lightening strikes on parched grass and wood. Over 3,600 individual fires consumed nearly 320,000 acres of woodlands. Major transportation corridors, such as I-95 in the east, I-75 in the west, and I-4 across the state, were intermittently closed due to the lack of visibility from smoke and haze. Figure 1 shows the location of significant fires (greater than 250 acres) during this six-month period.

Relevant to our study, the wildfires, combined with the regular mix of air pollutants found in the air of urban areas, created a dangerous condition for individuals with respiratory illnesses. In the Tampa Bay area alone, the American Lung Association estimated the presence of approximately 350,000 respiratory patients who could have been affected. Over the Memorial Day weekend of 2001, the Florida Department of Environmental Protection issued an air pollution alert for all of the counties in the I-4 corridor from Tampa Bay in the west to Daytona Beach in the east, including the Orlando area. Persons with respiratory problems were advised to stay inside during the long holiday weekend [5].

This health emergency, due to natural causes, holds great similarities to a potential biological or chemical attack via airborne agents. In a similar fashion, other researchers have used wildfires to learn valuable lessons on emergency response. For instance, the study of recent California wildfires highlighted both successes and problems, such as incompatible communication systems and business continuity challenges [1]. However, in this research we are using the wildfires as a context for understanding potential threats to human health. We propose to explore the data on hospital admissions due to respiratory illness during the time period encompassing these fires. As a preliminary investigation, we use a healthcare data warehouse and associated query tools to 'slice and dice' data to uncover patterns that might have provided alerts to the presence of hazardous agents in the environment. A retrospective study, such as this, where we know the cause of the illnesses, will inform the development of bioterrorism surveillance systems as we monitor real-time data for abnormal illness patterns that might indicate the presence of an unknown agent.

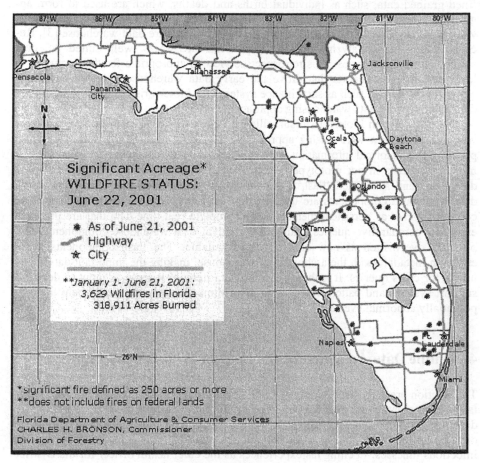

**Fig. 1.** Florida Wildfires of 2001

## 3 Bioterrorism Surveillance Using the CATCH Data Warehouse

Data warehousing technologies are a natural fit for many surveillance system requirements. In particular, the requirement for archiving both historical and real-time data is best accomplished using a data warehouse. In addition, any pattern recognition or data mining approaches to threat detection will require a data warehouse infrastructure. Our interdisciplinary team has amassed considerable experience in using data warehousing and data mining technologies for community health status assessment [2]. This experience has centered on supporting the Comprehensive Assessment for Tracking Community Health (CATCH) methodology with advanced data warehousing components and procedures.

The current CATCH data warehouse supports population-based health status assessments throughout Florida. The data warehouse serves as a historical repository of fined-grained data, such as individual births and deaths, which are used to form aggregate indicators of health status. We use a number of effective techniques to provide an adequate level of quality assurance in our healthcare data warehouse [3]. Reconstructing and analyzing historical patterns are tasks well suited to data warehousing technologies. This retrospective view is appropriate for the community-level health status reports that drove the early data warehouse development work. However, new tasks such as surveillance systems for bioterrorism require more timely data and real-time data warehousing approaches.

The challenge in bioterrorism surveillance lies in coupling historical perspectives with real-time data warehousing approaches. The existing CATCH data warehouse provides the historical information against which any new data can be compared. The new components in our prototype bioterrorism surveillance system are the real-time data feeds and associated 'flash' data warehouse components [4]. These innovative data warehouse components are used to store partially available real-time data. The components act as persistent memory for incomplete real-time data that are preprocessed for comparative queries against the archival data warehouse components, and possibly overwritten as new data become available. The flash components share common metadata with the archival data warehouse, making the important data items useful for cross queries. It is these common data items that serve as input to decision support systems and pattern recognition algorithms that may ultimately help identify potentially abnormal events.

# 4    Online Data Analytics for the Florida Wildfire Case Study

This section presents our exploratory online analytic processing (OLAP) of the hospital discharge data that cover the period of the Florida wildfires of 2001. We begin by describing the relevant data structures in the CATCH data warehouse and continue by developing the 'slice and dice' procedures for studying patterns of respiratory and infectious illnesses. In citing his experiences as the chief health officer for the District of Columbia, Dr. Walks notes that "the key to a successful response is the ability to communicate and share information quickly and fluidly with the appropriate people at the right time in order to make the critical decisions the situation demands" [7]. We consider data warehousing and OLAP technologies to be important methods for quickly analyzing and sharing information in support of critical decision-making activities. Surveillance personnel, such as epidemiologists and other healthcare professionals, can use integrated data warehousing technologies to rapidly analyze situations in ways that are currently very time consuming or simply not possible. Due to the sensitive nature of the data and potential costs of false alarms, fully automated pattern detection and alert mechanisms are unlikely to be implemented. Rather, systems that enable and accelerate analysis, feeding alerts to trained surveillance experts seem more likely. Again, data warehousing and OLAP tools are powerful techniques for constructing components of such surveillance systems.

This paper presents a preliminary case study using OLAP tools on an extended version of the CATCH data warehouse to capture respiratory illnesses patterns during selected Florida wildfires. In particular, the Florida hospital discharge data and specific respiratory illness categories are analyzed. While this preliminary approach will miss cases from physician offices, or even hospital visits with no overnight stay, the data is rich enough to provide realistic scenarios.

## 4.1  Hospital Discharge Star

The hospital discharge data discussed in this paper are used to derive CATCH indicators such as avoidable hospitalizations, which are among the types of data deemed appropriate for community assessment. However, the discharge transactions themselves can provide the flexibility for deeper analysis. For instance, the number of different procedures performed, volume estimates for institutions or integrated delivery systems, length of stay, and a fine-grained breakdown of charges are all possible targets of queries against this data warehouse component. Florida hospital discharge transactions are collected by the Agency for Health Care Administration (AHCA) from the more than 200 short-term acute care hospitals in the state. These hospitals report every discharge transaction, regardless of payer, throughout the state.

Figure 2 depicts the design of the hospital discharge star schema, showing the center fact table and selected radiating dimensions. The Florida hospital discharge transactions provide very useful numeric facts. For instance, length of stay is a particularly important measurement for analysis. There is also a measurement indicating elapsed days until the procedure. Finally, there is a total revenue item that provides important cost information. As it turns out, there is also a large text item with embedded revenue items that provides a breakdown of the various charges from room rates to laboratory fees. Procedures to parse this text item have been developed as part of the data staging activities and are used to extract two-dozen revenue items, providing nearly thirty interesting numeric facts for each transaction. This makes the hospital discharge star a very useful resource within the CATCH data warehouse.

The hospital discharge star has more than a dozen interesting discharge transaction dimensions, with more being added. One important dimension is the HOSPITAL table, with over 200 different hospitals identified as reporting institutions. Therefore, it is easy to generate reports and analyze data in terms of specific hospitals for surveillance. Several characteristics, such as number of beds, number of employees, type of corporate organization, and geographic location allow the hospitals to be grouped in a variety of ways. In addition, integrated delivery systems that form networks of hospitals provide a natural hierarchy along the hospital dimension.

## 4.2  Aggregate Data Cubes for Surveillance

In order to facilitate online analytic processing, an aggregate data cube is formed from the underlying hospital discharge data. This aggregate structure provides much improved performance for the roll-ups and drill-downs that characterize OLAP-style navigation. Of course, the true event-level data is still available for unanticipated queries, but many operations can be run against the pre-computed aggregate. Figure 3 depicts one such aggregate with hospital admissions organized by several dimensions, including specific hospitals, ICD (International Classification of Disease) diagnostic codes, dates, and patient age categories. As part of this case study, admissions with diagnoses from potential bioterrorism threats specifically related to respiratory and infectious illnesses were aggregated for OLAP analysis. (Table 1 contains the ICD codes used for the study.) The goal is to analyze the hospital admission patterns in the context of the Florida wildfires.

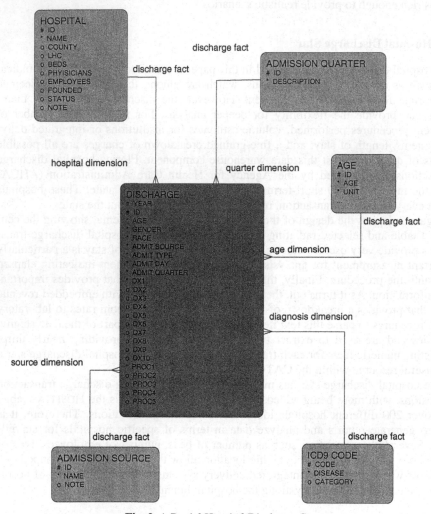

**Fig. 2.** A Partial Hospital Discharge Star

## 4.3 Data Drill-Down for Illness Patterns

Public reports discuss the individual wildfires with regard to time and location, which will inform much of the analysis. In fact, Governor Jeb Bush proclaimed a State of Emergency in accordance with Federal Emergency Management Agency (FEMA) guidelines for a collection of distinct areas from the middle of February through June of 2001. Some of these wildfires were near heavily populated areas and threatened major highways. Therefore, a selected set of wildfires offer the opportunity to study realistic scenarios that capture aspects of a biochemical attack.

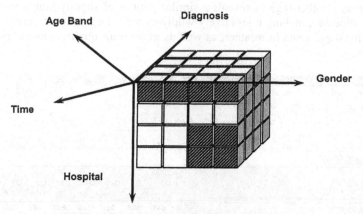

**Fig. 3.** Aggregate Data Cube for Surveillance

**Table 1.** Diseases (ICD Codes) Used in this Case Study - Diseases of the Respiratory System (ICD 460-519)

| Threat Indicators | ICD Codes | Comments |
|---|---|---|
| Acute Respiratory Infections | 460-466 | |
| Pneumonia and Influenza | 480-487 | |
| Pneumoconioses and Other Lung Diseases Due to External Agents | 500-508 | Respiratory Conditions Due to Chemical Fumes and Vapors (506) |

| Infectious and Parasitic Diseases (ICD 001-139) | | |
|---|---|---|
| Threat Indicators | ICD Codes | Comments |
| Intestinal Infectious Diseases | 001-009 | Cholera, Typhoid, Salmonella, Shigellosis, E. Coli |
| Zoonotic Bacterial Diseases | 020-027 | Plague, Anthrax |
| Viral Diseases Accompanied by Exanthim | 050-057 | Smallpox, Measles, Rubella |
| Other Diseases Due to Viruses and Chlamydiae | 070-079 | Viral Hepatitis, Infectious Mononucleosis |

In particular, a State of Emergency was declared for Brevard, Orange, Osceola, and Seminole counties (within the Division of Forestry, Orlando Fire District) from April 16th through June 26th of 2001. These wildfires will serve as the subject for several OLAP queries that allow us to 'drill down' into the data to explore illness patterns related to air pollution caused by the wildfires.

Figure 4 takes a regional perspective, showing the admissions associated with the potential threats (based on ICD codes) described in Table 1. This view rolls up several counties to form central Florida summaries. A few patterns do emerge from this coarse-grained overview. First, you can clearly see the seasonality in categories such as acute respiratory infections with the first and fourth quarters (the fall/winter) showing much higher numbers of cases. Secondly, the second quarter of 2001 does seem to have a somewhat higher rate of lung diseases due to external agents, as well as pneumonia and influenza. While this could simply be due to a nasty flu season, we will continue to drill-down to finer levels of granularity as part of our example. In fact, drilling across to other regions reveals a similar pattern of slightly higher volumes of respiratory illnesses, making it less likely wildfires had a large impact. Rather, natural variations for these years in weather, as well as general air quality may be more relevant factors.

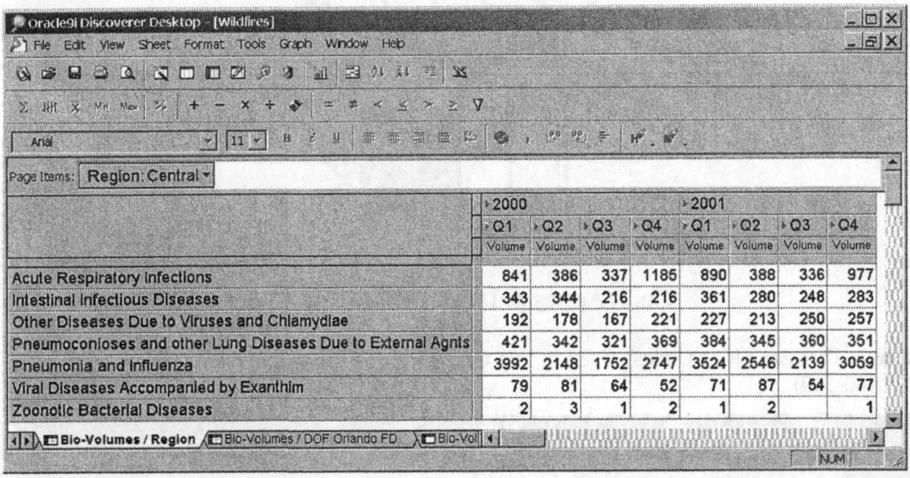

**Fig. 4.** Diseases by Quarter for 2000 and 2001

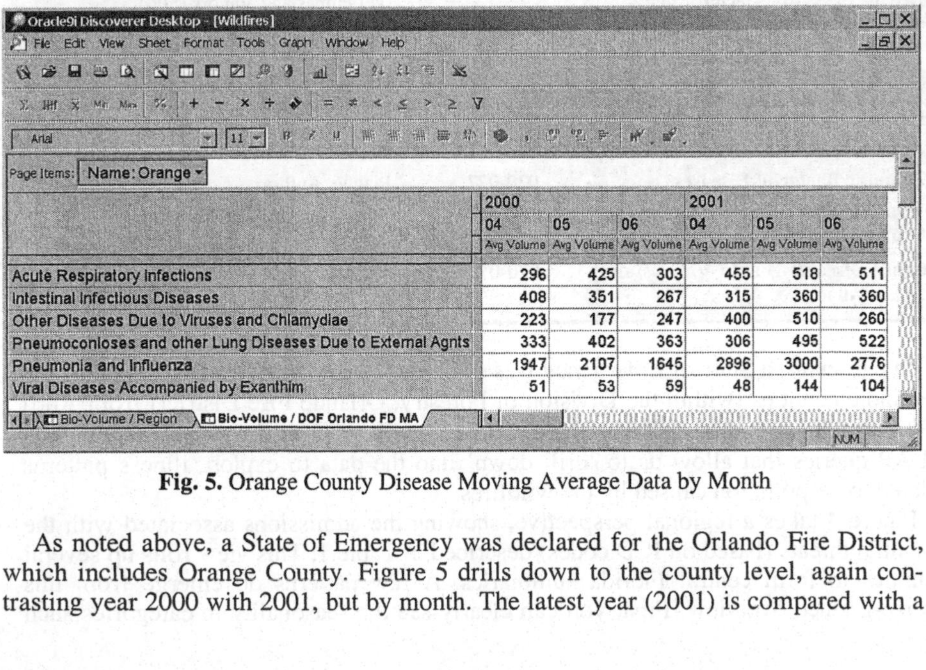

**Fig. 5.** Orange County Disease Moving Average Data by Month

As noted above, a State of Emergency was declared for the Orlando Fire District, which includes Orange County. Figure 5 drills down to the county level, again contrasting year 2000 with 2001, but by month. The latest year (2001) is compared with a three-year moving average in order to smooth out year-to-year variations. Additional values, such as expected values from regression equations or other predictive models are being incorporated into the data warehouse surveillance components for further analysis. At the county level, the pattern of somewhat higher rates remains for pneumonia and influenza, as well as acute infections for April and May.

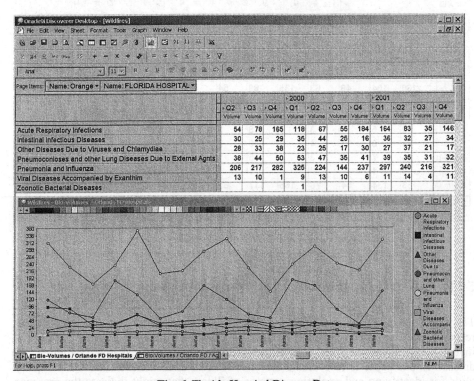

| | 2000 | | | | 2001 | | | | | | |
|---|---|---|---|---|---|---|---|---|---|---|---|
| | Q2 Volume | Q3 Volume | Q4 Volume | Q1 Volume | Q2 Volume | Q3 Volume | Q4 Volume | Q1 Volume | Q2 Volume | Q3 Volume | Q4 Volume |
| Acute Respiratory Infections | 54 | 78 | 165 | 118 | 67 | 55 | 184 | 164 | 83 | 35 | 146 |
| Intestinal Infectious Diseases | 30 | 25 | 29 | 35 | 44 | 25 | 16 | 36 | 32 | 27 | 34 |
| Other Diseases Due to Viruses and Chlamydiae | 28 | 33 | 38 | 23 | 25 | 17 | 30 | 27 | 37 | 21 | 17 |
| Pneumoconioses and other Lung Diseases Due to External Agnts | 38 | 44 | 50 | 53 | 47 | 35 | 41 | 39 | 35 | 31 | 32 |
| Pneumonia and Influenza | 206 | 217 | 282 | 325 | 224 | 144 | 237 | 297 | 240 | 216 | 321 |
| Viral Diseases Accompanied by Exanthim | 13 | 10 | 1 | 9 | 13 | 10 | 6 | 11 | 14 | 4 | 11 |
| Zoonotic Bacterial Diseases | | | | 1 | | | | | | | |

**Fig. 6.** Florida Hospital Disease Data

Within individual counties, it is possible to select specific hospitals. Florida Hospital is one of the major hospitals in Orange County and one of the largest institutions in the state. Figure 6 shows quarterly disease data from 2000 and 2001. Even at this finer level of detail, the somewhat elevated second (and possibly third) quarter data remains evident. The graphical capabilities of the OLAP tool are also used to present trend lines for visual analysis.

Finally, in Figure 7, we can incorporate another year and additional dimensions such as age into the query mix, explicitly selecting a county, hospital, and threat group. The age ranges are shown along the right-hand axis. Overall, the first and second quarters of 2001 are a bit higher, with most of the difference due to acute respiratory infections in the very young. While it would be hard to prove that such problems are directly related to the wildfires, the analytic process demonstrates how easily one can investigate patterns using OLAP technologies. Of course, more detailed study and confirmatory statistics must be used to complete any formal analyses. However, OLAP technologies can be used to rapidly uncover potential issues, prepare for further investigations, and plan for possible responses, all very important tasks for any surveillance system.

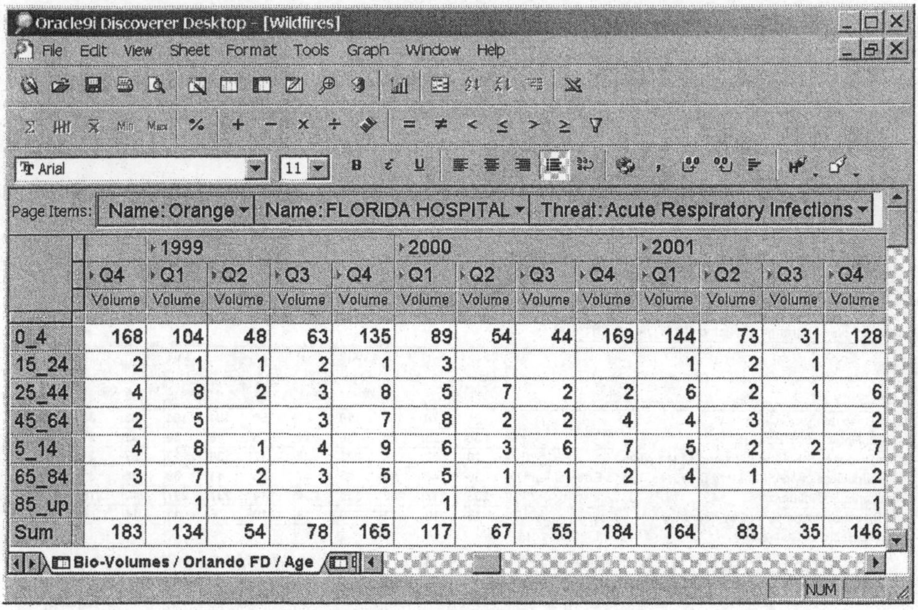

Fig. 7. Data Analysis of Respiratory Diseases

Page Items: | Name: Orange ▾ | Name: FLORIDA HOSPITAL ▾ | Threat: Acute Respiratory Infections ▾

| | 1999 | | | | 2000 | | | | 2001 | | | |
|---|---|---|---|---|---|---|---|---|---|---|---|---|---|
| | Q4 | Q1 | Q2 | Q3 | Q4 | Q1 | Q2 | Q3 | Q4 | Q1 | Q2 | Q3 | Q4 |
| | Volume | Volume | Volume | Volume | Volume | Volume | Volume | Volume | Volume | Volume | Volume | Volume | Volume |
| 0_4 | 168 | 104 | 48 | 63 | 135 | 89 | 54 | 44 | 169 | 144 | 73 | 31 | 128 |
| 15_24 | 2 | 1 | 1 | 2 | 1 | 3 | | | | 1 | 2 | 1 | |
| 25_44 | 4 | 8 | 2 | 3 | 8 | 5 | 7 | 2 | 2 | 6 | 2 | 1 | 6 |
| 45_64 | 2 | 5 | | 3 | 7 | 8 | 2 | 2 | 4 | 4 | 3 | | 2 |
| 5_14 | 4 | 8 | 1 | 4 | 9 | 6 | 3 | 6 | 7 | 5 | 2 | 2 | 7 |
| 65_84 | 3 | 7 | 2 | 3 | 5 | 5 | 1 | 1 | 2 | 4 | 1 | | 2 |
| 85_up | | 1 | | | | 1 | | | | | | | 1 |
| Sum | 183 | 134 | 54 | 78 | 165 | 117 | 67 | 55 | 184 | 164 | 83 | 35 | 146 |

◀ ▶ ▦ Bio-Volumes / Orlando FD / Age

# 5   Research Contributions and Future Directions

The urgent public need for effective bioterrorism surveillance systems has led our research team to extend the CATCH data warehouse with a focus on detecting and investigating abnormal illness patterns [4]. The important research challenge addressed in this paper is to evaluate the effectiveness of data warehouse OLAP query tools for identifying and exploring patterns of illness that might indicate the presence of a biological or chemical agent in the environment. OLAP tools are readily available and fairly easy to use yet still provide powerful query capabilities in a defined data warehouse environment. A retrospective analysis of the hospital admissions data surrounding the 2001 Florida wildfires illustrates the query techniques. The discovery of respiratory illness patterns during this time period provides some evidence that OLAP approaches may be useful in successfully detecting and analyzing future patterns.

Our OLAP procedures on the CATCH data warehouse hospital admissions data for the years 1998 through 2001 did discover some patterns of elevated respiratory illness during the wildfires. While we compared across regions (keeping the time period constant), used moving averages, and plan to incorporate other predictive models, the patterns could simply be natural variations. Further investigations at fine-grained levels of detail would be necessary to bolster any conclusions. The principal purposes of this study include the demonstration of our ability to rapidly and effectively use OLAP queries on the data warehouse to identify and analyze such illness patterns. As demonstrated in this case study, we are able to easily slice the data along dimensions of time (from days to years), illness (ICD codes for respiratory and infectious illnesses), geography (Orange County), hospital (Florida Hospital), and age. The developed queries then drilled down to finer and finer layers of detail as we investigated illness patterns.

Our future research directions on bioterrorism surveillance systems include:

- Identifying other key bioterrorism threat indicators that could be monitored as part of the prototype system.
- Expanding our development of data warehouse components and staging techniques for real-time data.
- Improving the capabilities of current pattern recognition algorithms that signal potentially abnormal events based on the selected threat indicators.
- Designing and implementing effective user interfaces or threat assessment dashboards for presenting the information.
- Evaluating our evolving prototype system using a panel of experts, soliciting feedback for further development activities.

Data warehousing technologies, including OLAP query tools, provide a powerful approach for bioterrorism surveillance. Furthermore, the data warehouse infrastructure enables research on new strategies for data mining and pattern recognition, as well as experimentation with real-time data feeds. All of these areas are critical components of emerging surveillance systems.

# References

1. Ballman, J., Case Study: When the Smoke Cleared, *Disaster Recovery Journal 17* 1 (2004), 16-20.
2. Berndt, D., Fisher, J., Hevner, A., and Studnicki, J. Healthcare Data Warehousing and Quality Assurance. *IEEE Computer 34* 12 (December 2001), 33-42.
3. Berndt, D., Hevner, A., and Studnicki, J. The CATCH Data Warehouse: Support for Community Health Care Decision Making. *Decision Support Systems 35* 6 (June 2003), 367-384.
4. Berndt, D., Hevner, A., and Studnicki, J. Bioterrorism Surveillance with Real-Time Data Warehousing. *Proceedings of First NSF/NIJ Symposium on Intelligence and Security Informatics (ISI 2003)*, Lecture Notes in Computer Science, LNCS 2665, Springer-Verlag (June 2003), 322-335.
5. Pittman, C. A Breath of Fresh Air Hard to Come by Here, *St. Petersburg Times*, May 26, 2001, 1.
6. Relman, D. and Olson, J. Bioterrorism Preparedness: What Practitioners Need to Know. *Infectious Medicine 18* 11 (November 2001), 497-515.
7. Walks, I., Preparing Your Organization for a Terrorist Attack, *Disaster Recovery Journal 16* 3 (2003), 34-38.

# West Nile Virus and Botulism Portal:
## A Case Study in Infectious Disease Informatics*

Daniel Zeng[1], Hsinchun Chen[1], Chunju Tseng[1], Catherine Larson[1],
Millicent Eidson[2], Ivan Gotham[2], Cecil Lynch[3], and Michael Ascher[4]

[1] Department of Management Information Systems
University of Arizona, Tucson, Arizona
{zeng,hchen,chun-ju,cal}@bpa.arizona.edu
[2] New York State Department of Health, SUNY, Albany
{mxe04,ijg01}@health.state.ny.us
[3] California Department of Health Services, UC Davis, Sacramento
clynch@dhs.ca.gov
[4] Lawrence Livermore National Laboratory
ascher1@llnl.gov

**Abstract.** Information technologies and infectious disease informatics are playing an increasingly important role in preventing, detecting, and managing infectious disease outbreaks. This paper presents a collaborative infectious disease
informatics project called the WNV-BOT Portal system. This Portal system
provides integrated, Web-enabled access to a variety of distributed data sources
related to West Nile Virus and Botulism. It also makes available a preliminary
set of data analysis and visualization tools tailored for these two diseases. This
system has helped to demonstrate the technological feasibility of developing a
cross jurisdiction and cross species infectious disease information infrastructure
and identify related technical and policy-related challenges with its national
implementation.

## 1 Introduction

Infectious disease outbreaks are critical threats to public health and national security
[1, 4, 12]. With greatly expanded trade and travel, infectious diseases, either naturally
occurred or caused by biological terror attacks, can spread at a fast pace within and
across country borders, resulting in potentially significant loss of life, major economic
crises, and political instability.

Information systems play a central role in developing an effective comprehensive
approach to prevent, detect, respond to, and manage infectious disease outbreaks of
plants, animals, and humans [2, 5]. Currently, a large amount of infectious disease
data is being collected by various laboratories, health care providers, and government
agencies at local, state, national, and international levels [11]. However, there exist a
number of technical and policy-related challenges hindering the effective use and
sharing of infectious disease data, especially datasets across species and across jurisdictions, in regional, national, and global contexts [3]. Several key challenges are
summarized below.

---

* Research reported in this paper has been supported in part by the NSF through Digital Government Grant #EIA-9983304.

H. Chen et al. (Eds.): ISI 2004, LNCS 3073, pp. 28–41, 2004.

- *Existing infectious disease information systems do not fully interoperate.* Most existing systems have been developed in isolation [8]. As such, when disease control agencies need to share information across systems, they may resort to using nonautomated approaches such as e-mail attachments and manual data (re)entry. In addition, much of the search and data analysis function is only accessible to internal users.

- *The information management environment used to analyze large amounts of infectious disease data and develop predictive models needs major improvements.* Current infectious disease information systems provide very limited support to professionals analyzing data and developing predictive models. An integrated environment that offers functionalities such as geocoding, advanced spatio-temporal data analysis and predictive modeling [6], and visualization is critically needed.

- *An efficient reporting and alerting mechanism across organizational boundaries is lacking.* Certain infectious disease information needs to be quickly propagated through the chain of public health agencies and shared with law enforcement and national security agencies in a timely manner. Certain models exist within the human public health community (e.g., the Centers for Disease Control and Prevention (CDC)'s ArboNet and Epi-X) and within certain states (e.g., New York State's Health Information Network (HIN)). However, in general the current reporting and alerting mechanism is far from complete and efficient, and may involve extensive and error-prone human interventions.

- *Data ownership, confidentiality, security, and other legal and policy-related issues need to be closely examined.* When infectious disease datasets are shared across jurisdictions, important access control and security issues need to be resolved between the involved data providers and users. Subsets of such data are also governed by relevant healthcare and patient-related laws and regulations. Negotiating the agreements that must be developed to govern access to and use of disease-related data by agencies and individuals can be labor and time-intensive [9].

This paper summarizes our ongoing research and system development effort motivated to address some of the above challenges. This effort is aimed at developing scalable technologies and related standards and protocols needed by the full implementation of the national infectious disease information infrastructure and at studying related policy issues. The resulting research prototype, called the *WNV-BOT Portal* system, provides integrated, Web-enabled access to a variety of distributed data sources related to West Nile Virus (WNV) and Botulism. It also provides information visualization capabilities as well as predictive modeling support. In this paper, we summarize the background and application context of our project and present the main technical components of WNV-BOT Portal. We also discuss broader technical and policy issues related to the design and development of a scalable national infectious disease infrastructure based on the lessons learned through our prototyping effort.

The rest of the paper is structured as follows. Section 2 discusses WNV and Botulism datasets and the related existing public health systems that WNV-BOT Portal is designed to integrate and interoperate. In Section 3, we present the overall system design and main technical components of WNV-BOT Portal. We conclude the paper in Section 4 by summarizing our research and discussing our ongoing activities and future plan.

## 2  West Nile Virus and Botulism Datasets and State Public Health Systems

The emergence of WNV in the Western Hemisphere was reported first in New York State in late summer 1999. This unprecedented event required rapid mobilization and coordination of hundreds of public health workers, expenditure of millions of dollars on an emergency basis, and immediate implementation of massive disease surveillance and vector control measures. The Health Information Network (HIN) system has been used by New York State to enable rapid and effective response to the WNV crisis. The HIN is an enterprise-wide information infrastructure for secure Web-based information interchange between the New York State Department of Health (NYSDOH) and its public health information trading partners, including local health departments and the New York State Department of Agriculture and Markets, New York State Department of Environmental Conservation, and the United States Department of Agriculture's Wildlife Services New York office [5]. This system currently supports 20,000 accounts and 100 mission critical applications, cross-cutting all key public health response partners in the state of New York. It implements sophisticated data access and security rules, allowing for real-time use of the data within the state while protecting confidentiality and scientific integrity of the data. The infrastructure is well suited to public health response, as illustrated by New York's ability to rapidly incorporate it into its plan to respond to the WNV outbreak in NY in 1999-2000 [5]. The system has evolved into an integrated surveillance system containing large quantities of real-time data related to WNV including (a) human cases, (b) dead bird surveillance data, (c) asymptomatic bird surveillance data, (d) mammal cases, and (e) mosquito surveillance data.

WNV has yet to manifest as an indigenous human disease in California, but the historical geographic spread of this disease and the fact that WNV has been detected in sentinel flocks of chickens and mosquito pools in California, would indicate the high likelihood that the state will have to deal with large numbers of cases later this year. Important as a cause of neurological morbidity and death, WNV is also a prototype of an emerging viral infection. The analysis of data collected regarding its occurrence and spread provides a basis for the development of predictive models for other emerging or as yet unidentified diseases. The California Department of Health Services (CADHS) has access to the detailed datasets from California's mosquito control districts and surveillance data on sentinel flock, dead bird, and equine specimens. In collaboration with USGS, we also have datasets concerning domestic and wild animal populations that might be exposed to WNV; some related data is available through CDC.

Botulism is a disease rarely seen in the United States with fewer than 200 cases per year reported to the CDC. Despite the low volume of cases, because of the risks associated with the possibility of a terrorist event utilizing botulinum toxin, the importance of having a system in place to identify and manage larger numbers of cases of the disease cannot be overestimated. The transactional data generated in such a system must also be available for post-event analysis in order to improve public health methods and responses. Both New York and California represent a significant part of the world economy and are high risk targets for bioterrorism due to the high level of international traffic into the states. NYSDOH has an internal database for botulism cases that occurred in New York State. In California, no computerized system currently exists that is capable of handling the information gathering, retrieval, and dissemination needs for a bio-terrorist event involving botulinum toxin. However, detailed paper-based information is available on both Botulism cases and antitoxin inventory. In addition, nationwide avian botulism data is maintained and updated by the National Wildlife Health Center.

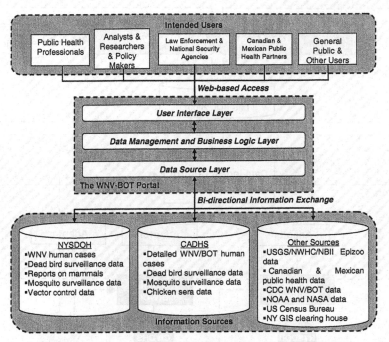

**Fig. 1.** Data Sources and Intended Users of the WNV-BOT Portal

# 3  WNV-BOT Portal System Development

The WNV-BOT Portal system has been developed to integrate infectious disease datasets on WNV and Botulism from New York, California, and several federal data sources. It also provides a set of data analysis, predictive modeling, and information visualization tools tailored for these two diseases. Figure 1 summarizes these datasets and intended users of WNV-BOT Portal.

## 3.1  WNV-BOT Portal System Design

As illustrated in Figure 2, from a systems perspective, WNV-BOT Portal is loosely-coupled with the state public health information systems in that the state systems will transmit WNV/BOT information through secure links to the portal system using mutually-agreed protocols. Such information, in turn, will be stored in the internal data store maintained by WNV-BOT Portal. The system also automatically retrieves data items from sources such as those from USGS and stores them in the internal data store.

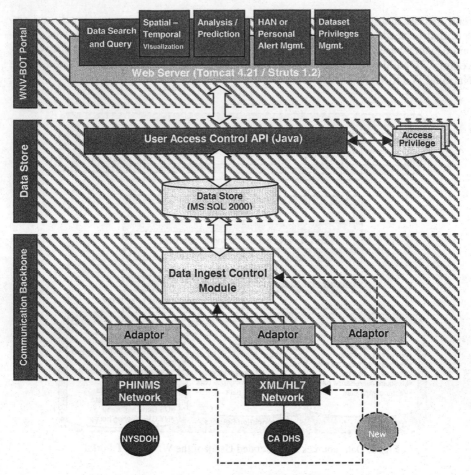

**Fig. 2.** Overall Architecture of the WNV-BOT Portal System

Architecturally, WNV-BOT Portal consists of three major components: a communication backbone, a data store, and a Web portal. Figure 2 illustrates these components and shows the main data flows between them and the underlying WNV/BOT data sources. The communication backbone module implements data transmission protocols. It normalizes data from various participating sources and is responsible for converting incoming data into a data format internal to the Portal system. The data store module receives normalized data from the communication backbone and stores it in a relational database. The data store module also implements a set of Java APIs that serves data requests from the user and imposes data access rules. The Web portal module implements the user interface and provides the following main functionalities: (a) searching and querying available WNV/BOT datasets, (b) visualizing WNV/BOT datasets using spatial-temporal visualization, (c) accessing analysis and prediction functions, and (d) accessing the alerting mechanism. The remainder of this section discusses the design considerations and technical details of these three major modules. A use scenario will be used to demonstrate how these modules work together to satisfy the user's information and analysis needs.

## 3.2  Communication Backbone

The communication backbone module enables data exchanges between WNV-BOT Portal and the underlying WNV/BOT sources. Several federal programs have been recently created to promote data sharing and system interoperability in the healthcare domain. The CDC's Electronic Disease Surveillance System (NEDSS) initiative is particularly relevant to our research. It builds on a set of recognized national standards such as HL7 for data format and messaging protocols and provides basic modeling and ontological support for data models and vocabularies. NEDSS and HL7 standards are having a major impact on the development of disease information systems. Although these standards have not yet been tested in cross-state sharing scenarios, they provide a solid foundation for data exchange standards in the national and international contexts. WNV-BOT Portal heavily utilizes NEDSS/HL7 standards.

WNV-BOT Portal currently supports two messaging systems: Public Health Information Network Messaging System (PHIN MS) which is developed by the CDC, and XML/HL7 Message Broker Network (MBN) which has been deployed in CADHS's California Public Health Information Network (CALPHIN). For illustration purposes, we use PHIN MS to describe the main components of these messaging systems. PHIN MS uses the Electronic Business Extensible Markup Language, ebXML, infrastructure to securely transmit public health information over the Internet. It is platform-independent and loosely coupled with systems that produce or receive messages. PHIN MS has three major components: Message Sender, Message Receiver, and Message Handler. The Message Sender sends ebXML messages to one or more Message Receivers; the Message Handler takes corresponding actions based on message types. Below is an example ebXML message sent from NYSDOH to the Portal following the PHIN MS system. CALPHIN has a similar architectural design but different applicable data formats:

```
- <Import>
  <Sending_Entity>NY</Sending_Entity>
  <Date_File_Created>2004-02-18</Date_File_Created>
  <Data_End_Date>2004-02-17</Data_End_Date>
  <NETSS_SiteID>36</NETSS_SiteID>
  <Number_Confirmed_Cases>3</Number_Confirmed_Cases>
  <Number_Probable_Cases>1</Number_Probable_Cases>
  <Number_Negative_Cases>1</Number_Negative_Cases>
  <Number_Indeterminate_Cases>0</Number_Indeterminate_Cases>
  <Number_NotDone_Cases>0</Number_NotDone_Cases>
  <Number_InProgress_Cases>0</Number_InProgress_Cases>
  <Number_Birds_Found>5</Number_Birds_Found>
- <Bird_Data>
  <Sending_Entity>NY</Sending_Entity>
  <Bird_ID>8444</Bird_ID>
  <Collection_Date>2002-01-01</Collection_Date>
  <Location_Address>9999 S Swan St</Location_Address>
  <Location_City>Albany</Location_City>
  <Location_Zip>12203</Location_Zip>
  <Location_County>Albany</Location_County>
  <Location_Latitude>42.659142</Location_Latitude>
  <Location_Longitude>-73.772406</Location_Longitude>
  <Bird_Species>WPU OTHER SPECIES</Bird_Species>
  <Number_Birds>1</Number_Birds>
  <WNV_Test_Results>P</WNV_Test_Results>
  <Captive_Or_Free_Ranging>F</Captive_Or_Free_Ranging>
  <Symptoms>Dead, trauma</Symptoms>
```

```
<Necropsy_Diagnosis>WPU diagnosis 1</Necropsy_Diagnosis>
<CDC_Week>1</CDC_Week>
</Bird_Data>
```

From an implementation perspective, the communication backbone module uses a collection of source-specific "adaptors" to communicate with underlying sources. We use the adaptor linking PHIN MS system and WNV-BOT Portal to illustrate a typical design of such adaptors. The data from NYSDOH to the portal system is transmitted in a "push" manner. NYSDOH sends secure PHIN MS messages to the portal nightly. The PHIN MS adaptor at the portal side runs a data receiver daemon listening for incoming messages. After a message is received, the adaptor will invoke the data ingest control module and stores the verified message in the portal's internal data store. The adaptor is also responsible for sending error and control messages back to PHIN MS if necessary. Other data sources (e.g., those from USGS) may have "pull" type adaptors which will periodically download information from the source systems and examine and store data in the portal's internal data store.

Another important function of the communication backbone module is data ingest control, which enforces different types of security checks ranging from account verification to data validation. The ingest control process is invoked by communication adaptors when a message is received. The first step of the process is to perform account authentication and ensure that the account is authorized to ingest data. (The HL7-based message/data payload is protected by public key encryption.) In the second step, the incoming message is examined by normalizing and cleansing subroutines before being saved in the portal data store. In this normalization and cleansing step, predefined dictionaries, taxonomy databases, and related string similarity measures such as Luvenshtein distance function, are used to identify possible typos in the incoming data. When typos are identified, the message is routed back to the data source for confirmation. At the end of the ingest control process, the message is converted into a standard HL7 XML format, ready to be stored in the Portal's internal data store.

### 3.3 Portal Data Store

A main objective of WNV-BOT Portal is to enable users from partnering states and organizations to share data. Typically data from different organizations has different designs and stored in different formats. To enable data interoperability, we use Health Level Seven (HL7) standards (http://www.hl7.org/) as the main storage format. In our approach, contributing data providers transmit data to WNV-BOT Portal as HL7-compliant XML messages through the secure communication backbone. After receiving these XML messages, WNV-BOT Portal will store them directly in its data store, a relational database built in Microsoft SQL server. This HL7 XML-based design provides a key advantage over an alternative design based on a consolidated database. In a consolidated database design, the portal data store has to consolidate and maintain all the data fields for all datasets. Whenever an underlying dataset changes its data structure, the portal data store needs to be redesigned and reloaded to reflect the changes. This severely limits system scalability and extensibility. Our HL7 XML-based approach does not have these limitations.

To alleviate potential computational performance problems associated with this HL7 XML-based approach while searching and querying, an index of stored XML objects is created. We have identified a core set of data fields based on which search will be done frequently and extracted these fields from all XML messages to be stored in separate database tables to enable fast retrieval. A flexible database schema is deployed to facilitate storage of different attributes from different datasets such as bird species from dead bird data and toxin types from Botulism cases. This design enables the Portal to dynamically generate customized search criteria for each dataset in the search process.

The access control API as part of the data store module is responsible for granting and restricting user access to sensitive data. To satisfy important data integrity and confidentiality requirements, we are implementing a central, role-based access control system. In this system, the owners of various WNV/BOT datasets specify explicitly the access privilege on datasets provided by them. To facilitate this access privilege elicitation process, we have developed a predefined set of privileges from which the data owners or providers can choose. Examples of such privileges include (a) "full visibility" indicating that all information is visible to any user; (b) "aggregation only at the county level" indicating that only aggregated information at the county level is visible to the user. There are two models to assign such privileges: the individual model and the trusted model. In the individual mode, the privileges are assigned directly to a specific individual user. In the trusted model, the data source administrator assigns access privileges to user roles as explained below.

In our current design, a user role is defined to have three parts: state, organization, and user type. For example, if user "John Smith" is from organization "AILab" in the state of Arizona and his type is "COORDINATOR," then the combination of Arizona, AILab and COORDINATOR is John's user role. A role can be represented by a string with various parts delimited by dots. For instance, the above role can be specified as "AZ.AILAB.COORINATOR." One user can have multiple roles in WNV-BOT Portal and these roles are assigned and managed by the administrator of each organization through a Web-based interface. Using the above system, the data owner/provider can easily specify which user roles are allowed to view the data, and which level of access privilege they may have. The access control API will ensure that these specified access control rules apply to all data access requests.

## 3.4  Web Portal

The WNV-BOT Portal website (http://wnvbot.eller.arizona.edu) is the main user interface, through which the user queries WNV/Botulism databases, analyses and visualizes datasets, and accesses alerting messages. Portal and site administrators also manage data access rules and user roles through the website. In this section, we present a use scenario to highlight the key data query and visualization functions provided by the Portal.

**3.4.1 Data Query and Search.** A typical data query process is comprised of five steps: (1) the user selects the disease of interest; (2) the user selects interested datasets; (3) the user specifies the time and geographic ranges of interest; (4) the system displays the returned query results; and (5) the user uses a visualization tool to summarize and explore interactively the returned results. We use the following example to illustrate how a user can access the Portal databases and perform basic searches and queries. Consider a user who is interested in WNV-positive, dead crow cases in New York State between 2001 and 2003. This example uses a test (not real) data set. After logging onto the Portal, the user first selects the disease of interest, in this case,

WNV. The Portal then presents a list of WNV-related datasets from which the user can choose. The metadata associated with the datasets is also shown next to the displayed dataset names. The datasets that the user does not have access privilege to will be listed at the bottom of the page. If the user needs to view the unprivileged datasets, he or she can request the access through the Portal. In the use scenario, the user selects the NY_DEADBIRD dataset to which the access privilege is available. By clicking the "advanced" button, the user accesses the "advanced search" mode. A list of source-specific attributes is presented and the user can submit fine-grained search criteria. In our example, the user selects the "Positive," "ND," and "unknown" statuses and the "crow" species. In addition, the user specifies the interested time range as that between "2001-01-01" and "2003-12-31," and the interested location as "All counties" from New York State.

After receiving all search criteria, the Portal system performs the searches and displays the query results in a table. Results are grouped by the dataset, and the name of the dataset and the number of the returned data items are shown in the title bar. The first row of the table shows the names of the various data fields returned. When the user moves the mouse over this first row, a pop-up tool-tip will be shown to provide a short description of the corresponding data field. (Note that depending on the access privilege the user or the associated user role has over the underlying datasets, this table may show data in different granularity even given the same search criteria). In our example, we assume the user has full access privilege and 475 data records in total are returned containing details such as case ID, date, state, county, status, and bird species. Figure 3 illustrates these four steps of the data query process discussed above.

**3.4.2 Spatial-Temporal Visualization.** This section focuses on Step 5 of the data query and analysis step, i.e., visualization. The role of visualization techniques in the context of large and complex dataset exploration is to organize and characterize the data visually to assist users in overcoming the information overload problem [13]. WNV-BOT Portal makes available an advanced visualization module, called the Spatial Temporal Visualizer (STV) to facilitate exploration of infectious disease case data and to summarize query results. STV is a generic visualization environment that can be used to visualize a number of spatial temporal datasets simultaneously. It allows the user to load and save spatial temporal data in a dynamic manner for exploration and dissemination. STV has three integrated and synchronized views: periodic, timeline, and GIS. The periodic view provides the user with an intuitive display to identify periodic temporal patterns. The timeline view provides a 2D timeline along with a hierarchical display of the data elements organized as a tree. The GIS view displays cases and sightings on a map. Figure 4 illustrates how these three views can be used to explore infectious disease dataset: The top left panel shows the GIS view. The user can select multiple datasets to be shown on the map in a layered manner using the checkboxes. The top right panel corresponds to the timeline view displaying the occurrences of various cases using a Gantt chart-like display. The user can also access case details easily using the tree display located left to the timeline display. Below the timeline view is the periodic view through which the user can identify periodic temporal patterns (e.g., which months have an unusually high number of cases). The bottom portion of the interface allows the user to specify subsets of data to be displayed and analyzed.

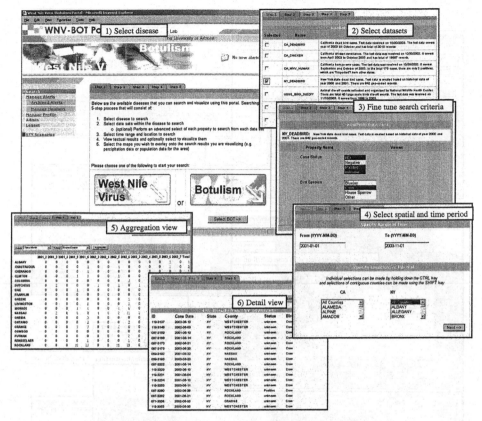

**Fig. 3.** Query West Nile virus Data through WNVBOT portal

We now illustrate how the user can use the visualization module for summarization and analysis purposes. Continuing from the scenario discussed in the previous section, the user clicks on the "visualization details" button to enter the visualization interface. Three background layers are available for the user to select: (1) geographic maps including national and state borders, rivers, and major roads, (2) land information including precipitation, temperature, and vegetation, and (3) demographic data such as population and unemployment rates. In Figure 4, the user has selected "New York State population 2000" and "major rivers" to observe possible correlations between dead crow cases and population/water distribution.

The user first selects to visualize all the cases from 2001-01-01 to 2003-12-31. This example uses a test (not real) data set. The periodic view indicates that in June there has been a surge of dead bird cases. By reducing and moving the time window, the user can further observe case distribution (by month) in each year using the periodic view. For instance, it can be observed that for each calendar year, all cases started in March and reached the climax in June. Using the GIS view, the user can selectively overlay case data on top of major rivers and population maps. It can be observed that many cases have been distributed along the populous areas along Hudson River.

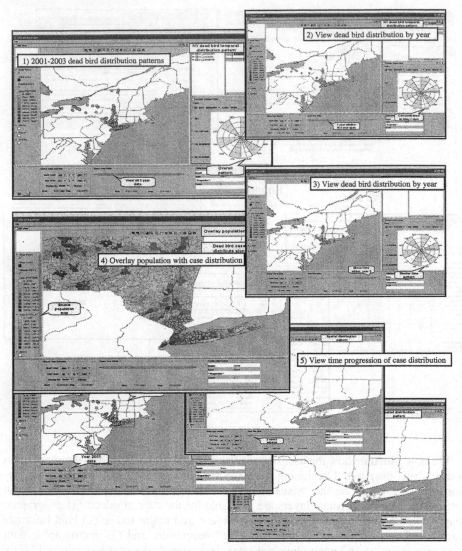

**Fig. 4.** Using STV to Visualize West Nile virus Data

Assume that the user now intends to find out more about case progression in the Long Island area in 2001. The user sets the global data time window to be from 2001-01-01 to 2001-12-31 and then zooms into the Long Island area using the zoom tool provided as part of the GIS view. By reducing the time window down to a two-week period and moving the time slider slowly from the beginning of the year to the end, the user can clearly see the case progression. In this example, the cases started in East Long Island around March and then gradually moved toward West and upstate. Internally, the STV tool has a scalable and flexible design to support its rich functionality. It has two main components: data preparation and user interface. The data preparation component requires an information source, a map server, and a conversion API to convert data into an XML-based format internal to the STV. The user interface component is implemented using Java WebStart™ technology which enables cross-platform, installation-free, and Web-based execution.

This component follows the standard Model-View-Control pattern (MVC) and uses a conversion API to convert XML input into an internal data model and an event-listener bridge to synchronize three views. Because of this flexible design, STV directly supports data feed from various methods including databases, flat files, among others. In WNV-BOT Portal, Microsoft SQL server is used to store the data and the ARCIMS map server is used as a map server. Incorporating new datasets for visualization can be done fairly efficiently. In a recent case, we successfully developed a visualization module for an air pathogen-sensing dataset within a week by one programmer.

**3.4.3 Alerting and Hotspot Analysis.** Our ongoing effort is focused on two aspects of infectious disease informatics: efficient alerting and hotspot analysis. For the past decades, alert dissemination networks such as Health Alert Network (HAN) systems are being developed and deployed in state public health agencies. However, there is a critical need to create cross-jurisdiction alerts and to automate the dissemination process. We are developing an advanced alerting module as part of WNV-BOT Portal to complement alerting and surveillance systems that already exist in various states. In our current design, alert messages can come from the following three sources: (a) The user can specify personalized triggering conditions (e.g., "notifying me if there are four Botulism cases within the past two days"), (b) The predictive models, as discussed later, will consider datasets from different origins and suggest with high confidence that a disease outbreak is in progress, (c) Public health officials may want to send alerts across organizational and state boundaries. Depending on the nature of the alert messages, some of them may be reviewed by designated personnel. The dissemination module will route the messages through state HAN systems to the public health professionals or send them via registered email address to Portal users when applicable.

In building predictive models for data with spatial and temporal attributes, Hotspot analysis is an approach widely applied in crime analysis and disease informatics applications. Hotspot is a condition indicating some form of clustering in a spatial and temporal distribution. For WNV, localized clusters of dead birds typically identify high risk disease areas. Automatic detection of dead bird clusters using hotspot analysis can help predict disease outbreaks and allocate prevention/control resources effectively. Most of existing disease informatics research uses the spatial scan statistic techniques to perform hotspot analysis. We are currently applying other hotspot analysis techniques (e.g., Risk-Adjusted Nearest Neighbor Hierarchical Clustering) that have been developed and successfully applied in crime analysis to disease informatics [7, 10]. Initial experimental results indicate that these techniques are complementary to the spatial scan techniques in many regards. In a broader context, we are pursuing research in vector borne emerging infection predictive modeling. In particular, we are (a) augmenting existing predictive models by taking additional factors (e.g., weather information, bird migration patterns) into consideration, and (b) tailoring data mining techniques for infectious disease datasets that have prominent temporal features.

## 4  Summary and Future Research

This paper presents a collaborative effort between IT researchers and public health agencies aimed at developing a scalable information sharing, analysis, and visualization environment in the domain of infectious diseases. The resulting prototype system, WNV-BOT Portal, focuses on two prominent disease types and has successfully demonstrated the technological feasibility of integrating and interoperating infectious disease datasets for multiple diseases and across jurisdictions. Our project has supported exploration of and experimentation with technological infrastructures needed for the full-fledged implementation of a national infectious disease information infrastructure and helped foster information sharing and collaboration among related government agencies at state and federal levels. In addition, we have obtained important insights and hands-on experience with various important policy-related challenges faced by developing a national infrastructure. For example, a nontrivial part of our project activity has been centered around developing data sharing agreements between project partners from different states.

We conclude this paper by discussing the pathway leading to the national infectious disease information infrastructure based on the lessons learned from our WNV-BOT project. Due to the complexity of such an infrastructure from both technical and policy standpoints, we envision that its development path will follow a bottom-up, evolutionary approach. Initially, each individual state will develop its own integrated infectious disease infrastructure for a limited number of diseases. Following successful deployment of such systems, regional nodes linking neighboring states can be established. Such regional nodes will leverage both state sources and data from federal agencies such as CDC, USGS, and USDA. National and international infrastructures will then become a natural extension and integration of these regional nodes, covering most infectious disease types.

## References

1. Berndt, D., Hevner, A. and Studnicki, J.: Bioterrorism Surveillance with Real-Time Data Warehousing. *NSF/NIJ Symposium on Intelligence and Security Informatics*, 2003.
2. M.Chang, M. Glynn, and S. Groseclose.: Endemic, notifiable bioterrorism-related diseases, united states, 1992-1999. *Emerging Infectious Diseases*, 9(5):556–564, 2003
3. Chen, H., Zeng, D., Atabakhsh, H., Wyzga, W. and Schroeder, J.: COPLINK: manging law enforcement data and knowledge. *CACM* 46(1), 28-34, 2003.
4. Damianos, L., Ponte, J., Wohlever, S., Reeder, F., Day, D., Wilson, G. and Hirschman, L.: MiTAP for Bio-Security: A Case Study. *AI Magazine*, 23(4), 13-29, 2002.
5. Gotham, I. J., Eidson, M., White, D. J., Wallace, B. J., Chang, H. G., Johnson, G. S., Napoli, J. P., Sottolano, D. L., Birkhead, G. S., Morse, D. L., and Smith, P. F.: West Nile virus: a case study in how NY State Health Information infrastructure facilitates preparation and response to disease outbreaks. *J Public Health Manag Pract*, 7(5), 75-86, 2001.
6. Hand, D. J.: *Discrimination and Classification*. Wiley, Chichester, U.K, 1981.
7. Jain, A. K., Murty, M. N., and Flynn, P. J.: Data clustering: a review. *ACM Computing Surveys*, 31(3), 264-323, 1999.
8. Kay, B. A., Timperi, R. J., Morse, S. S., Forslund, D., McGowan, J. J. and O'Brien, T.: Innovative Information-Sharing Strategies. Emerging Infectious Diseases, 4(3), 1998.

9. Kargupta, H., Liu, K. and Ryan, J.: Privacy Sensitive Distributed Data Mining from Multi-Party Data. *Proc. of ISI 2003*, 336-342, 2003.
10. Levine, N.: *CrimeStat: A Spatial Statistics Program for the Analysis of Crime Incident Locations (v 2.0)*. Ned Levine & Associates, Houston, TX, and the National Institute of Justice, Washington, DC. May 2002.
11. Pinner, R. W., Rebmann, C. A., Schuchat, A. and Hughes, J. M.: Disease Surveillance and the Academic, Clinical, and Public Health Communities. Emerging Infectious Disease, 9(7), 2003.
12. Siegrist, D. W.: The Threat of Biological Attack: Why Concern Now? *Emerging Infectious Diseases*, 5(4), 2002.
13. Zhu, B., Ramsey, M. and Chen, H.: Creating a Large-scale Content-based Airphoto Image Digital Library. *IEEE Transactions on Image Processing, Special Issue on Image and Video Processing for Digital Libraries*, 9(1), 163-167, 2000.

# A Novel Policy and Information Flow Security Model for Active Network

Zhengyou Xia[1], Yichuan Jiang[2], Yiping Zhong[2], and Shiyong Zhang[2]

[1] Department of computer, NanJing University of Aeronautics and Astronautics, China
Zhengyou_xia@yahoo.com
[2] Department of Computer information & technology, Fudan University, China
{jiangyc,zhongyp,shizhang}@fudan.edu.cn

**Abstract.** In this paper, we describe the active network security model from access control and information flow model. We present an access control policy called family tree policy for active network. The family tree policy can correctly represent active network that cannot be correctly modeled by BLP and Chinese wall model. At the same time, we further research the information flow security properties of active network and present the novel methods to research the information flow based on inheriting classes. The properties of information flow are described by properties of the inheriting class inner flow and flow among the different inheriting classes. Research For the inheriting class flow, the classic information flow model can be used. For the flow among the inheriting classes, we present a novel method to research it based on the conception of timestamp and flow.

## 1 Introduction

Active networks [1][2] provide a programmable platform on which network services can be defined or altered by injecting code or other information into the nodes of the network. This paradigm offers a number of potential advantages, including the ability to develop and deploy new network protocols and services quickly, and the ability to customize services to meet the different needs of the different classes of users.

Since the concept of the active network was put forward in 1996, the current active network research focuses on the support of flexible, dynamically changing [3][4], and fine-grained quality of service. Similar to traditional network security, it is crucial thing for active networks to protect its security. Active network security presents significant security challenges. There are a little research security features that exploit active networking. Despite significant energy devoted to security research in active networks [3][4][5], the issues of the security are by no means solved. This paper attempts to present active network security from access control policy and information flow model. Since the active network is different from the passive network, we present the novel access control policy (family tree policy) for active network. At the same time, we further research the information flow security properties of active network and present the novel methods to research the information flow based on inheriting classes.

H. Chen et al. (Eds.): ISI 2004, LNCS 3073, pp. 42–55, 2004.

## 2 Related Work and Motivation

The DARPA active network community has defined architecture for an active network node (ANN)[1][5]. That depicts a node as comprising a Node OS and one or more Execution Environments. The Execution Environments (EEs) provide a programming interface or virtual machine that can be programmed or controlled by the active packets. We briefly describe a simple threat model in figure1, which can be used to evaluate the effectiveness of our proposed solution to the active networks security problem.

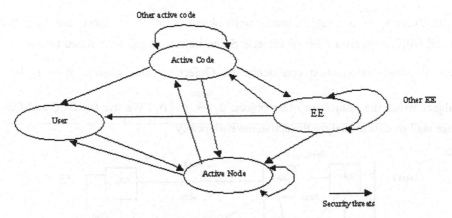

**Fig. 1.** Security threats model

**Node's viewpoint for threat:** The node hopes to protect its resource against unauthorized usage, protect the availability of its services, protect the integrity of the state that will allow it to continue to offer services, and protect its state against unauthorized exposure.

**EE's viewpoint for threat:** The EE can feel these threats coming from other EEs, from the senders of packets, and from the active code it hosts, Because others EEs may consume resources of active node that should allocated to EE. At the same time, packets may consume resource of EE.

**Active code/active packet's viewpoint for threat:** A node may wish to access an active code to install it, to retrieve it, to modify it, to terminate it, etc. Active code/packet may be able to create state that can be shared data and packet payload from unauthorized exposure or modification, to protect its services from unauthorized use, and to protect its resources against unauthorized usage.

**The sender's viewpoint for threat:** The sender of the active packet hope to protect the data being transmitted in the packet: ensure the integrity and confidentiality of the data in the packet and ensure other attributes of the packet not represented by the bits in the packet such as the latency through the network. The sender of the packet feels threats directly to the data in the packet from other active code in the node, from the execution environment and from the node itself.

Let S be a set of subjects, O be a set of objects. $s_i \in S, o_j \in O, (i, j = 1 \cdots n)$. AA is set of active applications that consist of active codes/packets and EE be set of execution environments. $AA_i \in AA, EE_j \in EE, (i, j = 1 \cdots n)$. We can define the following operations:

Subject can access object: $s_i \overset{access}{\sim} o_j$.    Subject cannot access object: $s_i \overset{access}{\nsim} o_j$. Subject can read object: $s_i \overset{read}{\sim} o_j$.    Subject cannot read object: $s_i \overset{read}{\nsim} o_j$. Subject can write object: $s_i \overset{write}{\sim} o_j$. Subject cannot write object: $s_i \overset{write}{\nsim} o_j$. Subject read the j BLP model [6][7] comprises a set of subjects S and objects O and formulated two principles to protect information confidentiality. Object or other object: $s_i \overset{read}{\sim} o_j | o_k$, subject writes the j object or other object: $s_i \overset{write}{\sim} o_j | o_k$. We use the BLP and Chinese wall models to analyze the active network policy.

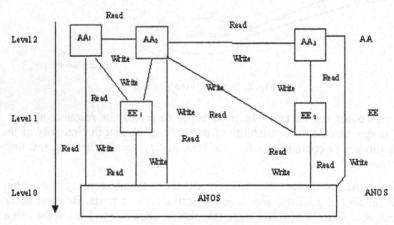

**Fig. 2.** BLP models active networks

## 2.1 BLP Model to Analyze Active Network

**The simple security property:** A subject s is allowed to read access to an object o if and only if C(s) dominates C (o).

**The *property:** A subject s is not allowed to write to an object o if and only if C (o) dominates C(s).

We analyze the result of BLP modeling active network policy .It is shown in figure 2 .In active node, there are three components. They are AA (active applications consist of active codes/active packets), EE (execution environment) and ANOS (active node OS). The level of different $EE_i$ is the same. Similarly, the level of different

$AA_j$ is also the same. According to BLP model, AA can read data from EE and ANOS; However, AA cannot write data into EE and ANOS. Similarly, EE can read data form ANOS and write data into AA; however EE cannot write data into ANOS and read data from AA. ANOS can write data into AA and EE and cannot read data from EE and AA. However, different $AA_j$ must be executed on the different $EE_i$ that corresponds with the $AA_j$ and the $EE_i$ only execute the corresponding $AA_j$.

If we apply the BLP model to the active network policy, we can get the following five results:

$$AA_1 \overset{read}{\sim} EE_1, AA_1 \overset{read}{\sim} EE_2, AA_2 \overset{read}{\sim} EE_1, AA_2 \overset{read}{\sim} EE_2, AA_3 \overset{read}{\sim} EE_1, AA_3 \overset{read}{\sim} EE_2,$$

$$AA_1 \overset{read}{\sim} ANOS, \quad AA_2 \overset{read}{\sim} ANOS, \quad AA_3 \overset{read}{\sim} ANOS$$

$$EE_1 \overset{write}{\sim} AA_1, EE_1 \overset{write}{\sim} AA_2, EE_1 \overset{write}{\sim} AA_3, EE_2 \overset{write}{\sim} AA_1, EE_2 \overset{write}{\sim} AA_2,$$

$$EE_2 \overset{write}{\sim} AA_3, EE_1 \overset{read}{\sim} ANOS, EE_2 \overset{read}{\sim} ANOS.$$

$$AA_1 \overset{access}{\sim} AA_2, AA_1 \overset{access}{\sim} AA_3, AA_2 \overset{access}{\sim} AA_1, AA_2 \overset{access}{\sim} AA_3, AA_3 \overset{access}{\sim} AA_2,$$

$$AA_3 \overset{access}{\sim} AA_1, EE_1 \overset{access}{\sim} EE_2, EE_2 \overset{access}{\sim} EE_1, ANOS \overset{write}{\sim} AA_1,$$

$$ANOS \overset{write}{\sim} AA_2, ANOS \overset{write}{\sim} AA_3, ANOS \overset{write}{\sim} EE_1, ANOS \overset{write}{\sim} EE_2$$

These operations are not all allowed in active network security architecture. According to the above security threat model of active network, the following operations must be ensured in active network secure architecture.

Secure operation requirement of Active network:

$$AA_1 \overset{read}{\sim} EE_1, AA_1 \overset{read}{\sim} EE_2, AA_2 \overset{read}{\sim} EE_1, AA_2 \overset{read}{\sim} EE_2, AA_3 \overset{read}{\sim} EE_1, AA_3 \overset{read}{\sim} EE_2,$$

$$AA_1 \overset{read}{\sim} ANOS, \quad AA_2 \overset{read}{\sim} ANOS,$$

$$AA_3 \overset{read}{\sim} ANOS \ EE_1 \overset{write}{\sim} AA_1, EE_1 \overset{write}{\sim} AA_2, EE_1 \overset{write}{\sim} AA_3,$$

$$EE_2 \overset{write}{\sim} AA_1, EE_2 \overset{write}{\sim} AA_2, EE_2 \overset{write}{\sim} AA_3, EE_1 \overset{read}{\sim} ANOS, EE_2 \overset{read}{\sim} ANOS.$$

$$AA_1 \overset{access}{\sim} AA_2, AA_1 \overset{access}{\sim} AA_3, AA_2 \overset{access}{\sim} AA_1, AA_2 \overset{access}{\sim} AA_3, AA_3 \overset{access}{\sim} AA_2,$$

$$AA_3 \overset{access}{\sim} AA_1, EE_1 \overset{access}{\sim} EE_2, EE_2 \overset{access}{\sim} EE_1, ANOS \overset{write}{\sim} AA_1,$$

$$ANOS \overset{write}{\sim} AA_2, ANOS \overset{write}{\sim} AA_3, ANOS \overset{write}{\sim} EE_1, ANOS \overset{write}{\sim} EE_2$$

If we use BLP to model the active network, we will violate secure operations of active network and cannot ensure the active network security. For example, $AA_1 \overset{access}{\nrightarrow} AA_2$, $EE_1 \overset{write}{\sim} AA_3$ $AA_3 \overset{access}{\sim} AA_1$ and $EE_1 \overset{access}{\sim} EE_2$, etc, are allowed by using BLP model. However, the operations are forbidden in active network secure architecture, because the AA sees the threat arising from the other AA and the EE can feel these threats from other EE. Therefore, we can assert that single BLP model cannot model the active network information flow.

## 2.2 Chinese Wall Model to Analyze the Active Network

We now apply the Chinese wall to model the active network policy. The Chinese wall model [8] has the following rules.

**The simple security:** People are only allowed to access information, which is not held to conflict with any other information that they already possess.

**\*Property:** write access is only permitted if

a)  Access is permitted by the simple security rule, and
b)  No subject can be read which is in a different company dataset to the one for which write access is requested and contains un-sanitized information.

According to Chinese wall model, we model active network policy. It is shown in figure3. There would be three conflicts of interest classes, one for AA (containing all active code executing on active node), one for EE (containing EE existing in active node) and the last for active node OS. If we apply Chinese wall model to active network, we can get the five results:

1) AA1, AA2 and AA3 belong to the same conflict of interest class. If users access any one of AA, they cannot access other AA. For example, if users execute AA1, they cannot access AA2 and AA3 ( $AA_1 \overset{access}{\nrightarrow} AA_2$, $AA_2 \overset{access}{\nrightarrow} AA_1$, $AA_1 \overset{access}{\nrightarrow} AA_3$,

$AA_3 \overset{access}{\nrightarrow} AA_1$, $AA_2 \overset{access}{\nrightarrow} AA_3$, $AA_3 \overset{access}{\nrightarrow} AA_2$ ).

2) EE1 and EE2 belong to the same conflict of interest class. If users access any one of EE, they cannot access other EE. For example, if users access EE1, they cannot access EE2 ( $EE_2 \overset{access}{\nrightarrow} EE_1$, $EE_1 \overset{access}{\nrightarrow} EE_2$ ).

3) EE, AA and ANOS belong to different conflict of interest class and User can access any one from different conflict of interest class.

4) When user accesses one AA from the first conflict of interest class, they still have freedom to access any one of EE from the second conflict of interest class. ( $AA_1 \overset{read}{\sim} EE_2 \mid EE_1, AA_2 \overset{read}{\sim} EE_2 \mid EE_1, AA_3 \overset{read}{\sim} EE_2 \mid EE_1$ ).

5) When user accesses some one EE from the second conflict of interest class, they still have freedom to access any one of AA from the first conflict of interest class.

$$( EE_1 \overset{write}{\sim} AA_2 \mid AA_1 \mid AA_3 \, , EE_2 \overset{write}{\sim} AA_2 \mid AA_1 \mid AA_3 ).$$

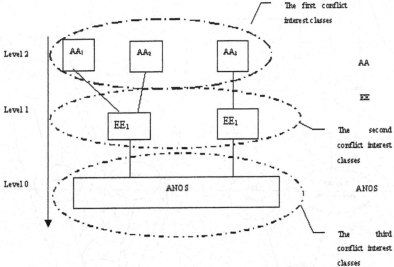

**Fig. 3.** Chinese wall models active network

According to active network security architecture and security threat model, the first and second results are accord with security requirement of active network. However, the fourth and fifth results are volatile with principle of active network security architecture and security threat model. In active network security architecture, $AA_i$ can only execute on $EE_j$ that is accord with the $AAi$. $EE_j$ can only access the $AA_i$ that is accord with $EE_j$ .For example when AA1 is forward to active node; the AA1 can only be executed on EE1 and cannot be executed by EE2.Though the EE and AA belong to different conflicts of interest class, according to active network secure architecture, when the user first accesses $AA_i$ or $EE_j$ from the one conflict of interest class, user doesn't have freedom to accesses $EE_j$ or $AA_i$ from the other conflict of interest class. Therefore, the single Chinese wall cannot model the active network policy. In order to model active network, we present a new kind of security policy, we called it Family Tree policy. The model is described detailed in the next section.

## 3   Family Tree Policies and Its Property

Access control is the process of mediating every request to resource and data maintained by an active node system and determining whether the request should be granted or denied. From the above section we assert that the BLP and Chinese wall cannot model the active network policy, then we presents the novel access control policy called family tree policy for active network.

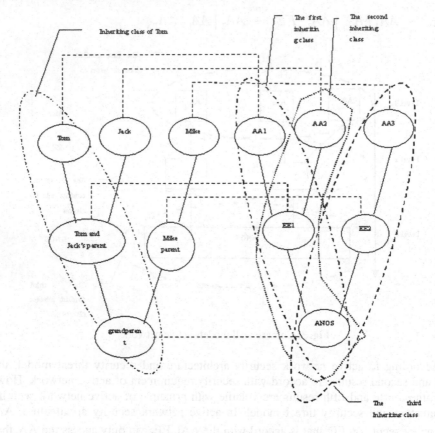

**Fig. 4.** Family tree policy for active networks

The family tree policy is shown in figure 4. Grandparent is the root of family tree. Tom and Jack inherit from their parent. Mike inherits from the parent. If we consider one inheriting class from view of Tom, the inheriting class includes {Tom, Tom and Jack's parent, grandparent}. Similarly, the inheriting class of Jack and Mike is respectively {Jack, Tom and Jack's parent, grandparent} and {Mike, Mike' parent, grandparent}. In the same inheriting class there is different level between components. We suppose the level of Jack, Tom and Mike as the second level. Their parent and grand parent is defined as the first level and zero level respectively. We now map family tree to the active network. That is. We can get the following:

$$f: family \ tree \rightarrow active \ network$$

$$f: grandparent \rightarrow ANOS \quad f: Tom \ and \ Jack's \ parent \rightarrow EE_1,$$

$$f: Mike'parent \rightarrow EE_2 \quad f: Tom \rightarrow AA_1, \ Jack \rightarrow AA_2, \ Mike \rightarrow AA_3,$$

Similarly, we can get the inheriting class of the AA1, AA2 and AA3.

$$AA_1 : \{AA_1, EE_1, ANOS\}; AA_2 : \{AA_2, EE_1, ANOS\}; AA_3 : \{AA_3, EE_2, ANOS\}$$

We consider the family tree policy to have the following two properties. That is simple property and * property.

**Simple property (Access Property):** A Subject cannot access the object of different inheriting class that doesn't belong to the subject inheriting class. Similarly, the subject of different inheriting class that doesn't belong to the object inheriting class cannot access the object. The subject in the same inheriting class can only access a Subject can only access the object in the same inheriting class and the object. All different inheriting classes have the same one ancestor. The ancestor can access any inheriting class and comply with BLP model.

**\* Property:** Write access is only permitted if

Access is permitted by the simple security rule, and a subject is allowed to write to an object o if and only if subject dominates object.

According to the properties of family tree policy, we analyze the active network policy to get the following conclusion:

In the inheriting class of AA1, we can get $AA_1 \overset{read}{\sim} EE_1$, $EE_1 \overset{read}{\sim} ANOS$,

$AA_1 \overset{read}{\sim} ANOS$, $ANOS \overset{write}{\sim} EE_1$, $EE_1 \overset{write}{\sim} AA_1$, $ANOS \overset{write}{\sim} AA_1$

In the inheriting class of AA2, we can get $AA_2 \overset{read}{\sim} EE_1$, $EE_1 \overset{read}{\sim} ANOS$,

$AA_2 \overset{read}{\sim} ANOS$, $ANOS \overset{write}{\sim} EE_1$, $EE_1 \overset{write}{\sim} AA_2$, $ANOS \overset{write}{\sim} AA_2$

In the inheriting class of AA3, we can get $AA_3 \overset{read}{\sim} EE_2$, $EE_2 \overset{read}{\sim} ANOS$,

$AA_3 \overset{read}{\sim} ANOS$, $ANOS \overset{write}{\sim} EE_2$, $EE_2 \overset{write}{\sim} AA_3$, $ANOS \overset{write}{\sim} AA_3$

According to access property, in the different inheriting class, we can get the following operations. $AA_1 \overset{read}{\nsim} EE_2$, $AA_2 \overset{read}{\nsim} EE_2$, $AA_3 \overset{read}{\nsim} EE_1$, $EE_1 \overset{access}{\nsim} EE_2$,

$EE_2 \overset{access}{\nsim} EE_1$, $AA_1 \overset{access}{\nsim} AA_2$, $AA_2 \overset{access}{\nsim} AA_1$, $AA_1 \overset{access}{\nsim} AA_3$, $AA_3 \overset{access}{\nsim} AA_1$,

$AA_2 \overset{access}{\nsim} AA_3$, $AA_3 \overset{access}{\nsim} AA_2$, $EE_1 \overset{write}{\nsim} AA_3$, $EE_2 \overset{write}{\nsim} AA_1$, $EE_2 \overset{write}{\nsim} AA_2$.

The above conclusion is accord with the secure operations requirement of active network security and security threat model. These can ensure security for the active network. Supposing, the AA1 is executing on active node and sends request to access EE2. If the active network is modeled by BLP or Chinese wall policy model, the request of AA1 is allowed. In fact this is forbidden in active network. If the active network is modeled by family tree policy, according to the access property of family tree policy, the request of AA1 is refused, because the EE2 is not in the same inheriting class of AA1. Supposing, the AA1 is executing on active node and send request access AA2 or AA3. If we use the BLP to model the active network, the request of AA1 is allowed. If Chinese wall is used to model the active network, the request of AA1 is refused. If the active network is modeled by the family tree, the request of the AA1 is refused.

Similarly, the EE1 sends request to access AA3. If the BLP and Chinese wall model is used to model active network policy, this request is allowed. However, the request is not allowed in active network secure architecture. If the family tree policy is used to model active network policy, the request of EE1 is not allowed.

In order to discuss other properties of family tree policy, Now we formalize these properties.

Let S be a set of subjects, O be a set of objects, FT be family Tree of system and root is the root of FT. $L_i$ be leaf of FT, ($i = 1, \cdots n$) and $n_i$ be node of family tree. $IC_{L_i}$ is defined as inheriting class of $L_i$.

The composing inheriting class algorithm is described as the following:

According to Subject and Object of system, a family tree (FT) is constructed.

Initial leaf $L_i$ ,(i=1)

Choose one leaf, $L_i$    $IC_{L_i}$ = $\{L_i\}$ .

$L_i = L_i.parent$

$IC_{L_i} = IC_{L_i} + \{L_i\}$

If Li<>root go to d
i++

     $i \leq n$

If        go to c

END


## 4   Information Flow Security

From the architecture of active network, we known there are five kinds of information flows in active network. It is shown as the figure 5.

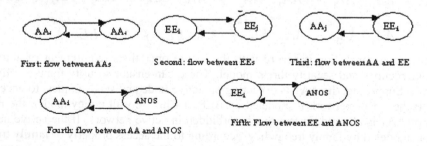

Fig. 5. Information flow in active network

In active network, the AA, EE and ANOS are let as the second level, the first level and the zero level. From the figure 5, the first and second flows belong to the same level. However the third fourth and fifth flows belong to the different level. In classic information flow security model, the subject and object is comparatively flow between the high level and low level. There is little research for the same level information flow. In the active network secure architecture, the first and second flow is prohibited. We cannot analyze the first and second information flow by using the classic information flow security properties. Therefore, we present a novel solution for analyze the information flow of the active network.

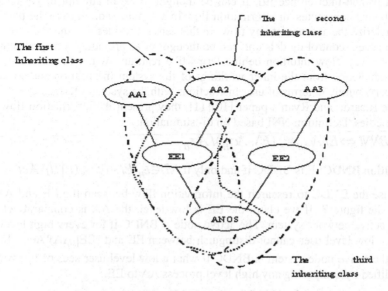

**Fig. 6.** Information flow based on inheriting class

We take figure 6 as an example. The first information flow in figure 4 is one among the AA1, AA2 and AA3. The second flow is information one between the EE1 and EE2. The third flow is the information one between $AA_i$ and $EE_j$ (i=1,2,3;j =1,2). The fourth flow is the information one between $AA_i$ and ANOS ((i=1,2,3). The fifth flow is information one between the $EE_j$ and ANOS. According to active network secure architecture, the AA1 and AA2 are only executed on EE1. The EE1 only supports the AA1 and AA2. The EE1 doesn't support the AA3. The AA3 is only executed on EE2. In order to analyze the information flow of active network, we introduce the ides of inheriting class of above section to analyze the information security properties of active network. We can get the three inheriting classes. The three inheriting classes is described as the following:

$$AA_1 : \{AA_1, EE_1, ANOS\}; AA_2 : \{AA_2, EE_1, ANOS\}; AA_3 : \{AA_3, EE_2, ANOS\}$$

From the above analyze, the information flows security properties of active network are researched as the flow of among the inheriting classes and the inheriting class inner flow. The first information flow is contained in the flow among the three different inheriting classes. The second information flow is contained in flow between the second and third inheriting classes. The third, fourth and fifth information flows are contained in the three different inheriting classes inner flow.

## 4.1 Information Flow Security Properties of Inheriting Class Inner

Since the inheriting class inner flow is relation of the high and low level, we can use the classic information flow security model to research the inheriting class inner flow.

Goguen and Meseguer based on some earlier work of Feiertag and Cohen proposed the idea of non-interference [9]. It can be thought of as an attempt to get to the essence of what constitutes an information flow in a system and, more to the point, how to characterize the absence of any flow. In this sense it resides at a more abstract level than the access-control models and can be thought of as providing a formal semantics to the one-way-.flow intuition behind terms like read and write. In particular, it abstracts completely from the inner workings of the system in question and formulates the property purely in terms of user interactions with the system interfaces.

In the Ricardo and Ryan's paper [10][11], they present the information flow security properties. Definition NNI based on bi- simulation:

$$E \in BNNI \Leftrightarrow E/Act_H \approx_B (E \backslash_I Act_H)/Act_H$$

**Proposition BNDC:** E is BNDC if and only if $\forall \Pi \in \varepsilon_H, E/Ac_H^t \approx_B (E|\Pi) \backslash Ac_H^t$.

We use the BNDC to research the information flow between the EE and AA. We can get the figure 7. If we claim the EE is low level, the AA is comparatively high level in active network system. The active node is BNDC if for every high level process AA a low level user cannot distinguish between EE and (EE| AA)\Act$_H$. In other words, the active node system is BNDC if what a low level user sees of the system is not modified by composing any high level process AA to EE.

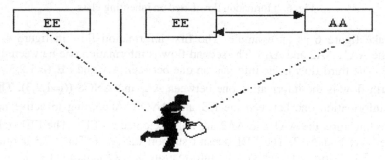

**Fig. 7.** Information flows between EE and AA based on BND C

## 4.2 Information Flow Security Properties between the Inheriting Flows

Information flow among the inheriting classes doesn't belong to flow between the high and low level. They are the same level, so we cannot use the classic information flow security properties to analyze them. In this section, we present a novel method to analyze them based on timestamp.

Let $IC_{it}$ ($i \in (1...n), t$ *denots time*) means the i inheriting class at t time. We hope the flow between the inheriting classes is independent.

$$P(^{IC_{it}}\!/_{IC_{jt}}) = P(IC_{it}) \quad i, j \in (1...n) \& i \neq j.$$

This means that the i inheriting class is independent from the j inheriting class at the t tine.

In order to ensure secure for active network, we can get the following requirement.

$$P(^{IC_{it}}\!/_{IC_{jt-1}}) = P(IC_{it}) \quad i, j \in (1...n) \& i \neq j.$$The requirement means that the i inheriting class at t time is independent from the j inheriting class at t-1 time. In other word, when an active application $AA_i$ is executing in executive environment at t time, $AA_i$ hopes that $AA_j$ that executing at t-1 time doesn't influence it.

Further, we consider the following condition.

$$P(^{IC_{it}}\!/_{IC_{jt}} \& IC_{it-1}) = P(IC_{it-1}) \quad and \quad P(^{IC_{it}}\!/_{IC_{jt-1}} \& IC_{it-1}) = P(IC_{it-1}).$$
$$i, j \in (1...n) \& i \neq j$$

It is that the i inheriting class at t time depends on the i inheriting class at t-1 time. This is accord with requirement of active network secure architecture, because an active application $AA_i$ executing at t time must depend on state of $AA_i$ executing in executive environment at t-1 time. In simple word, the state diversification of an inheriting class is only dependent on its state at t-1 time but independent on other classes' states at t or t-1 time.

If $P(^{IC_{it}}\!/_{IC_{jt}}) \neq P(IC_{it})$ $i, j \in (1...n) \& i \neq j$, it means the state diversification of inheriting class $IC_{it}$ at t time is depend on state of the $IC_{jt}$ at t time. At this condition, there are insecure information flows between the two inheriting classes. Let, a normal active application is executing in executive environment, at the same time, a malicious active application is executing in executive environment, too. If the state diversification of the normal active application is depend on state of malicious active application. The malicious active application will make unexpected harm on normal active application.

Similarly, $P(^{IC_{it}}\!/_{IC_{jt-1}}) \neq P(IC_{it})$ It means that the state diversification of $IC_{it}$ at t time is depend on state of $IC_{jt-1}$ at t-1 time, which denotes the flow among the inheriting classes at this condition is insecure. For example, when a normal active application is executing in executive environment, if the state of normal active application is depend on state of the malicious active application at the previous time, the normal active application will can be attacked by the malicious active application.

We further consider the complex condition, if the information flows between the inheriting classes satisfy the following condition.

$$P(^{IC_{it}}\!/_{IC_{jt-1}}) = P(IC_{it}) \quad and \quad P(^{IC_{it}}\!/_{IC_{jt}}) = P(IC_{it}) \quad i, j \in (1...n) \& i \neq j$$

And the information flows between the inheriting classes don't satisfy the following condition.

$$P(^{IC_{it}}/_{IC_{jt-1}} \ \& \ IC_{it-1}) \neq P(IC_{it-1}) \ \text{and} \ \ P(^{IC_{it}}/_{IC_{jt-1}} \ \& \ IC_{it-1}) \neq P(IC_{it-1}) \ \ i, j \in (1...n) \ \& \ i \neq j$$

At these conditions, the information flow among inheriting classes is insecure. However, these conditions are very strong restriction to design the monitor system of the active network. If we don't consider these conditions, it is necessary that the information flow among the inheriting classes ensure its security under the following conditions.

a) $P(^{IC_{it}}/_{IC_{jt}}) = P(IC_{it}) \ \ i, j \in (1...n) \ \& \ i \neq j$

b) $P(^{IC_{it}}/_{IC_{jt-1}}) = P(IC_{it}) \ \ i, j \in (1...n) \ \& \ i \neq j$

$$P(^{IC_{it}}/_{IC_{jt}} \ \& \ IC_{it-1}) = P(IC_{it-1}) \ \ \text{and} \ \ P(^{IC_{it}}/_{IC_{jt-1}} \ \& \ IC_{it-1}) = P(IC_{it-1})$$
$$i, j \in (1...n) \ \& \ i \neq j$$

## 5  Conclusion

In this paper, we describe the active network security model from access control and information flow model. Access control is the process of mediating every request to resource and data maintained by an active node system and determining whether the request should be granted or denied. We present an access control policy called family tree policy. The family tree policy can correctly represent active network that cannot be correctly modeled by BLP and Chinese wall model. In the family tree policy, the subjects and objects of the system are classified as different inheriting classes. A Subject cannot access the object of the different inheriting class. In the same inheriting class, the subject and object abide by the BLP model. All different inheriting classes have the same ancestor. The ancestor can access any inheriting class and comply with BLP model. In order to research the information flow security properties of active network, we use inheriting class ideas to analyze these information flows of active network. The properties of information flow are described by inner properties of the inheriting class and properties among different inheriting class. Using the properties between the different inheriting classes searches the first and second information flow of active network. The third, fourth and fifth information flow of active network is described by the inheriting class inner properties.

## References

1. Tennenhouse, D. and D. Wetherall.. Towards an Active Network Architecture. In Multimedia Computing and Networking. 1996. San Jose, CA.
2. D. Wetherall, John V. etc ANTS: A Toolkit for Building and Dynamically Deploying Network Protocols IEEE OPENARCH'98, San Francisco, CA, April 1998.

3. www.choices.cs.uiuc.edu/Security/seraphim/May2000/SecurityArchitecture.pdf a6AN Security working group. May 2000.
4. Roy H.Campbell, Zhaoyu Liu. Dynamic interoperable security architecture for active network. IEEE OPENARCH 2000, Israel, March 2000. 32-41.
5. K.L. Calvert, Architectural framework for active networks, version 1.0 University of Kentucky, July 1999. www.ccgatech.edu/project/canes/papers/arch-1-0.ps.gz.
6. D.E. Bell and L.J. LaPadula. Secure computer systems: Mathematical foundations.Technical Report ESD-TR-278, vol. 1, The Mitre Corp., Bedford, MA, 1973.
7. D. E. Bell. Secure computer systems: A re.nement of the mathematical model.Technical Report ESD-TR-278, vol. 3, The Mitre Corp., Bedford, MA, 1973.
8. D. F. C. Brewer and M. J. Nash. The Chinese wall security policy. In Proc. IEEE Symposium on Security and Privacy, pages 215–228, Oakland, CA, 1989.
9. A. Goguen and J. Meseguer, Security policies and security models, in: Proc. of the 1982 Symposium on Security and Privacy, pp. 11–20.
10. Focardi, R. and Gorrieri, R.: A Classification of Security Properties, JCS, 3(1):(1995) 5-33
11. Focardi, R., Gorrieri, R.: The Compositional Security Checker: A Tool for the Verification of Information Flow Security Properties. IEEE Trans. on Soft. Eng., 23(9): (1997) 550-571.

# A Novel Autonomous Trust Management Model for Mobile Agents*

Yichuan Jiang[1], Zhengyou Xia[2], Yiping Zhong[1], and Shiyong Zhang[1]

[1] Department of Computing & Information Technology, Fudan University
Shanghai 200433, P.R.China
jiangyichuan@yahoo.com.cn, {ypzhong,szhang}@fudan.edu.cn
[2] Department of computer, Nanjing University of Aeronautics and Astronautics,
Nanjing 210043, P.R.China
zhengyou_xia@yahoo.com

**Abstract.** Central trust mechanism and distributed trust mechanism are two dominant trust mechanisms. However, they are not well suited for mobile agent system since they can't achieve the trust management autonomy. To achieve the trust management autonomy, the paper presents a novel autonomous trust management model for mobile agents. In the presented model, every agent can implement trust management autonomously; agents can construct the global trust concept by the combination of trust information among agents; an agent can achieve the trust relation with other agent by trust path searching or trust negotiation. The simulation experiment results prove that our model is effective.

## 1 Introduction

Mobile agent technology is a research focus of artificial intelligence, which can make agents cooperate to perform the task. Mobile agent technology can support agent migration among hosts and make network application more flexible and effective [1]. However, the trust management of mobile agent remains as an unsolved question. If we don't solve such question well, the mobile agent technology can't achieve effective application in practice [2].

Now there have been some relative research works about the trust management of mobile agent, which are often based on the traditional security mechanism, such as access control list, role-based access control, PKI, etc.[3]. In those works, there always has a central repository to provide the access control and security trust information to individual agent or agents group, or has a trusted third party to provide the trust mechanism. We call those relative works as **Central Trust Mechanism**, which adopts the Trusted Authority (TA) or trusted third party to manage trust. Central Trust Mechanism is simple and effective, but it has many drawbacks, such as single point failure, the requirement of infrastructure, TA may become performance bottleneck, and so on. Obviously, the Central Trust Mechanism can't satisfy the requirement for the mobility and dynamics of mobile agent system.

---

* Supported by National High-Tech Research and Development Plan of China under Grant No. 2001AA142050

H. Chen et al. (Eds.): ISI 2004, LNCS 3073, pp. 56–65, 2004.

To solve the deficiency of Central Trust Mechanism, **Distributed Trust Mechanism** was proposed [5]. The well-known PGP trust model is a typical distributed trust one, which breaks the traditional hierachical trust architecture and does not need a central authorization organization to ensure the trust management, and the trust relation among entities is constructed by the credential signature [6]. Yosi Mass and Onn Shehory define and propose a distributed trust infrastructure in multi-agents system based on credential, which does not need a central credential mechanism or trusted third party [7], each agent can issue credential, an agent can be trusted if it can provide enough required credentials. However, in [7] only local trust can be realized and not global one. Moreover, [3] proposes a secure agent system model based on distributed trust and delegation mechanism, which integrates trust management and the delegation of permission trust together so as to provide effective security protection for agent.

Now distributed trust mechanism often constructs the trust relation by the valid credential signatures among agents, threshold cryptography and trust delegation. Though Distributed Trust Mechanism prevents single point failure, it increases the network load and delays service time, and it also deduces the success rate of constructing trust relation.

Autonomy is a characteristic and virtue of agent [8], so we should construct an autonomous trust management mechanism for mobile agent system. Though Distributed Trust Mechanism can be applied to mobile agent system in some degree, but they can't exert the autonomy of agent. The autonomous trust management should make each agent have the autonomous trust management function, which can make the trust mechanism of mobile agent more flexible and robust. Therefore, we launch the project of **Autonomous Trust Management** for Mobile Agents.

Srdjan Capkun, et al. presents a self-organized public-key management model for mobile ad hoc networks that allows users to generate their public-private key pairs, to issue certificates, and to perform authentication regardless of the network partitions and without any centralized services [9].

We refer the self-organization idea in [9] in some degree, and aiming at the characteristic of mobile agent system, propose an autonomous trust management model. In our model, every agent can make trust organization and management autonomously; agents can construct the global trust concept by the combination of trust information among agents. The model can well be suited for the mobile agent system.

The rest of the paper is organized as follows. Section 2 presents the related definition and makes a description for the question. Section 3 addresses the detail of autonomous trust management model. Section 4 makes simulation experiment. Then the paper concludes in Section 5.

## 2  Relative Definitions and Question Description

In [9], Srdjan Capkun, et al. presents the concept of certificate repository and certificate graph, referring to which, we present the concept of trust graph.

In mobile agent system, agents cooperate to perform tasks. Therefore, trust relation should be constructed among agents.

**Def 1. Agents Trust Relation Graph (ATRG):** ATRG denotes the trust relation among agents. ATRG= $(V, E)$ , where:

• $V$ denotes the agents;

• $E = V \times V$ denotes the trust relation among agents;

• $< v_1, v_2 >$ denotes that agent $v_1$ trusts $v_2$.

**Def 2. Agents Trust Sub-Graph (ATSG):** $\text{ATSG}_i$ denotes the trust information contained in agent i. $\text{ATSG}_i = (V', E')$ , where:

• $V' \subseteq V$ , which denotes the agents that have trust relation with agent i;

• $E' = V' \times V'$ denotes the trust relation among the agents of $V'$ , and $< v_1', v_2' >$

denotes that agent $v_1'$ trusts $v_2'$.

**Def 3. Agent Trust Path (ATP):** the trust path from agent i to j can be defined as an agent sequence $v_i, v_{i+1}, ..., v_n, ..., v_j$, where: $v_i$ trusts $v_{i+1}$, $v_{i+1}$ trusts $v_{i+2}$, ... , $v_{j-1}$ trusts $v_j$. The ATP denotes that agent i can get the trust relation with j after a series of trust delegation.

Each agent stores its own ATSG. In the initial phase of the system, each agent only holds the trust relations that it trusts or is trusted directly.

ATRG describes the global trust information of mobile agent system. In our model, in fact there isn't ATRG in the real mobile agent system, each agent only store the trust information related to itself. Only after continuous interaction and combination among agents, the concept of global trust can be achieved, and in real system such information doesn't exist really. Agents combine their trust sub-graphs by interaction, so the global trust concept can be achieved step by step. If agent i want to cooperate with j, i should find a trust path to j.

Fig 1 illustrates the relation of above concepts.

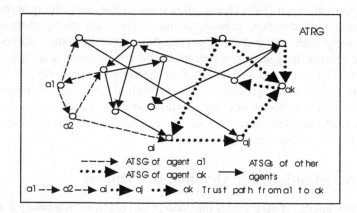

**Fig. 1.** Illustration of the Concept of ATRG, ATSG and ATP

Therefore, the question of this paper can be defined as:

- Each agent stores and manages its respective trust information (ATSG) autonomously;
- In the initial phase of the mobile agent system, the ATSG in each agent is very simple, each agent only holds the trust relations that it trusts or is trusted directly;
- Agents interact periodically and combine their ATSGs, therefore, the global trust information can be achieved gradually;
- If two agents want to construct trust relation, they should find a trust path from their ATSG2 after combination;
- If there aren't any paths between the two agents, then the two agents can construct trust relation by automated trust negotiation.

# 3 Autonomous Trust Management Model

## 3.1 Combination of Agent Trust Sub-graph

As said above, in the initial phase of the mobile agent system, the trust information in each agent is very simple, which are only trust relations that it trusts or is trusted directly. To achieve the global trust concept, agents need to combine their ATSGs.

The combination of ATSGs includes two kinds of situations: one is that each agent broadcast its trust information to the agents on neighboring nodes periodically, the broadcasting trust information contains the ATSG. The other is that agents exchange ATSG while they cooperates.

Each agent has a timer, the agent broadcasts trust information periodically (we can call the interval time as exchange period) to the agent on the neighboring hosts.

If two agents want to cooperate, they should construct their trust relation at first. At the same time, we can utilize the agents cooperation to exchange trust information for combination of ATSGs.

In the combination of ATSGs, each agent only absorbs the trust information that it hasn't and is relative to it. In this way, the global agents trust information can be achieved gradually.

Fig 2 is an example, in which we can see that the combination of ATSGs of a1 and a2.

The ATSG can be memorized as adjacency list which contains two kinds of nodes: headnode that denotes the agent, edgenode that denotes the one trusted by the agent of the corresponding headnode.

Next is the formal description of the data structure of ATSG.

```
typedef struct node
{agenttype trusting_agent;
 struct node *trust;
} edgenode;
typedef struct
{agenttype agent;
   edgenode *trust;
} headnode;
headnode ATSG[n];
```

Therefore, the ATSG memory structure of a1 after combination in Fig 2 is shown as Fig 3.

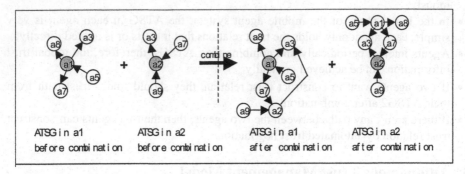

ATSG in a1
before combination

ATSG in a2
before combination

ATSG in a1
after combination

ATSG in a2
after combination

**Fig. 2.** Combination of ATSGs

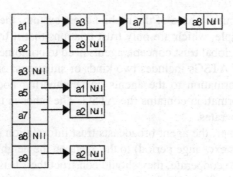

**Fig. 3.** Memory Structure of ATSG in a1

The combination algorithm can be seen in Algorithm 1.

*Algorithm 1.*

*Combination (headnode ATSG1[M],ATSG2[N]) /\*Comine ATSG2 into ATSG1\*/*

```
{
headnode ATSG1[m], ATSG2[n];
edgenode *temp, *point1;
edgenode *newedgenode;
headnode *newheadnode;
int k,b;
for (int i=0;i<n;i++)
{
/*Combine the agents trusted by ATSG1 into ATSG1*/
for (int j=0;j<m;j++)
 {if ATSG1[j].agent==ATSG2[i].agent
  {temp=ATSG2[i].trust;
  point1=ATSG1[j].trust;
  while temp <> null
   {b=0;
```

```
while (point1.trust <> null) && (b==0)
{if point1.trusting_agent == temp.trusting_agent
    b==1;
  point1=point1.trust;
  }
  if b==0
    {new newedgenode;/*create a new edgenode*/
    newedgenode.trusting_agent=temp.trusting_agent;
    newedgenode.trust=ADSG1[i].trust;
    ADSG1[i].trust=newedgenode;
    }
  point1=ATSG1[j].trust;
  temp=temp.trust;
  }
 }
}
/*Combine the agents that trust ATSG1 into ATSG1*/
temp=ATSG2[i].trust;
while temp<>null
{ for (j=0;j<m;j++)
  {if temp.trusting_agent==ATSG1[j].agent
    {m++;new newheadnode;/*create a new headnode*/
    newheadnode.agent=temp.trusting_agent;
    newheadnode.trust=ATSG2[i].trust;
    ATSG1[m]=newheadnode;
    temp=null;
    j=m;
    }
  };
  temp=temp.trust;
}}}
```

From the algorithm, we can see that the time complexity degree is $O(n^2m^2)$, so the algorithm can only perform well when the number of agents is few.

## 3.2  Construction of Trust Relation

If agent i wants to cooperate j, firstly it should construct a trust relation to j. The construction of trust relation has two kinds: one is that constructing relation by trust delegation among agents, i.e. looking for a trust path from i to j; other is that if there aren't any paths between the two agents, then the two agent can construct trust relation by automated trust negotiation.

**3.2.1 Searching for Trust Path.** Trust path is a structure based on trust delegation networks [11], which describes the trust relation delegated by a series of agents.

If agent i want to cooperate with j, i should firstly combine its ATSG with j's. Then i should search for a trust path to j in the new ATSG. Fig 4 shows a trust path searching process from a1 to a9.

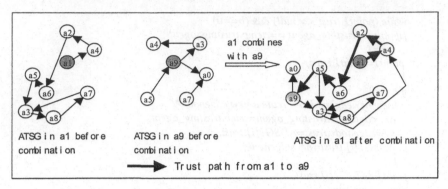

ATSG in a1 before combination

ATSG in a9 before combination

a1 combines with a9

ATSG in a1 after combination

→ Trust path from a1 to a9

**Fig. 4.** An Example of Searching for Trust Path

The algorithm that search for trust path can be seen in Algorithm 2.

*Algorithm 2.*
*int TrustPath_Searching (agenttype ai,aj; headnode ATSGi[m],ATSGj[n])*
*/\*for simplicity, next we denote the headnode or edgenode that contrains agent a as*
*node(a), and describe the data struct both of headnode and edgenode as node\*/*
*{node \*temp;*
*int b=0;*
*stack s; /\*define a variable of stack data structure\*/*
*combination (ATSGi, ATSGj);*
*push (s,node(a));*
*while (!empty(s) and (b==0))*
*{temp=pop(s);*
*if temp==node(aj)*
*b=1;*
*while temp<>null*
*{temp=temp.trust;*
*push(s,temp);} }*
*return (b);}*

If agent i can't find a trust path to agent j, then it concludes that it can't get the trust relation to j by trust delegation mechanism, so it may construct trust relation by automated trust negotiation, as shown in 3.2.2.

**3.2.2 Automated Negotiation of Trust.** If agent i can't find a trust path to j, then it can make automated negotiation with j about the trust relation.

Automated trust negotiation mainly manages the exchange of credentials between strangers for the purpose of property-based authentication and authorization when credentials are sensitive [13], which constructs trust relation if the credentials exchanged can satisfy the requirement of security policy. Credentials flow between i and j through a sequence of alternating credential request and disclosures, which we call a trust negotiation.

A credential is a digitally signed assertion by the credential issuer about the credential owner credentials can be made unforgeable and verifiable by using modern encryption technology: a credential is signed using the issuer's private key and verified using the issuer's public key [14]. If the exchanged credentials can satisfy the security polices of the two agents respectively, then a trust relation can be achieved.

Fig 5 is a simplified automated trust negotiation process.

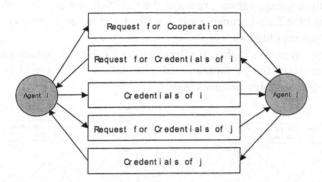

**Fig. 5.** Automated Trust Negotiation Process

If agent i can get trust relation with j by negotiation, then this new trust relation should be added into the ATSGs both of i and j.

### 3.3  Revocation of Trust

Each agent can revoke a trust relation related to itself if it confronts the following two situations: one is that the total AGST content exceeds the memory scope of the agent. Other is that the trust relation is damaged.

About the first situation, we should adopt some principles to realize the deletion of trust relations, such as FIFO (first in first out), NUR (Not used recently), LRU (Least recently Used), and so on.

About the second situation, if the trust relation between i and j is damaged, we not only revoke the it in the ATSG in i and j if the relation is damaged, but also revoke it in the ATSGs in all other agents.

## 4  Simulation Experiment

We make simulation experiment by C/C++ programming. We define the *performance* as the ratio between the successful trust construction number by path search or trust negotiation, and the total number of trust construction tests. In our simulation experiment, the memory size of agent is limitless. In the simulation experiment, when trust relation should be constructed among agents, the trust negotiation method can be used only after the trust path searching fails to find one path.

From the simulation result, we can conclude that:

- At the initial phase of system, since there is little information of ATSG in agent, so it is very difficult to find a trust path in ATSG. Therefore, the trust construction mainly adopts trust negotiation, so the *performance* of trust negotiation is more than the one of trust path searching;
- With the time going, agents exchange their ATSGs periodically. Therefore, the information of ATSG becomes more abundant and the *performance* of trust path searching becomes higher;
- When agents number is higher, the time cost of ATSGs combination also becomes higher. Therefore, the *performance* of trust path searching will become lower while the agents number becomes higher.

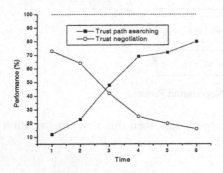

**Fig. 6.** Number of agents=5

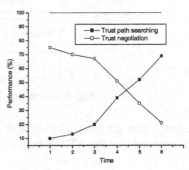

**Fig. 7.** Number of agents=10

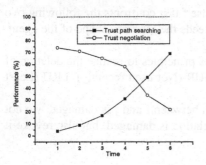

**Fig. 8.** Number of agents=15

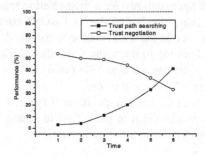

**Fig. 9.** Number of agents=20

## 5   Conclusion

In this paper, aiming at the characteristic of mobile agent autonomy, we presented a novel autonomous trust management model for mobile agents. The presented model can make mobile agent manage the trust information autonomously and exchange individual trust information to achieve the global trust information. Our model can exert the autonomy of mobile agent, which is more flexible and needn't any trusted authority. The simulation experiment proved that our model could perform well.

# References

1. SHI Zhong-Zhi. Intelligent Agent and Application (Science Press, 2000) 9-11. (in Chinese).
2. Yuh-Jong Hu. Some Thoughts on Agent Trust and Delegartion. AGENTS'01, May 28-June1, 2001, Montreal, Quebec, Canada.
3. L. Kagal, T. Finin, and A. Joshi. Developing Secure Agent Systems Using Delegation Based Trust Management. In Security of Mobile MultiAgent Systems (SEMAS 02) held at Autonomous Agents and MultiAgent Systems (AAMAS 02), 2002.
4. Stefan Poslad and Monique Calisti. Towards Improved Trust and Security in FIPA Agent Platforms. In Autonomous Agents 2000 Workshop on Deception, Fraud and Trust in Agent Societies, Spain, 2000.
5. A. Abdul-Rahman and S. Hailes, A distributed trust model, ACM New Security Paradigms Workshop, 1997
6. Alfarez Abdul-Rahman. The PGP Trust Model. EDI-Forum, April 1997. http://www.cs.ucl.ac.uk/staff/F.AbdulRahman/docs/
7. Yosi Mass and Onn Shehory. Distributed Trust in Open Multi-Agent Systems. In Workshop on Deception, Fraud and Trust in Agent Societies, Autonomous Agents 2000, 2000.
8. Michael N. Huhns. Trusted Autonomy. IEEE Internet Computing, 6(3):92-95, May-June 2002.
9. Srdjan Capkun, Levente Buttyan, Jean-Pierre Hubaux. Self-Organized Public-Key Managment for Mobile Ad Hoc Networks. IEEE Trans on Mobile Computing, Vol.2, No.1. Jan, 2003.
10. Srdjan Cpakun, Jean-Pierre Hubaux, and Levente Buttyan. Mobileity Helps Security in Ad Hoc Networks. In Proceedings of the ACM Symposium on Mobile Ad Hoc Networking and Computing (MobiHOC), June 2003.
11. Tuomas Aura. On the structure of delegation networks, Licentiate 's thesis. Technical Report A48, Helsinki University of Technology, Digital Systems laboratory, December 1997.
12. A. Jsang. An algebra for assessing trust in certification chains. In J. Kochmar, editor, Proceedings of the Network and Distributed Systems Security (NDSS'99) Symposium. The Internet Society, 1999.
13. W. Winsborough, K. Seamons, and V. Jones, Automated Trust Negotiation, DARPA Information Survivability Conference and Exposition (DISCEX '2000), January, 2000.
14. B.Schneier, Applied Cryptography, John Wiley and Sons, Inc., Second edition, 1996
15. William Ford, William Topp. Data Structures with C++. Prentice Hall,Inc. 1996.

# Privacy-Preserving Inter-database Operations*

Gang Liang and Sudarshan S. Chawathe

Computer Science Department
University of Maryland
College Park, Maryland 20742
{lg,chaw}@cs.umd.edu

**Abstract.** We present protocols for distributed computation of relational intersections and equi-joins such that each site gains no information about the tuples at the other site that do not intersect or join with its own tuples. Such protocols form the building blocks of distributed information systems that manage sensitive information, such as patient records and financial transactions, that must be shared in only a limited manner. We discuss applications of our protocols, outlining the ramifications of assumptions such as semi-honesty. In addition to improving on the efficiency of earlier protocols, our protocols are asymmetric, making them especially applicable to applications in which a low-powered client interacts with a server in a privacy-preserving manner. We present a brief experimental study of our protocols.

## 1  Introduction

**Motivating Applications.** We are witnessing a rapid rise in the number, size, and variety of databases maintained by organizations that must cooperate to a limited extent. In general, correlating data across two databases is likely to be beneficial to both parties. For example the motor-vehicle departments of two states may benefit from sharing information on recently issued drivers' licences, moving violations, and other records. However, regulations may require that one department divulge information about a person's moving violations to another department only if the other department also has some violations on record for that person. As another example, consider the information stored by various government agencies, such as the revenue service, the immigration service, and police departments at various levels. Correlating information across such databases is likely to be invaluable in preventing crime and tracking suspects. However, indiscriminate sharing will lead to serious violations of people's privacy. Again, laws or other guidelines may specify the circumstances under which these agencies may share information about a person or group of persons.

**Problem Definition.** In this paper, we focus on two 2-party privacy-preserving database operations: intersection and equi-join. More precisely, given relations

---

* This work was supported by the National Science Foundation with grants IIS-9984296 (CAREER) and IIS-0081860 (ITR).

H. Chen et al. (Eds.): ISI 2004, LNCS 3073, pp. 66–82, 2004.

$T_S(A, \beta)$ and $T_R(A, \gamma)$ at sites (parties) $S$ and $R$, respectively, we wish to compute the intersection $\pi_A T_S \cap \pi_A T_R$ or the equi-join $T_S \bowtie T_R$. (We use $\beta$ and $\gamma$ to denote the non-$A$-attributes of $T_S$ and $T_R$, respectively. For ease of presentation only, we assume that there is no overlap between $\beta$ and $\gamma$.) The intersection protocol should reveal only $|T_S|$ and $\pi_A S \cap \pi_A R$ to $R$ (and, similarly, reveal only $|T_R|$ and $\pi_A S \cap \pi_A R$ to $S$). Similarly, the equijoin protocol should reveal only $|T_S|$ and $T_S \bowtie T_R$ to $R$ (and $|T_R|$ and $T_R \bowtie T_S$ to $S$).

We assume that parties running the protocols are **semi-honest**, or *honest-but-curious*, meaning they execute the protocol exactly as specified, but they may attempt to glean more than the obvious information by analyzing the transcripts. In our example of the cooperating government agencies, this assumption means that the officials at one agency will attempt to make the best use possible of the information they are allowed to obtain, perhaps carefully choosing their queries and analyzing the results. However, they will not attempt to circumvent the protocol itself (for example, by sending incorrectly computed results or other false data).

To illustrate some of the issues, consider the following simple protocol, which seems reasonable at first glance: Site $S$ sends to $R$ the result of applying a one-way hash function $h$ to its $A$ values. That is, $S$ sends $h(\pi_A T_S)$ to $R$. In turn, $R$ applies the same hash function to its own $A$ values to yield $h(\pi_A T_R)$. By computing the intersection of the hashed sets, $h(\pi_A T_S) \cap h(\pi_A T_R)$, $R$ can determine the intersection $\pi_A T_S \cap \pi_A T_R$ (because the restriction of $h^{-1}$ to values in $R$'s database is known to $R$). Since $h$ is not easily invertible on arbitrary values, it seems that $R$ is unable to learn about $A$-values at $S$ that are not at $R$. Unfortunately, this simple protocol succumbs to the following simple attack: Given the set $h(\pi_A T_S)$ of hash values, $R$ can enumerate the domain of $A$ and compute $h(v)$ for each domain value $v$. When $h(v) \in h(\pi_A T_S)$, $R$ infers $v \in \pi_A T_S$. When $A$'s domain is not very large, this attack quickly discloses all of $\pi_A T_S$ to $R$, in violation of our privacy requirements.

Several approaches to solving such problems have appeared in prior work, and we mention a couple here: Perhaps the simplest solution is for $R$ and $S$ to relegate all computations to a third party trusted by both. While this approach may be workable in some situations, such *trusted third parties* are often hard to identify. Another alternative is to use one of the many *secure multi-party computation* protocols. Although these protocols present elegant and general-purpose solutions to our problem, they do so at the cost of very high computation and communication overheads. We discuss these ideas, along with other related work, further in Section 2.

Our protocols follow the general approach outlined by Agrawal, Evfimievski, and Srikant [13]. Unlike their symmetric use of a commutative encryption scheme to protect the privacy of both parties, our protocols are asymmetric: They use blind signatures to protect the privacy of one party and one-way hash functions to protect the privacy of the other. They incur smaller computation and communication overheads than those incurred by the earlier protocols and their asymmetric nature makes them especially interesting to commonly occurring applications consisting of a well-provisioned server communicating with clients of modest capabilities.

**Contributions.**    We may summarize the main contributions of this paper as follows:

- We present protocols for privacy-preserving computation of inter-database intersections and joins. Our protocols improve on the computation and communication overheads of prior work. An interesting feature of our protocols is that the overheads are asymmetric.
- We discuss applications of our protocols, highlighting ways to take advantage of their asymmetry and other features.
- We have publicly released our implementation of the protocols so that others may extend and experiment with it. The Java source code is available under GNU GPL terms at http://www.cs.umd.edu/~chaw/projects/pido/.
- We present a brief experimental study quantifying the performance of our protocols.

**Outline.**    We begin by discussing related work in Section 2. Section 3 presents some of the ideas upon which our work builds, including earlier work on similar protocols [1]. In Section 4, we present our protocols along with an informal analysis. In Section 5, we discuss applications, highlighting the ramifications of asymmetry and the assumption of semi-honesty. Section 6 presents the results of our experimental study. Section 7 summarizes our results and discusses future work.

## 2   Related Work

As noted in Section 1, the method closest to ours is that by Agrawal, Evfimievski, and Srikant [1], which is discussed in Section 3. In this section, we discuss some of the other work in the areas such as secure multiparty computation, privacy-preserving data mining, private information retrieval, and privacy-preserving recommender systems.

Du and Atallah's paper [11] provides a good review of secure multi-party computation (SMC) problems and develops a framework to identify new SMC problems. Yao first investigated the secure two party computation problem [24]. This problem was later generalized to multiparty computation. Chaum, Crepeau, and Damgard showed that essentially any multiparty protocol problem can be solved assuming only authenticated secrecy channels between pairs of participants [8].

Work in the area of privacy-preserving data mining focuses on problem of computing aggregate information from a very large amount of data without revealing individual data items. A commonly used idea is to introduce random perturbations to disguise the individual data items and to use reconstruction methods to recover the aggregated data or the distribution of the aggregation.

Agrawal and Srikant have proposed methods for numerical data that use Gaussian and uniform perturbation to disguise the data in the decision tree classifier model [2]. Canny has proposed methods for privacy-preserving collaborative filtering [6, 7]. The methods use homomorphic encryption to allow sums of encrypted vectors to be computed and decrypted without revealing individual data. In this scheme, a group of users can compute aggregations over all data without gaining knowledge of specific data about others. Methods for categorical data based on random response schemes have also been proposed. For example, Du and Zhan have modified the ID3 classification algorithm based on randomized response techniques [12]. They show that if the appropriate randomization parameters are used, the accuracy achieved is very close to that using the unmodified ID3 algorithm on the original data. Vaidya and Clifton have addressed privacy preservation in $k$-means clustering (a technique to group items into $k$ clusters) [22]. Their paper presents a method for $k$-means clustering when different sites contain different attributes for a common set of entities. Evfimvievski et al. have presented a method for association-rule mining in categorical data [13]. They describe the privacy leaks in the straightforward uniform randomization method and propose a class of randomization operations that are more effective. Iyengar has addressed the privacy protection problem in a data dissemination environment [19]. Transformation (generalization and suppression) is performed on the identifying content of data, such that no sensitive information is disclosed during dissemination. Unlike our methods in this paper, methods of the kind describe above permit inaccurate or modified data and a non-perfect result. The address an environment that consists of an information collector and several individual data sources, and privacy concerns are limited to the data sources, assuming a trusted collector.

The work on private information retrieval (PIR) is also related. A PIR protocol allows a user to access $k$ ($k > 1$) duplicated copies of data, and privately retrieve one of the $n$ bits of the data in such a manner that the databases cannot figure out which bit the user has retrieved. Chor and Gilboa have presented a method that focuses on computational privacy, rather then information-theoretic privacy [9]. This privacy is only guaranteed with respect to databases that are restricted to polynomial time computations. The paper shows that the computational approach leads to substantial savings. Di-Crescenzo, Ishai, and Ostrovsky have presented methods to reduce the communication overhead of PIR by using a commodity-based model [10]. In this case, one or more additional commodity servers are added to the PIR model. These servers may send off-line randomized messages to the user and databases. With the help of these servers, their schemes shift most of the communication to the off-line stage and are resilient against collusions of databases with more than a majority of the commodity servers. Beimel and Ishai have provided an efficient protocol for $t$-private, $k$-server PIR. that is secure despite $t$ of the $k$ servers colluding [4]. Gertner et al. present the Symmetrically-Private Information Retrieval (SPIR) model, which guarantees the privacy of the database as well as that of the user [15]. That is, a user learns only a single bit (the record) of $x$ (the database), but no other information about the data. Their paper also describes how to transform PIR schemes to SPIR schemes.

Huberman, Franklin, and Hogg have discussed a problem very similar to ours in the context of recommendation systems [17, 16]. Their protocol is used to find people with common preferences without revealing what the preferences. In a database context, Lindell and Pinkas have addressed the same privacy concerns as those in this paper [20]. Their paper addresses the privacy-preserving set-union problem. The central idea is to make all the intermediate values seen by the players uniformly distributed.

Protocols have also been proposed for a private equality test, which is a simplified version of intersection operation in which each of the two parties has a single record. Fagin, Naor, and Winkler have reviewed and analyzed dozens of solutions for this problem [14]. Vaidya and Clifton have presented a protocol for securely determining the size of set intersections in the multi-party case [23]. The main idea is to transform every party's database by applying a secure keyed commutative hash function and to calculate the intersection size on the transformed databases. Ioannidis, Grama, and Atallah have described a secure protocol for computing dot products, which can be used as a building block in many problems, such as the intersection size problem [18]. In contrast to conventional heavyweight cryptographic approaches, their protocol uses lightweight linear algebraic technique. Atallah and Du have addressed secure two-party computational geometry problems [3]. They present a secure scalar product protocol (with a slightly different definition of the scalar product problem) and secure vector dominance protocol. Using these as building blocks, they construct efficient protocols for the point-inclusion and polygon intersection problems.

## 3   Preliminaries

Recall from Section 1 that we are given relations $T_S(A, \beta)$ and $T_R(A, \gamma)$ at sites $S$ and $R$, respectively, where $\beta$ and $\gamma$ represent the non-$A$ attributes of the relations. For ease of presentation, we assume $A \notin \beta \cup \gamma$. The intersection protocol is required to compute $\pi_A T_S \cap \pi_A T_R$, revealing only $|T_S|$ and $\pi_A S \cap \pi_A R$ to $R$ and, similarly, revealing only $|T_R|$ and $\pi_A S \cap \pi_A R$ to $S$. The equijoin protocol is required to compute $T_S \bowtie T_R$, revealing only $|T_S|$ and $T_S \ltimes T_R$ to $R$ and revealing only $|T_R|$ and $T_R \ltimes T_S$ to $S$.

The protocols by Agrawal, Evfimievski, and Srikant [1] (henceforth, the **AES03 protocols**) use a commutative encryption scheme as a building block. A function $f$ is a commutative encryption function if $f_a(f_b(x)) = f_b(f_a(x))$, where $a$ and $b$ are two random keys. The **AES03 intersection protocol** may be summarized as follows:

1. Each of $S$ and $R$ applies a hash function $h$ to its data, to yield $X_S = h(V_S)$ at $S$ and $X_R = h(V_R)$ at $R$. Each also randomly generates a secret key. Let $e_S$ and $e_R$ denote the secret keys of $S$ and $R$, respectively.
2. Both sites encrypt their hashed data using their secret keys to yield $Y_S = f_{e_S}(X_S)$ at $S$ and $Y_R = f_{e_R}(X_R)$ at $R$.

3. Site $R$ sends $Y_R$ to $S$, after reordering the items in $Y_R$ randomly.
4. (a) Site $S$ sends $Y_S$ to $R$, after reordering the items in $Y_S$ randomly.
   (b) Site $S$ encrypts each $y \in Y_R$ using its private key $e_S$, generating tuples of the form $(f_{e_S}(y), y)$. We have
   $$Z'_R = \{(f_{e_S}(y), y) \mid y \in Y_R\} = \{(f_{e_S}(f_{e_R}(x)), y) \mid x \in X_R\}.$$
   (c) Site $S$ sends $Z'_R$ to $R$.
5. Site $R$ encrypts each $y \in Y_S$ with $e_R$, obtaining $Z_S = f_{e_R}(f_{e_S}(X_S))$
6. Finally, $R$ compares elements in $Z_S$ with the first components of the pairs in $Z_R$. When a match is found for some $(f_{e_S}(f_{e_R}(x)), y) \in Z_R$, $R$ determines that the element corresponding to $y$ (which is known to $R$) is in the intersection.

The **AES03 equijoin protocol** is similar to the above intersection protocol. The main difference is that, in step 4, $S$ also encrypts the non-$A$ attributes $\beta$ of each record with a new key that can be recovered only when the corresponding $A$ value is in the intersection. Thus, $S$ performs two commutative encryptions on each value of attribute $A$: The first is for the intersection and the second is to obtain the key used to encrypt the other attributes ($\beta$). Site $R$ first computes the intersection as in the intersection protocol. Then, it obtains the key for decrypting the corresponding equijoin results. For further details, we refer the reader to the original paper [1].

For the commutative encryption function, both AES03 protocols use the power function $f_e(x) = x^e \bmod p$, where $p$ is a safe prime number. In our implementation, $p$ is 1024 bits long.

**Blind Signatures.** As noted earlier, our protocols use blind signatures to help preserve the privacy of one party. Although our protocols do not depend on any particular blind signature scheme, for concreteness we will assume the RSA scheme in this paper [21]. Consider an RSA key pair: public key $(e, N)$ and private key $(d, N)$. In the following, we omit the modulus $N$ and refer to the keys as simply $e$ and $d$. To sign a message $m$ with private key $d$, one computes $sig = m^d \bmod N$. To check a signature, one computes $m' = sig^e \bmod N$, and checks whether $m = m'$. The blind signature scheme works as follows. Let $e$ and $d$ be the public and private keys of $S$. (As usual, $e$, but not $d$, is known to others.) Suppose $R$ would like to obtain $S$'s signature on a message $m$ without revealing $m$ to $S$. For this purpose, $R$ first chooses a random number $r$ and sends $x = m \times r^e$ to $S$. Site $S$ returns a signed version of $x$: $sig' = x^d = (m \times r^e)^d = m^d \times r$. Site $R$ computes $sig = sig'/r = m^d \times r/r = m^d$, which is message $m$ with $S$'s signature. All the above computations are modulo $N$, which we have omitted for brevity. In comparisons with the AES03 protocols, we assume $N$ is 1024 bits long.

## 4  Privacy-Preserving Protocols

**Intersection Protocol.** Using the notation described in Section 3, we describe our privacy preserving intersection protocol below. The protocol is also illustrated in Figure 1 (with the modulus $N$ omitted for simplicity).

1. Both $S$ and $R$ apply a hash function $h$ to their datasets to yield $X_S = h(V_S)$ and $X_R = h(V_R)$. Site $S$ generates an RSA key pair, $e$ and $d$ and publishes its public key $e$ to $R$.
2. Site $R$ blinds $X_R$ giving $Y_R = \{y = x \times r^e \mid x \in X_R\}$, where $r$ is a different random value for each $x$.
3. $R$ sends $Y_R$ to $S$.
4. $S$ signs $Y_R$ and gets the signature set $Z_R$. $S$ sends $Z_R$ back to $R$ without changing the order.
5. $R$ uses the set of $r$ values to unblind the set $Z_R$ and obtains the real signature set $SIG_R$.
6. $R$ then applies another hash function $H$ on $SIG_R$. $HSIG_R = H(SIG_R)$.
7. $S$ signs $X_S$ and gets the signature set $SIG_S$.
8. $S$ applies $H$ to $SIG_S$: $HSIG_S = H(SIG_S)$. $S$ sends $HSIG_S$ to $R$.
9. $S$ also signs the set $HSIG_S$ so that that, later on, $S$ cannot deny having sent this set and $R$ cannot forge items into this set. This step is optional, and is used only when the above protection is needed, for example in the equijoin protocol described later.
10. $R$ compares $HSIG_R$ and $HSIG_S$. Using the known correspondence between $HSIG_R$ and $V_R$, $R$ gets the intersection.
11. $SIG = SIG_R \cap SIG_S$. $R$ applies another one-way hash function $H'$ on $SIG$. $H'SIG = H'(SIG)$. $R$ then sends $HSIG$ to $S$, along with $H'SIG$. This step is optional, and is used only when $S$ needs to know the intersection, for example, in the following equijoin protocol.

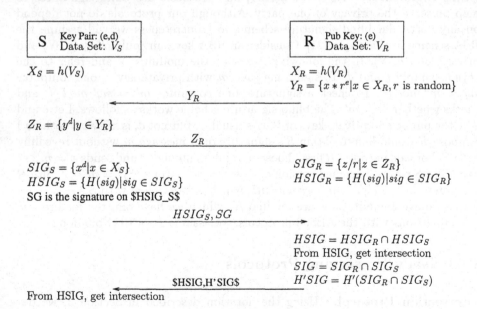

**Fig. 1.** Intersection protocol

**Analysis.** We now compare our intersection protocol (P2) with the AES03 intersection protocol (P1). We will not count the optional steps in P2, since the P1 does not provide the additional functionality they enable (verifiable messages and $S$'s knowledge about intersection). In any case, the additional computation and communication costs of these steps are small.

The number of communication rounds for both protocols is the same. Communication bandwidth used in the first two rounds of both protocols is $(1024 \times (N_S + N_R))$, where $N_S$ and $N_R$ are the sizes of the two relations. In the third round, $S$ only sends a set of hash value in P2. In P1, $S$ needs to send the set of commutative encryption blocks. Since the size of hash values (for example, 128 bits for MD5) is almost one order of magnitude shorter than the encryption block size (1024 bits), our protocol will use less communication. The communication savings are $(1024 - 128) * N_S$ bits.

In the commutative encryption scheme example described in the AES03 paper [1], the encryption function used is $f_e(x) = x^e \bmod p$. Here $p$ is a 1024-bit safe prime number. $e \in \{1, 2, \ldots, q-1\}$, where $q = (p-1)/2$. The computation of a single encryption is almost the same as a single RSA signature operation with a 1024-bit public number $N$. We performed some experiments on these two operations with Java. The result suggests that the commutative encryption requires about twice the running time of the RSA signature. We attribute this result to the use of an optimized RSA operation (Java API) vs. the unoptimized commutative encryption (implemented directly with the BigInteger class). For our analysis here, we assume one commutative encryption and one RSA signature operation take the same amount of time, $T$. Also, we assume that the hash operation is very fast compared with others, and we do not account for it. Our protocol requires blind/unblind operations. By our experiments, we found that the blind/unblind operation is also fast (about 100 times faster than the signature operation), due to the fact that $e$ is normally very small (3 or 65537). With the above assumptions, it is easy to determine that our protocol requires $(N_S + N_R) \times T$ time for signatures and $N_R \times 2 \times T/100$ for blind/unblind operations. Total time required is $(N_S + N_R)T + N_R T/50)$. In contrast, the AES03 protocol requires $2(N_S + N_R)T$ time.

Another property of our protocol is the highly asymmetric computation for $R$ and $S$. $S$ performs most of the computation ($N_S + N_T$ signatures plus some hash operations), while $R$ only performs $N_R$ fast blind/unblind operations. This feature makes the protocol very useful in an asymmetric environment, such as wireless hand-held device communicating with a powerful server.

There are two optional steps whose purpose will become clearer when we discuss the equijoin protocol. Step 11 enables $S$ to determine the intersection. In the AES03 protocol, only $R$ knows the intersection. In this step, another hash function ($H'$) is applied on the intersection's signature set, such that $R$ cannot send (fake) intersection items other than those in $V_R$, because $R$ can only generate the correct hash when the signature is known. Step 11 alone is not enough to prevent $R$ from adding fake items into intersection. $R$ can send to $S$ any value in $V_R - V_S$. To prevent this attack, at step 9, $S$ signature-protects the hash set, such that when $R$ sends a fake intersection item, $S$ can deny with proof that that hash value was not sent to $R$. With steps 9 and 11 together, $R$ cannot fake a larger intersection set. While $R$ can still send a smaller-than-true intersection set, we can use the protocol in such a way that $R$ has no incentives to do so, as discussed in Section 5.

If we do not count the optional steps then, after the protocol, $R$ learns the intersection set and $|V_S|$. $S$ learns $|V_R|$ only. It is difficult for $R$ and $S$ to learn other information such as other values from the other party not in the intersection. $R$'s privacy is protected by the blind operation. Due to blinding, $Y_R$ seems to be a random set to $S$. On the other hand, $R$ knows only signatures on $X_R$ after unblinding. It is very difficult for $R$ to forge signatures on other messages if we assume the secrecy of the blind signature scheme. $S$ protects the signature on $X_S$ by applying the one-way hash function $H$. Due to the one-way property, it is computationally difficult for $R$ to figure out the signature and thus the original message from hash value.

**Equijoin Protocol.**   Given our intersection protocol with the optional steps, the modifications needed for an equijoin are simple. At the end of the intersection protocol, both parties know the intersection. They only need to agree on a communication key to transfer the equijoin result. The equijoin protocol is described below and in Figure 2 (which omits the modulus $N$ for brevity).

1. Both $S$ and $R$ apply a hash function $h$ to their datasets to yield $X_S = h(V_S)$ and $X_R = h(V_R)$. Site $S$ generates an RSA key pair, $e$ and $d$ and publishes its public key $e$ to $R$.
2. Site $R$ blinds $X_R$ giving $Y_R = \{y = x \times r^e \mid x \in X_R\}$, where $r$ is a different random value for each $x$.
3. $R$ sends $Y_R$ to $S$.
4. $S$ signs $Y_R$ and gets the signature set $Z_R$. $S$ sends $Z_R$ back to $R$ without changing the order.
5. $R$ uses the set of $r$ values to unblind the set $Z_R$ and obtains the real signature set $SIG_R$.
6. $R$ then applies another hash function $H$ on $SIG_R$. $HSIG_R = H(SIG_R)$.
7. $S$ signs $X_S$ and gets the signature set $SIG_S$.
8. $S$ applies $H$ to $SIG_S$: $HSIG_S = H(SIG_S)$. $S$ sends $HSIG_S$ to $R$.
9. $S$ also signs the set $HSIG_S$ so that that, later on, $S$ cannot deny having sent this set and $R$ cannot forge items into this set. This step is optional, and is used only when the above protection is needed, for example in the equijoin protocol described later.
10. $R$ compares $HSIG_R$ and $HSIG_S$. Using the known correspondence between $HSIG_R$ and $V_R$, $R$ gets the intersection.
11. $SIG = SIG_R \cap SIG_S$. $R$ applies another one-way hash function $H'$ to $SIG$. $H'SIG = H'(SIG)$. $R$ then sends $HSIG$ to $S$, along with $H'SIG$.
12. On $S$'s side, let $sig_a$ be the signature on $a$, and $H''$ be another one-way hash function. $\forall a \in V_R \cap V_S$,
   $H''sig_a = H''(sig_a)$.

From $H''sig_a$, deterministically generate a key $k$ for some symmetric encryption function $E$.

$\gamma = E_k(\beta)$.

Send the tuple $(\gamma, Hsig_a)$ to $R$, where $Hsig_a = H(sig_a)$. If the order remains unchanged, $S$ can send $(\gamma)$ only.

13. From $Hsig_a$ and previously saved transcript, $R$ determines $sig_a$ and then computes $H''sig_a$ and $k$. After that, $R$ may decrypt $\gamma$, determine $\beta$, and obtain the equijoin result.

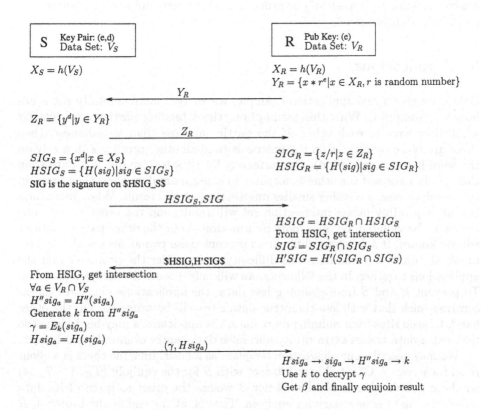

Fig. 2. Equijoin protocol

**Analysis.** Compared with the AES03 equijoin protocol, the above protocol only encrypts and sends non-$A$ attributes when necessary, i.e., for records in the equijoin result. The AES03 protocol encrypts and sends such attributes for every record in $T_S$, which can be very inefficient for large databases and large records. The AES03 protocol sends a total of $3N_R + N_S$ commutative cipher blocks (1024 bits each) and $N_S$ symmetric cipher blocks on other attributes over the network. Suppose the length of each record in $T_S$ is $L$. Then, the total communication is: $(3N_R + N_S) \times 1024 + N_S L$. In our protocol, only $2N_R + N_{RS}$ signature blocks (1024 bits each) and $3N_{RS}$ hash values (128 bits each) and $N_{RS}$ (the size of intersection) symmetric encryption blocks on other attributes are sent. So, the total communication is: $(2N_R + N_{RS}) \times 1024 + 3N_{RS} \times 128 + N_{RS}L$. For computation, the original protocol needs time $(2N_S + 5N_R) * T + (N_S + N_{RS})T'$, where $T'$ is the running time for each symmetric encryption block. Our protocol needs time $(N_S + N_R)T + N_R T/50) + 2N_{RS}T'$.

Our protocol enables $S$ to learn $N_R$ as well as values of $R.A$ that appear in the intersection, while in the AES03 protocol, $S$ only knows $N_R$. This extra information leakage not only makes the protocol much more efficient, but also enables the practical usage of our protocol without the semi-honest assumption, as explained in Section 5.

# 5   Applications

Before we give a real application example, we analyze more carefully the semi-honest assumption. With this assumption, the attending parties send exactly what they have to each other. If the parties are less than semi-honest, then there are two easy attacks on the protocols (and all other protocols that rely on the semi-honest assumption). One attack is for sites to give out less data than they really have and the other is for sites to claim more data than they have. In the less data case, a possibly smaller intersection set will result. When more data is sent, a possibly bigger intersection set will result, and the other party's privacy may be violated, because more information about the other party's dataset will be known. It seems very difficult to prevent these two attacks with the protocols themselves. To address this difficulty, we consider the protocols and the applications together. In the following, we will only discuss the equijoin protocol. To prevent $R$ and $S$ from claiming less data, the applications may provide incentives, such that with less-than-true data sites will be worse off. On the other hand, to keep sites from claiming more data, the applications may be designed so that extra data causes extra utility and false data causes eventual punishment.

We may describe our *application template* as follows. Imagine there is a client $R$ and a server $S$. Client $R$ is to interact with $S$ for the equijoin $(T_R.A = T_S.A)$ on these two databases. Neither $R$ nor $S$ wishes the other to learn of its data unless that data is necessary for equijoin. That is, at the end of the protocol, $R$ only knows the equijoin result and size of $S$'s database and $S$ only knows the size of $R$'s database and $T_R.A$ values that are in the equijoin result. Since the server's signature operations are expensive, the service is not free and the charge is based on the number of items $(|Y_R|)$ sent from $R$ to $S$ in step 3 of the equijoin protocol as well as the size of final equijoin result. We need the applications to run in such environment that if cheating is found, later punishment is possible. Certainly, we need to assume the equijoin result is useful to $R$, otherwise, there is no reason for $R$ to pay and run this protocol. We now assume that the parties are rational instead of semi-honest.

At step 3, $R$ has no incentives to send less data, since sending less data may result in a smaller equijoin result. $R$ has no incentives to send more data either, otherwise more money is paid to $S$. At step 4, $S$ has to send back the correct signature set, since $R$ can check with the given public key if desired. At step 8, $S$ will not send less data to $R$, since doing so may result in a smaller intersection and equijoin result, implying less money for $S$. $S$ does not have incentives to send more data, since the data which $S$ does not have may appear in the equijoin result. When $S$ cannot provide such data or provides false data, later punishment may occur. In step 11, $R$ will send exact intersection to $S$. The protocol doesn't allow $R$ to send a bigger set, and a smaller set leads to a smaller equijoin result to $R$. In step 12, $S$ has to send the correct equijoin result; otherwise, with the help of earlier transcripts, $R$ can prove that $S$ did not provide enough results. The above analysis assumes that each record in $S$'s database is of the same importance to $R$, and that the amounts of charge and punishment are appropriately set.

While there are several applications fitting the above application template, we present a typical one here: a credit query system. Consider several credit history authorities, each of which has credit histories for a large number of people, but none of which has the data for all people. There is also a large number of agents who query the credit histories of individuals The agents query the authorities in a batch mode, say, once per day. The query is based on the combination of several attributes, such as social security number, birth date, and name, such that it is not easy for an agent to fake a query. The authorities do not wish to divulge to agents credit records other than those queried; otherwise they are leaking information (the combination of SSN, birth date and name as well as the credit status) about individuals. For similar reasons, the agents do not wish the authorities to know all their client information unless the authorities have that information already. To prevent the agents from randomly combining SSN, birth date, and name and hopes of a lucky match with the authorities record, and as a reward for the authority's computation and information, the query is charged based on the size of the agent's query set and the final equijoin result. Mapping this application to our protocol, $V$ is the combination of three fields, SSN, birth date, and name. $X$ is the set of hash value on the combined attributes. The agents are $R$, and the authorities are $S$. The equijoin result should include not only the credit point, but also other information, say, the person's address, such that it is possible for the agent to check the validity of the returned data. The previous general incentive analysis applies to this application, so with proper setup and rational players assumption, the equijoin protocol is applicable here.

The server performs most of the asymmetric computation and gets paid. The charge here is both payment for the server's computations and incentive for the client's honest behavior. One problem with this approach is that when the number of simultaneous clients is large, the quality of the service may drop due to the intense server-side computation. One optimization is for the server to not compute the signatures on $V_S$ every time there is a client. Instead this computation is done for every, say, 100 clients. Then, most of the time, when a new client arrives, the only signatures computed are those on the client's data ($V_R$) which, in our setup, is small compared to the server's data.

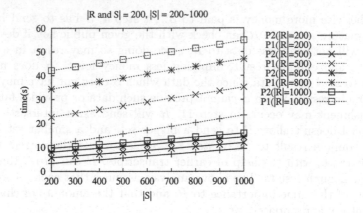

**Fig. 3.** Running time as a function of $|S|$, varying $|R|$ with $|R \cap S| = 200$

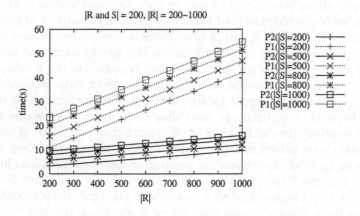

**Fig. 4.** Running time as a function of $|R|$, varying $|S|$ with $|R \cap S| = 200$

## 6   Experimental Study

We have implemented our protocols and the AES03 protocols [1] using Sun's Java SDK 1.4. RSA key length, as well as $p$'s length in the commutative encryption scheme, is set to 512 for the purpose of fast experimental runs. The commutative encryption key $e$ is randomly chosen from $\{1, 2, \ldots, q-1\}$, where $p = 2q+1$. The experiments were performed using synthetic data on GNU/Linux machines with dual Pentium III 1.6 GHz processors and 1 GB of RAM. In all the simulations, running time is measured from the first step to the last step of the protocols at the client $(R)$ side. The time to generate RSA key pairs and commutative encryption key pairs is not included.

We conducted five experiments, summarized in Figures 3–7. Each data point represents the average value measured over 14 runs. The 95% confidence interval for all points in Figures 3, 4, 5, 6, and 7 are smaller than 0.12%, 0.14%, 0.13%, 0.14%, and 0.18% of the corresponding mean values, respectively. In the figures,

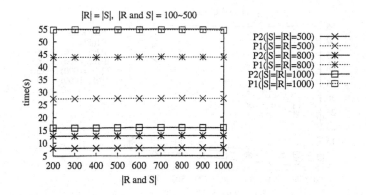

**Fig. 5.** Running time as a function of $|R \cap S|$, varying $|R|$ and $|S|$, with $|R| = |S|$

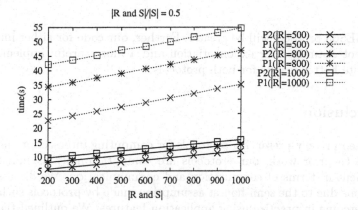

**Fig. 6.** Running time as a function of $|R \cap S|$, varying $|R|$, with $|R \cap S|/|S| = 0.5$

we use P1 to denote the AES03 protocols and P2 to denote our protocols. We use $N_R$, $N_S$, and $N_{RS}$ to denote $|R|$, $|S|$, and $|R \cap S|$, respectively.

The results indicate the performance benefits of our protocol. The benefit in scaling is greater for $R$ than for $S$. This trend can be observed in Figures 3 and 4. Curves for the AES03 protocol are steeper in Figure 4 because it performs encryption and decryption on $S$'s data twice but on $R$'s data five times. Figure 5 indicates that the two protocols are not sensitive to the intersection size. This result is expected for the AES03 protocol. Our protocol may be expected to fare worse with larger intersection sizes. However, since our experiments were run with $R$ and $S$ on the same machine, this effect is reduced and not noticeable. We note that the slopes of the lines for P1 are higher in Figure 7 than in Figure 6, confirming the higher sensitivity of the AES03 protocol to $R$'s size.

The above experiments assume that $S$ has only two attributes: one key attribute and one non-key attribute. In real applications, there may be a larger number of non-key attributes. In such a case, the improvement of our protocol

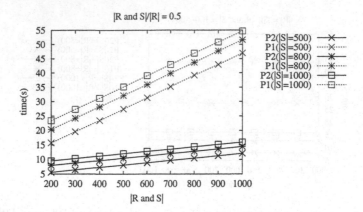

**Fig. 7.** Running time as a function of $|R \cap S|$, varying $|S|$, with $|R \cap S|/|R| = 0.5$

over the AES03 protocol will be greater. Further, our code for either implementation is not optimized for exponentiation and a more careful implementation will generate better results for both protocols.

## 7    Conclusion

We proposed privacy-preserving protocols for computing intersections and joins. Compared to prior work, our protocols are computationally asymmetric and more efficient in terms of computation and communication. We discussed how the problems due to the semi-honest assumption made by protocols such as ours can be overcome in practice using application features. We outlined the results of a brief experimental study of our protocols. Our implementation is publicly available.

As ongoing work, we are studying the the multi-party case. One possibility is running the two-party protocols repeatedly. However, we may be able to develop more efficient methods that take advantage of the asymmetry of our protocols. For example, in a 3-party scenario in which $A$ joins with $B$ and $C$ (using $A.a = B.b$ and $A.a' = C.c$), $A$ can run the 2-party protocol in parallel with $B$ and $C$, relegating the heavy computations (signatures) to them, performing only the two sets of light computations locally.

## References

1. R. Agrawal, A. Evfimievski, and R. Srikant. Information sharing across private databases. *In Proceedings of the ACM SIGMOD International Conference on Management of Data*, San Diego, CA, June 2003.
2. R. Agrawal and R. Srikant. Privacy-preserving data mining. *In Proceedings of the ACM SIGMOD International Conference on Management of Data*, pages 439–450. ACM Press, May 2000.

3. M. J. Atallah and W. Du. Secure multi-party computational geometry. In *Proceedings of the International Workshop on Algorithms and Data Structures*, 2001.
4. A. Beimel and Y. Ishai. Information-theoretic private information retrieval: A unified construction. *Lecture Notes in Computer Science*, 2076, 2001.
5. M. Ben-Or and A. Wigderson. Completeness theorems for non-cryptographic fault-tolerant distributed computation. In *Proceedings of the ACM Symposium on Theory of Computing*, pages 1–10, 1988.
6. J. Canny. Collaborative filtering with privacy. In *Proceedings of the IEEE symposium on Security and Privacy*, Oakland, CA, May 2002.
7. J. Canny. Collaborative filtering with privacy via factor analysis. In *Proceedings of the annual international ACM SIGIR conference on Research and Development in information retrieval*, Tampere, Finland, Aug. 2002.
8. D. Chaum, C. Crepeau, and I. Damgard. Multiparty unconditionally secure protocols. In *Proceedings of the ACM Symposium on Theory of Computing*, pages 11–19, 1988.
9. B. Chor and N. Gilboa. Computationally private information retrieval. In *Proceedings of the ACM Symposium on Theory of Computing*, pages 304–313, 1997.
10. G. Di-Crescenzo, Y. Ishai, and R. Ostrovsky. Universal service-providers for database private information retrieval. In *Proceedings of the ACM SIGACT-SIGOPS Symposium on Principles of Distributed Computing*, 1998.
11. W. Du and M. J. Atallah. Secure multi-party computation problems and their applications: A review and open problems. In *Proceedings of the Workshop on New Security Paradigms*, pages 11–20, Cloudcroft, New Mexico, USA, Sept. 2001.
12. W. Du and Z. Zhan. Using randomized response techniques for privacy-preserving data mining. In *Proceedings of the ACM SIGKDD International Conference on Knowledge Discovery and Data Mining*, Washington, DC, Aug. 2003.
13. A. Evfimievski, R. Srikant, R. Agrawal, and J. Gehrke. Privacy preserving mining of association rules. In *Proceedings of ACM SIGKDD International Conference on Knowledge Discovery and Data Mining (KDD)*, July 2002.
14. R. Fagin, M. Naor, and P. Winkler. Comparing information without leaking it. *Communications of the ACM*, 39(5):77–85, 1996.
15. Y. Gertner, Y. Ishai, E. Kushilevitz, and T. Malkin. Protecting data privacy in private information retrieval schemes. In *Proceedings of the ACM Symposium on Theory of Computing*, pages 151–160, May 1998.
16. T. Hogg, B. A. Huberman, and M. Franklin. Protecting privacy while sharing information in electronic communities. In *Proceedings of the Conference on Computers, Freedom and Privacy: Challenging the Assumptions*, Apr. 2000.
17. B. A. Huberman, M. Franklin, and T. Hogg. Enhancing privacy and trust in electronic communities. In *Proceedings of ACM Conference on Electronic Commerce*, pages 78–86, 1999.
18. I. Ioannidis, A. Grama, and M. Atallah. A secure protocol for computing dot products in clustered and distributed environments. In *Proceedings of the International Conference on Parallel Processing*, Vancouver, Canada, Aug. 2002.
19. V. S. Iyengar. Transforming data to satisfy privacy constraints. In *Proceedings of the ACM SIGKDD International Conference on Knowledge Discovery and Data Mining*, pages 279 – 288, Edmonton, Alberta, Canada, July 2002.
20. Y. Lindel and B. Pinkas. Privacy preserving data mining. In *Proceedings of Advances in Cryptology*, Aug. 2000.
21. W. Stallings. *Cryptography and Network Security*. Prentice Hall, New Jersey, 3rd edition, 2003.

22. J. Vaidya and C. Clifton. Privacy-preserving k-means clustering over vertically partitioned data. In *Proceedings of the ACM SIGKDD International Conference on Knowledge Discovery and Data Mining*, pages 206–215, Washington, DC, 2003.
23. J. Vaidya and C. Clifton. Secure set intersection cardinality with application to association rule mining, 2003. Manuscript.
24. A. C. Yao. How to generate and exchange secrets. In *Proceedings of the Annual Symposium on Foundations of Computer Science*, pages 162–167, Toronto, Canada, Oct. 1986.

# Finding Unusual Correlation
# Using Matrix Decompositions

David B. Skillicorn

School of Computing
Queen's University
skill@cs.queensu.ca

**Abstract.** One important aspect of terrorism detection is the ability to detect small-scale, local correlations against a background of large-scale, diffuse correlations. Several matrix decompositions transform correlation into other properties: for example, Singular Value Decomposition (SVD) transforms correlation into proximity, and SemiDiscrete Decomposition (SDD) transforms correlation into regions of increased density. Both matrix decompositions are effective at detecting local correlation in this setting, but they are much more effective when combined.

## 1 Introduction

Detecting terrorism can be posed as an unsupervised data-mining problem in which the goal is to separate individuals into two classes, threats and non-threats. However, it is unusual because the members of one class (the threats) are actively trying to look as similar to members of the other class as possible. Without information about the particular data-mining algorithm in use, the best strategy for doing this is to arrange for each of their attribute values to be modal (that is, typical).

This has two implications for the application of data mining to terrorism detection:

- Attributes collected should be those whose values are hard to manipulate; and
- The data-mining algorithms used should rely on the *relationships* between attributes, rather than simply the attribute *values*.

If attributes are chosen appropriately, then the activities of threats and threat groups may be visible as unexpected correlation, both among themselves and between the threats and their target. However, this correlation must be detected against a background of widespread diffuse correlation in the population at large, and this is what makes the problem difficult.

Matrix decompositions transform datasets to reveal properties that are latent or hard to see in their original form. Singular Value Decomposition (SVD) is a tool for detecting unusual correlation because it transforms variation into proximity. Both distance measures and visual inspection can detect proximity

H. Chen et al. (Eds.): ISI 2004, LNCS 3073, pp. 83–99, 2004.

far more easily than they can detect correlation directly. Semidiscrete decomposition (SDD) is a bump-finding technique – it detects regions of unusual density in data and repetitively removes them. SVD has high detection accuracy but relies on external inspection to determine the probable presence of a threat. SDD is able to identify threats directly using its own models.

We present results using artificial datasets. There is little experience to guide the form of such datasets, but we argue that the ones we use are plausible.

Section 2 discusses the goals of this work and the assumptions that we make about problems to be solved and the form of available data. Section 3 explains the way in which we generate datasets to test our approaches. Section 4 introduces singular value decomposition, particularly some of its less well-known properties that are useful in this setting. Section 5 introduces semidiscrete decomposition, a matrix decomposition that reveals regions of local homogeneity in datasets. Section 6 discusses the use of singular value decomposition and semidiscrete decomposition together, and introduces the JSS methodology. Section 7 explains the experiments that were performed to test our approaches. Section 8 discusses related work.

## 2    Goals and Assumptions

It seems implausible, given our present data-mining technologies and understanding of the problems of counterterrorism, that an individual data-mining technology will be able to be deployed as a frontline tool against terrorism. In particular, all individual data-mining techniques have non-zero false positive rates, so that they will all classify some non-threats as threats. False positives create irritation in those wrongly selected as potential threats, and distrust of the technology in those who use it – both of which weaken the effectiveness of a technology.

However, using a set of data-mining technologies, either as a pipeline or in other concerted ways, can mitigate the problem of false positives, and also some of the concerns about invasion of privacy. Two effective data-mining technologies are likely to report substantially the same true positives, but quite unlikely to report the same false positives. Hence the combination can be much more effective than either individually. Applying two or more data-mining technologies in sequence can reduce concerns about privacy. For example, the first technology may be applied to relatively public data, perhaps even anonymized. Those objects that the technology regards as suspicious can then be further examined using a different technology, perhaps using more information. Applying these techniques in sequence means that sensitive data needs only to be retrieved for a small fraction of the total number of objects. See Jensen *et al.* [9] for examples of this approach on real problems. Furthermore, the interval between the two processes provides a moment for intervention and oversight, perhaps formal permission to retrieve more confidential data. The role of access safeguards of this kind is discussed fully in [18].

Hence the role for a particular data-mining technology is a filter, winnowing a large dataset and selecting a manageable subset of individuals for further scrutiny using either downstream data-mining technologies, or traditional intelligence techniques.

We make the following assumptions about the problem setting:

- Datasets contain descriptions of the activities and attributes of individuals, but the threats among these individuals act in ways that are correlated, at least partially (that is, threats are cells). For example, datasets may contain information about locations visited over time, or location of residence. The work presented here cannot be used to address the 'lone terrorist' problem.
- The goal is either to identify *any* threat group (a hard problem) or to identify a threat group with a particular target individual whose properties are also part of the dataset (a slightly easier problem).
- A technique must have a false negative rate of zero (at least over a threat group; that is it may fail to detect some individuals but must detect at least one member of any threat group). Otherwise, it sometimes removes genuine threats, preventing them being detected in subsequent downstream analysis.

The choice of attributes is critical to the success of threat detection. Attributes in such datasets can be usefully divided into two kinds:

- *Incidental* attributes that describe properties and actions that may be *correlated* with terrorism. These may be static, such as country of citizenship, gender, income and so on; or based on actions such as purchasing particular kinds of plane tickets, or changing itinerary on the day of travel.
  Incidental attributes *happen* to have some predictive power for terrorism today, but this connection can be dissolved at any time.
- *Intrinsic* attributes that describe properties and, more commonly, actions that are *necessary* to carry out an attack, for example carrying out surveillance on a target site.
  Intrinsic attributes *necessarily* have some predictive power for terrorism and the connection cannot be dissolved, only diffused.

Intrinsic attributes are inherently better than incidental attributes because threats are *forced* to have certain values for them. Of course, some of the general public will also share these values; but such attributes allow datasets to be separated into those individuals who are *not* threats and those who *might be*. Incidental attributes cannot do this reliably. Moreover, the set of individuals who can be eliminated will tend always to be much larger than the set of possible threats who remain.

The use of intrinsic attributes forces threats to come under scrutiny. Their only remaining strategy is to conceal themselves among that part of the population who share the same attribute values – but this becomes harder and harder as the number of attributes increases, so there is a benefit to collecting wide-ranging data.

Concealing forced actions is difficult for two reasons:

- A threat group is forced to make coordinated actions, and such actions are potentially visible as correlations in the data. For example, if they meet to plan, then they are located at the same place at the same time. Even strategies to decouple simultaneous presence, such as letter drops, may fail if data is collected using time windows.
- A threat group is forced to carry out actions that are correlated with their target, and these actions are also potentially visible in the data. For example, they may travel the same route as the target but earlier in time.

If intrinsic attributes are used, threat groups cannot avoid correlations both among themselves and with their targets. It is these correlations, which reveal themselves as locally dense regions within appropriate representations of the dataset, that data mining must search for. Some evidence for this is provided by Krebs [12], who analyzed the connections among the group involved in the destruction of the World Trade Center. He showed that the members of the group were indeed tightly correlated. Of particular note is that a single meeting among a subset of them reduced the mean distance between members by 40% from its value given their relationships alone. Such is the power of intrinsic action attributes.

An immediate concern is that datasets describing any human population will be full of correlated subsets, and it might prove impossible to detect the correlations due to terrorism against such a noisy background. Consider the dentists of Pittsburgh[1]. We might expect that they would appear as a correlated group – they come from similar (educated) socioeconomic groups, they live in similar settings, and they travel to similar conferences and conventions. However, as we consider more aspects of their lives, these correlations begin to be diluted by others: they travel to differing parts of the country for family occasions, their children insist on holidays in different places, and they have different hobbies. The threats of Pittsburgh (should there be any) might also appear strongly correlated by a few attributes, but this correlation is much less likely to dilute as further attributes are considered.

More formally, the reasons why correlation in threat groups might be visible against a background of widespread correlation are these:

1. Most individuals are part of a fairly large number of subgroups with whom they are correlated – enough that the strength of membership in each one is quite small.

   Consider the folk theorem about six degrees of separation, the contention that a chain of acquaintances of length less than or equal to six can be built between any two people in some large population (originally the population of the U.S. in Milgram's original work, now often claimed for the total world population). If a given individual is acquainted with (say) $a$ individuals, then each of these $a$ individuals must be acquainted with a fairly large number of others outside the original set of $a$ or else the powers do not increase quickly enough (since $a^6 \approx$ the large population).

---

[1] Apologies to both dentists and Pittsburgh for this example.

This result contradicts our intuition that an individual's social circle tends to be small. The resolution (see, for example, [15]) is that such small social circles are bridged by rare, but not too rare, 'long-distance' connections.

Acquaintanceship is a reasonable, although not perfect, surrogate for correlation in the kind of datasets we are interested in – we would not be surprised that acquaintances would turn out to be fairly well correlated in large datasets – they live in similar places and have similar lifestyles, including travel arrangements. What is less obvious is that the 'long distance' connections in acquaintanceship are likely to produce strong correlations as well – for an acquaintanceship survives only if its members have 'something in common'. Hence the implication of six degrees of separation (and the existence of short paths in acquaintanceship graphs) is that correlation smears rapidly across subgroups because of the richness of cross-connections of common interests and behavior.

2. We might expect threats to be substantially less connected by correlation than most people because they have a much narrower focus. Informally, we might suspect that threats don't buy life insurance, don't take holidays, don't buy lottery tickets, and don't have children in Little League. We quote from Krebs [12, p49], relying on previous work on the social network structures of criminals: "Conspirators don't form many new ties outside of the network and often minimize the activation of existing ties inside the network". Baker and Faulkner [2] found that the need for secrecy distorts interactions between the parties.

These properties provide some assurance that a signature for threat actions exists in datasets that are sufficiently large and diverse. Note that, in this context, high dimensionality is a benefit because it acts to smear the background correlation in the population at large.

# 3  Data Generation Models

Since, for obvious reasons, real datasets containing threat actions are not available, the quality of detection models will be evaluated using artificial datasets. This immediately raises the question of what kinds of datasets are plausible and, of course, any choice is open to criticism.

Intrinsic attributes can be divided into those related to actions and those related to state. We now consider the properties of each.

For action attributes, an immediate issue is how to handle their temporal nature. Such attributes could be coded with time signatures attached and temporal data-mining techniques used – but I am not aware of any present data-mining technology powerful enough to detect temporal subsequences when different parts of them are carried out by different individuals (this is an interesting problem, though). It seems simpler, and perhaps more robust, to handle temporal properties by creating attributes for actions covering a period of time. For example, if visits to New York are an action of interest, then these can be converted into attributes as visits per month: January visits, February visits, and so on. It is also sensible to use overlapping time periods (creating partly correlated attributes) to avoid sensitivity to boundary choices.

Attributes representing actions will also be:

- Sparse, because only a small fraction of the total population of individuals will carry out any given task (e.g. only a small fraction of the U.S. travelling public visit New York in a given month).
- Have a frequency distribution whose mode is close to 1 and which decreases quickly (e.g. those people who visit New York in a given month mostly visit only once[2]).

Such attributes can plausibly be generated by introducing a high level of sparseness and by generating the nonzero values using a Poisson distribution with mean close to 1.

State attributes will have much flatter distributions. For example, the locations of residences of members of a threat group around a target might be expected to conform to a normal distribution because of the pressures for closeness to the target, counterbalanced by the pressure to remain far from each other. State attributes will also tend to be dense (everyone has to live somewhere).

It is, of course, arguable that other distributions are appropriate; for example, human intervention often creates distributions with heavy tails because humans deal quickly with the easy cases, leaving only harder ones.

## 4    Singular Value Decomposition

Singular value decomposition (SVD) [6] is a well-known technique for reducing the dimensionality of data.

Suppose that a dataset is represented as a matrix $A$ with $n$ rows (corresponding to individuals) and $m$ columns (corresponding to their attributes). Then the matrix $A$ can be expressed as

$$A = USV'$$

where $U$ is an $n \times m$ orthogonal matrix, $S$ is an $m \times m$ diagonal matrix whose $r$ non-negative entries (where $A$ has rank $r$) are in non-increasing order, and $V$ is an $m \times m$ orthogonal matrix. The superscript dash indicates matrix transpose. The diagonal entries of $S$ are called the *singular values* of the matrix $A$.

One way to understand SVD is as an axis transformation to new orthogonal axes (represented by $V$), with stretching in each dimension specified by the values on the diagonal of $S$. The rows of $U$ give the coordinates of each original row in the coordinate system of the new axes.

The useful property of SVD is that, in the transformed space, the maximal variation among objects is captured in the first dimension, as much of the remaining variation as possible in the second dimension, and so on. Hence, truncating the matrices so that $U_k$ is $n \times k$, $S_k$ is $k \times k$ and $V_k$ is $m \times k$ gives a

---

[2] The Zipf distribution is a plausible distribution for attributes such as these.

representation for the dataset in a lower-dimensional space. Moreover, such a representation is the best possible with respect to both the Frobenius and $L_2$ norms.

SVD has often been used for dimensionality reduction in data mining. When $m$ is large, Euclidean distance between objects, represented as points in $m$-dimensional space is badly behaved. Choosing some smaller value for $k$ allows a faithful representation in which Euclidean distance is practical as a similarity metric. When $k = 2$ or 3, visualization is also possible.

Another way to understand SVD is the following: suppose that points corresponding to both rows and columns are plotted in the same $k$-dimensional space. Then each point corresponding to a row is at the weighted median of the positions of the points corresponding to the columns and, simultaneously, each point corresponding to a column is at the weighted median of the positions of the points corresponding to the rows. Hence SVD can be viewed as translating correlation or similarity into proximity.

SVD measures variation with respect to the origin, so it is usual to transform the matrix $A$ so that the attributes have zero mean. If this is not done, the first transformed attribute dimension represents the vector from the origin to the center of the data, and this information is not usually particularly useful. For example, when $A$ is the adjacency matrix of a graph, it is the second transformed attribute dimension which describes the partitioned structure (if any) of the graph.

While SVD is a workhorse of data manipulation, it has number of subtle properties that are not well-known. We will use four of them.

*Fact 1:* The singular value decomposition of a matrix is insensitive to the addition (or subtraction) of independent zero-mean random variables with bounded variance [1]. This property has been used to speed up the computation of SVD by sampling or by quantizing the values of the matrix. In counterterrorism, the effect we are looking for is so small and the results so important that neither of these is attractive. However, the fact does explain why SVD is good at detecting clusters within clusters – the outer cluster representing the majority of the data has zero mean (by normalization) and so, by the *fuzzy central limit theorem*, increasingly resembles a normal distribution as the number of ordinary individuals (and the number of attributes) increases.

*Fact 2:* SVD is a numerical technique, and so the magnitudes of the attribute values matter. However, multiplying the attribute values of a row of $A$ by a scalar larger than 1 has the effect of moving the corresponding point further from the origin. Because the positions of all of the other points depend, indirectly, on their correlations with the scaled point, via their mutual interactions with the attributes, points that are correlated with the scaled point are pulled towards it. When there is little structure in the low-dimensional representation of a dataset, this scaling technique can be used to find the individuals who are (positively) correlated with a given individual. In practice, this often makes it easier to see a cluster that would otherwise be hidden inside another in a visualization.

*Fact 3:* The correlation between two objects is proportional to the dot product between their positions regarded as vectors from the origin. Two objects that are highly correlated have a dot product (the cosine of the angle between the two vectors) that is large and positive. Two objects that are highly negatively correlated have a dot product that is large and negative. Two objects that are uncorrelated have dot product close to zero.

The usefulness of this property comes because there are two ways for a dot product to be close to zero. The obvious way is for the vectors concerned to be orthogonal. However, when $m$ is less than $n$ (as it typically is) there are many fewer directions in which vectors can point orthogonally than there are vectors. Hence if most vectors are uncorrelated, they must still have small dot products but cannot all be orthogonal. The only alternative is that their values must be small. Hence vectors that are largely uncorrelated must have small magnitudes, and the corresponding objects are placed close to the origin in the transformed space. Hence, in a transformed space from an SVD, the points corresponding to objects that are 'uninteresting' (they are correlated either with nothing or with everything) are found close to the origin, while points corresponding to interesting objects are located far from the origin (potentially in different direction indicating different clusters of such objects).

The dot products between rows of a $U\Sigma$ matrix, even when truncated, capture these correlation relationships well because the neglected terms in the dot products are small.

*Fact 4:* The decomposition depends on all the data used, both normal and anomalous. The precise geometry of the detection boundary of SVD is hard to predict without performing the decomposition, and impossible without knowledge of the dataset. Hence, a threat group cannot reverse engineer the transformation to determine how they will appear, even knowing that SVD is being used. In particular, SVD is resistant to probing attacks since any attempt to probe cannot control for the innocent individuals considered at the same time.

The complexity of SVD is $\mathcal{O}(nm^2)$, where $n$ is the number of objects and $m$ the number of attributes. For dense data, such a complexity verges on impractical. However, for sparse data SVD can be computed with complexity $\mathcal{O}(rk)$ where $r$ is the number of nonzero entries in $A$ and $k$ is the number of dimensions retained. For example, for a dataset in which each row represents the travel patterns of an individual and the each column represent a visit to a particular city in a given week, the number of nonzero entries in each row would be small and the complexity would be linear in the number of people considered.

## 5    Semi-discrete Decomposition

Semidiscrete decomposition (SDD) [11] is superficially similar to SVD but is, underneath, a bump-hunting technique [13]. It finds regions of rectilinearly aligned locations in a matrix that contain elements of similar magnitude (the bumps).

Once again, given a matrix $A$ representing data, its SDD is

$$A = XDY$$

where $X$ is $n \times k$, $D$ is a $k \times k$ diagonal matrix, and $Y$ is $k \times m$. The differences from SVD are (a) $k$ can take any value, including $k > m$, (b) the entries on the diagonal of $D$ are non-negative but need not be decreasing, and (c) the entries of $X$ and $Y$ are all $-1$, $0$, or $+1$.

The easiest way to see what SDD is doing is to consider $A_i$ the (outer product) matrix obtained by multiplying the $i$th column of $X$ and the $i$th row of $Y$. Each such matrix has the same shape as $A$ and contains rectilinear patterns of $+1$s (representing positive bumps) and $-1$s (representing negative bumps) against a background of $0$s. Hence each $A_i$ represents the stencil of a region of similar (positive and negative value) and the value of $d_i$ represents its height. Note that $A$ is the sum of the $A_i$ weighted by the $d_i$.

It is natural to sort $X$ and $Y$ so that the corresponding entries of $D$ are in decreasing order, so that the most significant bumps are selected first. The $X$ matrix can then be naturally interpreted as a hierarchical ternary classification of the rows of $A$. The first column of $X$ classifies the rows of $A$ into three groups: those whose $X$ entry is $+1$, those whose $X$ entry is $-1$, and those whose $X$ entry is $0$. Those whose entries are $+1$ and $-1$ are similar but opposite, while those whose entries are $0$ are not in the bump being selected at this level.

Here is a small example:

$$\begin{bmatrix} 1 & 1 & 4 & 4 \\ 8 & 8 & 1 & 1 \\ 8 & 8 & 1 & 1 \\ 1 & 1 & 1 & 1 \end{bmatrix} = \begin{bmatrix} 0 & 1 & 0 & 1 \\ 1 & 0 & 1 & 0 \\ 1 & 0 & 1 & 0 \\ 0 & 0 & 1 & 1 \end{bmatrix} \begin{bmatrix} 8 & 0 & 0 & 0 \\ 0 & 4 & 0 & 0 \\ 0 & 0 & 1 & 0 \\ 0 & 0 & 0 & 1 \end{bmatrix} \begin{bmatrix} 1 & 1 & 0 & 0 \\ 0 & 0 & 1 & 1 \\ 0 & 0 & 1 & 1 \\ 1 & 1 & 0 & 0 \end{bmatrix}$$

There are no $-1$ values in this example. The product of the first column of $X$ and the first row of $Y$ is

$$\begin{bmatrix} 0 & 0 & 0 & 0 \\ 1 & 1 & 0 & 0 \\ 1 & 1 & 0 & 0 \\ 0 & 0 & 0 & 0 \end{bmatrix}$$

which is a stencil covering the region of the array where the elements have the value 8 (which is the value of $d_1$). The second outer product selects the regions where the elements have the value 2. The third and fourth outer products select regions where the elements have value 1. These two could not be selected as a single stencil because they cannot be rectilinearly aligned.

## 6  Using SVD, SDD, and Their Combinations

We use these matrix decompositions to look for groups with unusual correlation in the following ways:

- We perform an SVD, truncate the $U$ matrix to $k = 3$ and plot the resulting rows of $U$ as points in 3-dimensional space. Because of Facts 1 and 3 about SVD, we expect that points corresponding to tightly correlated groups will be far from the origin, while uncorrelated points will be close to the origin.

SVD can therefore be used as a ranking classifier, where the ranking is based on distance from the origin which, we have seen, is closely connected to 'interestingness'.

– We compute the distance from the origin of each row in the $U$ matrix, truncated to 10 columns. Those rows of the $U$ matrix that are greater than the median distance, and (respectively) greater than 1.3 times the median distance, from the origin are ignored, and the remaining rows plotted in three dimensions as before.

– Assuming knowledge of the target, those points in $U$ that are on the same side of the origin as the target point are plotted in three dimensions.

– The previous two techniques are combined so that only rows of $U$ corresponding to points far from the origin and on the same side of the origin as the target are plotted.

– The rows of $U$ are plotted in three dimensions but the points are labelled by their classification from the top three levels of the SDD hierarchical ternary classification. Color is used as the indicator for the first level (red = +1, green = 0, blue = −1) and shape as the indicator for the subsequent two levels like this:

| +1 +1 | dot | 0 +1 | + | −1 +1 | diamond |
|--------|--------|------|------|--------|---------------|
| +1  0 | circle | 0  0 | star | −1  0 | triangle down |
| +1 −1 | cross | 0 −1 | square | −1 −1 | triangle up |

In general, we expect that the classifications from SVD and SDD will agree; that is, points that are placed close together by SVD will be classified similarly by SDD and *vice versa*. In particular, it would be useful if the points corresponding to the threat group fell into a class of their own. In any case, points whose classification differs markedly between the two techniques may deserve further attention.

– SVD and SDD can be combined into a single technique called the JSS (Joint SVD-SDD) methodology. The following steps are performed:

• The SVD of $A$ is computed, the component matrices $U$, $\Sigma$ and $V$ are truncated at some $k$ (in this case $k = 15$), and the truncated matrices are multiplied to produce a matrix $A_k$. This matrix has the same shape as $A$.

• The correlation matrix $C = A_k A_k'$ is computed. This matrix is $n \times n$ and its entries represent the 'higher-order' correlation among objects. Some correlation due to 'noise' has been removed and some indirect correlation is now explicitly visible in this matrix (e.g. entries that would have been 0 in the correlation matrix of $A$ may now contain non-zero values).

• Each entry of $C$ is replaced by its signed square. Unlike SVD, SDD is not scale independent. The selection of a bump depends on both the average magnitude of the values it includes and also the number of array positions that it covers. Increasing the relative magnitude of the entries weights the selection towards bumps of high magnitude but low area, which is appropriate for this problem.

- The SDD of the scaled $C$ matrix is computed. This SDD finds regions of similar value in the matrix; since it is a correlation matrix, such regions correspond to correlated rows in the original matrix, $A$.

The results of SVD require inspection to determine the possible presence of a threat cluster; SVD transforms the data into a form where such anomalous clusters are more visible. On the other hand, SDD produces a hierarchical classification in which objects are allocated to clusters with a proximity structure (closeness in the classification tree). Hence the technique can sometimes identify a threat cluster itself, particularly if the target is known.

## 7  Experiment

In what follows, the part of the matrix $A$ representing normal individuals will consist of 1000 rows and 30 columns. The 30 columns represent a set of attributes about each individual – we assume that these are intrinsic attributes and that a threat is forced to correlate with a target in the values of at least some of these attributes. The dataset has 10 additional rows added to represent a threat group. The results are for the first random dataset generated – no selection of datasets to provide better than average results was made. Many of our experiments were more clear-cut than the examples reported here.

In plots of two- or three-dimensional space derived from SVD, points corresponding to normal individuals are shown as (blue) dots, the target is shown as a (red) star, and the points corresponding to threats as (blue) squares. In plots involving SDD, the color and shape coding comes from the SDD classification.

The dataset has 30 dimensions, with 1000 points normally distributed with variance 1, and a threat group of size 10 normally distributed with variance 0.5 centered at one of the points. Because the diameter of the threat cluster is only half of the diameter of the cluster of all data points, we expect points from the threat cluster to remain inside the background cluster on average.

The results for this dataset are shown in Figures 1, 2, 3, 4, 5, 6, 7, and 8. Figure 1 shows that the threat cluster is visible although there are other points that are quite far from the origin. If the threat cluster were unlabelled, the threat cluster would certainly arouse suspicion, but another 10–20 points would also require further investigation. About half the individuals are correlated with the target (Figure 2), about half are farther than the median distance from the origin (Figure 3), and about a quarter are both (Figure 5). When the required distance from the origin is increased, the set requiring further attention is reduced to about 6% of the dataset and includes all of the threat group.

The plot in Figure 7 labels each member of the threat group with the same symbol, but it would be hard to decide which symbol corresponded to the threat without other information. This seems to be characteristic of SDD applied directly to the dataset.

The plot in Figure 8 shows the classification by the JSS methodology in which the threat group is correctly identified, with one false positive. Note the presence of a cluster of two individuals labelled by a blue circle and a blue +.

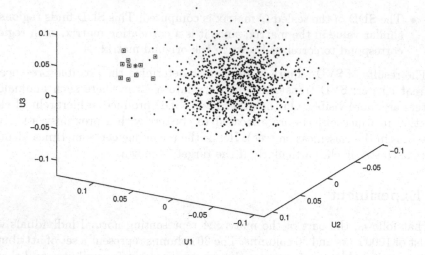

**Fig. 1.** SVD clustering showing positioning of the threat cluster

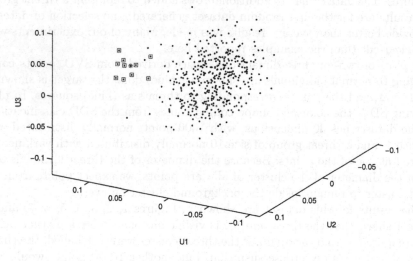

**Fig. 2.** 462 individuals correlated with the target

These represent the individuals who are most 'opposite' to the threat cluster. They therefore deserve special consideration because of the possibility that they represent alternative personas for members of the threat cluster – if two individuals are never at the same place at the same time, they may be two completely unconnected people – but the *may* be the same person using two identities.

This is arguably an easy dataset, but not entirely trivial because the fuzzy central limit theorem suggests that, given enough data, and given that normalization takes place after the data is collected, we can expect that many parts of a real dataset should look as if they were generated by a normal distribution.

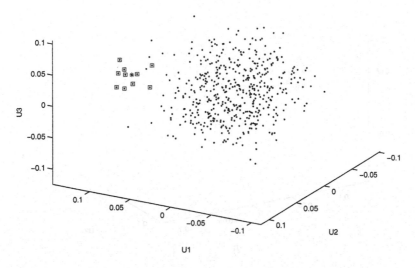

**Fig. 3.** 504 individuals greater than median distance from the origin

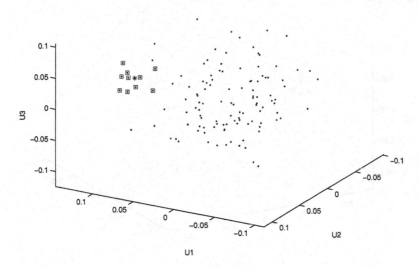

**Fig. 4.** 120 individuals greater than 1.3 times the median distance from the origin

The approach has been tried on datasets of greater complexity, datasets that are much larger, datasets that are sparse, and datasets that contain only binary values, but space prevents presenting the results here. In all cases, the techniques described here are able to distinguish the threat cluster.

SVD requires human analysis to detect clusters. Although this can be partly automated, for example by ranking points by their distance from the origin, this process loses the important directional information. Nevertheless, such a ranking could be used to generate a threat score for downstream analysis.

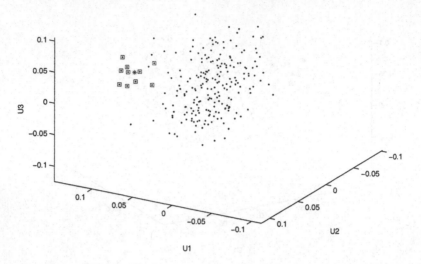

**Fig. 5.** 226 individuals greater than median distance from the origin and correlated with the target

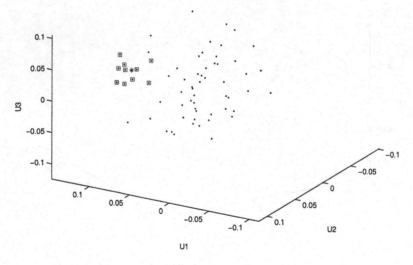

**Fig. 6.** 64 objects greater than 1.3 times the median distance from the origin and correlated with the target

The combination of SVD and SDD in the JSS methodology is the strongest of the analysis techniques. It exploits SVD's ability to detect correlation, but enhances it by using SDD's ability to detect regions of similar value in a correlation matrix. In general, the JSS methodology is better at partitioning objects into groups, and at identifying the group or groups that is most closely related to the target (when this is known).

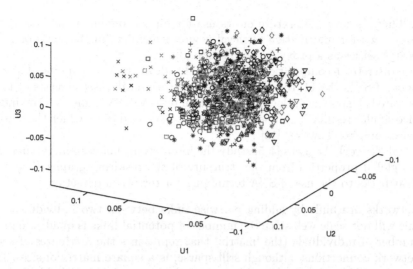

**Fig. 7.** Position from SVD, color and shape from SDD

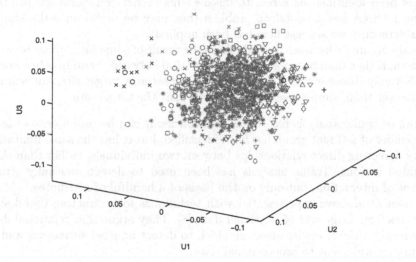

**Fig. 8.** Position from SVD, color and shape from JSS. The threat cluster is identified by the JSS hierarchical classification

## 8   Related Work

Techniques used for detecting outlying objects or outlying processes, for example Independent Component Analysis (ICA) [7], and 1-Class Classification [17, 19] seem less likely to provide good solutions for terrorism detection, although they may be effective when the *values* are completely beyond the control of individuals.

Singular value decomposition has been known since 1873, and used extensively in computing since Golub discovered an effective algorithm to compute it [6]. There is a vast literature on its use for dimensionality reduction; and it has been used for information retrieval where proximity (in the sense of cosine similarity) serves as a proxy for correlation [3].

Semidiscrete decomposition was originally developed as a reduced-storage analogue of SVD [10, 11, 16]. When the structure in a dataset consists of many well-isolated clusters, as it does in information retrieval, SVD and SDD do indeed produce similar results. This does not generalize well to data in which the clusters are more complex, however [13].

Social Network Analysis [4, 5] study the interactions between individuals and derives global properties from the structure of the resulting graphs. There are two drawbacks to the use of SNA techniques for terrorism detection:

- Networks are built by adding pairwise links between two individuals, and this will not scale well since the number of potential links is quadratic in the number of individuals (the 'matrix' that represents the attributes of social network connections, although still sparse, is a square matrix of size $n$). In practice, SNA seems to have been used when a particular individual threat has been identified as a tool to discover his or her collaborators. In other words, SNA has a bootstrap problem (but may be useful once the kind of prescreening we suggest here has been applied).
- Links are made between individuals as the result of some interaction between them, rather than because of some correlation between them. In other words, SNA may discover two collaborators who *meet* at a target site, but will not discover them simply because they both *visit* the target site.

Link or traffic analysis has similar drawbacks: it can be useful once at least one member of a threat group has been identified; but it has the same limitation of only detecting direct relationships between two individuals, rather than their correlated actions. Traffic analysis has been used to detect unusually strong patterns of interaction, but only on the basis of a handful of attributes.

Jensen *et al.* have experimented with techniques for extracting useful substructures from large sets of relational data [8]. They argue that relational data is inherently a richer environment in which to detect unusual situations, and so a natural complement to propositional data.

The paper [14] describes experiments using Inductive Logic Programming on relational datasets recording nuclear smuggling and contract killing. This work could presumably be generalized to counterterrorism.

## 9    Conclusion

We have shown that two matrix decompositions, SVD and SDD, are able to detect small correlated clusters, representing threats, against a variety of backgrounds representing degrees of innocent correlation. In particular, their use in combination using the JSS methodology is able to identify threat groups with very few false positives and (typically) no false negatives for threat groups as a whole.

These techniques represent the front line of data mining for counterterrorism. They are not strong enough to identify threats unambiguously, but they reduce the size of the problem for downstream techniques, often reducing the size of the datasets that need to be considered by 90%.

# References

1. D. Achlioptas and F. McSherry. Fast computation of low rank matrix approximations. In *STOC: ACM Symposium on Theory of Computing (STOC)*, 2001.
2. W.E. Baker and R.B. Faulkner. The social organization of conspiracy: Illegal networks in the heavy electrical equipment industry. *American Sociological Review*, 58:837–860, December 1993.
3. M.W. Berry, S.T. Dumais, and G.W. O'Brien. Using linear algebra for intelligent information retrieval. *SIAM Review*, 37(4):573–595, 1995.
4. T. Coffman, S. Greenblatt, and S. Marcus. Graph-based technologies for intelligence analysis. *CACM*, 47(3):45–47, March 2004.
5. L. Garton, C. Haythornthwaite, and B. Wellman. Studying online social networks. *Journal of Computer-Mediated Communication*, 3(1), 1997.
6. G.H. Golub and C.F. van Loan. *Matrix Computations*. Johns Hopkins University Press, 3rd edition, 1996.
7. A. Hyvärinen and E. Oja. Independent component analysis: Algorithms and applications. *Neural Networks*, 13(4–5):411–430, 2000.
8. D. Jensen and J. Neville. Data mining in social networks. Invited presentation to the National Academy of Sciences Workshop on Dynamic Social Network Modeling and Analysis, November 2003.
9. D. Jensen, M. Rattigan, and H. Blau. Information awareness: A prospective technical assessment. In *Proceedings of the 9th ACM SIGKDD International Conference on Knowledge Discovery and Data Mining*, 2003.
10. G. Kolda and D.P. O'Leary. A semi-discrete matrix decomposition for latent semantic indexing in information retrieval. *ACM Transactions on Information Systems*, 16:322–346, 1998.
11. T.G. Kolda and D.P. O'Leary. Computation and uses of the semidiscrete matrix decomposition. *ACM Transactions on Information Processing*, 1999.
12. V.E. Krebs. Mapping networks of terrorist cells. *Connections*, 24(3):43–52, 2002.
13. S. McConnell and D.B. Skillicorn. Semidiscrete decomposition: A bump hunting technique. In *Australasian Data Mining Workshop*, pages 75–82, December 2002.
14. R.J. Mooney, P. Melville, L.R. Tang, J. Shavlik, I de Castro Dutra, D. Page, and V.S. Costa. Relational data mining with Inductive Logic Programming for link discovery. In *Proceedings of the National Science Foundation Workshop on Next Generation Data Mining*, November 2002.
15. M. Newman and D. Watts. Renormalization group analysis of the small-world network model. *Physics Letters A*, 263:341–346, 1999,
16. D.P. O'Leary and S. Peleg. Digital image compression by outer product expansion. *IEEE Transactions on Communications*, 31:441–444, 1983.
17. B. Schölkopf, J.C. Platt, J. Shawe-Taylor, A.J. Smola, and R.C. Williamson. Estimating the support of a high-dimensional distribution. Technical Report MSR-TR-99-87, Microsoft Research, 1999.
18. K. A. Taipale. Data mining and domestic security: Connecting the dots to make sense of data. *Columbia Science and Technology Law Review*, 2, December 2003.
19. D.M.J. Tax. *One Class Classification*. PhD thesis, Technical University Delft, 2000.

# Generating Concept Hierarchies from Text for Intelligence Analysis

Jenq-Haur Wang, Chien-Chung Huang, Jei-Wen Teng, and Lee-Feng Chien

Institute of Information Science, Academia Sinica, Taiwan
{jhwang,villars,jackteng,lfchien}@iis.sinica.edu.tw

**Abstract.** It is important to automatically extract key information from sensitive text documents for intelligence analysis. Text documents are usually unstructured and information extraction from texts usually focuses on named entity extraction that is insufficient to reflect the concepts contained within documents. Other research on texts focuses on classifying the whole text into categories. However, texts might be diverse in subjects and suffer from classification accuracy. In this paper, our goal is to present a feasible approach to extract relevant information from texts and organize into concept hierarchies with the help of Web corpora. The approach is designed considering the need of information intelligence and the adaptation to different application domains.

## 1 Introduction

How to organize useful information in a form that facilitates observation of the embedded facts is an important problem that deserves investigation, especially in the field of intelligence analysis. In this paper, we intend to automatically organize a set of documents into a concept hierarchy, where an overall structure of them can be observed and important information summarized.

National security has become a critical issue in many countries since the tragic event of September 11. More and more suspected terrorist attacks such as car bombing or hijacking are being reported all over the world in the daily news. Besides terrorism, criminal activities such as financial frauds and cybercrimes are also becoming more common with the rapid increase of email and short message communications in people's daily life. These possible resources are usually in the form of unstructured text that should be carefully analyzed before suspected entities of security events could be identified. How to extract key information from these unstructured texts and digest it into useful information is a major challenge in intelligence information analysis.

Conventional research on information extraction (IE) from texts focuses on named entity extraction [1]. Named entities such as person names, places, and proper nouns are among the basic facts contained in documents, but they are insufficient to reflect the complete concepts within the documents. Key information such as relationships among these entities is more critical in better understanding the documents. Another research on texts is to classify the whole document into different categories. However, a document might contain text segments with very diverse subjects, and classification of the whole text could lead to classification accuracy problem.

H. Chen et al. (Eds.): ISI 2004, LNCS 3073, pp. 100–113, 2004.

In this paper, we intend to present a feasible approach to extract key information from texts. The approach is designed considering the need of information intelligence, and it is easily adapted to other applications and subject domains. The proposed approach is based on a Yahoo!-like concept hierarchy and text segments extracted from source documents as depicted in an example in Fig. 1.

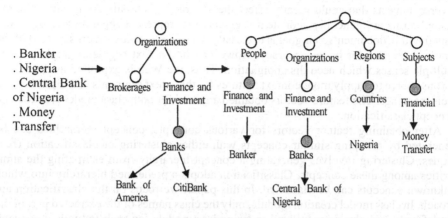

**Fig. 1.** A set of text segments extracted from source documents, an example concept hierarchy extracted from Yahoo! Directory, and the part of hierarchy with text segments classified

Fig. 1 shows a set of text segments extracted from a source document, in this case, an e-mail about financial fraud. A part of concept hierarchy is extracted from Yahoo! Directory for classifying the text segments. We intend to generate the part of concept hierarchy with text segments classified, which is the goal of the proposed approach.

For each sensitive document, we try to generate such a concept hierarchy with relevant text segments classified into meaningful parts (or nodes) of the hierarchy. This could be quite helpful in analyzing the common characteristics of the document sets. First, for human beings, it provides a natural perspective on viewing and browsing the data, whose meaning could be more easily grasped. Second, for database systems, such classification of textual data could help create meta-information, thus providing more flexible and powerful query options. For example, suppose there is a record of financial fraud in the database. After classifying the relevant facts, some meta-data can be created, e.g. the entities involved are: Banker (People), Nigeria (Regions), Money Transfer (Subjects), and Central Bank of Nigeria (Organizations). If all documents are classified in the above manner, the database system could provide concept-level search functions such as searching all records related to frauds about "Banking" in "West Africa", even though the text segments "Banking" or "West Africa" didn't actually appear within the source documents. Most important of all, the meta-information is automatically generated without human intervention.

The rest of this paper is structured as follows. The overall proposed approach is described in Section 2. Section 3 illustrates the concept extraction method. Section 4 details the process of concept hierarchy generation. Finally, discussions are given in Section 5, and Section 6 shows related works.

## 2   The Proposed Approach

The proposed approach consists of three separate modules: concept extraction, class model creation, and concept classification, as illustrated in Fig. 2. Concept extraction module uses term extraction methods such as PAT-tree-based approach [4] to extract relevant terms from a source document. The whole document usually contains very diverse subjects that could greatly affect the accuracy of classification. Since the extracted terms are generally short text segments that represent separate concepts contained within documents, our goal is to classify the separate text segments instead of the whole document for better accuracy. However, shorter text segments might contain multiple senses which need disambiguation. Thus, the Web is exploited as the largest corpus source to supply more context features for these text segments and disambiguate their meanings. The feature vectors obtained are used for both class model creation and concept classification.

After obtaining feature vectors for various concepts, concept hierarchies can be generated by grouping similar concepts with either clustering or classification techniques. Clustering involves generating a concept hierarchy from estimating the similarities among these concepts. Classification adopts a predefined hierarchy into which unknown concepts can be classified. In this paper, we focus on the classification approach. In class model creation module, only the class names of the extracted part of the predefined hierarchy were utilized to train class models for each individual concept. Thus our model training can be done without pre-arranged training sets.

For an unknown concept, concept classification module uses classification techniques to determine the most similar class in the hierarchy using the feature vectors obtained in the previous step. We discuss each module in more detail in the following sections.

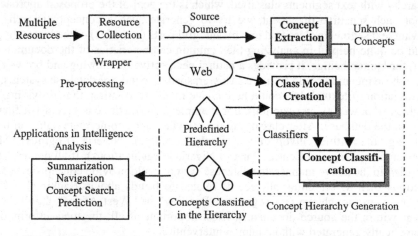

**Fig. 2.** An abstract diagram showing the concept of the proposed approach

As shown in Fig. 2, there are several issues in the process. (1) How to collect suitable resources for intelligence analysis? (2) Can all relevant concepts be effectively and efficiently extracted? (3) Is the created class model expressive enough for the concepts involved? (4) How can a concept hierarchy be generated? (5) What benefits will the concept hierarchy bring to intelligence analysis? Due to the page limitation, in the following sections, we will focus on the issues (2), (4), and (5).

# 3    Concept Extraction

The first issue of the proposed approach is how to efficiently and effectively extract relevant concepts from documents. Key information and important facts in a document such as person names, places, time, or proper nouns, are often short text segments that need to be extracted. Whether all relevant concepts could be extracted and their lexical boundaries correctly segmented is a challenge. In the proposed approach, term extraction methods are used to extract relevant text segments from source documents. The extracted text segments are considered to represent relevant concepts contained in the document.

Conventionally, there are two types of term extraction approaches. The first is language-dependent linguistics-based approach that relies on lexical analysis, word segmentation, and syntactic analysis for extracting named entities from documents. The second is language-independent statistics-based approach that extracts significant lexical patterns without length limitation, such as the local maxima method [15] and the PAT-tree-based method [4]. Considering diverse applications in intelligence analysis and Web environments, we adopt the second type of approach. Our proposed term extraction method, i.e. the PAT-tree-based local maxima method, is a hybrid of the above two method and has been found more efficient and effective.

First, we construct a PAT tree data structure for the corpus, in this case, a set of sensitive documents. Then by utilizing the PAT tree, we can efficiently calculate the association measure of every character or word $n$-gram in the corpus and apply the local maxima algorithm to extract the terms. The association measurement is determined not only by the symmetric conditional probability [15] but also the context independency ratio [4] of the $n$-gram. We detail the proposed method in the following subsections.

## 3.1    Association Measurement

The proposed association measurement, called $SCPCD$, combines the symmetric conditional probability $(SCP)$ [15] with the concept of context dependency $(CD)$ [4]. $SCP$ is the association estimation of its composed sub $n$-grams as defined below

$$SCP(w_1 \ldots w_n) = \frac{p(w_1 \ldots w_n)^2}{\frac{1}{n-1}\sum_{i=1}^{n-1} p(w_1 \ldots w_i) p(w_{i+1} \ldots w_n)} \tag{1}$$

where $w_1 \; w_n$ is the $n$ gram to be estimated, and $p(w_1 \ldots w_n)$ is the probability of the occurrence of the $n$-gram $w_1 \ldots w_n$.

Although $SCP$ can measure the cohesion holding the words together within a word $n$-gram to a certain degree, it cannot determine the lexical boundaries of the $n$-gram. An $n$-gram with complete lexical boundaries also implies that it tends to have free associations with other $n$-grams appearing in its context. Therefore, to further ensure that an $n$-gram has complete lexical boundaries, the concept of context dependency is introduced. Moreover, we consolidate the concept with *SCP* to form one association measurement. In order to achieve this goal, a refined measure, context independency ratio, which is a ratio value between 0 and 1, is extended from [4]. It is defined as follows

$$CD(w_1 \ldots w_n) = \frac{LC(w_1 \ldots w_n)RC(w_1 \ldots w_n)}{freq(w_1 \ldots w_n)^2} \qquad (2)$$

where $LC(w_1 \ldots w_n)$ is the number of unique left adjacent words in western languages or characters in oriental languages for the *n*-gram in the corpus, or equal to the frequency of the *n*-gram if there is no left adjacent word/character. Similarly $RC(w_1 \ldots w_n)$ is the number of unique right adjacent words/characters for the *n*-gram, or equal to the frequency of the *n*-gram if there is no right adjacent word/character. Using the ratio we are able to judge whether the appearance of an *n*-gram is dependent on a certain string containing it. For example, if $w_1 \ldots w_n$ is always a substring of string $xw_1 \ldots w_n y$ in the corpus, then $CD(w_1 \ldots w_n)$ is close to 0.

Combining formulae (1) and (2), the proposed association measure *SCPCD* is as follows

$$
\begin{aligned}
SCPCD(w_1 \ldots w_n) &= SCP(w_1 \ldots w_n) * CD(w_1 \ldots w_n) \\
&= \frac{LC(w_1 \ldots w_n)RC(w_1 \ldots w_n)}{\dfrac{1}{n-1}\sum_{i=1}^{n-1} freq(w_1 \ldots w_i)\,freq(w_{i+1} \ldots w_n)}
\end{aligned}
\qquad (3)
$$

Note that the difference between the formulae of *SCPCD* and *SCP* lies in their numerator items. For *SCP*, those *n*-grams with low frequency tend to be discarded, which is prevented in the case of *SCPCD*. The proposed new measure determines a highly cohesive term by the frequencies of its substrings and the number of its unique left and right adjacent words/characters.

## 3.2  Local Maxima Algorithm

The local maxima algorithm, called LocalMaxs [14], is based on the idea that each *n*-gram has a kind of cohesion holding the words together within the *n*-gram. This is a heuristic algorithm used to combine with the previous association measurements to extract *n*-grams which are supposed to be key terms from text. We know different *n*-grams usually have different cohesion values. Given that:

- An *antecedent* (in size) of the *n*-gram $w_1 w_2 \ldots w_n$, $ant(w_1 \ldots w_n)$, is a sub-*n*-gram of the *n*-gram $w_1 \ldots w_n$, having size $n$ - *1*. i.e., the $(n\text{-}1)$-gram $w_1 \ldots w_{n-1}$ or $w_2 \ldots w_n$.
- A *successor* (in size) of the *n*-gram $w_1 w_2 \ldots w_n$, $succ(w_1 \ldots w_n)$, is a $(n+1)$-gram $N$ such that the *n*-gram $w_1 \ldots w_n$ is an $ant(N)$. i.e., $succ(w_1 \ldots w_n)$ contains the *n*-gram $w_1 \ldots w_n$ and an additional word before (on the left) or after (on the right) it.

The local maxima algorithm extracts each term whose cohesion, i.e. association measure, is local maxima. That is the term whose association measure is greater than or equal to the association measures of its antecedents and is greater than the association measures of its successors.

## 3.3   The PAT-Tree Based Local Maxima Algorithm

Despite the usefulness of the local maxima algorithm, without a suitable data structure, the time complexity of the algorithm is high. The main time complexity problems occur in two places. One is to calculate the context independency ratio (CD) for each unique $n$-gram in the corpus and the other is to find the successor of an $n$-gram. And the two problems can be treated as one: finding the successors of an $n$-gram. An intuitive way to do so is to find out all $(n+1)$-grams and then to compare the $n$-gram with them sequentially to see if they are the successors of it which is time-consuming. Therefore, we introduce PAT tree as the data structure.

PAT tree is an efficient data structure. It was developed by Gonnet [6] from Morrison's PATRICIA algorithm (Practical Algorithm to Retrieve Information Coded in Alphanumeric) [9] for indexing a continuous data stream and locating every possible position of a prefix in the stream. This makes it easier and more efficient to find the successors of an $n$-gram. More details on the PAT tree can be found in [4].

By utilizing the constructed PAT tree for the corpus, we can efficiently retrieve all $n$-grams from the corpus, get frequencies and context dependency values, and then calculate the association measures, $SCPCD$, of all the $n$-grams.

## 3.4   Some Remarks on Term Extraction Performance

To determine the effectiveness of the proposed association measure $SCPCD$ and the efficiency of PAT-tree data structure, we conducted several experiments on Web search-result pages and scientific documents from the STICNET database[1] using the proposed PAT-tree-based local maxima algorithm.

First, we intended to realize whether the $SCPCD$ measurement could extract more text segments that are relevant to the document. As shown in Table 1, $SCPCD$ performed better than $SCP$ and $CD$ in terms of both precision and recall rates. The extraction accuracy was manually determined such that a term was taken as correctly extracted only if it was segmented at the correct lexical boundary.

**Table 1.** The obtained extraction accuracy including precision, recall, and average recall-precision of auto-extracted terms using different methods

| Association Measure | Precision | Recall | Avg. R-P |
|---|---|---|---|
| CD | 68.1 % | 5.9 % | 37.0 % |
| SCP | 62.6 % | 63.3 % | 63.0 % |
| SCPCD | 79.3 % | 78.2 % | 78.7 % |

On the other hand, to find out the efficiency of PAT tree data structure, we tested the speed performance of the local maxima method and the PAT-tree-based local maxima method. The results in Table 2 showed that PAT-tree data structure was efficient in term extraction. Although the PAT-tree construction phase took a little more time in small corpus, in the real-world case for large corpus where 1367 and 5357 scientific documents were tested, the PAT-tree-based local maxima method performed much better than the local maxima method.

---

[1] http://sticnet.stic.gov.tw/

**Table 2.** The obtained average speed performance of different term extraction methods

| Term Extraction Method | Preprocessing Time | Extraction Time |
|---|---|---|
| LocalMaxs (Web Queries) | 0.87 s | 0.99 s |
| PATtree+LocalMaxs (Web Queries) | 2.30 s | 0.61 s |
| LocalMaxs (1367 docs) | 63.47 s | 4851.67 s |
| PATtree+LocalMaxs (1367 docs) | 840.90 s | 71.24 s |
| LocalMaxs (5357 docs) | 47247.55 s | 350495.65 s |
| PATtree+LocalMaxs (5357 docs) | 11086.67 s | 759.32 s |

## 4 Concept Hierarchy Generation

With the extracted relevant concepts, the next challenge is to organize the relationships among them. Our approach is to generate a concept hierarchy where relevant concepts can be classified and easily observed.

The abstract diagram depicted in Fig. 3 shows the overall process of concept hierarchy generation, which is composed of three computational modules: context collection, class model creation, and concept classification. The approach exploits the highly ranked search-result pages retrieved from online search engines as the effective feature sources for training the concept classes contained in the hierarchy and each unknown text segment. The context collection module collects features for the concept classes and the unknown text segments. The feature sources are utilized in the class model training module to train statistical model for the concept classes. The concept classification module determines appropriate classes for the unknown text segment.

### 4.1 Class Model Creation

**4.1.1 Context Collection.** We adopt the vector-space model as the data representation for both unknown text segments and target concept classes. The contexts of a text segment are obtained from the highly ranked search-result pages (document snippets) returned by Web search engines, e.g., the titles and descriptions of search-result entries, and the texts surrounding the matched text segments. The features for a text segment are then extracted from the returned snippets. The same procedure is used to collect the training sets for the concept classes in the predefined concept hierarchy.

Using Web search engines as information sources has both disadvantages and advantages. Web contents are usually heterogeneous and noisy, and need careful treatment. However, with the presentation schemes of most search engines, the neighboring contents surrounding a matched query (text segment) in Web pages are selectively shown in the returned snippets. Therefore, features are extracted from the corresponding text segment's contexts instead of the whole Web page. Further, since a huge amount of pages have been indexed, most text segments can get sufficient search results for training. As a result of recent advances in search technologies, highly ranked documents usually contain documents of interest and can be treated, to some extent, as an approximation of the text segments' concept domains.

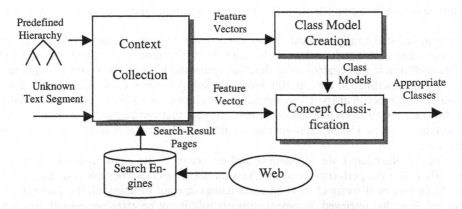

**Fig. 3.** An abstract diagram showing the process of concept hierarchy generation

**4.1.2 Representation Model.** Suppose that, for each text segment $s$, we collect up to $N_{max}$ search-result entries, denoted as $D_s$. Each text segment can then be converted into a bag of feature terms by applying normal text processing techniques, e.g., stop word removal and stemming, to the contents of $D_s$. Let $T$ be the feature term vocabulary, and $t_i$ be the $i$-th term in $T$. With simple processing, a text segment $s$ can be represented as a term vector $v_s$ in a $|T|$-dimensional space, where $v_{s,i}$ is the weight of term $t_i$ in $v_s$. The term weights in this work are determined according to one of the conventional $tf$-$idf$ term weighting schemes [11], in which each term weight $v_{s,i}$ is defined as $v_{s,i} = (1+log_2$ $f_{s,i}) * log_2 (n/n_i)$, where $f_{s,i}$ is the frequency of $t_i$ occurring in $v_s$ 's corresponding feature term bag, $n$ is the total number of text segments, and $n_i$ is the number of text segments that contain $t_i$ in their corresponding bags of feature terms. The similarity between a pair of text segments is computed as the cosine of the angle between the corresponding vectors, i.e., $sim(v_a, v_b) = cos(v_a, v_b)$. For the purpose of illustration, we define the average similarity between two sets of vectors, $C_i$ and $C_j$, as the average of all pairwise similarities among the vectors in $C_i$ and $C_j$:

$$sim_A(C_i, C_j) = \frac{1}{|C_i \| C_j|} \sum_{v_a \in C_i} \sum_{v_b \in C_j} sim(v_a, v_b). \qquad (4)$$

**4.1.3 Model Training.** In this research, we consider using a Yahoo!-like concept hierarchy for the problem of text-segment classification. It is a natural hierarchy of concepts, in which most of non-leaf classes contain an appropriate number of child classes. In most cases, manually constructing such a concept hierarchy for a certain IE task is not too difficult. For example, as will be shown in Section 4.3, based on the Yahoo! Directory, we can easily construct a hierarchy consisting of concept classes including People, Event, Time, and Place. For training a classification model for each concept class, such a hierarchy is useful, as its child classes offer ample information to characterize its concept. For example, in the People class, there are 55 sub-classes at the second level, e.g., Scientists and Politicians; and there are about hundreds of sub-classes at the third level, nine of which, e.g., Mathematicians and Physicians, are the sub-classes of the Scientists class; these sub-classes enrich the concept of the Scientists class.

In initial study, only non-leaf classes are considered as the target classes for classification. For each non-leaf class, its training set is the union of the document snippets obtained from search engines using the class name and its child class names as queries.

In our experiments, the top 100 document snippets were extracted as the feature source for a specific query. Using the Scientists class as an example, there were totally 1000 (i.e., 100+9*100) relevant document snippets that can be used to train its corresponding concept. Usually, it is not easy to obtain such amount of large training sets as the corpus.

On the other hand, the uniqueness and coverage of the child class names might greatly affect the performance of the class model. If a class does not contain enough child classes or if many of its child class names are not meaningful, the features extracted from the retrieved document snippets might not be effective enough to characterize the concept of the class. Obviously, not all semantic classes can use this kind of approach to train their class models. Also, not every unknown text segment can be classified with the proposed approach. In fact, the proposed approach is more suitable to classify the text segments that are more specific in their meaning and can retrieve more contextual information from the Web. Therefore, the proposed approach prefers classifying text segments into specific concept classes. It might not perform so well when classifying common text segments into a broader class.

## 4.2 Concept Classification

Given a new candidate text segment $s$, concept classification is to determine a set of classes $C_s$ that are considered as $s$'s related classes. With the same representation stated previously, the candidate text segment $s$ is represented as a feature vector $v_s$. We adopt a $k$NN ($k$-nearest neighbor) approach to classification.

$k$NN has been an effective classification approach to a broad range of text classification problems [13]. By $k$NN approach, a relevance score between $s$ and candidate cluster $C_i$ is determined by the following formula:

$$r_{kNN}(s, C_i) = \sum_{v_j \in R_k(s) \cap C_i} sim(v_s, v_j) \qquad (5)$$

where $R_k(s)$ are $s$'s $k$ most-similar objects, measured by *sim* function, in the whole collection. The classes that a text segment belongs are determined by either a predefined number of most-relevant classes or a threshold value of similarity scores. Different thresholding strategies have their advantages and disadvantages [19]. In this study, for evaluating the performance, we select the five most-relevant classes as candidates.

## 4.3 Experiments

To assess the performance of our approach, we have conducted several experiments. The Yahoo! Directory tree was used as our benchmark as it is readily available and well organized.

**4.3.1 Domain-Specific Term Categorization.** We first confined our attention to a specific domain, financial, and conducted an experiment to observe how well our approach could be applied. In the Yahoo! Finance & Investment Directory sub-tree, there are totally 40 first-level, 269 second-level, and 432 third-level classes. We used the first-level classes, e.g., "Banking" and "Mutual Funds," as the target classes and attempted to classify the class names at the third level, e.g., "Automated Teller Machines (ATMs)," onto it. For each target class, we took its class name and child class names at the second level, e.g., "Banks," "Credit Unions," and "Internet Banking," as the seed instances for model training. These class names could be taken as a kind of domain-specific facts extracted in an IE task. Table 3 shows the result of the achieved top 1-5 inclusion rates, where top-$n$ inclusion rate is the rate of text segments whose highly ranked $n$ candidate classes contain the correct class(es). To realize the effect of using second-level class names as seed instances in model training, the result was separated into two groups: with and without seed training instances.

**Table 3.** Top-$n$ inclusion rates for classifying Yahoo's Finance & Investment class names

| Yahoo! (Finance & Investment Class Names) | Top-1 | Top-2 | Top-3 | Top-4 | Top-5 |
|---|---|---|---|---|---|
| $k$NN- with Seed Training Instances | 0.71 | 0.86 | 0.90 | 0.92 | 0.94 |
| $k$NN – without Seed Training Instances | 0.40 | 0.57 | 0.66 | 0.71 | 0.75 |

**4.3.2 Named Entity Classification.** To observe how our technique performs in other circumstances, especially for named entities, we conducted another three experiments, i.e., using the sub-trees of "People" (People/Scientist), "Place" (Region/Europe), and "Time" (History-time Period) in Yahoo! Directory as our testbed. For these three cases, we randomly picked 100, 100, and 93 class names respectively, which can be considered as a kind of named entities, from the bottom-level and assigned them onto the top-level classes likewise. Table 4 and 5 respectively list the relevant information of the sub-trees employed and some samples of the test named entities, and Table 6 lists their respective classification results. It could be observed that in the "People" and "Place" cases, our technique obtained very satisfactory results, while in the "Time" case we cannot achieve similar result. The reason of its degradation seems that the concept of a time period, such as "Renaissance" and "Middle Ages", is too broad and too much noise is contained in the returned snippets, thus lowering the precision of our classification.

**Table 4.** The information of the three concept taxonomy trees extracted from Yahoo! Directory

| Hierarchy | # 1$^{st}$-level Classes (Target Classes) | # 2$^{nd}$-level Classes (Training Classes) | # 3$^{rd}$-level Classes (Text Segments) |
|---|---|---|---|
| People | 9 | 156 | 100 |
| Place | 44 | N/A | 100 |
| Time | 8 | 274 | 93 |

**Table 5.** Some samples of the test named entities randomly extracted from Yahoo! Directory

|  | Samples | Corresponding 1st -level Class |
|---|---|---|
| People | Curie, Marie (1867-1934)<br>Korzybski, Alfred (1879-1950)<br>Fulton, Robert (1765-1815)<br>Cantor, Georg (1845-1918) | Physicists<br>Linguists<br>Engineers & Inventors<br>Mathematicians |
| Place | Piraeus<br>Kannus<br>Vorchdorf<br>Grindavik | Greece<br>Finland<br>Austria<br>Iceland |
| Time | Glorious Revolution<br>Peloponnesian War<br>Hanseatic League<br>French Revolution | 17th Century<br>Ancient History<br>Middle Ages<br>18th Century |

**Table 6.** Top-$n$ inclusion rates for classifying Yahoo!'s People, Place, and Time class names

|  | Top-1 | Top-2 | Top-3 | Top-4 | Top-5 |
|---|---|---|---|---|---|
| Yahoo! People | 0.86 | 0.98 | 0.98 | 0.99 | 0.99 |
| Yahoo! Place | 0.87 | 0.95 | 0.97 | 0.97 | 0.98 |
| Yahoo! Time | 0.39 | 0.55 | 0.64 | 0.66 | 0.66 |

## 5  Discussion

With our preliminary experimental results on concept hierarchy generation, several issues remain to be addressed.

First of all, with the help of concept hierarchies, what benefits can we bring to intelligence analysis? It is important to organize documents in a form that facilitates overall observation and summarization of the embedded facts, especially in intelligence analysis. With the help of such concept hierarchy, irrelevant concepts in documents can be automatically filtered out, and intelligence analysts can quickly focus on concept space search of relevant associations. They can easily formulate their domain-specific queries for specific combination of facts and concepts in the documents, especially meta-classes information. For example, in our previous scenario, after generating concept hierarchies from each sensitive document on financial frauds, we can not only query all the "Money transfers" in "Nigeria", but also all "Banking" related types of frauds in "West Africa", even though the text segments "Banking" and "West Africa" didn't even appear in these documents.

For human beings, the concept hierarchy provides a natural and comprehensive perspective on viewing and browsing the documents. For database systems, such classification of textual data could help domain experts easily create meta-information, thus providing more flexible and powerful query options.

Secondly, there are other issues to be addressed. For instance, some form of wrapper functions could be needed in the resource collection module since a variety of document formats exist, e.g. HTML pages, e-mails, unstructured text reports, or structured databases.

In addition, there are some issues in term extraction step. For example, very short documents such as e-mails might be insufficient to extract enough relevant key terms (concepts). How to effectively extract relevant key terms from a relatively small document is a challenge to the success of our approach. In this case, we can use the whole document as the feature vector in both class model training and concept classification.

# 6   Related Work

**Information Extraction.** Document summarization is a popular information summarization approach, usually aiming at extracting important sentences as the abstract from single or multiple documents [10]. Organizing concept terms extracted from documents into a concept hierarchy is a useful approach to provide an overview of the information contained in the documents [12]. Different from previous works, our approach is focused on classifying concepts into a well-organized concept hierarchy without pre-arranged training sets.

**Text Classification and Information Filtering.** Text classification techniques are often used to analyze similarities among documents. In Sun et. al. [18], support vector machines were used for terrorism information extraction from free text collections, and Stolfo et. al. [17] proposed modeling user behavior from the mail server logs, thus forming a user profile of e-mail behavior. However, there is much difference between document classification and text segment classification. Documents normally contain more diverse concepts than text segments. The similarity between a document and a target class can be estimated using the distributions of the words; while the similarity between a text segment and a target class cannot apply the same approach because the text segment is usually very short. Therefore, in our approach, Web mining techniques are applied where the search-result snippets of the concepts are used as context features of the concepts.

**Web Mining.** Our research is related to Web mining [5] which mainly concerns about discovering useful information from huge amounts of semi-structured and unstructured data on the Web. There was some work that tried to discover rules for the extraction of specific information patterns [16]. Different from previous works, our approach uses search-result pages as the corpus for training concept classifiers.

**Link Analysis and Concept Space Approach.** Link analysis in intelligence domains aims to extract and search associations between entities. Lee [8] proposed a technique to extract association information from free texts. However, heavy dependence on Natural Language Processing (NLP) techniques and hand-crafted language rules limits its application to various forms of criminal data. The COPLINK Detect system [3] applied concept space approach [2] for association analysis, which has been found useful for crime investigation [7].

# 7  Conclusion

Information extraction from sensitive documents is important for intelligence analysis. In order to organize documents in a more comprehensive way, a concept hierarchy generation approach is proposed where key information is automatically extracted from texts. The approach is general and easily adaptable to other applications and subject domains. It is designed considering the need of intelligence analysis.

# References

1. Banko, M. and Brill, E. Scaling to Very Large Corpora for Natural Language Disambiguation. In *Proc. of the 39th Annual Meeting of the Association for Computational Linguistics (ACL 2001)*, 2001, 26-33.
2. Chen, H. and Lynch, K. Automatic Construction of Networks of Concepts Characterizing Document Database. *IEEE Transaction on Systems, Man and Cybernetics, 22 (5)*, 1992, 885-902.
3. Chen, H., Zeng, D., Atabakhsh, H., Wyzga, W., and Schroeder, J.: COPLINK: Managing Law Enforcement Data and Knowledge. *Communications of the ACM, 46 (1)*, 2003, 28-34.
4. Chien, L. F. PAT-Tree-based Keyword Extraction for Chinese Information Retrieval. In *Proc. of the 20th Annual International ACM Conference on Research and Development in Information Retrieval (SIGIR 1997)*, 1997, 50-58.
5. Feldman, R. and Dagan, I. KDT - Knowledge Discovery in Texts. In *Proc. of the 1st International Conference on Knowledge Discovery and Data Mining (KDD 1995)*, 1995.
6. Gonnet, G. H., Baeza-yates, R. A. and Snider, T. New Indices for Text: Pat Trees and Pat Arrays. *Information Retrieval Data Structures & Algorithms*, Prentice Hall, 1992, 66-82.
7. Hauck, R., Atabakhsh, H., Onguasith, P., Gupta, H. and Chen, H. Using Coplink to Analyze Criminal-Justice Data. *IEEE Computer, 35*, 2002, 30.37.
8. Lee, R. Automatic Information Extraction from Documents: A Tool for Intelligence and Law Enforcement Analysts. In *Proc. of 1998 AAAI Fall Symposium on Artificial Intelligence and Link Analysis*, 1998.
9. Morrison, D. PATRICIA: Practical Algorithm to Retrieve Information Coded in Alphanumeric. *JACM*, 1968, 514-534.
10. Radev, D. and McKeown, K. Generating Natural Language Summaries from Multiple On-line Sources. *Computational Linguistics, 24(3)*, 1998, 469-500.
11. Salton, G. and Buckley, C. Term Weighting Approaches in Automatic Text Retrieval. *Information Processing and Management, 24*, 513-523.
12. Sanderson, M. and Croft, B. Deriving Concept Hierarchies from Text, In *Proc. of ACM Conference on Research and Development in Information Retrieval (SIGIR 1999)*, 1999, 206-213.
13. Sasarathy, B. *Nearest Neighbor (NN) Norms: NN Pattern Classification Techniques*. McGraw-Hill. 1991.
14. Silva, J. F., Dias, G., Guillore, S., and Lopes, G. P. Using LocalMaxs Algorithm for the Extraction of Contiguous and Non-contiguous Multiword Lexical Units. *Lecture Notes in Artificial Intelligence, 1695*, Springer-Verlag, 1999, 113-132.
15. Silva, J. F. and Lopes, G. P. A Local Maxima Method and a Fair Dispersion Normalization for Extracting Multiword Units. In *Proc. of the 6th Meeting on the Mathematics of Language*, 1999, 369-381.

16. Soderland, S. Learning to Extract Text-based Information from the World Wide Web. In *Proc. of the 3rd International Conference on Knowledge Discovery and Data Mining (KDD 1997)*, 1997, 251-254.
17. Stolfo, S. J., Hershkop, S., Wang, K., Nimeskern, O., and Hu, C. Behavior Profiling of Email. In *Proc. of the 1st NSF/NIJ Symposium on Intelligence and Security Informatics (ISI 2003)*, 2003, 74-90.
18. Sun, A. Naing, M.-M., Lim, E.-P., and Lam, W. Using Support Vector Machines for Terrorism Information Extraction. In *Proc. of the 1st NSF/NIJ Symposium on Intelligence and Security Informatics (ISI 2003)*, 2003, 1-12.
19. Yang, Y. A Study on Thresholding Strategies for Text Categorization. In *Proc. of ACM Conference on Research and Development in Information Retrieval (SIGIR 2001)*, 2001, 137-145.

# Interactive Query Languages
# for Intelligence Tasks

Antonio Badia

Computer Engineering and Computer Science Department
University of Louisville
abadia@louisville.edu

**Abstract.** Counterterrorism and intelligence tasks rely on the efficient collection, analysis and dissemination of information. While information systems play a key role in such tasks, databases are ill-suited to support certain needs of the intelligence analyst, who many times needs to *browse* and *explore* the data in an interactive fashion. Since query languages are geared towards one-query-at-a-time exchanges, it is difficult to establish *dialogs* with a database. In this paper, we describe the initial phase of a project that focuses on designing and building a system to support interactive exchanges of information with a database, including the ability to refer to old results for new questions, and to play what-if scenarios. We describe our motivation, our formalization of the concept of dialog, and our initial design of the system. Further development is outlined.

## 1   Introduction

Recent world events (September 11, 2001, in the U.S.; March 11, 2004, in Spain) have made clear that sophisticated intelligence work is needed in order to deter and prevent terrorist threats. Such intelligence work relies on the efficient collection, analysis and dissemination of information. Clearly, information systems play a key role in such tasks: Michael Wynne, principal deputy under secretary of Defense for acquisition, technology, and logistics, has stated that *in the 21st century, the key to fighting terrorism is information*. Also, the paper [17] is significantly titled *Countering Terrorism Through Information Technology*. However, traditional databases are not specially suited for this environment, in which data access has special characteristics. One such characteristic is the need by intelligence analysts to *browse* and *explore* the data as it may not be clear which questions to ask. In a typical scenario, the analyst may ask questions from a database, examine the answers, go back for more information or play what-if scenarios *based on the answers obtained*.

Interaction with the database is hampered, since query languages are geared towards one-query-at-a-time exchanges, with limited information flow. Hence, it is difficult to establish *dialogs* with a database. In this paper, we describe a project on its beginning stages that focuses on designing and building a system to support interactive exchanges of information with a database, including the ability to refer to old results for new questions, and to play what-if scenarios.

H. Chen et al. (Eds.): ISI 2004, LNCS 3073, pp. 114–124, 2004.

In the next section, we describe the problem in detail, and give an example of the use that we envision for the system. Next, we formalize the notion of dialog, and show the initial design of the system. We then study some properties of our formalization and overview issues of implementation and efficiency. We close with some conclusions and outline further research in the project.

## 2    The Problem

It is clear that information and its flow are a powerful weapon that will play a key role in future adversarial scenarios. Managing this information (gathering it, organizing and fusioning it, and making it available to the parties that need it) is the goal of many ongoing projects within the Defense and Intelligence Communities[1]. Clearly, there is an important and real need for advanced information analysis tools for counter-intelligence -a central task in Homeland Security. In this section we explore some special requirements of intelligence works and show, via examples, that traditional database management systems do not address said requirements. Throughout the proposal, we use a database that contains information about flights that different airlines offer periodically (for instance, Air France may go from Paris to Washington, D.C. every week), and the passengers on each flight, including an **status** that indicates if the passenger is consider high, low, or medium risk. Many times, the way an intelligence analyst needs to operate is by exploring and interacting with the data. The analyst may have a clear, high-level goal in mind (i.e. find out if a suspected person 'X' is a member of a terrorist organization, or is in the United States right now), but such goal is not likely to be solved by a direct querying of any data base; rather, there will be a series of questions that will attempt to gather the information needed to fulfill the goal (for instance, is 'X' associated with any known member of terrorist organizations? Is he from a region known for recruiting? Has he (or anyone with an alias for him) traveled anywhere in the last six months?) ([12, 11, 7]). Hence, obtaining information one query at a time may be too time-consuming and complex, and may interrupt the flow of information between database and user. The overall goal of the project is *to improve the information flow between a particular type of user (an intelligence analyst) and database systems*. To see the need for such an improvement, assume the following dialog between an analyst (A) and a helper (H), with questions numbered in order:

- (A) What are the names of all passengers on Air France flights from Paris to D.C. during December 2003? (1)
- (H) Long list of names,,,
- (A) Of those, which ones are not French nationals? (2)
- (H) List of names...
- (A) Of those, which ones have status of high risk? (3)
- (H) None.

---

[1] See, for instance, the Advanced Question & Answering for Intelligence (AQUAINT) project funded by the Advanced Research and Development Agency (ARDA), or the Mercury project within the Joint Battlespace Infosphere (JBI).

- (A) Ok, then, which passengers are French nationals? (4)
- (H) Short list of names...
- (A) Of those, which ones are considered high risk? (5)

Note that the question in (2) refers to the answer for (1), the question in (3) refers to the answer for (2), but the question in (4) also refers to the answer for (1) (not to the answer for (3)!). Finally, the question in (5) refers to the answer for (4). If the analyst were using SQL or a similar query language to query a database (or even a menu-driven front end), instead of a helper, the results from previous queries would have to be saved explicitly by the user; otherwise they would be lost and must be reworked into further inquiries. Database queries happen *out of context*, and that is not how people operate. We would like a system that supports this kind of interactive process. We note, though, that dialog support can get very tricky. Assume that the question in (2) is *How many of those are not French nationals?*. Then the answer would be a number, but it still would make sense to ask (3)! In this case, (3) would not refer to the answer, but to the underlying set of names that the answer is counting.

Supporting dialogs is important for another reason: dialogs are the base for *what-if* type of reasoning. An intelligence analyst works many times with data that is not completely reliable or credible; alternatives must be considered, and their implications analyzed ([12, 11, 7]). Creating what-if scenarios is a helpful procedure in these cases; our approach will support this kind of reasoning.

## 3   Technical Approach

Support for dialogs has to carefully balance expressiveness, efficiency and flexibility. The reason is that, in an interactive mode, answers must be obtained *very fast*; however, the system should not burden the user in order to achieve fast response.

There is an obvious way to implement dialog support in relational databases: transform each SQL query from a `SELECT` statement to a `CREATE TABLE` statement, choose a name for each query, and then SQL takes care of the rest. Such approach is very inefficient for two reasons. First, the overhead in saving each result (overhead that grows as the number of queries in the dialog grows) may not be justified if only a few results are reused later on[2]. Second, on this scenario query answers are stored on disk, unindexed. However, we could achieve faster response times if some answers were kept in memory. Since it may not be possible to keep all answers in memory, a choice must be made. We would like a system that decides, for each answer, whether to keep it or not; if kept, in which format to keep it (see later about several options) and whether to keep it in disk or in memory. The system should take into account parameters like the size of the answer, the cost of recreating it (if not saved) and the probability of an answer being reused. Since it is impossible to determine, in a true ad-hoc

---

[2] In systems that are capable, a *materialized view* can be created instead; however, the efficiency problem persists.

dialog, whether an answer will be used again, we propose to have a system that archives dialogs per user, mines them to determine mode of interaction, and uses this information to decide when and how to store a result.

We now formalize the notion of dialog. Given a database $D$, we distinguish between the database schema $sch(D)$ and its extension $ext(D)$. It is well known that a database extension changes over time; however, for now we assume that the database remains fixed throughout a dialog. This will allow us to ignore difficult issues of time modeling and updating; getting around this simplification is left for further research.

Queries are assumed to be expressed in SQL, although the framework is mostly independent of the query language and can be extended[3]. Given query $q$, we write $q(D)$ to denote the application of query $q$ to database $D$ (i.e. running $q$ against $ext(D)$). Note that, while $q(D)$ is a relation, it has no name associated with it. For now, we will use *the expression $q(D)$* as the name of the relation. The expression $text(q)$ denotes the query itself, i.e. its SQL code. The relations mentioned in the FROM clause of $text(q)$ are denoted $from(text(q))$ -note that this is a set of names. A dialog with $D$, then, is seen as an ordered, finite sequence of queries $q_0, q_1, \ldots, q_n$, such that each query $q_i$ is run against database $D$ extended with the results of previous queries $q_j$, $0 \leq j < i$. $q_0$, called the *initial* query, is run against $D$. Formally, we associate with each query in the dialog a schema with function $sc$ as follows:

- $sc(q_0) = sch(D)$;
- $sc(q_{i+1}) = sch(D) \cup \bigcup_{0 \leq j \leq i} sc(q_j)$

Intuitively, in a dialog the relations created by running previous queries can also appear in a later query, i.e. for any query $q_i$, $from(text(q_i)) \in sc(q_i) = sch(D) \cup \bigcup_{0 \leq j < i} sc(q_j)$. Note that in a standard setting, $from(text(q_i))$ for any query $q_i$ can only mention relations appearing in the original database, (i.e. for all $i$, $from(text(q_i)) \in sch(D)$). If query $q_i$ mentions in its FROM clause the results from query $q_j$ (i.e. $q_j(D) \in from(text(q_i))$), we say that $q_i$ *uses* $q_j$. This creates a series of relationships among queries in a dialog which can be represented by a directed acyclic graph (DAG) as follows: each query is a node; a link from node $q_j$ to node $q_i$ exists if the query in $q_i$ uses the query in $q_j$. A DAG for our example of the previous section is shown in Figure 1, part (a) with each query represented by its number.

We call the set of nodes pointing to a node $q$ $in(q)$, and the set of nodes to which $q$ points, $out(q)$. Note that the resulting graph may not be a tree, but it has some common characteristics with a tree:

- there exists some nodes $q$ with $in(q) = \emptyset$. These nodes corresponds to query $q_0$ and to other queries which use only the database $D$. Such nodes are called the *roots* of the graph; the set of roots of graph $Q$ is denote $roots(Q)$.
- nodes in the graph can be grouped in *levels*, that denote where in the dialog they fit, as follows: $level(0) = roots(Q)$; $level(i+1) = \bigcup_{q \in level(i)} out(q)$.

---

[3] The only necessary characteristic is that the query language returns answers that can be integrated into the database. This is clearly the case with SQL.

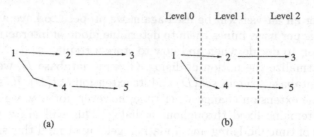

**Fig. 1.** Graph for example of section 2: (b), with levels added.

Note that if $q \in level(i)$ and $q$ uses $q'$ then $q' \in level(j)$ for some $j < i$. Note also that, for the finite graphs that represent dialogs, there is a $k$ such that $level(k) = \emptyset$, and therefore, for all $l > k$, $level(l) = \emptyset$. The smallest such integer $k$ is called the *length* of the graph. Given a graph $Q$, we create a pseudo-tree $Q_T$ as outline above, by grouping all nodes of $Q$ in levels (recall that level 0 corresponds to the roots of the graph). Analysis of $Q$ and $Q_T$ provide important clues about how to treat the queries in a dialog. Our previous graph example, divided into levels, is shown in Figure 1, part (b).

## 4    System Design and Implementation

We plan to implement a *dialog manager* as an interface between the user and the database system. The *dialog manager* will handle dialog support, build a dialog graph as defined above, and store it once the dialog is finished. To handle dialog support, the system will keep track of a user's questions, decide whether to store answers on disk or in memory, and in which form (see later for a discussion of options). The system will also allow the user to reuse results not only by name, but by using certain keywords in the From clause of the SQL query. In particular, assume we are in query $q_i$ of dialog (graph) $Q$. Then,

- keyword first always denotes $q_0$;
- keyword previous denotes $q_{i-1}$.
- keyword root n always denote the $n$-th query that is a root (i.e. the n-th element of $root(Q)$), with the order given by the order in which queries were produced.

The overall system, its modules and the flow of information are shown in Figure 2. When a user logs in, a *session* will be started. As far as the user does not log off, or explicitly terminates it, the session will continue. The user will be allowed to reuse results within a session. The dialog manager receives requests from the user in a slightly modified version of SQL (SQL plus the keywords introduced above). The Parser parses the incoming request, finds keywords (if any) and references to previous results, and makes appropriate substitutions to generate standard SQL. This is then sent to the database by the Wrapper. The Wrapper is designed to handle interaction with different databases and isolate

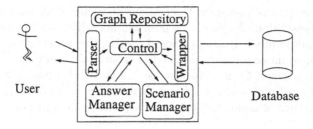

**Fig. 2.** Overall System Design.

the program from each database idiosyncrasies (it is planned to develop the Wrapper using JDBC). When an answer comes back, the manager checks the size of the answer, adds a node to the current dialog graph and decides, based on knowledge from previous graphs, the answer size, and the query text where and how to store the answer. The Answer Manager is in charge of storing the answer and keeping track of where each answer is, and in what representation. Once a dialog is over, the graph generated is stored in the Graph Repository, where it will be kept for further analysis and usage. Finally, an Scenario Manager handles what-if reasoning by receiving the changes to be made and the answer to be changed, and propagating the changes throughout the dialog graph. It also takes care of binding the original changes to the propagate changes, so that multiple scenarios can be supported.

We propose to collect all dialog graphs for a user or group of users, and mine some characteristics of them in order to improve dialog management. The intuitive idea is that past dialogs can help infer which answers are going to be reused (or, at least, the probability of this happening). Our working hypothesis is that users tend to reason and proceed in similar ways over time. Hence, mining graphs of past activities could provide useful indication of future actions[4]. The following are some characteristics of the graph $Q$ and the pseudo-tree $Q_T$ that are worth noting. The *(largest) smallest degree* of a level in $Q_T$ is the (largest) smallest node index in that level. The *jump* of $Q_T$ between two levels $i$ and $i + 1$ is the difference between the lowest degree in $i$ and the largest degree in $i + 1$. The jump of $Q$ is the largest jump in $Q_T$. Intuitively, the jump gives us an idea of how long it may take a user to go back to reuse an old result. A jump of 4, for instance, means that at some point a user did 3 different thing before coming back to use a result. If this is the longest a user took to reuse a result, it follows that all results that would have generated a longer jump were actually not reused, and therefore there was no need to save them. Assume, for instance, that a user has established $n$ dialogs $d_1, \ldots, d_n$ with a database, and the maximum jump is 6. Assume further that we are at dialog $n + 1$ in query $q_{10}$. Unless a further jump is taken in this dialog, this means that queries $q_0$ to $q_4$ can be forgotten, as chances are they will not be revisited. Of course, this is a heuristic, and it is perfectly possible for a user to keep on using increased

---

[4] Similar assumptions underlie other research ([1]).

jumps. However, psychological evidence about short term (or working) memory in humans suggests that the jump of a user will actually stabilize over time, and it may be a small number. If not to discard results, the information may be used to decide when to move some results to disk from main memory.

A node $q$ in a graph $Q$ such that $out(q) = \emptyset$ is called a *leaf*. Note that if $k$ is the length of $Q$, all nodes in $level(k)$ are leaves. The ratio of leaves in a graph to the total number of nodes helps us establish the probability of a result being reused.

Given a set of nodes $q_0, q_1, \ldots, q_m$, we say that the set forms a *chain* if $out(q_i) = \{q_{i+1}\}$ for $i = 0, \ldots, m-1$, and $in(q_j) = \{q_{j-1}\}$, for $j = 1, \ldots, m$. Given query $q_j$, a subgraph $Q$ rooted at $q_j$ such that there is a chain on it is called a *drill (or drill down)* on $q_j$. Intuitively, the chain represents a progressive refinement of the relation returned by $q_j$, without any further reference to the database. In our example, the sets $\{1, 2, 3\}$ and $\{1, 4, 5\}$ are both chains. Each relation in a chain is worth not only keeping, but keeping in memory if at all possible, since each subsequent question is computed from that answer alone (and therefore, keeping the answer in memory means that we do not need to access the disk at all!). If we relax the second requirement so that $in(q_j)$ contains only $q_{j-1}$ *and* relations from the database, we have a *pseudo-chain*. The results in a pseudo-chain are still worth keeping, and it may be a good idea to keep them in memory. This is due to the fact that the relations in the database and the previous answer $(q_{j-1}(sc(q_{j-1})))$ must be put together through some operation (most likely, though a join, although a set theoretic operation -union, difference, intersection- is also possible); if one of the operands is an in-memory table, the operation can be implemented much faster. Given query $q$, if $out(q)$ has more than one element, say $out(q) = \{q_1, \ldots, q_n\}$, we say that the elements of $out(q)$ are *complements* if $\bigcup_{1 \leq i \leq n} q_i(sc(q_i)) = q(sc(q))$ and the elements are pairwise disjoint. Note that this is the case of queries (2) and (4) in our example of the previous question. The interesting thing about such queries is that it may be easier to compute them all at once then separately; if a user tends to have queries that generate complements, it may be a good idea to compute complements when such a task is easy. For instance, for queries based on selection (say $\sigma_c(q)$, where $c$ is some condition), it is easy to compute a complement (computing $\sigma_{\neg c}(q)$). In our example, query 2 would select, from a certain list of passengers, those that are not French nationals. Later on, we come back to the same list and ask for those passengers which are French nationals. Clearly, both questions could have been computed at once with less effort.

We define, for a given node $q$ the *span of $q$* (in symbols, $Span(q)$) in a manner similar to the definition of levels: the span of a query $q$ in $i$ steps (in symbols, $span(q, i)$) is given by $span(q, 0) = out(q)$; $span(q, i+1) = \bigcup_{q' \in span(q,i)} out(q')$. Then, $Span(q) = \bigcup_i span(q, i)$[5]. The *span number* of query $q$ is simply the cardinality of $Out(q)$. Intuitively, the span number tells us how many results further down in the dialog use query $q$ *or* a result obtained by using $q$. The

---

[5] Note that, even though we do not limit our subscript, this is a finite, well defined process, bound by the length of the graph.

higher this number is, the more justified it is to materialize $q$ and to keep it in memory.

Finally, we can characterize *what if* analysis in this framework as follows. The result of changing a relation returned by a query (inserting, deleting or updating it) to further use the changed relation in a dialog is called creating a *scenario*. We need to track several scenarios, making the changes temporary, so that the same result can be changed in several ways (i.e. to support alternative analysis of the same data). We also need to propagate changes to results obtained from the changed result. Given query $q_i$, let $r'_i$ be the result of inserting, deleting, and/or updating $q_i(sc(q_i))$. Then, changes are not propagated back to relations in $from(text(q_i))$; rather, they are propagated forward to any $q_j$ such that $q_i(sch(q_i)) \in from(text(q_j))$. This is done iteratively, until all affected results are changed. Using our graph characterization of dialog, propagation proceeds using $out(q_i)$. Note that, given changes to $q$, the set of *all* nodes to which change should be propagated is exactly $Span(q)$. The changes are to be the result of reapplying queries to the new data. In our example of section 2, assume the analyst is surprised not to find a certain person's name in the answer to (4), and decides that the person is likely to be there under false identity (perhaps because other information supports this). Then, the analyst decides to change the answer to (4) and see what happens then. It is obvious, in this simple example, that the answer to (5) should also be changed accordingly (since $out(4) = \{5\}$), but that answers to (2) or (3) should remain untouched. Note that, had the analyst decided to change the answer to (2) for some reason, then the opposite would be true: the answer to (3) should change, but (4) and (5) should remain untouched. Note that the above simply characterizes the set of answers affected by a change; instead of an *eager* policy, changes can be propagated by a *lazy* (*on-demand, as-needed*) policy.

## 4.1   Implementation Issues

There is a clear need to make the system perform as fast as possible, given its goal of being interactive. In order to achieve the best possible response time, two techniques are adopted. The first technique consists of the graph analysis indicated above, in order to decide which answers to keep in memory, which ones to keep on disk and which ones can be disregarded. If the answer kept in memory is part of a larger computation, that computation can be sped up with memory-aware algorithms ([23, 21]). The second technique is to use several different representations for an answer, depending on factors like size, complexity of the query that produced it, etc. In particular, we will study three different representations for an answer: as a *virtual view*, in which case only the query itself, but not the results are not kept; as a *materialized view*, in which case the results are kept; and as a ViewCaches ([18, 19]). A ViewCache is an intermediate representation, between the virtual and the materialized one. Like virtual views, they do not need to be recomputed when there is a change in the base relations (i.e. for what-if reasoning). On the other hand, if the results of the view are needed, they can be materialized very efficiently. Unfortunately, ViewCaches can only be used with SQL queries that do not have aggregation, grouping or subqueries. While materialized views can be used in more cases, they must be recomputed whenever the base relations change. Fortunately, *incremental maintenance techniques* ([20, 9, 6, 13]) that were developed in the context of data warehousing can be used for this task.

## 5  Related Work

While the project is novel, it continues a long tradition in database research of trying to make databases more useful and user-friendly. Consequently, there has been considerable research on issues that are relevant, to some degree, to the present project, including efforts in flexible query answering (including natural language interfaces to databases), and query processing and optimization. Due to lack of space, we can only briefly mention some relevant references.

The motivation of Flexible Query Answering is in the flexibility of the data model more than flexibility at the query language level ([5]). Thus, flexible query answering usually addresses issues of querying semistructured data, or distributed databases, possibly with different data models. What this work has in common with our project is that there have been proposals of query languages that relax the need to know the structure of the database to some degree; such languages provide more flexible answers, but are not necessarily more user-friendly ([14]). An exception is the work of [15], which tries to increase the flexibility of the query language to allow naive users to recover from mistakes in writing queries.

Natural Language Interfaces for Databases (NLIDB) have a long tradition (see [2] for an introduction). While some ideas of this research provide inspiration for the present proposal, research in natural language has seen very limited commercial use, and is not directly applicable to the present project. Natural Language research has also generated (and interacted with) considerable research in *information retrieval* ([3]). Many modern RDMBS have an information retrieval component that implements some text retrieval functionality ([16]). However, even though there are techniques developed in this context that would contribute to a sophisticated dialog system ([8]), most of this research concentrates on retrieving information from text databases, and does not apply to structured databases. Also, it assumes a high degree of lexical analysis of the question, and does not take performance into account. Hence, such research is, by the most part, not directly applicable to the present project.

As for research in query processing and optimization, relevant research has been mentioned in the previous section. It is worth mentioning here that although the idea of dialog seems similar to existing OLAP systems, which support interactive analysis through, roll-up, drill-down, slice-and-dice queries ([10]), it goes beyond such systems in providing a dedicated architecture that studies past interactions in order to decide when and how to save and reuse past queries, and in supporting automatically what-if analysis. Also, the idea beyond our graph formalisms is obviously to provide us with a *caching strategy*, a well known and studied idea. However, unlike techniques like LRU (least recently used) and similar ones, our strategy is *semantic* in that it tries to take decisions based on issues like future use and role in the argument, and *adaptive*, in that it is not fixed in advance but depends on past behavior of a user or group of users.

Finally, we point out the strong connection to novel research that mines activity graphs in the context of workflow management to enhance user interaction ([1]).

# 6   Conclusion and Further Research

In this paper we have presented the initial concept for a project to provide relational databases with an interactive query capability, in the form of dialogs. After arguing the importance of this capability for intelligence and counter-terrorism tasks, we have shown how to formalize the concept, and some basic properties. We have also shown a design for a system that will implement these concepts, and discussed some alternatives for implementation.

We plan to design and implement such a system in the near future, as well as to explore extensions of the ideas proposed here. For instance, we plan to investigate if our techniques can be extended to the XML case, perhaps by considering XML as a nested view over an underlying relational database ([4]) and supporting dialogs in XQuery. We will set up experiments to determine the validity of our working hypothesis. We plan to use real users carrying out real-life tasks and study the set of graphs per user to determine how well the proposed measures reflect the user's behavior. Response time and user satisfaction (as determined by questionnaires) will be used to determine the system's degree of success.

One benefit of our graph representation is that it can be used to study the working habits of an analyst or group of analysts. This in turn can be used to pinpoint good and bad working habits, and to teach new analysts.

# References

1. van der Aalst, W.M.P.; Weijters, A.J.M.M. and Maruster, L., *Workflow Mining: Discovering Process Models from Event Logs*, to appear in IEEE TKDE, 2004.
2. I. Androutsopoulos, G. D. Ritchie, P. Thanisch, *Natural Language Interfaces to Databases: An Introduction*, Journal of Natural Language Engineering, vol.1, no.1, Cambridge University Press, 1995.
3. Baeza-Yates, R. and Ribeiro-Neto, B. *Modern Information Retrieval*, Addison-Wesley, 1999.
4. Braganholo, V., Davidson, S. and Heuser, C. *On the updatability of XML Views over Relational Databases*, in Proceedings of the Int'l Workshop on the Web and Databases (WebDB), 2003.
5. Chaudhri, V. and Fikes, R. Cochairs *Question Answering Systems: Papers from the AAAI Fall Symposium*, AAAI Press, 1999.
6. Colby, L., Griffin, T., Libkin, L., Mumick, I. S. and Trickey, H. *Algorithms for Deferred View Maintenance*, in Proceedings of ACM SIGMOD, 1996.

7. *A Compendium of Analytic Tradecraft Notes*, vol. I, edited by the Product Evaluation Staff, Directorate of Intelligence, Central Intelligence Agency.
8. Olivier Ferret, Brigitte Grau, Martine Hurault-Plantet, Gabriel Illouz, L. Monceaux, Isabelle Robba, Anne Vilnat *Finding An Answer Based on the Recognition of the Question Focus*, in Proceedings of TREC 2001, NIST, online publication (http://trec.nist.gov/pubs/trec10/t10_proceedings.html).
9. Gupta, A, Mumick, I. S. and Subrahmanian, V. S. *Maintaining Views Incrementally*, in Proceedings of the ACM SIGMOD Conference, 1993.
10. M. Jarke, M, Lenzerini, Y. Vassiliou and P. Vassiliadis, *Fundamentals of Data Warehouses*, Springer, 2000.
11. Krizan, L. *Intelligence Essentials for Everyone*, Joint Military Intelligence College, Washington, D.C., 1996.
12. *A Consumer's Guide to Intelligence*, Office of Public Affairs, Central Intelligence Agency.
13. *Materialized Views: Techniques, Implementations and Applications*, A. Gupta and I. S. Mumick, eds., MIT Press, 1999.
14. Alon Halevy, Oren Etzioni, AnHai Doan, Zachary Ives, Jayant Madhavan, Luke McDowell, Igor Tatarinov, *Crossing the Structure Chasm*, in Proceedings of CIDR 2003.
15. Motro, A *FLEX: A Tolerant and Cooperative User Interface to Databases*, IEEE TKDE 2(2), June 1990.
16. Oracle TechNet Homepage, http://technet.oracle.com/products/text.
17. Popp, R., Armour, T., Senator, T. and Numrych, K. *Countering Terrorism Through Information Technology, Communications of the ACM*, special issue on *Emerging Technologies for Homeland Security*, May 2004.
18. Nick Roussopoulos, Chung-Min Chen, Stephen Kelley, Alex Delis, Yannis Papakonstantinou *The ADMS Project: View R Us*, IEEE Data Eng. Bull. 18(2), pages 19-28, 1995.
19. Nick Roussopoulos *An Incremental Access Method for ViewCache: Concept, Algorithms, and Cost Analysis*, ACM Trans. Database Syst. 16(3), pages 535-563, 1991.
20. Xiaolei Qian, Gio Wiederhold *Incremental Recomputation of Active Relational Expressions*, IEEE Transactions on Knowledge and Data Engineering 3(3), Sept. 1991.
21. Jun Rao, Kenneth A. Ross *Cache Conscious Indexing for Decision-Support in Main Memory*, in Proceedings of VLDB 1999.
22. Guogen Zhang *Interactive Query Formulation Techniques for Databases* PhD thesis, University of California, Los Angeles, 1998.
23. Jingren Zhou, Kenneth A. Ross *Buffering Accesses to Memory-Resident Index Structures*, in Proceedings of VLDB 2003.

# Terrorism Knowledge Discovery Project: A Knowledge Discovery Approach to Addressing the Threats of Terrorism

Edna Reid[1], Jialun Qin[1], Wingyan Chung[1], Jennifer Xu[1], Yilu Zhou[1], Rob Schumaker[1], Marc Sageman[2], and Hsinchun Chen[1]

[1] Department of Management Information Systems, The University of Arizona, Tucson, AZ 85721, USA
{ednareid,qin,wchung,jxu,yiluz,rschumak,hchen}@bpa.arizona.edu
[2] The Solomon Asch Center For Study of Ethnopolitical Conflict, University of Pennsylvania, St. Leonard's Court, Suite 305, 3819-33 Chestmut Street, Philadelphia, PA 19104, USA
sageman@sas.upenn.edu

**Abstract.** Ever since the 9-11 incident, the multidisciplinary field of terrorism has experienced tremendous growth. As the domain has benefited greatly from recent advances in information technologies, more complex and challenging new issues have emerged from numerous counter-terrorism-related research communities as well as governments of all levels. In this paper, we describe an advanced knowledge discovery approach to addressing terrorism threats. We experimented with our approach in a project called Terrorism Knowledge Discovery Project that consists of several custom-built knowledge portals. The main focus of this project is to provide advanced methodologies for analyzing terrorism research, terrorists, and the terrorized groups (victims). Once completed, the system can also become a major learning resource and tool that the general community can use to heighten their awareness and understanding of global terrorism phenomenon, to learn how best they can respond to terrorism and, eventually, to garner significant grass root support for the government's efforts to keep America safe.

## 1 Introduction

Ever since the 9-11 incident, the multidisciplinary field of terrorism has experienced tremendous growth. The field has benefited greatly from increased national attention and a rich reservoir of knowledge accumulated through three decades of terrorism studies. Now, information-related issues, such as the communication and sharing of research ideas among counterterrorism researchers and the dissemination of counter-terrorism knowledge among the general public, become critical in detecting, preventing, and responding to terrorism threats. The recent advance in information technologies, especially Web technology, has alleviated the problems to some extent. However, more complex and challenging new issues keep emerging from numerous

H. Chen et al. (Eds.): ISI 2004, LNCS 3073, pp. 125–145, 2004.
© Springer-Verlag Berlin Heidelberg 2004

terrorism-related research communities as well as local, state, and Federal governments.

Terrorism threats have a wide range that spans personal, organizational, and societal levels and have far-reaching economic, psychological, political, and social consequences [14, 21]. A recent report from the National Research Council [12], *"Making
the Nation Safer: the Role of Science and Technology in Countering Terrorism,"* has
summarized the major issues and challenges as revolving around three different aspects: *Terrorism, Terrorist, and Terrorized (Victims).*

The first aspect (Terrorism) of the challenges is mainly associated with Information
searching and management and knowledge creation and dissemination issues in the
terrorism research domain. Currently, there are large and scattered volumes of terrorism-related data from diverse sources available to analyze terrorist threats and system
vulnerabilities [12]. However, maximizing the usefulness of the data is a challenge
because of: (1) the lack of counterterrorism-related databases that integrate these diverse sources and make them available to researchers, and (2) absence of advanced as
well as new methodologies to identify, model, and predict linkages among terrorists,
their supporters, and other perpetrators. Furthermore, for researchers new to terrorism,
information access and management is a major challenge, especially in reference to
identifying where to start, what to focus on, what types of data are available, where to
obtain such data, and whether empirical studies are available. Thus, advanced techniques to support intelligent information searching and techniques to analyze and map
terrorism knowledge domains are urgently needed.

The second aspect (Terrorist) of the challenges is mainly associated with how to
trace dynamic evolution of terrorist groups and how to analyze and predict terrorists'
activities, associations, and threats. While the Web has evolved to be a global platform
for anyone to use in disseminating, sharing, and communicating ideas, terrorists are
also using the Web to their own advantages. Terrorist-generated online contents and
the terrorists' Web usage patterns could be analyzed to enable better understanding
and analysis of the terrorism phenomena. Unfortunately, such terrorist-generated information has seldom been used in traditional terrorism research. On the other hand,
since the amount of terrorist-related information has well exceeded the capability of
traditional analysis methods, applying advanced techniques such as Social Network
Analysis may well provide a significant value-add.

The last aspect (Terrorized) of the challenges mainly involves how to successfully
give educators, students and the public systematic access to system-level thinking
about terrorism research. As recommended in the *"Making the Nation Safer"* report,
more research needs to be conducted on preparedness for terrorism attacks, human
responses to terrorism crises as well as the strategies for providing people with necessary knowledge of terrorism. Thus, how to utilize various information technologies in
achieving these goals remains an interesting and challenging problem.

To address the above challenges, the "Making the Nation Safer" report recommended establishing a terrorism research infrastructure that uses information fusion
techniques because all phases of counterterrorism efforts require that large amounts of
information from many sources be acquired, integrated, and interpreted. Information
fusion includes data mining, data integration, language technologies for information

extraction and multilingual retrieval, and data interpretation techniques such as visualization. These techniques would also be useful for evidence-based analysis in law enforcement, the intelligence community, emergency-response units, and other organizations involved in counterterrorism.

In the light of the foregoing, the University of Arizona's Artificial Intelligence (AI) Lab is developing Web-based counterterrorism knowledge portals to support the analysis of terrorism research, dynamically model the behavior of terrorists and their social networks, and provide an intelligent, reliable, and interactive communication channel with the terrorized (victims and citizens) groups. Specifically, the portals integrate terrorism-related multilingual datasets and use them to study advanced and new methodologies for predictive modeling, terrorist (social) network analysis, and visualization of terrorists' activities, linkages, and relationships.

The remainder of this paper is organized as follows. Section 2 reviews related research in information searching, analysis, and visualization techniques in relation to the counterterrorism domain. In section 3, we present our research questions. Section 4 describes the knowledge portals we are developing to address the three aspects of challenges in the counterterrorism domain, which include knowledge portals that help resolve the information access and management problems in terrorism research and support the exploration of knowledge creation patterns of contemporary terrorism researchers; knowledge portals that use advanced methodologies to analyze and visualize how the web is used by terrorist groups, how relations are formed and dissolved among terrorists, and detect organizational groups and their tasks; and a knowledge portal using the chatterbot framework to support citizens' and victims' responding to terrorism. The final section provides our concluding remarks in the interim.

## 2   Existing Approaches

Many information-searching and analytical approaches have been adopted in the academia and industries. The following sections review some of these techniques in relation to the counterterrorism domain.

### 2.1   General-Purpose and Meta-search Engines

Many different search engines are available on the Internet. Each has its own performance characteristics primarily defined by its algorithm for indexing, ranking and visualizing Web documents. For example, AltaVista and Google allow users to submit queries and retrieve Web pages in a ranked order, while Yahoo! groups Web sites into categories, creating a hierarchical directory of a subset of the Internet.

Internet spiders (a.k.a. crawlers), have been used as the main program in the backend of most search engines. These are programs that collect Internet pages and explore outgoing links in each page to continue the process. An example includes the World Wide Web Worm [27]. Most prevailing search engines, such as Google, are keyword-based. Although their search speeds are fast, their results are often overwhelming and imprecise. Low precision and low recall rates make it difficult to obtain specialized, domain-specific information from these search engines.

Selberg and Etzioni [37] have suggested that by relying solely on one search engine, users could miss over 77% of the references they might find most relevant because no single search engine is likely to return more than 45% of relevant results. A study by NEC Research Institute drew similar conclusions and revealed an alarming fact about Internet search engines: they cannot keep up with the net's dynamic growth, and each search engine covers only about 16% of the total Web sites [24].

The emergence of meta-search engines provides a credible resolution of the aforementioned limitations by triangulating outputs from several engines to arrive at relevant results. Several server and client-based meta-search engines, such as Copernic (http://www.copernic.com) "search the search engines" [37]. The results from other search engines are combined and presented to users. Although the information returned is comprehensive, the problem of information overload worsens if no post-retrieval analysis is provided.

## 2.2 Terrorism Research Centers' Portals

Web portal services provide another approach for retrieving information. For terrorism, there exists numerous information portals provided by specialized research centers such as the Center for the Study of Terrorism and Political Violence (CSTPV), located at St. Andrews University, Scotland, and directed by noted terrorism researcher, Professor Paul Wilkinson and formerly co-directed by Dr. Bruce Hoffman, Rand Corporation. These centers conduct terrorism research and provide portals that cater to the needs of academics, journalists, policymakers, students, and the general public. Terrorism research centers' portals are primarily providing information retrieval and dissemination services except for a few organizations such as the Terrorism Research Center (TRC) and the National Memorial Institute for the Prevention of Terrorism (MIPT) that have expanded their functions to include personalization (TRC) and the Emergency Responders Knowledge Base (MIPT). For example, the TRC, founded in 1996, has the highest number of portal features (31/61) including four terrorism databases and is highly recommended with about 5,000 incoming links [7].

The study by Kennedy and Lunn [21] generated lists of organizations conducting terrorism research and 28 different sources of terrorism databases and archives. Using their list of terrorism organizations and Carnegie Mellon University's [5] portal taxonomies, we analyzed terrorism research centers' portals to identify their features including the types of information and applications provided. Based on the analysis of 54 terrorism portals, the most frequently identified features were information retrieval and dissemination services. The information included full-text documents and archives (74%), links to other terrorism resources (54%), news (39%), and emergency preparedness materials (28%). Applications were limited to e-commerce services for selling terrorism books, reports, and multimedia resources (35%), and terrorism databases (22%) of groups, terrorist incidents, and bio-terrorism agents.

## 2.3  Information Analysis

Terrorism research centers' portals provide access to a diversity of unstructured (e.g., reports, news stories, transcripts) and structured (database) information but offer limited tools for integrating the resources and supporting information fusion (including post-retrieval analysis). After searching the terrorism portals, the user has to manually browse through the list of retrieved documents to locate relevant resources and establish relationships among the documents.

Automatic indexing algorithms have been used widely to extract key concepts from textual data. It has been shown that automatic indexing is as effective as human indexing [36]. Many proven techniques have been developed such as information extraction (IE). Information extraction techniques such as noun phrasing have been applied to perform indexing for phrases rather than just words [40]. These techniques are useful in extracting meaningful terms from text documents not only for document retrieval but also for further analysis.

There is, today, an increased interest in the use of data and web mining and machine learning techniques which focus on identifying terrorism-related patterns in data. These techniques have been applied to the analysis of news articles (such as in the Message Understanding Conference or MUC), online information sources (e.g., the Columbia University's Newsblaster system), and high-speed data streams that are processed and mined in a Distributed Mining and Monitoring System at Cornell University [31].

DARPA, for its part, is also supporting the development and integration of information fusion technologies such as data mining, biometrics, collaborative and knowledge discovery technologies that identify and display links among people, content, and topics [6] to counter "asymmetric threats" such as those found in terrorist attacks. For example, DARPA and other government agencies have solicited counter-terrorism proposals such as the Terrorism Knowledge Base project that was eventually approved for $9 million and is being developed by Cycorp Incorporated based in Austin, Texas, with the assistance of terrorism domain experts from the Terrorism Research Center [15]. The Terrorism Knowledge Base with its inference engine will support analysts in the intelligence community. However, these advanced technological systems are not available in most terrorism research centers or academic libraries that are used by terrorism researchers in the academic community.

## 2.4  Social Network Analysis

Existing terrorist network research is still at its incipient stage. Although previous research, including a few empirical ones, have sounded the call for new approaches to terrorist network analysis [4, 26, 39], studies have remained mostly small-scale and used manual analysis of a specific terrorist organization. For instance, Krebs [23] manually collected data from public news releases after the 9/11 attacks and studied the network surrounding the 19 hijackers. Sageman [35] analyzed the Global Salafi Jihad network consisting of 171 members using a manual approach and provided an anecdotal explanation of the formation and evolution of this network. None of these studies used advanced data mining technologies that have been applied widely in other domains such as finance, marketing, and business to discover previously unknown patterns from terrorist networks. Moreover, few studies have been able to systematically capture the dynamics of terrorist networks and predict terrorism trends. What is needed is a set of integrated methods, technologies, models, and tools to automatically mine data and discover valuable knowledge from terrorist networks based on large volumes of data of high complexity.

## 2.5  Chatterbot Techniques

The idea behind chatterbot techniques is to create an intimate atmosphere where individuals can converse with a natural language program (a chatterbot) and receive meaningful and immediate responses to their queries related to a certain domain without having to search the Internet for the answers themselves. Most chatterbot techniques rely on pattern matching algorithms which takes inputs from the user, parses and matches the input to one of the questions in their question/answer script, then picks out the appropriate response dictated by the script, and displays it to the user [42]. Examples include: ELIZA [42], Parry [11] and ALICE [16]. Previous studies on chatterbot have shown the potential of using chatterbot to provide people with easy access to domain-specific knowledge. We believe that chatterbot techniques can be used to provide the general public with necessary knowledge of the global terrorism phenomena.

## 3  Research Questions

Building on our research and system development experiences in portal collection building, text mining, information extraction, criminal network analysis and visualization, we propose to use an advanced knowledge discovery approach to design and develop a set of knowledge portals to address the challenges in the counter-terrorism domain. The research questions postulated in our project are:

1.  How can intelligent collection building, searching, text mining, and social network analysis techniques be used to help resolve the information access and management problems in terrorism research and support the knowledge creation and discovery patterns among contemporary terrorism researchers?
2.  How can intelligent collection building, searching, text mining with multi-lingual and translation capabilities, and social network analysis techniques be used to collect, analyze, and visualize Web contents created by terrorist groups so as to decipher the social milieu, network dynamics, and communication channels among terrorists?
3.  How can the chatterbot technology be used to support citizens' and victims' responding to terrorism and provide them with necessary knowledge of terrorism research?

# 4  An Advanced Knowledge Discovery Approach to Addressing Terrorism Threats

To help us systematically answer our research questions, we propose a project called Terrorism Knowledge Discovery Project. This project consists of several custom-built portals (testbeds): Terrorism Knowledge Portal (a prototype has already been created), Terrorism Expert Finder, Dark Web (consisting of Internet-based terrorist multilingual resources), Terrorist Network Portal, and Chatterbot Portal which will be organized around the three aspects of challenges associated with terrorism research, terrorists, and terrorized victims or target groups. Figure 1, in the next page, provides a summary of the all the portals.

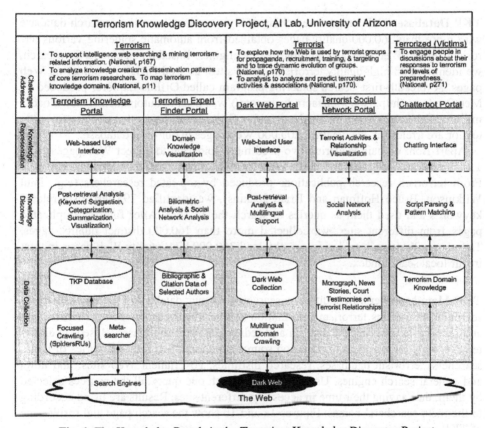

**Fig. 1.** The Knowledge Portals in the Terrorism Knowledge Discovery Project

In the following sections, we will describe the knowledge portals that address each of the three aspects of challenges in terms of the key components and techniques used in the portals.

## 4.1  Addressing Challenges Associated with Terrorism Research: Terrorism Knowledge Portal and Terrorism Expert Finder Portal

### 4.1.1 Terrorism Knowledge Portal

To address information access and management problems in the terrorism research domain, we developed the Terrorism Knowledge Portal, or TKP (http://ai.bpa.arizona. edu/COPLINK/tkp.html). The goal is to facilitate the searching and browsing of terrorism information on the Web. Developed based on an integrated knowledge portal approach [10], TKP consists of various components: searching of its own database, meta-searching other terrorism information sources, keyword suggestion, Web page summarization, categorization and visualization. Each sub-component is described below.

**TKP Database.** TKP supports searching of a customized terrorism research database with more than 360,000 quality pages obtained from automatic spidering various terrorism-related Web sites and multiple search engines. Based on an extensive research, we identified 38 high-quality terrorism Web sites as seed URLs for spidering Web pages. A breadth-first search spidering program called Offline Explorer produced by MetaProducts (http://www.metaproducts.com/) was used to automatically download 1 million Web pages using the seeds and after filtering out pages that contain too little text or are irrelevant, we obtained 200,000 Web pages in our local database.

Apart from domain spidering, we used meta-spidering to collect Web pages from 11 major search engines and news Web sites to provide rich terrorism information. From terrorism research publications produced by top-rated researchers (e.g., Paul Wilkinson, Bruce Hoffman and Brian Jenkins), we identified 795 terrorism-related keywords and used them as queries to search the 11 sites. After filtering duplicated pages from different sites, we collected more than 160,000 distinct quality pages. Together with domain spidering, we obtained 360,000 high-quality Web pages in total in our local search index.

**TKP Meta-searchers.** In addition to searching its own database, TKP supports meta-searching of various terrorism information sources. This ensures comprehensiveness and recency in covering the domain and reduces information biases. Based on an extensive study on terrorism information sources, we identified four categories of meta-searchers: terrorism databases, research institutes, government Web sites, and news and general search engines. Users can search with one query all the sources selected by them, thus saving their time in accessing different sites. Results are listed according to the meta-searchers' names. Figures 1a and 1b show the search page and result page of TKP.

**Keyword Suggestion.** To facilitate searching with different keywords, TKP provides keyword suggestion function, developed using the concept space approach [9]. It identified pairs of keywords co-occurring on the same pages and extracts them for use as thesaurus terms in our database. Each query to the TKP concept space thesaurus elicits a ranked list of keywords highly related to the input keyword. In addition, we used Scirus (http://www.scirus.com), a major Web site providing keyword suggestion of scientific terms, to retrieve more related terms.

**Document Summarization.** The TKP summarizer, a modified version of a text summarizer called TXTRACTOR, uses sentence-selection heuristics to rank text segments [28]. These heuristics strive to reduce redundancy of information in a query-based summary. The summarizer can flexibly summarize Web pages using three or five sentence(s). Users can invoke it by choosing the number of sentences for summarization in a pull-down menu under each result. After which, a new window is activated (shown in Figure 2c) that displays the summary on the left and the original Web page on the right.

**Document Categorization.** The TKP categorizer organizes the search results into various folders labeled by the key phrases appearing in the page summaries or titles (see Figure 2d), thereby facilitating the understanding of different groups of Web pages. We used the Arizona Noun Phraser (AZNP) to extract meaningful phrases from the titles and summaries of the search results. Developed at the Artificial Intelligence Lab of the University of Arizona, AZNP extracts all the noun phrases from each Web page automatically based on part-of-speech tagging and linguistic rules [40]. An indexing program calculates the frequency of occurrence of these phrases and selects the 20 most frequently occurring phrases to index the results. Each folder shown on Figure 2d is labeled by a phrase that appears in the pages categorized under it. As a page may contain more than one indexing phrase, the categorization is non-exclusive.

**Document Visualization.** The TKP visualizer was developed to reduce information overload when a large number of search results are obtained, which is a typical situation in many search scenarios. It has of two versions: the Jigsaw and Geographic Information Systems (GIS) versions. Web pages are clustered onto a map, generated using the Kohonen [22] self-organizing map (SOM) algorithm, which is a two-layered neural network that automatically learns from the input Web pages and clusters them into different naturally occurring groups. In the jigsaw SOM visualizer, key terms identified by AZNP were used to label map regions, where the sizes correspond to the numbers of pages clustered in them. Clicking on a map region brings up the list of pages on the right side of the pop-up window (see Figure 2e). Users can then open these pages by clicking on the links. In the GIS SOM visualizer, Web pages are shown as points on a two-dimensional map with their positions determined by the SOM algorithm. The map's background shows contour lines representing the varying values selected by users (e.g., frequency of occurrence of query terms in the Web pages) and is independent of the points' positions. Users can navigate on the map by clicking on the buttons and resize a certain part of the map by dragging a rectangle that will highlight the set of Web pages listed on the bottom right side of the pop-up window (see Figure 2f). Using the TKP visualizer, terrorism researchers can obtain a meaningful and comprehensive picture of a large number of search results.

**Fig. 2.** Major Components of the Terrorism Knowledge Portal

**Table 1.** List of Core Terrorism Authors Based on Times Cited in Citation Database

| Name | Organization | Specialty | Times cited | # pubs. | # years |
|---|---|---|---|---|---|
| 1. Wilkinson, Paul | St. Andrews Univ., Center for the Study Terrorism & Political Violence (CSTPV), UK | Terrorism, Europe | 229 | 87 | 31 |
| 2. Gurr, Ted | Univ. Maryland | Political violence | 214 | 52 | 40 |
| 3. Laqueur, Walter | Center for Strategic & Intl Studies (CSIS) (formerly) | Political violence, history | 191 | 38 | 27 |
| 4. Alexander, Yonah | Potomac Institute for Policy Studies, SUNY, Center for Strategic & Intl Studies (CSIS) (formerly) | International studies, media | 166 | 94 | 31 |
| 5. Bell, J.B. | Columbia Univ., Institute, War & Peace Studies (formerly) | Terrorist groups | 138 | 49 | 34 |
| 6. Stohl, Michael | Purdue University | Communication | 136 | 30 | 27 |
| 7. Jenkins, Brian | Rand Corporation (formerly), Kroll Associates, CSPTV council member. Founder terrorism program at Rand | Counterterrorism | 96 | 40 | 29 |
| 8. Ronfeldt, David | Rand Corporation | Cyberterrorism | 95 | 20 | 29 |
| 9. Crenshaw, Martha | Wesleyan Univ., CSTPV council member | Government | 90 | 40 | 34 |
| 10. Hoffman, Bruce | Rand Corporation, CSTPV (formerly) | Terrorist groups | 81 | 121 | 26 |
| 11. Arquilla, John | Naval Postgraduate School, Rand Corporation | Cyberterrorism | 75 | 20 | 29 |
| 12. Mickolus, Edward | National Foreign Assessment Center | Terrorist data | 73 | 26 | 27 |
| 13. Wardlaw, Grant | Australian Institute of Criminology | Criminology | 49 | 25 | 22 |
| 14. Hacker, F.J. | USC Medical & Law Schools | Psychology | 38 | 3 | 5 |
| 15. Rapoport, David | UCLA, Terrorism & Political Violence (founding editor) | Political violence | 37 | 33 | 33 |
| 16. Bassiouni, M.C. | DePaul Univ. | Law | 30 | 8 | 16 |
| 17. Kepel, Gilles | Institut d'Etudes Politiques, Paris | Religion & politics | 25 | 6 | 4 |
| 18. Kupperman, Robert | Kupperman & Associates, Center for Strategic & Intl Studies (CSIS) (formerly) | Crisis management | 25 | 20 | 19 |
| 19. Stern, Jessica | Harvard's Kennedy Institute, Council of Foreign Relations | Weapons mass destruction | 25 | 24 | 13 |

## 4.1.2 Terrorism Expert Finder Portal

Because of the information overload problem and the increasing number of dispersed researcher groups studying terrorism, we will build a collection containing data on core terrorism authors, their bibliographic citations, and their cited references in the Terrorism Expert Finder Portal. The portal will provide a much-needed mechanism for identifying, mapping, collaborating, and stimulating a convergence in thinking about research challenges such as terrorism definitions and theoretical models. Silke [38] described contemporary terrorism works as being characterized by a marked absence of conceptual agreement and a wide diversity of views on even basic issues. This portal is important because many researchers and students waste a lot of time since they often do not know where to start their terrorism research, who are the current experts, what are their empirical studies, and insights on specific issues. It provides a mechanism to map the terrorism knowledge domains and answer several research questions:

- Who are the core terrorism authors?
- What are their influential terrorism publications?
- What are the dominant knowledge creation, dissemination and communications processes used in terrorism research?

The portal is an extension of Reid's [32, 33, 34] research on identifying the invisible college of terrorism researchers and diffusion of their ideas. Reid, a former terrorism specialist at the Central Intelligence Agency, used bibliometric, citation and content analysis to identify and analyze core terrorism experts and their terrorism publications.

Of the 44 core terrorism authors identified, the top 19 authors are enumerated in Table 1 together with pertinent citation counts, number of terrorism-related publications, and number of years they authored terrorism publications. To calculate the number of years that an author has been writing terrorism publications (based on our database), his latest publication year is subtracted from his earliest publication year.

The core terrorism authors' data generated 1,324 records that covered about 35 years of research on contemporary terrorism. The data were parsed into many fields including author, title, journal, publication type, publication year, and the number of citations per title. The 44 core authors and their 250 coauthors published in 148 different journals, the largest number of which was published in *Terrorism and Political Violence* (141 articles).

We also conducted subject searches in ISI Web of Science to retrieve bibliographic and citation data on the topic: terrorism. About 7,590 records were retrieved and will be used to analyze citation, co-authorship, and social network patterns. The records were parsed into several fields such as author, cited author, cited source, and publication date of cited reference.

The data will be used for identifying, analyzing, summarizing, and visualizing core researchers' knowledge creation patterns. Table 2 presents methodologies that can be applied to the data. It is a revision of Boyack's [2] research that demonstrated the use of different techniques for analyzing 20 years of papers published in the *Proceedings of the National Academy of Sciences* (PNAS).

### 4.2  Addressing Challenges Associated with Terrorist: Dark Web Portal and Terrorist Social Network Portal

#### 4.2.1  Dark Web Portal Portal

In addition to analyzing terrorism research, we will also focus on the information access and methodological problems in analyzing terrorist groups. We propose to develop a Dark Web Portal which helps researchers locate, collect, and analyze Dark Web data. By "Dark Web", we mean the alternate side of the Web which is used by terrorist and extremist groups to spread their ideas.

**Table 2.** Summary of Methodologies for Analyzing the Terrorism Knowledge Domains

| Unit of Analysis | Methodology | Research question associated with: |
|---|---|---|
| Authors | Citation analysis, Co-authorship analysis, Content analysis, Factor analysis, Multidimensional scaling, Social network analysis | Communities of practices, Intellectual structure & history of terrorism, Levels & types of collaboration Pathfinder network for visualization Social structure of terrorism |
| Documents | Co-citation analysis, Content analysis, Various clustering methods | Development of paradigms |
| Journals | Co-citation analysis, Bradford distribution | Diffusion between fields, Sociology of science |
| Words | Content analysis, Relational extraction, Semantic analysis | Cognitive structure of terrorism Convergence in ideas Topical classification |
| Indicators such as economic activity level indicators (counts of papers, patents, & citations) | Combination of methodologies | Impact of scientific outputs & funding, Impact of scientific outputs on policy |

**Dark Web Testbed.** The goal of this part is to build a high-quality, up-to-date Dark Web testbed which contains multilingual information created by major terrorist groups in the world. We started the process by identifying the groups that are considered by reliable sources as terrorist groups. The main sources we used to identify US domestic terrorist groups include: Anti-Defamation League (ADL), FBI, Southern Poverty Law Center (SPLC), Militia Watchdog, and Google Directory. To identify international terrorist groups, we relied on the following sources: Counter-Terrorism Committee (CTC) of the UN Security Council, US State Department report, Official Journal of the European Union, and government reports from the United Kingdom, Australia, Canada, Japan, and P. R. China. These sources have been identified following the recommendations of core terrorism authors.

We manually identified the URLs of the web sites from the reports alluded to by the sources mentioned above then searched the web using the group names as queries. A total of 94 US domestic terrorist groups and 440 international terrorist groups have been identified. To ensure that our testbed covers all the major regions in the world, we sought the assistance of language experts in English, Arabic, Spanish, Japanese, and Chinese to help us collect URLs in different regions. After the URL of a group is identified, we used the SpidersRUs toolkit, a multilingual Digital Library building tool developed by our own group, to collect all the Web pages under that URL. So far, we have collected 500,000 Web pages created by 94 US domestic groups, 300,000 Web pages created by 41 Arabic-speaking groups, and 100,000 Web pages created by Spanish-speaking groups. The process of building the Dark Web testbed is ongoing.

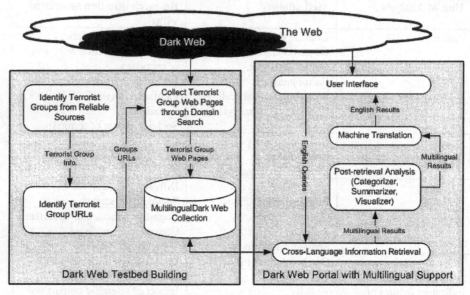

**Fig. 3.** The Components of the Dark Web Portal Project

**Intelligent Portal with Multilingual Support.** The purpose of the Dark Web Portal is to help terrorism researchers easily access, analyze, and understand the multilingual information in the Dark Web testbed. To address the information overload problem, the Dark Web Portal will be fitted with post-retrieval components (categorizer, summarizer, and visualizer) similar to those of the Terrorism Knowledge Portal. However, without addressing the language barrier problem, researchers are limited to the data in their native languages and cannot fully utilize the multilingual information in the testbed. To address this problem, we plan to add a Cross-language Information Retrieval (CLIR) component into the portal. CLIR is the study of retrieval information in one language through queries expressed in another language. Based on our previous research, we have developed a dictionary-based CLIR system for use in the Dark Web Portal. It currently takes English queries and retrieves documents in English, Spanish, Chinese, Japanese and Arabic. Another component that we will add to the Dark Web portal is a Machine Translation (MT) component, which will translate the multilingual information retrieved by the CLIR component back into the experts' native languages.

### 4.2.2 Terrorist Network Portal
Besides collecting terrorist data from the Web, we will also use an authoritative terrorism monograph and its articles as input data for our Terrorist Network Portal. The

monograph, entitled *"Understanding Terror Network"*, which analyzed the characteristics of 171 terrorists, was written by Dr. Marc Sageman, a forensic psychiatrist and expert on Al-Qaeda. Since terrorists are often unavailable for interviews, Crenshaw [13] recommended using case studies, diaries, and group histories as preferred sources of data for psychological analysis. By using the full-text version of Sageman's monograph and selective articles, we will have testbed data to design and analyze our terrorist network methodology for identifying and visualizing terrorist social networks.

Terrorists are not atomized individuals but actors linked to each other through complex networks of direct or mediated exchanges [26, 35]. Our terrorist network analysis research focuses on discovering and presenting previously unknown patterns in terrorist networks, which involve people, resources, and information tied together by family, religious, personal, financial, operational, and many other relationships. Specifically, we propose to analyze network members in terms of their personal, social, educational background. So, we want to identify how relationships among terrorists are formed and dissolved. To achieve this, we need to identify the relations' types, characteristics, and strengths, operational groups, their assigned tasks, and planned activities. This will enable us to discover the structure and organization of terrorist networks, capture network dynamics, and predict trends of terrorist attacks. We will employ various visualization techniques to intuitively present these patterns to facilitate the interpretation, comprehension, and application of the results.

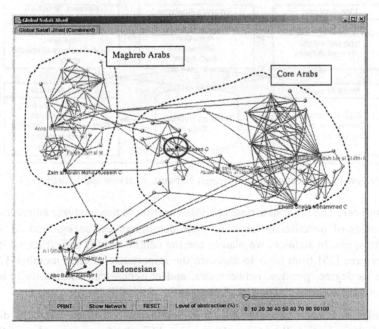

**Fig. 4.** Global Safafi Jihad Partition into Four Groups (red circle is Osama bin Laden)

We will design our Terrorist Network Analyzer and Visualizer (TNAV) using advanced social network analysis methodology. TNAV will provide statistical analysis, cluster analysis, social network analysis (SNA), and visualization. SNA has recently been recognized as a promising technology for studying criminal and terrorist networks [26, 39], which we plan to use in all five levels of analysis.

A network can be treated as a graph in which nodes represent individuals and links represent relations between the individuals. We propose to analyze terrorist networks at five different levels, namely, node, link, group, overall structure, and dynamics. For instance, Sageman partitioned the terrorist network, Global Salafi Jihad, into four groups: Central Staff, Maghreb Arabs, Core Arabs, and Indonesians. In each group, there are a hub and several gatekeepers. Figure 4 shows Osama bin Laden as the hub of the Central Staff cluster and issues commands to the whole network through his gatekeepers.

Figure 5 shows the system architecture of the TNAV. It consists of five analyzers corresponding to the five levels of analysis. The analyzers include:

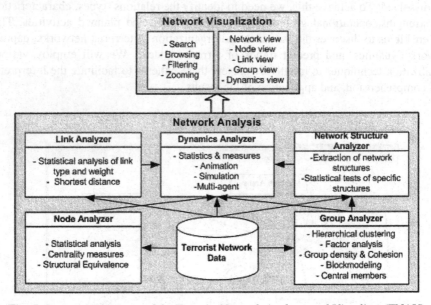

**Fig. 5.** System Architecture of the Terrorist Network Analyzer and Visualizer (TNAV)

**Node Analyzer.** The basic statistical analysis function in this analyzer summarizes the characteristics of terrorists in terms of their demographics, background, socio-economic status, etc. In addition, we plan to use the centrality [19] and structural equivalence measures [25] from SNA to measure the importance of each member. Centralities such as degree, prestige, betweenness, and closeness can automatically identify the leaders, gatekeepers, and outliers from a network [1, 39].

**Link Analyzer.** In addition to the statistical summary of link type and weight distribution, our link analyzer will measure the ease or difficulty for one member of the network to connect to other members. We plan to use traditional single source-destination

[17] and all-pair shortest-path algorithms [18] to identify this property of a terrorist network.

**Group Analyzer.** We plan to employ two methods to find groups in a terrorist network: hierarchical clustering [20, 30] and factor analysis. We will test which method is more likely to generate meaningful and valid groupings that match the actual organization of a terrorist network. In addition, with a rich set of approaches and metrics from SNA, we will extract interaction patterns between groups using blockmodeling approach [43], analyze and predict the stability of a terrorist group using group density and cohesion [41] measures, and detect the central members from a specific group.

**Network Structure Analyzer.** After the groups have been identified and their interaction patterns extracted, we will establish whether a terrorist network takes a specific structure (centralized or decentralized) and its degree of hierarchy. The structure found can help reveal the vulnerability of a terrorist organization.

**Dynamics Analyzer.** Adding a time dimension to all the statistics and measures in the previous levels, our dynamics analyzer will extract the patterns of change in terms of individual member's importance and operational roles; group(s) that are merging or splitting; and recruitment and turnover. We will also use animation to intuitively show how a network changes over time. More importantly, we hope to be able to predict the operations of a terrorist network based on the patterns extracted from historical data and use hidden Markov models, simulations, and multi-agent technology to foresee how a network reacts to changes such as removal of central members, disruption of certain groups, etc.

**GUI and Visualizer.** We propose to use several network layout algorithms such as multidimensional scaling (MDS) [3], pathfinder scaling [8], and force-directed spring algorithms to portray a terrorist network. Node view, link view, and group view can show the details of individual terrorists, their relations, and their group memberships. The dynamics view will present animated visualization of a network or a specific group over several periods of time. Statistical summary and test results will be presented in traditional formats such as charts and tables. The GUI will take user input such as a query for a seed terrorist and present the analysis result about the part of network surrounding the terrorist.

### 4.3 Addressing Challenges Associated with Terrorized Victims: Chatterbot Portal

In addition to supporting the analysis of terrorist groups, the Terrorism Knowledge Discovery Project will provide a testbed for victims and citizens who are trying to respond to terrorism. To help in the dissemination of information to the victims of terrorism, we will create a computer-driven natural language chatterbot that will respond to queries about the terrorism domain and provide real-time data on terrorism activities, prevention, and preparation strategies. The goal of this testbed is to create an intimate atmosphere where individuals can converse with the chatterbot and receive meaningful and immediate responses to their terrorism queries.

In our exploration of the chatterbot technology, we discovered that ALICE chatterbots could handle more domain-specific knowledge topics better than the general conversational chatterbots. After concluding tests using telecommunications domain knowledge, we decided that a chatterbot testbed would be appropriate for supporting general conversation and information exchange about terrorism.

The major thrust of the Chatterbot Portal segment is the development of the Terrorism Activity Resource Application (TARA). TARA uses a modified version of the ALICE engine to make the programming and maintenance of the system easier as well as providing some value-added features. The development phases of TARA are as the follows:

First, TARA will be benchmarked against search systems, such as Google, to explore the effectiveness and efficiency of using a natural language dialog system to return terrorism-related answers in a friendlier manner. This approach will eliminate some of the 'hunting and pecking' skills necessary for filtering out search engine information. Using the "official" websites that experts on terrorism deem to be trustworthy will ensure the reliability of TARA's responses.

Second, TARA will be built as a 'friend and a companion' to listen to users who have been affected by terrorism activities. We plan to define the knowledge in the Terrorism domain as static (e.g., 'Who is bin Laden?' or 'What should I do in case of a gas attack?'), and dynamic (e.g., 'What is the current Terror Threat Level?' or 'What has Hezbollah done recently?'). Because of TARA's genealogical relationship to ALICE, TARA possesses a natural language interface and all of the conversational dialogue components inherent in ALICE. We believe that these elements will be a vital part of TARA's flexibility in responding to queries that may not directly relate to Terrorism.

The last piece we envision applying is the use of multimedia content in conjunction with the conversational dialogue. We plan on using pictures, audio, and video feeds to enhance the knowledge delivery of the system.

## 5  Concluding Remarks

Information overload, uncertain data quality, and lack of access to integrated datasets and advanced methodologies for studying terrorism are major hurdles and challenges which both traditional and new counter-terrorism researchers have to overcome. Understanding the ramifications of each component hurdle and how existing information technology approaches can be used to address such hurdle is the over-arching objective of this project. In this report, we exhaustively analyzed component issues confronting contemporary approaches counter terrorism efforts and lined-up potent technology solutions to help fill in existing gaps. Taking the key suggestions from the report *"Making the Nation Safer"*, we are developing a Terrorism Knowledge Discovery Project that provides advanced methodologies for analyzing terrorism research, terrorist and their social networks, and the terrorized groups (victims and citizens).

The project consists of custom-built multilingual portals (testbeds): Terrorism Knowledge Portal, Terrorism Expert Finder, Dark Web (Web resources used by terrorists), Terrorist Network Portal, and Terrorism Activity Resource Application chatterbot.

Although the Terrorism Knowledge Discovery Project is aimed at supporting the counter-terrorism researcher community, we have reason to believe that the law enforcement, intelligence, and security communities can also benefit from using it. It is a critical first step in demonstrating the feasibility of developing a national terrorism research infrastructure. Most importantly, we believe that it will help facilitate knowledge creation and discovery processes because it will provide a seamlessly integrated environment of functional modules that fully support the collaborative efforts of various, culturally diverse terrorism research teams. Lastly, it can become the learning resource and tool that the general community can use to heighten their awareness of the global terrorism phenomenon, to learn how best they can respond to terrorism and, eventually, garner significant grass root support for the government's efforts to keep America safe.

## Acknowledgements

This research has been supported in part by the following grants:

- DHS/CNRI, "BorderSafe Initiative," October 2003-September 2004.
- NSF/ITR, "COPLINK Center for Intelligence and Security Informatics – A Crime Data Mining Approach to Developing Border Safe Research," EIA-0326348, September 2003-August 2005.

We would like to thank the officers and domain experts of Tucson Police Department, Arizona Department of Customs and Border Protection, and San Diego ARJIS for their support throughout the project. We would also like to thank all members of the Artificial Intelligence Lab at the University of Arizona who have contributed to the project, in particular Homa Atabakhsh, Cathy Larson, Chun-Ju Tseng, Ying Liu, Theodore Elhourani, Wei Xi, Charles Zhi-Kai Chen, Guanpi Lai, and Shing Ka Wu.

## References

1. Baker, W. E., Faulkner, R. R.: Social Organization of Conspiracy: Illegal Networks in the Heavy Electrical Equipment Industry. American Sociological Review 58(12) (1993) 837-860
2. Boyack, K. W.: Mapping Knowledge Domains: Characterizing PNAS. PNAS Early Edition (2003)
3. Breiger, R. L., Boorman, S., Arabie, P.: An Algorithm for Clustering Relational Data, with Applications to Social Network Analysis and Comparison with Multidimensional Scaling. Journal of Mathematical Psychology 12 (1975) 328-383
4. Carley, K. M., Lee, J. S.: Destabilizing Networks. Connections 24(3) (2001) 31-34

5. Carnegie Mellon University: Web Portal and Portal Taxonomies. Final Report of Consequence Management Program Integration Office (2001)
6. Cateriniccha, D.: Data Mining Aims at National Security. Federal Computer Week (2002)
7. Center, T. R.: About the Terrorism Research Center (2003)
8. Chen, C., Paul, R. J., O'Keefe, B.: Fitting the jigsaw of Citation: Information Visualization in Domain Analysis. Journal of American Society of Information Science and Technology 52(4) (2001) 315-330
9. Chen, H., Lynch, K. J.: Automatic Construction of Networks of Concepts Characterizing Document Databases. IEEE Transactions on Systems, Man, and Cybernetics 22 (5) (1992) 885-902
10. Chung, W., Zhang, Y., Huang, Z., Wang, G., Ong, T. H., Chen, H.: Internet Searching and Browsing in a Multilingual World: An Experiment on the Chinese Business Intelligence Portal (CBizPort). Journal of the American Society for Information and Science and Technology, Accepted for publication (forthcoming)
11. Colby, K. M. W., Sylvia, H., Dennis, F.: Artificial Paranoia. Artificial Intelligence 2 (1971) 1-25
12. Council, N. R.: Making the Nation Safer: the Role of Science and Technology in Countering Terrorism. Washington, D.C. (2002) 339
13. Crenshaw, M.: Psychology of Terrorism: An Agenda for the 21st Century. Political Psychology 21(2) (2000) 405-420
14. Cutter, S., T. J. Wilbank, (ed.): Geographical Dimensions of Terrorism, Taylor & Francis, Inc. (2003)
15. DARPA: Terrorism Knowledge Base Proposal. (2002)
16. De Angeli, A. J., Graham, I., Coventry, L.: The Unfriendly User: Exploring Social Reactions to Chatterbots. Proceedings of The International Conference on Affective Human Factors Design, London, Asean Academic Press. Han, S. K., YounGi (2001)
17. Dijkstra, E.: A Note on Two Problems in Connection with Graphs. Numerische Mathematik 1 (1959) 269-271
18. Floyd, R. W.: Algorithm 97: Shortest Path. Communications of the ACM 5(6) (1962) 345-370
19. Freeman, L. C.: Centrality in Social Networks: Conceptual Clarification. Social Networks 1 (1979) 215-240
20. Jain, A. K., Dubes, R. C.: Algorithms for Clustering Data. Upper Saddle River, NJ, Prentice-Hall (1988)
21. Kennedy, L. W., Lunn, C. M.: Developing a Foundation for Policy Relevant Terrorism Research in Criminology (2003)
22. Kohonen, T.: Self-organizing maps. Springer-Verlag, Berlin (1995)
23. Krebs, V. E.: Mapping networks of terrorist cells. Connections 24(3) (2001) 43-52
24. Lawrence, S., Giles, C. L.: Accessibility of Information on the Web. Nature 400 (1999) 107-109
25. Lorrain, F. P., White, H. C.: Structural Equivalence of Individuals in Social Networks. Journal of Mathematical Sociology 1 (1971) 49-80
26. McAndrew, D.: Structural Analysis of Criminal Networks. Social Psychology of Crime: Groups, Teams, and Networks, Offender Profiling Series, III. L. Allison. Dartmouth, Aldershot (1999)
27. McBryan, O.: GENVL and WWW: Tools for Taming the Web. Proceedings of the First International Conference on the World Wide Web, Geneva, Switzerland (1994)

28. McDonald, D., Chen, H.: Using Sentence-selection Heuristics to Rank Text Segments in TXTRACTOR. Proceedings of Second ACM/IEEE-CS joint conference on Digital libraries, Portland, Oregon, USA (2002)

29. Moore, R. G., Graham: Emile: Using a Chatbot Conversation to Enhance the Learning of Social Theory. Huddersfield, England, Univ. of Huddersfield (2002)

30. Murtagh, F.: A Survey of Recent Advances in Hierarchical Clustering Algorithms Which Use Cluster Centers. Computer Journal 26 (1984) 354-359

31. National Science Foundation: Data Mining and Homeland Security Applications. (2003)

32. Reid, E. O. F.: An Analysis of Terrorism Literature: A Bibliometric and Content Analysis Study. School of Library and Information Management. Los Angeles, University of Southern California (1983) 357

33. Reid, E. O. F.: Using Online Databases to Analyze the Development of a Specialty: Case Study of Terrorism. 13th National Online Meeting Proceedings, New York, NY, Learning Information (1992)

34. Reid, E. O. F.: Evolution of a Body of Knowledge: an Analysis of Terrorism Research. Information Processing & Management 33(1) (1997) 91-106

35. Sageman, M.: Understanding Terror Networks. Pennsylvania, University of Pennsylvania Press (2004)

36. Salton, G.: Recent Trends in Automatic Information Retrieval. Proceedings of the 9th Annual International ACM SIGIR, Pisa, Italy (1986)

37. Selberg, E., Etzioni, O.: Multi-service Search and Comparison Using the MetaCrawler. Proceedings of the 4th International World-Wide Web Conference (1995)

38. Silke, A.: Devil You Know: Continuing Problems with Research on Terrorism. Terrorism and Political Violence 13(4) (2001) 1-14

39. Sparrow, M. K.: Application of Network Analysis to Criminal Intelligence: An Assessment of the Prospects. Social Networks 13 (1991) 251-274

40. Tolle, K. M., Chen, H.: Comparing noun phrasing techniques for use with medical digital library tools. Journal of the American Society for Information Science (Special Issue on Digital Libraries) 51 (4) (2000) 352-370

41. Wasserman, S., Faust, K.: Social Network Analysis: Methods and Applications. Cambridge, Cambridge University Press (1994)

42. Weizenbaum, J.: Eliza - A Computer Program for the Study of Natural Language Communication between Man and Machine. Communications of the ACM 9(1) (1966) 36-45

43. White, H. C., Boorman, S. A. Breiger, R. L.: Social Structure from Multiple Networks: I. Blockmodels of Roles and Positions. American Journal of Sociology 81 (1976) 730-780

44. Vrajitoru, D.: Evolutionary Sentence Building for Chatterbots. Genetic and Evolutionary Computation Conference (GECCO), Chicago, IL (2003)

# The Architecture
# of the Cornell Knowledge Broker*

Alan Demers, Johannes Gehrke, and Mirek Riedewald

Department of Computer Science, Cornell University
{ademers,johannes,mirek}@cs.cornell.edu

**Abstract.** Intelligence applications have to process massive amounts
of data in order to extract relevant information. This includes archived
historical data as well as continuously arriving new data. We propose a
novel architecture that addresses this problem – the Cornell Knowledge
Broker. It will not only support knowledge discovery, but also security,
privacy, information exchange, and collaboration.

## 1 Introduction

A major challenge for intelligence agencies is to collect the relevant data. However, often an even greater challenge is to *analyze* that data and to draw conclusions from it. With increasing efforts for collecting more information, the data
analysis problem will be aggravated. For that reason the Knowledge Discovery
and Dissemination Working Group (KD-D) has initiated research on an information infrastructure that will meet the needs of U.S. intelligence and law enforcement agencies. This infrastructure will integrate new technology for online
analysis of incoming data streams as well as novel offline data mining approaches.
Based on discussions and projects within KD-D, we proposed the *information
spheres* architecture to address both operational and legal requirements for intelligence agencies [18]. The architecture consists of two components – *local* and
*global* information sphere.

A *local* information sphere exists within each government agency. In practice
it could correspond to even smaller units, depending on restrictions of access to
data. Its main goal is to support online analysis and data mining of multiple
high-speed data streams, with conceptually unrestricted local access to all data
managed by the system. Notice that information does not flow freely, i.e., the
local information sphere also enforces access control to ensure that an analyst
can only access what she *needs to know*.

The *global* information sphere spans multiple government agencies, and me-
diates inter-agency collaboration. It addresses the sometimes conflicting requirements of allowing analysts from different government agencies to efficiently share

---

* The authors are supported by NSF grants CCF-0205452, IIS-0121175, and IIS-
0084762. Any opinions, findings, conclusions, or recommendations expressed in this
paper are those of the authors and do not necessarily reflect the views of the sponsors.

H. Chen et al. (Eds.): ISI 2004, LNCS 3073, pp. 146–162, 2004.

information, hypotheses and evidence without violating applicable laws regarding privacy and civil rights. Hence the research challenges with respect to the global information sphere extend beyond efficient analysis and access control to privacy preserving data mining and information integration [2, 22, 27, 36, 43].

We propose the Cornell Knowledge Broker (CKB) which supports the functionality required for both information spheres: continuous processing of high-speed data streams from a variety of sources. This includes on-line data mining and trigger evaluation, deep offline analysis of archived data, as well as supporting interactive data analysis and exploration for analysts. The CKB will include novel techniques which are currently developed as part of the KD-D initiative, and it will follow the *plug-and-play* paradigm in order to support easy integration of new data mining and analysis operators and in order to be easily extended with new functionality. Already existing components are an adaptive subscription matcher, and a calculus for expressive subscriptions that can be stateful (across several documents, both temporally as well as content-wise). This will enable analysts to set up powerful filters for delivering relevant information from streams of incoming data in real-time. We are currently expanding the existing infrastructure to release a first version of the system in summer 2004.

## 2   System Architecture Overview

Figure 1 shows an overview of the information sphere architecture. Several local information spheres are connected with each other through a network. To preserve the privacy of individuals and also the privacy of the analyst (queries posed by an analyst might reveal that analyst's knowledge), access to a local sphere from the outside is restricted to privacy preserving technology. This technology is located in the Gateway Modules (GW). It allows analysts to leverage global knowledge within the bounds set by legal and security considerations.

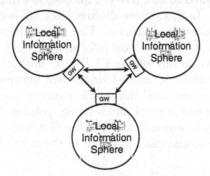

**Fig. 1.** Information sphere architecture

The local information sphere (cf. Figure 2) consists of one or more Cornell Knowledge Brokers, connected by a high-speed internal network (intranet). Each CKB has one or more processors with large main memory and essentially unrestricted archival capabilities, e.g., large hard disk drives or RAID arrays. We

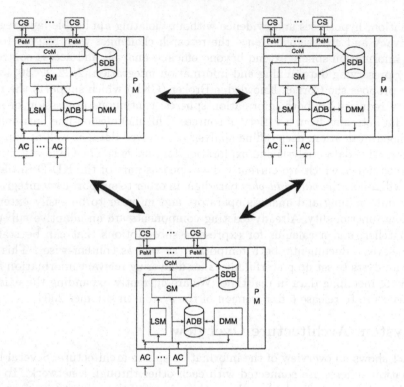

**Fig. 2.** Local information sphere

do not advocate any specific technology, e.g., a CKB unit could be a massively parallel machine or a cluster of PCs. Within a local information sphere information conceptually is allowed to flow freely. This does not imply that anybody can access any information. In fact, as we discuss later on, each CKB will support sophisticated access control mechanisms. The main difference from the global information sphere is that within a local information sphere data can essentially be stored and processed on any of the CKBs (by authorized users), requiring simpler interfaces that can be optimized for efficient information sharing. Stated differently, a user within the local information sphere can *trust* the system to enforce all applicable access control and security policies. Systems outside this trust boundary can only be accessed through the Gateway Modules. The Cornell Knowledge Broker will be discussed in detail in the next section.

## 3   The Cornell Knowledge Broker

The Cornell Knowledge Broker (see Figure 3) processes potentially massive streams of data, e.g., newsfeed data and continuously arriving measurements from sensors, but also reports from analysts, and other intelligence feeds. It supports on-line extraction of relevant information from streams in real-time, and

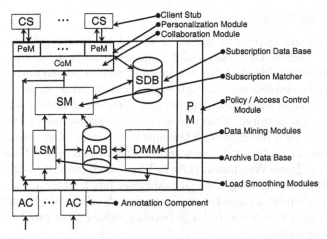

**Fig. 3.** Cornell Knowledge Broker

at the same time archives all incoming information for later deep offline analysis. Hence the CKB will ultimately combine the functionality of data warehouses [34] with that of data stream management systems (STREAM [5, 7], Aurora [12], TelegraphCQ [15], NiagaraCQ [16]) and sensor database systems [9, 37]. In the following sections we describe the components of the Cornell Knowledge Broker in more detail.

## 3.1    Annotation Component

The raw data that arrives at the knowledge broker might come in a variety of formats, e.g., streams of text data, relational data, images, voice recordings, sensor signals, and so on. Annotation Components (AC) transform this data into a coherent format which is amenable to data mining and stream processing techniques. For instance, an annotation module might parse incoming voice recordings and output the corresponding text. Another annotation module's task might be to analyze a plain text message and derive structural information from it like the topic of the text. Annotation modules hence add metadata to an item. This metadata will also describe in a uniform format where, when, and how this information was obtained or derived [10, 11].

In general we envision the annotation modules to annotate incoming data streams with XML metadata. XML is the ideal choice, because the majority of the data will be semi- or unstructured, typically plain text. Notice that this does not necessarily imply that the data be stored in native XML databases. Also, a mining tool might decide to first extract structured information from an XML document (certain attributes of interest) and then work on the structured information only.

## 3.2   Archiving Components

All incoming (annotated) information is stored for future reference and deep analysis in an Archive DataBase (ADB), shown in more detail in Figure 4. To support this functionality the CKB can initially rely on proven data warehousing technology. Data warehouses support sophisticated index structures and pre-computed summaries for efficiently answering complex analysis queries over very large data sets. The major disadvantage is that updates cannot be applied in real-time since they would interfere with the query processing and considerably slow it down. Hence the archive will use a combination of an online DataBase (DB) together with a Data Warehouse (DW). The (much smaller) online database keeps track of newly arriving data in real-time, but is typically not accessible for queries. The updates collected in the online database are then periodically moved to the data warehouse in large batches, where they can be accessed by the data mining modules.

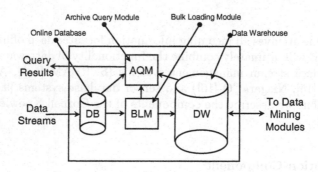

**Fig. 4.** Archive components

The Bulk Loading Module (BLM) controls the transfer of recent data from DB to DW. This setup is similar to current business architectures consisting of OLTP databases and data warehouses. BLM is fully aware of which data resides in DB and which has been moved to DW. It exports these statistics to the Archive Query Module (AQM), which handles queries from the Subscription Matcher (SM) and provides a consistent view of the archive database.

## 3.3   Data Mining Modules

Data Mining Modules (DMM) access the Data Warehouse in the archive to perform deep analysis over the collected information. Any technique for mining text data, images, numerical data, and so on, could be plugged in here. Data mining results need to be updated whenever a sufficient amount of new information has been moved from DB to DW. This update could be performed incrementally, or the data mining application computes a new result from scratch.

Within the context of the CKB the data mining modules are not just data consumers. They are also significant producers of new (derived) information.

The results produced by a DMM are fed back into the data processing life cycle within a CKB. In our current architecture data mining modules either generate (annotated) events or they populate relations (materialized views) in the archive. If events are generated, they can be processed in the Subscription Matcher like newly arriving information. The materialized views are available as input for other data mining applications.

The system can take advantage of this data cycle by incrementally extracting more detailed information from unstructured data, e.g., text and images, in a demand-driven manner. For example, assume in the beginning the metadata of a text consists only of the topic. In a first round of processing, a data mining tool determines the main keywords and adds them to the metadata. Based on this newly added information, the text could be labeled as "interesting" by an analyst's subscription (see discussion on Subscription Matcher below). This triggers another data mining application in the second round of processing to extract more detailed information with respect to some of the keywords, and so on.

The data analysis life cycle opens up several challenging research problems. First, how should different data mining applications be designed such that there is a maximum use of common intermediate results? Second, which of the intermediate results should be stored in the archive for later use? This problem is related to materialized view maintenance in data warehouses [29]. Third, how can events produced by diverse mining applications be efficiently processed such that large numbers of queries and high data arrival rates are supported?

## 3.4   Subscription Engine

The Subscription Matcher (SM) is part of the data processing cycle in the CKB. Its purpose is to analyze incoming data streams in real-time to alert analysts about relevant information and feed important data to data mining applications. For instance an analyst might set up a subscription that generates an alert whenever a document referring to a certain location or event is arriving. This would be a fairly simple subscription (filter predicate that compares an attribute value of incoming data with a given constant), like the ones supported by current publish/subscribe (pub/sub) systems [25].

For intelligence applications support for more complex subscriptions is required. This includes subscriptions concerning multiple events from multiple streams and temporal queries, e.g., discovery of temporal patterns. Similar to data mining applications (see Section 3.3), subscriptions can produce new events which are fed back into the system. For instance, there could be multiple low-level subscriptions that search for simple patterns in the incoming data. These patterns are then analyzed by more high-level subscriptions which discover more complex patterns consisting of simple patterns, and so on. Hence the subscription engine has to support *composite events*, i.e., queries can refer to events generated by other queries. Subscriptions are maintained in the Subscription DataBase (SDB).

Subscriptions may be defined such that their evaluation requires access to the archive. The main difference from data mining applications is the *real-time* requirement for processing subscriptions. The results of data mining applications could have considerable delay depending on the complexity of the algorithms.

Notice that there is an interesting duality between subscriptions and data mining. Subscriptions can be automatically generated by a data mining application, e.g., a mining workflow might have arrived at a stage where finding a new document mentioning A would result in a different next step than finding a document related to B. Hence the mining application would automatically generate a subscription to look for documents related to A or B. On arrival of a corresponding document, the mining application would be automatically notified and hence could continue its analysis appropriately. Similarly, a subscription set up by an analyst might trigger a deep analysis of historical information related to currently arriving data.

## 3.5 Load Smoothing

The Load Smoothing Module (LSM) ensures that the CKB does not collapse under sudden load spikes. As soon as LSM detects a possible overload situation, it pre-emptively eliminates some events from the data streams. Notice that the information is not lost, but its processing is deferred until the load on the system decreases.

LSM essentially works in two different modes. During load spikes it selects events to be removed from the system. Hence during that time only approximate results can be computed by those queries which are affected by dropped events. The goal of LSM during load spikes is to minimize given loss metrics for the currently active queries. Later, when the load returns to "normal" levels, LSM post-processes the initial approximate results until the exact results are obtained for all queries. As long as the system *in the average* has enough capacity to process incoming data, LSM smoothes load spikes by deferring computation.

The Load Smoothing Module addresses two challenging problems. First, it has to select which events to eliminate in order to cause the least loss in overall query accuracy during a load spike. Second, it has to decide which events to store in a fast database such that as soon as the load decreases, the exact result can be recovered. This is non-trivial, e.g., for joins not only the dropped events, but also matching partner-events need to be available for post-processing.

## 3.6 Personalization and Collaboration

The components related to personalization and collaboration are the SDB database, the Collaboration Module (CoM), and the Personalization Modules (PeM). The SDB database stores the personal profiles of analysts and applications. Here a personal profile contains metadata about current and past projects, keywords describing previous experience and expert knowledge, and of course the currently active subscriptions. This information affects the exchange of knowledge with other experts, but also between data mining applications. For instance, the semantics of a subscription or the importance of incoming data might be different depending on an analyst's background and her current projects and active subscriptions and data mining workflows.

Similarly, Personalization Modules (PeM) will support on-line re-organization and annotation of incoming data to take personalization information of the data consumer into account. For example, a PeM can automatically learn search preferences of an analyst for providing customized rankings of large query result sets (see also Section 4.4).

One of the most challenging modules to develop is CoM. Its main goal is to *automatically* enhance the collaboration between analysts. This includes meta-computing, meaning that CoM will search for commonalities in the different subscriptions and data mining workflows. Assume two analysts are working on different cases, but there is a connection between these cases. By identifying commonalities in their analysis setup, CoM would be able to alert the analysts. To simplify information exchange, CoM would generate a description of the encountered similarities and some of the most relevant differences (e.g., data one analyst was not aware of).

The second functionality of CoM is to support *introspection*, i.e., "mining for best practice." CoM keeps track of previous cases by storing in the SDB database which approaches had success in the past and which were not as effective (e.g., which mining models and parameters were selected, which subscriptions were used, which data sources were combined in which way). If in the future an analyst works on a problem which has a similar structure as a past one, CoM could recommend "good" approaches or even perform an initial automatic setup of the required data mining workflow and subscriptions.

### 3.7  Policy and Access Control

The Policy and Access Control (PM) module ensures that only authorized users have access to certain data, including subscriptions and personalization related information. PM also contains some of the privacy-preserving functionality needed for information exchange with other participants in a global information sphere. The functionality of PM therefore extends far beyond simple access control in operating systems, e.g., Windows or UNIX file ownership attributes. There has been work on security and access control for statistical and XML databases [1, 8, 45], but to date none of the proposed techniques provides a satisfactory combination of guaranteeing access restrictions while supporting desired analysis functionality.

We identified the following key features for PM. First, PM should support *fine-grained* access control, down to the level of single attribute values in documents. This results in potentially high overhead for enforcing policies, but will enable an analyst to access that and only that data that she needs to know. Second, there should be support for *dynamic* policies, i.e., the overhead for changing policies should be low. For instance, assume during an investigation an analyst detects a link between two documents in the database. Both documents are accessible to the analyst, but a third document which forms the link between the two currently is not. Depending on the case it might be necessary to extend the analyst's need-to-know in order to let her proceed with the investigation. Third, PM should support *adaptive content-based* access control. When new documents arrive at the system, it might not be initially clear which access policies apply. Only after several processing steps, when a document's content has been sufficiently analyzed, can proper access rights be assigned. In order to take as much of the computational burden away from human operators, PM should be able to automatically update access rights as the document is processed.

## 4    Current Status and Next Steps

We have available several techniques for the different modules, mostly for the Subscription Matcher, Load Smoothing and Data Mining Modules. In the following sections some of these techniques are surveyed, accompanied by a discussion how the different components will be connected in an initial version of the Cornell Knowledge Broker.

### 4.1    Techniques for the Subscription Matcher

The purpose of the Subscription Matcher is to analyze incoming data streams in real time to alert analysts about relevant information and feed important data to data mining applications. It is functionally similar to a continuous data stream query processor [5,7,12,15,16], a publish/subscribe system [25], or an event processing system [3,13,14,38,44]. However, there are significant differences.

In a conventional pub/sub system the query language typically consists of simple filter predicates–Boolean expressions evaluated on a single record of the publication stream [25]. Such queries lend themselves to efficient implementation. However, while they are able to select individual records or events of interest, they are obviously not able to identify spatial or temporal patterns, which involve multiple events, possibly from different input streams. We believe supporting such patterns is essential for intelligence applications. Thus, a more expressive subscription query language is required.

One very powerful approach is represented by the CQL Continuous Query Language implemented in the Stanford STREAM system [4]. In STREAM, data is modeled both as timestamped streams and as conventional relations. CQL includes the full SQL language, and performs the bulk of its data manipulation in the relational domain. In addition, there is a small set of stream-to-relation and relation-to-stream operators, used to translate stream data and query results between the stream and relational domains. While formally appealing, this approach has the drawback that it can easily express stream queries that are infeasibly expensive to execute; and there are no obvious criteria the user can apply to ensure her queries will be efficient.

We are taking a different approach. Instead of defining a single very powerful data stream query language, we are developing a *hierarchy* of query languages. At the bottom is a data stream query language that we already know how to implement very efficiently – simple attribute/value based publish/subscribe. Moving up in the hierarchy yields increasingly more expressive languages, with increasingly more expensive query execution. Instead of targeting one design point whose query language has great expressiveness, we are developing a "sliding scale" of expressiveness/performance design points which will allow us to control the tradeoff between expressiveness and performance.

The languages in our hierarchy are capable of defining "composite events" as discussed in Section 3.4. Query results produce events whose treatment by subsequent queries is indistinguishable from the treatment of primitive events arriving on the input data streams.

We are developing a general calculus for data stream queries. This calculus will provide the means for comparing the expressiveness and complexity of different query languages in a precise, formal way. Our preliminary results are quite encouraging, and we believe they validate our fundamental design choices:

- A data model comprising temporally-annotated data streams;
- A two-sorted first order logic including data terms and temporal terms, with strict limitations on the use of temporal terms;
- A specialized binding construct to allow parameterized aggregation.

Our calculus is powerful enough to simulate the majority of previous work in languages for data stream processing systems, pub/sub, and event processing systems. At the same time, we have been able to find fairly simple syntactic characterizations of subsystems that are semantically equivalent to the query systems we have examined, even systems that are much less expressive than our full calculus. The characterizations use properties such as nesting depth of operators and quantifiers, and the number of free variables in a formula – properties that intuitively have a natural relation to execution complexity, and in some cases translate directly to the structure of a message-oriented implementation of the subscription engine.

## 4.2  Techniques for the Data Mining Module

In the following we survey techniques that will be integrated as part of the Data Mining Module. Other data mining approaches can be easily added later on as the CKB evolves.

**Change Detection.** One of the major challenges presented by data streams is detecting a change. Up to now, work in this area has taken a parametric approach: the data has been modeled by prespecified families of distributions or Markov processes. A change is announced whenever an algorithm finds a model in this family that describes the current data better than the current model. We are working on a completely different, *nonparametric* approach. We make no assumptions about the distribution of data except that the records are generated independently; that is, the value of one record does not depend on the values of the records that appeared before it in the data stream. This technique has several advantages: it is intuitive, it is completely general (it is independent of the distributions that generate the data), works for discrete and continuous data, and shows good results experimentally.

Change has far-reaching impact on any data processing algorithm. For example, when constructing a data mining model over a data stream, old data before a change can bias a data mining model towards data characteristics that do not hold any longer. If we process queries over data streams, we may want to give separate query answers for each time interval where the underlying data distribution is stable. Our work is based on a formal definition of change and associated techniques for quickly detecting whenever statistically significant change has occurred.

Hopcroft et al. attack this problem for graph-structured data [30]. They examine how to detect communities in large linked networks, and how to track such communities over time. They focus in particular on data with a low signal-to-noise ratio.

**Detecting Bursts in Data Streams.** Kleinberg [35] proposes a framework for modeling "bursts" in temporal data, in such a way that they can be robustly and efficiently identified, and can provide an organizational framework for analyzing the underlying content. Many of the most widely used on-line media and Web information sources can be naturally viewed as continuous streams of information. Their time scales range from the minute-by-minute dynamics of usage at high-volume Web sites, to the hourly and daily evolution of topics in e-mail, news, and blogs, to the long-term research trends that are evident in research paper archives. Kleinberg's approach rests on the premise that the appearance of a topic or event is signaled by a "burst of activity," with certain features rising sharply in frequency as the topic emerges. The approach is based on modeling the stream using an infinite-state automaton, in which bursts appear as state transitions. The automaton also implicitly imposes a hierarchical structure on the bursts in a stream.

## 4.3    Techniques for the Load Smoothing Module

As discussed in Section 3.5, load smoothing consists of two different modes of operation: peak-load mode and low-load mode. During peak load, LSM removes events from the system in order to avoid thrashing. This is also referred to as *load shedding*. Most current approaches are based on random load shedding [6, 33, 42] (Tatbul et al. [42] also consider simple heuristics for semantic load shedding, where certain events have higher value to the query than others). Random load shedding works well for queries that compute aggregates, but as we show [17], random load shedding is inferior if we are concerned with the approximation quality of set-valued query results. In intelligence applications we expect a large fraction of the queries to have set-valued results, e.g., queries searching for certain documents or groups of similar documents from multiple input streams. Notice that we treat incoming documents as events with attached application data.

In [17] we propose novel approximation techniques for joins of data streams, i.e., where we are interested in finding matching (similar) documents or events in different data streams. We examine several popular and established approximation measures for sets. In our load shedding scenario most of these measures reduce to the MAX-subset measure: the best approximate result is the one which is the largest subset of the exact query answer. For MAX-subset we develop an optimal *offline* algorithm. For given input sets it determines in polynomial time (polynomial in parameters like input size, memory size, and size of the join window for sliding window joins [17]) the optimal strategy of keeping or dropping incoming events. This algorithm assumes complete future knowledge and hence is not applicable in a real system. However, it serves as a benchmark for comparing *any* practical online strategy with what is the best any such strategy could ever achieve with the given system resources.

As it turns out, as long as one can approximately predict future arrival probabilities of similar events, simple random load shedding is far inferior to semantic join approximation techniques like PROB [17]. PROB is a simple lightweight heuristic that in case of system overload drops the events with the lowest predicted arrival probability of a matching partner event in the other stream. PROB will therefore be added to LSM.

Unfortunately the optimization problem of minimizing result loss during peak load periods is very complex in general. To date there is no complete end-to-end load shedding approach except for simple random load shedding. The initial version of CKB therefore will support semantic join approximation as well as random load shedding for aggregation queries.

The second mode of operation of LSM, the low-load mode, presents new challenges which have not been sufficiently examined by the database community. In [17] we introduce the Archive-Metric (ArM) which measures the post-processing cost for the recovery of the exact result after a load spike. We have developed system models for optimizing different cost metrics related to accessing and processing all events that were dropped during peak load periods. Unfortunately optimal offline algorithms for this problem so far are too complex and hence not useful for benchmarking. We are currently developing efficient online heuristics that balance parameters like archive access cost, result latency, and total processing cost in terms of CPU and memory usage.

## 4.4   Techniques for Personalization and Collaboration

In recent work Joachims [32] proposes a novel approach to optimizing retrieval functions using implicit feedback. The main idea is to automatically learn functions that rank documents according to their relevance to a query. Taking an empirical-risk-minimization approach with Kendall's Tau as the loss function, a Support Vector algorithm is defined for the resulting convex training problem. An important property of this algorithm is that it can be trained with partial information about the target rankings like "for query Q, document A should be ranked higher than document B". In Web search applications such preference data is available in abundance, since it can be inferred from the clicking behavior of users. We expect similar properties to hold for intelligence applications, allowing the system to learn an analyst's preferences with respect to a certain query or project.

## 4.5  Privacy-Preserving Data Mining

As outlined in Section 1, a vital component of our system will be the capability to perform privacy-preserving computation and data mining in the global information sphere. Assume that there is an analyst in one local information sphere that initiates the privacy-preserving computation, and we call this information sphere the *server sphere*. We call the information spheres that participate in the computation by engaging in a protocol for privacy-preserving computation *client spheres*. For simplicity, we assume that there is one server and a set of clients, each having some data.

The usual solution to the above problem consists in having all client peers send their private data to the server sphere. However, the system that we are building will be able to accomplish this computation *without violating the privacy of individual clients*. In other words, if all the server needs is a data mining model, a solution is preferred that reduces the disclosure of private data while still allowing the server to build the model. Similarly, if all the server needs is the answer to an aggregate query, the computation of this query should not disclose anything beyond the answer to the query (and what can be concluded from the query answer).

One possibility is as follows: before sending its piece of data, each client sphere perturbs it so that some true information is taken away and some false information is introduced. This approach is called *randomization*. Another possibility is to decrease precision of the transmitted data by rounding, suppressing certain values, replacing values with intervals, or replacing categorical values by more general categories up the taxonomic hierarchy, see [19, 31, 40, 41].

The usage of randomization for preserving privacy has been studied extensively in the framework of statistical databases [20, 21, 26, 28, 39]. In that case, the server has a complete and precise database with the information from its clients, and it has to make a version of this database public, for others to work with. One important example is census data: the government of a country collects private information about its inhabitants, and then has to turn this data into a tool for research and economic planning. However, it is assumed that private records of any given person should not be released nor be recoverable from what is released. In particular, a company should not be able to match up records in the publicly released database with the corresponding records in the company's own database of its customers.

Our recent work in this area has addressed the problem of privacy-preserving association rule mining, and we introduced a novel notion of *privacy breaches*, a formal definition of how much privacy is compromised for a given privacy-preserving data mining method [24, 23].

## 4.6  How to Connect the Different Modules

At first glance, implementing the infrastructure that connects the different modules of the CKB might appear to be a substantial effort. We believe this is not the case. While the CKB's infrastructure does have some unusual requirements, it is fundamentally similar to many high-performance enterprise applications. The requirements are generally quite close to what is provided in existing J2EE implementations.

We propose to start from an existing open-source J2EE system such as JBoss (http://sourceforge.net/projects/jboss). Rather than building new infrastructure, we view ourselves as building a medium-size J2EE application, possibly with minor enhancements to a few of the APIs – e.g., enhancing JMS to support our richer subscription semantics. Developing a CKB prototype in this way should be well within the capabilities of a university research group. Stated differently, by relying on J2EE technology we can concentrate our efforts on the design of the CKB modules and their interaction.

## 5  Conclusion

The major challenge for intelligence applications is to find relevant information in massive amounts of available data, both data which is already archived as well as newly arriving data. We have presented the Cornell Knowledge Broker, which constitutes the information processing unit of the information sphere architecture. The CKB takes a unique approach to combining offline deep analysis (traditional data mining) with real-time online processing, while at the same time providing support for access control and privacy-preserving technology.

We do not claim that the Cornell Knowledge Broker and the Information System architecture are the only possible way to support analysts in processing massive amounts of data. Indeed, the architecture itself leaves room for alternative implementations. Our main goal is to create an infrastructure that integrates novel data mining techniques to maximize their effectiveness.

Our future work will therefore follow two directions. First, we will continue to develop novel techniques for mining large data sets and data streams. These techniques lie at the heart of the actual data processing task performed by an analyst. Second, we will extend the system architecture to integrate these techniques to maximize their effectiveness, enabling them to interact with each other and with system services such as access control. We are currently implementing several of the CKB's modules and expect a first prototype of the system to be ready in the second half of 2004. Once a prototype system is available, we will be able to evaluate our architecture design decisions and to make quantitative comparisons to alternative approaches.

## References

1. N.R. Adam and J.C. Wortmann. Security-control methods for statistical databases: A comparative study. *ACM Computing Surveys*, 21(4):515–556, 1989.
2. R. Agrawal and R. Srikant. Privacy-preserving data mining. In *Proc. ACM SIG-MOD Int. Conf. on Management of Data*, pages 439–450, 2000.
3. M. K. Aguilera, R. E. Strom, D. C. Sturman, M. Astley, and T. D. Chandra. Matching events in a content-based subscription system. In *Proc. ACM Symp. on Principles of Distributed Computing (PODC)*, pages 53–61, 1999.

4. A. Arasu, S. Babu, and J. Widom. The CQL continuous query language: Semantic foundations and query execution. Technical report, Stanford University, 2003.
5. B. Babcock, S. Babu, M. Datar, R. Motwani, and J. Widom. Models and issues in data stream systems. In *Proc. Symp. on Principles of Database Systems (PODS)*, pages 1–16, 2002.
6. B. Babcock, M. Datar, and R. Motwani. Load shedding techniques for data stream systems (short paper). In *Proc. Workshop on Management and Processing of Data Streams (MPDS)*, 2003.
7. S. Babu and J. Widom. Continuous queries over data streams. *ACM SIGMOD Record*, 30(3):109–120, 2001.
8. E. Bertino, S. Jajodia, and P. Samarati. Database security: Research and practice. *Information Systems*, 20(7):537–556, 1995.
9. P. Bonnet, J. Gehrke, and P. Seshadri. Towards sensor database systems. In *Proc. Int. Conf. on Mobile Data Management (MDM)*, pages 3–14, 2001.
10. P. Buneman, S. Khanna, K. Tajima, and W. C. Tan. Archiving scientific data. In *Proc. SIGMOD*, pages 1–12, 2002.
11. P. Buneman, S. Khanna, and W. C. Tan. Why and where: A characterization of data provenance. In *Proc. Int. Conf. on Database Theory (ICDT)*, pages 316–330, 2001.
12. D. Carney, U. Çetintemel, M. Cherniack, C. Convey, S. Lee, G. Seidman, M. Stonebraker, N. Tatbul, and S. Zdonik. Monitoring streams – a new class of data management applications. In *Proc. Int. Conf. on Very Large Databases (VLDB)*, 2002.
13. A. Carzaniga, D. S. Rosenblum, and A. L. Wolf. Achieving scalability and expressiveness in an internet-scale event notification service. In *Proc. ACM Symp. on Principles of Distributed Computing (PODC)*, pages 219–227, 2000.
14. S. Chakravarthy, V. Krishnaprasad, E. Anwar, and S.-K. Kim. Composite events for active databases: Semantics, contexts and detection. In *Proc. Int. Conf. on Very Large Databases (VLDB)*, pages 606–617, 1994.
15. S. Chandrasekaran, O. Cooper, A. Deshpande, M. J. Franklin, J. M. Hellerstein, W. Hong, S. Krishnamurthy, S. R. Madden, V. Raman, F. Reiss, and M. A. Shah. TelegraphCQ: Continuous dataflow processing for an uncertain world. In *Proc. Conf. on Innovative Data Systems Research (CIDR)*, 2003.
16. J. Chen, D. J. DeWitt, F. Tian, and Y. Wang. NiagaraCQ: A scalable continuous query system for internet databases. In *Proc. ACM SIGMOD Int. Conf. on Management of Data*, pages 379–390, 2000.
17. A. Das, J. Gehrke, and M. Riedewald. Approximate join processing over data streams. In *Proc. ACM SIGMOD Int. Conf. on Management of Data*, pages 40–51, 2003.
18. A. Demers, J. Gehrke, and M. Riedewald. Research issues in mining and monitoring of intelligence data. In H. Kargupta, A. Joshi, K. Sivakumar, and Y. Yesha, editors, *Data Mining: Next Generation Challenges and Future Directions*. MIT/AAAI Press, 2004. To be released.
19. George T. Duncan, Ramayya Krishnan, Rema Padman, Phyllis Reuther, and Stephen Roehrig. Cell suppression to limit content-based disclosure. In *Proceedings of the 30th Hawaii International Conference on System Sciences*, volume 3. IEEE Computer Society Press, 1997.
20. George T. Duncan and Sumitra Mukherjee. Optimal disclosure limitation strategy in statistical databases: Deterring tracker attacks through additive noise. *Journal of the American Statistical Association*, 95(451):720–729, 2000.

21. Timothy Evans, Laura Zayatz, and John Slanta. Using noise for disclosure limitation of establishment tabular data. *Journal of Official Statistics*, 14(4):537–551, 1998.

22. A. Evfimievski, R. Srikant, R. Agrawal, and J. Gehrke. Privacy preserving mining of association rules. In *Proc. ACM SIGKDD Int. Conf. on Knowledge Discovery and Data Mining*, 2002.

23. Alexandre Evfimievski, Johannes Gehrke, and Ramakrishnan Srikant. Limiting privacy breaches in privacy preserving data mining. In *Proceedings of the 22nd ACM SIGACT-SIGMOD-SIGART Symposium on Principles of Database Systems (PODS 2003)*, 2003.

24. Alexandre Evfimievski, Ramakrishnan Srikant, Rakesh Agrawal, and Johannes Gehrke. Privacy preserving mining of association rules. In *Proceedings of the 8th ACM SIGKDD International Conference on Knowledge Discovery in Databases and Data Mining*, pages 217–228, Edmonton, Alberta, Canada, July 23–26 2002.

25. F. Fabret, H.-A. Jacobsen, F. Llirbat, J. Pereira, K. A. Ross, and D. Shasha. Filtering algorithms and implementation for very fast publish/subscribe. In *Proc. ACM SIGMOD Int. Conf. on Management of Data*, pages 115–126, 2001.

26. Stephen E. Fienberg, Udi E. Makov, and Russel J. Steele. Disclosure limitation using perturbation and related methods for categorical data. *Journal of Official Statistics*, 14(4):485–502, 1998.

27. J. Gehrke, editor. *Special Issue on Privacy and Security*, volume 4 of *SIGKDD Explorations*, 2002.

28. J.M. Gouweleeuw, P. Kooiman, L. C. R.J. Willenborg, and P.-P. de Wolf. Post randomisation for statistical disclosure control: Theory and implementation. *Journal of Official Statistics*, 14(4):463–478, 1998.

29. A. Gupta and I. S. Mumick, editors. *Materialized Views: Techniques, Implementations, and Applications*. MIT Press, 1998.

30. J. E. Hopcroft, O. Khan, B. Kulis, and B. Selman. Natural communities in large linked networks. In *Proc. ACM SIGKDD Int. Conf. on Knowledge Discovery and Data Mining*, pages 541–546, 2003.

31. Vijay S. Iyengar. Transforming data to satisfy privacy constraints. In *Proceedings of the 8th ACM SIGKDD International Conference on Knowledge Discovery in Databases and Data Mining*, pages 279–288, Edmonton, Alberta, Canada, July 23–26 2002.

32. T. Joachims. Optimizing search engines using clickthrough data. In *Proc. ACM SIGKDD Int. Conf. on Knowledge Discovery and Data Mining*, pages 133–142, 2002.

33. J. Kang, J. F. Naughton, and S. D. Viglas. Evaluating window joins over unbounded streams. In *Proc. Int. Conf. on Data Engineering (ICDE)*, 2003.

34. R. Kimball. *The Data Warehouse Toolkit*. John Wiley and Sons, 1996.

35. J. M. Kleinberg. Bursty and hierarchical structure in streams. *Data Mining and Knowledge Discovery*, 7(4):373–397, 2003.

36. Y. Lindell and B. Pinkas. Privacy preserving data mining. *Journal of Cryptology*, 15(3):177–206, 2002.

37. S. Madden, M. J. Franklin, J. M. Hellerstein, and W. Hong. The design of an acquisitional query processor for sensor networks. In *Proc. ACM SIGMOD Int. Conf. on Management of Data*, pages 491–502, 2003.

38. I. Motakis and C. Zaniolo. Formal semantics for composite temporal events in active database rules. *Journal of Systems Integration*, 7(3-4):291–325, 1997.

39. Sumitra Mukherjee and George T. Duncan. Disclosure limitation through additive noise data masking: Analysis of skewed sensitive data. In *Proceedings of the 30th Hawaii International Conference on System Sciences*, volume 3, pages 581–586. IEEE Computer Society Press, 1997.
40. Pierangela Samarati and Latanya Sweeney. Generalizing data to provide anonymity when disclosing information. In *Proceedings of the 17th ACM Symposium on Principles of Database Systems*, Seattle, Washington, USA, June 1–3 1998.
41. Pierangela Samarati and Latanya Sweeney. Protecting privacy when disclosing information: k-anonymity and its enforcement through generalization and suppression. In *Proceedings of the IEEE Symposium on Research in Security and Privacy*, Oakland, California, USA, May 1998.
42. N. Tatbul, U. Çetintemel, S. Zdonik, Mitch Cherniack, and Michael Stonebraker. Load shedding in a data stream manager. In *Proc. Int. Conf. on Very Large Databases (VLDB)*, pages 309–320, 2003.
43. J. Vaidya and C. Clifton. Privacy preserving association rule mining in vertically partitioned data. In *Proc. ACM SIGKDD Int. Conf. on Knowledge Discovery and Data Mining*, pages 23–26, 2002.
44. A. Yalamanchi, J. Srinivasan, and D. Gawlick. Managing expressions as data in relational database systems. In *Proc. Conf. on Innovative Data Systems Research (CIDR)*, 2003.
45. T. Yu, D. Srivastava, L. V. S. Lakshmanan, and H. V. Jagadish. Compressed accessibility map: Efficient access control for xml. In *Proc. VLDB*, pages 478–489, 2002.

# Computer-Based Training for Deception Detection: What Users Want?

Jinwei Cao, Ming Lin, Amit Deokar, Judee K. Burgoon,
Janna M. Crews, and Mark Adkins

Center for the Management of Information
University of Arizona, Tucson, AZ, 85721, USA
{jcao,mlin,adeokar,jburgoon,jcrews,madkins}@cmi.arizona.edu

**Abstract.** Training humans in detecting deception is as much a difficult and important problem as detecting deception itself. A computer-based deception detection training system, Agent99 Trainer, was built with a goal to train humans to understand deception and detect deception more accurately. Based on the previous studies, a newer version of this system was designed and implemented not only to overcome the limitations of the earlier system, but also to enhance it with additional useful features. In this paper, we present a usability study to test the design of this system from a users' perspective. The findings of this study, based on quantitative and qualitative data, demonstrate good usability of the training system, along with providing a better understanding of what users want from such a deception detection training system.

## 1 Introduction

In the past two years, a curriculum for deception detection training and two prototypes of computer-based deception detection training systems called Agent99 Trainer have been developed in a southwest research university for US Air Force officers. Reported in many literatures, human's deception detection accuracy rates are only slightly better than chance level (around 50%) [3], [14], [16]. The goal of the Agent99 Trainer, therefore, is to train people (such as Air Force security officers) to understand deception and enable them to detect deception more accurately, along with providing the advantages of computer-based training such as ease of access and low cost. The first prototype of Agent99 Trainer was designed as a Web-based multimedia training system, and it has been shown effective in deception detection training [4]. It was also demonstrated that users had a good experience with this first prototype [5].

However, several limitations of the first prototype were discovered when the prototype was evaluated [5]. These limitations, including security concerns with Web-based implementation and insufficient functionalities, indicated the need for a new design of Agent99 Trainer. Hence, based on the experiences from developing the first prototype, we designed a new one in which, the major design of the first prototype was retained, but the Web-based implementation was changed to CD-ROM implementation, and some advanced features such as search functionality and assessment tool were added. A recent experiment showed that the new prototype also effectively improved people's deception detection accuracy [13]. However, in order to judge the success of the system, we also need to evaluate the usability of the system, which can be measured based on attributes such as system effectiveness, user satisfaction and

H. Chen et al. (Eds.): ISI 2004, LNCS 3073, pp. 163–175, 2004.

system ease of use [17]. In this paper, we will focus on evaluating the usability of the new prototype of Agent99 Trainer, and study what system features affect the system's usability. More broadly, we want to investigate what users really want in a computer-based training system for deception detection.

The remainder of the paper is organized as follows. We first review the deception detection training literature briefly, followed by the design of the new prototype of Agent99 Trainer. We then describe the usability measures and evaluation instrument; present the analysis, results and lessons learned. Finally, we conclude the paper with a list of suggestions for future development of the system.

## 2    Agent99 Trainer – A Computer-Based Training System for Deception Detection

Many previous research studies have shown that properly designed training can help people better detect deception [20], [10], [11], [12]. Our previous research has identified three critical components of effective deception detection training: explicit instructions on cues of deception, practice judging the veracity of real communication, and immediate feedback on the judgment [15], [6]. Although these three components can be easily implemented in a traditional classroom training environment, the shortage of qualified deception detection instructors and the consequent high cost of traditional classroom training call for a more efficient and cost-effective alternative. As a result, a computer-based training system, Agent99 Trainer, was developed for deception detection training.

The first prototype of Agent99 Trainer was designed and implemented as a Web-based multimedia training system. The three critical components of deception detection training were implemented in two modules in this prototype: *Watch Lecture* and *View Example with Analysis*. The *Watch Lecture* module presented a deception detection lecture through a combination of synchronized media including the expert video of the lecture, PowerPoint slides, and lecture notes. The lecture was segmented into different topics and a pull down menu was provided so that users can jump to any topic during the training. The *View Example with Analysis* module linked practice examples to the deception cues taught during the lecture. Users could view those examples and click on a link to receive analytical feedbacks on the deception cues illustrated.

Experiments have shown that this first prototype was effective in deception detection training: users' detection accuracy was significantly improved [6]. However, some problems of this prototype were also pointed out [5], such as insufficient interaction, lack of assessment capability, and bandwidth restriction. In addition, implementing the Web-based prototype in the Air Force training site was revealed to be troublesome because of the networking security concerns from the military. Therefore, the second prototype of the Agent99 Trainer was developed to address these problems by changing the delivery method and adding new functionalities.

The new prototype was delivered on CD-ROMs, which enabled us to carry high quality audio/video without the networking bandwidth restrictions. The major design of the *Watch Lecture* and *View Example* modules in the old prototype was retained in this new prototype, but the two previously separated modules were combined into a single *Virtual Classroom* (Fig 1) module. The lecture video, slides and notes were structured in a very similar fashion as in the old prototype, and they were still synchronized. Examples were now embedded in the lecture video, as subtopics under certain concepts or cues of deception detection. An outline-type navigation menu (upper right in Fig 1) replaced the pull down menu in the old prototype, in order to give users a clear framework of the lecture throughout their training process. Users were able to choose any particular lecture topic or example they wanted to watch from the navigation menu.

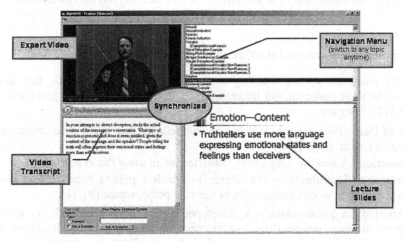

**Fig. 1.** The Virtual Classroom

Besides the *Virtual Classroom*, two new modules were added into the new prototype: *Search Tools* and *Assessment Tool*. The *Search Tools* (Fig. 2) was designed to better support just-in-time training. It allowed users to look for specific information using two methods: *Keyword Search* and *Ask A Question (AAQ)*. AAQ allowed the user to ask a question regarding the subject matter using everyday English (e.g. *what is deception detection?*) Search results returned by the system would be a list of the relevant video segments in the lecture video. The *Assessment Tool* was designed to popup quizzes at certain breakpoints in the lecture, to test users' understanding of the lecture until then (Fig. 3). The correct answer would be given to users as feedback, each time after they answered the question.

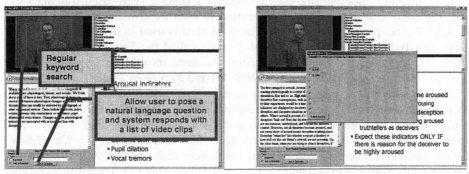

**Fig. 2.** Search Tools                                    **Fig. 3.** Assessment Tool

# 3  Study Design

Since the objective of this study is to evaluate the usability of the new prototype of Agent99 Trainer, a usability questionnaire was given to the users during an experiment conducted at an Air Force training center. The responses to this questionnaire were collected together with the learning performance data in the same experiment for convenience. However, only the usability data will be analyzed and interpreted in this study.

## 3.1  Usability Measures and the Questionnaire

There are many measurable usability attributes described in literature, but three of them are the most common and important ones used to measure any given system's success [17]. They are:

- **Ease of Use** – The degree to which a person believes that using a particular system would be free of effort [9].
- **Satisfaction** – Users are subjectively satisfied when using the system [17].
- **Effectiveness/Usefulness** – The degree to which a person believes that using a particular system would enhance his or her task performance [9], [1].

In this study, a questionnaire was developed to test these three usability attributes from many different perspectives. For example, in terms of user satisfaction, questions were asked about whether the users feel the overall training content interesting; whether they like the major features of the system, such as the self-paced control and/or the structured and synchronized multimedia; whether the new functions such as Ask A Question (AAQ) or Popup Quizzes made them feel more satisfied; how they feel about the quality of audio and video in this system; and whether they would consider using the system again. According to Weisberg's guidelines [18] on how to develop questionnaires to avoid invalid questions and improve reliability, we designed both closed-ended and open-ended questions in our questionnaire, so that users can both choose from given alternatives as well as have the freedom to answer in their own words. Negatively worded items were also provided to avoid any bias caused by different wording.

The development of the questionnaire was an incremental process. Starting with a previous usability questionnaire used for testing a general Web-based training tool [19], the questionnaire was iteratively revised in each experiment when the earlier Agent99 Trainer prototype was tested. The final version used in this study contained items directly from an existing validated measure called the *System Usability Scale* (*SUS*) [2]; items adapted from other existing validated measures such as *Questionnaire for User Interface Satisfaction* (*QUIS*) [7] and *Perceived Usefulness and Ease of Use* [9]; as well as items developed by us regarding some specific system features. There were twenty nine closed-ended questions rated on a 7-point Likert-type scale (*1 = Completely Disagree; 2 = Mostly Disagree; 3 = Slightly Disagree; 4 = Neither Agree nor Disagree (Neutral); 5 = Slightly Agree; 6 = Mostly Agree; 7 = Completely Agree*). However, seven questions among them were about certain system functions that were only available in certain treatment groups (see Table 2). Therefore an eighth choice "*N/A*" (not applicable) was added to deal with this situation. Six open-ended questions were given to users after the closed-ended questions. They were as follows: 1) *Please describe any problems that you experienced using this system*; 2) *What do you like about the system?* 3) *What do you dislike about the system?* 4) *How can the system be improved to better help you learn?* 5) *In what learning situations do you think you would like to use this type of learning system?* 6) *Other comments*. The questionnaire was evaluated by several graduate students prior to conducting the study to avoid any possible misunderstanding.

## 3.2  Experiment

The usability questionnaire was given in an experiment conducted at an Air Force training center. The major purpose of this experiment was to test the effectiveness of Agent99 Trainer by measuring users' learning performance. For this purpose, pre- and post-tests on deception knowledge and deception judgment accuracy were given before and after training respectively. The usability questionnaire was deployed after the post-test. To understand the relationship between the different combinations of system functions and the system usability, we compared the Agent99 Trainer prototype with full functions to the ones with partial functions. The experimental conditions are described in section 3.2.3.

### 3.2.1  Participants
The participants were 180 Air Force officers who were receiving general training at a large US Air Force training center. Deception detection training was considered part of their training program and they were given credits for participating in the experiment. The participants were randomly assigned to 5 treatment groups and scheduled to several different sessions; however, the number of participants per group varied due to some technical difficulties we encountered during the experiment. For example, in the first few sessions, some users had to be changed to a different treatment group due to a computer problem.

### 3.2.2  Experimental Conditions and Procedure
The experimental conditions were arrayed from least to most amount of functions as follows (in ascending order):

*Video Only.* In this condition, users watched a video of an expert talking about deception, with PowerPoint slides and examples cut in the video. The presentation order in this video is pre-determined by the instructor.

*Linear A99.* In this condition, lecture outline, expert video, PowerPoint slides and lecture notes were shown on the Agent99 Trainer interface. PowerPoint slides and lecture notes were synchronized with the lecture video. However, users could not click on the lecture outline to change topics. They still had to follow the pre-determined instruction pace and sequence.

*A99 + AAQ.* This condition had almost all function of Agent99 Trainer except for the popup quizzes. Users could control their own learning pace by clicking on the lecture outline. They could also look for specific topics by using keyword search or AAQ.

***A99 + AAQ + Content.*** This condition was almost the same as the previous, except that links to more examples of deception detection were provided at the bottom of the lecture outline.

***A99 + AAQ + Content + Quizzes.*** This condition deployed the complete functional implementation of Agent99 Trainer. Additionally, more examples of deception detection were also given in this condition.

The procedure of the experiment is summarized in Table 1. There were two training sessions in this experiment. The first session was an introductory lecture about basic deception detection knowledge and the second session was a lecture teaching the specific cues of deception. Every user completed both sessions under the same experimental conditions. Since the introductory lecture had less content than the cues lecture, the usability questionnaire was given after the post-test at the end of the first session to prevent participants from getting fatigued. Finally the two sessions had about the same duration: one and half hours.

**Table 1.** Experiment design

| Training Sessions | Treatment Conditions | | | | |
|---|---|---|---|---|---|
| | Video Only | Linear A99 | A99 + AAQ | A99 + AAQ + content | A99 + AAQ + content + quizzes |
| Intro | Pre-tests | Pre-tests | Pre-tests | Pre-tests | Pre-tests |
| | | | Instruction | | |
| | Post-tests | Post-tests | Post-tests | Post-tests | Post-tests |
| | Usability Questionnaire | Usability Questionnaire | Usability Questionnaire | Usability Questionnaire | Usability Questionnaire |
| Cues | Pre-tests | Pre-tests | Pre-tests | Pre-tests | Pre-tests |
| | | | Instruction | | |
| | Post-tests | Post-tests | Post-tests | Post-tests | Post-tests |

In the *Intro* session where the usability questionnaire was given, every participant in all groups was given a CD-ROM containing the entire session. They were instructed to start the Agent99 Trainer program from the CD-ROM at the same time, and the entire procedure was then controlled by the program. Participants first watched a short video on the introduction to the Agent99 Trainer and the procedure of the experiment. They would then be given the pre-tests. The Agent99 Trainer counted time for users and would force them into the training step if they didn't finish the test on time. After one hour of training, participants would be given the post-tests. The one hour training time was designed to be slightly longer than the length of the basic lecture video so that participants could have time to explore more contents and try out more system functions in the last three conditions. However, the training time and the time for completing pre- and post-tests were the same across conditions in order to control the variance among treatment conditions. Finally, all participants were asked to complete the usability questionnaire.

# 4 Results

## 4.1 Factor Loading and Responses to Specific Items

Factor analysis was conducted to reduce the twenty two close-ended items (applicable to all five conditions) into a smaller number of composite variables that represent the major usability attributes. Using principle component analysis extraction with vari-max rotation and Kaiser normalization, five factors were extracted, which are as follows.

**Perceived Learning Effectiveness** (Alpha = .8400): captures users' perception on how effectively the system helped them learn about deception detection;

**General Satisfaction** (Alpha = .7803): captures users' overall satisfaction with the system;

**Audio/Video Quality Satisfaction** (Alpha = .7722): captures users' satisfaction with the quality of the audio and video used in this system;

**Ease of Use/Learning to Use** (Alpha = .7804): captures users' perception on how easily they could learn to use the system and how easily they actually used the system;

**Comparison With Traditional Classroom Learning:** captures users' views on their experience with Agent99 as compared to the traditional classroom. This factor contains only one item, so it needs to be refined in the future to improve its reliability.

These five factors correspond well to the three usability measures proposed in section 3.1, since we believe that the audio/video quality and the comparison to classroom training are also different perspectives of user satisfaction. Mean and standard deviation of each factor in each experimental condition and in total are shown in Table 4. In brief, the usability attributes were measured positive across all conditions, with most means close or more than 5 (Slightly agree). This indicates that the participants agreed that the Agent99 Trainer system had good usability even with just partial functions. Among the five extracted factors, only the last one, *comparison with traditional classroom learning*, had average neutral responses. However, this result is consistent with other distance learning research findings [8]. It indicates that online training would rather be complementary to classroom training than a complete replacement.

As described in section 3.1, seven closed-ended items could only apply to certain conditions and the responses to these specific items were shown in Table 2.

As shown in Table 2, most of the items related to specific features of Agent99 Trainer got positive responses. For example, the synchronized multimedia presentation and the self-paced learning method were both viewed as effective in helping users learn to detect deception. Although some students experienced the information overload problem caused by multiple multimedia displays, most of them did not view it as a significant issue. The newly-added function, popup quizzes, was also rated as very helpful in supporting learning. However, for the three items measuring users' attitudes towards the search tools, almost all users selected "N/A". After carefully analyzing the responses to the open-ended questions, we realized that most users had no time to use these new functions because of the time constraint on the lecture and because they were not **forced** to use these functions (not as the popup quizzes, which were mandatory to be taken during the training). In fact, the following comment was very representative of this situation: "I didn't use the keyword or AAQ feature because I barely had the time". This indicates that although the training time had been designed to be slightly longer than the training video, the actual individual learning time could be even longer than the designed time, because the self-paced control in condition 3, 4, and 5 allowed users to replay video segments as many times as they want. Therefore, the responses for these three items could not represent the real usability of the search tools, and we need to re-test the search tools in the future.

**Table 2.** Responses to the items related to specific features of Agent99 Trainer[1]

| Items | N | Mean (Std.) | Applicable Conditions |
|---|---|---|---|
| The synchronous display of video, slides and notes helped me understand the subject matter. | 162 | 5.32 (1.61) | 2, 3, 4, 5 |
| It was hard for me to concentrate with so much information (ask a question, keyword search, video, slides and notes) on the screen. † | 157 | 5.03 (1.62) | 2, 3, 4, 5 |
| I liked being able to select any part of the lecture or examples at any time. | 122 | 5.42 (1.36) | 3, 4, 5 |
| The "Keyword Search" helped me find specific information easily. | 52 | 3.75 (1.57) | 3, 4, 5 |
| The "Ask a Question" helped me find specific information easily. | 46 | 3.52 (1.46) | 3, 4, 5 |
| The natural language based "ask a question" was better than the "keyword search" function when I wanted to find specific information. | 44 | 3.89 (1.04) | 3, 4, 5 |
| The Popup Quiz helped me learn deception detection concepts. | 40 | 5.60 (1.41) | 5 |

## 4.2 Comparison among Different Conditions

To understand the relationship between the different combinations of system functions and the system usability, we conducted a planned contrast analysis. We noted that the time constraints restricted users from using the search tools, and hence the actual usage of the system in conditions 2, 3, and 4 was similar to some extent. Therefore, we planned the contrasts as in Table 3.

Contrast 1 compares the Video Only condition with all the other conditions. The hypothesis is that the partial or complete implementation of Agent99 Trainer (A99) is better than a simple linear lecture video.

Contrast 2 compares the three actually similar A99 groups with the one having full functionalities. We predicted that the popup quizzes could bring more positive usability.

Contrast 3 compares the Linear A99 with the non-linear A99 groups (users can control their own learning pace). We hypothesize that non-linear A99 will have more positive usability.

---

[1] The responses to the negatively worded item (labeled with †) were reverse-coded; therefore, for all the items listed, larger numbers indicate more positive response.

Finally, contrast 4 tests whether the addition of more examples in A99 can make better usability.

**Table 3.** Contrast coefficients

| | System Features | | | | |
| Contrast | Video Only | Linear A99 | A99 + AAQ | A99 + AAQ + content | A99 + AAQ + content + quizzes |
| --- | --- | --- | --- | --- | --- |
| 1 | -4 | 1 | 1 | 1 | 1 |
| 2 | 0 | -1 | -1 | -1 | 3 |
| 3 | 0 | -2 | 1 | 1 | 0 |
| 4 | 0 | 0 | -1 | 1 | 0 |

ANOVA tests with planned contrasts above were conducted for each of the five factors extracted from the factor analysis. Mean and standard deviation of each factor are shown in Table 4.

**Table 4.** Means and standard deviations of the five factors

| | N | Learning mean (std) | Satisfaction mean (std) | AV mean (std) | Ease of Use mean (std) | Online/Class mean (std) |
| --- | --- | --- | --- | --- | --- | --- |
| Video | 30 | 4.96 (1.03) | 4.83 ( .99) | 4.75 (1.41) | 5.90 ( .74) | 3.67 (2.11) |
| Linear A99 | 37 | 5.26 (1.21) | 5.08 ( .96) | 5.05 (1.12) | 5.96 ( .79) | 3.50 (1.74) |
| A99 + AAQ | 30 | 5.44 (1.09) | 5.20 (1.28) | 4.88 (1.35) | 6.18 ( .75) | 4.10 (2.11) |
| A99 + AAQ + content | 43 | 5.03 ( .99) | 4.76 (1.04) | 4.96 (1.10) | 5.87 ( .80) | 4.07 (1.78) |
| A99 + AAQ + content + quizzes | 40 | 5.60 (1.10) | 5.49 (1.18) | 5.03 (1.22) | 6.10 (1.01) | 3.97 (1.87) |
| Total | 180 | 5.26 (1.10) | 5.07 (1.11) | 4.95 (1.22) | 6.00 ( .83) | 3.90 (1.89) |

Results of these contrast analysis and explanations to these results, supported by the responses to the open-ended items, are discussed below for each factor.

### 4.2.1 Perceived Learning Effectiveness

The planned contrasts were significant for both contrast 1 (t = 1.697, p = .046, one-tailed) and contrast 2 (t = 1.730, p = .043, one-tailed). It indicates that the Agent99 Trainer (with full or partial functions) was better than a simple linear lecture video, and that the Agent99 Trainer with full functions was better than the one with partial functions. By analyzing the responses to the open-ended items, we found that the following features of the system could explain these contrast results.

- **Structured and synchronized multimedia lecture:** Except for condition 1 (Video Only), the following response was very representative for all other 4 conditions: "The video, slide and notes/commentary combine to give you the visual as well as audio aspects that reinforces the learning material being presented very effectively". The obvious difference between the comments in condition 1 and the other 4 conditions indicated that the synchronized multimedia display did improve users' experience on learning as we predicted.

- **User self-paced control:** The following response was very representative in condition 1 (Video Only) and 2 (Linear A99): "I was unsure how to go back so I couldn't relearn what I had missed". On the other hand, in the rest of the conditions, users reacted with positive comments such as "liked the ability to go to different sections at any time by using the top right screen", "allows one to backtrack and see sections again", and "it allowed you to learn at your own pace". Therefore, user self-paced control played a key role in improving users' learning experience.

- **Popup quizzes:** In the condition where the popup quizzes were used, i.e. condition 5 (A99 + AAQ + content + quizzes), users gave comments such as: "I liked the pop up questions most because of the feedback it provided". Noticing that in other conditions users complained about **lacking of immediate feedback** in comments like: "there was no immediate feedback", we conclude that the immediate assessment and feedback provided with popup quizzes made the difference between condition 5 and the other Agent99 Trainer conditions.

Besides these features that determined the differences among conditions, we found that users' overall perceived learning effectiveness in Agent99 Trainer was positive, as shown in the following representative comment: "I imagine coursework taught through Agent99 would be easier to understand and lead to better results than other types of media." A key contributor to this positive learning effectiveness across all conditions was the use of **video/audio/text examples for practice**. Not only the closed-ended item for this feature got the highest mean response (mean = 5.90), but there were also a lot of positive user comments about this feature in all five conditions, such as "the examples were very helpful" and "Examples of what you are trying to teach are good".

### 4.2.2 General Satisfaction

The planned contrast for contrast 2 was significant ($t = 2.366$, $p = .010$, one-tailed). Similar to the results for *Perceived Learning Effectiveness*, the Agent99 Trainer with full functions is better than the one with partial functions. Again, this could be due to the addition of **popup quizzes** which provided assessment and immediate feedback. Although contrast 4 was not statistically significant, from the qualitative data it appears that the Agent99 Trainer with more content had worse usability than the one with less content. One possible explanation for this anomaly would be **cognitive overload**. Users in condition 4 found the training session very lengthy. This was suggested by the user suggestions such as "reduce the amount of information in the program; I realize there is a lot to be delivered, but take it in phases", and "it was kind of long and stressful". Possibly users in this condition were exposed to information overload in the given time frame. Although users in condition 5 were also given more examples as in condition 4, the user comments in condition 5 showed that most users did not avail the additional content provided because of the time spent in answering the popup quizzes. One representative comment from condition 5 is: "I could not take benefit of the complete information provided because of the time constraints". Therefore, the users in condition 5 did not have the information overload problem as in condition 4. Thus, lengthiness and cognitive load affect the perceived satisfaction of the system, in that, the higher the cognitive load, the lesser the perceived satisfaction.

Although no statistical significance was shown between the first condition and the rest, the user comments indicated a preference for the **synchronized multimedia lecture** and the **user self-paced control**, such as "liked the combination of audio and video presentation along with slideshow and text" and "liked the ability to go to different sections at any time by using the top right screen". Consistent with the findings for *Perceived Learning Effectiveness*, we observed that the perceived user satisfaction was positively related to these two features.

### 4.2.3  Audio/Video Quality Satisfaction

There was no significant planned contrast for this factor. The satisfaction level for audio/video quality was not very high (mean = 4.99) for all groups. The following comments expressed the users' concerns on audio and video quality, and explained a possible reason for the low score: "the video window is too small to pick enough details on the examples", "audio levels wasn't consistent across all examples", "some of the audio/video was cutoff at the end of clip before completely finishing", and "sound quality can be improved". Each of these representative comments address different issues involved in the quality of audio and video presented. These definitely need to be considered in the improved version of the system.

### 4.2.4  Ease of Use/Learning to Use

Again, we did not observe any statistically significant differences between the different conditions. This result is good because it indicated that the addition of system functions did not make the system too complex to use. The perceived ease of use for the Agent99 Trainer was the highest among all five usability factors ($M_{total}$ = 6.00, $M_{condition5}$ = 6.10). Positive comments were representative across all five conditions, such as: "It was easy to use and very informative", "Simple to understand and easy to follow along", and "Extremely easy to use..."

### 4.2.5  Comparison with Traditional Classroom Learning

There were no significant differences among any conditions on users' opinions about comparing Agent99 training system with the traditional classroom. Majority of the users liked Agent99 Trainer as compared to the traditional classroom learning. This was evident from their comments such as: "Agent99 Trainer would be good in any academic setting", and "can be used in a at home-based environment where I can take my time with it, stop and replay info as needed". Some comments indicated a preference for the traditional learning system as compared to the Agent99 Trainer system and suggested improvements to the Agent99 Trainer. This was very helpful and was seen from comments like "I think this is an excellent way to conduct distance learning courses; however there should be an option to be able to actually communicate with an instructor for more specific questions". Still others commented on disliking this system compared to the classroom learning, mainly because of the lack of interaction and feedback. Example comments include "certain topics like the one we went over require discussion and personal explanation to sometimes see complex details that aren't obvious the first time you look at it". Interestingly, such responses were mainly from users in conditions 1 through 4, but not from condition 5. This also indicated support for the effectiveness of the feedback provided by the popup quizzes in condition 5.

# 5   Conclusion: A Checklist for Future Developers

Resulting from both the quantitative and qualitative data collected in this exploratory study, findings of this study demonstrate that the Agent99 Trainer has good usability. More importantly, these findings provide future developers a better understanding of what users want in such a deception detection training system, which are summarized in the following list:

- **Synchronized multimedia lecture.** A special feature of the Agent99 Trainer, the synchronized multimedia lecture, was well embraced by most users. The combination of the video, slides, and text give users multiple channels of learning so that an individual can choose his or her favorite channels to focus on. This presentation also gives users a vivid simulation of the typical classroom instruction they are familiar with. However, some users may face an information overload problem with the multiple presentations. A user configurable GUI that allows users to choose their own combination of displays could be a solution to tackle this problem.
- **Ample real-world examples.** For a training program about deception detection, real-world examples are the most effective ways for helping users learn different deception scenarios and the respective detection strategies. This is not only preferred by the users, but also demonstrated in many previous research studies.
- **Assessment and immediate feedback.** Users need assessments to test their understanding on the subject matter. However, without immediate feedback, they cannot know how well they learned and hence cannot effectively adjust their learning process. Therefore, any assessment provided in the training system needs to be accompanied by an immediate feedback to the users. If the assessments are used for experiment measures, the users need to be informed before the experiment that they will not get feedbacks on these tests; otherwise the satisfactory level towards the system could be decreased.
- **User self-paced control.** Users most likely want to control the training program so that they can learn on their own pace. At the least, they should be given an opportunity to go back to a specific topic they do not understand. The navigable lecture outline provided in the Agent99 Trainer is a good example for the implementation of user self-paced control.
- **High quality audio/video.** For any training system that uses lots of video or audio presentations, the quality of the audio/video clips can greatly affect the system usability. Professional production of the lecture video and the example video or audio clips is highly desired.
- **Sufficient training time.** Finally, the training time for using such a training system should not be restricted. Clearly shown in this study, too much training content with insufficient training time will lead to the cognitive overload problem and will hence decrease the system usability. Ideally, users want to use such a training system as a supplementary tool for just-in-time learning.

This list provides us a guideline for future development. This can also be a guideline for any developers who want to design an information system for deception detection training with good usability. Based on this list of what users want, we will improve our current prototype by providing configurable user interface, improving audio/video quality, providing more immediate feedback, and providing more real-world examples. Since unlimited training time could add difficulty in controlling variances in a controlled experiment, we plan to conduct a field study to test the learning effectiveness and users' experience in using the system without time limitation.

# References

1. Bevan, N. and Macleod, M.: Usability measurement in context. Behaviour and Information Technology, Vol. 13. (1994) 132-145
2. Brooke, J.: SUS: A "quick and dirty" usability scale. Usability Evaluation in Industry. Taylor and Francis (1996)
3. Buller, D. B., Burgoon, J. K.: Interpersonal Deception Theory. Communication Theory, Vol. 6. (1996) 203-242
4. Cao, J., Crews, J., Lin, M., Burgoon, J. K., and Nunamaker, F. J.: Designing Agent99 Trainer: A Learner-Centered, Web-Based Training System for Deception Detection. NSF/NIJ Symposium on "Intelligence and Security Informatics", Tucson, AZ (2003) 358-365
5. Cao, J., Crews, J., Burgoon, J. K., and Nunamaker, F. J., Lin, M.: User Experience with Agent99 Trainer: A Usability Study. 37th Annual Hawaii International Conference on System Sciences (HICSS 2004)
6. Cao, J., Crews, J., Lin, M., Burgoon, J. K., and Nunamaker, F. J.: Can people be trained to detect deceptions? Americas Conference on Information Systems (AMCIS 2003), Tampa, Florida
7. Chin, J. P., Diehl, V. A., and Norman, K. L.: Development of an instrument measuring user satisfaction of the human-computer interface. Proceedings of the CHI `88 Conference on Human Factors in Computing Systems. (1988)
8. Croson, D. C. and Westerman, G.: Distance learning over a short distance. Working paper. (2004)
9. Davis, F. D.: Perceived Usefulness, Perceived Ease of Use, and User Acceptance of Information Technology. MIS Quarterly, Vol. 13. (1989) 319-340
10. DeTurck, M. A., Harszlak, J. J., Bodhorn, D., Texter, L.: The Effects of Training Social Perceivers to Detect Deception from Behavioral Cues. Communication Quarterly, Vol. 38. (1990) 1-11
11. Fiedler, K., Walka, I.: Training Lie Detectors to Use Nonverbal Cues Instead of Global Heuristics. Human Communication Research, Vol. 20. (1993) 199-223
12. Frank, M. G., Feeley, T. H.: To Catch a Liar: Challenges for Research in Lie Detection Training. Journal of Applied Communication Research. (2002)
13. George, J. F., Biros, D. P., Adkins, M., Burgoon, J. K., Nunamaker, F. J.: Testing Various Modes of Computer-Based Training for Deception Detection. Submitted to the 2nd NSF/NIJ Symposium on "Intelligence and Security Informatics", Tucson, AZ (2004)
14. Kraut, R.: Humans as Lie Detectors. Journal of Communication, Vol. 30. (1980) 209-216
15. Lin, M., Cao, J., Crews, M. J., Nunamaker, F. J., and Burgoon, J. K.: Agent99 Trainer: Design and Implement a Web-based Multimedia Training System for Deception Detection Knowledge Transfer. Americas Conference on Information Systems (AMCIS 2003), Tampa, Florida
16. Miller, G. R., Stiff, J. B.: Deceptive Communication. Sage Publications, Inc. (1993)
17. Nielsen, J., Usability Engineering. Boston: Academic Press, 1993.
18. Weisberg, H. F., Krosnick, J. A., and Bowen, B. D.: An introduction to survey research, polling, and data analysis. Thousand Oaks, CA: Sage. (1996)
19. Zhang, D. S.: Virtual Mentor and Media Structuralization Theory. PhD dissertation in the MIS Department, University of Arizona, Tucson, AZ. (2002)
20. Zuckerman, M., Koestner, R., Alton, O. A.: Learning to Detect Deception. Journal of Personality and Social Psychology, Vol. 46. (1984) 519-528

# Identifying Multi-ID Users in Open Forums*

Hung-Ching Chen, Mark Goldberg, and Malik Magdon-Ismail

Rensselaer Polytechnic Institute, 110 8th Street, Troy, NY 12180, USA
{chenh3,goldberg,magdon}@cs.rpi.edu

**Abstract.** We describe a model for real-time communication exchange in public forums, such as newsgroups and chatrooms, and use this model to develop an efficient algorithm which identifies the users that post their messages under different IDs, *multi-ID users*. Our simulations show that, under the model's assumptions, the identification of multi-ID users is highly effective, with false positive and false negative rates of about 0.1% in the worst case.

## 1 Introduction

It is well known that some users, or *actors*, in communication networks, such as newsgroups and chatrooms, post messages using different actor IDs. We denote such actors as *multi-ID actors* or *multi-ID users*. As a rule, these actors attempt to hide the fact that one person is operating using multiple IDs. The reasons for an actor to use multiple IDs are varied. Sometimes, an actor who has become a pariah of a certain public forum may try to regain his/her status using a different ID; sometimes, Actors may post messages under different IDs in order to instigate debate or controversy; sometimes, actors may pose as multiple IDs in order to sway democratic processes in their favor in certain voting procedures on Internet forums, such as a leadership election. In general, the identification of an actor who posts under several IDs should have important forensic value. At a very least, flagging IDs as possibly belonging to the same actor of a public forum can justify further investigation of the posts under those IDs.

A variety of approaches could be adopted to identifying multi-ID actors. Though tracing the source of an Internet packet is not trivial, it is technically possible to identify the IP address of the packets sent by different IDs. While this certainly help with the identification, this information is often insufficient, since a single IP address could represent a cluster of computers on a local network. Furthermore, access to those computers could be available to different people, as is the case for computer laboratories in universities. Another approach would be to analyze the semantics of the messages. For example, a particular actor may use a particular phrase in all of the IDs that it operates. Semantic analysis would attempt to discover stylistic similarities between posts of the same actor using different IDs. This entails sophisticated linguistic analysis that is generally not efficient, and may not be easy to automate, which becomes a serious obstacle if

---

* This research was partially supported by NSF grants 0324947 and 0346341.

H. Chen et al. (Eds.): ISI 2004, LNCS 3073, pp. 176–186, 2004.
© Springer-Verlag Berlin Heidelberg 2004

the task is to identify multi-ID users operating in several out of potentially many thousands of communication networks. Below is a sample log from a chatroom, which illustrates the difficulty of any form of linguistic analysis.

```
[20 : 01 : 18]  <id₁> I shall powerful fart from apple pie, than from hamburger
[20 : 01 : 41]  <id₂> some girls who want to chat with a male with webcam??
[20 : 01 : 55]  <id₃> I shall powerful fart from mom beans than from american taco
[20 : 01 : 57]  <id₃> hahahahahahahah
[20 : 02 : 18]  <id₄> hey <BB> id₁₁ <AB> : i'm happy :P
[20 : 03 : 35]  <id₁> Big farting from salad Olivier!
[20 : 03 : 40]  <id₅-> be nice id₄
[20 : 03 : 47]  <id₅-> or be gone
[20 : 04 : 18]  <id₇> still searching for guys between 35 nd 45
[20 : 04 : 23]  <id₄> <BB> id₅- <AB> : did i talked to yu
[20 : 04 : 26]  <id₄> did i say somthing bad
[20 : 04 : 30]  <id₈> id₉@hotmail.com
[20 : 04 : 30]  <id₈> id₉@hotmail.com
[20 : 04 : 30]  <id₈> id₉@hotmail.com
[20 : 04 : 40]  <id₄> she know what she do if she want to kick me she will
[20 : 04 : 49]  <id₁₀> hello any hot girl that wanna chat pick me
```

In this paper, we present an altogether different approach, based upon statistical properties of the posts. To take the chatroom as an example, each post has three tags associated with it, $<t,\text{id},\text{message}>$: $t$ is the time of the post; id is the ID posting the message; and message is the message that was posted. The question we address is whether it is possible to identify the multi-ID users based only on the times and IDs of the posts, *i.e.*, ignoring the actual message texts.

We describe a model that provides a realistic emulation of a live public forum, such as a chatroom or a newsgroup. This model is based on viewing each actor as a queue of "posts-in-waiting." Based upon the messages that are delivered by the server and the list of its "friends", every actor builds up its queue of jobs–the replies to messages received by the actor. The actor processes each of these messages one by one and submits each reply to the server; these messages then generate reply-jobs in queues of other IDs (the friends), and so on. Using such a model as a foundation, we discover statistical parameters that differentiate between multi-ID actors and single-ID actors. These parameters are the result of numeric and combinatorial analysis of the sequence of posts which (the analysis) does not use semantic information regarding the texts of the posts. The main observation, which forms the basis of our algorithm, is that the pots tagged with an ID operated by a multi ID actor do not appear as frequently as do the posts of single-ID users. Furthermore, all posts of multi-ID users are correlated, in particular, they do not occur too close together. Our algorithm detects the IDs whose posts display such statistical anomalies and identify them as coming from multi-ID users. statistical characteristics and identify them.

Our experiments based upon the model of an open forum establish the feasibility of the statistical identification of multi-ID users. The accuracy of our algorithm depends on the length of time over which data is collected, and as expected, the more data is collected, the more accurate the results of the algorithm. Our error rates over long time periods are under 1%.

*Related work.* Very little work exists on determining the multi-ID users from open forum logs, such as chat rooms. However, a number of researchers have mined for various other information on chat rooms, instant messenging forums and internet relay forums, [1–7]

*Paper outline.* The remainder of this paper is as follows. First we introduce some preliminary definitions, followed by a model for generating forum logs (message postings). Section 3 contains a description of a multi-user identification algorithms and Section 4 presents the results of numerical simulations. We present the results with model-generated newsgroup as well as real newsgroup logs.

*Acknowledgment.* We would like to thank Ahmet Camptepe who was responsible for collecting the chatroom logs that were used to illustrate some of the results in this paper. We would also like to thank Mukkai Krishnamoorthy, Sergej Roytman and Bülent Yener for useful conversations.

## 2  Preliminaries

In order to make the discussion more precise, we will introduce some definitions here. We use small letters $i, j, k, \ldots$ to denote specific IDs that post on the open forum, and capital letters $A, B, C, \ldots$ to denote specific actors. There is a (many to one) mapping $\mathcal{A}$ that associates IDs with actors, thus $\mathcal{A}(i) = A$ means that actor $A$ is operating ID $i$. We use id to denote the inverse of $\mathcal{A}$, thus $\mathsf{id}(A) = \{i, j, k, \ldots\}$ is the set of IDs that that actor $A$ is operating. The number of IDs that $A$ is operating is given by $|\mathsf{id}(A)|$. If $|\mathsf{id}(A)| > 1$, then $A$ is a multi-ID actor; otherwise, if $|\mathsf{id}(A)| = 1$, $A$ is a single-ID actor.

We assume that there are relationships among the IDs, *i.e.*, an ID $i$ can be the "friend" of one or more other IDs, $j_1, \ldots, j_k$. All these relationships are represented by the *friendship-graph G*, which is a graph in which all the IDs correspond to a vertex. There is an edge between two IDs if they are friends. We assume that, on the open forum, messages are only exchanged among friends. Two IDs that are not friends do not communicate during the time-period in question. We do not have access to the friendship graph, even though this graph governs the communication dynamics. We assume that every ID knows its friends.

A message posted by an ID has four attributes $\{t, \mathsf{id}_S, \mathsf{txt}, \mathsf{id}_R\}$. Here $t$ is the time at which the message was posted; $\mathsf{id}_S$ is the source-ID that is posting the message; txt is the text of the message; and $\mathsf{id}_R$ is the set of IDs for the intended receivers of the message. For simplicity, assume that $\mathsf{id}_R$ always contains exactly one intended receiver. Our results, however, apply to the more general case. The time stamp is given by the server at the time it posts the message onto the screen.

We assume that the receiver-ID, upon seeing the message posted, knows that the message was intended for that ID. Not all four attributes are necessarily

posted on the open forum. For example, in chatrooms, $\mathrm{id}_R$ is not posted and
the receiver-ID knows implicitly if a message is meant for him/her from the text
and context. In newsgroups, the $\mathrm{id}_R$ is often included in the post. We define the
*forum log* $\mathcal{L}$ as the sequence of posts in the form $\{<t, \mathrm{id}_S>_i\}_{i=1}^{N}$, where $N$ is the
number of posts that were made. Note that we ignore the possible information
that is present in the message texts, even though in some cases, the message
reveals the receiver ID.

Our goal is to construct an algorithm to determine multi-ID actors using
only the information in the forum log.

## 3   A Model of an Open Forum

We assume that the messages appear on a virtual screen in a sequence, and that
they are accessible to all actors participating in the forum. In the reality though,
these messages may appear on different physical screens. We do not address the
motivation or the semantics of the messages, rather the stochastic process that
generates the messages.

Underlying the communication is the friendship graph. For illustration, consider the friendship graph illustrated in the figure below.

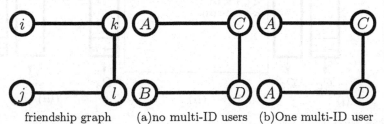

friendship graph     (a)no multi-ID users   (b)One multi-ID user

In (a), we show the graph after mapping each ID to its corresponding actor,
thus for example, $\mathcal{A}(()j) = B$. In (b), we show a second scenario, in which now
$A$ is a multi-ID actor, thus $\mathrm{id}(A) = \{i, j\}$. Our main concern in this paper is
to determine how the forum log will be different when the IDs are operated by
actors as in (a) versus (b). The fundamental observation that will aid us toward
this goal is that an actor has a finite bandwidth, i.e., it takes a user some amount
of time to process messages onto the server. Thus, in (a), the messages for IDs
$i$ and $j$ are processed by different actors, whereas in (b), a single actor has to
divide her bandwidth between the two IDs. In particular, we will investigate
the statistical consequences of this division of bandwidth among the IDs of a
multi-ID actor.

To make this notion of bandwidth division more formal, we associate to each
actor $A$, a processing queue, $\mathcal{Q}_A$. The messages that this actor wishes to post are
placed in the queue, and are processed in FIFO order. Further, after completing
a message, the actor submits it to the server, which is also implementing a queue.
We assume that messages that arrive at the same time are places in any queues
in a random order. To illustrate, notice that according to the friendship graph,
three conversations are going on, namely $(i, k), (j, l), (k, l)$. Suppose that $i, j$ and

$k$ choose to initiate these conversations. When the actor graph is as in (a), the initial queue status is shown in the ($i$) in the figure below. ($ii$) shows the server messages after each actor has processed one message and ($iii$) shows the resulting queues after the actors see the messages and initiate replies into their queues.

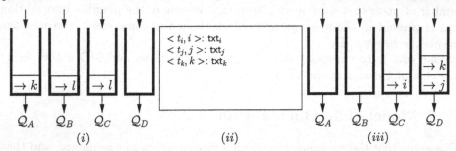

The next figure shows the same evolution for the actor graph in (b). Notice how the forum log will be different solely on account of the fact that actor $A$ is now operating more than one ID.

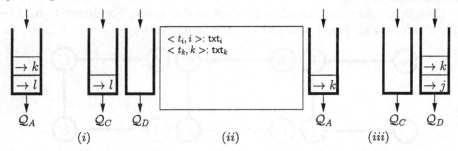

We now describe a forum log *generator* that implements such a model. Our generator can be made very general, but for illustration, we present one of the simplest versions. There are three components:

**Initialization.** Let $\{e_1, e_2, \ldots, e_m\}$ be a sequence of the edges in $G$ (randomly ordered). For every actor $A$, a queue $\mathcal{Q}_A$ is defined; initially, all $\mathcal{Q}_A$s are empty. For every edge, one of its endpoints is randomly selected as *the source* $s$ and the other endpoints is determined as the *recipient* $r$. Note that $s$ and $r$ are IDs, not actors. A reply message to $r$ is pushed onto the queue $\mathcal{Q}_{A(s)}$, i.e., onto the queue of the actor corresponding to the source ID. The result of the initialization step is an array of queues, $[\mathcal{Q}_{A_1}, \mathcal{Q}_{A_2}, \ldots, \mathcal{Q}_{A_n}]$, where each queue corresponds to unique actor operating on the forum. A queue may correspond to multiple IDs in the friendship graph $G$. Note that some queues may be empty.

**Processing by Actors.** Every actor $A_i$:

1. Processes and removes the first message on its queue. The time to process this message $\tau$ could be set randomly to simulate long and short messages. After processing this message, the actor submits it to the forum.

2. Scans the forum postings for any messages that are addressed to any ID in id($A_i$). Each such message generates a reply to the poster of the message. This reply is pushed onto $Q_{A_i}$.

**Processing by Forum.** The forum has a global queue $Q_F$ of messages to be posted. The messages arrive according to the times they were submitted to the forum by actors; if a posts arrive at the same time, the forum sorts them into an arbitrary (random) order. The forum processes its queue using FIFO order, taking a time of 1 unit to post a message.

## 4 Algorithms

The input to the multiuser-identification algorithm is a the forum log $\mathcal{L} = \{<$ $t, id_S >_i\}_{i=1}^N$, the times of the postings and the IDs that made the postings. To design an identification algorithm, we need to determine a statistical property of the communication exchange which separates multi-users from users that employ one ID only. The intuition behind out algorithm is that since a user has only one queue, it can only process messages sequentially. This is independent of whether she is operating one ID or multiple IDs. Suppose that, on average, it takes an actor $\tau_0$ to complete a message. Then, the time gap between two messages posted under different IDs but by the same actor will on average be $\tau_0$ time units. On the other hand, if two different actors are posting messages for a pair of IDs, then this restriction does not hold. In fact, over a long enough time period, one expects that the posts of these two IDs may arrive arbitrarily close to each other.

Let $i, j$ be two IDs, and consider the two subsequences of the forum log consisting only of the posts of each of these IDs: $\{< t_i, i >\}$ and $\{< t_j, j >\}$. Define the set of separation times, $\{D_{ij}\}$, as the set of time differences between *consecutive* posts of the two IDs – i.e., for every pair of times $t_i, t_j$ at which $i$ posts followed by $j$ or $j$ followed by $i$, and there are no posts made in between these two posts, then $|t_j - t_i| \in \{D_{ij}\}$. We define two separation indices, the *mean separation index* $M(i, j)$ for IDs $i, j$, and the *minimum separation index* $\min D(i, j)$:

$$M(i, j) = \text{mean}\{D_{ij}\}$$
$$\min D(i, j) = \min\{D_{ij}\}$$

We expect that if $\mathcal{A}(i) = \mathcal{A}(j)$, then these separation indices will be significantly larger that if $\mathcal{A}(i) \neq \mathcal{A}(j)$. More specifically, if $M(i, j)$ and $\min D(i, j)$ are small, then it is not possible that $\mathcal{A}(i) = \mathcal{A}(j)$. On the other hand, if they are large, then it would be extremely unlikely that $\mathcal{A}(i) \neq \mathcal{A}(j)$ on account of the independence of the actors behind the IDs, and hence it is likely that $\mathcal{A}(i) = \mathcal{A}(j)$. The intuition we have described would hold for any model of the forum log that assumes a finite bandwidth for the actors, as well as sequential processing of messages. The quantities that would vary from model to model would be exactly how large the separation indices would have to get before one could declare that a pair of IDs is suspicious and is probably from a multi-ID actor. In order to test these hypotheses, we simulate a forum log according to the model in the previous section and compute the statistics $M(i,j)$ and $\min D(i,j)$ for every pair of IDs. We give, in the Table 1 below, the averages of these statistics over pairs of IDs from the same actor versus pairs from different actors separately. The statistics in Table 1 were obtained assuming that the time $\tau$ that an actor takes to prepare a post is 250 units. It is clear that the separation indices are drastically different depending on whether the pair of actors is on the same versus on different actors. Further, the histograms in Figure 1 indicate that not only are the separation indices different on average, but the distributions are also well separated. We are thus led to the following algorithm for identifying multi-ID actors:

1: //**Algorithm to identify multi-ID actors**
2: //**Input:** Forum Log $\mathcal{L} = \{< t, \mathrm{id}_S >_i\}_{i=1}^N$.
3: //**Output:** Pairs of IDs on the same actor.
4: For every pair of IDs $i, j$, compute $\min D(i,j)$;
5: Cluster the values of $\min D(i,j)$ into two groups, $G_{large}$ containing the large values, and $G_{small}$ containing the smaller. Every pair $(i,j)$ belongs to one of these groups.
6: **return** all the pairs $(i,j) \in G_{large}$;

Defining the equivalence relation $i \equiv j$ iff $(i,j) \in G_{large}$, the equivalence classes of the IDs then partitions the IDs into sets, each of which are operated by

Table 1. Some statistical properties of the $\{D_{ij}\}$

|  | $\mathcal{A}(i) = \mathcal{A}(j)$ | $\mathcal{A}(i) \neq \mathcal{A}(j)$ |
|---|---|---|
| $\text{mean}_{i,j}\{M(i,j)\}$ | 382.79 | 264.63 |
| $\text{mean}_{i,j}\{\min D(i,j)\}$ | 156.36 | 3.22 |

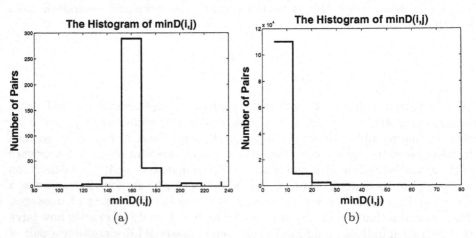

Fig. 1. Histograms of $\min D(i,j)$. In (a), $\mathcal{A}(i) = \mathcal{A}(j)$; in (b), $\mathcal{A}(i) \neq \mathcal{A}(j)$

one actor. Thus we can identify all the IDs common to a given actor from the algorithm above.

## 5   Experiments

The model for the dynamics of the forum log has the following parameters

*del*: The average time for an actor to compose a message and submit it to the forum server. Although, in general, this average composition time can be time and/or actor dependent, for our simplified model, we assumed it to be a constant.

*wid*: A parameter specifying how much the actual time to compose a message can vary from the average time *del*. If $\tau$ is the time to compose a message, then we assume that $\tau$ is uniformly distributed in $\left[del - \frac{1}{2}wid, del + \frac{1}{2}wid\right]$. In general, *wid* can be time and/or actor dependent, but for our simplified model, we keep *wid* fixed. *wid* can be viewed as a noise parameter that introduces some non-determinism into the forum log.

*len*: the length of a post by a actor; it is assumed that *len* determines the minimal time-period needed for a actor to compose the message; in general, *len* is time- and actor-dependent, but for this model, *len* is a constant.

*run*: the total number of time units for which the forum log is generated.

*nID*: the total number of IDs participating in the communication exchange.

*maxID*: the maximum number of IDs employed by a single actor – a *k-ID actor* operates *k* IDs.

*nFriend*: the average number of friends an ID has in the friendship graph.

In our simulations, we fixed $nID = 500$, with about an equal number of 1-ID actors, 2-ID actors, 3-ID actors and 4-ID actors, thus $maxID = 4$. We fixed $nFriend = 5$, and used different values of *del*, *wid* and *run* to determine how these three parameters influence the accuracy of the detection algorithm, which we define as the percentage of pairs of IDs that are assigned to the correct group (multi or single).

$$Accuracy = \frac{\text{The number of pairs (i,j) assigned into correct group}}{\text{The total number of (i,j) pairs}}$$

To implement step 5 of the algorithm, we used a standard $K$-means algorithm [8], with $K$ set to 2.

The details of the simulation are as follows. First randomly generate a friendship graph with average degree 5. Using this friendship graph, we run the forum generator for *run* timesteps, to generate a forum log. We then implement the detection algorithm to determine which ID's are from single-ID actors and which IDs are on the same actor. We then compute the accuracy, and repeat this entire simulation over 10 times to get a more accurate estimate of the average accuracy.

Table 2 illustrates how the accuracy depends on *wid* and *del* when $run = 1,000,000$ and when $run = 10,000$. When the observation sequence is long

**Table 2.** The dependence of the Accuracy (in %) on $del, wid, run$

| $del$ | wid | | | | $del$ | wid | | | |
|---|---|---|---|---|---|---|---|---|---|
| | 0 | 50 | 100 | 250 | | 0 | 50 | 100 | 250 |
| 250 | 99.9992 | 99.9998 | 99.9999 | 99.9996 | 250 | 98.1425 | 97.98 | 97.8906 | 98.0964 |
| 500 | 99.9995 | 99.9997 | 99.9993 | 99.9993 | 500 | 96.2923 | 96.634 | 96.6173 | 96.8459 |
| 1000 | 99.9976 | 99.9972 | 99.9979 | 99.9972 | 1000 | 91.6025 | 92.3209 | 92.3017 | 92.2991 |
| 5000 | 99.7129 | 99.7452 | 99.7740 | 99.7695 | 5000 | — | 84.8614 | 82.3213 | 79.4296 |

(a) $run = 1,000,000$                    (b)$run = 10,000$

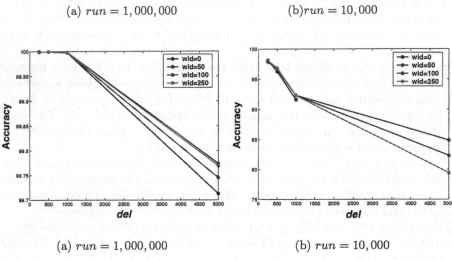

(a) $run = 1,000,000$                    (b) $run = 10,000$

**Fig. 2.** The dependence of the Accuracy (in %) on $del$ and $wid$

enough ($run = 1,000,000$), the accuracy is almost 100% and is not influenced much by $wid$, i.e, the fact that messages take random amounts of time to compose does not seem to heavily affect the algorithm's accuracy. However, there is a slight decrease in performance when $del$ increases. This is mostly due to the fact that there are fewer posts (data) when $del$ increases, as the observation period is fixed. Showed in *Figure* 2 is the dependence of the accuracy on $del$, the time to compose a message, for different value of the noise parameter $wid$.

Notice that when $run$ is small, i.e., the observation period is small, the accuracy considerably drops. This is due to the significant drop in the amount of data available for the classification into single versus multi-ID actors. This is illustrated in Table 3, where we show the number of posts that the various types of actors make. Also illustrated in Table 3 is the effect of the limited bandwidth assumption that we place on the actors. The 4-ID actors post less frequently than the 1-ID actors. While one would expect the frequency of posting to have dropped by a factor of 4 in going from the 1-ID actors to the 4-ID actors, it is not quite a factor of 4. The reason is that some of the 1-ID actors are friends with IDs belonging to 4-ID actors, which means that the frequency of posting of

**Table 3.** The average number of messages posted by different types of actors

| del | # of IDs operated by an actor | | | | del | # of IDs operated by an actor | | | |
|---|---|---|---|---|---|---|---|---|---|
|  | 1 | 2 | 3 | 4 |  | 1 | 2 | 3 | 4 |
| 250 | 2876.6 | 1910.8 | 1326.4 | 1015.9 | 250 | 23.95 | 18.89 | 13 | 9.75 |
| 500 | 1436.6 | 954.8 | 663.3 | 507.3 | 500 | 12.41 | 9.18 | 6.31 | 4.75 |
| 1000 | 717.1 | 477.2 | 331.5 | 253.8 | 1000 | 5.39 | 4.23 | 2.98 | 2.25 |
| 5000 | 142.9 | 95.7 | 66.6 | 50.7 | 5000 | 0.38 | 0.49 | 0.33 | 0.25 |

(a) $run = 1,000,000$              (b) $run = 10,000$

these 1-ID actors will be slowed down by the fact that they have to wait longer for the responses from the 4-ID actors.

In principle the average number of posts could be used to discriminate between multi-ID actors and single-ID actors, however the distributions of this statistic are not as separated as with min$D$.

# 6 Conclusions

We have presented an algorithm to identify multi-ID users, the justification of which is based on a novel and reasonable model of communication exchange on a public forum. Along this direction, the model could be considerably expanded to include more realistic and nondeterministic phenomena, such as multi-party exchange; server delays; and different composition time distributions for each actor. Further, one could allow the friendship graphs and the general communication dynamics on the forum to be time varying. It is also possible to incorporate statistical parameters of the real communication forum into the model.

What we have demonstrated is that under the broad assumption of a finite processing power for each actor, and the fact that messages are processed sequentially, an actor operating multiple IDs will give itself away by the fact that those IDs will have different posting statistics to the normal, single-ID actors. In particular the posts of these IDs will not be independent, nor as frequent. We see that introducing randomness into the time to compose a message does not have much effect on the algorithm, nor did changing the average time to compose a message – i.e., the algorithm is quite robust to the specific details of the model, which is comforting. Our simulations show that if the time to compose a message is 5000 units (a unit being the time for the server to process a message), then with 1,000,000 time units of observation, we can essentially obtain 100% accuracy. To put this in perspective, in a chatroom if it takes about 10 seconds to compose a message, then we need under 1 hour of observation.

It is, of course, important to realize that every identification algorithm can potentially be deceived by a skillful actor who intends to hide its multiple IDs. However the attempt to deceit our algorithm will likely cause a time delay in the postings of the user (or other irregularities). A systematic delay in a user's activity may in turn be employed for the identification purposes.

# References

1. Nardi, B.A., Whittaker, S., Bradner, E.: Interaction and outeraction: instant messaging in action. In: Computer Supported Cooperative Work. (2000) 79–88
2. We, T., Khan, F.M., Fisher, T.A., Shuler, L.A., Pottenger, W.M.: Error-driven boolean-logic-rule-based learning for mining chat-room conversations (2002)
3. Khan, F.M., Fisher, T.A., Shuler, L., Wu, T., Pottenger, W.M.: Mining chat-room conversations for social and semantic interactions (2002)
4. Budzik, J., Bradshaw, S., Fu, X., Hammond, K.: Clustering for opportunistic communication. In: Proceedings of WWW 2002, ACM Press (2002)
5. Elizabeth, R.: Electropolis: Communication and community on internet relay chat (1992)
6. Whittaker, S., Jones, Q., Terveen, L.: Contact management: Identifying contacts to support long-term communication (2002)
7. Isaacs, E., Kamm, C., Schiano, D.J., Walendowski, A., Whittaker, S.: Characterizing instant messaging from recorded logs (2002)
8. Bishop, C.M.: Neural Networks for Pattern Recognition. Clarendon Press, Oxford (1995)

# Self-efficacy, Training Effectiveness, and Deception Detection: A Longitudinal Study of Lie Detection Training

Kent Marett[1], David P. Biros[2], and Monti L. Knode[3]

[1] MIS Department, College of Business
Florida State University, Tallahassee FL 32306, USA
lkm7032@cob.fsu.edu
[2] Information Assurance Division, USAF Chief Information Office
Washington DC, USA
David.Biros@pentagon.af.mil
[3] HQ Air Force Special Operations Command, Hurlburt Field, FL, USA
Monti.Knode@hurlburt.af.mil

**Abstract.** Studies examining the ability to detection deception have consistently found that humans tend to be poor detectors. In this study, we examine the roles of self-efficacy and training over time. We conducted a field experiment at a military training center involving 119 service members. The subjects were given two sessions of deception detection training. Their performance history, perceived effectiveness of the training, and perceived self-efficacy were measured over time. Two significant findings were identified. First, training novelty and relativity played a noticeable role in the subjects' perceptions of effectiveness. Second, influencing subject self-efficacy to detect deception requires time and multiple iterations of the task so as to allow the subjects the opportunity to calibrate their skills. We believe that continued research along this line will ultimately results in marked improvement in deception detection ability.

## 1 Introduction

Though rooted in earliest recordings of human history, deception, and its detection thereof, has only recently been the focus of research in communication methods and media. Marked by an interest to examine the acts of both deception and its detection, researchers have embarked on a quest to investigate the communicative interaction between those people who lie and those who are the targets of those lies. In prior studies, subjects have demonstrated an ability to identify certain cues exhibited by deceivers and more effectively detect deceptive communications [1, 2]. However, results indicate that one could flip a coin and just as accurately detect deception if directly lied to in a face-to-face conversation [3]. Such results have confounded researchers attempts at developing a singularly accurate model for identifying predictive causal constructs in deceptive communications. Certainly, some people are better at detecting lies than others, and there may be many individual differences that explain detection success. Among these differences are a person's self-efficacy pertain-

H. Chen et al. (Eds.): ISI 2004, LNCS 3073, pp. 187–200, 2004.

ing to the accomplishment of a task, such as lie detection. Self-efficacy is a dynamic quality that presumably fluctuates over time, due to personal experience with the task in question or tasks similar to it.

This paper reports on a longitudinal study that investigates some cognitive differences that may impair or improve a person's ability to detect deception, as well as a person's belief in their lie detection abilities. Specifically, we investigate the effect that one's self-efficacy to detect lying in others has on their actual performance doing so, and how the results from that performance in turn effects one's self-efficacy. Predictors of the changes to self-efficacy were examined in this study, including the influences of training, feedback, and perceived training effectiveness.

The rest of the paper is organized as follows. First, the prior relevant theory and literature on deception detection are reviewed. A research model for the current study is presented along with the appropriate testable hypotheses. The method for data collection is described, followed by a summary of the data analysis and results. The results are then discussed, and finally the implications for future research are presented.

## 1.1 Background

Several models and theories have emerged regarding deception, its detection, and lack thereof. Deception has been defined in several ways, both in message content and delivery. For the purposes of this study, we use the definition developed by Buller and Burgoon [4], "a message knowingly transmitted by a sender to foster a false belief or conclusion by the receiver" (p.205). This definition rules out honest mistakes and errors, and focuses on communication that is intentionally faulty. In order to instill a false conclusion in conversational partners, a deceiver must have sufficient communicative skill as to make bad information seem legitimate. Communicative experience [5], poise [6], control [7], motivation [8], the expectation of successful deception [9], and even physical attractiveness [10] have all shown to increase sender believability.

However, communication is not a one-way street. Receivers react, respond, and create feedback that may create a reflective response from a deceiver, and this is the basis of what has been termed *interpersonal deception theory* [4], hereafter referred to as IDT. Based on the principle that during normal communication, conversational partners judge, adapt to, and reciprocate the behavior and norms of others, IDT holds that deceivers are especially interested in the reactions of others to their lies. After assessing the responses of receivers, the deceiver may decide to reinforce their lies with additional misinformation, continue with their initial behavior, or even curtail their deception. Obviously, a change in a deceiver's behavior may be such that it catches the attention of the receiver, making them suspicious. This behavior includes commonly-held indicators that deception is taking place, like pupil dilation and higher voice pitch [8]. These indicators have not always proven to be reliable in every situation which may lead some deceivers to believe they are better lie detectors than they actually demonstrate (see [1] for a recent meta-analysis of behavioral indictors of deception). Ekman [8] explains that the receiver can misinterpret many of these indicators as betraying deception, when in fact they are actually signs of nervousness. In short, a receiver's perceived ability to detect lies, or their self-efficacy, could be based on a false understanding of human behavior.

Self-efficacy is founded in social cognitive theory, specifically the concept of triadic reciprocality where social factors (environment), self-influences (personal), and outcomes (behavior) interact in a reciprocal fashion [11]. Self-efficacy centers around the belief in one's ability to be cognizant of one's self and the surrounding environment, and the use of that belief to judge capabilities to organize and execute courses of action to achieve a certain performance level. Bandura [11] identifies personal efficacy as perhaps the single-most influential factor in determining an individual's behavior because the individual internalizes their surroundings and then sets parameters on themselves based on their findings. Efficacy has been studied and shown as a highly causal factor of personal behavior and performance in disparate environments such as computer use [12], neighborhood socioeconomic status [13], and in performance-related efficacy in sports [14], thus illustrating its considerable application. Prior studies have demonstrated a reciprocating link between efficacy and performance, providing evidence of a positive correlation between the two [15, 16, 17]. However, with regard to the ability and performance involved with detecting deception, the longitudinal effect of efficacy has gone unexplored.

## 1.2  Self-efficacy, Lie Detection, and Training

The ability to detect lies is hindered human biases that are relevant to this study. The first of these was named (appropriately enough) the *lie-detection bias*. Vrij [18] describes this as the overly inflated belief in one's ability to detect lies, usually based on faulty heuristics like those described in the previous section. An example given by Vrij includes the tendency of people to judge strange or out-of-character behavior displayed by others as being deceptive, when there may actually be an innocent explanation for that behavior. Moreover, the ability to proficiently detect lies can be a matter of personal pride. As Elaad [19] suggests, social norms stipulate that people do not want to be known as being gullible or easily misled, thus the ability to detect lies is a desirable trait. It has been shown that the lie-detection bias can be overcome with the use of performance feedback. Of sixty participants in a study involving feedback, Elaad found that forty subjects initially rated themselves above average as lie detectors. After receiving positive feedback (regardless of actual performance), their perceived detection abilities were reinforced, but the efficacy of those receiving negative feedback was significantly affected, disconfirming their perceived abilities. People generally tend to firmly believe in their detection abilities until given reason to believe otherwise, an inherent bias.

Another naturally-occurring bias affecting lie detection that has been noticed by deception researchers is the *truth bias*. McCornack and Parks [20] describe this bias as the inherent belief that conversational partners behave honestly, at least until proven otherwise. The truth bias has been observed in relationships ranging from those between romantic couples to those among perfect strangers. This often impedes the ability to judge incoming communication as being deceptive. Stiff and colleagues [21] found that inducing suspicion in receivers can offset the truth bias, but detection rates nevertheless remain poor. A better solution for overcoming the truth bias may lie in training receivers to be aware of possible deception.

Training goes beyond simply inducing suspicion in communicators, in that it also instills a state of vigilance in the receiver [22]. Prior studies on detection training have shown that it is most effective when explicit instruction on nonverbal cues is coupled with repetitive exercises that allow trainees to evaluate examples of honesty and deception, as well as the availability feedback on their performance [23]. Biros, George, and Zmud [24] found that training at or near the time of the incident improves human sensitivity to the possible existence of deception, and combined with periodic warnings, training is effective for improving deception detection accuracy. Further, Ekman and O'Sullivan [25] observed that trained Secret Service agents maintain a high state of vigilance to nonverbal cues pointing to deception. It remains to be seen, however, how training eventually affects a person's self-efficacy for lie detection.

Finally, training has long been envisioned as having a dramatic effect on a person's self-efficacy, especially when the training is perceived to have been effective. Bandura [11] theorizes that changes in efficacy not only occur following personal attempts to perform an action or behavior, but changes also take place as a consequence of enactive attainment of the pertinent skills. This is primarily due to the acquisition of new knowledge, skills, experience with a task, and performance-based feedback that a quality training program provides [26]. Typically, prior research focusing on the effects of training toward one's self-efficacy has centered around gaining occupational skills, but training can also relate to the lifetime development of psychosocial skills (such as those involved with deceptive communication). Of course, the benefits of training are somewhat limited by the perceptions and motivations of those being trained. Noe's [27] model of training effectiveness illustrates the importance of making the skill sets being delivered to trainees salient to their careers and lives. Trainees also perceive training transfer as being effective when the organization appears committed to the program and when their own productivity shows a noticeable increase [28].

In summary, this study was conducted to determine the effects on deception detection performance and detection self-efficacy during the course of a training program intended to improve those abilities in trainees. This section reviewed some of the relevant prior literature from deceptive communication and training. The following section presents the research model and develops the hypotheses tested in the present study.

## 2 Research Model and Hypothesis Development

Prior studies have typically taken a snapshot measurement of an individual's general or specific self-efficacy and draw correlations without regard for possible reasons of individual perceptions *at that time* [11]. In other words, individual efficacy can – and will – change relative to their surroundings and cognition of personal history. Confidence in one's detection abilities may fluctuate at times, but it should remain largely unchanged until either confronted or confirmed. The model below follows the assumption that performance feedback will affect efficacy and personal factors, and via triadic reciprocality [11], alter future behavior and detection performance. The relationships in question are analyzed at multiple points during the study, and the predicted directions of these relationships are illustrated in Figure 1.

The first two hypotheses presented speculate on how perceived detection capability will inevitably influence detection performance. Because of the theorized dynamic relationship between self-efficacy and performance, it is expected that there will be a reciprocating influence on both over time. Based on the feedback that is provided to an individual, deception detection performance presents a confrontation to personal belief, thus having a direct influence on individual belief and capabilities [11]. In

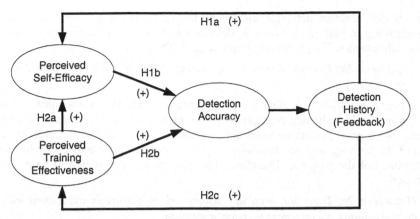

**Fig. 1.** Research Model

essence, detectors will base their perceived efficacy on a history of performance standards, provided such feedback can be given [18]. Detection accuracy history becomes the realized confirmation of a receiver's attempts to discern between truth and falsehoods. Thus, the following hypothesis is presented:

*Hypothesis 1a: Receiver detection accuracy history will positively influence perceived self-efficacy to detect deception.*

Given that the relationship between self-efficacy and task performance has long been believed to be reciprocating, it follows that self-efficacy should influence future detection performance, as prior research investigating other individual abilities has shown. Viewed in this way, an individual's confidence in his ability to detect lies is expected to become a sort of self-fulfilling prophecy, as those who come to strongly believe in their abilities will improve their accuracy over time, and vice versa. Thus:

*Hypothesis 1b: Receiver perceived self-efficacy to detect deception will positively influence detection accuracy.*

The final three hypotheses deal with the effect that deception detection training has on the relationship between self-efficacy and detection performance. More specifically, we posit that as long as trainees believe they are receiving quality training for lie detection, their perceived self-efficacy will show significant increases. This relationship is expected to exist throughout the entire training program, as has been found in prior research examining self-efficacy and learning at both early and late periods in a training program [29].

*Hypothesis 2a: Perceived training effectiveness will be positively related to receiver perceived self-efficacy to detect deception.*

The perceived effectiveness of lie detection training is predicted to be related with actual lie detection performance. As prior studies have shown, training a subskill such as detection deception will aid a receiver's detection accuracy and contribute to a receiver's perceived capability. This improvement has been demonstrated in both content-analysis training [30] and cues-based training [31, 32]. The effect of the training itself is not in dispute here, however; rather we are interested in the trainees' quality assessments of the training and how that may be tied to performance. It is believed that, should deception detection training be perceived as being salient and important to improving an individual's own lie detection abilities, the detection performance of those individuals will significantly improve [27]. Therefore:

*Hypothesis 2b: Perceived training effectiveness will be positively related to detection accuracy.*

Finally, feedback regarding the performance of individuals attempting to detect deception should influence perceptions of the effectiveness of the training program. Feedback on good performance should give the trainees belief in the high effectiveness of the training, whereas feedback on poor detection performance should result in disapproval of the program. Therefore, this relationship is predicted to be positive in direction.

*Hypothesis 2c: Detection accuracy history will be positively associated with perceived training effectiveness to detect deception.*

The constructs introduced in the model and hypothesis will be operationalized in a later section.

## 3   Research Methodology

To test the hypotheses above, a field experiment was conducted at a military training installation in the southeastern United States using 128 personnel enrolled in an introductory communications career-track training course. Because the curriculum takes place in one location over a period of up to four months, the venue provided several subjects for participation in the study over its duration. Participation was voluntary, though recommended by the director of the training course. To avoid compromising the study, participants were informed that this research was being collected in order train personnel on deception detection and then evaluate said training based on improvements in results. A total of 119 personnel opted to continue with the study through its seven-week entirety. At the conclusion of the experiment, the true reasons for the study were debriefed to all subjects.

The authors (one was a former military training instructor) and their respective research teams developed the training curriculum jointly, with an emphasis placed on incorporating explicit instruction, skill practice, and feedback [23]. Instruction was provided by one doctoral student from a US business school and three officers completing their masters degrees at a US military graduate school. The trainers were initially introduced by the subjects' regular instructors and were informed that the training sessions were sponsored by a military service office of scientific research, thus driving home the support of the training from those higher in command. In order to reinforce the salience of deception detection training to the subjects, and in line with previous findings the trainers repeatedly used examples from real world scenarios in military and non-military settings.

Subjects were already assigned to "blocks" or classes of 16 trainees each, for the purposes of their communications career path training. The blocks were randomly assigned to either deception training exposure or to a control group receiving no training. Training sessions began with an initial performance test, in which subjects were required to make judgments of veracity for each of six communication events. A training presentation followed the performance test. Each presentation was supplemented by a Powerpoint slideshow provided by both traditional lecture and electronic delivery modes (see [33]), and each presentation was designed to last for one hour. Lectures included deceptive communication examples used by the instructors to illustrate the cues, and included samples of text, audio, and video communication. Most examples came from past studies of deception detection, consisting of experimental subjects trying to deceive their interviewers. Other examples were specifically created and recorded for this study as they focused on real world military events to add a sense of realism for the subjects. The subjects then engaged a post-training performance test made up of six more communication events, after which the correct answers for both the pre-training and post-training performance tests were provided by the instructors. The sessions concluded with a measurement of each subject's perceived self-efficacy. Blocks in the control treatment received none of the training, and were limited to merely the detection performance tests and other measures.

Although each session followed the same sequence of activities, the content presented in each session differed. The first lecture involved an introduction to the topic of deception detection, but this took place a week after pre-training measures were taken from the sample. Two weeks after the first lecture, a lecture devoted solely to deceptive cues was presented. Both lectures included examples, opportunities for the participants to practice the skills that were discussed, evaluation of those skills, and feedback of the performance. Each lecture also included a post-lecture questionnaire (described later) assessing each subject's perceived self-efficacy. A timeline of the experiment is presented in Figure 2 below.

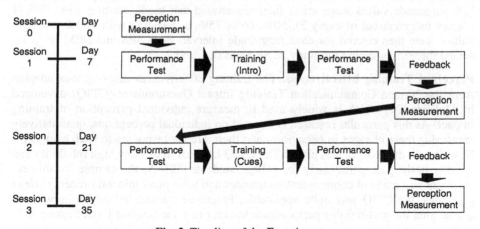

**Fig. 2.** Timeline of the Experiment

At the conclusion of the experiment, subjects were debriefed as to the nature of the study and its conclusions, and subjects were allowed to ask questions and make comments pertaining to the research.

## 3.1 Measurement

Measuring for much of this research was developed to be web-based in order to ease data collection and examination. Web-based questionnaires were created to foster a sequential format and further minimize errors in data collection. Each questionnaire was provided with an instruction set and completed in the presence of one of the administrators in order to ensure honesty, individual effort, and to answer any questions that may have been raised. The performance tests were web-based as well. Each instructor was given a list of exact survey procedures and timelines to follow. A group reference number and the last four digits of a subject's social security number were used as a primary to mark individual performance and perceptions for longitudinal study as they were stored in an off-site database. The measures used for the dependent variables are as follows:

**Self-efficacy.** The self-efficacy measure (questionnaire) used in this study is based off the methodology prescribed by Bandura [11] and has shown both valid and reliable results in prior research [34, 35]. Self-efficacy was measured in two ways: self-efficacy magnitude (SEM) and self-efficacy strength (SES). Both SEM and SES items were modified in a similar fashion to those used by Betz and Hackett [36]. With respect to magnitude, subjects were first asked to indicate whether they could achieve an identified level of lie detection proficiency, to which they either respond with a "yes" or a "no". Subjects were then asked to identify their degree of confidence in their ability to perform at that level (the strength dimension of self-efficacy); subjects were asked to respond with a numerical value between "0" (impossible) and "100" (complete confidence). SEM was presented to subjects as a measure of overall accuracy – detecting both "truths and deceptions". Because research has repeatedly shown people's ability to detect deceptive communications to only be roughly 50% accurate [3], magnitude values were set at intervals around that mark, starting with 33% (1 correct judgment out of every 3), 50%, 66%, 75%, and ending with 100%. Strength values were then entered for each magnitude interval. Both SES and SEM were assessed three times during the study, at Sessions 0, 1, and 2.

**Perceived Training Effectiveness.** The training effectiveness measure was adapted from the 20-item Communication Training Impact Questionnaire (CTIQ) developed by DeWine [37] which is widely used to measure individual perception of training impact. As this particular research is focused on individual perceptions, quantitatively measuring these changes in behavior – and therefore the responses to such a survey – fit well with the goals of this effort. The CTIQ has proven to show high reliability and validity in the past, particularly for college students [38]. As the sample for this experiment was made of communication trainees and were predominantly recent college graduates, the CTIQ was quite applicable. Perceived training effectiveness was assessed after the post-training performance tests for both the Session 1 and Session 2.

**Deception Detection Performance.** Both the pre-training and post-training detection performance tests consisted of 6 separate communication examples, two each in text, audio, and audio-video formats. In each test, half of the examples were deceptive and half were not. After witnessing each example, subjects were asked to make a judgment about a potentially deceptive event. Performance was therefore assessed as the number of correct judgments made by each participant. Detection performance was measured at four different times during the study, in forms of pre-training and post-training tests during Sessions 1 and 2. For the analysis of the research model presented earlier, only the pre-training and Session 1 and 2 post-training performance data was used.

**Detection Accuracy History.** This measure represented the cumulative detection performance of the subjects over the two sessions. The performance scores that were obtained before the end of each session were averaged for each subject. In other words, the history score for Session 1 was made up of the scores for the pre-training and post-training tests for Session 1, while those two test scores were combined with the pre-training and post-training scores from Session 2 for its history average. Subjects were given explicit feedback on their performance on all tests and were also asked following each test whether their performance had improved or not, and the researchers made a point of ensuring each subject was aware of their performance trend.

A pilot study was conducted out approximately three weeks before the main experiment, with 19 volunteer military graduate students. The pilot study included the training session on cues, judgment pretests and posttests, and a survey resembling the final all-inclusive survey of Session 2. The pilot study allowed us to check the validity of the above measures, to assess the technical feasibility of the data-gathering techniques, and to gather feedback on the test and survey. Instrument reliabilities were determined for the self-efficacy and perceived training effectiveness measures during the main experiment, the results of which are located in Table 1.

**Table 1.** Instrument reliabilities

| Instrument | Session 0 | Session 1 | Session 2 |
|---|---|---|---|
| Self-efficacy | $\alpha = .83$ | $\alpha = .71$ | $\alpha = .74$ |
| Perceived Training Effectiveness | -- | $\alpha = .79$ | $\alpha = .82$ |

## 4 Analysis and Results

The research model presented earlier was analyzed twice, for sessions 1 and 2 respectively, via structural equation modeling using LISREL. The results of each analysis are presented in Figure 3 below, and the descriptive statistics are provided in Table 2. Using a predetermined $\alpha$-level of .05, none of the hypothesized paths were found to be statistically significant at session 1. However, the effect of an individual's accumulated performance history begins to make a significant impact on self-efficacy in session 2, lending support to hypothesis 1A. Further, the individual's perception of the training he or she has received also has some significant bearing on detection performance in session 2. There are significant links between detection performance and history for both sessions, but these relationships are naturally interrelated and were therefore not hypothesized.

## 5 Discussion

The primary focus of this study was to understand the relationship between a person's history of success at detecting deception and the perceived self-efficacy to accomplish the task. Further, this study employed a deception detection training program and measured the subjects' perceived effectiveness of the training. It was hypothesized that the training would improve detection accuracy and, in turn, improve the subjects' detection histories so as to improve their overall self-efficacy. A longitudinal study was developed whereby subjects were given training and were assessed on their ability to detect deception over time.

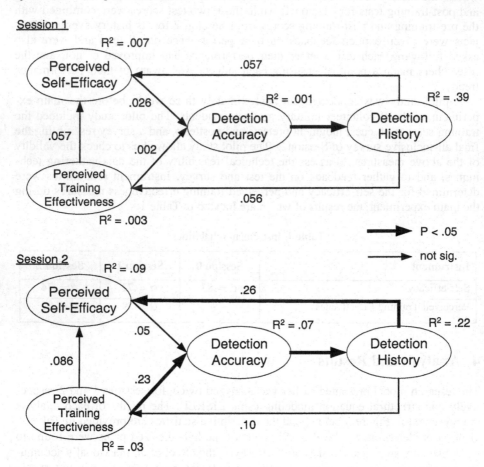

**Fig. 3.** Structural Model Results for Sessions 1 and 2

**Table 2.** Descriptive statistics

| Measure | Mean (SD) | Measure | Mean (SD) |
|---|---|---|---|
| Self-Efficacy SES0 | .583 (.18) | Accuracy 2A | .716 (.19) |
| Self-Efficacy SES1 | .580 (.19) | Accuracy 2B | .580 (.15) |
| Self-Efficacy SES2 | .554 (.21) | History Session 2 | .606 (.01) |
| Accuracy 1A | .503 (.21) | Train Eff. Session 1 | 3.30 (.43) |
| Accuracy 1B | .622 (.17) | Train Eff. Session 2 | 3.41 (.44) |
| History Session 1 | .562 (.13) | | |

Interestingly, the first round of training and testing was unsuccessful. However, the training was incorporated within the course's standard training regimen and the subjects did not have enough experience to form a history. Further, the first round of training involved an introductory course in deception detection. The subjects, as part of their military training, recently had a course in basic information security called Network User Licensing (NUL). Apparently, the NUL training included concepts related to the introductory training of the study resulting in few usable findings.

In round two, training about deception detection cues was introduced. This training was new whereas the first round of training was somewhat similar to the NUL. The cue training was novel and taught the subjection new concepts toward deception detection. Over time and with the addition of the new training material and exercises, the subjects began to develop a history of detection success. This is consistent with Gist's findings on training novelty [26]. And, as hypothesized, this success led to a greater perceived self-efficacy of the subjects toward their ability to detect deception. Table 3 depicts the findings of the two studies. Unfortunately, no other hypotheses were supported. This may be due, in part, to the limited number of examples the subjects had to rely on to build a detection accuracy history.

These are interesting findings due to the longitudinal nature of the study. It appears detectors must be given an opportunity to calibrate their detection abilities before they can develop a perception of their capabilities.

## 5.1  Limitations and Implications

While this study identified some interesting findings, it was not without its limitations. The instruction provided in this study was only a small part of the overall curriculum of the course taken by the subjects. It is possible that the overall learning task may have reduced the effectiveness of the deception detection training. This, along with the limited number of examples may have stifled the effects on detection accuracy history until time two (T2). It is also possible that the subject did not learn to the level needed to improve detection accuracy. Unfortunately due to time constraints, a manipulation check was infeasible.

**Table 3.** Summary of Findings

| Hypothesis | Session 1 | Session 2 |
|---|---|---|
| 1a. Detection accuracy history will positively influence perceived self-efficacy to detect deception | Not Supported | Supported |
| 1b. Perceived self-efficacy to detect deception will positively influence detection accuracy | Not Supported | Not Supported |
| 2a. Perceived training effectiveness will be positively related to perceived self-efficacy to detect deception | Not Supported | Not Supported |
| 2b. Perceived training effectiveness will be positively related to detection accuracy. | Not Supported | Supported |
| 2c. Detection accuracy history will be positively associated with perceived training effectiveness to detect deception | Not Supported | Not Supported |

Researchers and managers alike can benefit from the results of this study. Researchers need to understand and appreciate the roles of performance history and self-efficacy in deception detection training and the task of deception detection itself. Further, the use of a longitudinal study highlights the importance of long term exposure to the training subject matter. Similarly, managers must understand that deception detection training may require iterations of both training and demonstration/performance activities to enable employees to build a deception detection history of success.

## 5.2 Summary

The roles of self-efficacy and training effectiveness are curious with respect to detection accuracy. While it is logical to surmise that self-efficacy would positively influence deception detection accuracy, we did not find support for that assertion in this study. Yet, this is consistent with the concept of truth bias. The perceived effectiveness of the training in the later half of the study suggests an opportunity for future investigation. Training that is novel and interesting seems to stimulate a subject's desire to achieve more accurate results with respect to deception detection. Regardless of the findings, this study demonstrated the need for continued investigation of self-efficacy and perceived training effectiveness on deception detection performance.

## Acknowledgment

Portions of this research were supported by funding from the U. S. Air Force Office of Scientific Research under the U. S. Department of Defense University Research Initiative (Grant #F49620-01-1-0394). The views, opinions, and/or findings in this report are those of the authors and should not be construed as an official Department of Defense position, policy, or decision.

## References

1. DePaulo, B., J. Lindsay, B. Malone, L. Muhlenbruck, K. Charlton, and H. Cooper, Cues to deception. *Psychological Bulletin*, (2003). 129(1): p. 74-118.
2. Zuckerman, M., B. DePaulo, and R. Rosenthal, Verbal and nonverbal communication of deception, in *Advances in experimental social psychology*, L. Berkowitz, Editor. (1981), Academic Press: New York. p. 1-59.
3. Miller, G. and J. Stiff, *Deceptive communication*. (1993), Newbury Park, CA: Sage Publications, Inc.
4. Buller, D. and J. Burgoon, Interpersonal deception theory. *Communication Theory*, (1996). 6: p. 203-242.
5. Riggio, R. and H. Friedman, Individual-differences and cues to deception. *Journal of Personality & Social Psychology*, (1983). 45(4): p. 899-915.
6. Burgoon, J. and D. Buller, Interpersonal deception: III. Effects of deceit on perceived communication and nonverbal behavior dynamics. *Journal of Nonverbal Behavior*, (1994). 18(2): p. 155-184.

7.  Burgoon, J., D. Buller, L. Guerrero, and C. Feldman, Interpersonal deception: VI. Effects of preinteractional and interactional factors on deceiver and observer perceptions of deception success. *Communication Studies*, (1994). 45: p. 263-280.
8.  Ekman, P., *Telling lies: Clues to deceit in the marketplace, politics, and marriage*. Vol. 2. (1992), New York: WW Norton and Company.
9.  DePaulo, B., C. LeMay, and J. Epstein, Effects of importance of success and expectations for success on effectiveness at deceiving. *Personality and Social Psychology Bulletin*, (1991). 17(1): p. 14-24.
10. DePaulo, B., J. Tang, and J. Stone, Physical attractiveness and skill at detecting deception. *Personality and Social Psychology Bulletin*, (1987). 13(2): p. 177-187.
11. Bandura, A., *Social Foundations of Thought and Action*. (1986), Englewood Cliffs, NJ: Prentice Hall.
12. Compeau, D. and C. Higgins, Computer self-efficacy: Development of a measure and initial test. *MIS Quarterly*, (1995): p. 189-211.
13. Boardman, J. and S. Robert, Neighborhood socioeconomic status and perceptions of self-efficacy. *Sociological Perspectives*, (2000). 43(1): p. 117-136.
14. Weinberg, R., Relationship between self-efficacy and cognitive strategies in enhancing endurance performance. *International Journal of Sport Psychology*, (1986). 17(4): p. 280-292.
15. Shea, C. and J. Howell, Efficacy-performance spirals: An empirical test. *Journal of Management*, (2000). 26(4): p. 791-812.
16. Harrison, A., K. Rainer, W. Hochwarter, and K. Thompson, Testing the self-efficacy performance linkage of social-cognitive theory. *Journal of Social Psychology*, (1997). 137(1): p. 79-87.
17. Gist, M., C. Stevens, and A. Bavetta, Effects of self-efficacy and post-training intervention on the acquisition and maintenance of complex interpersonal skills. *Personnel Psychology*, (1991). 44(4): p. 837-861.
18. Vrij, A., *Detecting Lies and Deceit*. (2000), Chichester: John Wiley.
19. Elaad, E., Effects of feedback on the overestimated capacity to detect lies and the underestimated ability to tell lies. *Applied Cognitive Psychology*, (2003). 17: p. 349-363.
20. McCornack, S. and M. Parks, Deception detection and relationship development: The other side of trust, in *Communications Yearbook 9*, McLaughlin, Editor. (1986), Sage Publications: Beverly Hills, CA.
21. Stiff, J., H. Kim, and C. Ramesh, Truth biases and aroused suspicion in relational deception. *Communication Research*, (1992). 19(3): p. 326-345.
22. Buller, D., K. Strzyzewski, and F. Hunsaker, Interpersonal deception: II. The inferiority of conversational participants as deception detectors. *Communication Monographs*, (1991). 58: p. 25-40.
23. Vrij, A., The impact of information and setting on detection of deception by police detectives. *Journal of Nonverbal Behavior*, (1994). 18: p. 117-136.
24. Biros, D., J. George, and R. Zmud, Inducing sensitivity to deception in order to improve decision making performance: A field study. *MIS Quarterly*, (2002). 26(2): p. 119-144.
25. Ekman, P. and M. O'Sullivan, Who can catch a liar? *American Psychologist*, (1991). 46: p. 913-920.
26. Gist, M. and T. Mitchell, Self-efficacy: A theoretical analysis of its determinants and malleability. *Academy of Management Review*, (1992). 17: p. 183-211.
27. Noe, R., Trainee attributes and attitudes: Neglected influences of training effectiveness. *Academy of Management Review*, (1986). 11: p. 736-749.
28. Facteau, J., G. Dobbins, J. Russell, R. Ladd, and J. Kudisch, The influence of general perceptions of the training environment on pretraining motivation and perceived training transfer. *Journal of Management*, (1995). 21(1): p. 1-25.

29. Lee, S. and H. Klein, Relationships between conscientiousness, self-efficacy, self-deception, and learning over time. *Journal of Applied Psychology*, (2002). 87(6): p. 1175-1182.
30. Landry, K. and J. Brigham, The effect of training in criteria-based content analysis on the ability to detect deception in adults. *Law and Human Behavior*, (1992). 16(6): p. 663-676.
31. Fiedler, K. and I. Walka, Training lie detectors to use nonverbal cues instead of global heuristics. *Human Communication Research*, (1993). 20(2): p. 199-123.
32. deTurck, M. and G. Miller, Training observers to detect deception: Effects of self-monitoring and rehearsal. *Human Communication Research*, (1990). 16(4): p. 603-620.
33. George, J., D. Biros, J. Burgoon, and J. Nunamaker. Training professionals to detect deception. in *1st NSF/NIJ Symposium on Intelligence and Security Informatics*. (2003). Tucson AZ.
34. Wood, R. and E. Locke, The relation of self-efficacy and grade goals to academic performance. *Educational and Psychological Measurement*, (1987). 47(4): p. 1013-1024.
35. Bandura, A. and D. Cervone, Self-evaluative and self-efficacy mechanisms governing the motivational effects of goal systems. *Journal of Personality & Social Psychology*, (1983). 45(5): p. 1017-1028.
36. Betz, N. and G. Hackett, The relationship of career-related self-efficacy expectations to perceived career options in college women and men. *Journal of Counseling Psychology*, (1981). 28: p. 399-410.
37. DeWine, S., Evaluation of organizational communication competency: The development of the communication training impact questionnaire. *Journal of Applied Communication Research*, (1987). 15: p. 113-127.
38. Lester, P. and L. Bishop, *Handbook of tests and measurement in education and the social sciences*. (2001), Lancaster PA: Technomic Publishing Co.

# Composite Role-Based Monitoring (CRBM) for Countering Insider Threats*

Joon S. Park and Shuyuan Mary Ho

School of Information Studies
Center for Science and Technology
Syracuse University
Syracuse, New York 13244-4100
{jspark,smho}@syr.edu

**Abstract.** Through their misuse of authorized privileges, insiders have caused great damage and loss to corporate internal information assets, especially within the Intelligence Community (IC). Intelligence management has faced increasing complexities of delegation and granular protection as more corporate entities have worked together in a dynamic collaborative environment. We have been confronted by the issue of how to share and simultaneously guard information assets from one another. Although many existing security approaches help to counter insiders' unlawful behavior, it is still found at a preliminary level. Efficiently limiting internal resources to privileged insiders remains a challenge today. In this paper we introduce the CRBM (Composite Role-Based Monitoring) approach by extending the current role-based access control (RBAC) model to overcome its limitations in countering insider threats. CRBM not only inherits the RBAC's advantages, such as scalable administration, least privilege, and separation of duties, but also provides scalable and reusable mechanisms to monitor insiders' behavior in organizations, applications, and operating systems based on insiders' current tasks.

## 1 Introduction

The greater an individual's knowledge of corporate internal resources, the greater the potential threat from that person. Statistically, the cost of insider threats exceeds that of outsider threats. Insiders are not interested in damaging systems or applications, but in obtaining critical information and accessing the internal level of resources. Many examples are found in government reports and news [2, 4, 5, 12, 19]. For instance, in 1985, Jonathan Pollard, who had high-level security clearance, was arrested for passing tens of thousands of pages of classified U.S. information such as satellite photographs, weapon systems data, etc., to Israelis. In 1988, a Libyan intelligence agent obtained the U.S. Military's officers' directory through his wife, who worked at the Department of Transportation and had access to the database of the Metropolitan Washington Council. In 1993, the General Accounting Office (GAO) reported that insiders' abusive use of the National Crime Information Center (NCIC) for personal

* This work was supported by the "Information Assurance for the Intelligence Community (IAIC)" program of the Advanced Research and Development Activity (ARDA).

H. Chen et al. (Eds.): ISI 2004, LNCS 3073, pp. 201–213, 2004.

reasons or profits had threatened the safety of U.S. citizens. In one case an NCIC terminal operator conducted an unusual amount of background search on her boyfriend's business clients. In 1998, the Social Security Administration (SSA) revealed that unethical employees had sold SSA records to a West African credit card fraud association. From the above, we certainly can see that insiders are not always friends who would benefit organizational business operation, but may be significant threats to the corporate assets.

According to the 2002 CSI/FBI Annual Computer Crime and Security Survey [12], insider misuse of authorized privileges or abuse of network access has caused great damage and loss to corporate internal information assets for many reasons, including acts of human error or failure, ignorance of top-level management, lack of enforcement of the SETA (Security Education, Training and Awareness) program with information security knowledge and awareness, ambiguous definition of policy management in a collaborative workplace, network and system vulnerabilities, an inappropriate software development control cycle that could cause an intentional or unintentional backdoor to be implanted within the systems or applications, incomplete configuration management of systems and networks, inefficient intrusion detection tools, inappropriate network infrastructural design, all-powered system administrative privileges, infrequent review of the system audit logs, and so on.

To mitigate insider threats, both technical and procedural methodologies in deterring insiders' attempts to obtain unauthorized access to internal assets in a sensitive organization, such as the Intelligence Community (IC) should be planned and deployed. Intelligence management has faced increasing complexities of delegation and granular control as more and more entities have worked together in a dynamic collaborative environment. We today are confronted by the issue of how to share and simultaneously guard information assets from one another in sensitive organizations. Many security technologies have been invented to prevent threats from outsiders, but they have limited use in countering insiders' abnormal behavior. For instance, cryptography protects information from an outsider attack trying to obtain unauthorized access to it. Signature-based network intrusion detection sensors and honeypot technology [15] monitor and log network activities, and send alerts to the administrator for early warning of flooding or denial-of-service attack. However, none of these approaches can provide an effective countermeasure against malicious insiders who already have authorized access to internal assets. Although some existing security approaches help counter insiders' unlawful behavior, they are still considered as being done at a preliminary level and efficiently prohibiting privileged insiders from internal assets remains a challenge today.

In this paper we introduce the CRBM (Composite Role-Based Monitoring) approach that is accomplished by extending the current role-based access control (RBAC [8, 11, 13]) model to overcome its limitations for countering insider threats. CRBM not only inherits RBAC's advantages such as scalable administration, least-privilege, and separation of duties, but also provides scalable and reusable mechanisms to monitor insiders' behavior, including access to resources and activities within organizations, applications, and operating systems based on insiders' current tasks. It defines a role structure in each domain and provides mappings between them. Those role mappings are not only horizontal (among domains at the same level; e.g., between two different organizations), but also vertical (among domains at different levels; e.g., between an organization and its applications).

We begin by identifying potential threats exploited by insiders. In particular, we provide problem analyses on insider threats to the Intelligence Community (IC). A typical scenario of how to generate intelligence reports after analyzing different sections of corporate security is given. Following this section is some related work focusing on insider threats within technical and procedural methodologies. We then describe a CRBM approach that can be used to monitor insiders' behavior based on their roles in organizations, applications, operating systems, and current tasks. We conclude by identifying plans for our future work and its possible research areas.

## 2  Typical Operational Scenario in IC

In this paper, we consider a scenario that fits into the typical operation of the Intelligence Community (IC). The scenario is a workflow that produces information reports and starts with the senior analyst (SA) receiving the task assignment. In the task-assignment phase, the SA decomposes the task into a number of sub-questions, which it assigns to other analysts who analyze the information requirements, collect information, analyze and produce reports, and disseminate the final reports. Individual tasks can be subdivided into a number of sub-tasks. The process involves cooperation and coordination between multiple users (insiders) with different roles spanning multiple organizations. Insiders use various applications and operating systems to fulfill their tasks. Those applications and operating systems are under different policies. Some of them are not interoperable. In the collection phase, the analyst seeks information from multiple resources that may span various organizations. It is assumed that each user must possess an organizational role in order to utilize the applications and operating systems within the IC. An analyst in a collaborative IC environment is expected to work within other roles and to become involved in different stages of the work. According to each task assignment, an analyst may need to access various areas of information.

## 3  Problem Analysis

Based on the above scenario we have discovered and identified three major problems in the current operation of IC: complexity, scalability, and reusability. As we explain in the following sections, we believe the CRBM approach can solve the above problems in countering insider threats by using separate role structures in organizations, applications, and operating systems, while providing mappings between them based on the insider's current task.

### 3.1  Complexity

In IC, there may be many users assigned to various job functions across multiple organizations. A user's *current* job functionality can be dynamically changed, based on the context. Multiple applications and systems span multiple domains of work. For example, a junior analyst, Max, who is responsible for Project A, may not be able to gain access to other internal resources (say, of Project B) that are outside his current duties. If there are many different projects being assigned to many different insiders who belong to multiple departments within IC, there will be a complex web of assigned duties among projects, analysts, departments and/or divisions. Such a web of identities (especially with many users joining in or signing out), tasks with different status and rates of progress, and access permissions become complicated to manage and could easily cause falsely granted accessibility. For instance, the right person might not be given the right permission, or an unauthorized person could be given permission to access resources (projects) that are not part of his/her duty. Furthermore, the entire procedure is vulnerable to users' mistakes because of the complex web of users, jobs, permissions, and other constraints. For instance, a user may execute a behavior that is unrelated to his or her current task. Due to such increasing complexity in the IC, being able to control and monitor insiders' activities becomes critically important and has created huge overheads on insider threat monitoring.

## 3.2  Scalability

A common phenomenon in the IC is that people join in and sign out of jobs frequently, based on their current task. For example, Bob is responsible for ten projects as a senior analyst in the IC. If, one day, Bob resigns from the IC, John has to come in to partially take over what Bob previously worked on, say five projects. Alice, a junior analyst, is assigned to work on two of those tasks that Bob has left. Thomas, a director, may come in to work on the three tasks that are about to be delivered to the customer. Those ten projects were supposed to be finished by Bob alone if he were still with the IC; however, ten projects now have to be split into three groups owned and supervised by three different personnel within the IC. Obviously, we need a more scalable management in this case. Furthermore, changing one user's permissions for the distributed resources is very tricky in the conventional identity-based approach (e.g., there may be permission revocation from many different files that are distributed in various places) because of the direct mapping of identity and permission. Typically, therefore, a system administrator cancels a resigned user's account or changes the user's passwords for this purpose, which implies that the identity-based approach (revocation in the example) is not reliable. In order to strengthen the competitiveness of the IC so that it provides the best quality of service, it has to overcome the scalability problem when there is a dilemma concerning the management of identities, permissions, controlling the accessibility of the resources, and providing other constraints.

## 3.3  Reusability

Whenever there are multiple applications and systems used within an organization in order to counter insider threats, there is a need to provide effective and powerful monitoring mechanisms for each and every single domain (e.g., various applications and systems) that is being used in the organization. However, we must assume that the organization will update or change some of those applications or systems in the future. If we had to modify each monitoring mechanism or strategy whenever we change a system or an application, it would be too costly and complex, which could cause technical or procedural errors in monitoring. This obviously does not fit into the IC operational environment, where many applications are dynamically installed and uninstalled, and systems are frequently added to or removed from the domain. Furthermore, an entire organization may join or leave the community with its own applications and systems. Hence, there is a pressing need for a reusable monitoring mechanism for each domain that can be easily integrated with other domains. In other words, if each application, system, or even organization has its own monitoring structure with a well-defined interface, we can simply integrate it with others.

## 4 Management vs. Technology for Countering Insider Threats

We briefly describe what some other scholars had in mind regarding insider threats. Although various aspects such as policy administration, SETA, and detective and preventative technology have been discussed, we divide this topic into management and technology viewpoints.

### 4.1 Management Approaches

Peter Neumann states that a large percentage of threats are caused by insiders' misuse of information and by privileges being improperly authorized [6]. Even audit trails are inadequate to monitor unauthorized access because privileged insiders have the potential to compromise systems. Some risks to insider threats are identified as (1) no fine-grained access control system is implemented, (2) all-powerful administrator root privileges are given, and (3) no serious authentication mechanism is practiced. Techniques such as separation of duties, split-key encryption, and enlightened management are urgently required to implement and guard corporate information security,

Whitman has pointed out the top 12 information security threats named in the CSI/FBI Annual Computer Crime and Security Survey and compared the 2002 statistics with those of 2001 [12, 19]. The comparison identified an increasing awareness of insider threats. From the statistics, the threat of "insiders' abuse of net access" ranked in second place in 2001 and continued to rank second in 2002. The threat of "unauthorized access by insiders" ranked in fourth place in both 2001 and 2002. In addition, Whitman identified 12 categories of new threats from a survey. Among these, the top six threats are all related to unethical human behavior such as human error or failure, intellectual property violation, deliberate acts of espionage or trespass, information extortion, sabotage or vandalism, and theft. From such identification, Whitman has indicated that a consistent security policy and ethical training are critical to the prevention of malicious insider acts. Unfortunately, neither the information security policy nor ethical training is being practiced by the corporation as protection mechanisms. Thus, Whitman promotes the importance of the SETA (security education, training, and awareness) program because any security profile begins with a valid security policy. Such policy is then translated into action through an effective security plan that focuses on the prevention, detection, and correction of threats.

Quigley has shown how dangerous it can be for ex-employees who, out of greediness and revengefulness, hack into a corporate internal network [17]. Many businesses have moved toward a collaborative setup with downstream distributors and resellers, and therefore upstream vendors and suppliers, employee screening, interviewing and background checking have become vitally important to the prevention of insider sabotage incidents. Not only because of the employee's ethics issue, a company itself also has to maintain an upscale secure operation because ex-employees are often allowed to continue to access the company's internal resources, database, file servers, intranets and email, along with their remote access to VPN and dial-in accounts. Such "back doors" to the corporate network should be thoroughly examined and restricted. Network monitoring services have gradually become popular as more and more businesses are willing to hire professional companies to monitor their business networks and catch saboteurs. An emphasis on information security from different management angles such as laws and regulations, network monitoring services, risk assessment, and cyber insurance practices has become substantial for countering insider threats.

## 4.2 Technical Approaches

As a technical countermeasure at the network level, Vetter, Wang, and Wu have mentioned that providing security in a routing protocol must involve the protection of authenticity and integrity of routing protocol messages [18]. There has been a consideration of using cryptography; however, it comes to a performance trade-off when the encrypting and decrypting packets dramatically slow down the network transmission rate. Even if the cryptographic authentication does prevent forging, replay, and modification of protocol messages by outsiders, the threat still exists when an intruder is able to block or delete messages transmitted on the link. Regarding the internal threats, it is still not practical to use conventional cryptographic solutions since there is a need for a pair of routers to share a secret key. The insider here is defined as a protocol participant; any router that exchanges routing information internally is viewed as the insider. The authors mentioned that the OSPF (their proposed routing protocol) does provide some inherent protections. For example, bad information flooded into one area does not affect routing in other areas. Several routers that have access to the same set of information do check each other for corroboration.

Honeypot technology is an approach that has been used to detect and decoy outsider threats deployed at the perimeter network and now can be used to identify, trace and gather information related to insider threats [15]. Since honeypots collect much smaller data sets compared to the millions of logs and thousands of alerts generated by traditional technology, they reduce false positives compared to the anomaly-based IDS technologies, and catch false negatives that could not be detected by traditional signature-based IDS. Honeypot creates a trap, a disguised environment to entice illegal users and their improper and unlawful behavior. Not only honeypots can trace and gather information for forensics. Spitzner has also mentioned that honeytokens could work as digital entities that lure intentional insiders to the honeypots [15]. Spitzner has specified that simply deploying honeypots on the internal network would not be likely to detect advanced insiders, since most of them would already have proper privileges to such critical resources. The strategy here is to use thousands of honeypots as small as honeytokens, instead of just one, to interact with attackers. This would dramatically increase the likelihood of capturing attackers.

There are many other technical approaches to monitoring insider threats [1, 7]; however, none of those approaches as yet provide a comprehensive solution to IC.

## 5 The CRBM (Composite Role-Based Monitoring) Approach

### 5.1 Role-Based Access Control (RBAC)

RBAC has rapidly emerged in the 1990s as a technology for managing and enforcing security in large-scale enterprise-wide systems. The basic notion of RBAC is that permissions are associated with roles, and users are assigned to appropriate roles, thereby acquiring the roles' permissions. Figure 1 shows a simplified RBAC model. RBAC ensures that only authorized users are given access to certain data or resources. From the initial conceptions of RBAC, a family of RBAC models (RBAC'96 Model) was developed in 1996 by Ravi Sandhu and associates [14]. This model was in turn adapted to be the NIST unified standard RBAC model in 2000 [3]. The NIST model outlines cumulative levels within the 1996 model, characterizing them as flat, hierarchical, constrained, and symmetric. Park identified the user-pull and server-pull RBAC architectures and implemented them with secure cookies and digital certificates [9, 10, 11].

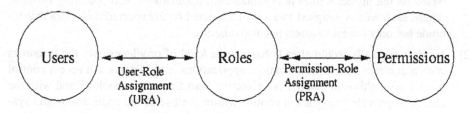

**Fig. 1.** A Simplified RBAC Model

In RBAC, a role is a semantic construct forming the basis of an access control policy. System administrators can create roles, grant permissions to those roles, and then assign users to the roles on the basis of their specific job responsibilities and policy. RBAC provides the mapping between users and permissions through User-Role Assignment (URA) and Permission-Role Assignment (PRA). Usually, PRA is more stable (of course, it can be changed if necessary) than URA, because job responsibilities in an organization do not change frequently, while users' job functions change quite often. The system makes access control decisions based on the users' roles instead of their identities. This provides an efficient access control mechanism to the system and resolves the scalability problem.

## 5.2  RBAC Enhancements for CRBM

Although many researchers have suggested various ways to prevent insider threats, most of those approaches have been limited to applying within a single domain or between domains at the same level (e.g., between organizations or between systems, not between an organization and a system). The reality is that an organization is not only composed of a single domain, but has become a collection of different domains (including organizations, applications, and operating systems) out of the business inter-cooperativeness in nature. Thus, in order to provide a robust and comprehensive monitoring mechanism for countering insider threats, we introduce the CRBM approach, which would map out the authorization in one domain with another vertically (such as role mappings among domains of systems, applications and organizations) as well as horizontally (such as role mappings among different organizations). This approach maps out the roles among various domains in a concrete authorization and monitoring system.

The CRBM approach is based on the extended concepts of RBAC. We still provide the inherent benefits of the role-based approach, but we would like to discuss the limitations of the original RBAC that are enhanced for CRBM.

1) RBAC was originally designed for strong, effective, and scalable access control. It provides scalable administration, least privilege, and separation of duties to the target domain for its access control. However, the scope of insider threats is broader than that of access control. Access control is a critical component for countering insider threats, but we also need to monitor other insider behavior such as communication patterns, frequencies, areas of topics, areas or interests, etc. Therefore, CRBM provides a comprehensive behavior-monitoring mechanism based on the insider's roles in organizations, applications, and operating systems, where each role is assigned to a set of expected or unexpected behaviors that include not only access to assets but also others.

2) Insiders normally would already have some level of privileges over the resources within domains such as organization, applications, and systems. An access control mechanism, although much more effective than firewall technology and with the ability to provide fine-granted control within the use of the applications and systems of organizations, cannot provide full security control to privileged insiders and thus is not sufficient to counter an insider's misuse of information. Suppose a malicious system administrator, Bob, were to arbitrarily release users' ids, passwords, SSNs or contact information to his external partners, his action would infringe upon the current access control mechanisms. An insider's misbehavior cannot be detected by the RBAC approach or any other security mechanisms if the insider is a privileged user. Obviously, Bob has abused his privileges in the example, but with current access control or monitoring technology, such behavior cannot be monitored or detected because most security models and mechanisms, including RBAC, are designed to detect unauthorized users' abnormal access. Once users are granted privileges, they are lawful and powerful insiders, and their misbehavior is not monitored at all. Therefore, by comparing the insider's actual behavior and the set of expected or unexpected behavior defined, based on the in-

sider's roles and current work, CRBM provides stronger and more accurate monitoring mechanisms than those of existing approaches for the purpose of countering insider threats.

3) In the original RBAC approach, a user (insider with granted privileges, in our case) can choose one or more roles (among his or her assigned roles) that he or she is going to use in the session (known as a set of activated roles in RBAC). RBAC would offer least privilege via using the concept of the session in order to make systems more secure. However, the RBAC approach assumes and trusts that the privileged user always activates necessary roles in a particular session for specific tasks. Still, once the user is granted certain privileges, there is basically no mechanism to control behavior as being rightful or not. Say a user, Alice, is assigned to Administrator, Analyst, and Employee roles, and her current task is to generate a survey report that requires the Analyst role. It is the most reasonable behavior if Alice activates the Analyst role and uses the role's corresponding privileges. However, she could activate the Administrator role as well as the Analyst role in the same session and misuse her privileges (e.g., change the system configuration files with the permission associated with the Administrator role). The concept of a session in current RBAC approaches can be exploited by insiders to misuse their privileges. Thus, CRBM provides the mappings between the sessions of organizational, application, and operating systems roles. These mappings can be dynamically changed based on the user's current task, which can prevent an insider from abusing his or her roles across the domains.

4) RBAC approaches typically consider the role structures within a single domain or multi-domains at the same horizontal level (e.g., between organizations or between systems). The abstraction of the role structure for a single domain is certainly simple and of great benefit, but it does not provide the essential explicitness of a complicated inter-related organizational or system structure. In order to make the abstraction of the role structure more applicable to multiple domains so that it can counter insider threat effectively in a reusable manner, the need is pressing to consider role structures among multi-domains at different levels (e.g., between an organization and a system) as well as at the same level. This makes the current role-based approaches much more scalable, effective, and reusable. CRBM satisfies these requirements by separating the role structures of organizations, applications, and operating systems, and by providing mappings between them. Those role mappings are not only horizontal (among domains at the same level) but also vertical (among domains at different levels).

## 5.3  CRBM Architecture

Figure 2 depicts the CRBM architecture used to monitor the behavior of an insider (Alice). In summary, the behavior of the insider is being monitored in the organization to which she belongs, in the software application she is using, and in the operating system of Alice's machine. All of Alice's monitored behavior in those domains is analyzed based on her current task [16] and roles in order to detect if she has misused her privileges.

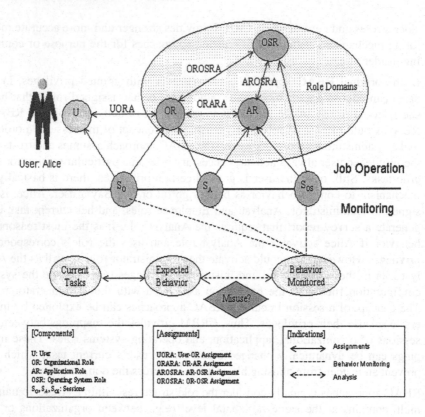

**Fig. 2.** CRBM Approach

The CRBM approach to monitoring insider threats maps role structures into three independent domains: organization role (OR), application role (AR), and operating system role (OSR). OR depicts the roles defined at the organization level. Likewise, AR depicts the roles defined in the application and OSR in the operating system. We assume that a user (U) is assigned to organizational roles before the operation by the global policy to perform his/her duties. S depicts a session, which is a set of activated roles. In the figure, for example, the $S_O$ is the set of organization roles activated by Alice. $S_A$ is the set of application roles activated for Alice, and $S_s$ is the set of OS roles activated for Alice. OR are assigned to the insider's identity (e.g., OR Employee is assigned to Alice), while AR and OSR are assigned to the corresponding OR (not the insider's identity directly). For instance, AR Reader can be assigned to OR Employee, not to Alice. As a result, Alice has AR Reader in the application because she is an employee of the organization, not because she is Alice. Typically, to use an application or a system in an organization, the user should first be assigned to some organizational roles such as Employee. Likewise, OSR is assigned to AR, which allows the user to run the applications in the operation systems, based on the user's OR. If a user's current task requires direct access to the OS (not through any applications–but, for instance–file management in the user's machine), we need to provide a direct mapping between OR and OSR.

Users in an organization are commensurate with their job functions as well as with their positions within the organizational role structure (e.g., role hierarchy). The process of assigning users to organizational roles is called user-OR-assignment (UORA). Likewise, target applications and operating systems may have independent role structures (AR and OSR, respectively). OR and AR are bridged by the OR-AR-assignment (ORARA). We believe each application should have its own role structure that is independent of other domains in order to provide more scalable and reusable monitoring mechanisms. As with application roles, each OS has its own role structure. This creates an OS role structure (OSR) in the figure. AR and OSR are bridged by AR-OSR-assignment (AROSRA). The role structure from each domain can be used as a monitoring interface for that domain when one role structure is integrated with others. Likewise, OR and OSR are bridged by OR-OSR-assignment (OROSRA), which increases the reusability of the monitoring mechanism. The assignments among users, organizational roles, application roles, operating system roles, and their sessions have effectively formed a scalable and reusable net to monitor insiders' behavior.

The user activates the sessions (the organizational session is usually activated first, which triggers the activation of other sessions manually or automatically). Based on her current task in the domains, she is allowed to use the corresponding privileges in the domains. A detailed description of the session activations and their interdependencies are found in [8]. In CRBM, the user's behavior in three different sessions (organization, application, and OS) are monitored. Finally, the monitored behavior is compared with the expected or unexpected behavior, which is defined based on the user's current task, to find out if the user misused her privileges. For instance, let us say that an authorized user (insider), Alice, is assigned to organizational roles (OR) such as Employee, Analyst, and Administrator, and her current task is to generate a survey report, which requires the Analyst role. Suppose Alice activates the Administrator role as well as the Analyst in the same session $(S_O)$, which automatically generates the corresponding $S_A$ and $S_{OS}$ and misuses her administrative privileges while finishing her current task (e.g., she changes some sensitive configuration files in the system). This situation can be detected by CRBM if the insider's behavior (i.e., changing the system configuration) is not defined in the current task's expected behavior set. This can work even when the insider abuses her privileges under her current task. In the example, Alice activates just the Analyst role, which is required for her current task, makes a copy of sensitive information, and emails it to her external partner. This behavior can also be detected by CRBM by comparing Alice's behavior in $S_A$ and $S_{OS}$ with the set of expected and unexpected behavior that were defined based on the policies.

## 6 Conclusions and Future Work

In this paper we identified the generic problems for countering insiders' behaviors in IC with respect to complexity, scalability, and reusability. After coming to an understanding about how other scholars have analyzed threats by advanced insiders at both management and technical levels, we introduced our CRBM approach by extending existing RBAC approaches with separate role structures of organizations, applications, and operating systems, and mappings among them. We explained each component that participates in the correlation of role domains and how the mappings of role structure and activation of sessions have come into the picture.

In our future work, we will attempt to apply the CRBM approach to a real IC scenario and we hope to shape our approach into a firm model. By using the delegation monitoring mechanism, we should be able to monitor users' behavior and identify users' improper intension on the internal network according to their delegated roles. We will also attempt to apply this approach to monitoring the all-powerful system administrators' activities. Possible integration with other technologies such as firewalls, intrusion detection systems, and the application of honeypot/honeytoken decoying technologies for monitoring insider threats will be further considered.

## Acknowledgments

The authors are grateful to Eric Brown, Bob Delzoppo, Matt Downey, Liaquat Hossain, Elizabeth Liddy, Anand Natarajan, and Svetlana Symonenko for their useful discussions and comments.

## References

1. Robert H. Anderson, Thomas Bozek, Tom Longstaff, Wayne Meitzler, Michael Skroch, Ken Van Wyk. *Research on Mitigating the Insider Threat to Information Systems - #2*: Proceedings of a Workshop Held, August 2000.
   http://www.rand.org/publications/CF/CF163.
2. Dorian Benkoil, *An Unrepentant Spy: Jonathan Pollard Serving a Life Sentence.* ABCNEWS.com Oct. 25, 1998.
3. David F. Ferraiolo, Ravi Sandhu, Serban Gavrila, D. Richard Kuhn and Ramaswamy Chandramouli, *Proposed NIST Standard for Role-Based Access Control.* ACM Transactions on Information and System Security (TISSEC), Vol. 4, No. 3, August 2001, Pages 224–274.
4. Michale V. Hayden. *The Insider Threat to U. S. Government Information Systems.* National Security Telecommunications and Information Systems Security Committee (NSTISSAM) INFOSEC 1-99, July 1999.
   http://www.nstissc.gov/Assets/pdf/NSTISSAM_INFOSEC1-99.pdf
5. Jacob V. Lamar Jr. *Two Not-So-Perfect Spies; Ronald Pelton is Convicted of Espionage as Jonathan Pollard Pleads Guilty.* Time 16 June, 1986.
6. Peter G. Neumann. *Risks of Insiders.* Communications of the ACM, Volume 42, Issue 12, December 1999. ISSN: 0001-0782.
7. Nam Nguyen, Peter Reiher, and Geoffrey H. Kuenning, *Detecting Insider Threats by Monitoring System Call Activity.* Proceedings of the IEEE Workshop on Information Assurance, West Point, NY June 2001.

8. Joon S. Park, Keith P. Costello, Teresa M. Neven, and Josh A. Diosomito. *A Composite RBAC Approach for Large, Complex Organizations*. 9th ACM Symposium on Access Control Models and Technologies (SACMAT), Yorktown Heights, New York, June 2-4, 2004.
9. Joon S. Park, Ravi Sandhu, and SreeLatha Ghanta. *RBAC on the Web by Secure Cookies*. 13th IFIP WG 11.3 Working Conference on Database Security, Seattle, Washington, July 26-28, 1999.
10. Joon S. Park and Ravi Sandhu. *Secure Cookies on the Web*. IEEE Internet Computing, July-August 2000.
11. Joon S. Park, Ravi Sandhu, and Gail-Joon Ahn. *Role-Based Access Control on the Web*. ACM Transactions on Information and System Security (TISSEC), Volume 4, Number 1, February 2001.
12. Richard Power. *CSI/FBI Computer Crime and Security Survey*. Computer Security Issues & Trends, 2002.
13. Ravi S Sandhu, Edward J Coyne, Hal l. Feinstein and Charles E. Youman, *Role-Based Access Control Models*. IEEE Computer, Volume 29, Number 2, February 1996.
14. Ravi Sandhu, David Ferraiolo and Richard Kuhn. *The NIST model for Role Based Access Control: Towards A unified standard, Proceedings*. Proceedings of the 5th ACM Workshop on Role Based Access Control, July 26-27, 2000.
15. Lance Spitzner. *Honeypots: Catching the Insider Threat*. Proceedings of the 19th Annual-Computer Security Applications Conference, 2003.
16. Roshan K. Thomas and Ravi Sandhu. *Conceptual Foundations for a Model of Task-based Authorizations*. In Proceedings of the IEEE Computer Security Foundations Workshop (CSFW), Franconia, New Hampshire, June 1994.
17. Ann Quigley. *Inside Job*. netWorker, Volume 6, Issue 1, Pages: 20 – 24, March 2002. ISSN: 1091-3556.
18. Brain Vetter, Feiyi, S. Felix Wu. *An Experimental Study of Insider Attacks for OSPF Routing Protocol*. IEEE International Conference on Network Protocols, pp. 293 - 300, October 1997.
19. Michael E. Whitman. *Enemy at the Gate: Threats to Information Security*. Communications of the ACM, Vol. 46, No. 8., August 2003.

# Critical Infrastructure Integration Modeling and Simulation

William J. Tolone[1], David Wilson[1], Anita Raja[1], Wei-ning Xiang[2],
Huili Hao[2], Stuart Phelps[2], and E. Wray Johnson[3]

[1] Department of Software and Information Systems, College of Information Technology
University of North Carolina at Charlotte, 9201 University City Blvd, Charlotte, NC 28223
{wjtolone,davils,anraja}@uncc.edu
[2] Department of Geography and Earth Sciences, College of Arts and Sciences
University of North Carolina at Charlotte, 9201 University City Blvd, Charlotte, NC 28223
{wxiang,hhao}@uncc.edu, sphelps@carolina.rr.com
[3] IntePoint Solutions, LLC. 9201 University City Blvd, Charlotte, NC 28223
Wray.Johnson@IntePoint.com

**Abstract.** The protection of critical infrastructures, such as electrical power grids, has become a primary concern of many nation states in recent years. Critical infrastructures involve multi-dimensional, highly complex collections of technologies, processes, and people, and as such, are vulnerable to potentially catastrophic failures on many levels. Moreover, cross-infrastructure dependencies can give rise to cascading and escalating failures across multiple infrastructures. In order to address the problem of critical infrastructure protection, our research is developing innovative approaches to modeling critical infrastructures, with emphasis on analyzing the ramifications of cross-infrastructure dependencies. This paper presents an initial overview of the research and of the modeling environment under development.

## 1 Introduction

The protection of critical infrastructures, such as electrical power grids, has become a primary concern of many nation states in recent years - particularly within the U.S. Critical infrastructures involve multi-dimensional, highly complex collections of technologies, processes, and people, and as such, are vulnerable to potentially catastrophic failures (intentional or unintentional) on many levels. A pointed recent example can be seen in the August 2003 blackout in the northeastern U.S. and eastern Canada. A series of unintentional events led to a loss of power for millions of businesses and homes. Moreover, failure in the electrical power infrastructure had serious impacts on other critical infrastructures. For example, the loss of power also led to a loss of water in many communities, as water systems depend heavily on power to operate the pumping systems that deliver water for consumption. The tight couplings within and across infrastructures and the brittleness that can result were clearly evident in the length of time it took to restore power to the affected region. It also was evident that failure isolation is a difficult task within complex infrastructures, let alone across infrastructures. While the August 2003 blackout may not be considered catastrophic from a human perspective, it was clearly catastrophic from an economic perspective.

H. Chen et al. (Eds.): ISI 2004, LNCS 3073, pp. 214–225, 2004.

Given the breadth and depth of critical infrastructures, one can readily observe characteristics that make the problem of protecting a nation's critical infrastructures, in general, intractable. Key among these characteristics is the inherent complexity of the infrastructures, each defining a unique field of research with numerous open problems regarding organization, operation, and evolution. For example, electric power systems are complex, semi-redundant networks of power generation, transmission, and distributions facilities relying upon technologies that may vary in age in excess of twenty years. Rinaldi et. al. [22] refer to such infrastructures as complex adaptive systems. Furthermore, many of these critical infrastructures were designed and constructed over several decades with few, if any, security considerations in mind. Aside from nuclear power generation facilities, this is particularly true of the energy sector. As a result, each of these critical infrastructures faces a clear and present danger of failure by accident or design.

Magnifying these challenges and the dangers that arise are numerous inherent interdependencies that exist among critical infrastructures. Electric power systems depend upon transportation networks to deliver fuel to generation facilities. These same generation facilities often depend upon water systems for cooling purposes. In addition, electric power systems depend heavily upon telecommunication networks to support the Supervisory, Control and Data Acquisition (SCADA) systems that manage power transmission and distribution. The list of interdependencies among the critical infrastructure sectors is long and in some cases, poorly understood. Furthermore, many interdependencies are very strong, time-sensitive, and essential. The result is a brittle "system of systems" that could lead to catastrophic occurrences as a failure (intentional or unintentional) cascades and escalates across infrastructures.

Our research is helping to address the crucial and daunting task of infrastructure protection by developing innovative infrastructure modeling approaches in order to help identify and understand vulnerabilities. In particular, we are interested in explicitly modeling and exposing the impact that failures in one infrastructure may have on connected and related infrastructures. Our approach also contributes to current understanding of the design and application of intelligent agent-based systems as applied to geographic information system (GIS) environments. This paper presents an initial overview of our work in developing a modeling and simulation environment to help nations, states, and regions better understand the vulnerabilities within their critical infrastructures, particularly those vulnerabilities that are due to cross infrastructure dependencies. Section 0 provides a brief background on the notion of critical infrastructure and highlights the current research in modeling and simulating cross-infrastructure dependencies. Section 0 presents our approach to this challenging modeling and simulation problem, including a brief overview of the simulation architecture. Section 0 demonstrates our initial results via an example simulation scenario, and Section 0 summarizes our work and identifies future research opportunities.

# 2  Background

We begin by developing a working definition of what constitutes a critical infrastructure and providing some background on infrastructure modeling. We have chosen to adopt the definition put forth by the U.S. Patriot Act, which identifies a critical infrastructure to be:

> systems and assets, whether physical or virtual, so vital to the United States that the incapacity or destruction of such systems and assets would have a debilitating impact on security, national economic security, national public health or safety, or any combination of those matters [2]

Under this definition, critical infrastructures may be organized according to the following sectors: agriculture, food, water, public health, emergency services, government, defense industrial base, information and telecommunications, energy, transportation, banking and finance, chemical industry and hazardous materials, postal and shipping, and national monuments and icons [2].

The problem of understanding the behavior of critical infrastructures and their interdependence is an integral part of many well-established disciplines, such as urban and regional planning, civil and environmental engineering, operations research, landscape architecture, and emergency management [14]. More recently, as a key area of inquiry, it is receiving increasing attention from the emerging field of geographic information science and technology (GI S&T) [24, 26].

Researchers in the GI S&T community have primarily approached the study of the behavior and spatial interdependence of critical infrastructures from three distinct vantage points. The first stream of inquiry examines the interdependence of critical infrastructures with tools from spatial statistics and econometrics, and identifies their approach as spatial data analysis (SDA) [6, 13]. The second approach depicts geographic correlations among critical infrastructure components by using traditional map overlay methods for spatial data aggregation in GIS environments [4, 10, 11]. The third approach uses rule-based inference engines, usually fueled by human expert's knowledge, in the delineation and manipulation of interdependence [12, 28]. Each of these approaches, while informative, does not in isolation adequately address the problem regarding the impact of critical infrastructure interdependencies.

Consequently, many respected authors, such as Getis [9] and Sinton [24], have advocated a multi-dimensional approach to the study of behavior and spatial interdependence of critical infrastructures. Instead of "divide-and-conquer," they suggested a strategy that combines strengths of the three intellectual streams of inquiry and investigates the matter of interdependence from all three vantage points. Despite some genuine efforts [1, 7, 9, 18], progress along this route has yet to meet the advocates' expectations. The status quo is exemplified by some most recent publications in which little if any multi-dimensional results were reported [16, 29].

Thus, the problem of understanding the behavior of critical infrastructures and their interdependence remains a difficult, open problem. The limitations of single-dimensional approaches are by no means trivial. Multi-dimensional approaches, while theoretically promising, have produced few results. In the following sections, we present our approach to cross-infrastructure modeling and simulation, which leverages the strengths of a multi-dimensional approach. We believe our approach provides an appropriate foundation for multi-dimensional analyses of critical infrastructure interdependencies. We include some initial results to demonstrate the kinds of analyses and subsequent understandings to be gained from our work.

# 3  Our Approach

In this section, we present our approach to infrastructure and cross-infrastructure modeling and simulation. Fundamentally, the problem of enabling cross-infrastructure simulations is one of proper integration of individual critical infrastructure behavior models. Different approaches were considered regarding how to perform this integration. The approaches and the problem of integration can be considered along two dimensions: the *level of integration* and the *methodology of integration*. Linthicum describes the problem of integration [15] in terms of four levels: data level, application interface level, method (i.e., business process) level, and the user interface level. These levels represent common practices of enterprise integration.

Data level integration is a bottom-up approach that creates "integration awareness" at the data level by extending data models to include integration data. For example, infrastructure models are extended to include explicit infrastructure interdependency data. Application level integration creates "integration awareness" at the application level, which in our case refers to the infrastructure models. At this level, behavioral analysis constructs for each infrastructure are adapted to recognize and interact with other infrastructures. Method level integration develops "integration awareness" external to the infrastructure models - that is, infrastructure models remain unaware of one another. This cross-infrastructure awareness is encapsulated and managed at a level above the infrastructures. The final level of integration creates "integration awareness" at the user interface level. This level of integration, through techniques such as "screen scraping," is often used to integrate legacy systems. In our work, we need to draw on a potentially diverse set of individual infrastructure models, which has led us to adopt a method level approach.

The methodology dimension of integration refers to the method by which integration occurs given an integration level. Integration methodologies may be partitioned into two categories: peer-to-peer integration and brokered integration. Peer-to-peer integration is most common and effective for data and application level integration. These methodologies essentially support fire-and-forget or request-response remote procedure calls among applications. Brokered integration is most common and effective for method level integration. Different approaches to brokered integration include agent-based integration and workflow-based integration. Each of these approaches depends upon meta-knowledge to enable the integration. Agent-based integration utilizes contextual meta-knowledge represented in the form of facts and rules while workflow-based integration utilizes procedural knowledge represented in the form of process models. Because user interface level integration is a technique for opening up legacy systems, this level may participate equally within both methodology categories (see Table 1). In our work, the focus on cross-infrastructure interaction has led us to adopt a brokered approach.

**Table 1.** Level and Methodology of Integration

|  | Data | Application | Method | User Interface |
|---|---|---|---|---|
| Peer-to-peer | X | X |  | X |
| Brokered |  |  | X | X |

In particular, our approach to integrating critical infrastructures for the purpose of cross-infrastructure modeling and simulation utilizes an intelligent agent-based, brokered methodology designed for method level integration. The following sections detail and motivate our design choices and present our architecture for agent-based critical infrastructure integration.

### 3.1 Intelligent Software Agents for Integration, Modeling, and Simulation

In order to ground the discussion of our agent-based approach, we first clarify the notion of agents as employed in our research. The term software agent, though commonplace, does not have a common definition. Many definitions have been proposed, often reflecting the purpose(s) of their application. Our preferred definition is an adaptation of Weiss [27] and Franklin and Graesser [8].

> *Definition 1*. A **software agent** is an autonomous program, or program component, that is situated within, aware of, and acts upon its environment in pursuit of its own objectives so as to affect its future environment.

Software agents can be further categorized, according to Weiss [27], by their degree of autonomy and intelligence, and the type of environment within which they may be situated. *Autonomy* refers to an agent's ability to sense and act upon its environment without intervention (e.g., human intervention) - the more autonomous an agent, the less need for intervention. *Intelligence* refers to an agent's ability to be reactive, proactive, and social (i.e., converse with other agents). *Agent environments* are characterized based on issues of accessibility, determinism, dynamism, continuity, and their episodic nature (i.e., whether agents must consider past and future actions when reasoning about current actions). These environment characteristics shape an agent's required capabilities[1].

Our decision to utilize intelligent software agents to support critical infrastructure integration, modeling, and simulation is based primarily on three motivating factors. First, we examined the types of critical infrastructure models we desired to integrate. It was clear from this examination that neither data nor application level integration would provide the appropriate level of extensibility and scalability that our modeling and simulation environment requires. Data and application level integration could be accomplished for specific infrastructure models that are well-scoped and fully populated. However, we desire an ability to perform simulations across multiple, potentially sparse infrastructure models. As such, method level integration, and therefore brokered integration, is the most promising approach.

Second, we examined the meta-knowledge necessary to support cross-infrastructure simulations. This examination focused on the contextual versus procedural characteristics of the meta-knowledge and revealed that infrastructure interdependency data are highly contextual. Our conclusion is further supported by the contention that agent-based systems are a promising approach to modeling complex adaptive systems

---

[1] Another characteristic frequently discussed is agent mobility - the ability of an agent to migrate among machines. We view agent mobility as an architectural characteristic derived from agent environment characteristics such as accessibility.

[22]. Consequently, we capture meta-knowledge using a rule-based, declarative approach rather than a procedural representation such as hierarchical state transition diagrams or Petri nets.

Third, we examined the desired simulations. This examination revealed a strong need for multiple types of simulations. We organize these simulation types along the following three dimensions of analyses. Each has been shown to be supported effectively by agent-based solutions. The nature of these analyses also suggests an agent design that embodies a strong notion of intelligence as previously described.

1. Predictive ("what if") and prescriptive ("goal-driven") analyses - these types of analyses are complementary and often used simultaneously. They are used during simulations to determine the consequences of vulnerability exploitation or if there are vulnerabilities that might lead to an undesirable outcome. [5, 19, 20, 23]
2. Discovery based analyses - these types of analyses examine infrastructure models and the supporting meta-knowledge to discover new knowledge (e.g., uncover unidentified infrastructure interdependencies) and identify data set inconsistencies. [17, 25]
3. Probabilistic analyses - these types of analyses introduce variability into simulations in order to provide better approximations of infrastructure behavior. [3, 21]

Thus, in order to best address the problem of critical infrastructure integration, modeling, and simulation, we are developing an intelligent agent-based system that provides a brokered methodology for method level integration. This system will afford a better understanding of critical infrastructure vulnerabilities, particularly those due to cross-infrastructure dependencies, as a means to provide better protection to a nation's critical infrastructures. In the following, we provide an overview of our system architecture and demonstrate our current results via an example simulation.

### 3.2 Modeling and Simulation Architecture

The architecture of our modeling and simulation environment (see Fig. 1) is designed to allow end users to execute simulations seamlessly within the context of a GIS environment. Users initiate simulations by selecting and disabling infrastructure features and then viewing the impacts of those actions through the GIS visualization support.

In order to support cross-infrastructure simulations, we have developed a community of intelligent software agents that register interest in the critical infrastructure models of concern. These agents collectively sense changes within infrastructures, reason about the changes using meta-knowledge that includes cross-infrastructure dependency data, communicate within the community of agents, and based upon the outcome of the collective reasoning, potentially affect change back to and across the infrastructures of concern.

Currently, two types of change may be affected by the agents. First, agents, having sensed an infrastructure state change (e.g., a transmission line has failed due to contact with a tree branch), may reason about the impacts of this event upon all infrastructures based upon the meta-knowledge available and affect changes in state within and across infrastructures. Second, agents, having sensed change, may utilize GIS supported network analyses to reason about and affect changes within infrastructures. This latter feature allows agents to leverage specialized functionality to enhance simulations.

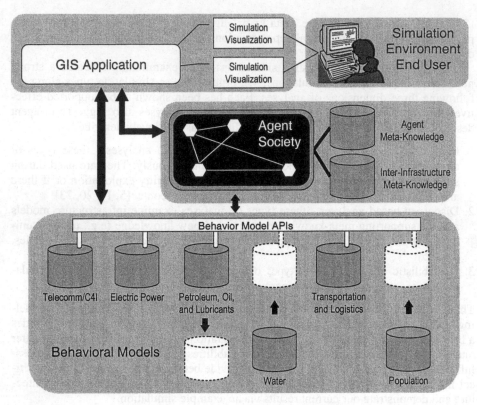

**Fig. 1.** Simulation Environment Architecture

Three important characteristics of our architecture are its flexibility, scalability, and extensibility. Our architecture is *flexible* in that it allows the 'plug and play' of different models of the same infrastructure for a given region. Our architecture is *scalable* in that multiple models of the same infrastructure type (e.g., models of adjacent transportation systems) may simultaneously participate in a single simulation. Our architecture is *extensible* in that new infrastructure model types may be easily incorporated into the simulation environment.

## 4   Example Results

In this section we provide a demonstration of our simulation environment. We begin by discussing the critical infrastructure models in question. This example simulation contains four critical infrastructures for a fictional town: electrical power transmission and distribution, gas distribution, telecommunications, and transportation (see Fig. 2). The land area for the region in question is roughly four square miles. However, we have successfully conducted simulations on regions with land area well in excess of 500 square miles. In fact, our simulation environment operates independent of region size. Furthermore, it is not a requirement that the infrastructure models completely overlap one another. Infrastructure models may overlap very little, if at all.

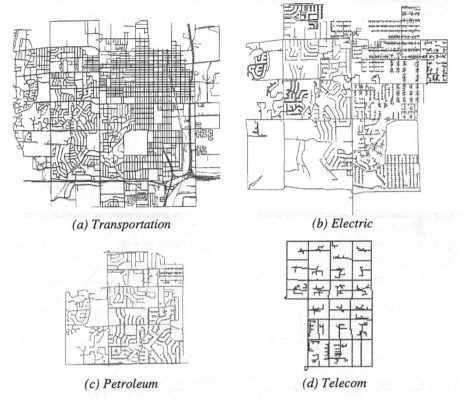

(a) Transportation                    (b) Electric

(c) Petroleum                         (d) Telecom

**Fig. 2.** Example simulation infrastructures

For simplicity in presentation, we further scope the example simulations by focusing our simulation on an area roughly eight city blocks in size and limit the number of infrastructures to two: gas and electric power. Fig. 3 contains four screen captures of the example simulation. While both the electric power and gas distribution infrastructures are visualized in all four screen shots, we have configured the GIS display to depict the electric power impacts and gas distribution impacts separately. Thus, Fig. 3 (a) and (b) are time sequenced visualizations of changes to the electric power infrastructure while Fig. 3 (c) and (d) are time sequenced visualizations of changes to the gas distribution infrastructure.

The type of simulation presented in this example is a predictive (i.e., "what-if") analysis. To begin the simulation, the end user selects and disables a feature of interest. Fig. 3 (a), identifies this feature as a small segment of the power distribution network. Once disabled, the feature is highlighted through color change and increased thickness. This change to the infrastructure, which is part of the agent environment, is sensed by the agent community. The agent community reasons that downstream power distribution might be affected and thus requests the GIS network analysis support to analyze the downstream impacts. These downstream impacts are accepted and rendered (see Fig. 3 (b)).

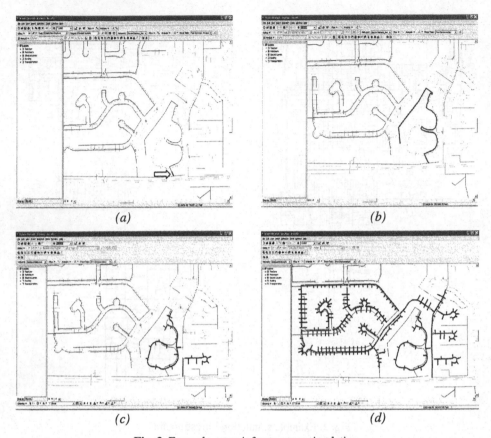

*(a)*    *(b)*

*(c)*    *(d)*

**Fig. 3.** Example cross infrastructure simulation

At the same time, the agent community reasons that disabling that same initial power distribution feature may also impact gas distribution infrastructure due to a nearby electric powered gas pump. Thus, the agent community affects the gas infrastructure by disabling the gas pump. Once the gas pump is disabled the agent community reasons that downstream gas distribution may be affected and requests the GIS network analysis support to analyze downstream impacts. These downstream impacts are accepted and rendered (see Fig. 3 (c)). The agent community further reasons that downstream power disruptions, as depicted in Fig. 3 (b), impact additional gas distribution due to cross-infrastructure dependencies. As a result, additional segments of the gas distribution infrastructure are disabled and subsequent analyses renders downstream effects as shown in Fig. 3 (d). Thus, disabling a small segment of the electric power infrastructure has left a small region without power, but an even larger region without gas. Such a conclusion may not be easily predicted without the aid of proper modeling and simulation support.

Other visualization techniques are also possible. For example, depicts an elevated rendering of three of the critical infrastructures (gas, electrical power, and transportation - top to bottom). Such renderings are supported by many GIS systems. By augmenting this visualization with extruded renderings of the disabled infrastructure, additional perspective and understanding may emerge.

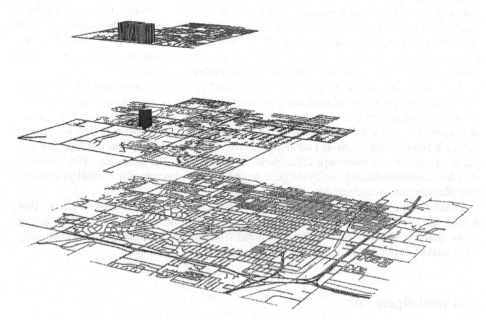

**Fig. 4.** Three-dimensional, extruded renderings for additional analyses

## 5  Summary and Future Work

Protecting critical infrastructures remains a difficult open problem, in part due to the multitude of complex interdependencies that exists among infrastructures. Our research is helping to address the crucial and daunting task of infrastructure protection by developing innovative infrastructure modeling approaches in order to help identify and understand vulnerabilities. In this paper, we presented the initial results of our approach, which utilizes communities of intelligent software agents to model and simulate cross-infrastructure dependencies. We demonstrated, by way of an example, that the behavior of critical infrastructures may be better understood through multi-infrastructure simulations.

We have identified several areas of future work based upon the initial research presented here. First, we are expanding our environment to support discovery-based analyses such as constraint-based conformance analyses to identify inconsistencies within and across infrastructure models and their representations. Furthermore, we plan to investigate additional discovery-based analyses including: i) case-based reasoning, which can extract meta-knowledge from simulation execution, and ii) spatial inference analysis, which draws upon the correlation, or even causal relationship, between land use patterns for an area and the spatial patterns of infrastructure networks.

A second area of future work is to incorporate probabilistic representations of infrastructure dependencies and failures, where the fuzzy effects of probabilistic events will require agents to use more complex reasoning processes. We also plan to scale our approach to common cause failures, where multiple infrastructures are disabled because of a common cause. These studies will provide us a good understanding of the nature of cascading and escalating failures among critical infrastructures. In addition, we expect to use our work to study the possible organizations of agents, their communication protocols, and resource-bounded adaptive behavior.

A third area of future investigation is the interface between our simulation models and decision-making or plan-making models that various government agencies and private organizations use in their practice of homeland security planning, emergency management, and counter-terrorist drills. This requires an approach that brings together a broader spectrum of knowledge, skills, and expertise to study the policy impacts of critical infrastructure assessment, management, and planning. The outcome will be recommendations for developing sound support systems for critical infrastructure planning and management.

Finally, ongoing research is required to validate not only the meta-knowledge that agents utilize, but also the methodology for representing, organizing, and reasoning about that knowledge. We believe that these studies will eventually lead to our long term goal of better protecting critical infrastructures.

## Acknowledgements

The authors would like to thank the following people for their contributions to the project: Bei-tseng Chu, Mirsad Hadzikadic and Vikram Sharma of the Department of Software and Information Systems, UNC Charlotte; Mark Armstrong, Michael Russell, and Robert Vaessen of IntePoint Solutions, LLC; and Qianhong Tang of the Department of Geography and Earth Sciences, UNC Charlotte.

## References

1. Anselin, L., Getis, A.: Spatial statistical analysis and geographic information systems. Annals of Regional Science. Vol. 26 (1992) 19-33
2. As cited in: The President's National Strategy for Homeland Security (2002)
3. Bar-Shalom, Y.: Multitarget Multisensor Tracking: Advanced Applications. Artech House (1990)
4. Burrough, P.A.: Methods of spatial analysis in GIS. International Journal of Geographical Information Systems. Vol. 4. No. 3. (1990) 2-21
5. Chu, B., Long, J., Tolone, W.J., Wilhelm, R., Peng, Y., Finin, T., Matthews, M.: Towards intelligent integrated planning-execution. International Journal of Advanced Manufacturing Systems. Vol. 1. No. 1. (1997) 77-83
6. Cressie, N.: Statistics for Spatial Data. John Wiley, Chichester (1991)
7. Flowerdew, Green: A real interpolation and types of data. In, FotheringHam, S. and Rogerson, P. (Editors), Spatial Analysis and GIS Taylor & Francis, London (1994) 121-145

8. Franklin, S., Graesser, A.: Is it an agent, or just a program?: a taxonomy for autonomous agents. 3rd International Workshop on Agent Theories, Architectures, and Languages. Springer-Verlag, (1996)
9. Getis, A.: Spatial dependence and heterogeneity and proximal databases. In, Fothering-Ham, S. and Rogerson, P. (Editors), Spatial Analysis and GIS Taylor & Francis, London (1994) 105-120
10. Goodchild, M.F., Kemp, K.K.: NCGIA core curriculum. University of California at Santa Barbara, CA (1990)
11. Greene, R.W.: Confronting Catastrophe: a GIS Handbook. ESRI Press, Redlands CA (2002)
12. Gronlund, A.G., Xiang, W.-N., Sox, J.: GIS, expert systems technologies improve forest fire management techniques. GIS World, Vol. 7. No. 2. (1994) 32-36
13. Haining, R.: Spatial data analysis in the social and environmental sciences. Cambridge University Press, Cambridge, UK (1990)
14. Kaiser, E.J., Godschalk, D.R., Chapin, F.S., Jr,.: Urban Land Use Planning. 4th Edn. University of Illinois Press, Urbana, IL (1995)
15. Linthicum, D.S.: Enterprise Application Integration. Addison-Wesley, New York (2000)
16. Mitchell, A.: The ESRI Guide to GIS Analysis. ESRI Press, Redlands, CA (1999)
17. Moukas, A., Maes, P. Amalthaea: an evolving multi-agent information filtering and discovery systems for the WWW. Autonomous agents and multi-agent systems. Vol. 1. (1998) 59-88
18. Openshaw: Two exploratory space-time-attribute pattern analysers relevant to GIS. In , FotheringHam, S. and Rogerson, P. (Editors), Spatial Analysis and GIS Taylor & Francis, London (1994) 82-104
19. Pearl, J.: Probabilistic Reasoning in Intelligent Systems: networks of plausible Inference. Morgan Kaufmann, San Mateo, CA (1988)
20. Peng, Y., Finin, T., Labrou, Y., Cost, S., Chu, B., Tolone, W.J., Long, J., Boughanam, A.: An agent-based approach to manufacturing integration: the CIIMPLEX experience. Applied Artificial Intelligence, An International Journal. Vol. 13. No. 1-2. (1999) 39-64
21. Rao A.S., Georgeff, M.P.: Modeling rational agents within a BDI-architecture. In J. Allen, R. Fikes, and E. Sandewall, editors, Proceedings of the Second International Conference on Principles of Knowledge Representation and Reasoning. Morgan Kaufmann (1991) 473-484
22. Rinaldi, S.M., Peerenboom, J.P., Kelly, T.K.: Identifying, understanding, and analyzing critical infrastructure interdependencies. IEEE Control Systems Magazine. December (2001) 11-25
23. Russell, S.J., Wefald, E.H.: Do the Right Thing: Studies in Limited Rationality. MIT Press, Cambridge, MA (1991)
24. Sinton, D.F.: Reflections on 25 years of GIS. GIS World. Vol. 5. No. 2. (1992) 1-8
25. Sycara, K., Decker, K., Pannu, A., Williamson, M., Zeng, D.: Distributed intelligent agents. IEEE Expert. Vol. 11 No. 6. (1996) 36-46
26. University Consortium for Geographic Information Science (2003)
27. Weiss, G. ed.: Multiagent Systems. MIT Press (1999)
28. Xiang, W.-N.: Knowledge-based decision support by CRITIC. Environment and Planning B: Planning and Design, Vol. 24. No. 1. (1997) 69-79
29. Zeiler, M.: Modeling Our World. the ESRI Guide to Geodatabase Design. ESRI Press, Redlands, CA (1999)

# Mining Normal and Intrusive Activity Patterns
# for Computer Intrusion Detection

Xiangyang Li[1] and Nong Ye[2]

[1] University of Michigan – Dearborn, 4901 Evergreen Rd., Dearborn, Michigan 48128, USA
xylum@umich.edu
[2] Arizona State University, Box 875906, Tempe, Arizona 85287, USA
nongye@asu.edu

**Abstract.** Intrusion detection has become an important part of assuring the computer security. It borrows various algorithms from statistics, machine learning, etc. We introduce in this paper a supervised clustering and classification algorithm (CCAS) and its application in learning patterns of normal and intrusive activities and detecting suspicious activity records. This algorithm utilizes a heuristic in grid-based clustering. Several post-processing techniques including data redistribution, supervised grouping of clusters, and removal of outliers, are used to enhance the scalability and robustness. This algorithm is applied to a large set of computer audit data for intrusion detection. We describe the analysis method in using this data set. The results show that CCAS makes significant improvement in performance with regard to detection ability and robustness.

## 1 Introduction

Intrusions into computer and network systems have presented significant threats to these systems for providing continued service. There exist two general categories of intrusion detection techniques: anomaly detection and misuse detection (signature recognition) [1]. Anomaly detection techniques first build a profile of a subject's normal activities and then signal observed activities as intrusive if there is significant deviation. Signature recognition techniques first learn signature patterns of intrusive (and normal) activities from training data, and then in detection match these patterns with incoming data of observed activities. Anomaly detection is capable of detecting novel attacks, while signature recognition is accurate in detecting known attacks. Anomaly detection and signature recognition often co-exist in an intrusion detection system to complement each other.

Intrusion detection through signature recognition can be considered as a classification problem. A set of attribute or predictor variables, $X = (X_1, X_2, ..., X_p)$, can be used to describe the data record collected in normal and intrusive activities. A target variable, $Y$, can be used to represent class (normal/intrusive or finer categories) corresponding to the nature of activities. Given a data record of observed activities, intrusion detection is a classification relying on a function, $f: X \rightarrow Y$, which can be learned from training data.

Intrusion detection algorithms must handle the complex data from computer systems. First of all, activity data from a computer and network system can easily contain millions of records per day. In addition, each record may have hundreds of data fields. A data mining algorithm to learn signature patterns from such large amounts of data must be scalable. Secondly, patterns of normal and intrusive activities very likely

H. Chen et al. (Eds.): ISI 2004, LNCS 3073, pp. 226–238, 2004.

change over time, and new forms of attacks emerge everyday. Hence, a data mining algorithm must have the incremental learning ability to update signature patterns as more training data become available. Lastly, the distribution for normal and intrusive data may be unclear. Various types of variables of numerical, ordinal and nominal values may appear in data. The data structure may range from well-structured to less-structured and to unstructured.

Many data mining techniques, such as decision trees [8,15], association rules [7], artificial neural networks and genetic algorithms [13], and Bayesian networks [14], have been used for intrusion detection through signature recognition. However, in many cases, these existing data mining techniques are not capable of learning signature patterns in a scalable, incremental manner. And several of them including Bayesian networks require the understanding of specific domain knowledge and data distribution.

This paper focuses on signature recognition techniques to meet the identified requirements in the above. We have developed an innovative data mining algorithm, called Clustering and Classification Algorithm – Supervised (CCAS) [9], which specifically aims at the scalable, incremental learning ability. CCAS is based on two concepts: supervised clustering for learning signature patterns of normal and intrusive activities during a training phase, and instance-based classification for using these signature patterns to classify observed activities. We choose clustering because it relies very little on the distribution models of data. This is very suitable for intrusion detection where underlying distribution models of both normal and intrusive data are unclear. During the training phase, the value of the target variable for each data record in the training data is known and is used to supervise the clustering of normal and intrusive data records. The resulting clusters represent signature patterns. In addition, we also use the redistribution of training data points, the supervised hierarchical grouping of clusters, and the removal of outliers as the post-processing approaches to adjust the cluster structure. These approaches overcome the sensitivity of pattern structure to the input order of training data, a common problem to incremental algorithms, and thus make CCAS a robust algorithm.

## 2   A Brief Review of Clustering and Instance-Based Learning

Cluster analysis places data points into clusters based on their similarity. Cluster analysis relies on attribute values of data points to partition data points into clusters such that a given objective function is optimized. Among well-known heuristics algorithms are hierarchical clustering algorithms and partitioning clustering algorithms such as the $K$-means method [6]. For example, the hierarchical clustering algorithm uses a nested sequence of partitions, which can be agglomerative or divisive. Partitioning algorithms construct a partition of the data points into clusters such that the data points in a cluster are more similar to each other than to the data points in different clusters. Both the hierarchical and partitioning clustering algorithms require a complete matrix of pair-wise distances between all data points before the clustering can proceed. This creates difficulty in incremental learning that must update clusters when new data points become available, and is not scalable when we deal with large amounts of data.

A simple way of incrementally clustering data points is to process data points one by one and group the next data point into an existing cluster that is closest to this data point. However, there exists a problem of "local bias of input order". When a new data point is incorporated, the existing clusters only give the distribution of past data points. Therefore different input orders of the training data points produce different cluster structures. Recently, the methods applied by [16,2,12,4] to enable scalable, incremental learning have been reported to overcome this problem. In grid-based clustering method the data space is partitioned into a number of non-overlapping regions or grids. A histogram is then constructed to describe the density of the data points in each grid cell. Only data points in the same grid cell can be clustered together. Subspace clustering is a grid-based method. It is a bottom-up method of finding dense units in lower dimensional subspaces and merging them to find dense clusters in higher dimensional subspaces. This method is based on the concept that if a dense cell exists in $k$ dimensions then all its projections in a subset of $k$ dimensions are also dense. Density-based clustering uses a local cluster criterion. It requires that a cluster should contain a certain number of points within some radius. Hence, density-based methods consider clusters as regions of data points with high density, and clusters are separated by regions of data with low density or noise.

CCAS is built on a number of concepts in the above scalable cluster analysis and instance-based classification [10], together with several innovative concepts that we develop. Different from other clustering algorithms, CCAS is a supervised learning algorithm. Compared with instance-based learning, it improves learning accuracy and scalability by the use of clusters instead of original instances.

## 3   CCAS Algorithm

### 3.1   Cluster Representation and Distance Measures

Following the notation in the previous section, each data record, with the attribute vector $X$ in $p$ dimensions and the target variable $Y$, is a data point in a $p$-dimensional space. Each attribute or predictor variable is numeric or nominal. $Y$ can be a binary variable with value 0 or 1, or a multi-category nominal variable. $Y$ is known for each record in training data. In classification, $Y$ is determined from the attribute vector. In this paper, we only consider numeric attributes and binary target variable. Variations of CCAS for dealing with other types of predictor variables and target variable will be presented in future reports.

In CCAS, a cluster $L$ containing a number of data points is represented by the centroid (with coordinates $XL$) of all the data points in it, the number of data points $(N_L)$, and the target class $(YL)$. The distance from a data point to a cluster can be calculated using different distance measures. The weighted Euclidean distance is used in this study of applying CCAS to intrusion detection:

$$d(X,L) = \sqrt{\sum_{i=1}^{p}(X_i - XL_i)^2 r_{iY}^2} \qquad (1)$$

where $X_i$ and $XL_i$ are the coordinates of the data point $X$ and the cluster $L$'s centroid in the $i$th dimension, and $r_{iY}$ is the correlation coefficient between the prediction variable $X_i$ and the target variable $Y$.

In CCAS, we also use the distance between two clusters. This is calculated using the above distance measure except that the coordinates of a data point are replaced by the coordinates of a cluster centroid.

## 3.2 Training – Supervised Clustering

We need to group $N$ training data points into clusters, supervised by the target variable information. CCAS performs a grid-based non-hierarchical clustering based on the distance information as well as the target class information of data points. There are two steps involved.

**Data Space Division.** Firstly we divide the space of data points into grid cells. Each dimension is divided into a set of intervals along the range limited by the minimum and maximum values appearing in the training data points. The whole space is separated into "cubic" cells indexed by these intervals. Each data point or cluster belongs to one grid cell and can be assigned a reference index.

Obviously we bring in subjective impact because of the introduction of a parameter, i.e., the number of grid intervals in each dimension. How to choose this parameter makes difference on the performance of this algorithm. Different training may have different data points and distribution, and thus should have different settings of this parameter. The number of intervals can be different for each dimension and unequal intervals could be used in one dimension. In our study and experimentation, we simplify our work by using a same number of equal grid intervals for all dimensions. After a set of experiments, we choose one best setting of 11 intervals in the experimentation.

**Incremental and Supervised Clustering.** We use a heuristic to absorb data points one by one into a cluster structure, supervised by the target class information. The clustering procedures are shown in the pseudo program code below.

Basically, we search the existing clusters to look for the nearest cluster to each coming data point in the same grid cell. If this nearest cluster has the same target class as this data point, this data point is adopted into this cluster and the centroid is updated. If there is no cluster in the grid cell or the target class of the nearest cluster is different, a new cluster is created with this data point as the centroid and has the same target class. This process repeats until all data points in the training data set are incorporated into the cluster structure.

```
For each data point X in training data
     Calculate the grid index for X;
     For each existing cluster L
               If X and L have the same grid index
               determine if L is the nearest cluster to X;
     End;
     If there is a nearest cluster L with same class as X
               incorporate X into L;
               update the centroid coordinates of L;
               increment the number of points in L by 1;
        Else
               create a new cluster containing only X;
               its centroid is X;
               its target class is same as the label of X;
End;
```

## 3.3  Post-processing of the Cluster Structure

As described, at any time, the existing cluster structure reflects only a local view of the training data points that have been processed. Presenting the data points in a different order may result in a quite different cluster structure, and consequently different performance in classifying new data. To improve the robustness, we use additional steps to post-process the above cluster structure, shown in the table.

**Table 1.** Problems addressed by the additional steps and the grid-based clustering method.

|                      | Incremental learning | Scalability | Robustness |
|----------------------|:--------------------:|:-----------:|:----------:|
| Grid-based clustering | ✓ | ✓ | ✓ |
| Redistribution |  |  | ✓ |
| Supervised Grouping |  | ✓ | ✓ |
| Outlier removal |  |  | ✓ |

**Redistribution of Training Data Points.** Using the redistribution method, all data points in the training data set are clustered again using the existing clusters as the seed clusters. The clustering procedure is same, except that when a seed cluster is found to be the nearest cluster to a data point, the seed cluster is discarded and is replaced with a new cluster with the data point as the centroid. In the redistribution, we allow new clusters to emerge and thus allow adjustment of the cluster structure. Obviously this redistribution process can be repeated many times. Classification performance is expected to improve with repetition but at computation cost. Our experiments show that usually one time of redistribution is sufficient for improving robustness.

**Supervised Grouping of Clusters.** A natural cluster may correspond to several produced clusters falling into different grid cells in a neighborhood. Very like a traditional hierarchical clustering algorithm, we use a supervised grouping procedure to check if any two clusters nearest to each other have the same target class and thus can be grouped into one cluster. In this grouping procedure, a single linkage method [6] is used in calculating the distance between two clusters, where the distance between two clusters is defined as the distance between their nearest "points", the original clusters in our case. The application of the supervised hierarchical clustering algorithm to the original clusters not only improves the robustness of the cluster structure but also reduces the number of clusters.

**Removal of Outliers.** Clusters that have very few data points may represent noises in training data samples and thus outliers. Hence, clusters with fewer data points than a threshold value could be removed. The threshold on the minimum number of data points that a cluster must have can be chosen based on the average number of data points in the produced clusters. However this threshold is closely dependent on the specific training data. For example, there may be very few instances of certain type of attack. This threshold value can be different for clusters with different target classes. In this study of application to intrusion detection data, we set this threshold value to 2, based on a set of experiments.

## 3.4  The Working Flow

The following figure shows the five phases used in our application to intrusion detection. Phase 1 is necessary because we need to calculate the correlation coefficients and information entropies used in the distance measure and record the value range of each predictor variable. In phase 3, we use the output from the grid-based clustering in phase 2 as the seed clusters to redistribute the training data points in order to get a more accurate cluster structure. In phase 4, we first apply the supervised grouping. After this, outliers become more obvious and are removed. We apply the supervised grouping in phase 5 again to get a more compact and accurate cluster structure.

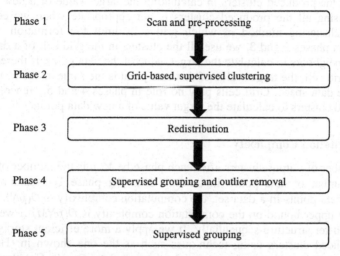

**Fig. 1.** Workflow in our application, which uses two rounds of supervised grouping.

CCAS supports the incremental update of the clusters with new training data. We easily see that each approach could function independently, linked by the input and output clusters. The initial clustering and redistribution are incremental algorithms. The outlier removal method does not impact incremental learning. The supervised grouping changes the original cluster structure. But we could still use the new cluster structure to incrementally incorporate the new data. Another advantage of CCAS is that it easily supports the local adjustment of the cluster structure. Thus we could implement and maintain models in a parallel computing environment. The above two features bring the flexibility in the management of intrusion detection system.

## 3.5  Classification

In training the data points are mapped into a cluster structure with clusters of different classes. In classification, we use these clusters to distinguish intrusive activities from normal activities. Based on instance-based classification, we classify a new data point by comparing the data point with the clusters. We assign the distance-weighted average of the target values of the $k$ nearest clusters, $L_1, ..., L_k$, to the target value of the data point $X$ as follows:

$$W^j = \frac{1}{d^2(X,L^j)}, \qquad Y = \frac{\sum_{j=1}^{k} YL^j W^j}{\sum_{j=1}^{k} W^j} \qquad (2)$$

where $L_j$ is the $j$th nearest cluster, $W^j$ is the weight for the cluster $L^j$ based on its distance to $X$; the target class values of this cluster and $X$ are $YL^j$ and $Y$. $Y$ falls in $[0,1]$ to describe the closeness of this data point to the two target classes of 0 and 1.

There are differences in the classification stage after each of the major phases. We may use all the produced clusters in calculating the target value of a new data point. However, using all the produced clusters is not appropriate when we consider the grid-based clustering method in which grid cells limit the formation of clusters. Therefore, in phases 2 and 3, we use all the clusters in the grid cell of a data point as the nearest neighbors to calculate the target value of the data point. If there is no cluster in this grid cell, the target value of this data point is the same as the nearest cluster in the entire data space. Grid cells play no role in phases 4 and 5. Hence, we use all the produced clusters to calculate the target value of a new data point.

### 3.6  Computation Complexity

Let the number of output clusters after each phase be $M$. $p$ is the number of attributes. $N$ is the number of data points in training data. For phase 1 - scanning and pre-processing data points in a data set, the computation complexity is $O(pN)$. For phases 2 and 3, the upper bound on the computation complexity is $O(pNM)$ if we search the produced cluster structure sequentially. If we apply a more efficient storage structure of the produced clusters using techniques such as the one shown in (Huang et al, 1992), the computation complexity can be improved to $O(pN)$. For the supervised grouping of clusters in phases 4 and 5, the computation complexity has a constant as the upper bound, depending on the number of input clusters. The complexity of computing pairwise distances of clusters traditional hierarchical clustering is $O(M_I(M_I-1)/2)$, where $M_I$ is the number of initial clusters. In our implementation, the computation takes less time because many distances are not used and can be ignored. The computation complexity of removing outliers in phase 4 is $O(M)$. The computation complexity of classifying a data point is $O(pM)$. Again this computation complexity can be reduced to $O(p)$ if we use a more efficient technique to store and search the cluster structure.

## 4  Application to Intrusion Detection

### 4.1  Data Representation

The data used in this application consist of computer audit records for a sequence of audit events by the Basic Security Module (BSM) from a host machine with a Solaris operating system. Each audit record has a number of attributes, including event type, user ID, process ID, command type, time, remote IP address, and so on. The target class of an audit event is 1 if the event is from an attack and 0 otherwise.

In this study, we use only the information of event type from each audit record. It is discovered that the short sequences of audit event types, especially those produced from system calls, made by a program during its normal executions are very consistent, and different from the sequences of its abnormal executions as well as the executions of other programs [3]. Therefore a data set containing these normal sequences can be used as the baseline of the normal behavior of a program, and as the basis to detect anomalies. This also provides the foundation for signature recognition.

There are in total 284 different types of audit events in this Solaris operating system. These audit events include system calls such as those operations to access files, directories, or other system resources, and events generated by application software. We use 284 attribute variables to represent their frequencies respectively. Given a stream of audit events, we use an exponentially weighted moving average (EWMA) technique [11] to obtain a smoothed frequency distribution of every event type in the recent past of the current audit event, using the following formula:

$$\begin{cases} X_i(t) = \lambda \times 1 + (1 - \lambda) \times X_i(t-1) \text{ if the current event is the ith event type} \\ X_i(t) = \lambda \times 0 + (1 - \lambda) \times X_i(t-1) \text{ if the current event is not the ith event type} \end{cases} \quad (3)$$

where $X_i(t)$ is the smoothed observation value of the $i^{th}$ predictor variable for the current event, and $\lambda$ is a smoothing constant which determines the decay rate.

With this EWMA method, we add the temporal characteristic into the values of the predictor variables. In our study, we initialize $X_i(0)$ to be 0 for $i = 1,...,284$. We let $\lambda$ be 0.3 -- a common value for the smoothing constant [11]. Hence, for each event in the training and testing data set, we obtain a vector of $(X_1,..., X_{284})$.

## 4.2  Training and Testing Data

We use the MIT Lincoln Laboratory's 2000 DARPA Intrusion Detection Evaluation Data (http://ideval.ll.mit.edu/) to create our training and testing data. The data are generated in a local-area network (LAN) at the MIT Lincoln Laboratory by simulating activities in a typical U.S. Air Force LAN. The data includes several phases of a distributed denial of service (DDoS) attack. This attack scenario is carried out over multiple network sessions. These sessions have been grouped into 5 attack phases, over the course of which the attacker probes, breaks in via some Solaris vulnerability, installs Trojan DDoS software, and finally launches a DDoS attack. There are 15 normal sessions and 7 attack sessions in the data stream from the host machine called "Mill," and 63 normal and 4 attack sessions in the other data stream from host machine "Pascal". All the data records in a normal session have target value of 0 while they have target value 1 in intrusive sessions. The sessions are arranged in a sequential mode, i.e., the data points of different sessions are not mixed in time. Each of the two event streams has over a hundred thousand audit records. There are 104,907 events in the Mill data set. Among them, there are 36,036 intrusive events, and all other events are normal. There are 114,082 events in the Pascal data set. Among them, there are 32,327 intrusive events, and all other events are normal. We use the data from Pascal as the training data and the data from Mill as the testing data. In this way, we build up the signatures from the data collected on one machine and try to detect the attacks when they are applied in a similar scenario.

To examine the robustness of CCAS, we use two different input orders of the training data. In the 2000 DARPA Intrusion Detection Evaluation Data, the attack sessions are mixed with normal sessions. In addition to the original input order, we create a reversed input order by reversing the order of sessions while maintaining the order of audit events in each session. Since we do not change the order of audit events in a session, the coordinates of data points (frequency vectors) keep the same values as the original input order. We refer to the original and reversed input orders as input orders 1 and 2 respectively.

## 4.3   Analysis Method

In this study the target value of each audit record in the testing data falls in [0, 1] and indicates the intrusiveness of the corresponding audit event. Given a signal threshold, we signal an event as intrusive if the target value is greater than or equal to this signal threshold; otherwise we claim the event as normal. A signal on a truly normal event is a false alarm. A signal on a truly intrusive event is a hit. A false alarm rate is the ratio of the number of signals on all the normal events in the testing data to the total number of normal events in the testing data. A hit rate is the ratio of the number of signals on all the intrusive events in the testing data to the total number of intrusive events in the testing data. Hence, given a signal threshold, we obtain a pair of the false alarm rate and the hit rate. We then plot a ROC (Receiver Operating Characteristics) curve using pairs of false alarm rate and hit rate that are generated by varying the value of the signal threshold. In a ROC curve, $X$-axis represents the false alarm rate while $Y$-axis represents the hit rate. The closer the curve is to the top-left corner (100% hit rate/0% false alarm rate) of the plot, the better the detection performance. Such a ROC analysis is based on the target value of each audit event in the testing data for evaluating detection performance on individual audit events. Hence, it is called the event-based ROC.

However, it is not appropriate to detect intrusions in this data based on individual events, because the same audit event may be common in both normal and intrusive activities. To reduce the false alarm rate as much as possible, it is important to examine aggregate sets of individual events.

If we consider the audit record captures the features of normal and intrusive activities adequately, and a functional intrusion detection algorithm can distinguish normal or intrusive activities by the difference of target values of audit records representing them, in most cases this predicted target value of those intrusive data records should be greater than that of normal data records. As we discussed before, audit records are arranged into sessions. All the audit records in one session are either normal or intrusive. So we could comfortably assume that a good performance will show higher predicted target values for most audit data records in an intrusive session than the values of audit data records in a normal session. Based on this assumption, we use a statistic on all the data records of a session, called signal ratio, instead of the predicted target value of an individual event, as the more helpful information in classifying sessions. The session-based ROC analysis includes the following steps:

1. Calculate a signal threshold to determine if we should signal an individual event based on its predicted target value. There are several ways to determine this signal threshold. In our study we calculate the average $\mu$ and the standard deviation $\sigma$ of predicted target values for all the normal events in the training data. The signal

threshold is set as $\mu+a\sigma$, because we are mainly interested in detecting a large predicted target value close to 1 which indicates a possible intrusion, where $a$ is a coefficient to adjust the signal threshold.

2. Compute a "session table" containing a session signal ratio for each session. For each session we calculate the ratio of the number of signals to the total number of events as the session signal ratio for a given signal threshold.

3. Similarly, plot the ROC curve based on the session signal ratios of all the sessions in the testing data.

We expect that session signal ratios for normal sessions are lower than session signal ratios for intrusive sessions. In this study, we experiment with various values of $a$, and it appears that small $a$ values of 0.5, 0.6, and 0.7 produce the best performance from our experimentation. This possibly is due to the fact that normal clusters dominate the produced cluster structure because of the majority of normal data points in the training data. This feature makes the predicted target value of intrusive points in testing data shift to the average of $\mu$ calculated for all normal data points in training data.

For the different data input orders used to examine the robustness of CCAS, the best way should be investigating the generated cluster structures directly. However since we have a high-dimensional data space in this study, and we get quite a few clusters from each phase, such "best" way is not feasible in practice. In our study we will compare the performance to provide a picture about the robustness of CCAS.

## 4.4  Result Analysis

Figure 2 shows the ROC analysis of the testing results from phases 2, 3, 4, and 5 using input order 1 of the training data. The grid-based clustering and the post-processing redistribution in phases 2 and 3 respectively detect only about 60% of the attack sessions when no false alarms are produced on normal sessions. This indicates that 5 of the 7 attack sessions are detected. After phase 4 using the supervised grouping and the outlier removal, we obtain a 100% detection rate with no false alarms for two signal thresholds. After phase 5, all the three signal thresholds produce the 100% detection rate and the 0% false alarm rate.

In Figure 3, we can see that the input order of the training data has impact on the grid-based clustering in phase 2 and the redistribution in phase 3. The ROC curves for input order 2 are worse than those for input order 1, especially in phase 3. After phase 4, the detection performance becomes a little better. One signal threshold produces a detection rate of a little above 70% without false alarms. After phase 5, again two signal thresholds produce the 100% hit rate and the 0% false alarm rate. Hence, the additional post-processing steps in CCAS have made detection performance of CCAS robust to the different input orders of the training data.

## 5  Conclusion

In this paper we present CCAS -- a scalable data mining algorithm with incremental learning ability. This algorithm uses several post-processing approaches to improve the robustness. CCAS is tested using a large set of computer audit data for intrusion detection. The results show significant improvement in detection performance and robustness to input order of training data and noises.

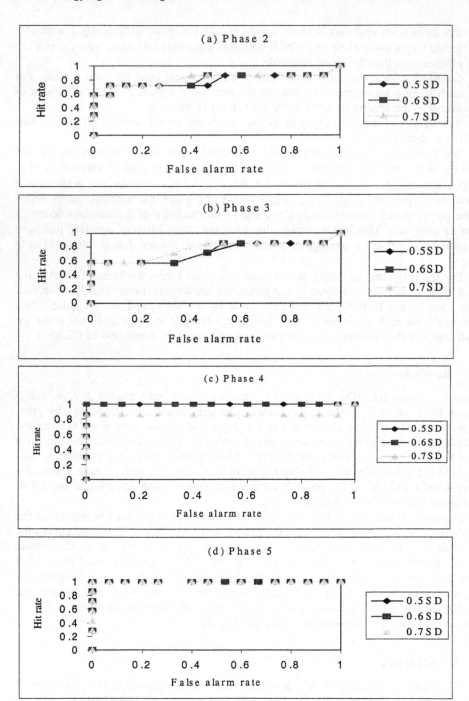

**Fig. 2.** ROC analysis for CCAS using 11 grid intervals and input order 1.

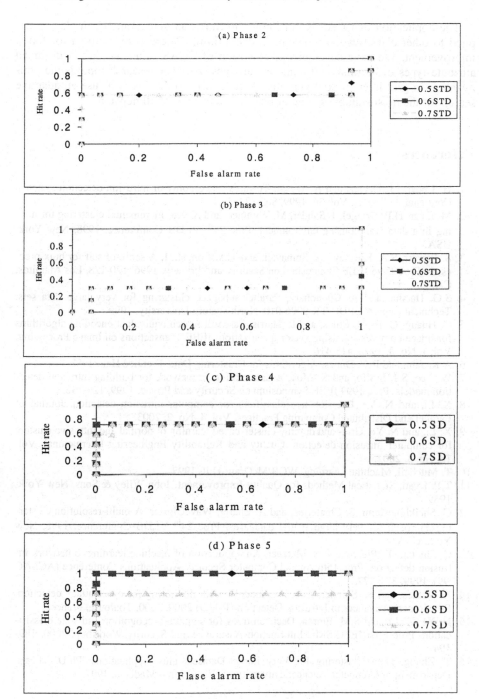

**Fig. 3.** ROC analysis for CCAS using 11 grid intervals and input order 2.

The application of CCAS is not limited to intrusion detection. It can also be applied to other classification problems in data mining. There is more room for future improvement. We have developed an extension of CCAS to handle data with mixed attribute types of nominal and numeric variables. Another research topic is the optimization in grid interval configuration. A good way to do this is to use an adaptive search for the most suitable setting of this parameter in each dimension.

# References

1. H. Debar, M. Dacier, and A. Wespi, Towards a taxonomy of intrusion-detection systems, Computer Networks. Vol. 31. 1999, 805-822.
2. M. Ester, H.P. Kriegel, J. Sander, M. Wimmer, and X. Xu, Incremental clustering for mining in a data warehousing environment. Proc 24th VLDB Conference. 1998, New York, USA.
3. S. Forrest, S.A. Hofmeyr, A. Somayaji, and T.A. Longstaff, A sense of self for unix processes. Proc 1996 IEEE Symposium on Security and Privacy. 1996, 120-128, Los Alamitos, CA.
4. S.G. Harsha, and A. Choudhary, Parallel subspace clustering for very large data sets. Technical Report, CPDC-TR-9906-010. Northwestern University, 1999.
5. C. Huang, Q. Bi, R. Stiles, and R. Harris, Fast full search equivalent encoding algorithms for image compression using vector quantization. IEEE Transactions on Image Processing, Vol. 1, No. 3. 1992, 413-416.
6. A.K. Jain, and R.C. Dubes, Algorithms for Clustering Data. Prentice Hall, 1988.
7. W. Lee, S.J. Stolfo, and K. Mok, A data mining framework for building intrusion detection models. Proc 1999 IEEE Symposium on Security and Privac. 1999, 120-132.
8. X. Li, and N. Ye, Decision tree classifiers for computer intrusion detection. Journal of Parallel and Distributed Computing Practices, Vol. 4, No. 2. 2003.
9. X. Li, and N. Ye, Grid- and dummy-cluster-based learning of normal and intrusive clusters for computer intrusion detection. Quality and Reliability Engineering International, Vol. 18, No. 3. 2002.
10. T. Mitchell, Machine Learning. WCB/McGraw-Hill, 1997.
11. T.P. Ryan, Statistical Methods for Quality Improvement. John Wiley & Sons, New York, 1989.
12. G. Sheikholeslami, S. Chatterjee, and A. Zhang, WaveCluster: A multi-resolution clustering approach for very large spatial databases. Proc 24th VLDB Conference. 1998, New York, USA.
13. C. Sinclair, L. Pierce, and S. Matzner, An application of machine learning to network intrusion detection. Proc 15th Annual Computer Security Applications Conference (ACSAC '99). 1999, 371-377.
14. A. Valdes, and K. Skinner, Adaptive, model-based monitoring for cyber attack detection. Proc Recent Advances in Intrusion Detection (RAID) 2000. 2000, Toulouse, France.
15. N. Ye, X. Li, and S.M. Emran, Decision trees for signature recognition and state classification. Proc First IEEE SMC Information Assurance and Security Workshop. 2000, 189-194.
16. T. Zhang, Data Clustering for Very Large Datasets plus Applications. Ph.D. Thesis. Department of Computer Science, University of Wisconsin – Madison, 1997.

# The Optimal Deployment of Filters
# to Limit Forged Address Attacks
# in Communication Networks*

Enock Chisonge Mofya and Jonathan Cole Smith

Department of Systems and Industrial Engineering
The University of Arizona
P.O. Box 210020
mofya@email.arizona.edu
cole@sie.arizona.edu

**Abstract.** We consider forged address attacks in communication networks, wherein an attacking node forges the address of communication requests sent to a victim node. Unless the victim can ascertain the origin of the attack, it must cease to respond to communication requests until the attack subsides. We examine the problem of identifying a minimum cardinality subset of nodes on a network, such that placing route-based filters on these nodes provides a prescribed level of security. We model the problem as an integer program and illustrate its performance on randomly generated networks. Next, we develop a greedy heuristic to deploy filters in these networks, and compare its solution quality to that of the integer programming approach. These findings are then used to motivate both the importance of addressing this problem by optimal techniques and to motivate future research approaches for solving such problems.

## 1 Introduction

In this paper, we consider the following scenario that describes a class of communication network attacks. Let a communication network be represented by a directed graph $G(N, A)$ with node set $N = \{1, ..., n\}$ and arc set $A$. A node $s \in N$ may send a series of communication requests (e.g., network packets) to another node $d \in N$, but with a forged address of $o \in N$. Node $d$ has no choice but to ignore requests from $o$, which effectively disables communication from $o$ to $d$. Should $s$ choose to forge its address using multiple false origin addresses, it can practically shut down the effective operation of node $d$ altogether.

In the context of Internet communication, these attacks are called *Denial of Service* (DoS) attacks. When the attacks simultaneously originate from several locations, they are termed Distributed Denial of Service (DDoS) attacks [2, 3]. To protect nodes against these attacks, some mechanism must be in place to verify whether or not the purported origin of a communication request matches

---

* Dr. Smith gratefully acknowledges the support of the *Defense Advanced Research Projects Agency* under Grant #N66001-01-1-8925.

H. Chen et al. (Eds.): ISI 2004, LNCS 3073, pp. 239–251, 2004.

the true origin of the request. If a node can somehow verify that the purported origin of a communication request is false, it can halt the attack and perhaps even identify the attacking node.

The general context of such problems can be envisioned as verifying the origin of communication requests. This is becoming an increasingly vital problem in situations such as ascertaining the identity of certain transmitters in hostile environments and tracing the sender of harmful packages through a postal system. These concepts also extend to the strategic deployment of sensor networks in settings such as transportation networks.

The problem of locating the attack source in the context of DDoS attacks is called *IP Traceback*, and has recently been an active area of research. Our approach is based on *route-based distributed packet filtering* [1, 6]. In this approach, a filter placed on some node in the network analyzes traffic flows entering the node via some arc. If the filter can determine that a request (or in this specific case, a packet) has forged its origin address, given its current position in the network and its destination, it drops the request from the network. Otherwise, the request continues on its path through the system. A packet flowing through several nodes in a network may have to pass many such tests, or maybe none at all, before it reaches its destination.

In this type of situation, any packet having a valid origin address will never be dropped by a filter. (This requirement is called *safety*.) However, a filter may indeed fail to drop a packet with a forged origin address, if it is impossible for a filter to prove that the origin of an incoming packet must have been forged. Moreover, each validity check that a filter makes incurs some delay in the network. Hence, we wish to minimize the number of filter placements in the network, while retaining some overall measure of security in the network.

A prior study by Armbruster, Smith, and Park [1] proved that this problem is strongly NP-hard, even when *perfect security* is enforced in the network, i.e., no node can attack any other node, using any false address. Regrettably, the authors demonstrate that many filters must typically be deployed under such stringent security systems. Instead, we may wish to simply bound the amount of work necessary for a node under attack to determine the attacking node. For instance, suppose that for any node $d$ currently under attack from purported node $o$, the true origin of the attack must come from no more than $b$ nodes. In this case, node $d$ can investigate these $b$ candidates one-by-one to ascertain which node is attacking. Accordingly, we call $b$ the *traceback number* for the address/victim pair $(o, d)$. In this paper, we identify the optimal placement of filters throughout the network, such that the traceback number of any address/victim pair is no more than $b$. (Thus, in this paper, $b$ takes on a global definition as the maximum traceback number for any such node pair.)

In the perfect security problem posed in [1] (i.e., $b = 0$), a two-stage algorithm is developed to solve the problem to optimality. In the first stage, the authors state several necessary conditions for feasible solutions to the problem. These conditions imply a preprocessing step that requires the assignment of filters to several nodes. After this processing, the problem decomposes to a set of

Minimum Vertex Cover (MVC) problems (see for instance [5]) that must be solved in a second stage. While MVC is strongly NP-hard in the worst case, many problems either do not require any second-stage solution, or require the solution of "easy" second-stage MVC instances. In fact, a greedy vertex cover heuristic employed by [6] provably yields an optimal solution for a class of practical large-scale communication network systems.

However, when generalizing this problem for traceback values of $b > 0$, the necessary conditions of Armbruster et al. [1] no longer hold true, and thus the relationship between our filter placement problem and MVC is no longer clear. Hence, a new approach must be taken to solve the problem.

The rest of the paper is organized as follows. In Sect. 2, we provide a formal statement of our problem. We then state an integer programming model to solve the problem to optimality, and describe a heuristic algorithm to quickly obtain good solutions to the problem. We report computational results on a set of randomly generated networks with varying values of $b$ in Sect. 3 to demonstrate the value of using exact optimization approaches as opposed to heuristic strategies, and the computational effort required to solve such problems to optimality. Finally, we summarize our work and examine directions for future research in Sect. 4.

## 2   Problem Statement and Algorithmic Approach

We begin in Sect. 2.1 by specifically defining the filter placement problem that we address in this paper. Following the problem statement, we describe an integer programming formulation for the problem in Sect. 2.2, and a greedy vertex-cover-based heuristic in Sect. 2.3.

### 2.1   Problem Statement and Notation

We follow the notation given in [1] to define the filter placement problem. Define the *communication set* $C \subseteq N \times N$ such that $(u, v) \in C$ if and only if node $u \in N$ is permitted to send packets to node $v \in N$. We say that $C$ is complete if $(u, v) \in C$ for all node pairs $u \in N$ and $v \in N - \{u\}$. Packets sent to any node $d \in N$ with purported address $o$ such that $(o, d) \notin C$ will automatically be dropped by the network without the need for a filter. The routing policy of the network that ignores packets with $(o, d)$ pairs outside the set $C$ is referred to as a "trivial filter."

Next, let $R$ be a function defined on all node pairs $(o, d) \in C$, such that $R(o, d)$ returns a set of paths that a packet from $o$ to $d$ may take. For the purposes of this paper, we will assume that only one path is specified for each node pair. (In fact, this is not a restricting assumption on our methodology, although the complexity that we claim for some of our operations does depend on the number of paths that exist between node pairs.) We denote a set of nodes in a path $p$ by $N(p)$ and a set of arcs in $p$ by $A(p)$.

We can consider two types of filters for deployment in a network: *maximal* and *semi-maximal* filters. Although the algorithms described in this paper are valid for either choice, we focus on maximal filters in this study. A maximal filter can be defined by the following function:

$$F^m(o, a, d) = \begin{cases} 0 & \text{if } a \in A(p) \text{ for some } p \in R(o, d) \\ 1 & \text{otherwise.} \end{cases} \tag{1}$$

The function in (1) returns a 0 if a packet travelling from $o$ to $d$ could possibly use arc $a$, and 1 otherwise. By contrast, a semi-maximal filter is defined by the function:

$$F^s(o, a) = \begin{cases} 0 & \text{if there exits a } d \text{ such that } a \in A(p) \text{ for some } p \in R(o, d) \\ 1 & \text{otherwise.} \end{cases} \tag{2}$$

The semi-maximal filter returns a 0 if $o$ could use arc $a$ when forwarding packets to *any* of its destinations. Each filter establishes a lookup table for each arc on which packets arrive. A maximal filter requires the use of $O(n^2)$-size lookup-tables, since they reference both $o$ and $d$, while semi-maximal filters require only $O(n)$-size look-up tables, since they only need to reference node $o$. However, the filtering capability of the maximal filter is more than that of the semi-maximal filter, since $F^m(o, a, d) \geq F^s(o, a)$ for all $o \in N$, $a \in N$, and $d \in N$. For example, consider a path $p \in R(o, \bar{d})$ for some $\bar{d} \in N - \{d\}$ with $a \in A(p)$ such that no path in $R(o, d)$ containing arc $a$ exists. The maximal filter will drop a packet going to $d$ with purported address $o$, since $o$ does not use arc $a$ when routing to $d$. However, the semi-maximal filter would not drop such a packet, since $o$ uses arc $a$ when routing to some path (namely, $\bar{d}$).

In this study, we assume that a filtered node may not attack other nodes, i.e., it cannot forge its origin address. We further assume that packet attributes (purported origin and destination node) may only be set by the sending node. Once the packet is sent, none of its attributes may be changed.

Given these considerations, suppose a set of filters has been deployed on the network. Define $N_{od} \subseteq N$ for all $(o, d) \in C$ to be the set of all nodes other than $o$ that can send packets to $d$ with purported address $o$, such that no filters established on the network will drop these packets. For a given traceback number $b \geq 0$, the *Generalized Minimum Filter Placement Problem* (GMFPP) identifies a minimum cardinality subset of nodes $F$ on the network such that placing filters on $F$ ensures that $|N_{od}| \leq b$ for all $(o, d) \in C$. Observe that $b \in \{0, ..., n - 2\}$, where $b = 0$ represents the perfect security case, and $b = n - 2$ means that there exists a node $d \in N$ such that any node $s \in N - \{o, d\}$ can attack $d$ using address $o$ (also, this implies that $(s, d) \in C$ $\forall s \in N - \{d\}$). The practical nature of this problem is that any node $d$ under attack with purported address $o$ can reply to the attack by investigating only the $b$ suspects that may be launching the attack.

We provide two solution methodologies to the GMFPP: a 0/1 integer programming model that can be solved by the branch-and-bound method, and a modified greedy vertex cover heuristic. The integer programming model guarantees an optimal solution, but becomes computationally prohibitive as the problem size grows large. On the other hand, our heuristic is capable of providing solutions to large problem instances in polynomial time, but without any guarantee on optimality.

## 2.2   Integer Programming Model

In this section, we model the GMFPP as a 0/1 integer program. Consider a packet originating from $s \in N$ with destination $d \in N$ having a forged address $o \in N$, such that $(o, d) \in C$ and $(s, d) \in C$. Given our filtering mechanism, define the set of nodes $G_{sod}$ such that $v \in G_{sod}$ if and only if a filter placed on node $v$ will drop these packets. Observe that $s \in G_{sod}$ for all possible choices of $o$ and $d$, since a filtered node cannot attack other nodes.

To compute the set of nodes in $G_{sod}$, we compare the path $p_s$ taken from $s$ to $d$, to the path $p_o$ taken from $o$ to $d$. All nodes that are on path $p_s$ but not on $p_o$ are added to the set $G_{sod}$. Furthermore, for a node $v$ belonging to both $p_s$ and $p_o$, we check to see if the node that precedes $v$ in $p_s$ is the same node that precedes $v$ in $p_o$. If the two nodes are different, $v$ is added to $G_{sod}$, since a maximal filter placed on $v$ would indeed be able to stop this attack. The complexity for computing $G_{sod}$ is $O(n)$, and thus the computation of all $G_{sod}$ sets is $O(n^4)$.

Given this information, we define binary variables $y_i$ for each node $i \in N$ in the network. Our integer program will set $y_i = 1$ if a filter is placed on node $i$ in the solution, and $y_i = 0$ otherwise. We also define a set of auxiliary variables $w_{sod}$ for each possible attack on node $d \in N$ by node $s \in N$ with forged address $o \in N$, with $o \neq s$, $(s, d) \in C$, and $(o, d) \in C$. The variable $w_{sod}$ equals to 1 if an attack on $d$ by $s$ using forged address of $o$ might not be stopped by the set of deployed filters, and equals to 0 if this attack will definitely be stopped by a filter. (The $w$-variables allow us to verify that we have obeyed the traceback number restrictions. The rather unusual definition of these variables is addressed following the statement of this formulation.) We formulate the GMFPP as:

$$\text{Minimize} \sum_{i \in N} y_i \tag{3a}$$

$$\text{s.t.} \sum_{s:(s,d) \in C, o \neq s} w_{sod} \leq b, \; \forall (o, d) \in C \tag{3b}$$

$$w_{sod} + \sum_{i \in G_{sod}} y_i \geq 1 \; \forall (o, d) \in C, \forall s \neq o : (s, d) \in C \tag{3c}$$

$$y_i, \; w_{sod} \text{ binary.} \tag{3d}$$

The objective function (3a) minimizes the total number of filters placed in the network. Constraints (3b) limit the number of nodes $s$ that can successfully send packets to node $d$ with purported address $o \neq s$ to at most the traceback number $b$. Constraints (3c) state that node $s$ must be allowed to attack node $d$ by sending packets with purported address $o$, unless a filter is placed on one of the nodes in $G_{sod}$ that prevents such an attack. Finally, (3d) state the logical restrictions on the variables $y$ and $w$.

The integer programming formulation given in (3) must yield an optimal objective function value and set of filter placements. However, it is possible that some $w_{sod}$ variable equals to 1 in an optimal solution for a node $o$ that actually can *not* attack $d$ using forged address $s$. To see this, observe that if $w_{sod} = 0$ for some $(s, o, d)$ node triple defined for (3c), then $\sum_{i \in G_{sod}} y_i \geq 1$ necessarily, and thus cannot attack $d$ using address $o$. However, examining the converse of this statement, it is possible that even though $\sum_{i \in G_{sod}} y_i \geq 1$, $w_{sod} = 1$ is still possible. However, this situation only occurs if the traceback constraint for node pair $(o, d)$ is not a binding constraint (i.e., the actual number of nodes that can attack $d$ with forged address $o$ is strictly less than $b$), which permits the optimization process to arbitrarily set $w_{sod}$ to 0 or 1.

We can address this situation, if desired, by stating the following constraints.

$$y_i + w_{sod} \leq 1 \ \forall (o, d) \in C, \ \forall s \neq o : (s, d) \in C, \ \forall i \in G_{sod}. \tag{4}$$

These constraints impose the restriction that $w_{sod} = 1$ *if and only if* $s$ can attack $d$ using address $o$. However, (4) constitutes an $O(n^4)$ set of constraints to the model, and does not affect the optimality of the filter placements. Hence, we omit these constraints in our study.

A more practical remedy to this problem would be to modify the objective function (3a) to include a term that would penalize the number of positive $w$-variables as a secondary consideration. This hierarchical approach reflects the following philosophy: first, minimize the number of filters placed in the solution, and second, out of all alternative optimal solutions, minimize the total sum of $w_{sod}$ variables. The objective function would then be given as:

$$\text{Minimize} \sum_{i \in N} M y_i + \sum_{\text{all } (s,o,d) \text{ triples}} w_{sod} \tag{5}$$

where $M$ is a value such that $M$ is a number greater than the total number of $(s, o, d)$ sets (e.g., $M = 1 + n^3$ is sufficiently large). This would force the model to ignore any solution that uses more filters than absolutely necessary, given the preemptive weight of $M$ on the number of filters selected. However, given this objective, no $w_{sod}$ will be set equal to 1 at optimality unless an attack prescribed by this triple can indeed occur (or else, a better solution would exist in which $w_{sod} = 1$). Hence, employing (5) as our objective function also serves to define $w_{sod} = 1$ if and only if an attack can occur from $o$ to $d$ using address $s$. However, such an objective function also requires the integer program to exert even more computational effort, since an additional "tie-breaking" requirement is incorporated into the model. We leave the investigation of this more complex model for future research.

Finally, note that if we implement the model with the binary restrictions on $w$ relaxed to $0 \leq w_{sod} \leq 1$, there exists a solution to this relaxed problem in which all $w$-variables are binary. The argument to verify this claim starts by observing that any optimal solution to the relaxed problem still requires binary $y$-variables. Consider any optimal solution having some fractional variable, $w_{sod} = f$. Then according to constraints (3c), we must have $y_i = 1$ for some $i \in G_{sod}$. Hence, revising this $w_{sod}$ variable to equal 0 instead of $f$ retains feasibility with respect to (3c). Furthermore, decreasing this variable value does not affect its feasibility with respect to (3b). Since the objective function (3a) does not involve any $w$-variables, this revised solution must also be optimal. (Note that if we used the objective (5) in lieu of (3a), we could use the foregoing argument to show that all $w$-variables are binary in *any* optimal solution.) This observation is important, because although the number of variables in (3c) is $O(n^3)$, only $O(n)$ of these variables are restricted to be binary, and thus the worst-case performance of this NP-hard problem is governed by $O(2^n)$ behavior rather than $O(2^{n^3})$ behavior. Hence, our implementation of the integer programming algorithm assumes that $w$-variables are continuously defined on the interval [0,1].

## 2.3   A Modified Vertex Cover Heuristic

We now describe a heuristic that estimates the solution of the GMFPP in polynomial time. The heuristic is based on a greedy vertex cover heuristic that was described in [6]. A *vertex cover* on a graph is a set of nodes $C$ such that each edge in the graph is incident to at least one node in $C$. Finding the minimum such cover is well-known to be NP-hard [4].

The heuristic that we describe below can be can be viewed as a two-phase algorithm, in which the first phase establishes filters on nodes according to a classical greedy vertex cover heuristic until either $|N(u,v)| \le b$ for all $(u,v) \in C$, or until a vertex cover is established. In the latter case, a second phase is examined in which filters are greedily placed on additional nodes until a feasible solution is determined for the problem. The algorithm is given as follows.

**Step 1.** The algorithm is initialized by setting the solution $F = \emptyset$. Convert $A$ into an undirected graph by including a single edge $(i,j)$ in $A$ if and only if either $(i,j)$ or $(j,i)$ was previously in $A$. For each $i \in N$, set $d_i$ equal to the degree of node $i$ (i.e., the number of arcs incident to node $i$). Establish a list $L$ of node pairs in the communication set $C$.

**Step 2.** If $L$ is empty, go to Step 8. Otherwise, choose the next pair $(u,v) \in L$, and execute Step 3.

**Step 3.** If $|N_{uv}| > b$, execute Step 4. Otherwise, remove $(u,v)$ from $L$ and return to Step 2.

**Step 4.** Identify node $i \in \text{argmax}_{k \in N}\{d_k\}$. If $d_i = 0$, go to Step 5, and otherwise, go to Step 6.

**Step 5.** Find a node $\ell \notin F$ such that placing a filter on $\ell$ will stop the most number of attacks on $v$ with purported address $u$. Add $\ell$ to $F$. Go to Step 7.

**Step 6.** Add node $i$ to $F$. Reduce $d_i$ and $d_j$ by 1 for all $j$ such that $(i,j) \in A$ or $(j,i) \in A$. Go to Step 7.

**Step 7.** Update $N_{uv}$, and return to Step 3.

**Step 8.** Return $F$ as the heuristically generated feasible solution to the GMFPP.

Note that the inner loop of the algorithm, consisting of Steps 4 - 7, must be executed no more than $n$ times, since a filter is located on the network at each of these iterations. The most time-consuming step in this inner loop is encountered in Step 5, which takes $O(n^2)$ operations. (The algorithm must examine all possible attacking origins, and compare the nodes on the paths from those destinations to $v$ with the path from $u$ to $v$, as done in the calculation of the $G$ sets mentioned for the integer programming model.) Hence, the overall complexity for this heuristic is $O(n^3)$.

## 3   Computational Results

In this section, we present computational results for both the integer programming model and the heuristic algorithm given in Sect. 2. In particular, we wish to obtain initial results regarding the computational time of the integer programming algorithm, and the typical degree of suboptimality encountered due to using heuristic versus optimal solutions.

We first describe the random generation of three sets of problem instances, which we solve in this section by the methods presented earlier. For each instance, we generate a graph of a given size and density. An edge is placed randomly between each pair of nodes $(i, j)$ with probability given by the specified edge density. The first set of instances was generated with 15 nodes and an edge density of 0.4. The second set of instances was generated with 20 nodes and an edge density 0.4, and lastly, the third set of instances contained 30 nodes and an edge density of 0.2. We refer to these sets of instances as "small", "medium", and "large" instance sets, respectively. For each instance set, 10 instances were generated, for a total of 30 instances.

In all the instances, we assume complete communication (i.e., each node can send packets to every other node). The routing policy $R(u, v)$ for each pair of nodes $u, v \in N$ returns a single shortest path from node $u$ to node $v$ (assuming equal weights on the edges) for all communication pairs.

All implementations were performed using the C++ programming language, and the integer programming models were implemented using CPLEX 8.1 via ILOG Concert Technology 1.3. All computations were performed on a SUN UltraSparc–III with a 900 MHz processor and 2.0GB RAM Unix machine.

As a visual illustration of the differences possible in using exact versus heuristic solutions, we solved a 13-node problem with $b = 3$ using both methods. Figure 1 shows this network topology, in which every node communicates with all other nodes along shortest paths. A minimum cardinality set of nodes that must be filtered is shown as the set of double-circled nodes in the figure. The solution obtained from the integer programming model shows that the minimum number of filters required is five.

We then solved the same problem using the heuristic algorithm, whose solution is displayed in Fig. 2. Note that the heuristic solution required two more filters than the optimal solution from the integer program, which is a significant increase for a problem of this size.

The primary issue regarding the integer programming algorithm is its practicality on solving problem instances of varying sizes. We display the average execution time and standard deviation required for solving (3) by CPLEX in Figures 3-5 for each of the three test sets, varying $b$ from its lower limit to its

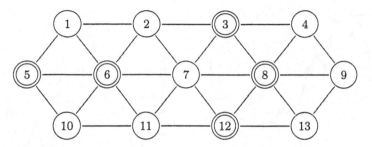

**Fig. 1.** Integer Programming Solution, with $b = 3$

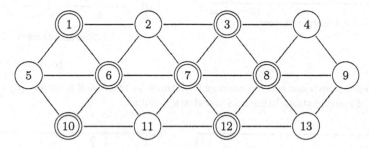

**Fig. 2.** Heuristic Solution, with $b = 3$

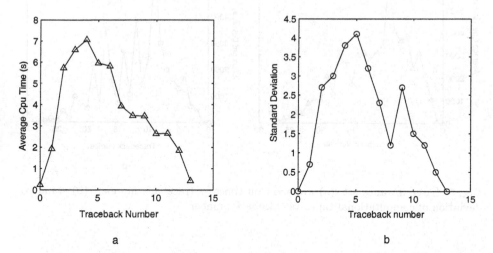

a                                                                                  b

**Fig. 3.** Small instance set. (a) average Cpu times vs traceback number. (b) standard deviation of computational times vs traceback number

upper limit. Observe the sharp rate of increase in the computational time required to solve these instances as the problem size grows from small (15 nodes) to medium (20 nodes) to large (30 nodes). Hence, without further modification to this algorithm, a heuristic strategy must be employed to solve problems larger than the ones investigated in this preliminary study.

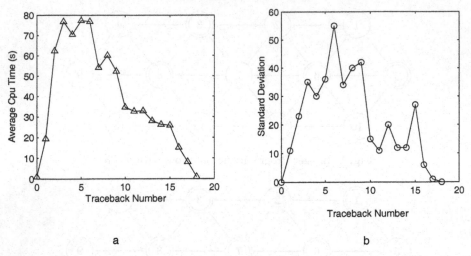

a                                   b

**Fig. 4.** Medium instance set. (a) average Cpu times vs traceback number. (b) standard deviation of computational times vs traceback number

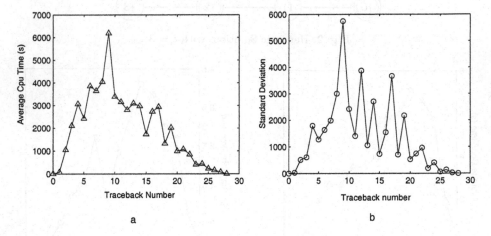

a                                   b

**Fig. 5.** Large instance set. (a) average Cpu times vs traceback number. (b) standard deviation of computational times vs traceback number

Another important observation regards the peak of the computational times when $b$ is roughly equal to 30% of $n$. This is due to the fact that few filters are in fact required when $b$ becomes moderately large, and many small subsets of $N$ serve as alternative optimal solutions. (As is typical of most integer programming problems, the vast majority of computational effort is spent in proving the optimality of a solution obtained very early in the algorithm.) On the other hand, when $b$ is very small, the problem is easier to solve, because several filters are fixed early in a preprocessing stage. The truly difficult problems seem to be those for which $b$ lies in between these values. Given the motivation for heuristic

**Table 1.** Quality of heuristic solutions compared to optimal solutions for the small instance set

| $b$ | $z_1^*$ | $z_2^*$ | $z_3^*$ | $z_4^*$ | $z_5^*$ | $z_6^*$ | $z_7^*$ | $z_8^*$ | $z_9^*$ | $z_{10}^*$ | 0 | 1 | 2 |
|---|---|---|---|---|---|---|---|---|---|---|---|---|---|
| | | | Optimal Number of Filters | | | | | | | | Suboptimality | | |
| 0 | 11 | 12 | 12 | 10 | 10 | 12 | 13 | 13 | 12 | 11 | 3 | 5 | 2 |
| 1 | 8 | 9 | 8 | 8 | 9 | 9 | 9 | 9 | 10 | 9 | 5 | 3 | 2 |
| 2 | 7 | 8 | 7 | 6 | 8 | 7 | 8 | 8 | 8 | 7 | 8 | 2 | 0 |
| 3 | 6 | 7 | 6 | 6 | 7 | 6 | 7 | 7 | 7 | 7 | 7 | 3 | 0 |
| 4 | 5 | 6 | 6 | 5 | 6 | 5 | 6 | 6 | 6 | 6 | 5 | 5 | 0 |
| 5 | 5 | 5 | 5 | 5 | 6 | 4 | 5 | 6 | 6 | 5 | 5 | 5 | 0 |
| 6 | 5 | 5 | 4 | 3 | 5 | 4 | 5 | 5 | 5 | 4 | 5 | 4 | 1 |
| 7 | 4 | 4 | 4 | 3 | 4 | 4 | 4 | 5 | 4 | 4 | 4 | 6 | 0 |
| 8 | 4 | 3 | 3 | 3 | 4 | 3 | 4 | 4 | 4 | 3 | 5 | 4 | 1 |
| 9 | 3 | 3 | 3 | 3 | 3 | 3 | 3 | 4 | 4 | 3 | 6 | 4 | 0 |
| 10 | 3 | 3 | 3 | 2 | 3 | 3 | 3 | 3 | 3 | 3 | 7 | 3 | 0 |
| 11 | 2 | 2 | 2 | 2 | 3 | 3 | 2 | 3 | 3 | 2 | 8 | 2 | 0 |
| 12 | 2 | 2 | 2 | 2 | 2 | 2 | 2 | 2 | 2 | 2 | 10 | 0 | 0 |
| 13 | 0 | 0 | 0 | 0 | 0 | 0 | 0 | 0 | 0 | 0 | 10 | 0 | 0 |

**Table 2.** Quality of heuristic solutions compared to optimal solutions for the medium instance set

| $b$ | $z_1^*$ | $z_2^*$ | $z_3^*$ | $z_4^*$ | $z_5^*$ | $z_6^*$ | $z_7^*$ | $z_8^*$ | $z_9^*$ | $z_{10}^*$ | 0 | 1 | 2 | 3 |
|---|---|---|---|---|---|---|---|---|---|---|---|---|---|---|
| | | | Optimal Number of Filters | | | | | | | | Suboptimality | | | |
| 0 | 20 | 16 | 16 | 16 | 17 | 18 | 17 | 17 | 16 | 15 | 5 | 3 | 0 | 2 |
| 1 | 12 | 14 | 13 | 13 | 12 | 13 | 14 | 14 | 13 | 12 | 4 | 4 | 2 | 0 |
| 2 | 11 | 12 | 11 | 11 | 11 | 11 | 12 | 12 | 11 | 10 | 3 | 7 | 0 | 0 |
| 3 | 10 | 11 | 10 | 10 | 9 | 10 | 11 | 10 | 11 | 9 | 2 | 8 | 0 | 0 |
| 4 | 9 | 10 | 9 | 9 | 8 | 8 | 10 | 9 | 10 | 8 | 1 | 6 | 3 | 0 |
| 5 | 8 | 9 | 9 | 9 | 7 | 8 | 9 | 9 | 9 | 7 | 1 | 6 | 3 | 0 |
| 6 | 7 | 9 | 7 | 8 | 7 | 7 | 8 | 8 | 8 | 6 | 0 | 3 | 6 | 1 |
| 7 | 7 | 8 | 7 | 7 | 6 | 6 | 8 | 7 | 7 | 6 | 0 | 5 | 4 | 1 |
| 8 | 7 | 7 | 6 | 7 | 6 | 6 | 7 | 6 | 6 | 6 | 1 | 4 | 4 | 1 |
| 9 | 6 | 7 | 5 | 6 | 5 | 5 | 6 | 6 | 5 | 5 | 0 | 5 | 4 | 0 |
| 10 | 5 | 6 | 5 | 5 | 5 | 5 | 6 | 5 | 5 | 5 | 1 | 4 | 3 | 2 |
| 11 | 4 | 5 | 5 | 5 | 4 | 5 | 5 | 5 | 4 | 4 | 1 | 3 | 3 | 3 |
| 12 | 4 | 5 | 4 | 5 | 4 | 4 | 5 | 5 | 4 | 4 | 1 | 4 | 3 | 2 |
| 13 | 4 | 4 | 4 | 4 | 4 | 4 | 4 | 4 | 4 | 4 | 1 | 4 | 5 | 0 |
| 14 | 3 | 4 | 4 | 4 | 4 | 4 | 4 | 4 | 3 | 3 | 1 | 8 | 1 | 0 |
| 15 | 3 | 4 | 3 | 3 | 3 | 3 | 4 | 3 | 3 | 3 | 4 | 6 | 0 | 0 |
| 16 | 2 | 3 | 3 | 3 | 2 | 3 | 3 | 3 | 3 | 2 | 7 | 3 | 0 | 0 |
| 17 | 2 | 2 | 2 | 2 | 2 | 2 | 2 | 2 | 2 | 2 | 10 | 0 | 0 | 0 |
| 18 | 0 | 0 | 0 | 0 | 0 | 0 | 0 | 0 | 0 | 0 | 10 | 0 | 0 | 0 |

study, we then briefly examine the quality of heuristic solutions on the problems generated. Tables 1-3 display the results of our experiments, where the solution obtained by the heuristic is compared against the known optimal solution obtained from our prior experiments with the integer programming formulation.

**Table 3.** Quality of heuristic solutions compared to optimal solutions for the large instance set

| $b$ | Optimal Number of Filters | | | | | | | | | | Suboptimality | | | |
|---|---|---|---|---|---|---|---|---|---|---|---|---|---|---|
| | $z_1^*$ | $z_2^*$ | $z_3^*$ | $z_4^*$ | $z_5^*$ | $z_6^*$ | $z_7^*$ | $z_8^*$ | $z_9^*$ | $z_{10}^*$ | 0 | 1 | 2 | 3 |
| 0 | 29 | 27 | 27 | 29 | 28 | 27 | 29 | 27 | 29 | 28 | 4 | 4 | 2 | 0 |
| 1 | 19 | 19 | 18 | 20 | 18 | 19 | 20 | 18 | 18 | 18 | 0 | 7 | 3 | 0 |
| 2 | 16 | 17 | 16 | 17 | 16 | 16 | 17 | 15 | 16 | 16 | 2 | 4 | 3 | 1 |
| 3 | 14 | 15 | 14 | 15 | 15 | 15 | 15 | 15 | 15 | 15 | 2 | 5 | 3 | 0 |
| 4 | 13 | 14 | 13 | 14 | 14 | 14 | 13 | 13 | 13 | 13 | 0 | 8 | 0 | 2 |
| 5 | 12 | 13 | 12 | 13 | 12 | 13 | 12 | 12 | 12 | 12 | 1 | 6 | 3 | 0 |
| 6 | 12 | 12 | 12 | 12 | 11 | 12 | 12 | 11 | 11 | 12 | 4 | 4 | 2 | 0 |
| 7 | 11 | 11 | 11 | 12 | 10 | 11 | 11 | 11 | 11 | 10 | 3 | 3 | 4 | 0 |
| 8 | 10 | 10 | 10 | 11 | 10 | 10 | 11 | 10 | 10 | 9 | 2 | 4 | 4 | 0 |
| 9 | 9 | 10 | 10 | 10 | 10 | 10 | 10 | 10 | 9 | 9 | 3 | 5 | 2 | 0 |
| 10 | 9 | 9 | 9 | 10 | 9 | 9 | 9 | 9 | 9 | 9 | 3 | 5 | 1 | 1 |
| 11 | 9 | 9 | 9 | 9 | 8 | 9 | 9 | 9 | 8 | 8 | 3 | 5 | 1 | 1 |
| 12 | 8 | 8 | 8 | 8 | 8 | 8 | 9 | 8 | 8 | 8 | 3 | 4 | 2 | 0 |
| 13 | 7 | 8 | 8 | 8 | 7 | 8 | 8 | 8 | 8 | 7 | 2 | 6 | 1 | 1 |
| 14 | 7 | 7 | 7 | 7 | 7 | 7 | 7 | 8 | 7 | 7 | 1 | 6 | 2 | 0 |
| 15 | 6 | 7 | 7 | 7 | 6 | 6 | 7 | 7 | 7 | 6 | 0 | 6 | 2 | 1 |
| 16 | 6 | 7 | 6 | 7 | 6 | 6 | 7 | 7 | 6 | 6 | 1 | 7 | 2 | 0 |
| 17 | 6 | 6 | 6 | 6 | 6 | 6 | 7 | 6 | 6 | 6 | 1 | 7 | 2 | 0 |
| 18 | 5 | 6 | 6 | 6 | 5 | 5 | 6 | 6 | 6 | 5 | 1 | 6 | 3 | 0 |
| 19 | 5 | 5 | 5 | 6 | 5 | 5 | 6 | 6 | 5 | 5 | 3 | 4 | 3 | 0 |
| 20 | 5 | 5 | 5 | 5 | 5 | 5 | 5 | 5 | 5 | 4 | 2 | 6 | 2 | 0 |
| 21 | 5 | 5 | 4 | 5 | 4 | 4 | 5 | 5 | 5 | 4 | 2 | 6 | 2 | 0 |
| 22 | 4 | 5 | 4 | 4 | 4 | 4 | 4 | 4 | 4 | 3 | 1 | 5 | 4 | 0 |
| 23 | 4 | 4 | 4 | 4 | 3 | 4 | 4 | 4 | 4 | 3 | 3 | 4 | 3 | 0 |
| 24 | 3 | 3 | 3 | 3 | 3 | 3 | 3 | 3 | 4 | 3 | 1 | 7 | 2 | 0 |
| 25 | 3 | 3 | 3 | 3 | 3 | 3 | 3 | 3 | 3 | 3 | 4 | 6 | 0 | 0 |
| 26 | 2 | 2 | 2 | 2 | 2 | 2 | 2 | 2 | 3 | 2 | 2 | 8 | 0 | 0 |
| 27 | 2 | 1 | 2 | 2 | 1 | 2 | 2 | 2 | 2 | 2 | 8 | 2 | 0 | 0 |
| 28 | 0 | 0 | 0 | 0 | 0 | 0 | 0 | 0 | 0 | 0 | 10 | 0 | 0 | 0 |

The column labelled $b$ again displays the traceback numbers for which the problem was run. The columns $z_i^*$, $i = 1,...,$ 10 represent the optimal number of filters for instance $i$ determined by the integer program. The "suboptimality" columns $q = 0, 1, 2,$ and 3 (for the last two cases) indicate the number of instances, out of 10, for which the heuristic solution was worse than the optimal solution by $q$ filters. (Thus, column 0 is the number of times that the heuristic correctly identified the optimal solution.) The heuristic solution was always within 3 filters of the optimal solution for each instance examined. The execution time for these heuristics is not recorded, since all terminated in under 1 second of CPU time. Observe that the suboptimality of the heuristic tends to become more severe as the problem instances become more difficult for the integer programs to solve. Indeed, there seems to be a direct correlation between the CPU seconds required for CPLEX to solve instances to optimality and the suboptimality encountered by the heuristic approach.

## 4   Conclusions and Future Research

In this paper we stated the *Generalized Minimum Filter Placement Problem* and presented an integer programming model to solve it to optimality. We also presented an $O(n^3)$ heuristic for this problem based on a greedy vertex cover heuristic. Our preliminary studies on this problem indicate that solving the integer programming model will not be practical on larger instances (say, $n \geq 40$), unless some significant work is performed in strengthening the linear programming relaxation to the problem or improving the overall algorithmic approach to solving this model. Moreover, while the basic model presented in this paper performs well on some of the easier instances, it tends to yield suboptimal solutions in more challenging instances. These challenging instances arise when the traceback number is about 30% of the number of nodes in the problem.

Future tasks motivated by the computational results presented in this paper include findings ways of strengthening the integer programming model to improve on the computation times. We will investigate valid inequalities that can be derived from the routing information and the architecture of the network topology. The performance of the heuristic can also be improved by taking routing information into consideration, and by attempting to simultaneously reduce the traceback number for all nodes, rather than one communication pair at a time as done by our algorithm once a vertex cover is established on the network. We leave these developments for future research.

## References

1. B. Armbruster, J.C. Smith, and K. Park, A packet filter placement problem with application to defense against Distributed Denial of Service attacks, Working Paper, The University of Arizona, Tucson, AZ, 2004.
2. Computer Emergency Response Team (CERT), CERT Advisory CA-2000-01 Denial-of-service developments, January 2000.
   http://www.cert.org/advisories/CA-2000-01.html.
3. P. Ferguson and D. Senie, Network ingress filtering: Defeating denial of service attacks which employ IP source address spoofing, May 2000. RFC 2827.
4. M. Garey and D. Johnson, Computers and Intractability: A Guide to the Theory of NP-Completeness, W. H. Freeman, San Francisco, 1979.
5. G.L. Nemhauser and L. Wolsey, Integer and Combinatorial Optimization, John Wiley & Sons, Inc, New York, NY, 1988.
6. K. Park and H. Lee. On the effectiveness of route-based packet filtering for distributed DoS attack prevention in power-law internets. In *Proc. ACM SIGCOMM '01*, pages 15–26, 2001.

# A Tool for Internet Chatroom Surveillance

Ahmet Çamtepe, Mukkai S. Krishnamoorthy*, and Bülent Yener**

Department of Computer Science, RPI, Troy, NY 12180, USA
{camtes,moorthy,yener}@cs.rpi.edu

**Abstract.** Internet chatrooms are common means of interaction and communications, and they carry valuable information about formal or ad-hoc formation of groups with diverse objectives. This work presents a fully automated surveillance system for data collection and analysis in Internet chatrooms. The system has two components: First, it has an eavesdropping tool which collects statistics on individual (chatter) and chatroom behavior. This data can be used to profile a chatroom and its chatters. Second, it has a computational discovery algorithm based on Singular Value Decomposition (SVD) to locate hidden communities and communication patterns within a chatroom. The eavesdropping tool is used for fine tuning the SVD-based discovery algorithm which can be deployed in real-time and requires no semantic information processing. The evaluation of the system on real data shows that (i) statistical properties of different chatrooms vary significantly, thus profiling is possible, (ii) SVD-based algorithm has up to 70-80% accuracy to discover groups of chatters.

## 1   Introduction and Background

Internet chatrooms provide for an interactive and public forum of communication for participants with diverse objectives. Two properties of chatrooms make them particularly vulnerable for exploitation by malicious parties. First, the real identity of participants are decoupled from their chatroom nicknames. Second, multiple threads of communication can co-exists concurrently. Although human-monitoring of each chatroom to determine *who-is-chatting-with-whom* is possible, it is very time consuming hence not scalable. Thus, it is very easy to conceal malicious behavior in Internet chatrooms and use them for covert communications (e.g., adversary using a teenager chatroom to plan an unlawful act). In this work, we present a fully automated surveillance system for data collection and analysis in Internet chatrooms. Our system can be deployed in the background of any chatroom as a *silent listener* for eavesdropping. The surveillance is done in the form of statistical profiling for a particular chatter, a group of chatters or for the entire chatroom. Furthermore, the statistical profiles are used to devise algorithms which can process real-time data to determine chatters and their partners. Thus, the proposed system could aid the intelligence community

---

* This research is supported by NSF ITR Award #0324947.
** This research is supported by NSF ITR Award #0324947.

H. Chen et al. (Eds.): ISI 2004, LNCS 3073, pp. 252–265, 2004.

**Table 1.** Top five IRC networks

| network | users | channels | servers |
|---------|-------|----------|---------|
| QuakeNet | 212005 | 184108 | 38 |
| Undernet | 144138 | 50720 | 38 |
| IRCnet | 117820 | 56550 | 44 |
| GamesNET | 45722 | 44521 | 22 |
| BRASnet | 43927 | 16523 | 34 |

to discover hidden communities and communication patterns within a chatroom without human intervention.

IRC (Internet Relay Chat) [1–5] is the original and the most widely used Internet chat medium. Currently there are *675* IRC networks distributed all around the world. There are total of *5290* servers within these networks having *1219906* users on *591257* channels [6]. IRC is a multi-user, multi-channel and multi-server chat system which runs on a Network. It is a protocol for text based conferencing and provides people all over the world to talk to one another in real time. Conversation or chat takes place either in private or on a public channel called as chat room.

IRC follows a client/server model. Server can be running on many machines, in a distributed fashion on a network, where each server has a copy of the global state information of the entire network. IRC client communicates with an IRC server through Internet. Client logs on to a server, picks a unique nickname and selects one or more channels to join. A channel is a group of one or more users who receive all messages addressed to that channel. A channel is characterized by its name, topic, set of rules and current members. Basically, there are two types of channels: *standard channels* and *safe channels*. Standard channels are created implicitly when the first user joins it, and cease to exist when the last user leaves it. Creation and deletion of the safe channels are made by the servers upon request and that is why they are named as *safe channels*. In order for the channel members to keep some control over a channel, some channel members are privileged and called as channel operators. They can perform actions such as setting the topic, ejecting (kicking) a user out of the channel, banning a users or all users coming from a set of hosts, and sharing their privileges with other users.

Server is part of a global IRC server network. When a client sends a message to a channel, server sends this message to all other servers and each server submits the message to people who are part of the same channel. This way, users of a channel, who are distributed all over an IRC network, can communicate in broadcast manner within a channel. In this work, we select Undernet because it is one of the biggest IRC networks with its *38* servers, *50000* channels and more than *100000* users. Table 1 lists top five IRC networks in the world [6].

## 1.1    Multiple Nicknames Authentication in IRC

IRC is not a secure protocol since all the messages and other information are transmitted in clear text. Authentication is also not reliable since servers authenticate clients: (i) by plain text password, and (ii) by DNS lookups of source IP addresses which are subject to spoof. Multiple nick names further compicate the authenticity of users while analyzing chat room data. During an IRC session a client can change its nickname on the flight. Although such changes are visible from *change nickname* messages, once clients are disconnected, they can use any nicknames they like when they login to server again. Furthermore, a client can access IRC from different hosts under different nicknames. In such situations, it is impossible to decide whether given two nicknames belong to same or different person. We note that some of the channels introduce an additional security by sending an "ident" query to the "identd" service running on client hosts. The Identification Protocol [5] provides a mechanism to determine the identity of a user using a particular TCP connection. Given a TCP source and destination port pair of a TCP socket, Identification Protocol running on client host can first locate the process which has created the socket. Then, it can find the owner of the process and return the user id as the response to the ident query. Identification Protocol itself is not secure and can not be accepted as a trusted authority for this functionality. It is possible to implement a fake *identd* software. Actually, some IRC clients come with their own fake identity services with which client can hide its identity or initiate impersonation attacks.

The multiple nicknames problem is out of the scope of this work. In our system we simply maintain a list of nicknames that a client used in the channel. (Note that this information is available in the messages logs as mentioned above). For a new client, we check nickname against these nickname lists, if it is in a list of a person, we assume that person has disconnected and connected again.

## 1.2    Related Work

In this work, we focus on IRC networks and build a system for data collection and identification of hidden communication patters and groups. There are several spy tools to listen IRC channels. PieSpy [7, 8] is an IRC program (bot) that logins to IRC servers, joins and listens to IRC Channels. PieSpy is used to collect messages and extract information to visualize social networks in a chatroom. It has simple set of heuristic rules to decide who is talking to who. These rules include direct addressing (destination nickname is written at the beginning of the message). *Direct addressing* is simple and most reliable method to set relation between users, but it can not be used always. *Temporal Proximity* is another approach. If there is a long period of silence before a user sends a message and this message is immediately followed up by a message from another user, then it is reasonable to imply that the second message was in response to the first. Temporal Proximity searches for such cases to infer a relationship between the users. *Temporal Density* is an approach when Temporal Proximity is not applicable. Basically, If several messages have been sent within a time period all

**Table 2.** Example Data Matrix

| $ID\backslash Time$ | 1 | 2 | 3 | 4 | 5 | 6 | 7 | 8 | 9 | 10 | 11 | 12 | 13 | 14 | 15 |
|---|---|---|---|---|---|---|---|---|---|---|---|---|---|---|---|
| 1 | 0 | 0 | 1 | 2 | 0 | 1 | 0 | 0 | 0 | 0 | 0 | 0 | 1 | 0 | 2 |
| 5 | 0 | 0 | 0 | 0 | 0 | 0 | 0 | 0 | 0 | 0 | 0 | 0 | 0 | 0 | 0 |
| 6 | 0 | 0 | 0 | 0 | 0 | 0 | 0 | 0 | 1 | 2 | 0 | 1 | 0 | 1 | 0 |
| 7 | 0 | 0 | 0 | 1 | 0 | 1 | 0 | 1 | 0 | 1 | 0 | 2 | 0 | 0 | 0 |
| 10 | 0 | 0 | 0 | 0 | 0 | 0 | 0 | 0 | 0 | 0 | 0 | 0 | 0 | 0 | 0 |
| 12 | 0 | 0 | 0 | 0 | 0 | 0 | 1 | 0 | 0 | 3 | 1 | 0 | 0 | 0 | 0 |
| 13 | 0 | 0 | 0 | 0 | 0 | 0 | 0 | 0 | 0 | 0 | 1 | 0 | 0 | 0 | 0 |
| 14 | 0 | 0 | 0 | 0 | 0 | 0 | 0 | 0 | 0 | 0 | 1 | 0 | 1 | 0 | 0 |
| 15 | 0 | 0 | 0 | 0 | 0 | 0 | 0 | 0 | 0 | 0 | 0 | 0 | 0 | 0 | 0 |

of them are originating only from two users, then it is assumed that there is a conversation between these two users. This idea is similar to our fixed window approach; however, there is no verifiable performance study of PieSpy nor the impacts of these parameters to the discovery of communication patterns.

*Chat Circle* [9] is an abstract graphical interface for synchronous conversation which aims to create a richer environment for online discussions. This approach is based on graphical visualization and does not provide eavesdropping capability.

There are several proposals for discovering hidden groups and communication patterns in social networks (see [10–12] and references therein). For example Social Network Analysis (SNA) [10] is a software tool which considers relationships between people, groups, organizations, computers or other information/knowledge processing entities. The nodes in the network are the people and groups while the links are the relationships between the nodes. SNA is based on computing the metrics: degrees, betweenness, closeness, boundary spanners, peripheral players, network centralization, structural equivalence and cluster analysis. Since defining an accurate graph for IRC is a hard problem, the results based on a graph construction may have high noise.

**Organization of the Paper.** This paper is organized as follows. In Section 2 we describe how to access and collect data in IRC. In Section 3 we explain a computational discovery algorithm, based on the Singular Value Decomposition (SVD), for locating groups of chatters. In Section 4 we present the experimental results and finally conclude in Section 5.

## 2  Data Acquisition

In this work, we have implemented a simple IRC client which logs to a server, selects a unique nickname and joins to a given channel. Program silently listens to the channel (i.e., it is a *silent listener*) and logs all the messages.

Our IRC client continuously collects data. In this work, we used ten days of channel logs for the statistical analysis. For our algorithm, we used two busiest four-hour periods in a day (i.e., from 08:00 to 12:00, and from 20:00 to 24:00).

Each four hour period is divided into eight 30-minute intervals called *sampling windows* (e.g., 08:00 to 08:30, 08:30 to 09:00, etc).We also used other sampling window sizes, i.e. $15, 30, 45, 60, 75, 90$-min. We further divide the sampling windows into *time slots* of sizes 15, 30, 45, 60, 75 or 90 seconds. For each time slot, we count number of messages of each user. We construct data matrices $C$ where each row corresponds to a user and each column to a time slot. Entry at $c_{ij}$ in the matrix is the number of messages of user $i$ in time slot $j$. An example of data matrix is shown in Table 2 assuming the time slot to be 15 sec.

The first column of each row gives an identity number of the chatter. $i, j$-th entry of the matrix gives the number of messages that chatter $i$ sent during the $j^{th}$ instance (time slots). In this example, the first chatter (identity 1) is sending two messages at the $4^{th}$ time slot. Similarly the $4^{th}$ row chatter (identity 7) is sending one message at the $4^{th}$ time slot. Our algorithm hypothesizes that possibly chatter 1 and chatter 7 are communicating. This hypothesis gets stronger upon observing the message posting in the time slots 6 and 12. Thus, persistence of co-existence of posting chat messages in the time scale indicates a correlation among chatters. We use Singular Value Decomposition algorithm to quantify such relations as explained later in the paper.

## 2.1 Generating Data Matrices

We use two methods to generate data matrices. In *fixed window* matrix generation method, the sampling windows do not overlap (e.g., 08:00 to 08:30, 08:30 to 09:00, etc). However, there is a chopping of the conversation at the allotted time interval with the fixed window scheme. Thus, we consider *sliding window* method in which the windows overlap as shown in Figure 1. For example, in sliding window method for window overlap of 15 minutes, we generate matrices for time intervals of 08:00-08:30, 08:15-08:45, 08:30-09:00, etc. This method generates sixteen matrices for 4 hour period for window size of 30 minutes. In the experiments, we investigate the impact of both sliding and fixed window methods, as well as the size of time slots on the quality of the solutions obtained by our algorithm.

## 2.2 IRC Selection and Noise Filters

We decided to listen three channels in Undernet Network. These are channels *USA*, *Philosophy* and *Political* where the language is English. Each of these channels represents a different communication style and different user profiles. Channel *USA* is a recreation channel which contains large amounts of junk messages. Messages are short, conversations are short-lived, and people tend to jump from one short non-brainy conversation to another. We consider messages as *noise* if they have no value in chatroom analysis. We observed the following properties of such messages: (i) they are short broadcasts, (ii) they have sexual, offensive, annoying or abusive content, (iii) they are irrelevant with the topics in the channel, and (iv) they usually do not get any response. Usually, owners of such messages are kicked out of the channel by the channel operators. We apply some simple

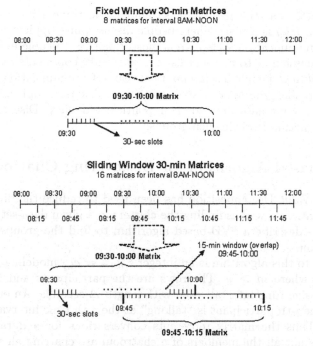

**Fig. 1.** The Fixed and Sliding Window Time Series

set of rules to filter out the noise. These rules are based on our preliminary observations and worked fine for our case. First, we eliminate the messages of the *kicked-out-users* with the assumption that they are kicked out because their messages are considered as noise. Next, we eliminate messages of the non-English speakers. This can be achieved by using some frequent non-English (Spanish, Italian, French, German, ...) keywords. We also eliminate users who send messages which include words like *"wanna chat"*, *"cares to chat"*, *"care to chat"*, *"any girls"*, *"some girls"*, *"anyone wants"*, *"anyone who wants"*, *"anyone with webcam"*, *"Chat anyone"*, *"Anyone want to"*, *"someone to talk"*, *"someone want to talk"*, *"someone wanna talk"*, *"someone to chat"*, *"someone want to chat"*, *"someone in usa"*, *"someone from"*, *"looking for someone"*, *"aslpls"*, *"asl pls"*, *"asl please"* Note that such word sequences mean that the chatter is looking for some private chat, and the chatter's intention is not to join a decent conversation within the channel.

*Stopword Elimination* can be considered as a better technique to clean noise from a chatroom data. Stopwords are a list of common or general terms that appears frequently in a language. Analysis on word frequencies shows that there are few words that appear often and carry really little information. Many search engines don't index stopwords because they're expensive to index, i.e. there are so many of them, and they carry little useful information. For the case of chatroom analysis, it is possible to generate stopword lists for chatrooms based on the topics, the communication styles, and user profiles.

258 Ahmet Çamtepe, Mukkai S. Krishnamoorthy, and Bülent Yener

Channel *USA* has the highest noise among the three IRCs we examined. Channel *Philosophy* is a place where people discuss philosophical subjects with low noise. Communication style here is mostly pairwise, people either select to be part in discussion or to be silent listener and make comments rarely. Finally, in channel *Political*, people discuss political issues. Communication style in this channel is more like groupwise. Two or more users discuss a topic and users may separate into groups according to their political tendency. Discussions occurs among and sometimes within such groups.

# 3 SVD-Based Algorithm for Discovering Chatter Groups

The Singular Value Decomposition has been used to reduce the dimensionality of the data-matrix as well as finding the clusters in a given data-set [13]. In this subsection, we describe a SVD-based algorithm to find the groups in the chat room discussion.

The input to this algorithm is an integer $C_{n \times m} = c_{i,j}$ modeling a chat room conversations where $m \geq n$. The rows are the participants and the columns are the successive time intervals each with length $\Delta$ seconds. An entry $c_{i,j} = k$ means that the $i$-th participant is "talking" at the $j$-th time interval by posting $k$ messages. Thus the matrix represents conversations for a duration of $m\Delta$ seconds. Since not all the members of a chatroom are chatting all the time the matrix $C$ is quite sparse.

If a set of participants $i_1, i_2, \cdots, i_k$ are *chatting* as a group, we expect them to carry on their conversations over multiple $\delta$ units. Thus, there will be many nonzero entries in the corresponding rows for many of the columns. We propose an algorithm to identify such groups.

**Algorithm:**

### Compute SVD

Compute the Singular Value Decomposition of $C$. This gives three matrices, $U, D$ and $V$, where $D_{n \times m}$ is a diagonal matrix and $U_{n \times n}$ and $V_{m \times m}$ are orthogonal matrices (i.e., $UU^T = U^TU = I$ and $VV^T = V^TV = I$) such that $C = UDV^T$.

### Low Rank Approximation

The diagonal entries of D (by the property of SVD) are nonnegative and decreasing values. By considering the successive rations of the diagonal entries, we chose the first $k$ dimensions. The choosing the first $k$ dimensions contribute an error, which is= $E_k = \sum_{i=1}^{n} d_{j,j}^2 - \sum_{j=1}^{k} d_{j,j}^2$. We normalize the error and choose largest $k$ such that $E_k/E_n \leq \eta$ is minimized for a given relative error bound $\eta$.

### Clustering the Low Dimension

**Table 3.** Chatroom Statistics: Message Size and Interarrival Time

| Metric | Philosophy Msg Size | Political Msg Size | USA Msg Size | Philosophy Arr. Time | Political Arr. Time | USA Arr. Time |
|---|---|---|---|---|---|---|
| MEDIAN | 49 | 61 | 19 | 61 | 64 | 41 |
| AVERAGE | 55 | 68 | 40 | 66 | 69 | 57 |
| STD DEV | 34 | 38 | 66 | 37 | 34 | 54 |
| VARIANCE | 1210 | 1466 | 4456 | 1430 | 1216 | 2965 |
| SKEWNESS | 1 | 1 | 3 | 1 | 1 | 1 |
| KURTOSIS | 1 | 8 | 13 | 2 | 5 | 3 |

Cluster the points $d_{1,1}u_1, d_{2,2}u_2, \cdots, d_{k,k}u_k$ (in reduced dimension) of the given matrix. Cluster these points (in each of the dimensions)[1].

*Report the Clusters*

Output the participants in the clusters as groups.

# 4  Experimental Results

There are several objectives of the experimental study. First, a statistical quantification of chatroom communications is obtained. The statistics are collected both for the entire chatroom and for the pairwise communications as well. Second, we measure the performance of our SVD-based clustering algorithm by checking the accuracy of its results against to a verification tool.

## 4.1  Statistical Profiling of Chatrooms

We have collected data from three chatrooms over 10-days (10K to 20K messages per day) of time period to determine the message interarrival distribution and message size distributions. In Table 3, we present the overall statistical properties. The table shows that the *USA* chatroom has the most noise and the *Philosophy* chatroom is the least one (based on the second moment information). Similarly the distribution for *USA* chatroom is skewed most (the third moment) and it diverges from the normal distribution the most (the fourth moment information). These two measures indicate long tailed distributions. The table also shows that, in average the messages and the interarrival time of the messages are shortest in the *USA* and longest in *Political*.

In Figure 2, we show the histograms of message interarrival time and message size information for all three chatrooms over 10-days of data. In Figure 3, we apply curve fitting to message size distributions and discover a surprising result that *USA* chatroom message size distribution follows a power law.

---

[1] There are several choices of clustering algorithms. In our experiments we applied a thresholding scheme on the first dimension.

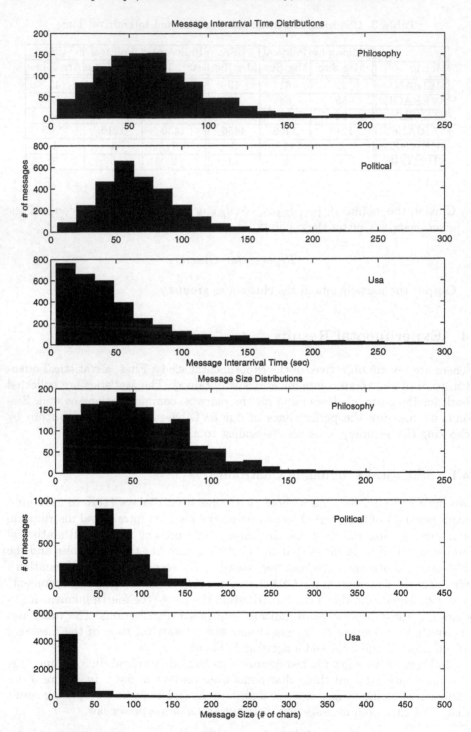

**Fig. 2.** Message arrival and message size histograms for all three chatrooms

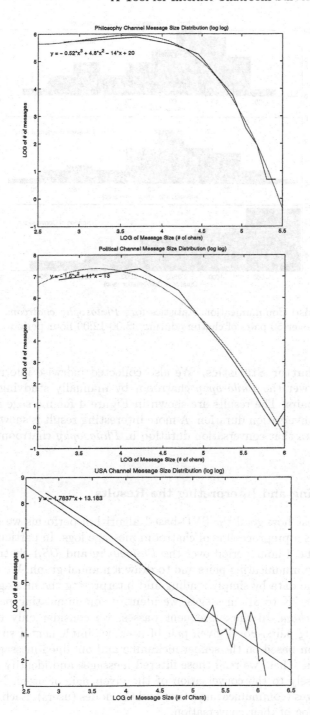

**Fig. 3.** Message size (log-log) distributions for all three chatrooms. The USA chatroom obeys the power-law

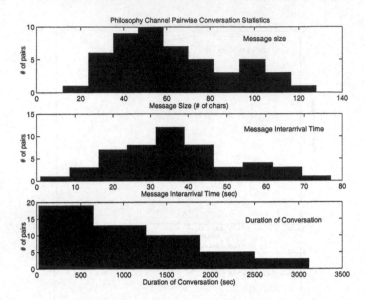

**Fig. 4. Pairwise** Communication Statistics for *Philosophy chatroom*. The statistics are computed over 50 pairs of chatters during 08:00-12:00 hour period

**Pairwise Chatter Statistics.** We also collected pairwise information for 4-hour period over the *Philosophy* chatroom by manually studying the data to identify the pairs. The results are shown in Figure 4 for message size, message arrival and conversation duration. A more interesting result is shown in Figure 5 which indicates that conversation duration in *Philosophy* chatroom has a linear decline.

## 4.2   Verifying and Interpreting the Results

In order to test how good the SVD-based algorithm performs we design a tool which requires a preprocessing of chatroom message logs. In particular, we manually study the 4-hour period over the *Philosophy* and *USA* chatroom data to identify the communicating pairs and to draw a manual-graph. We made several passes over the data by simply reading and interpreting the messages. With the first pass over 2K to 3K messages, we identify communicating pairs, i.e. *who-is-talking-to-whom*. In the subsequent passes, we consider only the identified communicating pairs. For a given pair of user, we implement a simple message filter operation based on the sender nickname and obtained messages belonging to either users. Then, we read those filtered messages and identify messages belonging precisely to the conversation of the given pair of users. Manual-graph consists of edges (communicating pairs) and the nodes (users). Each pairs (edges) has message log of their conversation.

The verification tool takes (i) the edges and nodes of the manual-graph graph, and (ii) clusters of nodes generated by the SVD-based algorithm (i.e. the output

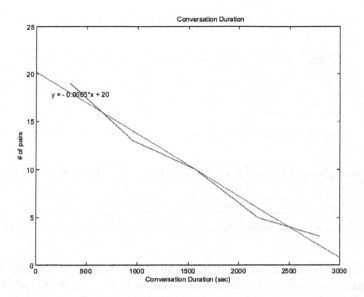

**Fig. 5. Pairwise** Communication Durations in *Philosophy chatroom* 8:00-12:00

of the algorithm). Program first merges clusters sharing at least one node. We assume that these clusters are cliques and we list all possible edges in these cliques. The nodes and edges induced by the clusters of the SVD-based algorithm are compared with the edges and nodes of the manual-graph. Any node which is in the manual-graph but not a member of any cluster produced by the SVD algorithm is assumed to be missed by the algorithm. Similarly, any edge of the manual-graph which is not a member of any cluster is assumed to be missed by the SVD. Program outputs missed and found edges and nodes.

Message logs produced during manual-graph generation process are used to calculate pairwise statistics. They are also used to calculate weights for the edges and nodes of manual-graphs. Weight of an edge is the number of messages exchanged during the conversation of node pairs. Weight of the node is the total number of messages send by this node. Verification program outputs edges and nodes sorted in their weights. Miss of an edge or a node with high weight is not desirable and can be used as a performance metric for evaluating the algorithm.

**Interpretation.** We examine the impacts of (i) time slots, and (ii) disjoint vs sliding windows on the performance of the algorithm. In Table 4, we show the results obtained from a large matrix which is obtained from 4-hour data. There is only one matrix corresponding to window of size 240-min (4-hour) over 4-hour data. We experimented different time slots, i.e. 15, 45 and 90 sec. Evidently the longer the time slot the better the results are. Figure 4, presents histogram of message interarrival time for pairwise communications in *philosophy* channel. Interarrival times almost always fall below 90-sec, which we assume is the reason for the performance increase as time slots gets larger. As the time

**Table 4.** Philosophy chatroom: 240-min (4-hour) window over 4-Hour data with various time slots

| Time Slots | % of Missed Edges | % of Missed Nodes |
|------------|-------------------|-------------------|
| 15 sec     | 71 %              | 69%               |
| 45 sec     | 55 %              | 44%               |
| 90 sec     | 44 %              | 28%               |

**Table 5.** Philosophy chatroom: Non-overlapping windows over 4-Hour data with 30-second time slots

| Sampling Window | % of Missed Edges | % of Missed Nodes |
|-----------------|-------------------|-------------------|
| 15 min          | 47%               | 36%               |
| 30 min          | 42%               | 65%               |
| 90 min          | 26%               | 20%               |

slot gets smaller, number of the columns in the matrix increases yielding more sparse matrix. Moreover, the impact of the noise in the computations is reduced by larger time slots.

In Table 5, we fixed time slot as 30-sec and divided the 4-hour time interval into various window sizes. We would like to examine the impact of time various (15, 30, 90 min) window sizes. Here, we have the same tendency as we reported above. As the window size increases, the performance of the SVD algorithm increases. We claim that results here are strongly related to the duration of the conversation metric presented in Figure 4. Simply, some of the conversations might get chopped at the allotted time interval. Certain duration of conversation values for communicating pairs might create such an increase in the number of chopped messages for certain window sizes. A conversation falling on two or more window might be missed by SVD algorithm. Therefore the larger the window size, the better the results are.

Finally, in Table 6, we compare the performance of our algorithm as a function of different sliding window schemes with fixed time slot of 15-sec. The results show that overlap size does not have any significant impact. The difference among the results of *Philosophy* and *Political* channel is caused by the nature of the chatroom. Since there is a chopping of the conversation at the allotted time interval with the fixed window scheme, our sliding window approach provides an increase in performance of the SVD algorithm. When we compare results in Table 6 and 5, we see that percentage of missed nodes decreases with overlapping; even though time slot used in Table 6 is 15-sec which has been shown to have highest miss rates in Table 4.

## 5    Conclusions

The Internet chatrooms can be abused by malicious users who can take advantage of its anonymity to plan for covert and unlawful actions. We presented a fully automated system for data collection and discovery of chatter groups

**Table 6.** Philosophy and Political chatroom: 30-Minute overlapping windows (sliding windows) over 4-Hour data with 15 second time slots. The performance of the SVD-based algorithm varies depending on the nature of the chatroom

| Sliding window overlap | % of Missed Edges | % of Missed Nodes |
|---|---|---|
| Phil. 15 min. | 42% | 28% |
| Phil. 10 min | 42% | 28% |
| Polit. 15 min | 58% | 41% |

and implicit communication patterns in IRC without semantic information or human intervention. We have shown that the chatroom traffic characteristics changes significantly from one chatroom to another. However, quantifying such characteristics enables us to build novel tools that can not only eavesdrop into a chatroom but also it can discover sub-communities and hidden communication patterns within the room.

This work could aid intelligence community to eavesdrop in chatrooms, profile chatters and identify hidden groups of chatters in a cost effective way. Our future work focuses on enhancing the SVD algorithm working in the time domain with topic based information. Our preliminary results show that such enhancement is possible.

# References

1. Kalt, C.: RFC 2810 Internet Relay Chat: Architecture (2000)
2. Kalt, C.: RFC 2811 Internet Relay Chat: Channel management (2000)
3. Kalt, C.: RFC 2812 Internet Relay Chat: Client protocol (2000)
4. Kalt, C.: RFC 2813 Internet Relay Chat: Server protocol (2000)
5. Johns, M.S.: RFC 1413 Identification Protocol (1993)
6. Gelhausen, A.: IRC statistics. http://irc.netsplit.de (1998) (accessed 10 February 2004).
7. Mutton, P., Golbeck, J.: Visualization of semantic metadata and ontologies. In: Seventh International Conference on Information Visualization (IV03), IEEE (2003) 300–305
8. Mutton, P.: Piespy social network bot. http://www.jibble.org/piespy/ (2001) (accessed 14 October 2003).
9. Viegas, F.B., Donath, J.S.: Chat circles. In: CHI 1999, ACM SIGCHI (1999) 9–16
10. Krebs, V.: An introduction to social network analysis. www.orgnet.com/sna.html (2004) (accessed 10 February 2004).
11. Magdon-Ismail, M., Goldberg, M., Siebecker, D., Wallace, W.: Locating hidden groups in communication networks using hidden markov models. In: NSF/NIJ Symposium on Intelligence and Security Informatics (ISI 03), Tucson, PA, ISI (2003)
12. Goldberg, M., Horn, P., Magdon-Ismail, M., Riposo, J., Siebecker, D., Wallace, W., Yener, B.: Statistical modeling of social groups on communication networks. In: First conference of the North American Association for Computational Social and Organizational Science (CASOS 03), Pittsburgh PA, CASOS (2003)
13. Golub, G.H., Loan, C.F.V.: Matrix Computations. 3rd edn. The Johns Hopkins University Press, Baltimore, MD (1996)

# ChatTrack:
# Chat Room Topic Detection Using Classification

Jason Bengel, Susan Gauch, Eera Mittur, and Rajan Vijayaraghavan

Information & Telecommunication Technology Center
University of Kansas, 2335 Irving Hill Road,
Lawrence Kansas 66045-7612
{jasonb,sgauch,eerakm,rajan}@ittc.ku.edu

**Abstract.** The traditional analysis of Internet chat room discussions places a resource burden on the intelligence community because of the time required to monitor thousands of continuous chat sessions. Chat rooms are used to discuss virtually any subject, including computer hacking and bomb making, creating a virtual sanctuary for criminals to collaborate. Given the upsurge of interest in homeland security issues, we have developed a text classification system that creates a concept-based profile that represents a summary of the topics discussed in a chat room or by an individual participant. We then discuss this basic chat profiling system and demonstrate the ability to selectively augment the standard concept database with new concepts of significance to an agent. Finally, we show how an investigator can, once alerted to a user or session of interest via the profile, retrieve details about the chat session through our chat archiving and search system.

## 1 Introduction

One rapidly growing type of communication on the Internet is Instant Messaging (IM) and Internet Relay Chat (IRC). Once primarily popular with teenagers, its use has exploded among adults and it is quickly expected to surpass electronic mail as the primary way in which people interact with each other electronically by the year 2005 [7]. Online chat provides a mode of talking to others using a keyboard as in e-mail, but it has the spontaneity of real-time human interaction much like that of a telephone call. The fame of IM has been sparked by the ability to stay connected with associates, friends, and family, and its entertainment value through meeting new people, swapping files, and participation in town-hall style chat rooms to discuss virtually any imaginable topic. Unfortunately, criminals have also migrated to the electronic chat havens, sneaking into homes to lure children [5], committing corporate and homeland espionage [4], and even discussing terrorist plots with other outlaws [3, 15].

Instant messaging is defined as a client-based peer-to-peer chat discussion occurring between small numbers of participants. Client-based chat software revolves around direct connections between users; and a central directory server is used to broadcast the availability of each client. Since chat traffic is not broadcast through a centralized server, no central authority exists to monitor or enforce good behavior. Popular IM products include MSN Messenger, Yahoo Messenger, and Trillian. In contrast to IM, server-based chat takes place on one or more dedicated servers, where all chat traffic is first transmitted through a server that then transmitted to the appro-

H. Chen et al. (Eds.): ISI 2004, LNCS 3073, pp. 266–277, 2004.
© Springer-Verlag Berlin Heidelberg 2004

priate recipients. IRC is server-based, wherein participants log in with client software such as XChat or mIRC. One server is capable of handling hundreds of simultaneous users and chat rooms.[1] Participants join and create new rooms to chat with groups and also to privately whisper with one another.

While most participants in chat rooms are engaged in legitimate information exchanges, chat rooms can also be used as a forum for discussions of dangerous activities. By detecting discussions associated with terrorism or illegal activities, crime prevention abilities may be enhanced. For example, a terrorist may be looking to recruit like-minded people to his cell, or child predators may be attempting to lure children. To automatically identify suspicious conversations and/or individuals, intelligence workers need an archive of online chat discussions and sophisticated tools to help them filter and process the large quantity of collected information. Human monitors could actively watch and decide when chat is of concern to law enforcement, but that would be prohibitively expensive and people are unlikely to participate in a chat system that is openly scrutinized by human agents.

Online chat provides a new tool to support criminal collaborations. Intelligence agencies need tools to analyze and archive suspicious subjects' online chat, whether it is obtained in public chat rooms or through covert analysis of all chat data passing through a particular server via packet sniffing [11]. Since chat sessions can span several days or even months, agents need a way of recording and tracking topics generated from chat discussions, analogous to FBI analysis of e-mail [17]. With the increased emphasis on security issues since September 11, 2001, agencies would benefit from identifying suspicious electronic conversations automatically.

Our goal is to assist in crime detection and prevention by automatically creating concept-based profiles summarizing chat session data. We have created *ChatTrack*, http://www.ittc.ku.edu/chattrack, a system that can generate a profile on the topics being discussed in a particular chat room or by a particular individual. This summary allows analysts to focus their attention on people or discussions whose profiles intersect with domains of national security interest. For example, a profile showing active participation in topics of "bacteria cultures/anthrax" and "water reservoirs" could be significant to counterterrorism intelligence, whereas an individual pursuing the topic of "instruments/violins" could be disregarded (unless investigating a Stradivarius heist). Because the profiles created are summaries, individual privacy is not violated unless further investigation of the session is conducted, requiring further permissions. We discuss our method of profiling chat conversations and the search mechanism utilized for more in-depth analysis, and provide sample results from data collected on IRC.

## 2  Literature Review

Topic identification from text documents is a longstanding problem. However, since online chat is structured differently from written discourse, this poses new challenges

---

[1] A February 10, 2004 sampling of chat networks indicates 131,832 clients in 46,345 rooms on EFnet; 125,350 clients in 47,080 rooms on Undernet; and 107,832 clients in 54,536 rooms on IRCnet. Most people do not remain connected 24/7, so the user base is several times larger.

for classification systems. Because chat sessions do not contain linear discussions of single topics, but rather partially threaded, interwoven topics that oscillate in short, incomplete utterances, topic detection is even more difficult for chat sessions. Studies have started to look at the current problems facing chat room topic detection and monitoring.

A chat room's topics vary based on its participants' current interests, so it is impossible for a person to know what topics are being discussed in a chat room without first joining it to observe its contents. A conversation-finding agent called Butterfly aims to resolve this by visiting rooms to sample thirty seconds of data that is then used to create a simple term vector [15]. People searching for chat topics request recommendations by querying with words in which they are interested, also represented as a term vector. An "interest profile" is generated by summing the weights of the dot product of the two vectors; and when the sum is above a threshold, the chat room is recommended. One limitation is that Butterfly visits only rooms it can see; however, it is the "secret rooms" that are considered the most useful and interesting to the intelligence community.

E-mail messages are typically threaded; i.e., a reply to a message is grouped with the original message. Conversely, chat turns are not taken between participants. A response to one utterance may come several minutes after it is spoken, opening the potential for confusion if a large number of people are present. [17] looks at automatic techniques for discovering, threading, and retrieving material in streams of data. Topic detection and tracking aims to discover the tracking of topics and new events. Segmentation is used to find boundaries between topics, followed by a logistic regression to combine probabilities obtained from a language model built from concatenated training events. These topics are then clustered to determine new events from pre-existing ones. Since news events were used as test data, it is reasonable to suspect that chat utterances may not provide sufficient keywords. Additional studies using techniques borrowed from text classification may assist on threading chat utterances.

Comprehending the interests and interactions between the participants of chat rooms can be used to create a profile of an individual's behavior. [19] uses a metaphor for creating individual visual data portraits and to represent the interactions between users. The data portrait combines attributes of user activity such as utterances spoken, the rate of responses, and relationships between users, such as groups of users avoiding outsiders. Attributes such as timing between utterances, responses, initial chat vs. reply, are included in the portrait, and change over time to represent a temporal view. A garden metaphor represents one group, and groups are visually compared to indicate how interactions differ, such as a dominating voice or a democratic group with equal participation.

Topic classification requires a domain of expertise for each concept. IBM has developed WebFountain, which makes use of chat room archives, web pages, e-mail, and so on, which can then be queried for knowledge of a specific domain [2, 14]. This could provide intelligence agents a means for assembling bodies of knowledge on concepts of national security interest, such as a terrorist organization. [6] evaluated text classification techniques (Naïve Bayes, k-nearest neighbor, and support vector machine) to find suitable methods of chat log classification to assist in automated crime detection. Training data was limited to four categories, limiting topic distinctions to law enforcement analysis. [1] looks at topic identification in chat lines and news sources using complexity pursuit. This algorithm separates interesting components from a time series of data, identifying some underlying hidden topics in streaming data. The authors report that their results could complement queries with other topic segmentation and tracking methods on text streams.

Our work complements the above systems. If PeopleGarden were combined with a concept-based profiler such as ChatTrack, this would be a tremendously useful security tool – closed groups discussing topics of national security could be flagged for analysis by intelligence agents. We focus on topic detection performed by an individual on chat data. Combining information from multiple sources, such as is done in WebFountain, would increase the accuracy of the profiles and being able to track the profiles over time, as is done by topic tracking systems, would also be a valuable enhancement.

## 3  Topic Detection for Security Analysis

We have developed ChatTrack, a collective set of applications and tools for the analysis and archival of electronic chat room discussions. As shown in Figure 1, ChatTrack archives the contents of chat room discussions in XML format. Subsets of this data can be classified upon request to create profiles for particular sessions or particular users. The classifier is pre-trained on over 1,500 concepts, and it can also be extended to include concepts of interest to a particular analyst. Thus, the profiles created can be easily adapted to a variety of domains. The data is also indexed for quick search by speaker, listener, keyword, session, and/or date and time.

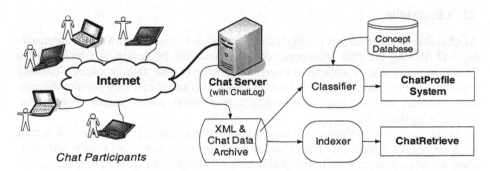

**Fig. 1.** The ChatProfile and ChatRetrieve systems are major components of ChatTrack and provide Web-based user interfaces

### 3.1  Archiving

There are two perspectives from which one can choose to log activity on server-based systems; the first uses an autonomous bot agent, and the second uses a modified chat server. To collect samples for testing, we obtained chat session data from public chat rooms on various IRC networks and from our own modified server.

ChatTrackBot is designed to silently record activity from chat rooms of which it is a member. It is controlled by the owner, who sends it commands indicating the room names to join and part. The bot appears as a normal user but, unlike some chatbots, it does not attempt to fool others into thinking it is human by responding to participants' queries, and appears as an end-user IRC client program when queried by the IRC client-to-client protocol. For testing purposes, we augmented an IRC server to record all chat activities (including public and whispered utterances). While bots are limited to recording only the activity visible to them, a modified server is capable of logging all system activity. Users of our chat server were made fully aware that their content was being logged by a notice on the login screen.

Both ChatTrackBot and our modified IRC server store the archived data in XML format. We designed our own XML schema to identify essential chat actions such as sending/receiving a message, joining/parting a chat room, logging on/off a server, nickname changes, and so on. The XML chat data is parsed to extract the chat utterances, and then each utterance is parsed and stored into three files, separately storing the speaker and receiver names and the utterance. The receiver name consists of either the public chat room in which the utterance was spoken or the username to which the utterance is being privately sent. These files are placed in a directory hierarchy archive that encodes the date and room name identifier, and the filenames encode the utterance transmission time.

The ChatTrack project page makes many of these products available. The XML schema, modified IRC server, and ChatTrackBot are all available there. In addition, we developed and distribute ChatLog, a library written in "C," that can be used by chat developers to extend their own client and/or server-based chat software to create XML log files.

## 3.2  ChatProfile

As chat data is archived, an intelligence agent needs an automated way of summarizing and filtering the chat utterances. We addressed this by designing ChatProfile, a system that uses text classification to create a profile of chat data, in essence creating a summary of the chat. Profiles indicating topics of concern can then prompt the analyst to explore the associated chat session in more detail using ChatRetrieve, as discussed in Section 3.3.

As the basis of ChatProfile, we used a vector space classifier developed as part of the KeyConcept project [8]. The classifier must first be *trained*, i.e., taught what concepts are to be searched for in the chat sessions. During training, the classifier is provided with a set of pre-defined concepts and example text that has been classified into the concepts, taken from of the Open Directory Project (ODP)[2]. Then, for each category, the classifier creates a vector of representative keywords and their weights based upon the *tf\*idf* (term frequency * inverse document frequency) formula developed for vector space search engines [12]. We trained our classifier on 1,565 concepts from the top three levels of the ODP hierarchy. These were selected because they had a minimum of 28 training documents, found through empirical studies to provide adequate training data for accurate classification [10].

---

[2] See http://dmoz.org

To create a profile from chat data, an analyst selects the criteria of interest using any combination of session name, speaker/receiver names, and a date/time range, as depicted by the web-based interface in Figure 2. A *user* profile focuses on one chat participant by filtering based on a speaker name only, whereas a *session* profile filters by chat room name only. The chat utterances fulfilling the analyst's criteria are then collected from the archive and prepared for classification by removing high frequency (stop) words and stemming by the Porter stemmer. The classification of several hundred chat utterances generally completes in under a minute.

The classifier then creates a vector of keywords extracted from the chat data and calculates the similarity between this vector and the vectors for each trained concept using the cosine similarity measure [12]. The concepts are then sorted by their similarity values in decreasing order, and the top-matching concepts and their similarity values are returned as the result of classification. Concepts are visually represented in a hierarchical fashion using a Web interface, with asterisks shown next to each concept to indicate the *relative* concept weights at each level of the hierarchy. Profile accuracy has been tested in [13], but needs to be retested for chat data.

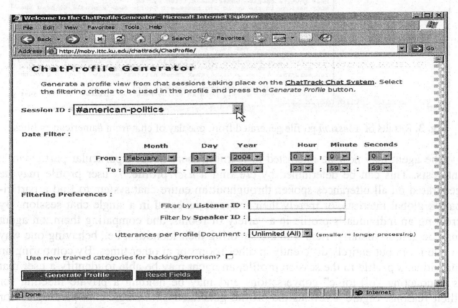

**Fig. 2.** The ChatProfile filtering interface allows an agent to select criteria of interest for inclusion in a user or session profile

Envision a scenario in which an agent wishes to generate a *session* profile on the #american-politics chat room. (Test data was obtained from a public IRC server and includes 7,612 utterances from 225 chat participants.) As depicted in Figure 2, the #american-politics session is selected from the drop-down session list, and the agent selects filtering for activity occurring on February 3, 2004. Listener and Speaker ID fields are left blank so as to include all participants, and a profile is then generated. Examining the results shown in Figure 3, the three asterisks next to News (compared to one or zero asterisks for all other top level concepts), indicate that the majority of the chat falls under the "News" concept. When the News concept is expanded, we find that the most highly weighted sub-concepts are Politics and Alternative Media. Further expansion reveals that the profile for the chat room is heavily weighted in "US Election 2004" and "Conservative and Libertarian."

**Fig. 3.** Results of a *session* profile generated from one day of chat from #american-politics

The agent may now be interested in learning more about a particular participant's interests. This can be determined by creating a *user* profile. A user profile may be generated on all utterances spoken throughout an entire chat system to find a participant's global interests, or merely their interests revealed in a single chat session. By creating an individual's profile in a variety of rooms, and comparing them, an agent may be able to identify users who are spoofing their identities, i.e., behaving one way in one room but entirely differently in other rooms or at other times. By comparing an individual's profile to the session profile, an agent may be able to identify a user that is conducting "off-topic" conversations and may be holding a private meeting for illicit reasons. Figure 4 reveals the profile generated on a single chat participant for the same session used in Figure 3. This particular participant spoke 46 utterances in the session, shown in the right hand pane, and his/her profile interests seem focused on societal issues dealing with abortion. All actual usernames in the utterances have been masked for privacy.

The interests of intelligence agencies evolve as world events take place and new homeland security threats appear. To deal with this reality, ChatProfile has been designed to allow new concepts to be added to the concept database for profile recognition. To demonstrate this ability, we added training documents for the concepts of terrorism and hacking. Training documents were selected from various websites that seemed authoritative on their respective topics. An agent would typically make use of a concept database that has been tuned for category recognition for the subjects of interest, omitting uninteresting concepts. A session profile created on #hackphreak (14,367 utterances from 270 unique participants) indicates a profile in the "Arts" category of music and writing (Figure 5). Using the enhanced concept database for terrorism/hacking increases the strength of the "Computers" top-level category, and identifies the secondary level of hacking (Figure 6). The terrorism concept is not shown as an example, but was successfully identified in experiments.

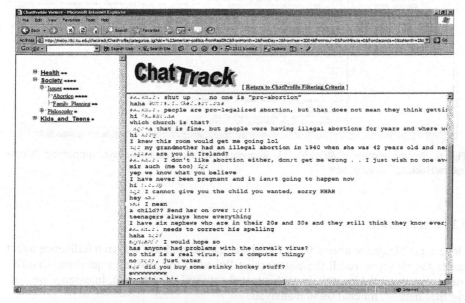

**Fig. 4.** Results of a *user* profile on one chat participant, restricted to #american-politics

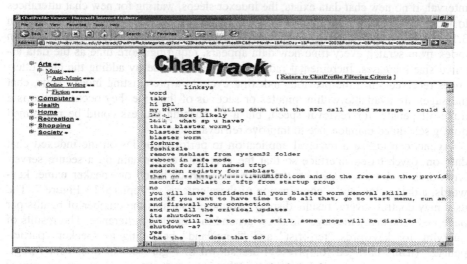

**Fig. 5.** Session profile of #hackphreak

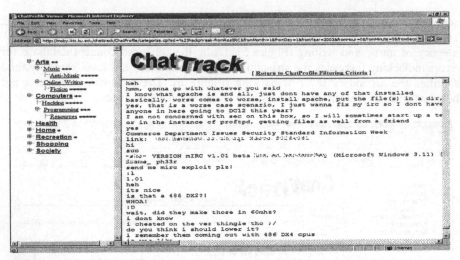

**Fig. 6.** Session profile of #hackphreak augmented with concept database, supporting "Computers/Hacking" as a concept

### 3.3 ChatRetrieve

Once a profile that warrants further analysis has been identified, an intelligence agent needs the ability to recall the chat session linked to the profile in question. ChatRetrieve was designed to provide sophisticated retrieval of chat data, in essence providing the "details" for chat session analysis.

In order to keep chat session archive up to date, indexing takes place concurrently as users chat. We use an incremental indexer that runs continuously at a predefined interval. If no new chat data exists, the indexer sleeps, waiting for new chat utterances to index. When new XML data appears, the logs are parsed as described in Section 3.1, and the output is added to the inverted indices. Traditional indexers create an index from scratch every time new data appears, requiring more time as the data archive size increases. Incremental indexing solves this issue by adding the chat utterances received since the previous indexing cycle to a pre-existing index. Thus, chat messages are available within minutes or seconds of the time they occur. There is a trade-off penalty for retrieval speed, but a re-indexing process could be performed during scheduled maintenance to improve retrieval times.

Agents can utilize a retrieval application to perform queries on the indexed chat data on a web-based interface so that the chat data can remain on a secure server. Keywords retrieval is based on $tf*idf$. Queries can be based on speaker name, keywords, a date range, and a combination of these criteria, as depicted by Figure 7. The user may control several results display parameters such as the number of results per page and how many messages to show around the matching utterance. The results of querying for keywords "terrorist" and "homeland" belonging to speaker "participant42" (name changed for privacy) are shown in Figure 8. On this results page, clicking on a room name link performs a chat session replay that includes utterances spoken by all participants of that session.

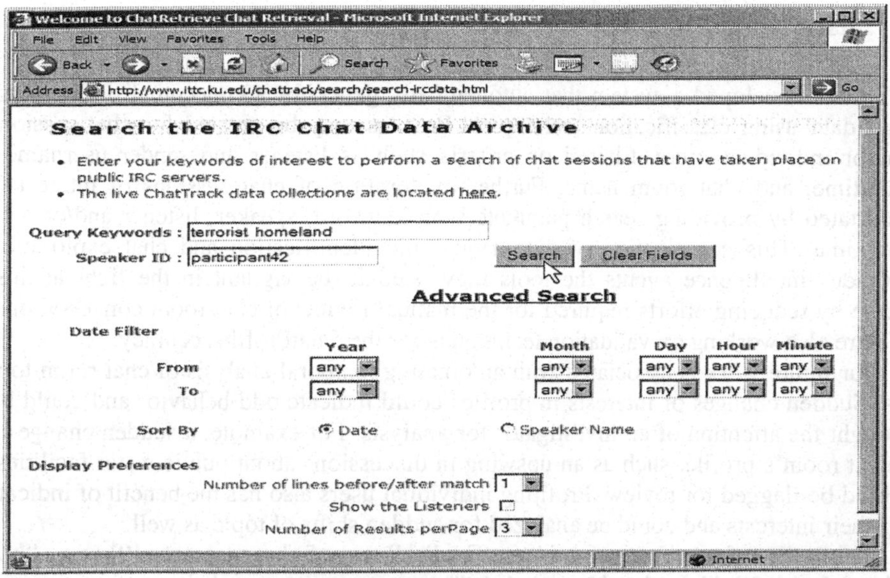

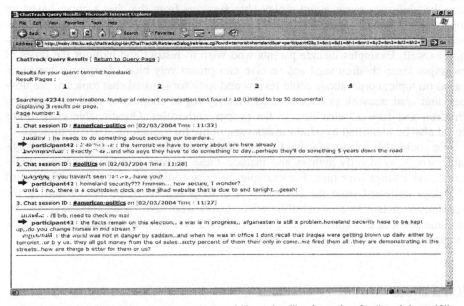

**Fig. 7.** Screenshot of ChatRetrieve interface

**Fig. 8.** Results of searching for "terrorist" and "homeland" only spoken by "participant42"

One unique feature of the ChatRetrieve system is that we track all the chat room participants even if they do not contribute to the discussions. The agent may choose to display the listeners who heard particular messages. We are currently working on the ability to search by listener and/or profile by listener to allow analysis of users who choose to eavesdrop on certain discussions but not actually exchange messages.

## 4   Discussion and Future Work

We have developed a system that automatically generates a conceptual profile from chat data using classification techniques. Profiles may be created for chat sessions and/or individual users, filtered on criteria such as listener and sender usernames, date/time, and chat room name. Further exploration of chat sessions of interest is facilitated by providing search parameters on keyword, speaker, listener and/or date and time. This combination of automatic topic identification and chat exploration provides intelligence agents the tools they need to be vigilant in the fight against crime by reducing efforts required for the manual review of chat room conversations. We are also working on validation techniques for the ChatProfile accuracy.

Our future work is associated with automating temporal analysis of chat room topics. Sudden changes of interests in profiles could indicate odd behavior and could be brought the attention of an investigator for analysis. For example, a sudden change in a chat room's profile, such as an upswing in discussions about public water facilities, should be flagged for review. Profiling individual users also has the benefit of indicating their interests and could be analyzed for sudden shifts of topic as well.

Due to the informal nature and "non-English" text of chat messages [9] (e.g., "*brb* – be right back", "*lol* – laughing out loud"), preprocessing may help to extract meaningful words from the seemingly meaningless chatter. We hope to provide investigators the ability to retrieve and replay chat sessions from the chat archive based on topics (e.g., "bomb making") rather than specific words (e.g., "nitroglycerin" or "pipe bomb"). Chat topic classification has applications outside of the intelligence community as well. Examples include parents who wish to restrict and monitor the types of messages their children send and receive can proactively block dangerous messages based on topic; corporations could review and look for unusual chat topics of employees; and chat network providers could identify rogue chatters or predators stalking children and forward chat data to the proper authorities. Questionable chat rooms could also be identified by administrators searching for violations of server policies.

We could also consider factors like metrical habits, rhetorical devices, and polysyllabic words to identify authors and include these in user profiles, since chat nicknames can change over time. For example, priority could be given to investigation of chat logs collected from the utterances of a supposed child, yet demonstrating the vocabulary or language model of an adult. Users who have "adult" language models in some sessions and child-like language models in others may indicate a child predator, and can be identified in this manner.

## References

1. Bingham, E., Kab, A., and Girolami, M., "Topic Identification in Dynamical Text by Complexity Pursuit." In *Neural Processing Letters* 17: 1-15, 2003, 69–83.
2. Cass, S., "A Fountain of Knowledge." IEEE Spectrum Online, Jan. 4, 2004. http://www.spectrum.ieee.org/WEBONLY/publicfeature/jan04/0104comp1.html, last accessed Feb. 4, 2004.
3. "AOL reports alleged chat room terrorist threat." CNET News.Com. http://news.com.com/2100-1023-234832.html, last accessed Jan. 29, 2004.

4. "Soldier held on suspicion of aiding al Qaeda." CNN News,
   http://www.cnn.com/2004/US/02/13/natl.guard.arrest/, last accessed Feb. 13, 2004.
5. "Ex-Marine admits child abduction." CNN News.
   http://www.cnn.com/2004/WORLD/europe/02/12/britain.marine/, last accessed Feb. 12, 2004.
6. Elnahrawy, E., "Log-Based Chat Room Monitoring Using Text Categorization: A Comparative Study." In *Proceedings of the International Association of Science and Technology for Development Conference on Information and Knowledge Sharing (IKS 2002).* St. Thomas, US Virgin Islands, USA, November, 2002.
7. "Instant Messaging." Gartner Consulting.
   http://www3.gartner.com/3_consulting_services/marketplace/instMessaging.jsp
8. Gauch, S., Madrid, J., Induri, S., Ravindran, D., Chadlavada, S., "KeyConcept: A Conceptual Search Engine." *Information and Telecommunication Technology Center, Technical Report: ITTC-FY2004-TR-8646-37,* University of Kansas, USA.
9. Komando, Kim., "Using IM: Know the Lingo (and 4 other tips)."
   http://www.bcentral.com/articles/komando/119.asp, last visited Jan. 14, 2004.
10. Madrid, J., Gauch, S., "Incorporating Conceptual Matching in Search." In *Proceedings of the 11th Conference on Information and Knowledge Management (CIKIM '02).*
11. Meehan, A., Manes, G., Davis, L., Hale, J., and Shenoi, S., "Packet Sniffing for Automated Chat Room Monitoring and Evidence Preservation." In *Proceedings of the Second annual IEEE Systems, Man, and Cybernetics Information Assurance Workshop,* West Point, New York, June 5-6, 2001.
12. Salton, G., and McGill, M. J. *Introduction to Modern Retrieval.* McGraw-Hill Book Company, 1983.
13. Trajkova, J., Gauch, S., "Improving Ontology-Based User Profiles." Computer Assisted Information Retrieval (RIAO 2004), University of Avignon (Vaucluse), France. April 26-28, 2004.
14. Tretau, R., Chiang, D., Grelsokh, D., Leman, S., Shekhtmeyster, R. "WebFountain Guide." IBM Redbooks. October 13, 2003.
   http://www.redbooks.ibm.com/redbooks/pdfs/sg247029.pdf, last accessed Feb 10, 2004.
15. "Agents pursue terrorists online." USA Today.
   http://www.usatoday.com/news/world/2002/06/21/terrorweb-usat.htm, last accessed Mar. 12, 2004.
16. Van Dyke, N. W., Lieberman, H., and Maes, P., "Butterfly: A Conversation-Finding Agent for Internet Relay Chat." In *Proceedings of the 1999 International Conference on Intelligent User Interfaces.* 39–41, 1999.
17. "Inside the FBI: DCS-1000 (Carnivore) Diagnostic Tool." Washingtonpost.com Live Online, September 27, 2000. http://www.fbi.gov/chat/chat2000.htm, last accessed Feb. 5, 2004.
18. Wayne, C. L., "Topic Detection and Tracking in English and Chinese." In *Proceedings of the 5th International Workshop Information Retrieval with Asian Languages,* 165–172, September 2000.
19. Xiong, R. and Donath, J., "PeopleGarden: Creating Data Portraits for Users." In *Proceedings of the 12th Annual ACM Symposium on User Interface Software and Technology.* 37–44, 1999.

# *SECRETS*: A Secure Real-Time Multimedia Surveillance System*

Naren Kodali[1], Csilla Farkas[3,4], and Duminda Wijesekera[1,2]

[1] Dept of Info. and Software Eng.,
George Mason University, Fairfax, VA 22030–4444,
{nkodali,dwijesek}@gmu.edu
[2] Center for Secure Information Systems,
George Mason University, Fairfax, VA 22030–4444,
[3] Information Security Laboratory,
University of South Carolina, Columbia, SC-29208
farkas@cse.sc.edu
[4] Dept of Computer Science and Eng.,
University of South Carolina, Columbia, SC-29208

**Abstract.** We propose a surveillance framework (*SECRETS*: SECure Real-time ElecTronic Surveillance) that is a practical solution to safeguarding sensitive physical facilities like command and control centers, missile storage facilities, by providing controlled secure distribution of live multimedia data recorded on-site onto display devices with different access permissions in a multi-level secure environment. *SECRETS* uses cameras and microphones as input devices and handheld radio linked displays as output devices. The geographical location of an input device determines its security level and the classification of the holder determines the security level of an output device. In *SECRETS* only those recipients with corresponding security classifications receive live media streams, but during emergencies, they can receive pre-computed emergency instructions and/or cover stories. We use SMIL [Aya01] formatted, multimedia feeds including cover stories, and explain how *SECRETS* can compose necessary multimedia documents, compute views for each security classification, enforce access control and deliver media to the handheld devices while respecting both wealthy run time semantics [KFW03b] of multimedia as well as MLS security [KFW03a].

## 1 Introduction

Safeguarding facilities by monitoring them with electronic audio/video devices has been widely implemented in recent times. [Spy,VCM]. The monitored areas are accessible only to predefined groups of people and therefore the same condition holds for the disclosure of live surveillance records to the same set of people, when they are remotely located. Consider an airport in which passengers and

---

* This work was partially supported by the National Science Foundation under grants CCS-0113515 and IIS-0237782.

H. Chen et al. (Eds.): ISI 2004, LNCS 3073, pp. 278–296, 2004.
© Springer-Verlag Berlin Heidelberg 2004

employees can enter common areas, like transportation facilities, and waiting areas. However, secured areas, like luggage transport and service stations, are available for authorized employees only. The highest security areas, such as the air traffic control room, are accessible to specialized personnel who are appropriately authorized. The keyword here is "authorization", meaning that people who are not authorized to access a physical location should not be allowed physical or electronic access to that location. In the surveillance world, the exact same rules apply and the potential recipient of the surveillance data must have the same authorization that an ordinary person of any trade would have to be physically or electronically present at that location. However, during emergency operations, controlled dissemination of sensitive data may become necessary in order to obtain support services or to prevent panic. Therefore, it is necessary to develop methods and tools to allow selective access to surveillance feeds during normal and emergency operations.

The primary motive of this paper is the development of a surveillance system referred to as *SECRETS* that enables the expression, broadcast and secure retrieval at remote locations of SMIL-formatted multimedia compositions with their rich runtime semantics.

Secondly, we propose techniques to enforce access control, and exploitation of cover stories to disseminate relevant material to unauthorized users during emergencies. We then show how normal and emergency operations of a MLS secure facility can be composed as a SMIL document enriched with proposed extensions. We take such a composition and construct views appropriate for different security classes, referred to as a MLS normal form of a SMIL document with appropriate security decorations.

Thirdly, given the runtime delays of an operational platform, we show how to generate an executable appropriate for that runtime, which we call a display normal form of a SMIL document. We then encrypt media streams and transmit them to intended recipients under normal and emergency operating conditions. For simplicity, we assume a multilevel security classification of physical areas and their corresponding surveillance data. Similarly, people accessing these facilities have security clearances. Employees and visitors are allowed to enter or view the surveillance feeds of a particular location (e.g., via broadcasts) only if they have the appropriate security clearance. We enforce that requirement on guarding personnel during normal operations. We propose that *SECRETS* be equipped with a semantically rich, pre-orchestrated multimedia cover story repository, so that in emergencies cover stories can be released to lower security levels. A detailed deployment infrastructure along with its compliance with present day standards, COTS products and commercially available authoring and display devices is provided.

We use SMIL-based multimedia composition framework adapted for multilevel physical surveillance. The reason for selecting SMIL is guided by recent industrial trends. First, many browsers and off-the-shelf display and communication devices are becoming SMIL compliant [VSA,Nok]. Secondly, as mobile communication, using SMIL, becomes faster and more integrated, mobile de-

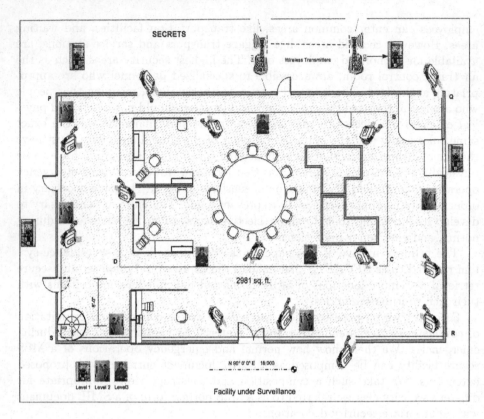

**Fig. 1.** A hypothetical facility under Surveillance with *SECRETS*

vices are becoming available [Spy,VCM]. Thirdly, toolkit support is becoming available to integrate XML compliant services [PCV02,Bul98]. Therefore, with the right technological framework, our solution becomes portable to a wide range on-site surveillance activities.

The rest of the paper is organized as follows Section 2 presents some related work, Section 3describes SMIL, Section 4 discusses the architecture and general requirements of a general problem domain. In Section 5, we present preprocessing fundamentals in the MLS domain and the associated normal form. Section 6 and Section 7 deals with the runtime operations and real-time deployment issues respectively. Section 8 concludes the paper.

## 2    Related Work

SMIL has been the focus of active research [RvOHB99,RHO99,SSC00], and many models for adaption to real world scenarios have been provided. Multilevel security (MLS) has been widely studied to ensure data confidentiality, integrity, and availability . MLS systems provide controlled information flow(from higher level to the lower level) based on the security classification of the protection objects (e.g., data items) and subjects of the MLS system (e.g., applications running in behalf of a user). Damiani et al [DdV03] discuss controlled dissemination of sensitive data within an *Scalable Vector Graphics*(SVG) image used to render the map of a physical facility and propose an access control model with complex filtering conditions. Bertino at al [BHAE02] provide a security framework to model access control in video databases, where objects are sequences of frames or particular objects within frames. The access control model is based on security objects, subjects, and permitted access modes, such as viewing and editing. The proposed models provide a general framework of the problem domain, however they do not explain how access control objects to be released are formalized and enforced. While most models addresses the need of multimedia, their approach does not incorporate runtime semantics of multimedia. They primarily address textual documents and exploit the granular structure of XML documents. In Multimedia there is a sense of temporal synchrony and continuity thereby synchronization and integration of different and diverse events is necessary to produce sensible information. The process of retrieval needs sophisticated techniques and algorithms which all of the above models do not completely address.

The authors have proposed semantic constructs [KFW03a] for MLS-SMIL formatted multimedia documents used in the domain of physical surveillance, and the related algebra involving construction,transfer and display of the SMIL fragments that represent live audio and video surveillance feed. Additionally [KW02] proposes methods for enforcing discretionary access control for SMIL formatted pay-per-view movies on the Internet . The cinematic structure consisting of acts, scenes, frames of actual movies are written as a SMIL document without losing the sense of the story. A secure and progressively updatable SMIL document [KWJ03] is used to enforce RBAC and respond to traffic emergencies. In an emergency response situation, different recipients of the live feeds have to be discriminated to people playing different roles. This paper proposes a practical application that can be deployed by implementing the algebra, theoretical results and algorithms that have been extensively discussed in the earlier papers.

A distributed architecture for multi-participant and interactive multimedia that enables multiple users to share media streams within a networked environment is presented in [Sch99]. In this architecture, multimedia streams originating from multiple sources can be combined to provide media clips that accommodate look-around capabilities. In addition, Quality of Service (QoS) is an integral part of multimedia. Wijesekera et al. [WS96] proposed properties of quality metrics associated with continuous media and Gu et al. [GNY+01] propose *HQML*, a language to negotiate some QoS parameters between clients and server.

## 3    SMIL: Synchronized Multimedia Integration Language

SMIL [Aya01] is an extension to XML developed by W3C to author multimedia presentations with audio, video, text and images to be integrated and synchronized. The distinguishing features of SMIL over XML are the syntactic constructs for timing and synchronizing live and stored media streams with qualitative requirements. In addition, SMIL provides a syntax for spatial layout including non-textual and non-image media and hyperlinks. We do not address the later aspects of SMIL in this paper. Consequently we explain those SMIL constructs that are relevant for our application.

SMIL constructs for synchronizing media are ⟨ seq⟩, ⟨ excl ⟩ and ⟨ par⟩. They are used to hierarchically specify synchronized multimedia compositions. The ⟨ seq⟩ element plays its children one after another in sequence. ⟨ excl⟩ specifies that its children are played one child at a time, but does not impose any order. The ⟨ par⟩ plays all children elements as a group, allowing parallel play out. For example, the SMIL specification ⟨ par⟩ video src=camera1 ⟩ ⟨ audio src=microphone1⟩ ⟨ /par⟩ specify that media sources camera1 and microphone1 are played in parallel.

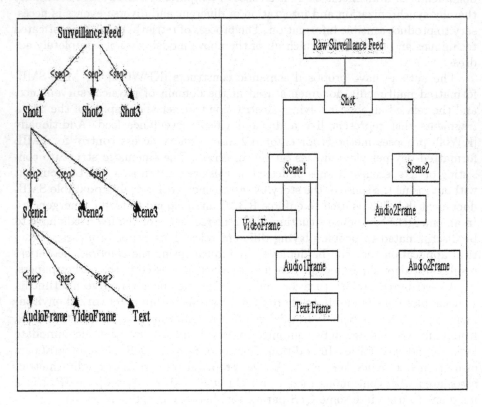

**Fig. 2.** Representation of SMIL Constructs

In SMIL, the time period that a media clip is played out is referred to as its *active duration*. For parallel play to be meaningful, both sources must have equal active durations. When clips do not have equal active durations, SMIL provides many constructs to equate them. Some examples are begin (allows to begin components after a given amount of time), dur (controls the duration), end (specifies the ending time of the component with respect to the whole construct), *repeatCount* (allows a media clip to be repeated a maximum number of times). In addition, attributes such as *syncTolerance* and *syncMaster* controls runtime synchronization, where the former specifies the tolerable mis-synchronization and the latter specifies a master-slave relationship between synchronized streams. An important construct that we use is ⟨switch⟩ allowing one to switch among many alternatives compositions listed among its components. These alternatives are chosen based on the values taken by some specified attributes. For example, ⟨switch⟩ ⟨audio src="stereo.wav" systemBitrate⟩25⟩⟨audio src="mono.wav" systemBitrate ⟨ 25⟩⟨/switch⟩ plays stero.wav when the SMIL defined attribute systemBitrate is at least 25 and mono.wav otherwise. We use this construct to specify our surveillance application. In order to do so, we define two custom attributes customTestMode that can take values "normal" and "emergency" and customTestSecurity that take any value from ("TS","S","UC"). The first attribute is used to indicate the operating mode that can be either normal or emergency and the second attribute indicates the security level of streams that can be top secret, secret or unclassified.

# 4   *SECRETS* Architecture

Figure 1 shows a hypothetical military facility with varying levels of sensitivity based on geographic location. Assume that the area enclosed by the innermost rectangle ABCD contains weapons with highest degree of sensitivity and is accessible (and therefore guarded by) personnel with the highest level of clearance, say top secret (TS). The area between the rectangles PQRS and ABCD is classified at medium level of sensitivity and therefore requires personnel with secret (S) security clearances. The area external to PQRS contains least sensitive material, and can be accessed by unclassified personnel, like visitors and reporters. We classify the areas into Top-Secret (TS), Secret (S) and Unclassified (UC) security levels with application domains. Security labels form a lattice structure. For simplicity, we omit the application domain and use TS, S, and UC as security labels. The area inside ABCD is TS, the area inside of PQRS, but outside of ABCD is S, and the area outside PQRS is UC. Employees, guards, support services personnel, and general public have TS > S > UC clearances, where " > " corresponds to the dominance relation defined in MLS systems. As depicted in Figure 1, an area with higher level of sensitivity is a sub-part of areas with all lower levels of sensitivities. Therefore, a guard with top-secret clearance may be used in the classified area, but not vice versa. For electronic surveillance purposes, cameras (infrared and normal light) and other devices such as microphones are situated throughout the facility and are regulated based on geographical co-ordinates as shown in 3.

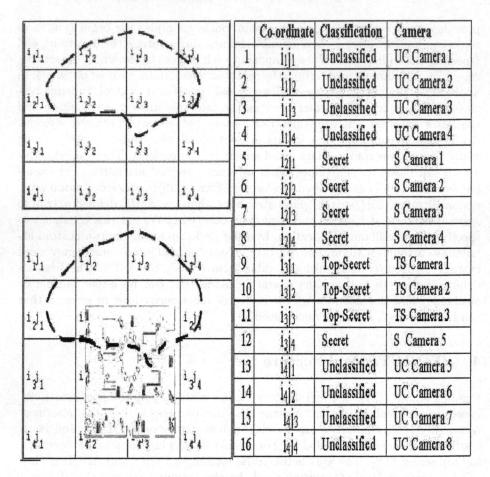

| | Co-ordinate | Classification | Camera |
|---|---|---|---|
| 1 | $i_1\|_1$ | Unclassified | UC Camera1 |
| 2 | $i_1\|_2$ | Unclassified | UC Camera2 |
| 3 | $i_1\|_3$ | Unclassified | UC Camera3 |
| 4 | $i_1\|_4$ | Unclassified | UC Camera4 |
| 5 | $i_2\|_1$ | Secret | S Camera1 |
| 6 | $i_2\|_2$ | Secret | S Camera2 |
| 7 | $i_2\|_3$ | Secret | S Camera3 |
| 8 | $i_2\|_4$ | Secret | S Camera4 |
| 9 | $i_3\|_1$ | Top-Secret | TS Camera1 |
| 10 | $i_3\|_2$ | Top-Secret | TS Camera2 |
| 11 | $i_3\|_3$ | Top-Secret | TS Camera3 |
| 12 | $i_3\|_4$ | Secret | S Camera5 |
| 13 | $i_4\|_1$ | Unclassified | UC Camera5 |
| 14 | $i_4\|_2$ | Unclassified | UC Camera6 |
| 15 | $i_4\|_3$ | Unclassified | UC Camera7 |
| 16 | $i_4\|_4$ | Unclassified | UC Camera8 |

**Fig. 3.** Geographic grid representing capture locations

## 4.1   Information Flow in *SECRETS*

The capture and the ensuing transfer of sensitive information within *SECRETS* is regulated via an Client-Server architecture as shown in Figure 4. Multimedia streams emanating from strategically located devices are continuously used are continuously captured and transmitted to a centralized control facility for dissemination and then directed to handheld devices of appropriate security personnel.

As we observe in Figure 4 The server consists of a Camera Manager and an Audio Manager which are integrated based on a system clock with the help of a synchronization manager. These empirical needs of synchronization and integration are also the foundations of the SMIL language. The repositories of captured information and cover stories is resident in a database that communicates with the synchronization manager via the buffer manager during the preprocessing and formatting of real time data in to SMIL documents. The transfer is handled by Network Manager and could be wired( if within the facility) or through wireless radio links. The Network manger as an dual interface at both the client and the server locations to facilitate secure and effective communication.

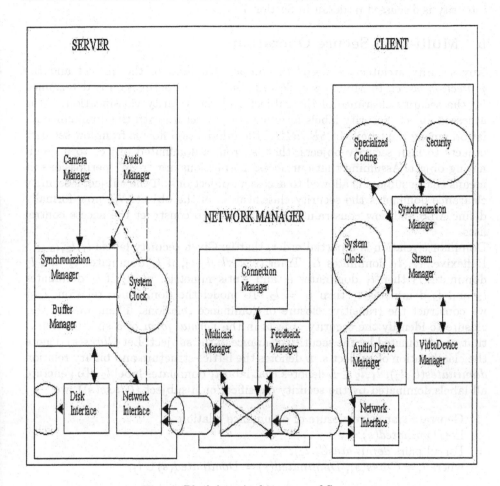

**Fig. 4.** Black-box Architecture of Secrets

In *SECRETS* the clients could be stationary on-site personnel or guards equipped with display devices and performing duties at remote locations. At the client location there are audio and video managers to enable the stream integration based on the system clock. The access/release control of the documents is controlled via specialized coding or hardware devices, collectively called *smartcards* within the display device that can interpret the encryption and release only the allowed views corresponding to the privileges of the client.

An inbuilt Cryptix Parser that is programmed in firmware (or in software) exists within the smartcard to handle the decryption process and enable selective decryption of the appropriate view based on the access privileges as defined in the smartcard. All transmissions of media files to various people in the hierarchy use standard hypertext transfer protocol (HTTP) web protocol or the Wi-Fi (802.11) wireless transfer protocol. The encryption mechanism to enforce integrity is discussed in detail in Section 7

## 5  Multi-level Secure Operations

Any security architecture needs the proper definition of the *subject* and the *protection object*. In Multi Level Security each access permission is determined by the security clearance of the subject and the security classification of the accessed object. Security labels form a lattice structure with the dominance relation among the labels. In *SECRETS* the information flow is from low security objects to high security objects, that is, from a dominated object to a dominating object. Assuming that our access permissions are "read" permissions, it means that a subject is allowed to access an object only if the subject's security clearance dominates the security classification of the object. We now formally define MLS and how constraints could be used to construct the access control lists.

Dominance relation is a partial order, that is: Given security labels $l_1, l_2, l_3$ : Reflexive: $\forall l_1, l_1$ dominates $l_1$, Transitive: $\forall l_1, l_2, l_3$, if $l_1$ dominates $l_2$ and $l_2$ dominates $l_3$ then $l_1$ dominates $l_3$ and Antisymmetric: $\forall l_1, l_2$ if $l_1$ dominates $l_2$ and $l_2$ dominates $l_1$ then $l_1 = l_2$. To model the dominance relation, first we construct the transitive closure of dominance relations. Then, we use this closure to identify the security objects in the *normal form* of a specification $S$ that are dominated by the security clearance of the subject. Let $Class(s)$ denote the classification of subject $s$. $L$ denotes the lattice structure and binary relation $dominates(l_1, l_2)$, $l_1, l_2 \in L$ denotes that label $l_1$ dominates label $l_2$. To generate all labels dominated by the security classification a subject $(Class(s))$, we

1. Generate transitive closure of dominance relation
2. Let $Dominated(s) = \emptyset$
3. For all pairs $dominates(l_i, l_j)$,
   where $l_i = Class(s)$, $Dominated(s) = Dominated(s) \cup l_j$

To permit accesses for a subject to objects, we use the set *Dominated* to determine the appropriate data items. That is, a subject is granted the access $a$ to an object $o$ if the security clearance of the subject dominates the security classification of the object.Therefore MLS could be stated as an (s,o,a) triple. $\forall s$, if $Class(s)$ and $\{l_{i_1}, \ldots, l_{i_n}\} \in Dominated(s)$ and $o \in Cl_{i_k}$ $k = 1, \ldots, n$ then $(s, o, a)$.

### 5.1  MLS SMIL Fragment with Security Attributes

The sample SMIL fragment shown below is a simplified example derived from a complex SMIL specification using the defined attributes. As the figure shows, the file consists of two sections, where the first section defines the custom attribute customTestMode with values "Normal" and "Emergency". Because the second and the fourth lines of Figure 2 specifies that customTestMode is hidden, the value of this attribute corresponding to each stream cannot be reset later. The second part of the file consists of a switch statement consisting of collection of media streams connected by ⟨par⟩ constructs. Notice that the ⟨switch⟩ statement consists of two sections where the first one begins with the line ⟨par customTestMODE= "Normal"⟩ and the second one begins with the line ⟨par customTestMODE= "Emergency"⟩. That specifies that the streams inside be shown under normal and emergency operating conditions. In this example, each area has a camera and a microphone to record audio and video streams . They are named CameraTS1.rm, CamerU1.wav etc. The security classification of each source is identified by the application defined SMIL attribute customTestSecurity. For example, ⟨video src="CameraTS1.rm" channel="video1" customTestSecurity="TS"/⟩ specifies that the video source named CameraTS1.rm has the Top Secret security level. The main composition is encoded using a ⟨switch⟩ statement that is to be switched based on the operating mode (normal or emergency).

```
<smil xmlns="http://www.w3.org/2001/SMIL20/Language">
<customAttributesMODE>
      <customTestMode="Normal" title="Normal Mode"
        defaultState="true" override="hidden"
       <customTestMode id="Emergency" title="Emergency Mode"
        defaultState="true" override="hidden"
<customAttributesMODE> <customAttributesSecurity>
      <customTestSecurity id="TS" title="Top-Secret"
        defaultState="true" override="hidden"/>
      <customTestSecurity id="S" title="Secret"
        defaultState="true" override="hidden"/>
      <customTestSecurity id="UC"  title="Unclassified"
        defaultState="true" override="hidden"/>
</customAttributesSecurity> <body> <switch>
//Classification is TS(Top-Secret)
<par customTestMODE= "Normal"> <video src="CameraTS1.rm"
channel="video1" customTestSecurity="TS"/> <audio
src="CameraTS1.wav" customTestSecurity="TS" />
//Classification is S(Secret)
<video src="CameraS1.rm" channel="video1" customTestSecurity="S"/>
<audio src="CameraS2.wav" customTestSecurity="S"/>
//Classification is U(Unclassified)
<video src="CameraU1.rm" channel="video2" customTestSecurity="S"/>
<audio src="CameraU1.wav" customTestSecurity="S" /> </par> <par
customTestMODE= "Emergency">
//All 3 above together (Total of 6 feeds)
    </body>
</smil>
```

## 5.2   Normal Form and Operational Semantics

The MLS Normal Form of a SMIL specification S as the one in Section 5.1 called *mlsNF* is one that is parallel composition of at most three specifications, where each specification belongs to one security class, that are said to be the views corresponding to the respective security classes. We now give a formal definition of mlsNF.

**Definition 1 (MLS Normal Form)** *We say that a SMIL specification (s) is in the mlsNF(MLS Normal Form) if it is of the form* $\langle$ *seq* $\rangle$ $\langle$ *par* $\rangle$ $C_t s(s) \langle$ */par* $\rangle$ $\langle par \rangle$ $C_s(s) \langle$ */par* $\rangle$ $\langle$ *par* $\rangle$ $C_u(s)$ $\langle$ */par* $\rangle$ $\langle$ */seq* $\rangle$ *where all Security classifications in* $C_t s$ *(s),* $C_s(s)$, $C_u$ *(s)are respectively Top-Secret, Secret and Unclassified.*

In the most general case, a SMIL specification in mlsNF is of the form $\langle$par $\rangle$ Cts Cs Cu Cod Cud $\langle$/par$\rangle$ where Cts Cs Cu Cod and Cud respectively have top secret, secret, unclassified, over specified and under specified security levels. How one resolves under specification and over specification is a matter of policy, and is not addressed in this paper. Independently, Cts, Cs, Cu are to be shown to guards with top secret, secret, and unclassified clearances. A detailed discussion of the *normal form*,the algorithm for conversion of an arbitrary SMIL fragment to its mlsNF, the operational semantics based on the normal form and its proof of correctness can be obtained from our previous papers [KFW03a,KFW03b].

## 6   Runtime Operations

In order to respond to emergencies, the SMIL specifications have a mode switch encoded using a custom attribute attributeTestMode. As observed in the SMIL fragment, this attribute is to be evaluated at the beginning of a $\langle$switch$\rangle$ statement. This is unsatisfactory for the intended surveillance purposes, because the operating mode could vary many times after the switch is initially evaluated. If the $\langle$switch$\rangle$ is evaluated only once, the SMIL specification is now oblivious to such changes in application situations. In this section, we show how to rewrite a SMIL document with one $\langle$switch$\rangle$ statement for changing a mode to that one that makes the attributeTestMode be evaluated at regular intervals. Although in theory any system could switch its operating mode in an arbitrarily small time intervals, practical considerations limits this interval to a minimum. This minimum switching granularity may depend upon many parameters such as hardware, software and the inherent delays in of switching on fire-fighting and other emergency related equipment. Therefore, given a switching delay D, we rewrite the given SMIL document so that the mode attribute attributeTest-Mode re-evaluated every D time units as discussed in the next section.

The Figure 5 pictorially represents the process of generating and encrypting the views and the black-box architecture for deployment in *SECRETS* that will be discussed in the Sections 6 and 7.

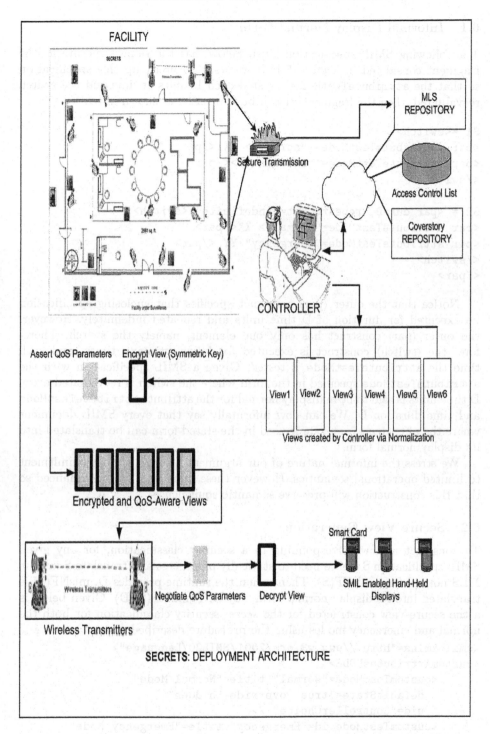

**Fig. 5.** View Generation and Deployment Architecture

## 6.1   Informal Display Normal Form

The following SMIL specification given below, has the same structure as the fragment considered in Section 5.1. If we want to break up this specification so that the `attributeTestMode` is tested each D units of time and the switch reevaluated, then the fragment S1 can be translated as shown in S2.

```
S1 =<switch>
<par  attributeTestMode= "normal"> XX </par>
<par attributeTestMode= "emergency"></par>
</switch>

S2 = <par dur=D, repeatCount="indefinite"><switch>
<par attributeTestMode="normal"> XX</par>
<par attributeTestMode="emergency">YY </par>
</switch>
</par>
```

Notice that the outer ⟨par⟩ construct specifies that enclosing specification be executed for duration of D time units and repeated indefinitely. However, the outer ⟨par⟩ construct has only one element, namely the switch. Therefore, the ⟨switch⟩ construct is executed for infinitely many times, and each time the `attributeTestMode` is tested. Given a SMIL specification with the `attributeTestMode` specified in the form where the switch is reevaluated every D time units is said to be in display normal for the attribute `attributeTestMode` and time duration D. We can now informally say that every SMIL document where the `attributeTestMode` is used in the stated form can be translated into its display normal form.

We stress the informal nature of our argument because of our commitment to limited operational semantics. However these semantics can be enhanced so that this construction will preserve semantic equivalence.

## 6.2   Secure View Generation

To construct a view corresponding to a security classification, for any given SMIL specification S for we need to statically preprocess and translate S into its MLS normal form mlsNF(S). Then, when the runtime provides D, mlsNF(S) is translated into its display normal form, say DNF(mlsNF(S),D). Given below is a the secure view constructed for the *secret* security classification for both the normal and emergency modes using the procedure described above.

```
<smil xmlns="http://www.w3.org/2001/SMIL20/Language">
<customAttributesMODE>
      <customTestMode="Normal" title="Normal Mode"
        defaultState="true" override="hidden"
        uid="ControllerChoice" />
      <customTestMode id="Emergency" title="Emergency Mode"
      --------
```

```
</customAttributesMODE>
<customAttributesSecurity>
------
</customAttributesSecurity>
  <body>
    <switch>
<ref src="ModeNClassS.smil"
customTestMode ="Normal" customTestSecurity="S"/>
<ref src="ModeNClassS.smil"
customTestMode ="Emergency" customTestSecurity="S"/>
    </switch>
  </body>
</smil>
```

The *SECRETS* runtime takes each the set of streams within the switch that has duration of D, evaluates the switch, and depending upon the mode encrypts and transmits either the streams corresponding to normal operating mode or those that correspond to the emergency operating mode. The mode evaluation procedures for setting of the MODE value associated with a `customTestMODE` is as follows:

1. The initial setting is taken from the value of the `defaultState` attribute, if present. If no default state is explicitly defined, a value of false is used.
2. The URI (Controller Choice) defined by the uid attribute is checked to see if a persistent value has been defined for the custom test attribute with the associated id (Normal, Emergency). If such a value is present, it is used instead of the default state defined in the document (if any). Otherwise, the existing initial state is maintained.
3. As with predefined system test attributes, this evaluation will occur in an implementation-defined manner. The value will be (re) evaluated dynamically.

## 6.3   Quality of Service Issues

The SLA (Service Level Agreement determines the specifications and restrictions that have to be communicated between the client and the server in order to maintain good quality [WS96]. The requirements of the processors and memory (primary and secondary), and other technicalities such as tolerable delay, loss, pixels have to be negotiated prior or sometimes during the transfer process. HQML [GNY+01] proposes an XML based language for the exchange of processor characteristics. The most important characteristic is the amount of buffer, in terms of memory that the recipient device should have in order to maintain continuity. These specifications would be represented within the SMIL document, so that the recipient device will first prepare or disqualify itself for a reception. In *SECRETS*, the QoS parameters are generally negotiated prior to the display. They could be set as custom defined attributes that have to resolve to true for the display to happen. We could use some of the standard attributes of the switch statement `systemRequired`, `systemScreenDepth`, and `systemScreenSize` to enforce regulation.

```
<App name = "Surveillance Facility#3">
    <Configuration id = "Level1Guard">
            <UserLevelQoS> high </UserLevelQoS>
            <UserFocus> memory </UserFocus>
    </Configuration>
    <Configuration id = "Level2Guard">
            <MemUnit mem = "Mbytes"> 5MB </mem>
            <UserLevelQoS> Average </UserLevelQoS>
            <UserFocus> Delay </UserFocus>
            <Delayunit del = "Minutes"> 7 </del>
            <SLAModel> Conform SLA </SLAModel>
    </Configuration>
    <Configuration id = "Level3Guard">
            <UserLevelQoS> high </UserLevelQoS>
            <UserFocus> clarity </UserFocus>
            <Clarityunit clar= "pixels/inch"> 200 </clar>
    </Configuration>
</App>
```

The HQML fragment above describes QoS declaration and negotiation. The mobile or stationary device on receiving this file should be able to make decisions based on the user/server defined thresholds.

# 7   Client-Server Deployment

Mobile handheld viewing devices that have embedded SMIL players are the recipients in *SECRETS*. A smartcard, which enforces access control, is embedded into the display device [KW02,KWJ03]. Each display device has a unique smartcard depending on the classification of the guard that utilizes it and his classification and any other rules set by the controller. A decryption key associated with the privileges of the guard is also embedded in the smartcard thereby effectively transferring the load from the server onto the recipient device. When a display device receives an encrypted SMIL document, the smartcard decrypts the appropriate segment depending on the available decryption key. We use XML Encryption for encrypting the views as well as transferring the keys, embedded in the SMIL document. as represented below . An inbuilt Cryptix Parser handles the decryption process would enable selective decryption of the appropriate view based on the access privileges as defined in the smartcard. All transmissions of media files to various people in the hierarchy use standard hypertext transfer protocol (HTTP) web protocol or the Wi-Fi (802.11) wireless transfer protocol. In the SMIL document, each view is encrypted with an unique SymmetricKey depending on the security classification and the process is repeated for all the views within the document. All the encrypted views have a corresponding symmetric decryption key (which is the same as the encryption key) and the recipient smartcard. Figure 6 summarizes the details of the process and provides a run-time algorithm for *SECRETS*.

```
<smil>
-----
<switch>
<par>
 <media src= "ModeNClassS.smil" customTest3 = "Emergency"/>
      <EncryptedData xmlns='http://www.w3.org/2001/04/xmlenc#'>
      <CipherData>
      <CipherValue>MAabaVaAnTeNaaKisTAM</CipherValue>
      </CipherData>
      </EncryptedData>
</par>
<par> <media src=" ModeNClassTS.smil" customTest3="Normal"/>
      ------
</par>
//Other SMIL views.
      ------
 <\smil>
```

The fragment above represents the encryption procedure embedded in SMIL and is explained as below

1. The granularity of encryption in SCERETS is a view
2. The Symmetric key cipher is (3DES CBC)
3. The Symmetric key has an associated Class based on the intended recipient "SymmetricKey Class [TS,S,UC]".
4. CipherData contains a CipherReference, a reference which helps in the transformations necessary to obtain the encrypted data

# 8   Conclusions

We have presented *SECRETS*, a surveillance framework for audio-video surveillance of multi-level secured facilities during normal and pre-envisioned emergencies. We enhanced the SMIL specification with security decorations in order to achieve our goal of being able to satisfy MLS constraints during normal operations and provide controlled declassification during emergencies. Then we showed how to transform such a SMIL composition to its MLS normal form that preserve runtime semantics intended by SMIL constructs while creating views compliant with MLS requirements. Given the delay characteristics of a runtime, we show how to transform a SMIL document in MLS normal form so that the operating mode can be switched with the minimum delay while respecting runtime

| At Server(Processing center) | At Client( Display devices): |
|---|---|
| start; | start; |
| while(Repository != NULL) | //Negotiate Modality parameters |
| initiate toMLSNF; | //Negotiate QoS parameters |
| normalize( ); | if (QoS = FALSE) |
| *define customAtrributeMode* | exit(); |
| define customTestMode = " Normal" | if (QoS == TRUE) |
| define customTestMode = " Emergency" | while (timedDisplay instance = 1) |
| | switch(MODE on case) |
| *define customAttributeSecurity* | (case 1) Mode == "N") |
| define customTestSecurity = " TS(Top-Secret)" | decrypt Normal View; |
| define customTestSecurity = " S(Secret)" | else if |
| define customTestSecurity = " UC(Unclassified)" | (case 2  Mode == "E") |
| | decrypt Emergency View; |
| while(customTestMode = "Normal") | timedDisplayInstance ++; |
| for  customTestSecurity = values(TS,S,UC) | //Re-evaluate Mode at every timed |
| generate view; | //display |
| | end; |
| while(customTestMode = "Emergency" ) | |
| customTestSecurity = "Secret"; | |
| generate coverstory ( Coverstory TS-S1.ram); | |
| //This coverstory would mask the TS data for a | |
| S guard | |
| //Repeat for Unclassified// | |
| | |
| encrypt (Normal View and Emergency View) | |
| state Modality Parameters using Layout | |
| state Resource and QoS Parameters using HQML | |
| transmit() | |
| end; | |

Fig. 6. *SECRETS* Run-time Algorithm

semantics of SMIL. Our ongoing work extends this basic framework to incorporate richer multimedia semantics as well as diverse security requirements such as non-repudiation of media evidence, two-way media channels and incorporate them in SMIL metamodels. Finally, this paper focuses on confidentiality issues. Although our approach to provide controlled information flow in real-time multimedia systems is based in concepts similar to MLS, the developed methods and techniques are also applicable in other security models, like Role-Based or

Discretionary Access Control models. However, it is also important to address data integrity and source authentication issues. These issues, along with the development of a complete and comprehensive prototype system are part of our future work.

# References

[Aya01]     Jeff Ayars. *Synchronized Multimedia Integration Language*. W3C Recommendation, 2001. http://www.w3.org/TR/2001/REC-smil20-20010807.

[BHAE02]    Elisa Bertino, Moustafa Hammad, Walid Aref, and Ahmed Elmagarmid. An access control model for video database systems. In *Conference on Information and Knowledge Management*, 2002.

[Bul98]     David Bulterman. Grins: A graphical interface for creating and playing smil documents. In *Proc. of Seventh Int'l World Wide Web Conf. (WWW7)*. Elsevier Science, New York, April 1998.

[DdV03]     Ernesto Damiani and Sabrina De Capitani di Vimercati. Securing xml based multimedia content. In *18th IFIP International Information Security Conference*, 2003.

[GNY+01]    Xiaohui Gu, Klara Nahrstedt, Wanghong Yuan, Duangdao Wichadakul, and Dongyan Xu. An xml-based quality of service enabling language for the web, 2001.

[KFW03a]    Naren Kodali, Csilla Farkas, and Duminda Wijesekera. Enforcing integrity in multimedia surveillance. In *IFIP 11.5 Working Conference on Integrity and Internal Control in Information Systems*, 2003.

[KFW03b]    Naren Kodali, Csilla Farkas, and Duminda Wijesekera. Multimedia access contol using rdf metadata. In *Workshop on Metadata for Security, WMS 03*, 2003.

[KW02]      Naren Kodali and Duminda Wijesekera. Regulating access to smil formatted pay-per-view movies. In *2002 ACM Workshop on XML Security*, 2002.

[KWJ03]     Naren Kodali, Duminda Wijesekera, and J.B.Michael. Sputers: A secure traffic surveillance and emergency response architecture. In *submission to the Journal of Intelligent Transportaion Systems*, 2003.

[Nok]       Mobile Internet Toolkit: Nokia. www.nokia.com.

[PCV02]     Kari Pihkala, Pablo Cesar, and Petri Vuorimaa. Cross platform smil player. In *International Conference on Communications, Internet and Information Technology*, 2002.

[RHO99]     L. Rutledge, L. Hardman, and J. Ossenbruggen. The use of smil: Multimedia research currently applied on a global scale, 1999.

[RvOHB99]   Lloyd Rutledge, Jacco van Ossenbruggen, Lynda Hardman, and Dick C. A. Bulterman. Anticipating SMIL 2.0: the developing cooperative infrastructure for multimedia on the Web. *Computer Networks (Amsterdam, Netherlands: 1999)*, 31(11–16):1421–1430, 1999.

[Sch99]     B. K. Schmidt. An architecture for distributed, interactive, multi-stream, multi-participant audio and video. In *Technical Report No CSL-TR-99-781, Stanford Computer Science Department*, 1999.

[Spy]       Spymake. Integrated surveillance tools http://www.spymakeronline.com/.

[SSC00]     Paulo Nazareno Maia Sampaio, C. A. S. Santos, and Jean-Pierre Courtiat. About the semantic verification of SMIL documents. In *IEEE International Conference on Multimedia and Expo (III)*, pages 1675–1678, 2000.

[VCM]      Mobile VCMS. Field data collection system http://www.acrcorp.com.

[VSA]      VSAM. Video surveilance and monitoring webpage at http://www-2.cs.cmu.edu/ vsam/.

[WS96]     Duminda Wijesekera and Jaideep Srivastava. Quality of service (qos) metrics for continuous media. *Multimedia Tools and Applications*, 3(2):127–166, 1996.

# Studying E-Mail Graphs
# for Intelligence Monitoring and Analysis
# in the Absence of Semantic Information*

Petros Drineas, Mukkai S. Krishnamoorthy,
Michael D. Sofka, and Bülent Yener

Department of Computer Science, RPI, Troy, NY 12180, USA
{drinep,moorthy, sofkam,yener}@rpi.edu

**Abstract.** This work describes a methodology that can be used to identify structure and communication patterns within an organization based
on e-mail data. The first step of the method is the construction of an
e-mail graph; we then experimentally show that the adjacency matrix
of the graph is well approximated by a low-rank matrix. The low-rank
property indicates that Principal Component Analysis techniques may be
used to remove the noise and extract the structural information (e.g. user
communities, communication patterns, etc.). Furthermore, it is shown
that the e-mail graph degree distribution (both with respect to indegrees
and outdegrees) follows power laws; we also demonstrate that there exists
a giant component connecting 70% of the nodes.

## 1 Introduction and Motivation

E-mail communications play an important role in information society as a means
for collaboration and knowledge exchange. It dominates business, social and
technical transactions and it is an attractive area for research on community
formation and evolution in the social networks context. Since individuals in an
organization create formal or adhoc groups, their e-mail communication patterns usually carry implicit information regarding their common activities and
interests.

This paper describes an experiment conducted in our institution (RPI) using
e-mail message logs obtained over several days. Using this data we construct an
*e-mail graph* that captures the communication patterns. In our work we examine the properties of e-mail graphs and study a variety of metrics; first of all,
we validate that the distributions of the indegrees and outdegrees in our graph
follow power laws. Next, we present a spectral analysis of the graph based on
the Singular Value Decomposition (SVD) and demonstrate that the adjacency
matrix of the graph is quite low rank. The low-rank property and the existence
of power laws in the e-mail graph indicate that Principal Component Analysis
techniques can be used for the discovery of user communities and communication patterns. Additionally, we observe that the graphs have a giant connected
component, which could be used to help reduce the complexity of our algorithms.

---

* This research is supported by NSF ITR Award #0324947.

H. Chen et al. (Eds.): ISI 2004, LNCS 3073, pp. 297–306, 2004.

Our work essentially validates the use of models such as the ones proposed in [1, 2] to model the e-mail graph. Thus, from such models, we can easily estimate the probability that a user sends/receives $k$ e-mails within a period of time $T$ (i.e. $p(k)$ will be $k^{-\alpha}$ for suitable choices of the exponent $\alpha$, as we shall demonstrate in the experimental results section). We can also predict how the e-mail graph evolves over time, thus predicting future e-mail communications. Finally, such models might be used to design and evaluate strategies for the spreading of infectious software, such as worms and viruses, in the Internet via e-mail.

## 1.1  Related Work

Understanding on-line social networks and analyzing their structures has been a focus of intense research in both Social Science and Computer Science (please see [3] and references therein). E-mail is the predominant means of communication in on-line society. Most works have focused on information flow via e-mail and, in particular, the spread of a viral epidemic and the design of effective strategies to prevent such a spread. In [4] the authors analyze e-mail logs and constructed the corresponding e-mail graph over a period of 2 months for senders sending e-mail to or from the HP lab e-mail server; they demonstrate a power law distribution for the outdegrees of this graph (the exponent of the power law was close to 2.0). Similar work was done in [5]; the e-mail graph was generated from the address books of users in a large university system. The authors demonstrate that the degree distributions follow exponential distributions; notice though that they examine a different graph, since the address book of an e-mail user does not necessarily generate links to all e-mail recipients.

In [6], the authors analyze e-mail communication between members of an HP lab over a period of 2 months; their goal is to identify efficient strategies for searching such networks for a specific individual (node). They form a "social network" from this graph by putting an edge between two users if and only if the two users exchanged at least 6 e-mail messages. The resulting graph exhibits an exponential (and not a power law) distribution on the degrees of its nodes. However, in [7], the authors analyze a similar e-mail log, again from the HP labs, over a period of 2 months; they explicitly state that the "raw" data (namely, the graph created by adding an edge between user $i$ and user $j$ if user $i$ sent an e-mail to user $j$) exhibits power-law degree distributions. Results of [8] imply that such graphs consist of a giant connected component and many smaller isolated components. Also, results of [9] imply that the eigenvalues of the adjacency matrix of the graph follow a power law distribution; we expand on these points in section 3.1.

Finally, we note that e-mail communications can be addressed at the organizational or workgroup level as suggested in [10]. Furthermore, application of SVD to social networks are previously considered for discovering communities [11][1].

---

[1] The authors thank to the anonymous referees for pointing out additional references.

**Our Contribution.** The main contribution of our work is the application of SVD on a graph created from e-mail data and the spectral analysis of this graph. By showing existence of the power law and low-rank properties on e-mail graphs, we establish a basis for using SVD based data mining approaches to discover hidden communities in e-mail communications.

# 2   Model and Methodology

## 2.1   Data Collection and Processing

Data for the e-mail samples were taken from a full SMTP (Simple Mail Transport Protocol) feed at Rensselaer Polytechnic Institutes' central mail servers from one full week.

The SMTP protocol minimally identifies a connecting SMTP relay, the envelope sender, the envelope recipients and the DATA. The DATA contains the e-mail message body and additional e-mail headers. Sendmail logs a "from" line for the envelope sender and a series of "to" lines for each message recipient. These appear in the log file in the order that multiple, parallel, sendmail dae-mons processed the messages. When a new SMTP connection is established, sendmail assigns a unique queue id to the message. The queue id can be used to extract the linked log entries corresponding to a single e-mail message.

Logging is further complicated by e-mail forwarding, and alias expansion, which result in "ctladdr" and "clone" entries, respectively. RPI's e-mail logs also record the results of virus and Unsolicited Commercial E-mail (spam) filtering.

It is important to make clear the distinction between envelope sender and recipients, and the e-mail "From" and "To" headers. E-mail headers are DATA as far as the SMTP protocol is concerned, and are not recorded sendmail. Sendmail logs the envelope information, which appears in the SMTP dialog, and which may differ from the message headers. For example, a message sent with a Blind Carbon Copy (bcc) header will have envelope recipients which do not appear in the message headers. Likewise, a mailing list may use a envelope sender which is a special bounce detection address with a unique identification tag, while the message header provides the true list name and reply-to address. The provided data included only envelope information.

Personally identifiable information in the logs was obscured using the HMAC message authentication protocol with a 128bit SSH1 hash. Identifying information included the envelope sender and recipients, the connecting mail relay, the message id (a unique id generated by e-mail clients), and delivery status information.

Information about spam scores and viruses were not included in the logs used for the study. The format of virus and spam messages has gone through numerous changes over the past year, making relatively safe obfuscation error prone. In addition, messages from spammers and virus infected machines is intentionally misleading, and attempt to exploit bugs in client e-mail readers. As a result, the log entries often contain non-standard characters (especially in envelope sender, and message id and attachment names) making consistent parsing difficult. However, such messages can often be inferred from delivery status errors, unknown users and missing recipients (when the spam is dropped by Rensselaer's spam filter).

## 2.2 The E-Mail Graph

From the e-mail data we construct a graph represented by an adjacency matrix $A$. In the graph each node corresponds to a concealed e-mail address (i.e., the rows and columns of $A$) and there is an edge $(i, j)$ in the graph if node $i$ sends an e-mail to node $j$.

## 2.3 SVD and Spectral Analysis

We briefly review the singular value decomposition of matrices; we will use some of its properties in our discussion in Section 3.1. Any $m \times n$ matrix $A$ can be expressed as

$$A = \sum_{t=1}^{r} \sigma_t(A) u^{(t)} v^{(t)^T},$$

where $r$ is the rank of $A$, $\sigma_1(A) \geq \sigma_2(A) \geq \ldots \geq \sigma_r(A) > 0$ are its singular values and $u^{(t)} \in \mathcal{R}^m, v^{(t)} \in \mathcal{R}^n, t = 1, \ldots, r$ are its left and right singular vectors respectively. The $u^{(t)}$'s and the $v^{(t)}$'s are orthonormal sets of vectors; namely, $u^{(i)^T} u^{(j)}$ is one if $i = j$ and zero otherwise. We also remind the reader that

$$\|A\|_F^2 = \sum_{i,j} A_{ij}^2 = \sum_{i=1}^{r} \sigma_i^2(A),$$

$$\|A\|_2 = \max_{x \in \mathcal{R}^n : \|x\|=1} \|Ax\| = \max_{x \in \mathcal{R}^m : \|x\|=1} \|x^T A\| = \sigma_1(A).$$

In matrix notation, SVD is defined as $A = U \Sigma V^T$ where $U$ and $V$ are orthogonal (thus $U^T U = I$ and $V^T V = I$) matrices of dimensions $m \times r$ and $n \times r$ respectively, containing the left and right singular vectors of $A$. $\Sigma = \mathbf{diag}(\sigma_1(A), \ldots, \sigma_r(A))$ is an $r \times r$ diagonal matrix containing the singular values of $A$.

One of numerous applications of SVD is in recovering the structure of matrices and in noise removal in a variety of settings. The underlying idea is very simple: since $A = \sum_{t=1}^{r} \sigma_t(A) u^{(t)} v^{(t)^T}$, we can create approximations to $A$ by keeping only the top $k$ "principal components" (i.e. the top $k$ $\sigma_t(A) u^{(t)} v^{(t)^T}$) for various values of $k$. Essentially, discarding the "smallest" principal components (the ones corresponding to the smallest singular values), results in a small loss in accuracy, and we might justifiably consider these components as "noise". This procedure is commonly referred to as "Principal Component Analysis" and the following theorem (usually attributed to Eckart and Young [12]) quantifies the loss of accuracy incurred by keeping only the top $k$ components for various values of $k$.

**Theorem 1.** *Let $A_k = \sum_{t=1}^{k} \sigma_t u^{(t)} v^{(t)^T}$ (for any $1 \leq k \leq r$). $A_k$ is the "best" rank $k$ approximation to $A$ with respect to the 2-norm and the Frobenius norm; namely, for any matrix $D$ of rank at most $k$,*

$$\|A - A_k\|_2 \leq \|A - D\|_2 \quad and \quad \|A - A_k\|_F \leq \|A - D\|_F.$$

*Also,*

$$\|A - A_k\|_F^2 = \sum_{t=k+1}^{r} \sigma_t^2(A) \quad and \quad \|A - A_k\|_2 = \sigma_{k+1}(A).$$

We say that a matrix $A$ has a "good" rank $k$ approximation if the 2-norm and the Frobenius norm of $A - A_k$ is small; for a detailed treatment of Singular Value Decomposition see [12].

## 3 Experimental Results

### 3.1 Spectral Analysis of the E-Mail Graph

Not surprisingly, the e-mail graphs exhibit low-rank structure. As a result, Principal Component Analysis techniques would be successful if applied on such graphs to extract communities of users, remove noise, etc. In Figure 3 we plotted the spectral characteristics of the 3 graphs. The graphs are obtained from splitting one week mail logs into three sets for managing the complexity of SVD algorithm. More specifically, the plot demonstrates how accurately we can approximate the given graphs by keeping a small percentage of the maximal number of principal components (see Section 2.3 for background) that comprise the graphs; notice that for a graph with $n$ vertices, we might have up to $n$ principal components.

We now describe the findings of Figure 3. Notice that the $x$-axis represents the percentage of principal components (out of the maximal possible number of principal components) that are kept, while the $y$-axis represents the percentage of the spectrum of the graph contained within these principal components; more specifically, let $A$ denote the adjacency matrix of a graph. Then, the $y$-axis represents the ratio

$$\frac{\|A - A_k\|_F^2}{\|A\|_F^2},$$

which may be viewed as the relative error of the approximation $A_k$ to $A$ using a certain percentage of the maximal number of principal components. Recall that the above ratio is equal to

$$\frac{\sum_{t=k+1}^{r} \sigma_t^2(A)}{\sum_{t=1}^{r} \sigma_t^2(A)}.$$

Thus, in order to compute the ratio, we computed a large number of singular values for the adjacency matrix $A$ of each graph using MatLab. Notice that a very small percentage (say 5%) of the principal components is enough to cover almost 80% of the spectrum for all three graphs. Thus, we conclude that the

Table 1. E-mail Graph Properties

| E-mail Graph Size | Giant Component (GC) Size | GC Clustering Coefficient | GC Diameter |
|---|---|---|---|
| 22776 | 15260 | 0.0013 | 23 |
| 21614 | 14996 | 0.0025 | 20 |
| 21732 | 15400 | 0.0012 | 26 |

graphs have a low-rank property, which directly implies that Principal Component Analysis could be used to remove the noise and extract their structure. We should also mention that our findings are consistent with the power-law distribution of the indegrees and outdegrees of the graph nodes. In [9], the authors studied the distribution of the eigenvalues of graphs whose degree distributions (on the nodes) follow power laws, and they demonstrated that the eigenvalues exhibit a power law distribution themselves; we defer a more thorough analysis of this connection to the full version of the paper.

### 3.2 Power Laws in E-Mail Graph

In this section we show that (i) degree distribution of e-mail graph obeys power laws, (ii) there is a giant component within each graph that spans approximately 70% of the nodes, (iii) the diameter of the giant component is small, and (iv) the neighborhood connectivity of a node is quite sparse.

The **diameter** is the longest shortest path between any pair of nodes in a connected graph. It reflects how far apart two nodes are (from each other) in the e-mail graph. We computed the diameter of the giant component and the results are shown in Table 1.

The **clustering coefficient** reflects the connectivity information in the neighborhood environment of a node [13]. It provides the transitivity information [14], since it controls whether two different nodes are connected or not, assuming that they are connected to the same node. The clustering coefficient $C_i$ is defined as the percentage of the connections between the neighbors of node $i$, i.e.

$$C_i = \frac{2 \cdot E_i}{k \cdot (k - 1)}, \tag{1}$$

where $k$ is the number of neighbors of node $i$ and $E_i$ is the number of existing connections between its neighbors. We compute $C_i$ for all nodes $i$ in the giant component and take the average to get a global value. Table 1 shows that the overall clustering coefficient is quite low.

In Figures 1 and 2 we show that there exists a giant component, and that both the whole graph and the giant component have power law degree distributions. For the whole graph, the in-degree exponent is around 1.9, while for the giant component it is approximately 1.7. The out degree exponents of the giant component and the whole graph are also close (3.1 and 3.2, respectively).

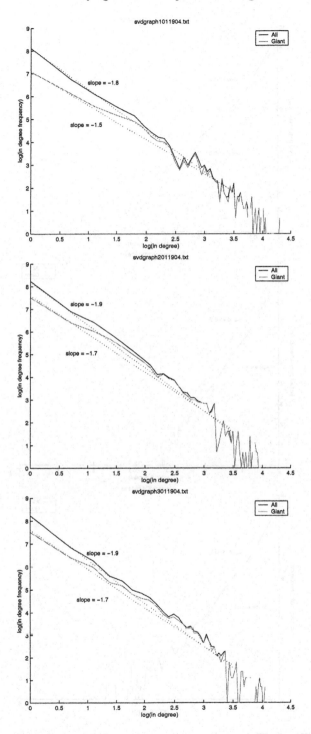

**Fig. 1.** The in-degree distribution of e-mail graph

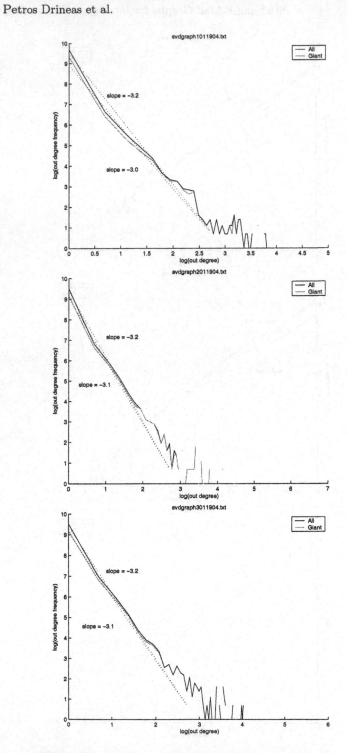

**Fig. 2.** The out-degree distribution of the e-mail graph

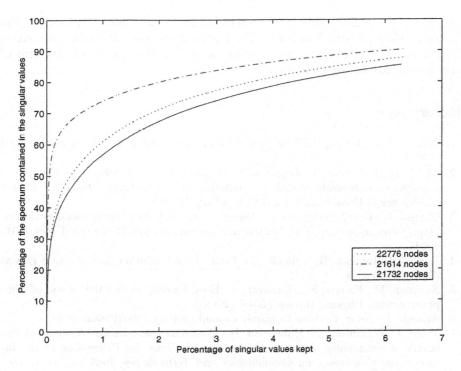

**Fig. 3.** Adjacency matrix spectrum vs. rank

The power-law distribution and the in-degree, out-degree exponent difference intuitively emerge from the observation that there are a few individuals inside the organization getting many external e-mails (e.g., member of mailing lists), and there are also some individuals inside the organization sending out announcements to many people, thus having very high outdegrees (e.g., program committee members for a conference, etc.).

## 4   Discussion and Conclusions

This work establishes a basis for applying Principal Component Analysis (PCA) to e-mail communication graphs, to discover groups and communication patterns, by showing existence of the low-rank property and power laws in these graphs. It also shows existence of the giant component property which helps identifying the groups in other connected components thus reduces the complexity of the data mining algorithms. Based on the power laws one can now determine the probability that a user sends/receives $k$ e-mails with in a period of time $T$. This probability can be used to model how e-mail graphs evolve over time (i.e., prediction of future e-mail communications).

However, we also note the limited applicability of this approach to discovering malicious groups such as terrorist cells (a.k.a., the adversary in security jargon). In particular, the adversary may use freely available e-mail servers like Yahoo or Hotmail with fake e-mail IDs. Furthermore, the adversary can conceal its communication patterns by inducing noise into the system in the form of unsolicited mail or self e-mailing.

# References

1. Babarasi, A., Albert, R.: Emergence of scaling in random networks. Science **286** (1999)
2. Kleinberg, J., Kumar, S., Raghavan, P., Rajagopalan, S., Tomkins, A.: The web as a graph: measurements, models and methods. In: Proceedings of the International Conference in Combinatorics and Computing. (1999)
3. Garton, L., Haythornthwaite, C., Wellman, B.: Studying online social networks. http://www.ascusc.org/jcmc/vol3/issue1/garton.htm (1997) (accessed March 16, 2004).
4. Wu, F., Huberman, B., Adamic, L., Tyler, J.: Information flow in social groups (2003) manuscript.
5. Newman, M., Forrest, S., , Balthrop, J.: E-mail networks and the spread of computer viruses. Physical Review **(E)66** (2002)
6. Adamic, L., Adar, E.: How to search a social network (2003) manuscript.
7. Tyler, J., Wilkinson, D., Huberman, B.: E-mail as spectroscopy: Automated discovery of community structure withing organizations. In: Proceeding of the International Conference on Communities and Technologies, Netherlands, Kluwer Academic Publishers (2003)
8. Aiello, W., Chung, F., Lu, L.: A random graph model for massive graphs. In: STOC. (1999) 171–180
9. Chung, F., Lu, L., Vu, V.: Eigenvalues of random power law graphs. Annals of Combinatorics **7** (2003)
10. Nonaka, I.: A dynamic theory of organizational knowledge creation. Organization Science **5** (1994) 14–37
11. Freeman, L.C.: Visualizing social groups. In: 1999 Proceedings of the Section on Statistical Graphics, American Statistical Association (2000) pp:47–54
12. Golub, G., Loan, F.V.: Matrix Computations. Johns Hopkins University Press (1984)
13. Dorogovtsev, S.N., Mendes, J.F.F.: Evolution of Networks. Advances in Physics **51** (2002) 1079–1187
14. Newman, M.: Who is the best connected scientist? a study of scientific coauthorship networks. Physical Review (2001)

# THEMIS: Threat Evaluation Metamodel for Information Systems

Csilla Farkas[1], Thomas C. Wingfield[2],
James B. Michael[3], and Duminda Wijesekera[4]

[1] Dept. of Computer Science and Engineering, USC, Columbia, S.C. 29208
farkas@cse.sc.edu
[2] The Potomac Institute for Policy Studies, Arlington, Va. 22203
twingfield@potomacinstitute.org
[3] Dept. of Computer Science, Naval Postgraduate School, Monterey, Calif. 93943
bmichael@nps.edu
[4] Dept. of Information and Software Engineering, GMU, Fairfax Va. 22030
dwijesek@gmu.edu

**Abstract.** THEMIS (**T**hreat **E**valuation **M**etamodel for **I**nformation **S**ystems) is a description logic-based framework to apply state, federal, and international law to reason about the intent of computer network attacks with respect to collateral consequences. It can be used by law enforcement agencies and prosecutors to build legally credible arguments, and by network designers to keep their defensive and retaliatory measures within lawful limits. THEMIS automates known quantitative measures of characterizing attacks, weighs their potential impact, and places them in appropriate legal compartments. From the perspective of computer networks, we develop representations and a way to reason about the non-network related consequences of complex attacks from their atomic counterparts. From the perspective of law, we propose the development of interoperable ontologies and rules that represent concepts and restrictions of heterogeneous legal domains. The two perspectives are woven together in THEMIS using description logic to reason about and guide defensive, offensive, and prosecutorial actions.

## 1 Introduction

Conventional security measures are designed to prevent attacks and to discourage attackers from continuing their attacks. Once an intrusion into a system or misuse of the a system is detected, the system response is to disengage itself from the rogue processes performing the intrusion or misuse actions. Current efforts aim to capture behavioral information about malicious users that can be used as the basis for developing sophisticated responses to intrusions, and to establish guilt of supposed intruders. Software and hardware decoy systems have been developed [12, 11, 16, 5] that allow observation and recording of attackers' activities as a form of counterintelligence in support of countermeasures.

In addition to the decoy systems, various organizations collect cyber crime related data, ranging from system log records to outputs of sophisticated intrusion detection systems. However, only a few attempts have been made to

H. Chen et al. (Eds.): ISI 2004, LNCS 3073, pp. 307–321, 2004.

develop an integrated framework to analyze these data [1] and to incorporate legal restrictions [15, 13] regarding data collection, dissemination, usability, and response [23].

In this paper we focus on the specific problem of evaluating the "intent" and the consequences of computer network attacks from the perspective of national security. This evaluation is especially important to justify retaliatory actions and ensure their lawfulness while providing maximal defense against an adversary. Judging attackers' intent and evaluating the consequences of the attacks are difficult tasks because both the attackers and the consequences of attacks can be categorized into diverse domains. For example, an attacker may be a "script kiddie," a hacker, or a member of a cyber terrorist group, and the consequences (effects) of a computer attack may range from mere inconvenience to human injuries and threats to national security. Coincidently, judging intent requires system-level evidence to be collected, assimilated and maintained to satisfy legal definitions and standards of acceptability, non tampering, and non-repudiation. We propose an approach that relies on legal guidelines to evaluate computer attacks.

With respect to determining intent and damage caused by cyber attacks, from a legal perspective, Schmitt [18] and, subsequently, Wingfield [23] propose seven factors to distinguish between economic and political coercion (non-armed) and armed coercion. These factors (explained in detail in section 2.1) are: severity, immediacy, directness, invasiveness, measurability, presumptive legitimacy, and responsibility. Evaluation of cyber attacks, using these factors, is referred to as the Schmitt Analysis. Michael et al. [14] demonstrate, via a case study of kinetic and cyber attacks on a safety-critical software-intensive system, the applicability of the Schmitt Analysis to determine whether an attack has risen to the level of "use of force" under international law. However, subjective and ad-hoc evaluation of the Schmitt factors can be erroneous with widely varying results, and may not be able to handle large-scale, distributed attacks. It is necessary, therefore, to develop systematic and automated methods for Schmitt Analysis.

This paper presents our current results in developing a metamodel to evaluate characteristics of computer network attacks, and to reason about legal aspects of these attacks and their responses. In particular, we propose a formalism to represent the characteristics of an attack as stated in [14, 18, 23] so that they can be effectively used in an automated reasoning system.

We present a rudimentary policy specification language using the Rule Markup Language [2] syntax. Rules are developed to express legal and military constraints, and the evaluation criteria for the Schmitt Analysis. Reasoning based on these rules will allow the classification of an attack (or coordinated attacks) and support the formulation of counter actions. Our aim is to develop THEMIS using the latest Semantic Web standards such as SWRL (A Semantic Web Rule Language combining OWL and RuleML [4]). These techniques are shown to be promising to support interoperation and reasoning over heterogeneous data domains.

The organization of the paper is as follows. Section 2 contains background information. Section 3 contains the overview of the THEMIS framework. Description of the components of THEMIS are presented in Section 4, where Section 4.1 describes the ontology representation, Section 4.2 the policy specification, and Section 4.3 the conflict resolution and default strategy. Finally, we conclude in Section 5.

## 2   Background Information

### 2.1   Schmitt Analysis

Factors, to distinguish between military (armed), and economic and political coercion of computer network attacks, were identified by Schmitt [18] and Wingfield [23]. Analysis of computer network attacks based on these factors results in justifications that are considered *use of force* under Article 2(4) of the United Nation's Charter. In the perspective of increased attacks and state sponsored attacks against national resources, the Schmitt analysis represents a crucial step to ensure preservation of international law while allowing maximal level of defense. Details of the factors are:

**Severity:** Measure of physical damage and human casualties. For example, value of compromised resources, human injuries, size of the affected area, etc.

**Immediacy:** Time period before the effect is observed, and how long it lasts. For example, effects can be observed (occurred) minutes after the attack, system is unavailable for a week, etc.

**Directness:** Whether the attack caused the results directly (e.g., DDOS attack against Navy communication system) or indirectly (e.g., disabling the Internet to support attack on a particular system).

**Invasiveness:** Did the attack require crossing national boundaries?

**Measurability:** Can the characteristics (damage) of the attack be easily measured? (e.g., physical or financial damage, lost system time, etc.)

**Presumptive Legitimacy:** Is the action analogous to actions (such as large scale application of violence) that could only be presumed legitimate if undertaken by a state?

**Responsibility:** Is a nation-state responsible, and is it publicly stating this?

### 2.2   Semantic Web

The need for interoperation and reasoning over heterogeneous data and knowledge sources is not unique to our application area. The WWW Consortium is developing a standard referent known as the *Semantic Web* for which humans specify the rules of engagement in their own language which in turn will be automatically translated into machine-executable instructions for exchanging self-describing information. Our framework conforms to the existing technologies on the Semantic Web and can be fully integrated with them.

The Semantic Web [7] is envisioned as several, interconnected layers. The lowest layer (XML and namespace) consists of machine-readable code. The next layers, RDF and ontologies, consists of resource definitions available at the machine level. The level on top of the ontologies consists of rules. The top layers consist of logical reasoning engines that would assist in constructing proofs. The main lesson learned from the Semantic Web is that the ontologies provide the crucial translation between applications within a domain.

Using Semantic Web [3] technologies seem to be promising for a variety of domains, like e-business rules [10], intrusion detection [20], and agent-based systems [9]. Most of our proposed legal formulations relate to the ontology and rules layers. For the framework to function, a representative of each legal jurisdiction must publish its own ontologies and rules, making them available for viewing by other communities. For example, if the Federal Bureau of Investigation (FBI) is investigating a cyber attack launched from a site in the European Union (EU), it could consult the EU rules repository to determine the extent of permissible legal countermeasures. By using the ontology layer, different law enforcement agencies could publish their own conceptualization (ontologies), so that they could be seamlessly compiled to fight anticipated cyber crimes.

### 2.3 Legal Reasoning

Developing legal reasoning models is not new. With the increased computational power and the expressiveness of the representational techniques several reasoning models have been developed. Most contributions are based on artificial intelligence. A difficult problem here is to handle so called *open-textured* concepts, i.e., lack of clear definition of legal concepts, requiring experience and common sense to determine their applicability. Nevertheless, several models have been developed. The main categorization of these models are rule-based (logical), case-based, and adversarial reasoning.

Case-based reasoning models rely on previous experiences, maintained as distinct cases, to analyze current cases. Examples of case-based legal reasoning systems are HYPO [17, 6] and GREBE [8]. Some of the systems combine rule-based and case-based methods, like the CABARET [19] system. The two methods are also used for legal argumentation.

A relatively new area of legal reasoning research is to develop ontologies to represent conceptualization of legal domains. Visser et al. [21, 22] give an overview of the roles ontologies may play in the legal contexts. These roles include knowledge sharing, verification of knowledge base, software engineering, knowledge acquisition, knowledge reuse, and domain-theory development. However, none of these works address the legal aspects of cyber attacks or the assessment of the attack consequences from the legal perspective.

## 3  THEMIS Framework

Cyber activities are rarely contained within geographical borders, therefore the identification of presumed violators and preservation of legal evidence require coordinated efforts in multiple jurisdictions, each of which has its own set of legal standards. To support this coordinated effort, it is necessary to enable knowledge sharing and reasoning over diverse knowledge bases. Ontologies, developed by each jurisdiction, support this need by giving explicit specification of the concepts and the relationships assumed to exist among them. In addition to the local ontologies, we propose the development of meta-ontologies which relate various local ontologies. This high-level representation allows the user to compare, analyze, and reason with the legal domain of the different jurisdictions.

Concepts and their relationships, provided by the ontologies, are captured by the formal syntax of the Attack Response Policy (ARP) specification language. The ARP language is a logical language allowing to express legal and response policies. For this, we define the precise alphabet for ARP and a set of predicates (originating from the ontologies) to create policies for legal reasoning, argumentation, attack evaluation, and response.

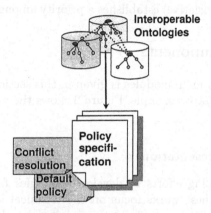

**Fig. 1.** Components of the THEMIS Framework

The two main components of THEMIS are: 1) Legal, military, and computer network attack concept ontologies, and 2) the ARP specification language, capable of reasoning with these ontologies. In addition, THEMIS is capable of resolving conflicts and applying default policies. Figure 1 shows the components of THEMIS.

## 3.1   Network Attack Example

The complexity of formulating the proper rule of law, deconflicting areas of overlap with other such rules, and correctly applying it to the facts at hand is a subtle and complex process. However, it is possible to construct several general principles of application. One such principle is that for any given problem, there is a hierarchy of laws which prevents a logical impasse with apparently conflicting laws. It is not always clear, but almost always possible to establish such a priority in the application of multiple rules.

Consider the following example showing the cascading nature of the network attacks, and the legal restrictions governing the investigation. Assume, that the computer system of the air traffic control tower of Airport XX in state X is attacked, causing the system to malfunction. Due to erroneous information, two airplanes crash, causing physical damage to the planes and the nearby buildings, and loss of human life.

Investigators in state X would be permitted to use all the means at their disposal to identify, locate, and apprehend the perpetrators because the intrusion to a computer system took place in state X. Assume, that the investigation of the air traffic system reveals that the network attack originated from state Y. This requires to acquire the appropriate permissions from the jurisdiction of state Y. Without evidence of the attack origin and permissions, a violation of the US Constitution (e.g., an unreasonable search or seizure, prohibited by the Fourth Amendment and extended to the states through the Fourteenth Amendment) would occur. This priority of law (federal constitutional, federal legislative, state constitutional, state legislative) establishes a priority among the applicable rules.

## 4    THEMIS Components

An overview of the two main modules is given in this section, using the Schmitt Analysis as a representative example. Figure 2 shows the workflow of the attack analysis and response.

### 4.1    Ontology Representation

There are several ongoing efforts to develop ontologies for cyber attacks [20, 9]. However, most of these works focus on the technical aspects of the attack (e.g., type of attack, system components exploited by the attacks, means of

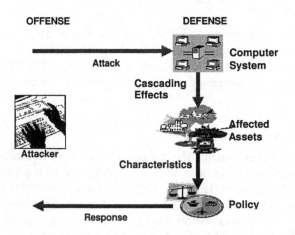

**Fig. 2.** Attack Analysis Model

exploitation) and are limited in describing the legal characteristics of the attacks and their non-network related cascading consequences. To strengthen security and to provide efficient and lawful response it is necessary to evaluate auxiliary consequences that may reach out of the domain of computer systems, and develop measurements of the damage caused by cascading effects.

Our ontology representation is compatible with current work but extends it in four respects: 1) provides measurements of damage assessment, 2) represents cascading and escalating effects of cyber attacks, 3) represents legal concepts, and 4) provides metadata necessary for distributed legal reasoning. Figure 3 shows the graphical representation of computer network attacks from the perspective of consequences. Figure 4 shows a sample of the corresponding OWL representation.

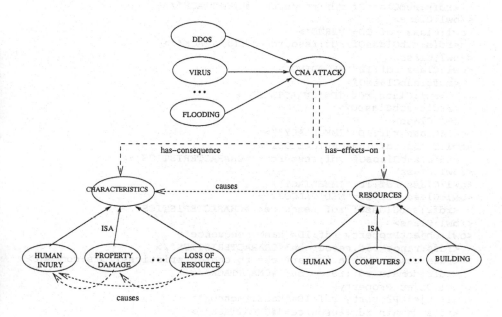

**Fig. 3.** Computer network attacks and their characteristics

Figure 5 shows the relationship between the consequences and the factors used in the Schmitt Analysis. Figure 6 shows a sample of the corresponding OWL representation.

## 4.2 Attack Response Policy (ARP)

To determine the lawfulness of the responses to computer attacks, we need to evaluate the direct and indirect damages caused by the attacks and generate policies for handling them. This includes damage to the target system (usually a computer network and its components) and the cascading effects of the

```
<?xml version="1.0"?>
<rdf:RDF
    xmlns:rss="http://purl.org/rss/1.0/"
    xmlns="http://a.com/ontology#"
    xmlns:jms="http://jena.hpl.hp.com/2003/08/jms#"
    xmlns:rdf="http://www.w3.org/1999/02/22-rdf-syntax-ns#"
    xmlns:rdfs="http://www.w3.org/2000/01/rdf-schema#"
    xmlns:owl="http://www.w3.org/2002/07/owl#"
    xmlns:vcard="http://www.w3.org/2001/vcard-rdf/3.0#"
    xmlns:daml="http://www.daml.org/2001/03/daml+oil#"
    xmlns:dc="http://purl.org/dc/elements/1.1/"
  xml:base="http://a.com/ontology">
  <owl:Class rdf:ID="CNAATTACK"/>
  <owl:Class rdf:ID="CHARACTERISTICS"/>
  <owl:Class rdf:ID="RESOURCES"/>
  <owl:Class rdf:ID="DDOS">
    <rdfs:subClassOf rdf:resource="#CNAATTACK"/>
  </owl:Class>
  <owl:Class rdf:ID="VIRUS">
    <rdfs:subClassOf rdf:resource="#CNAATTACK"/>
  </owl:Class>
  <owl:Class rdf:ID="FLOODING">
    <rdfs:subClassOf>
      <owl:Class rdf:ID="CNAATTACK"/>
    </rdfs:subClassOf>
  </owl:Class>
  <owl:Class rdf:ID="IMMEDIACY"/>
  <owl:Class rdf:ID="MEDICALCOST">
    <rdfs:subClassOf rdf:resource="#CHARACTERISTICS"/>
  </owl:Class>
  <owl:Class rdf:ID="IMMEDIACY"/>
  <owl:Class rdf:ID="MEDICALCOST">
    <rdfs:subClassOf rdf:resource="#CHARACTERISTICS"/>
  </owl:Class>
  <owl:ObjectProperty rdf:ID="hasConsequence">
    <rdfs:range rdf:resource="#CHARACTERISTICS"/>
    <rdfs:comment>Relating attacks to characteristics</rdfs:comment>
    <rdfs:domain rdf:resource="#CNAATTACK"/>
  </owl:ObjectProperty>
  <owl:ObjectProperty rdf:ID="hasEffectsOn">
    <rdfs:domain rdf:resource="#CNAATTACK"/>
    <rdfs:range rdf:resource="#RESOURCES"/>
    <rdfs:comment>Attacks having effects on Resources</rdfs:comment>
  </owl:ObjectProperty>

      ...
```

**Fig. 4.** OWL representation of computer network attacks and their characteristics

compromised assets, caused by limited availability, integrity, or confidentiality. Cascading effects of an attack may reach out of the cyber domain, resulting in damage to physical and human assets. Attack consequences are categorized according to the levels and types of the incurred damages. Note, that "attack consequences" refer to non-computational consequences (i.e., different from log-

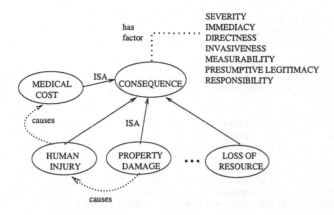

**Fig. 5.** Attack characteristics

ical consequence). They refer to the results of the attacks in the target system, and their cascading and escalating effects. Given the aforementioned requirements, our goal is to develop language for specifying policy and law governing attack assessment and response. Technically, law governs human and automated-system behavior, whereas policy defines the latitude with which the law can be applied. In this paper, however, we use the term "policy," to encompass both law and policy as defined above. Ontologies supply the intra- and interdependencies of the affected assets. We are developing the basic alphabet and predicates for our Attack Response Policy (ARP) specification language.

We are planning to use SWRL [4] rules to reason about the attacks, their characteristics, and legality of responses. For the Schmitt Analysis, THEMIS reaches a classification of the attacks into three categories: "use of force," "arguable use of force," or "not a use of force" according to Article 2(4) of the UN Charter.

**Attack Response Policy (ARP) Specification Language.** Our goal is to develop a set of symbols that can be used to build rules expressing policy and assessment requirements. The ARP specification language defines basic alphabet and predicate symbols. The alphabet of ARP language includes constant symbols, variables, functions, and terms. Constant symbols correspond to elementary concepts of the ontologies, like *computer, human, attack, etc.*. Variables range over the domain of these concept. Function symbols map related concepts, determine quantitative relations, and used to construct terms.

We also define predicates, necessary to build rules expressing attack assessment requirements, legal and response policies. For example, the 4-ary predicate symbol *attack* has the following form:

$$attack(a - id, a - name, orig, targ)$$

where the first argument is an attack identification number, the second is the name of the attack, the third is the originator of the attack, and the fourth argu-

...

```
<owl:Class rdf:ID="CHARACTERISTICS">
  <owl:Class rdf:ID="LOSSOFRESOURCE">
    <rdfs:subClassOf rdf:resource="#CHARACTERISTICS"/>
  </owl:Class>
  <owl:ObjectProperty rdf:ID="hasFactor">
    <rdfs:comment>Relating characteristics with their factors</rdfs:comment>
    <rdfs:domain rdf:resource="#CHARACTERISTICS"/>
    <rdfs:range>
      <owl:Class>
        <owl:unionOf rdf:parseType="Collection">
          <owl:Class rdf:about="#SEVERITY"/>
          <owl:Class rdf:about="#IMMEDIACY"/>
          <owl:Class rdf:about="#DIRECTNESS"/>
          <owl:Class rdf:about="#INVASIVENESS"/>
          <owl:Class rdf:about="#MEASURABILITY"/>
          <owl:Class rdf:about="#RESPONSIBILITY"/>
          <owl:Class rdf:about="#PRESUMPTIVELEGITIMACY"/>
        </owl:unionOf>
      </owl:Class>
    </rdfs:range>
  </owl:ObjectProperty>
  <owl:ObjectProperty rdf:ID="causes">
    <rdfs:domain>
      <owl:Class>
        <owl:unionOf rdf:parseType="Collection">
          <owl:Class rdf:about="#HUMANINJURY"/>
          <owl:Class rdf:about="#PROPERTYDAMAGE"/>
          <owl:Class rdf:about="#LOSSOFRESOURCE"/>
          <owl:Class rdf:about="#RESOURCES"/>
        </owl:unionOf>
      </owl:Class>
    </rdfs:domain>
    <rdfs:comment>Relation between different kinds of
characteristics</rdfs:comment>
    <rdfs:range>
      <owl:Class>
        <owl:unionOf rdf:parseType="Collection">
          <owl:Class rdf:about="#MEDICALCOST"/>
          <owl:Class rdf:about="#HUMANINJURY"/>
          <owl:Class rdf:about="#PROPERTYDAMAGE"/>
          <owl:Class rdf:about="#CHARACTERISTICS"/>
        </owl:unionOf>
      </owl:Class>
    </rdfs:range>
  </owl:ObjectProperty>
```

...

**Fig. 6.** OWL representation of attack characteristics

ment is the target of the attack. For example, the fact that a distributed denial-of-service (DDOS) attack was launched from IP address 129.167.2.5 against IP address 168.145.21.26, and the attack was detected and numbered with attack identification number 29 can be represented with the ground fact (i.e., predicate with constant symbols only)

$$attack(29, DDOS, 129.167.2.5, 168.145.21.26)$$

The consequence predicate is a 3-ary predicate, with arguments attack ID, consequence type, and target.

$$consequence(a - id, c - type, targ)$$

Each Schmitt factor is represented as a predicate, with attack ID, target, and value arguments. For example, the predicate corresponding to factor *severity* is

$$severity(a - id, targ, val)$$

The 4-ary predicate *causes* captures dependencies between cascading consequences

$$causes(c - type_1, targ_1, c - type_2, targ_2)$$

where $c - type_i$ corresponds to the consequence type on the asset $targ_i$ ($i = 1, 2$).

**Policy Rules.** Using the predicates of the ARP language, we can build rules to reason about the damages, express legal restrictions, and determine legitimacy of counter actions. Each rule has the following form:

$$head \leftarrow body_1, body_2, \ldots, body_n$$

where $body_1$, $body_2$, ... , $body_n$ is referred to as the body of the rule. Intuitively, if there is a valuation to the symbols of the *body* such that all predicates are true, then the head must also be true. We restrict our rules to use only the symbols of the ARP language, atomic datatypes, and ARP predicates, and to be bounded, that is, all symbols of the head must appear in the body.

The following example shows the rules to derive cascading consequences of an attack.

$$attack(a - id, a - name, orig, targ_1) \leftarrow attack(a - id, a - name, orig, targ),$$
$$consequence(a - id, c - type, targ),$$
$$causes(c - type, targ, c - type_1, targ_1)$$

$$consequence(a - id, c - type_1, targ_1) \leftarrow attack(a - id, a - name, orig, targ),$$
$$consequence(a - id, c - type, targ),$$
$$causes(c - type, targ, c - type_1, targ_1)$$

The two rules state that if there is an attack on the *targ* asset, and the consequence *c-type* of the attack causes a consequence $c$-$type_1$ on asset $tarq_1$, then the attack is considered an attack on $targ_1$ and the consequence of the attack is $c$-$type_1$.

Rules to evaluate attacks from the perspective of the Schmitt Analysis can be created in a similar fashion. Predicate, generated for each factor, are used in rules implementing the Schmitt Analysis.

Consider the effects of the distributed denial-of-service attack (DDOS) on the computer system of an air traffic control tower. Let us assume, that the attack may cause damage to the network components (e.g., unavailability of the system), cascade to damage to physical resources (e.g., crash of the airplane due to missing control data), and human injuries (e.g., result of the crash) [23]. To perform the Schmitt Analysis we need measurements of the factors, like severity. For example, we can state that the severity of the attack is "high" if its cascading effects cause injuries to more than 10 non-military, i.e., civilian, people. This can be represented with the following rule:

$$severity(a - id, targ, high) \leftarrow injured(x),\ x > 10,\ rank(civilian)$$

We may have several rules with the same head. Depending on the prerequisites of the rule (i.e., predicates of the body), more than one rule may be applicable. We briefly discuss how to handle logical inconsistencies (contradictory rules) and nondeterminism (ambiguity) in a subsequent section.

**Damage Assessment.** First, we presents a way of calculating attack characteristics, using the concepts and their properties in the interoperable ontology and the formalization provided by ARP. We assume that each atomic resource (e.g., computer CPU unit) has a corresponding value and measure of atomic damage (i.e., the direct damage to this resource without the consideration of other resources). Damage to a complex asset, say a personal computer, is calculated recursively, based on the damages of atomic resources. That is,

$$damage_c = f(f(damage_{c_1}), \ldots, f(damage_{c_l}))$$

where $c_1, \ldots, c_l$ are immediate subclasses or instances instances of the class $c$, and $f$ is a function that defines how the damages to $c_1, \ldots, c_l$ contribute to the total damage. The recursion uses the ontology concept hierarchy to identify subcomponents of the assets.

Intuitively the calculation of the total damage of a system incorporates damages to the different components of the system. For example, a virus attack on the system may damage different software components, as well as cause damage because of the loss of production time, and the cost of recovery (software, human time, etc.)

Consequences of attacks rarely remain isolated. Cascading effects of cyber attacks must be addressed to gain a realistic evaluation of the damage caused by the attacks. See [14] for examples of cascading effects from kinetic and cyber attacks on a subway system. The total damage caused by a computer network attack, denoted as $DAMAGE_{attack}$, is calculated as

$$DAMAGE_{attack} = F[damage_{C_1}, damage_{C_2}, \ldots, damage_{C_j}]$$

where $damage_{C_1}$ is the damage on the original target computer system, $damage_{C_i}$ ($i = 2, \ldots, j$) represent the damage to the indirectly effected assets. The function $F$ determines how to combine the individual damages. As the simplest solution, both $f$ and $F$ may be defined as simple additions; that is, the total damage of an attack is the sum of the direct and indirect damages to the affected resources.

## 4.3   Conflict Resolution and Default Policy

Conflict resolution strategies are necessary if the overlapping concepts of the ontologies and the corresponding law create legal ambiguities (nondeterminism), illogical statements (inconsistencies), or no applicable law exists. A legal ambiguity may occur when more than one restrictions exist on the same concept. These restrictions are not conflicting but differ in other aspects (e.g., scope). In the logic framework this would result in nondeterministic behavior. Although the removal of such behavior is not the ultimate goal of our system, THEMIS will indicate such occurrences. This allows human experts to compensate for this ambiguity inside or outside the legal framework. A simple method to eliminate ambiguity is by assigning precedence criteria to the rules, which in turn allows to deterministically select the most prominent rules.

Inconsistencies occur when two contradictory restrictions can be derived over the same concept. Selection of the most prominent restriction may be similar to the ones mentioned for ambiguous restrictions. We are using legal hierarchy and rule-precedence settings to derive consistent decisions. Non-automated resolution of inconsistencies requires cooperation of legal expert and decision makers as well as technologies to handle exceptions. Another conflict resolution strategy used by attorneys is called "most specific takes precedence." For instance, there is a general prohibition against shooting another citizen. This rule applies in almost all places at almost all times, but narrow exceptions do exist for self-defense and the defense of others. This structure ensures that *lacunae* in the law are kept to an absolute minimum.

A general principle is that there need not be any areas left uncovered by a rule of law. Most laws are not formulated to apply to narrow fact patterns, but rather to broad areas of similar circumstances. An entire field may be covered by a relatively simple rule, with narrowly defined subsets having specific rules to cover exceptional circumstances. THEMIS can be used to verify this desirable property. In encountering a situation that is not covered, THEMIS will generate and alert. An alert may indicate an incomplete policy specification in THEMIS or the nonexistence of law with regard to this policy. Human analysis is recommended for further evaluation of the cause of an alert.

## 5   Conclusions

Computer attacks, due to their distributed nature, usually span multiple jurisdictions. Therefore, the evaluation of attacks, for the purpose of prosecution or response, requires the cooperation of each of the jurisdictions that the attack touches. THEMIS is an automated system whose purpose is to assist attorneys and those responsible for defending computing assets. THEMIS consists of legal ontologies which represent and retrieve domain knowledge about state, federal, and international law. We established the following requirements for THEMIS: it must address legal ambiguities with nondeterminism, it must provide a mechanism for identifying and resolving conflicts between laws, and it should allow for specifying default rules to capture the manner in which attorneys handle situations in which the law does not address one or more aspects of an attack. We intend to address each of the aforementioned requirements as we continue to refine our ontologies.

## Acknowledgement

This work was partially supported by the National Science Foundation under grants IIS-0237782, CCR-0113515, the Department of Homeland Security through the Naval Postgraduate School Homeland Security Leadership Development Program, and the Critical Infrastructure Protection Project of the George Mason University.

## References

1. Automated incident reporting (airCERT). Technical report, Carnegie Mellon Software Engineering Institute, Cert Coordination Center.
2. The rule markup initiative. http://www.ruleml.org/, 2004.
3. The Semantic Web. http://www.w3.org/2001/sw/, 2004.
4. Joint US/EU ad hoc Agent Markup Language Committee. SWRL: A semantic web rule language combining OWL and RuleML. http://www.daml.org/2003/11/swrl/, 2003.
5. P. Ammann, D. Wijesekera, and S. Kaushak. Scalable, graph based network vulnerability analysis. In *Proc. of the 9th ACM Conference on Computer and Communications Security*, pages 217–224, 2002.
6. K.D. Ashley. *Modeling Legal Argument: Reasoning with Cases and Hypotheticals*. Bradford Books/MIT Press, Cambridge, MA, 1990.
7. T. Berners-Lee, J. Hendler, and O. Lassila. The Semantic Web. *Scientific American*, 2001.
8. K. Branting. Reasoning with portions of precedents. In *Proc. 3rd Intl. Conf. on Artificial Intelligence and Law*, pages 145–154. ACM Press, New York, 1991.
9. Harry Chen, Tim Finin, and Anupam Joshi. Using OWL in a pervasive computing broker. In *Workshop on Ontologies in Open Agent Systems, AAMAS*. citeseer.nj.nec.com/583175.html.
10. Benjamin N. Grosof. Representing e-business rules for the semantic web: Situated courteous logic programs in RuleML. In *Proc. Workshop on Information Technologies and Systems (WITS '01)*, 2001.
11. Auguston M. Rowe N. Michael, J. B. and R. D. Riehle. Software decoys: Intrusion detection and countermeasures. In *Proc. Workshop on Information Assurance*, pages 130–139. IEEE, 2002.
12. J. B. Michael. On the response policy of software decoys: Conducting software-based deception in the cyber battlespace. In *Proc. of the 26th Annual International Computer Software and Applications Conference*, pages 957–962. IEEE, 2002.
13. J. B. Michael, G. Fragkos, and M. Auguston. An experiment in software decoy design: Intrusion detection and countermeasures via system call instrumentation. In di Vimercati S. D. C. Samarati P. Gritzalis, D. and S. Katsikas, editors, *Security and Privacy in the Age of Uncertainty*, pages 253–264. Norwell, Mass.: Kluwer Academic Publishers, 2003.

14. J. B. Michael, G. Fragkos, and D. Wijesekera. Measured responses to cyber attacks using schmitt analysis: A case study of attack scenarios for a software-intensive system. In *Proc. Twenty-seventh Annual Int. Computer Software and Applications Conf.*, pages 621–627. IEEE, 2003.

15. J. B. Michael and T. C. Wingfield. Lawful cyber decoy policy. In di Vimercati S. D. C. Samarati P. Gritzalis, D. and S. Katsikas, editors, *Security and Privacy in the Age of Uncertainty*, pages 483–488. Norwell, Mass.: Kluwer Academic Publishers, 2003.

16. The Honeynet Project. *Know your Enemy - Revealing the Security Tools Tactic, and Motives of the Blackhat Community*. Addison-Wesley, 2002.

17. E. L. Rissland and K.D. Ashley. A case-based system for trade secrets law. In *Proc. 1st Intl. Conf. on Artificial Intelligence and Law*, pages 61–67. ACM Press, New York, 1987.

18. M.N. Schmitt. Computer network attack and the use of force in international law: Thoughts on a normative framework. Research Publication 1, Information Series, 1999.

19. D. B. Skalak and E. L. Rissland. Argument moves in a rule-guided domain. In *Proc. 3rd Intl. Conf. on Artificial Intelligence and Law*, pages 1–11. ACM Press, New York, 1991.

20. J. L. Undercoffer, A. Joshi, T. Finin, and John Pinkston. A target-centric ontology for intrusion detection: Using DAML+OIL to classify intrusive behaviors. *Knowledge Engineering Review – Special Issue on Ontologies for Distributed Systems*, 2004.

21. P. Visser and T. Bench-Capon. The formal specification of a legal ontology. In *Legal Knowledge Based Systems; foundations of legal knowledge systems. Proceedings JURIX'96. R.W.*, 1996. citeseer.ist.psu.edu/visser96formal.html.

22. P. Visser and T. Bench-Capon. A comparison of two legal ontologies. In *Working papers of the First International Workshop on Legal Ontologies*. University of Melbourne, Melbourne, Australia, 1997. citeseer.ist.psu.edu/visser97comparison.htm.

23. T. Wingfield. *The Law of Information Conflict: National Security Law in Cyberspace*. Aegis Research Corp., 2000.

# Balancing Security and Privacy in the 21st Century

Chris C. Demchak[1] and Kurt D. Fenstermacher[2]

[1] School of Public Administration and Policy
[2] Department of MIS, Eller College of Business and Public Administration
University of Arizona, Tucson, Arizona, 85721, USA
{cdemchak,kurtf}@eller.arizona.edu

**Abstract.** The policy steps taken after 9/11 have fomented a particularly intense and often bitter national debate on privacy versus security. We offer a framework for a middle ground that views privacy as an aggregate of two unrelated concepts: knowledge of behavior and knowledge of identity. We offer a visual metaphor for considering government policy in these two dimensions and argue that the default policy should be one that supports intensive monitoring of behavior with limited knowledge of identity until there is reasonable cause to reveal additional information about identity. Moreover, we argue that whenever behavior and identity are considered together, institutions must have safeguards in place to validate the data and offer an appeals process to redress errors in information systems.

## 1  Privacy and Security: A Conflict in Policy

Following the tragic events of September 11th, the United States government has implemented substantial changes in policy with regard to national security, many of which have implications for personal privacy. To date, the polar debate has had few participants in the middle ground. The New York Times published articles entitled "Pentagon Plans a Computer System That Would Peek at Personal Data of Americans" [1] and "A Safer Sky or Welcome to Flight 1984?" [2]. Meanwhile Admiral John Poindexter, who led the Total Information Awareness project, stated, "We must become much more efficient and more clever in the ways we find new sources of data, mine information from the new and old, generate information, make it available for analysis, convert it to knowledge, and create actionable options" [1], Marc Rotenberg, director of the Electronic Privacy Information Center (http://www.epic.org/) said of the same project, "This could be the perfect storm for civil liberties in America." [1] In the crisis atmosphere following the attack of September 11th and the continued anti-terrorism actions, the balance has tipped to favor security over privacy. After an initial reaction, privacy rights have been restored after past crises. However, today's contradictions between existing privacy legislation and recent security policies may make this normally transient imbalance longer and possibly permanent.

While both sides of this debate have entrenched themselves, we argue that the question is not, "How can citizens enjoy total privacy?", but instead, "In an open society, what is the right balance of security and privacy?" We begin by proposing that the usual notion of privacy – the inability of others to know what we do – con-

H. Chen et al. (Eds.): ISI 2004, LNCS 3073, pp. 322–330, 2004.
© Springer-Verlag Berlin Heidelberg 2004

founds two simpler notions: knowing what we do (behavior) and who we are (identity). By separating behavior and identity, we propose a compromise that enables effective security policies while protecting the rights of the individual. Figure 1 illustrates the separation of knowledge about behavior (the horizontal axis) and knowledge about identity (the vertical axis). Recent government policies and many government officials argue that we should value security over privacy, and this weighting places such policies in the upper right-hand region, where there is extensive knowledge of individuals' behavior and identity. Privacy advocates look to shield individuals from prying eyes and advocate that knowledge of either behavior or identity is unacceptable. The debate to date is captured in the diagonal line labeled "Security-privacy debate line", where advocates try to push along the line toward their position.

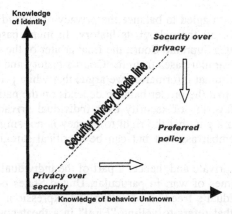

**Fig. 1.** Separating knowledge of identity from knowledge of behavior allows the consideration of anonymity and privacy separately

We argue new thinking is needed on both sides and that an optimal balance of security and privacy lies not on the line of the current debate, but below it. The preferred policy region (in the lower right of Fig. 1) favors knowledge of behavior over knowledge of identity. Because it is ultimately actions that concern security personnel, they can capture the most relevant information by monitoring behavior. Privacy advocates can be assured that institutional safeguards will ensure that monitoring organizations cannot associate an identity with an individual without a reasonable suspicion of a past or future crime. While we argue that the default policy should be that security organizations cannot associate extensive data on identity with deep knowledge of behavior, there must be some provision for doing so. We propose that security organizations must meet a minimal threshold to obtain identifying information. In addition, we argue that because errors are inevitable, organizations that can join data on identity and behavior must support rapid procedures for validation and appeal.

As an example, we consider the ubiquitous video cameras that pervade American life today. By themselves, video cameras enable security personnel in store, parking garages and office buildings monitor behavior, but a standard closed-circuit television (CCTV) system does not reveal identity. However, a face recognition system [3] that attempts to match images from the same video cameras threatens anonymity, but does not monitor behavior. During Super Bowl XXXV in Tampa, Florida, officials used a face recognition system to scan the crowd in attendance and identified 19 petty criminals. [4] By linking a CCTV system with a face recognition system, an organization ties identity and behavior together. While this potentially offers the greatest value to law enforcement, it is also fraught with the most danger for the average citizen.

In the following sections, we discuss the conflict in policies recently implemented in the United States and explore these policies in the context of our behavior-identity knowledge (BIK) framework.

## 2 Historical Perspectives on the Privacy and Security Conflict in the US

The United States has struggled to balance the privacy of individuals against the need to secure the liberty of all throughout its history. In many cases, this struggle has reached the United States Supreme Court, the final arbiter of the Constitution's meaning. By reviewing two similar cases from the Court's history and the recent expansion of a key database of criminal information we argue that while privacy and security do conflict in some cases that the proper balance depends on the national context and the government's recent favoring of security over individual privacy strikes the wrong balance. Moreover, we argue that the right to privacy is not simply a convenience or mechanism to avoid embarrassment but can be a critical safeguard against government misfeasance.

What is considered private and, hence, a part of the individual's sovereignty varies with the context. In times of war, in particular, United States policy has been more restrictive of an individual's freedom of action and expression. The famed U.S. Supreme Court opinion that refers to yelling "Fire!" in a theater was written in a case that stemmed from the search and seizure of anti-draft publications produced by the Communist Party during the First World War. In writing the majority opinion, Justice Holmes stated the Court's principle of context in balancing security and privacy [5]:

> We admit that, in many places and in ordinary times, the defendants, in saying all that was said in the circular, would have been within their constitutional rights. But the character of every act depends upon the circumstances in which it is done. *Aikens v. Wisconsin*, 195 U.S. 194, 205, 206. The most stringent protection of free speech would not protect a man in falsely shouting fire in a theatre and causing a panic. It does not even protect a man from an injunction against uttering words that may have all the effect of force. *Gompers v. Bucks Stove & Range Co.*, 221 U.S. 418, 439. The question in every case is whether the words used are used in such circumstances and are of such a nature as to create a clear and present danger that they will bring about the substantive evils that Congress has a right to prevent. It is a question of proximity and degree. When a nation is at war, many things that might be said in time of peace are such a hindrance to its effort that their utterance will not be endured so long as men fight, and that no Court could regard them as protected by any constitutional right.

In short, some actions (in this case, speech calling on young men to resist the draft and the planned distribution of such speech) may be restricted as circumstances warrant. While the Court's opinion specifically mentions "a nation at war", presumably the Court would recognize a spectrum of context in which the threat might vary from global peace to imminent, massive armed invasion – and so too would the actions allowed in such times. However, the Court has also ruled that even in times of war, restrictions on action are not absolute.

Another law passed during the First World War criminalized threats against the President of the United States. Certainly society has a reasonable goal in ensuring that the President can serve without threat of physical harm – even if those threats do not come to fruition. In *Watts v. United States*, a young man was charged with violating the statute barring threats against the President when he stated in a small group at a Washington anti-war rally in 1966, "They always holler at us to get an education. And now I have already received my draft classification as 1-A and I have got to report for my physical this Monday coming. I am not going. If they ever make me carry a rifle the first man I want to get in my sights is L. B. J. They are not going to make me kill my black brothers." [6] The Court stated that:

> [T]he statute initially requires the Government to prove a true "threat." We do not believe that the kind of political hyperbole indulged in by petitioner fits within that statutory term. For we must interpret the language Congress chose "against the background of a profound national commitment to the principle that debate on public issues should be uninhibited, robust, and wide-open, and that it may well include vehement, caustic, and sometimes unpleasantly sharp attacks on government and public officials." *New York Times Co. v. Sullivan*, 376 U.S. 254, 270 (1964)."

While the Court has recognized that the government must balance privacy and security, it also argued for the necessity of debate even in times of crisis. For example, sedition laws (such as the Sedition Acts of 1798 and the Espionage Act of 1917) are prohibitions against kinds of speech that are acceptable as long as the nation is not at war as discussed in the Supreme Court's opinion in *Schneck* [7]. In the US, even if the laws remain on the books, without another similar crisis, they are rarely enforced – in fact, the Espionage Act originally passed in June of 1917 was amended the next May in 1918 and again in 1940 and 1970 [8], although it is rarely applied today.

Today's world is not the world of 1919, or even 1966, because today devastating attacks that kills thousands or perhaps tens of thousands can be conducted in only a few hours. While it was once possible to let events unfold before responding to them, today the possibility of sudden, massive destruction requires preemption as well as reaction. This shift from reaction to preemption is only increases the tension between privacy and security, because preemptive action requires greater invasions of privacy – preemption requires identifying those planning action, which requires knowledge and hence necessitates studying the identity and behavior who have not yet committed an overt act. From the early days of the Cold War, many privileges of privacy have been undermined by institutional developments typically unnoticed by most citizens. For example, since its founding in 1967 by the Federal Bureau of Investigation (FBI) the National Crime Information Center (NCIC) has been steadily expanding. While originally intended to link local police departments' arrest records across the country for FBI use, NCIC now links over 80,000 agencies – at the state level and below as well as some foreign agencies.[9] The current edition (NCIC 2000) includes "data on wanted persons, missing persons, gang members and individuals with arrest records, as well as records about stolen cars, boats, and other information." [10]

While malicious use of criminal history data is clearly a significant problem, much more likely is the inaccuracy of the data. Therefore, such databases should have well-defined procedures for ensuring the accuracy of the data and correcting erroneous information. While the potential burden of incorrect security information is potentially much higher than with common business databases (for example, the database of a credit reporting bureau), the correction processes in security databases are less rigorous than those of credit bureaus. In fact, in 1982, the Los Angeles Police Department entered an arrest warrant for T. D. Rogan, a robbery suspect. The individual in custody was not Mr. Rogan, but instead a criminal who had stolen his wallet. The police did not enter a physical description, however. Even after the LAPD realized the error, it was not corrected and the real Mr. Rogan was arrested four times over two years – three times at gunpoint. [11]

Moreover, credit reporting agencies are bound by the rules of the Privacy Act of 1974[1]; however, government's unique status as the maker of rules enables it to exempt itself from those same rules. The Justice Department announced in March 2003 that "it would no longer comply with the obligation under the 1974 Privacy Act to ensure the accuracy, completeness and timeliness of the 39 million criminal records maintained in the NCIC system." [10] In addition to drawing a distinction between privacy and anonymity, we also mean privacy to encompass the notion of an individual's control over information. When information is secretly collected and disseminated, those affected have little recourse to correct inevitably incorrect information. Therefore, we argue that a debate on striking a balance between security and privacy must recognize incorporate polices for individuals' access to relevant information and procedures for the rapid appeal and correction of inaccurate information.

The existence of the NCIC and the erosion of citizens' rights with respect to information maintained about them is a canonical example of the state of the conflict between security and privacy. After 9/11, for example, NCIC's existence promised the possibility of knowledge-generating mechanisms that could aid in finding those who would do harm to Americans. This crisis-born legitimacy has institutionalized this network and whatever reduction in individual privacy its expansion entails. In Westernized nations where the police enjoy high levels of trust by the citizens, there is an underlying acceptance of government control of these files, even if the data never proves necessary in pursuing criminals.

## 2.1 Recent Privacy-Related Legislation in the United States

Beyond institutional evolutions, there is an emerging more direct conflict between existing privacy legislation – a right not granted in the Constitution explicitly – and post-9/11 security policies. The privacy legislation directly affected includes the Family Educational Rights and Privacy Act (FERPA) of 1974, the Health Insurance Portability and Accountability Act (HIPAA) of 1996, the Financial Services Modernization Act (FSMA) of 1999 and the more recent Fair and Accurate Credit Transactions Act (FACT) of 2003. Each of these acts regulated the collection of databases that link individuals and information about their lives in the education, health, and credit sectors, respectively. These acts recognize the need for some institutions to collect and use data but limit their ability to secretly collect that information or to refuse to cor-

---

[1] The Privacy Act of 1974, 5 U.S.C. § 552a (2000), which has been in effect since September 27, 1975, can generally be characterized as an omnibus "code of fair information practices" that attempts to regulate the collection, maintenance, use, and dissemination of personal information by federal executive branch agencies. [9]

rect their files when challenged. The security legislation and implementing policies most in conflict are the post-9/11 USA-PATRIOT (2001) and the Homeland Security (HAS) 2002. These acts seek foreknowledge of dangerous individuals by collecting information on a wide population of non-citizens and citizens from many sources to identify potential terrorists or (importantly) their accomplices. With both privacy-protecting and security-enhancing legislation operating, the experience for citizens will be confusing at a minimum. For example, one can challenge a credit company for inaccurate data eventually but, when that inaccurate data is passed to security agencies, one cannot challenge the airport security guard in any reasonable time if one is wrongly accused.

## 3   Disaggregating Privacy for a Practical Privacy-Security Balance

This history suggests a middle ground is needed to institutionally balance the individual's control of, and the security institution's access to, knowledge about that individual. In devising a framework to accomplish this balance, we considered the range of possibilities in what knowledge about a person the wider society tends to have by law, by common practice, and by accident. In a mass society, one could argue that the continuum of disclosure ranges from the person being *public* to being *invisible*. That is, personal exposure to external review varies from having both identity and behavior widely known to having nearly no knowledge of the individual's behavior or identity available to the surrounding society. Figure 1 presents this conceptual framework with illustrative technologies.

To strike the right balance, however, policymakers and citizens must jointly consider this continuum as decomposable into two aspects – identity and behavior, which can be regulated separately to modulate the overall balance of privacy and security. The pure cases not only are highly politically divisive; they are not desirable in mass societies. Invisibility of individuals imposes unacceptable risks in a large-scale inter-dependent society facing global interactions in the emerging age of information and terrorism and vulnerable to the catastrophic ripple effects of mass destruction devices. Complete publicness is equally undesirable, not only due to the perils of some actors accumulating extensive data stores, but also due to historical aversion of US citizens to broad societal exposure without safeguards. Hence, we believe that it is better to focus on one aspect or the other of this continuum and construct a satisficing compromise using technological advances appropriately can be devised to broadly meet the concerns of both the pro-security and pro-privacy interests in society.

### 3.1   Understanding Behavior Distinctly from Identity

In common language, a "very private man" would be someone whose name is known, but whose actions are not. Equally common understood is that an anonymous person's actions may be known but not who they are. If we can institutionalize this distinction in policy, agencies and technologies, we can provide a way in which security against harmful behavior may be tracked while intrusions into personal identity for no good cause can be blocked.

We take our point of departure from evident public acceptance of behavior monitoring if identity is not readily available. The prevalence of security cameras in

American society now means that in most retail stores, cameras monitor all spaces within the store. As customers wander about a store, security personnel monitor them and so have intimate knowledge of their actions – which clothes they remove the rack, which magazines they browse and the products they buy. However, store security personnel often do not know who a particular individual is, only what he or she does in the store. Within such stores customers retain control of their identity, but cede knowledge of their behavior to protect the store, other citizens and themselves.

Conversely, national identification cards reveal identity but not behavior. One may know that Joe Smith lives here but has no way of knowing what he is doing now or at any other time. The imposition of such cards has always been exceptionally bitter and divisive in the United States. Furthermore, there is the accuracy problem found in the use solely of names to tag individuals, as shown in the Rogan example. As a practical matter, we infer that seeking this balance by making identity easy to obtain but behavior more difficult will be more politically unacceptable than the converse.

We argue that the real danger to citizens and to security is when individuals or organizations have extensive information on both behavior and action. Compared to video surveillance, an individual's credit report conveys knowledge of behavior and identity. As a summary of individual's past credit-related actions, a credit report offers little privacy among those with access to it. In addition, credit reports carry extensive identifying information to ensure that a credit history is correctly associated with the described individual, which removes anonymity. Most people expect that a credit report would be relatively "private". As long as such information is closely held within a few organizations and there are known and enforced procedures for correcting errors and mitigating the consequences to the individual the extensive information maintained by credit bureaus is not necessarily problematic. In our compromise, therefore, it is possible to have both identity and behavior but only if necessary and extensive safeguards are in place to guard against both mistakes and abuses.

The challenge is to translate this distinction into policy and agency guidelines and appropriate technologies. Implementing a more refined concept beginning with governmental databases is essential because, despite the rise of corporate data gathering, government information collection is fundamentally different from corporate (private) information collection due to the power that governments wield over the lives of their citizens as illustrated in the case of Mr. Rogan's mistaken identity – having an officer un-holster a weapon because of identity inaccuracies in a nationally shared database is particularly risky and unnerving. With modern database techniques, collating existing information sources generates new information. Today, as envisioned by government policymakers these data collection efforts would track identity and behavior, but without the common safeguards such invasions of privacy demand.

We propose the data collection efforts should respect the division between identity and behavior by allowing the government to collect information on behaviors, but must place identity knowledge behind shields that can only be breached with cause and with validation and appeal processes built into the systems from the outset. While race, ethnicity, education and religion are poor predictors of intent to harm, behavior offers clues not found in identity. The fact that an individual purchases a one-way airline ticket with cash is worthier of suspicion than another individual whose parents emigrated from Saudi Arabia. Only under legally defined procedures open to rapid validation and appeal, would agencies be able to match identity with behavior. A one-way ticket bought with cash should trigger a cascade of associations as the buyer's identity is revealed to the system and further associated with previously anonymous actions such as an expired visa and recent pilot training. In this way, while the potential of information technology to ruin lives in a moment is redirected into tracking threatening behaviors rather than disliked religions, ethnicities, names, or regional origins. Behavior is not constrained, identity is shielded and yet security knowledge development is also possible.

# 4  Future Work on the Interplay among Anonymity, Privacy and Technology

The potential speed, ubiquity and comprehensiveness of information technologies play a critical role in the balance between security and privacy. With the ability to track millions of people and their activities and recognize complex patterns of behavior among different people in different places, security is enhanced. The same technologies are available to force validation and appeal processes. In the emerging Information and Terrorism Age, this effort to keep the right balance will be a continuous struggle in innovation and flexibility. With regard to privacy and security, technology cuts both ways in an interdependent world. Those who would harm others can use bleeding edge technologies that make it difficult to track suspicious individuals, e.g., pre-paid cell phones[2], encryption and known vulnerabilities of networked computer systems. Networked computers enable people to masquerade as someone else, or in the words of a now famous *New Yorker* cartoon, "On the Internet, nobody knows you're a dog!" [13]. Understanding that the goal is not to track people, but instead behavior, narrows the task technically as well as politically.

While the scope of this paper limits extensive discussion of the next steps in this research, we are investigating how the behavior-identity knowledge framework might be implemented both in policy settings and in nationally networked information systems. We recognize that while our recommendations might provide some guidance for policymakers, we must also propose an implementation that will enable agencies to gather information in accord with the framework, but still serve their own needs for surveillance and analysis. To that end, we are currently exploring a key escrow system that would enable agencies to collect behavior-based information and associate that behavior with a unique identifier, representing the monitored individual. Identifying information such as names, aliases, known associates, photos, fingerprints and genetic markers, would be encrypted and the encryption key stored separately. With a showing of cause, agencies could request the release of the appropriate key, which would enable them to associate the monitored behavior with a specific individual.

For example, suppose that an airline traveler pays cash for a round-trip ticket and boards a plane. As the traveler's boarding pass is scanned at the gate, identifying information such as the traveler's name is sent to a central server that retrieves an encryption key that is indexed by identifying information. The encrypted identifica-

---

[2] A recent article from the New York Times cast doubt on the success of this strategy by explaining how international law enforcement used Al Qaeda operatives' preference for a particular cell phone chip to track Al Qaeda communications that Al Qaeda believed to be anonymous and untraceable. [12]

tion information is then used to store behavioral information, such as the flight number, the aircraft, seat assignment and a note that this was a cash purchase. If the United States Transportation Security Administration analyzes the behavioral information tied to the passenger and determines that she represents a security threat, the TSA can petition for the release of identifying information. While we work to refine the implementation model, we believe that separating tracking and storage of behavior and identity will help chart a middle ground between the extremes of the current privacy -security debate – both technically and institutionally.

# References

1. J. A. Markoff, "THREATS AND RESPONSES: INTELLIGENCE; Pentagon Plans a Computer System That Would Peek at Personal Data of Americans," *The New York Times*, November 9, 2002,Online, National Desk
2. J. Sharkey, "BUSINESS TRAVEL: ON THE ROAD; A Safer Sky or Welcome to Flight 1984?," *The New York Times*,
3. W. Zhao, R. Chellappa, P. J. Phillips, and A. Rosenfeld, "Face recognition: A literature survey," *ACM Computing Surveys*, vol. 35, 2003.
4. V. Chachere, "Snooper Bowl? Biometrics Used at the Super Bowl to Detect Criminals in Crowd," ABCNews.com. Last accessed: March 3, 2004. Available at: <http://abcnews.go.com/sections/scitech/DailyNews/superbowl_biometrics_010213.html> 2001.
5. "Schenck v. United States," in *U.S.*, vol. 249: United States Supreme Court, 1919, pp. 47.
6. "Watts v. United States," in *USSC*, vol. 394: United States Supreme Court, 1969, pp. 707.
7. "Espionage Act," in *U. S. C.*, vol. Title 1, 1917.
8. "Espionage Act of 1917," Microsoft Corporation. Last accessed: March 1, 2004. Available at: <http://encarta.msn.com/encyclopedia_761554217/Espionage_Act_of_1917.html>.
9. E. P. I. C. , "EPIC - SIGN-ON LETTER: Require Accuracy for NCIC,"Electronic Privacy Information Center. Last accessed: February 29, 2004. Available at: <http://www.epic.org/privacy/ncic/>. 2004.
10. E. P. I. C. , "EPIC Alert 10.07," Electronic Privacy Information Center. Last accessed: February 29, 2004. Available at: <http://www.epic.org/alert/EPIC_Alert_10.07.html>. 2003.
11. E. Alderman and C. Kennedy, *The Right to Privacy*. New York, NY, USA: Alfred A. Knopf, 1995.
12. D. Van Natta, Jr. and D. Butler, "Tiny Cellphone Chips Helped Track Global Terror Web," *The New York Times*, March 1, 2004. Late Edition - Final, A1, Col. 1.
13. P. Steiner, "On the Internet, Nobody Knows You're a Dog," in *The New Yorker*, vol. 69, 1993, pp. 61.

# IT Security Risk Management under Network Effects and Layered Protection Strategy

Wei T. Yue, Metin Cakanyildirim, Young U. Ryu, and Dengpan Liu

Department of Information Systems and Operations Management,
School of Management,
The University of Texas at Dallas
Richardson, Texas 75083-0688, USA
{wei.yue,metin,ryoung,freeme}@utdallas.edu

**Abstract.** This paper considers the implications of network effects and distinction of security measures in the risk management procedure. We compare three models in the risk management procedure: without network effects and general protection measures, without network effects but with general protection, and with both network effects and general protection measures. The paper details the impact in terms of security risks, investment levels, and benefits of security investment, in the three models. We show that the preferable way to conduct risk management procedure is to follow the latter of the three models.

## 1 Introduction

In recent years information technology (IT) security has become an essential issue as business operations and transactions are increasingly performed with digital assets. Various studies have documented huge amounts of losses in security breaches due to cyber attacks [1, 2]. Modern businesses rely on integrated IT systems from different business units inside and outside of the organization to promote flexibility and productivity. As a result, IT security professionals are faced with the daunting task of protecting multiple IT systems that are dispersed at different networks.

To protect valuable IT assets, an organization needs to invest in security protection measures to reduce the likelihood of security breaches and the subsequent losses resulted from attacks. The National Institute of Standards and Technology (NIST) risk management guide advocates the practice of security risk identification and classification so that protection resources can be allocated to the appropriate security measures to defend our IT systems [3]. The computer security risk management procedure comprises two important goals: risk assessment and risk mitigation. According to the guide, the relative risks of different IT systems first have to be established for an organization. IT systems that possess the higher risks will be given higher protection resource and priority. The security risk of an IT system is determined by estimating its threat level, vulnerability level, and the values to the organization. While the guide provides

H. Chen et al. (Eds.): ISI 2004, LNCS 3073, pp. 331–348, 2004.

a good guidance to the IT security professionals, two issues command more attention: i)the network effects in IT security risk assessment and mitigation and ii)the distinction between general and system-specific protection measures.

Nowadays, system network security risks arise for a system from multiple sources, because a system is connected to multiple systems. From the risk assessment standpoint, it is important to consider risks from all the connected systems. In addition to that, an attack can be carried out from one compromised system to compromise another system. This type of successive attack creates network effects in security risks in which the security threat for one system is not confined to that system. To properly estimate security risks, the secondary effects generated by attackers treat IT systems as an *object* and a *subject* of attack must be incorporated into the risk management procedure.

The importance of the network effects is not not limited to the risk assessment stage. Risk mitigation calls for protection priority to the higher risk IT systems. However, under this scheme the extended protection effects of one system on the other connected systems are not included. To properly account for protection benefits, the protection planning for one system also extends to plannings for other systems. Because of the network effects in protection, risk mitigation plan that yields maximum benefits should consider all systems instead of just focusing on the few high risk systems during the risk mitigation stage.

The main goal of risk mitigation involves selecting appropriate security protection strategy. Security measures nowadays can be classified as either general or system-specific purposes. In other words, there are security measures that protect multiple (or single) IT systems while others can only be applied to specific IT assets. These two groups of protection measures are commonly used in parallel to achieve layered security protection scheme. It is beneficial to make a protection measures distinction in the risk mitigation process, because the complementary effects between general and system-specific measures are not only limited to the tradeoffs in protection effectiveness. General protection measures often provide the "scale effect" in protection that does not exist in system-specific measures. To optimize risk mitigation strategy, the "scale effect" introduced by the the general protection measures has to be considered in conjuncture with the tradeoffs in security measures effectiveness.

Despite the increased awareness of the computer security issues, there are very few discussions about the practical issues regarding computer security risk management. There were several studies focused on the security issues from the economics and managerial perspectives [4–8], in which the main delivery of the risk management exercise, i.e., the returns on security investment (ROSI), is discussed. However, none considered the network effects in security and distinction in security measures. In this paper, we examine three types of risk management models. The first case ignores both general protection measures and network effects, and only considers system-specific protection. The second model includes general protection measures but ignores the network effects. In the third case, both types of protection measures and network effects are considered. We assume a problem of protecting multiple systems of different values with a given security protection resource. The goal is to compare the optimal protection decisions under the three cases.

## 2   Problem Description

Security practitioners have long described IT assets as being "as secure as the weakest link," which essentially alluded to the need of protecting a network of systems instead of only protecting the few important systems. The weakest link concept is intuitive, because with system interdependencies the defeat of one weak spot could lead to the defeat of the entire security initiatives. In this paper, our study is pertained to the elimination of the weakest link under layered protection measures.

**Table 1.** Definition of Variables

| Notation | Description |
|---|---|
| $V_i \in (0,1]$ | Initial vulnerability for IT system $i$ |
| $p(x_i, y) \in [0,1]$ | Security vulnerability on IT system $i$ from external attackers given investment $x_i$ and $y$ |
| $q(x_i) \in [0,1]$ | Security vulnerability on IT system $i$ from internal attackers given investment $x_i$ |
| $S_i$ | Expected losses under successful attack on IT system $i$ |
| $\bar{S}_i$ | Total expected losses due to successful attack on IT system $i$ and IT system $k$ from IT system $i$ |
| $N$ | Total number of attacking incidents |
| $y \in [0, Q]$ | Investment on general security measures |
| $x_i \in [0, Q]$ | Investment on system-specific security measures for IT system $i$ |
| $\theta \in [0,1]$ | Fraction of attack incidents originated by external attackers |
| $\rho_i \in [0,1]$, $\sum_{i=1}^{m} \rho_i = 1$ | Fraction of attack incidents on IT system $i$ out of all external attacks |
| $\gamma_i \in [0,1]$, $\sum_{i=1}^{m} \gamma_i = 1$ | Fraction of attack incidents on IT system $i$ out of all internal attacks |
| $\phi_{ik} \in [0,1]$ | Expected probability of successful successive attacks from IT system $i$ to IT system $k$ by the external attackers |
| $\mu_{ik} \in [0,1]$ | Expected probability of successful successive attacks from IT system $i$ to IT system $k$ by the internal attackers |
| $\sigma_i \in [0,1]$ | Relative attack difficulty on IT system $i$ attacks between internal and external given y $= 0$ |

We study a problem of protecting $m$ IT systems for a given budget resource $Q$. All systems are connected to each other with a link. Each pair of systems have their dedicated link. For instance, system $i$ is connected to system $j$ through link $ij$. Essentially, we do not assume any network topology or architecture. System $i$ $(i = 1, 2, \ldots, m)$ is assumed to have an initial vulnerability level $0 < V_i \leq 1$. Attackers are classified as either external or internal attackers. The distinction here is that external attackers have no access rights to IT systems, while internal attackers are legitimate users who have ties to the organization. Even though external attacks are commonly reported in the media, an Internet security threat report [9] found a substantial number of security incidents that involved internal threats. Internal attackers also have more flexibility in carrying out attacks due to the close proximity and knowledge in the IT systems. Hence, a system $i$ is more vulnerable to internal attacks than external attacks. That is, system $i$ has an initial vulnerability of $\sigma_i V_i$, ($0 < \sigma_i \le 1$) for external attackers but initial vulnerability of $V_i$ for internal attackers. The security protection measures can be categorized into general or system-specific purposes. The internal attackers only have to defeat the system-specific protection to compromise information assets. External attackers need to defeat general and system-specific protections. Here we adopt a narrow view of the general protection measures by representing them as perimeter defense measures.

There is a total of $N$ number of attack attempts over the given budget cycle. Out of all attack attempts, $\theta \in [0,1]$ fraction belong to external attacks. Among the external attacks, there is $\rho_i \in [0,1]$ fraction of external attacks on system $i$, and $\gamma_i \in [0,1]$ fraction of internal attacks is directed to system $i$. All attacks are homogeneous. We do not model any attack side behaviors by assuming that attacks are homogeneous. When the network effect is not considered, a successful attack on system $i$ incurs losses of $S_i$. Since all attacks are the same, the differences in losses can be attributed to the differences in system values.

Furthermore, we make the following assumptions regarding the protection measures. Investments of $x_i$ in system-specific protection and $y$ in the general protection measures reduce system $i$ 's vulnerability to $p(x_i, y) \in [0,1]$ against external attackers. System-specific investment of $x_i$ also reduces the vulnerability to $q(x_i)$ against internal users.

$\mathcal{A}$1. $0 \le p(x_i, y) \le 1$; $0 \le p(x_i) \le 1$
$\mathcal{A}$2. $p(x_i = 0, y = 0) = \sigma_i V_i$; $p(x_i, y = 0) = \sigma_i q(x_i)$; $p(x_i, y = \infty) = 0$
$\mathcal{A}$3. $q(x_i = 0) = V_i$; $q(x_i = \infty) = 0$
$\mathcal{A}$4. $p_y < 0, p_{yy} > 0$ [1]; $p_{x_i} < 0, p_{x_i x_i} > 0$
$\mathcal{A}$5. $q_{x_i} < 0$; $q_{x_i x_i} < 0$

The vulnerability functions $p(x_i, y)$ and $q(x_i)$ are decreasing convex functions with investments. Previous studies have found/used similar functions [10, 6]. When there is no investment on any security measures, vulnerability remains the same as initial vulnerability. It is also more difficult for external attackers than for internal attackers to successfully attack a system when there are system-specific protections but no general protections. Furthermore, the only way to achieve absolute security is when security investment is infinity.

## 3   Model Development

We present three different IT security risk management models. The outcome of a risk management exercise is security investment levels in security measures.

---

[1] $p_y$ denotes $\frac{\partial p}{\partial y}$; $p_{yy}$ denotes $\frac{\partial^2 p}{\partial y^2}$

Security risks are defined as vulnerability × losses. We do not model the type of losses incurred in attacks. In general, losses incurred because of the breach of confidentiality, integrity, and availability of IT assets. The benefits are the reduced amount of expected losses/risks. The presence of network effects and the use of general security measures are the two factors that draw the distinctions among the three models.

## 3.1   Single-Tier Security Measures

The first case does not consider the presence of network effect or the use of general protection measures. Essentially, investment in general protection measures is assumed to be zero ($y = 0$). The problem of maximizing the expected benefits is presented in (1)

$$b(x_i) = \max \ N \sum_{i=1}^{m} \left( \theta \rho_i \Big( \sigma_i V_i - \sigma_i q(x_i) \Big) S_i + (1 - \theta)\gamma_i \Big( V_i - q(x_i) \Big) S_i \right) - \sum_{i=1}^{m} x_i$$

$$\text{subject to } \sum_{i=1}^{m} x_i = Q$$

$$x_i \geq 0 \quad \text{for } i = 1, 2, \ldots, m$$

$$y \geq 0 \ .$$

The formulation shows that the initial risk in IT asset for system $i$ is

$$N\big(\theta \rho_i \sigma_i + (1 - \theta)\gamma_i\big)V_i S_i \ . \tag{1'}$$

The organization wide initial risks in IT asset are

$$N \sum_{i=1}^{m} (\theta \rho_i \sigma_i + (1 - \theta)\gamma_i) V_i S_i \ . \tag{1''}$$

## 3.2   Two-Tier Security Measures

The risk management procedure also accounts for the use of general protection measures in this case. This problem differs from problem (1) only in the protection effort against external attackers, as general defense is assumed to be perimeter defense.

We model two separate cases under this framework. They are with and without the consideration of network effects in the risk management procedure. In the presence of network effects, successful attacks on one system will lead to further attacks on other systems.

**Without Network Effects.** The problem is formulated in (1). In the presence of general protection measures, the consequences of using protection against external attacks are represented by vulnerability function $p(x_i, y)$.

$$b^g(x_i, y) = \max \; N \sum_{i=1}^{m} \left( \theta \rho_i \big( \sigma_i V_i - p(x_i, y) \big) S_i + (1 - \theta) \gamma_i \big( V_i - q(x_i) \big) S_i \right)$$

$$- \left( \sum_{i=1}^{m} x_i + y \right) \tag{1}$$

$$\text{subject to} \quad \sum_{i=1}^{m} x_i + y = Q$$

$$x_i \geq 0 \quad \text{for } i = 1, 2, \ldots, m$$

$$y \geq 0 .$$

The initial security risks under system and organization levels are defined the same as in Eqns. 1' and 1''.

**With Network Effects.** In the context of network effects in IT security, security risks of one system affect the security risks of the other systems. Moreover, the protection of one system also affects the protection levels of the other connected systems. For simplicity, we assume here that the propagation of attacks only occurs once from the original attack. When an external attacker compromises a system $i$, there is an expected probability of continued successful attacks $\phi_{ik} \in [0, 1]$ on system $k$. For internal attackers, the expected probability is $\mu_{ik} \in [0, 1]$. The expected losses for an original attack on system $i$ become

$$\bar{S}_i = \left[ S_i + \sum_{\substack{k=1 \\ k \neq i}}^{n} \phi_{ik} S_k \right] .$$

The same attack propagation formulation can also be used for internal attacks by replacing the expected probability of successful subsequent attacks with $\mu_{ik}$.

The problem with network effects can be written as

$$b^n(x_i, y) = \max \; N \sum_{i=1}^{m} \left( \theta \rho_i \big( \sigma_i V_i - p(x_i, y) \big) \left( S_i + \sum_{\substack{k=1 \\ k \neq i}}^{m} \phi_{ik} S_k \right) \right. \tag{2}$$

$$\left. + (1 - \theta) \gamma_i \big( V_i - q(x_i) \big) \left( S_i + \sum_{\substack{k=1 \\ k \neq i}}^{m} \mu_{ik} S_k \right) \right) - \left( \sum_{i=1}^{m} x_i + y \right)$$

$$\text{subject to} \quad \sum_{i=1}^{m} x_i + y = Q$$

$$x_i \geq 0 \quad \text{for } i = 1, 2, \ldots, m$$

$$y \geq 0 .$$

Under the possibility of successive attack, it is no longer possible to write the individual risks for a system because any such risks comprise the risks from another system. Basically, the risks that arise from successive attack can be accounted for by adding the risks into the system that *originates* the attacks or *receives* the attack. At the end, all the network risks are borne by the organization. Hence, here we only write the organization risks

$$N \sum_{i=1}^{m} \left[ (\theta \rho_i \sigma_i + (1-\theta)\gamma_i) V_i \left( S_i + \sum_{\substack{k=1 \\ k \neq i}}^{m} \phi_{ik} S_k \right) \right] . \tag{2'}$$

If we relax the assumption of only one additional attack after a successful attack on the first system, and allow the attacker to subsequently attack from the second compromised system, the expected loss associated with the original attack on system $i$ is

$$\bar{S}_i = \left[ S_i + \sum_{\substack{k=1 \\ k \neq i}}^{n} \phi_{ik} \left( S_k + \sum_{\substack{l=1 \\ l \neq i,k}}^{n} \phi_{kl} S_l \right) \right] . \tag{3}$$

The formulation can be extended to include further subsequent attacks from the $2^{nd}$, $3^{rd}$, and so forth, compromised systems.

From our formulation, we can obtain the following results.

**Proposition 1.** *Risk assessment without the consideration of network effect in the presence of successive attacks underestimates expected IT security risks for the organization.*

*Proof (of proposition).* The difference in initial risks with and without network effects = Eqn. 2' minus Eqn. 1'' > 0 if $\exists \phi_{ik} > 0$ for $k \neq i$ & $k = 1, 2, \ldots, m$.    □

The results are not surprising because when there are secondary attacks spawn from the original attacks, the actual number of attacks to the IT assets for the organization increases. If we compare the two models with the same number of attacks, we get the result of Prop. 2.

**Proposition 2.** *The organization-wide expected risks under the risk assessment model with network effects are lower, equal, or higher than under the risk assessment model without network effects depending on*

$$\sum_{i=1}^{m} \left( \theta \rho_i \sigma_i + (1-\theta)\gamma_i \right) V_i \sum_{\substack{k=1 \\ k \neq i}}^{m} \phi_{ik} S_k \lesseqgtr \sum_{i=1}^{m} \left( \theta \rho_i \sigma_i + (1-\theta)\gamma_i \right) V_i S_i$$

*respectively, when the total numbers of attacks are equal for the two models.*

*Proof (of proposition).* Since every system generates one additional attack in the presence of network effects, there are $2N$ instead of $N$ attacks without network effects. Then, the difference in initial risks between having and not having network effects with the same number of total attacks is $b^n(x_i, y) - 2b^g(x_i, y) =$

$$N \sum_{i=1}^{m} \left( \left( \theta \rho_i \sigma_i + (1-\theta)\gamma_i \right) V_i \left( \sum_{\substack{k=1 \\ k \neq i}}^{m} \phi_{ik} S_k - S_i \right) \right) \lessgtr 0 \quad \text{iff}$$

$$\sum_{i=1}^{m} \left( \theta \rho_i \sigma_i + (1-\theta)\gamma_i \right) V_i \sum_{\substack{k=1 \\ k \neq i}}^{m} \phi_{ik} S_k \lessgtr \sum_{i=1}^{m} \left( \theta \rho_i \sigma_i + (1-\theta)\gamma_i \right) V_i S_i \; . \qquad \square$$

The result shows that when the aggregate expected losses from successive attacks are larger than the original attack, the model without networks effects underestimate security risks. It is conceivable to have security risks overestimated when network effects are not considered. This is likely when additional attacks on another system from a compromised system become very difficult to succeed.

We can also come to some conclusions regarding risk mitigation.

**Proposition 3.** *The risk mitigation approach that considers general and system-specific protection measures performs no worse than the approach that only makes use of system-specific protection measures.*

*Proof (of proposition).* The optimal expected benefits $E[b(x_i^*, y^*]$ can be achieved in problem 1 with $y^* \in [0, Q]$. Since problem 1 is a special case of problem 1 with $y = 0$, the expected benefits for problem 1 will be no worse than problem 1, i.e., $E[b(x_i^*, y^*] \geq E[b(x_i^*, y = 0]$ $\qquad \square$

**Proposition 4.** *The risk mitigation approach that considers general and system-specific protection measures, and is done individually and sequentially on each system, performs no better than the approach that considers all systems at the same instance.*

*Proof (of proposition).* The ad hoc consideration of general measures determines an investment level for one system at a time. The realized investment $y' \in [0, Q]$ in the general measures can only be increased, but cannot be decreased when the future systems are considered. Therefore, an approach that can increase and decrease the investment level when a system is under consideration cannot do worse in selecting the optimum $y^*$ $\qquad \square$

The implication from the above propositions is that a risk mitigation process should make a distinction on general and system-specific protection measures; and the way to optimally do this is by having all systems under consideration in the process.

The issues regarding the reduced risk levels and the optimal distribution of resources for the different models require additional definitions. For further analysis, we define

$$p(x_i, y) = \sigma_i V_i e^{-(\alpha x_i + \beta y)} \qquad (4)$$

where $\alpha > 0$ and $\beta > 0$, and

$$q(x_i) = V_i e^{-\alpha x_i} \; . \qquad (5)$$

Coefficients $\alpha$, $\beta$ represent factors that influence the effectiveness of the security measures.

We now look at a special case in which the given budget ensures positive investments in system-specific measures for all systems and general measures (if available), i.e., $x_i \geq 0$, $y \geq 0$. We simplify the model by assuming $\gamma_i = \rho_i$, $\phi_{ik} = \mu_{ik}$ and $\sigma_i = \sigma$. Essentially, the probabilities of attacking system $i$ from the external and internal attack pools are the same. Both the internal and external attackers have the same success probability in a successive attack from system $i$ to system $k$. Furthermore, the difficulty levels, i,e., the additional attack difficulty of an external attack over an internal attack on a system, are the same for all systems.

Solving all three cases yield the following results where the superscripts s, g, n denote the cases of single-tier, two-tier without network effects and two-tier with network effects respectively. (All derivations are in the appendix)

*Single-Tier Security Measures*
Let $c_i = N\rho_i V_i S_i$.

$$x_i^{s*} = \frac{1}{m}\left[ Q + \frac{1}{\alpha}\sum_{j=1}^{m} \ln\left(\frac{c_i}{c_j}\right) \right] \tag{6}$$

*Two-Tier Security Measures without Network Effects*

$$x_i^{g*} = \frac{1}{m}\left[ Q + \frac{1}{\alpha}\sum_{j=1}^{m} \ln\left(\frac{c_i}{c_j}\right) - \frac{1}{\beta}\ln\left(\frac{\theta(m\beta - \alpha)}{(1-\theta)\alpha}\right) \right] \tag{7a}$$

and

$$y^{g*} = \frac{1}{\beta}\ln\left(\frac{\theta\sigma(m\beta - \alpha)}{(1-\theta)\alpha}\right) \tag{7b}$$

*Two-Tier Security Measures under Network Effects*
Let $d_i = N\rho_i V_i\left(S_i + \sum_{\substack{k=1 \\ k \neq i}}^{m} \phi_{ik} S_k\right)$

$$x_i^{n*} = \frac{1}{m}\left[ Q + \frac{1}{\alpha}\sum_{j=1}^{m} \ln\left(\frac{d_i}{d_j}\right) - \frac{1}{\beta}\ln\left(\frac{\theta(m\beta - \alpha)}{(1-\theta)\alpha}\right) \right] \tag{8a}$$

and

$$y^{n*} - \frac{1}{\beta}\ln\left(\frac{\theta\sigma(m\beta - \alpha)}{(1-\theta)\alpha}\right) \tag{8b}$$

The optimal solutions for all three models illustrate that the distribution of security resources follows the relative risks of the systems with higher risks systems receiving more resources. In cases where both types of security measures are considered, a fraction of security resources is allocated to the general protection measures. The amount of resources allocated depends on the number of internal and external attackers ($\theta$), the difficulty of attack for external attackers

($\sigma$), the number of IT systems ($m$), and the relative effectiveness in the two types of security measures ($\alpha$ and $\beta$). We can make the following observation regarding the distribution of system-specific resources when we do not consider the network effects.

**Observation 5.** *In the presence of general protection measures, less security resources are allocated to system-specific protection. The spread of resources among system-specific measures is more even with general protection than without general protection.*

The result that the an outcome of general security measures provides a uniform protection over a range of IT systems, and generates larger amount of benefits to the higher risks IT systems. We also see that the "scale effect" is controlled by the number of IT systems and the relative effectiveness of security measures.

When we consider the network effects, the spread of resources among system-specific measures becomes more even (with general measures).

**Observation 6.** *The spread of security resources among system-specific measures is more even with network effects than without network effect considerations when the risks generated by the successive attacks are spread evenly among all systems.*

We have pointed out that the initial risks are different between the cases with network effects and without network effects. However, when the expected losses from successive attacks are similar for every system, the distribution of resource among systems is more even with network effects. Essentially, the difference in relative risks among systems is reduced, which indicates that security risks are accounted for as network risks instead of system-specific risks.

Next, we provide a numerical example to illustrate the results of our models.

### 3.3 Numerical Example

The numerical exercise was conducted using Matlab v6.5. We used the following parameter values for the numerical example.

- $V_i = 0.9$, for $i = 1, 2, \ldots, m$, $\sigma = 0.9$
- $\theta = 0.3$, $m = 100$, $N = 1000$, $Q = 200$
- $\alpha = 0.5$, $\beta = 0.3$
- $\rho_i = \gamma_i = 1/100$ for $i = 1, 2, \ldots, m$
- $\phi_i = \mu_i = e^{-\alpha Q/m}$ for $i = 1, 2, \ldots, m$
- $S_i$ is generated using Matlab's normal density function *normpdf*
  $S_i = 500*normpdf(\text{i},50,30)$

We generated the expected losses in system values based on the normal density function. In this example, the expected losses from successive attacks are set to be the same. The expected probability is assumed to be $e^{-\alpha Q/m}$, and the attack target is the highest value system for all systems. There are three

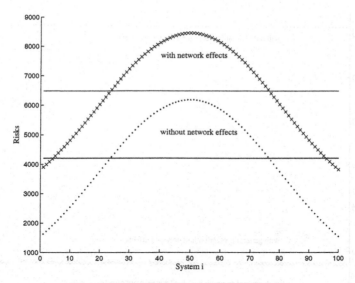

**Fig. 1.** Initial Risks Levels for System $i$

IT systems that share the same highest value; one highest value system is the target of all other systems, and it targets another highest value system in the successive attack.

We have indicated in previous section that when there are network effects, it is not possible to account system risk individually for each system, because it consists of additional risks from other systems. The method that we used to account for system risk in the network case is shown in our formulation, i.e., according to the system that *contributes* to the security risks. Hence, the initial security risks curve for all systems with network effects as shown in Fig. 1, is similar to the curve without network effects. The straight line in Fig. 1 represents the average initial risks for the two cases.

The security risks after security investment are shown in Fig. 2. Note that the overall security risks are higher in the network case (from Fig. 1). As a result, the lowest security risks case shown in Fig. 2 belongs to the case without network effects but with general protection. The level of security risks is much lower with general protection than without general protection, demonstrating the contribution of using general protection measures. The security risks levels after investment are the same for all systems in all three cases. This is the effect of having enough budget to protect all systems, as the marginal benefits for all systems are equal to the marginal costs for all systems. When budget is limited, the distribution of risks among systems will not be uniform since priorities can only be given to the higher risk systems.

When we normalized the protection improvements brought by security investment, we see then in Fig. 3 that under network effects, the distribution of improvements are more evenly spread. Compared to the case without network effects, there are lower percentage of improvements over some higher risks sys-

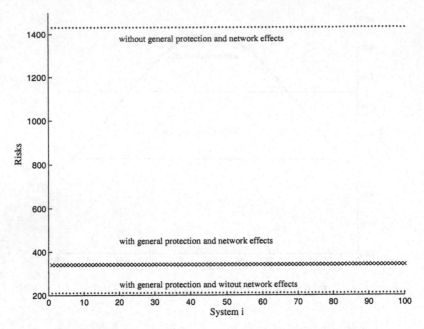

**Fig. 2.** Risk Levels for System $i$ after Security Investment

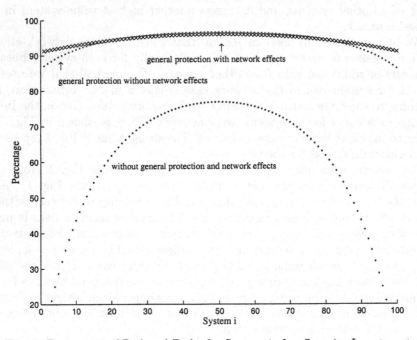

**Fig. 3.** Percentage of Reduced Risks for System $i$ after Security Investment

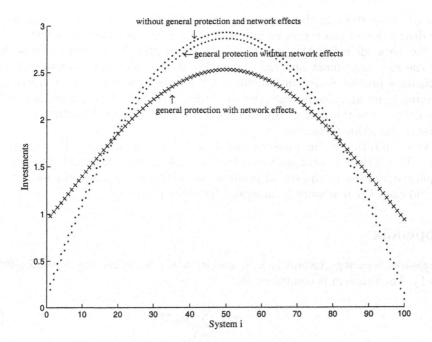

**Fig. 4.** Investment Levels for System $i$

tems but higher percentage of improvements over the low risk systems in the case with network effects. The result indicates that security risks are treated more from the perspectives of organization rather than from individual systems. When general protections are not considered, we see a diverse improvement levels for different systems.

The displays of protection improvements are reflected on the system-specific investment levels as shown in Fig. 4[2]. The figure shows that investment resources are more evenly spread among systems in the case with network effects. In the presence of general protection measures, less system-specific resources are allocated; the reduction is more significant for the higher value systems than the lower-value systems.

## 4  Conclusion and Limitations

The computer security risk management is a critical process in the protection of organization's information asset. Under the overall IT security protection scheme, the main contributions by the risk management exercise are the determination of security risks for systems and the development of protection strategy

---

[2] The general protection investment amount is not shown in this figure, but is found to be 6.498 for the two cases that consider general protection measures

to reduce the risks. In this paper we explored the issues of network effects and the distinction of protection measures in the risk management procedure.

We have identified the importance of accounting for network effects during the risk assessment and risk mitigation stages. Moreover, conducting risk mitigation process under an individual system basis is shown to be inferior to accounting for all systems concurrently during the process. One main reason for this outcome is the lack of consideration regarding the contribution from the general protection measures.

One limitation in the presented models is the simplification of many conditions. This is the first attempt to model the problem and it is intended to provide a qualitative view to the stated problem. In addition, we have only analyzed a special case. Current work is underway for other cases.

# Appendix

*Single-tier Security:* Assume $\rho_i = \gamma_i$, and $\sigma_i = \sigma$, and define $c_i = N\rho_i V_i S_i((\theta\sigma - \theta + 1)$. The problem is equivalent to:

$$\min \sum_{i=1}^{m} c_i e^{-\alpha x_i} \tag{9}$$

$$\text{subject to } \sum_{i=1}^{m} x_i = Q$$

$$x_i \geq 0 \quad \text{for } i = 1, 2, \ldots, m$$

We also scale the problem such that $c_i\alpha \geq 1 \Leftrightarrow \ln c_i\alpha \geq 0$. Construct the Lagragean:

$$L(x_i, \mu_i, \lambda) = \sum_{i=1}^{m} c_i e^{-\alpha x_i} + \lambda\left(\sum_{i=1}^{m} x_i - Q\right) + \mu_i\left(\sum_{i=1}^{m} -x_i\right) \tag{10}$$

The Kuhn-Tucker conditions are

**i** $\frac{\partial L}{\partial x_i} = -c_i\alpha e^{-\alpha x_i} + \lambda - \mu_i = 0$

**ii** $\sum_{i=1}^{m} x_i = Q, \quad x_i \geq 0$

**iii** $\mu_i \geq 0$

**iv** $\mu_i(-x_i) = 0$

(i.)We get $x_i = \frac{1}{\alpha} \ln \frac{\alpha c_i}{\lambda - \mu_i}$ and the condition $\lambda \geq \mu_i$ has to be satisfied.
(ii)

$$\text{If } x_i > 0 \Rightarrow \mu_i = 0 \text{ (by iv) } \Rightarrow x_i = \frac{1}{\alpha} \ln \frac{\alpha c_i}{\lambda}. \tag{11}$$

$$\text{If } \mu_i > 0 \Rightarrow x_i = 0 \text{ (by iv) } \Rightarrow \mu_i = \lambda - \alpha c_i. \tag{12}$$

Let us order $c_1 \geq c_2 \geq \ldots \geq c_m$ then by (11), $x_1 \geq x_2 \geq \ldots \geq x_m$.
Let $\bar{m} = \min\{i : x_{i+1} = 0, i \geq 1\}$. If $x_m \geq 0$, then set $\bar{m} = m + 1$.
Using (11) and (12), with $c_i \geq c_{i+1}$,

$$x_1 \geq x_2 \geq \ldots \geq x_{\bar{m}} > 0 = x_{\bar{m}+1} = \ldots = x_m$$
$$\mu_1 \leq \mu_2 \leq \ldots \leq \mu_{\bar{m}} < 0 = \mu_{\bar{m}+1} = \ldots = \mu_m$$

All that remains is finding $\bar{m}$.
For the purpose, define $\lambda$, for $1 \leq n \leq m$,

$$\ln \lambda(n) := \frac{1}{n} \left( \sum_{i=1}^{n} \ln \alpha c_i - \alpha Q \right) \tag{13}$$

Since $c_i \geq c_{i+1}$, we know $\ln \lambda(n)$ is decreasing in $n$.
Since $\frac{1}{\alpha} \ln \lambda(1) \leq \frac{1}{\alpha} \ln \alpha c_1$, $\bar{m} \geq 1$, consider the following algorithm to find $\bar{m}$:

**Set** $\bar{m} = 1$, Found $= 0$
**Repeat** until Found $= 1$ or $\bar{m} > m$
      **if** $\frac{1}{\alpha} \ln \lambda(\bar{m} + 1) < \frac{1}{\alpha} \ln \alpha c_{m+1}$
      **Set** $\bar{m} = \bar{m} + 1$
     **else** Found $= 1$

To solve the KKT set,

$\lambda = \lambda(\bar{m})$
For $1 \leq i \leq \bar{m}$, $x_i = \frac{1}{\alpha}(\ln \alpha c_i - \ln \lambda)$
       $\mu_i = 0$

For $\bar{m} < i \leq m$, $x_i = 0$
       $\mu_i = \lambda - \alpha c_i$

Now we show that this solution satisfies KKT.
For condition (i): For $1 \leq i \leq \bar{m}$: Since $\mu_i = 0$, (i) reduces to $-c_i \alpha e^{-\alpha x_i} + \lambda = 0$, which is solved by $x_i = \frac{1}{\alpha}(\ln \alpha c_i - \ln \lambda)$.
For $\bar{m} < i \leq m$: Since $x_i = 0$, (i) reduces to $-\alpha c_i + \lambda - \mu_i = 0$, which is the definition of $\mu_i$.

For condition (ii): By (19), $\sum_{i=1}^{m} x_i = \sum_{i=1}^{\bar{m}} x_i = \sum_{i=1}^{\bar{m}} \left( \frac{1}{\alpha}(\ln \alpha c_i - \ln \lambda) \right) = \frac{1}{\alpha} \left( \sum_{i=1}^{\bar{m}} \ln \alpha c_i - \bar{m}(\frac{1}{\bar{m}} \sum_{i=1}^{\bar{m}} \ln \alpha c_i - \alpha Q) \right) = Q$.

Since $x_{\bar{m}} \leq x_i$ for $i \geq \bar{m}$, we show $x_{\bar{m}} \geq 0$ to conclude $x_i \geq 0$ for $i \leq \bar{m}$. By the "if" condition in the algorithm $\frac{1}{\alpha} \ln \lambda(\bar{m}) < \frac{1}{\alpha} \ln \alpha c_{\bar{m}} \Rightarrow x_i = \frac{1}{\alpha} \ln \alpha c_{\bar{m}} - \frac{1}{\alpha} \ln \lambda > 0$. For $i > \bar{m}$, by our choice $x_i = 0$.

For condition (iii): For $1 \leq i \leq \bar{m}$, $\mu_i = 0$ by our choice. For $m \leq i \leq m$, $\mu_i = \lambda - \alpha c_i$. Since $\mu_i \geq \mu_{\bar{m}+1}$ for every $i > \bar{m}$, we show $\mu_{\bar{m}+1} \geq 0$ to conclude $\mu_i \geq 0$ for $i > \bar{m}$.
By the "if" condition in the algorithm $\frac{1}{\alpha} \ln \lambda(\bar{m} + 1) \geq \frac{1}{\alpha} \ln \alpha c_{\bar{m}+1}$.
Combining with $\lambda(\bar{m} + 1) \leq \lambda(\bar{m})$, we obtain, $\frac{1}{\alpha} \ln \lambda(\bar{m}) \geq \frac{1}{\alpha} \ln \alpha c_{\bar{m}+1} \Rightarrow \mu_{\bar{m}+1} = \lambda - \alpha c_{\bar{m}+1} \geq 0$

For condition (iv): This condition is trivially satisfied by the definition of $x_i$ and $\mu_i$. $\qquad \square$

*Two-tier Security:* Assume again $\rho_i = \gamma_i$, and $\sigma_i = \sigma$, and define $d_i = N\rho_i V_i S_i$. The problem is equivalent to:

$$\min \ \sum_{i=1}^{m} d_i \theta \sigma e^{-\alpha x_i - \beta y} - d_i(1-\theta)e^{-\alpha x_i} \tag{14}$$

$$\text{subject to} \ \sum_{i=1}^{m} x_i + y = Q$$

$$x_i \geq 0 \quad \text{for } i = 1, 2, \ldots, m, \quad y \geq 0$$

$$L(x_i, y, \mu_i, \lambda, \gamma) = \sum_{i=1}^{m} d_i \theta \sigma e^{-\alpha x_i - \beta y} + \sum_{i=1}^{m} d_i(1-\theta)e^{-\alpha x_i}$$

$$+ \lambda \left( \sum_{i=1}^{m} x_i + y - Q \right) + \mu_i \sum_{i=1}^{m} \left( -x_i \right) + \gamma(-y) \tag{15}$$

The Kuhn-Tucker conditions are

**ia** $\frac{\partial L}{\partial x_i} = -d_i \sigma \theta \alpha e^{-\alpha x_i - \beta y} - d_i(1-\theta)\alpha e^{-\alpha x_i} + \lambda - \mu_i = 0$

**ib** $\frac{\partial L}{\partial y} = -\sum_{i=1}^{m} d_i \sigma \theta \beta e^{-\alpha x_i - \beta y} + \lambda - \gamma = 0$

**ii** $\sum_{i=1}^{m} x_i + y = Q, \quad x_i \geq 0, \quad y \geq 0$

**iii** $\mu_i \geq 0, \quad y \geq 0$

**iv** $\mu_i(-x_i) = 0, \quad \gamma(-y) = 0$

(i.) We get $x_i = \frac{1}{\alpha} \ln \frac{\alpha d_i(\sigma \theta e^{-\beta y} - \theta + 1)}{\lambda - \mu_i}$, $y = \frac{1}{\beta} \ln \frac{\sum_i^m d_i \sigma \beta \theta e^{-\alpha x_i}}{\lambda - \gamma}$, and the conditions $\lambda \geq \mu_i$, $\lambda \geq \gamma$ have to be satisfied.

(ii)

$$\text{If } x_i > 0 \Rightarrow \mu_i = 0 \ (\text{by iv}) \ \Rightarrow x_i = \frac{1}{\alpha} \ln \frac{\alpha d_i(\sigma \theta e^{-\beta y} - \theta + 1)}{\lambda}. \tag{16}$$

$$\text{If } x_i = 0 \Rightarrow \mu_i > 0 \ (\text{by iv}) \ \Rightarrow \mu_i = \lambda - \alpha d_i(\sigma \theta e^{-\beta y} - \theta + 1). \tag{17}$$

If $\gamma > 0$, it has already been solved in the previous case because $y = 0$

$$\text{Without Loss of Generality } \gamma = 0, y = \frac{1}{\beta} \ln \frac{\sum_i^m d_i \sigma \beta \theta e^{-\alpha x_i}}{\lambda}. \tag{18}$$

From (16) and (18), we get $e^{-\beta y} = \frac{\alpha(1-\theta)}{\theta \sigma(m\beta - \alpha)}$, $y > 0 \Rightarrow \ln(m\beta - \alpha) > \ln \alpha(1 - \theta) - \ln \sigma \theta$ has to be satisfied.

Let us order $d_1 \geq d_2 \geq \ldots \geq d_m$ then by (16), $x_1 \geq x_2 \geq \ldots \geq x_m$.

Let $\bar{m} = \min\{i : x_{i+1} = 0, i \geq 1\}$. If $x_m \geq 0$, then set $\bar{m} = m + 1$.

Using (16) and (17), with $d_i \geq d_{i+1}$,

$$x_1 \geq x_2 \geq \ldots \geq x_{\bar{m}} > 0 = x_{\bar{m}+1} = \ldots = x_m$$

$$\mu_1 \leq \mu_2 \leq \ldots \leq \mu_{\bar{m}} < 0 = \mu_{\bar{m}+1} = \ldots = \mu_m$$

All that remains is finding $\bar{m}$.

For the purpose, define $\lambda$, for $1 \leq n \leq m$,

$$\ln \lambda(n) := \frac{1}{n}\left( \sum_{i=1}^{n} \ln \alpha d_i(\sigma\theta e^{-\beta y} - \theta + 1) - \alpha(Q - y) \right) \qquad (19)$$

Since $d_i \geq d_{i+1}$, we know $\ln \lambda(n)$ is decreasing in $n$.

Since $\frac{1}{\alpha} \ln \lambda(1) \leq \frac{1}{\alpha}\alpha \ln d_1(\sigma\theta e^{-\beta y} - \theta + 1)$, $\bar{m} \geq 1$, consider the following algorithm to find $\bar{m}$:

**Set** $\bar{m} = 1$, Found $= 0$
**Repeat** until Found $= 1$ or $\bar{m} > m$
    **if** $\ln((\bar{m}+1)\beta) > \ln \alpha(1 - \theta) - \ln \sigma\theta$
        $y = \frac{1}{\beta} \ln \frac{\theta\sigma(\bar{m}\beta - \alpha)}{\alpha(1-\theta)}$
    **else** $y = 0$
    **if** $\frac{1}{\alpha} \ln \lambda(\bar{m}+1) < \frac{1}{\alpha} \ln \alpha d_{m+1}(\sigma\theta e^{-\beta y} - \theta + 1)$
        **Set** $\bar{m} = \bar{m} + 1$
    **else** Found $= 1$

To solve the KKT set,

$\lambda = \lambda(\bar{m})$
For $1 \leq i \leq \bar{m}$, $x_i = \frac{1}{\alpha}(\ln \alpha d_i(\sigma\theta e^{-\beta y} - \theta + 1) - \ln \lambda)$
    $\mu_i = 0$
    $y = \frac{1}{\beta} \ln \frac{\theta\sigma(\bar{m}\beta - \alpha)}{\alpha(1-\theta)}$
    $\lambda = \sum_{i=1}^{\bar{m}} d_i \sigma\theta\beta e^{-\alpha x_i - \beta y}$
For $\bar{m} < i \leq m$, $x_i = 0$
    $\mu_i = \lambda - \alpha d_i(\sigma\theta e^{-\beta y} - \theta + 1)$
    $y = \frac{1}{\beta} \ln \frac{\theta\sigma(\bar{m}\beta - \alpha)}{\alpha(1-\theta)}$
    $\lambda = \sum_{i=1}^{\bar{m}} d_i \sigma\theta\beta e^{-\beta y}$

Now we show that this solution satisfies KKT.

For condition (ia): For $1 \leq i \leq \bar{m}$: Since $\mu_i = 0$, (ia) reduces to $-\alpha d_i(\sigma\theta e^{-\beta y} - \theta + 1)e^{-\alpha x_i} + \lambda = 0$, which is solved by $x_i = \frac{1}{\alpha}(\ln \alpha d_i(\sigma\theta e^{-\beta y} - \theta + 1) - \ln \lambda)$.

For $\bar{m} < i \leq m$: Since $x_i = 0$, (ia) reduces to $-d_i\sigma\theta\alpha e^{-\beta y} - d_i(1 - \theta)\alpha + \lambda - \mu_i = 0$, which is the definition of $\mu_i$

For condition (ib): For $1 \leq i \leq \bar{m}$:, (ib) reduces to $-\sum_{i=1}^{\bar{m}} d_i\sigma\theta\beta e^{-\alpha x_i - \beta y} + \lambda = 0$, which is solved by $y = \frac{1}{\beta} \ln \frac{\theta\sigma(\bar{m}\beta - \alpha)}{\alpha(1-\theta)}$.

For $\bar{m} < i \leq m$: Since $x_i = 0$, (ib) reduces to $-\sum_{i=1}^{\bar{m}} d_i\sigma\theta\beta e^{-\beta y} + \lambda$, which is the definition of $\lambda$

For condition (ii): By (19), $\sum_{i=1}^{m} x_i = \sum_{i=1}^{\bar{m}} x_i = \sum_{i=1}^{\bar{m}} \frac{1}{\alpha}(\ln \alpha d_i(\sigma\theta e^{-\beta y} - \theta + 1) - \ln \lambda) =$

$$\frac{1}{\alpha}\left( \sum_{i=1}^{\bar{m}} \ln \alpha d_i(\sigma\theta e^{-\beta y} - \theta + 1) - \bar{m}\left(\frac{1}{\bar{m}} \sum_{i=1}^{\bar{m}} \ln \alpha d_i(\sigma\theta e^{-\beta y} - \theta + 1) - \alpha(Q - y)\right) \right) = Q - y.$$

Since $x_{\bar{m}} \leq x_i$ for $i \geq \bar{m}$, we show $x_{\bar{m}} \geq 0$ to conclude $x_i \geq 0$ for $i \leq \bar{m}$. By the "if" condition in the algorithm $\frac{1}{\alpha} \ln \lambda(\bar{m}) < \frac{1}{\alpha} \ln \alpha d_{\bar{m}}(\sigma \theta e^{-\beta y} - \theta + 1) \Rightarrow$ $x_i = \frac{1}{\alpha}(\ln \alpha d_m(\sigma \theta e^{-\beta y} - \theta + 1) - \ln \lambda) > 0.$

For $i > \bar{m}$, by our choice $x_i = 0$.

For condition (iii): For $1 \leq i \leq \bar{m}$, $\mu_i = 0$ by our choice.

For $\bar{m} \leq i \leq m$, $\mu_i = \lambda - \alpha d_i(\sigma \theta e^{-\beta y} - \theta + 1)$. Since $\mu_i \geq \mu_{\bar{m}+1}$ for every $i > \bar{m}$, we show $\mu_{\bar{m}+1} \geq 0$ to conclude $\mu_i \geq 0$ for $i > \bar{m}$.

By the "if" condition in the algorithm

$$\frac{1}{\alpha} \ln \lambda(\bar{m} + 1) \geq (\frac{1}{\alpha} \ln \alpha d_{\bar{m}+1}(\sigma \theta e^{-\beta y} - \theta + 1)).$$

Combining with $\lambda(\bar{m} + 1) \leq \lambda(\bar{m})$, we obtain, $\frac{1}{\alpha} \ln \lambda(\bar{m}) \geq \frac{1}{\alpha} \ln \alpha d_{\bar{m}+1}$ $(\sigma \theta e^{-\beta y} - \theta + 1) \Rightarrow \mu_{\bar{m}+1} = \lambda - \alpha d_{\bar{m}+1}(\sigma \theta e^{-\beta y} - \theta + 1) \geq 0$

For condition (iv): This condition is trivially satisfied by the definition of $x_i$ and $\mu_i$; $y$ and $\gamma$.     □

# References

1. Ernst, Young: Global information security survey 2003. Technical report, Ernst and Young LLP (2003)
2. Richardson, R.: 2003 CSI/FBI computer crime and security survey. Technical report, Computer Security Journal (2003)
3. Stoneburner, G., Goguen, A., Feringa, A.: Risk management guide for information technology systems. Special Publication 800-30, National Institute of Standards and Technology (NIST), Technology Administration, U.S. Department of Commerce (2002)
4. Cavusoglu, H., Raghunathan, S.: Configuration of intrusion detection systems: A comparison of decision and game theory approaches. In: Proceedings of the International Conference on Information Systems. (2003)
5. Cavusoglu, H., Mishra, B., Raghunathan, S.: Optimal design of information technology security architecture. In: Proceedings of the Twenty-Third International Conference on Information Systems, Barcelona, Spain (2002) 749–756
6. Gordon, L.A., Loeb, M.P.: The economics of information security investment. ACM Transactions on Information and System Security 5 (2002) 438–457
7. Straub, D.W., Welke, R.J.: Coping with systems risk: Security planning models for management decision-making. MIS Quarterly 22 (1998) 441–469
8. Straub, D.W.: Effective is security: An empirical study. Information Systems Research 1 (1990) 255–276
9. Higgins, M.: Symantec Internet security threat report: Attack trends for Q3 and Q4 2002. Symantec Corporation (2003)
10. Moitra, S.D., Konda, S.L.: A simulation model for managing survivability of networked information systems. SEI/CERT Report CMU/SEI-2000-TR-020, Carnegie Mellon University (2000)

# Mind the Gap: The Growing Distance between Institutional and Technical Capabilities in Organizations Performing Critical Operations

Gene I. Rochlin

Energy and Resources Group: 310 Barrows Hall
University of California, Berkeley, CA 94720
armsis@socrates.berkeley.edu

**Abstract.** Although there are many reasons to seek to augment the capacity of crisis management and response organizations with various forms of information technology (IT), it is not clear that they will be able to adapt organizationally or institutionally to make effective use of the new capabilities. The behavior of organizations responsible for large, complex and tightly coupled systems is already known to be very difficult to predict reliably, due to their complexity, coupling, and nonlinear interactions. Historically, they are subject to a range of pathologies that are difficult to predict, ranging from self-organizing disasters to rigid and insensitive response. IT intensive organizations add to this the potential for unprecedented incoherence of tasks and task monitoring, leading to possible displacement of the locus of administration or the dissipation of task responsibility in ways that are still poorly understood, and badly in need of further intensive study[1].

## 1 Introduction

When asked to present a paper on how information technology might be used to augment American security, I was not at first sure how or where my own research on organizational reliability and information infrastructures would fit in. Most of my research has centered on the problems that managers of complex systems performing critical tasks face when their response to emerging crises is mediated by technologies whose capabilities and limitations they do not fully understand [1]. There is a long history of misadaptation and failures in the introduction of what are loosely called "information and telecommunication" (IT) systems into complex organizations [2], including a recent article speculating on future accidents and disasters that might occur from institutional inability to recognize the long-term vulnerabilities and unanticipated consequences of embedding IT and/or computer systems [3] into critical operations. Some of the concerns that have been raised in the past about the problems of relying on more traditional, hard-wired or localized IT systems, especially under emergency conditions or other situations of high stress, and of maintaining infrastructure under the strain of constant adaptation and change (National Research Council 2000 [4]), may be extendable to systems that extend to, incorporate, or are replaced by those based on extended and distributed webs such as the internet, but there is very little experience to date upon which to base a more systematic analysis.

---

[1] This paper is dedicated to the memory of Rob Kling, one of the founders of the study of the effects of IT on organizational performance and social behavior.

H. Chen et al. (Eds.): ISI 2004, LNCS 3073, pp. 349–358, 2004.
© Springer-Verlag Berlin Heidelberg 2004

## 2  Context

The major focus of the conference was on security and response, broadly defined. To some extent, this encompasses the means and methods for reacting to emergencies, disasters, or imminent threats, all of which entail dependence on the performance of complex, IT-dependent organizations. Much of the discussion also centered on anticipating rather than reacting to a wide variety of threats ranging from criminal activity to terrorist attacks, through the use of data mining, behavioral profiles, and other forms of data analysis and manipulation. While there is far less experience with the latter, many of the proposed strategies for data mining and surveillance will almost certainly require a high degree of organizational and administrative centralization, whatever the shape and design of the technical infrastructure. To the extent that this is the case, some of what can be learned from response organizations may reasonably be generalized. In particular, there was some concern expressed over the ability, or inability, of organizations to maintain either the infrastructure or the trained personnel to achieve the degree of cross-organizational collaboration that would be required to achieve the results that are sought.

Designs for the integration and coordination of a wide variety of traditional emergency response organizations – police departments, fire departments, hospitals, and medical services – by means of advanced information technologies, under the aegis of a superordinating agency such as the State of California's Office of Emergency Services, or Federal units subordinated to or integrated with the Department of Homeland Security, have a way of looking neat and orderly on paper. But in a phrase familiar to all working engineers, there are two kinds of technology design: the ones that work on paper, and the ones that work in practice. All too often, they do not overlap.

Based on past experience, there is a significant gap between the expectations of many of the promoters of integration and coordination through IT and the reality shaped by the resources, experience, and culture of those organizations [4-6]. Can their performance in an extended and large-scale crisis match the expectations of those designing the newly extended and extensively networked systems of integration and coordination? The empirical evidence is at best ambiguous, and in many ways contradictory. The purpose of this paper is to expand upon my concern, and that of many colleagues who work on organizational performance, that insufficient attention has been paid to the gap between what could be and what probably is.

## 3  Problems of Advanced IT in "Traditional" Emergency Response Organizations

By characterizing fire departments, police departments, ambulance systems, and hospitals as "traditional," I do not mean to imply that they are backwards, or unwilling to adopt new means and methods of operation, communication, or integration via IT. Rather, I mean that it is necessary to understand their histories and culture, the ways in which they adapt to and perceive the tasks and risks that shape their lives.

This was brought home to me most forcefully when discussing the tragic losses of the New York Fire Department on September 11, 2001 with several personnel of local fire departments, as part of my own research on organizational reliability and performance. During the second day and night of the Berkeley-Oakland Hills fire of

1991, the Oakland Fire Department held back a fairly considerable reserve of personnel and equipment just below the fire zone (and just above my own house). Obviously concerned, many of the residents both of the burning zone and the one adjacent to it, demanded to know why this equipment was not being used to fight the fire. The Chief defended his decision, in the face of often hostile criticism, on the grounds that he needed a reserve in case the fire jumped over the firebreak they were seeking to establish around the grounds of a large resort hotel. Using this as an example, I was seeking to determine whether the people I was interviewing could estimate what kind of improvements in means of communications or revamping of command and control systems could have avoided the rush of firemen into the twin towers on Sept. 11.

Much to my surprise, the folks I was talking to did not think that much could have been done under the circumstances. One quote from a colleague who is also a fireman haunts me still: "You can't ask firemen not to rush into a burning building to save people." At the most basic level, it's what they do. It's what gives meaning and purpose to their professional lives. It's what they did in the first day of the Berkeley Hills fire as well. Holding equipment back was possible on day 2 because the emergency response phase was over and the immediate risk to lives had diminished.

Command does not always mean control [7]. In an emergency, professionals will do what they are trained to do, and that training is embedded at least as deeply by socialization and culture as it is by organization charts and command hierarchies [8]. Unless one is prepared to scrap history and tradition and rebuild the organizations from scratch, what advanced IT should be doing is working with and supporting the grunts who take the risks on the front lines of emergencies. But this has not always been the case.

Consider, for example, the effects of the QuesTec system for monitoring umpire's calls at baseball games. One of the complaints that umpire's have had about the QuesTec system is that they are beginning to think more about the monitoring than the pitch in front of them. The *New York Times* reported an umpire as saying:

In a QuesTec city, you say, 'What is the machine going to say?' not 'What was that pitch?' Pretty soon you're umpiring a video game, not a baseball game. It affects your mindset of what you're doing out on the field [9].

In a recent article, *The Economist* had a rather pessimistic take on the increased use of government IT projects in Britain, using as examples such cases as the chaos caused by the failure of the Passport Office's new computer system in 1999 and the long delays in implementing new air traffic control systems [5]. The reasons given are apt for what we are considering here. Government agencies are poor at oversight of projects, and often incapable of providing informed scrutiny. The specifications tend to be rigid, and "set in stone" by authorizing bodies. And trial and error learning is usually *not* an option. Moreover, each added layer of oversight simply creates new modes of systemic failure, and less responsiveness to the needs and requirements of those who actually have to perform the tasks themselves. What happens next exhibits a pattern that has been empirically observed in many cases.

There is constant pressure from both inside and outside the organization to "improve" or "modernize" the system in the name of efficiency. Often, this means the introduction of advanced and centralized IT systems with manuals several inches thick, and an attendant requirement to take many hours of classes in preparation for the changeover. Unable to "anchor" their primary task to their historical experience, workers are under constant stress, often expressed as being trapped forever on the steep part of the learning curve. At the same time, their work becomes devalued as they shift from operators of a complex task environment to operators of the equipment that performs the actual operations [10, 11]. As a result, many long-time employees retire early, taking with them the institutional memory that is an essential building block of reliable system performance.

## 4 Networks and Complexity

The complex, tightly coupled heterogeneous networks of interdependence that are central to the anticipated performance of these various missions and pursuit of this highly diverse range of objectives have only been in existence for a relatively short time. Even so, a great deal of that experience has been interpreted as a warning about the consequences of increased system complexity. As Charles Perrow pointed out in his well-known book *Normal Accidents*, and in other events analyzed by me and by Scott Sagan, among others, in other contexts [12-14], high complexity and tight coupling can lead to event sequences where the organization can not understand, analyze, or respond correctly in the time it has available to it [15]. High complexity combined with organizational heterogeneity can also lead to the sorts of event sequences pointed out by Diane Vaughan in her study of the *Challenger*, where differences in organizational culture and structure led to a fatal misdiagnosis of launch risk, even with ample time and superb IT and communications at its disposal [16]. What is more, the report of the *Columbia* accident investigation board shows that despite its dedication to adaptation and learning, NASA remains an organization that not only failed to achieve what Karl Weick has characterized as the "requisite variety" needed to manage complexity [17], but actively moved in the other direction as it turned critical tasks over to contractors [18].

Dramatic cases that end in disasters are of course well documented, but there is not much in the way of systematic empirical analysis of complex, decentralized organizations. A great deal of what passes for "social" theorizing about reliability and stability of complex socio-technical systems seeks instead to transcend attempts at extrapolation from past behavior by searching for analogies and metaphors – often from purely physical systems. In the past, it was assumed in both social and physical cases that systems that "succeed" are driven by negative feedback processes toward predictable states of adaptation to the environment. Success was equated with equilibrium, and therefore stability, regularity, and predictability. These assumptions, which were drawn from Newtonian physics and Darwinian evolution are now being challenged at the fundamental level by the new "sciences of complexity," concerned with the dynamical properties of non linear and network feedback systems [19, 20].

One example of new thinking on this subject is a recent book by Russ Marion that does set out to apply newer theories of complexity to organizations [21]. Using Kauffman's formulations – in particular the notion that systems need to be near the "edge of chaos" to be adaptive [22], he finds that there are optimal levels and intensities of interaction in complex organizations. Too much, and the system moves towards chaos, too little and it is overly stable and unable to adapt. But he has no idea of what would constitute the proper tools for analysis, let alone for design. Few of us do.

Even research that attempts to deal with networked organizations and complexity in terms of life at the edge of chaos rarely deals with heterogeneity, or with the poten-

tial role of IT in heterogeneously complex organizations. The only theoretical literature I could find on analogically similar systems dealt, interestingly enough, with
biology – studies of complex, diverse, heterogeneous, and tightly coupled food webs[2].
Models of biosystems having these characteristics showed that they can maintain
stability and reliability over time only if they remained flexible and adaptable, which
in turn requires both fungible resources and units in the web capable of using these
resources in innovative ways [23]. All of which sounds quite familiar to students of
organizational reliability, who have long questioned both the assumption of negative
feedback towards some equilibrium point (the ideal of rational systems analysis) and
the abstract theoretical literature that deals primarily with the structure of open systems rather than operational dynamics.

## 5  The Internet

Emergency response is not the only mission of homeland security. There a variety of
others, such as responding to widespread civil disorder, or the consequences and af-
termath of military or terrorist attacks, that will require the coordination of a wide
variety of organizations having vastly different resources, capabilities, and missions.
And there is the growing problem of trying to monitor and anticipate potential threats,
many of which may be designed and organized by groups who never meet face to
face, or communicate over traditional hardwired telecommunications, but instead
make efficient use of the internet [24]. This is not a new agenda – it has been developing gradually over the past ten years or more–but recent events in the United States
and overseas have raised both the stakes and the demands for a more fully integrated
and controllable means for inter-agency coordination, cooperation, and response.

Not that much is known empirically about organizations that are designed around
internet technologies rather than more traditional forms of IT. The only examples of
long-standing come from health services and hospitals [4]. Even here, where there is
considerable accumulated experience, the prognosis for organizational adaptation to
deal with complexity is mixed. As the National Research Council reported:

Despite the promise of many Internet-based applications, health care organizations
can be expected to encounter many obstacles as they attempt to apply these technologies to realize their strategic visions. They will face barriers to, and constraints on,
organizational change, as well as uncertainty about the efficacy and effects of Internet-based applications. A resistance to change might come from denial of the need to
change, the inability to manage change, uncertainties about the types of changes
needed and how best to make them, mistaken assessments of optimal changes, and
failures in executing changes. These issues are not unique to the adoption of the Internet and could arise in many other areas of organizational change, including those
driven by other types of information technology. What makes Internet-driven change
different is its magnitude and the high degree of uncertainty. Organizations that have
difficulty making the necessary investments in, and managing, information technology in general will have even more difficulty adapting to the Internet [4].

---

[2] Of course, much of the foundational work on this was done by Ilya Prigogine some thirty
years ago on self-organizing and self-designing systems. When asked about his Nobel Prize
winning work, Prigogine uses the example of two cities, one of which was closed with
guards and gates, and the other of which was open to trade and ideas. The first one, he said,
would wither and die, the second one thrive.

Those uncertainties are compounded in the case of 'virtual' organizations – organizations that have no physical infrastructure, but are constituted entirely over networked communications [25]. The analytic problem is that the communicative and performative structures of virtual organizations may differ radically from those of more conventional organizations, making their behavior more difficult to predict [26]. There are also questions about failure modes that remain unanswered. Whereas many organizations performing critical tasks have gone to great lengths to secure those communication links that are most central to their functions, there is really no way to secure links that are wholly external to the organization. In one rather famous case, failure of the Galaxy satellite in 1998 caused many hospitals to lose their internal communications completely [27]. Even the Internet, with its famous designed-in redundancy, remains external to the organization, and therefore yet another source of uncertainty as to whether it can be relied upon in a crisis.

## 6  Problems of Network Integration

This last point leads to the next – the problems of integrating the various components of the proposed super-agency or super-organization into a coherent whole subject to centralized decision-making and resource allocation and consistent behavior and response. What is envisioned is not at all along the models of the military, which has a well-defined and quite deliberately homogeneous and hierarchical system of training and acculturation. Rather, it is made up of heterogeneous networks of behaviorally and culturally diverse organizations that are not easily subjected to the kinds of integration and standardization that would make their response in a crisis predictable – especially under circumstances that put them under immediate stress.

Moreover, many of them – perhaps most, in these financially troubled times – have limited resources and limited existing IT capabilities, and little prospect of being given additional resources to bring them up to performative expectations. In my own state, California, we do have a very professional statewide Organization of Emergency Services (OES), which must deal with the comparatively high probability of an extensive disaster in the form of a major earthquake at some time in the not-too distant future. And you must understand that it began from a typical basis, where different cities, and even different agencies within cities, operated on different communications frequencies and with different equipment, where the fire hydrants of adjacent cities often had different couplings and the police forces different behavioral cultures. The difficulties in implementing joint command and mutual response in the Berkeley-Oakland Hills fire of 1991 produced a statewide Standardized Emergency Management System (SEMS) and, in 1995, a means for integrating and automating SEMS response by means of a Response Information Management Service (RIMS).

At first, RIMS worked by conventional means of communication. But as the number of participating agencies grew from just a few to over 2,000, OES moved it from telephone and fax to the Internet. In so doing, they faced some intriguing challenges. Some of the response organizations and forces they were trying to integrate had almost no computer facilities (of the type needed), and those that did had very uneven operator capabilities. Many of the organizations had no backup power supplies for their communication equipment, and, in earthquake country, almost none of them had their equipment solidly bolted down. Realizing that the system would be vulnerable to the loss of landlines, or even transmission towers, they do have satellite communication as a backup – although there are only 58 terminals, and they are controlled at the county or regional level. Moreover, telephone interviews produced no "standardized" answer as to the operational role of RIMS other than the general statement that it was intended to provide a means for inter-agency and inter-organizational communication.

Small departments utterly dependent on mutual aid have welcomed it, and some firefighters have had special training to become part of a strike team to fight wildland fires. But the SEMS/RIMS system is complicated, and has never really been tested in full (even in the recent spate of wildfires in Southern California in 2003). Larger departments have the equipment for training, but it is often resented, and resisted, and its integration through RIMS is familiar only to those at the top of the department who are formally responsible for inter-agency communication. Some departments that have acquired SEMS simulators have in fact never used them – and some, I was told, are busy dusting them off to see if they can be used to help with new cooperation mandates concerning homeland security.

Why are some organizations so slow to adapt to the new systems of networking and integration, and so resistant to changes that incorporate major networking and efforts at joint response (which is far more than the usual and familiar forms of "mutual aid")? Many of them are already understaffed and overburdened, lacking the time and "slack" to rehearse and perfect their roles, or to run realistic crisis exercises. And even if the exercises are "realistic," just what does that mean? In May of 2003, the Department of Homeland Security organized the most extensive drill in American history – simulating nearly simultaneous attacks on Seattle and Chicago. Government officials ranging from Tom Ridge to the mayors of Seattle and Chicago were ready and on call, and the relevant fire and police departments had been briefed. All were expecting the exercise, which went off "satisfactorily." Even so, many weaknesses were exposed – most notably the limitations in communication capacity [9].

During research on nuclear power plant operations, I was privileged to sit in at the emergency response coordination center during such a "realistic" exercise. Using a worst-case scenario, the accident was assumed to take place in mid-afternoon of a school day. The plan called for the police to redistribute themselves in the area to direct traffic and coordinate evacuation, for the fire department to move downwind of the plant to wash down contamination from people and from still-occupied facilities, and for the drivers of school buses to take their buses in, *towards* the plant, to get the children out. My research team asked some rather mild questions. Would the bus drivers really drive into an area of potentially higher risk to evacuate the children? Would they need a police escort in a real situation? Could they get one? Would any equipment at all be able to move if a panic set in? Are fire department personnel comfortable with their role? Would the emergency response command center really have the authority to order other units about? The questions seemed to cause discomfort to the managers, but were met with amused and knowing (and often cynical) comments by those who would have to carry out the operations in the real world, under real world conditions.

This is not to say that the organizations will not react well, or bravely, in a real emergency. In crises and disasters that are of relatively limited scope and duration, these organizations have often responded heroically and dramatically, often by improvising, and more often at tremendous cost in organizational resources – the most dramatic, of course, being the incredible loss of life among firemen and other emergency response workers in the attack on the World Trade Center. But as indicated previously, what they were doing is what they were trained to do, as individuals and teams, not what was expected of them by an outside organization.

Some elements of the military now pride themselves on the way in which they used IT for flexible and adaptive combat in Iraq. The examples tend to be of situations where IT was used to reduce a fighting unit's dependence on the networks in which it is embedded – in formal terms, to "decompose" the command and control network and "decouple" the unit from it. If that is how IT would be used for homeland security and disaster response, to provide more accurate, more timely information to units operating semi-autonomously within their own bounded rationality and scope, that would be something of surprise. A forensic analysis of past versions of information-rich networks does not give us great confidence in the ability of those who design and implement them to let them decompose under stress.

Moreover, as I pointed out earlier, decomposition under stress might not be the correct action at all. At times, it might be wiser to hold resources back until the full scope of the event was known, and resources could be intelligently allocated. But as we all know from movies and novels, as well as "real life," that would lead to a real tension with the operating organizations, who would worry that the command and control system was more interested in maintaining order, and control, than in events taking place on the ground. Those of us who work on disaster research are very familiar with the importance of self-organization in early situation assessment and response – and with the tendency of system designers to neglect it. If, as is more than likely, the culture of the networking organization places a premium on control of resources and command of situations, while the culture of the various operating organizations call for action, there would certainly be a clash. If the organizations being networked are also heterogeneous in their approaches and cultures, and had differential access to partial information, it would require considerable wisdom and experience to manage and balance all of this. It is hard to be optimistic.

## 7  Conclusion

These emergency and crisis anticipation and response systems need to remain stable and reliable over long periods of time, even when little used or seldom activated. We do know from studies of simpler organizations operating under more benign conditions and performing less demanding tasks that organizations faced with long periods of inaction tend to lose their entrepreneurs and cease to innovate, and either die outright or become living fossils. Do our expectations match this reality? Or are we arbitrarily declaring that IT will move reality to conform with expectations?

IT could be a means for innovation and adaptation, but it could also be a source of rigidity and obsessive standardization. It could be used to watch for and seek to address signs of obsolescence and decay, but it could just as easily exacerbate the process by labeling innovation as deviance. It could be used to protect the life and liberty of a society, but it could also be used to control and dominate it. And to be more specific, data mining and communication monitoring could be used to seek out rare and threatening circumstances, or deteriorate into efforts to see threats in the most commonplace of events.

"Virtual" organizations – ephemeral networks such as e-mail, ad-hoc user groups, and other means of virtual networking over the Internet (including potential terrorist networks) – are complex and difficult to analyze. And so are the equally virtual systems set up to monitor and police them. Empirical work on virtual organizations has shown that whereas task-structure usually predicted perceived performance, it often did not predict objective performance [25, 26]. That is, results indicate that the fit between structure and task routineness may increase perception that the organization is performing well without providing a measure of actual performance. This is disturbing.

Data mining and other forms of electronic prying and eavesdropping have far more profound effects on social life and civil liberties than baseball. It is not a video game – but there is great danger that the system's 'operators' will increasingly treat it as one – without realizing it. This is a new form of organizational pathology, to be added to an already long list that includes, inter alia:

• Overconcern with strict adherence to regulations at the expense of social goals.

• Red tape, overly complex regulations, and proliferation of special interests.

• Goal displacement towards organizational rather than political/social purpose.

• Inability to measure or evaluate overall (as opposed to task) effectiveness.

Which can lead in turn to social pathologies:

• Indispensable bureaucracies that are increasingly resistant to external control

• Exploitation and dehumanization, leading to feelings of powerlessness, meaninglessness, normlessness, cultural estrangement, self-estrangement, and social isolation

In sum, large, high-tech (complex and tightly coupled) systems are already known to be very difficult to measure (or control) due to their complexity, coupling, and nonlinear interaction, and subject to a range of difficult to predict pathologies ranging from self-organizing disasters to rigid and unwarranted response. IT intensive organizations add to this the potential for unprecedented incoherence of tasks and task monitoring, displacement and even dissipation of responsibility, and increased dependence on the "invisible infrastructure" – other organizations that may not even be aware of their own role in overall performance.

Human systems are open and natural systems. They thrive through adaptation, learning, and flexibility in the search for the more ephemeral goals of satisfaction, liberty, and survival. Unlike previous methods of interaction, human-machine systems that make extensive use of the Internet are also, in many ways, "open" systems, flexible and able to learn and to adapt quickly to circumstances. But the systems that are being put into place to perform the many tasks set out in the extensive set that ranges from emergency response to anticipative monitoring and detection will have little opportunity to learn, since the ultimate basis for learning is trial and error, and these agencies are being designed to eliminate the prospect for error from the outset. Such systems are more than usually subject to the organizational distortion that focuses performance criteria and evaluation on rational means for achieving narrowly defined goals, and tend to become rigid and non-adaptive with age. And that gap, between the nature of the threat and the evolution of the agencies, may be the greatest gap of all.

# References

1. G. I. Rochlin, "Essential Friction: Error Control in Organizational Behavior," in *The Necessity of Friction*, N. Akerman, Ed. Heidelberg: Springer/Physica-Verlag, 1993, pp. 196-234.

2. G. I. Rochlin, *Trapped in the Net: The Unanticipated Consequences of Computerization.* Princeton, NJ: Princeton University Press, 1997.
3. G. I. Rochlin, "Future IT Disasters: A Speculative Exploration," in *Managing Crises: Threats, Dilemmas, Opportunities,* U. Rosenthal, R. A. Boin, and L. K. Comfort, Eds. Springfield IL: Charles C. Thomas, 2001, pp. 251-266.
4. National Research Council, *Networking Health: Prescriptions for the Internet.* Washington D.C.: National Academy Press, 2000.
5. Economist, "The Health Service's IT Problem," in *The Economist,* 2002.
6. C. Perrow, "Organizing to Reduce the Vulnerabilities of Complexity," *Journal of Contingencies and Crisis Management,* vol. 7, pp. 150-155, 1999.
7. M. Landau and R. Stout, jr., "To Manage Is Not To Control: Or the Folly of Type II Errors," *Public Administration Review,* vol. 39, pp. 148-156, 1979.
8. K. E. Weick and K. M. Sutcliffe, *Managing the Unexpected.* San Francisco: Jossey-Bass, 2001.
9. S. Kershaw, "Terror Scenes Follow Script of Never Again," in *The New York Times.* New York, 2003, pp. A19.
10. J. Novek, "IT, Gender, and Professional Practice: Or, Why an Automated Drug Distribution System Was Sent Back to the Manufacturer," *Science, Technology, &Human Values,* vol. 27, pp. 379-403, 2002.
11. S. Zuboff, *In the Age of the Smart Machine: The Future of Work and Power.* New York: Basic Books, 1984.
12. C. Perrow, *Normal Accidents: Living With High-Risk Technologies.* New York: Basic Books, 1984.
13. G. I. Rochlin, "Iran Air Flight 655: Complex, Large-Scale Military Systems and the Failure of Control," in *Responding to Large Technical Systems: Control or Anticipation,* T. R. La Porte, Ed. Amsterdam: Kluwer, 1991, pp. 95-121.
14. S. D. Sagan, *The Limits of Safety: Organizations, Accidents, and Nuclear Weapons.* Princeton: Princeton University Press, 1993.
15. K. E. Weick, "The Collapse of Sensemaking in Organizations: The Mann Gulch Disaster," *Administrative Science Quarterly,* vol. 38, pp. 628-652, 1993.
16. D. Vaughan, *The Challenger Launch Decision: Risky Technology, Culture, and Deviance at NASA.* Chicago: University of Chicago Press, 1996.
17. K. E. Weick, *The Social Psychology of Organizing.* New York: Random House, 1979.
18. Columbia Accident Investigation Board, "Final Report." Washington DC: U. S. Government Printing Office, 2003.
19. T. I. Sanders, *Strategic thinking and the new science : planning in the midst of chaos, complexity, and change.* New York: Free Press, 1998.
20. M. M. Waldrop, *Complexity : the emerging science at the edge of order and chaos,* 1st Touchstone ed. New York: Simon & Schuster, 1993.
21. R. Marion, *The Edge of Organization: Chaos and Complexity Theories for Formal Social Systems.* Thousand Oaks, Calif.: Sage Publications, 1999.
22. S. A. Kauffman, *The origins of order : self-organization and selection in evolution.* New York: Oxford University Press, 1993.
23. M. Kondoh, "Foraging Adaptation and the Relationship Between Food-Web Complexity and Stability," *Science,* vol. 299, pp. 1388-1391, 2003.
24. J. Stern, *The ultimate terrorists.* Cambridge, MA: Harvard University Press, 1999.
25. U. J. Franke, *Managing virtual web organizations in the 21st century : issues and challenges.* Hershey, PA: Idea Group Pub., 2002.
26. M. K. Ahuja and K. M. Carley, "Network Structure in Virtual Organizations," *Organization Science,* vol. 10, pp. 693-703, 1999.
27. R. Cook, "Galaxy IV and the Risks of Efficient Technologies," in *Risks 19.75,* 19.75 ed. http:/catless.ncl.ac.uk: Forum on Risks, 1998.

# Analyzing and Visualizing Criminal Network Dynamics: A Case Study

Jennifer Xu, Byron Marshall, Siddharth Kaza, and Hsinchun Chen

Department of Management Information Systems,
University of Arizona, Tucson, AZ 85721
{jxu,byronm,sidd,hchen}@eller.arizona.edu

**Abstract.** Dynamic criminal network analysis is important for national security but also very challenging. However, little research has been done in this area. In this paper we propose to use several descriptive measures from social network analysis research to help detect and describe changes in criminal organizations. These measures include centrality for individuals, and density, cohesion, and stability for groups. We also employ visualization and animation methods to present the evolution process of criminal networks. We conducted a field study with several domain experts to validate our findings from the analysis of the dynamics of a narcotics network. The feedback from our domain experts showed that our approaches and the prototype system could be very helpful for capturing the dynamics of criminal organizations and assisting crime investigation and criminal prosecution.

## 1 Introduction

In intelligence and law enforcement domains investigators have long used "networks" to refer to criminal or terrorist organizations. This is because offenses such as terrorist attacks, narcotic trafficking, and armed robbery depend, to a large extent, on the collective efforts of multiple, interrelated individuals. When analyzing such crimes investigators not only examine the characteristics and behavior of individual offenders but also pay much attention to the organization, structure, and operation of groups and the overall network. Knowledge and insights gained from these analyses may help intelligence and law enforcement agencies identify the target offenders for removal or select effective strategies to disrupt a criminal organization.

Although it is promising, criminal network analysis faces many challenges especially when a criminal organization's dynamic nature is taken into consideration. A criminal organization is not a static system but keeps changing over time: members may leave or join the network; they may change their roles, gain more power, or lose power; relations may form among members or dissolve; groups may merge or split; the overall network may evolve from a centralized, hierarchical structure to a decentralized, flat one or vise versa. All these changes add high complexity to the analysis. Unfortunately research in criminal network analysis is rather scarce, let alone dynamic network analysis. It is a pressing need to identify appropriate methodologies and techniques to capture dynamic patterns of criminal networks, thereby aiding crime investigation and disruptive strategy selection.

H. Chen et al. (Eds.): ISI 2004, LNCS 3073, pp. 359–377, 2004.

In this paper we propose to employ several quantitative methods and measures from the area of social network analysis (SNA) to study the dynamics of criminal networks. These measures and methods can be used to detect and describe the changes in network members' individual characteristics and social roles (e.g., leader and gate-keeper) and capture the dynamic patterns of group membership and structure. In addition, we employ the animation method to visualize the evolution of a criminal network in terms of its changes in members, relations, groups, and the overall structure. In order to evaluate the usefulness of the proposed quantitative methods and the visualization approach, we conducted a field study and asked domain experts to validate the findings from our analysis of the evolution of a narcotics network.

The remainder of this paper is organized as follows. Section 2 briefly introduces the research background. Section 3 reviews SNA literature regarding the methods and visualization techniques for analysis of network dynamics. Section 4 proposes the quantitative methods and visualization approach. The evaluation results from the field study are presented in Section 5. Section 6 concludes the paper and discusses future research directions.

## 2  Research Background

A criminal network is primarily a social network in which individuals connect with one another through various relations such as kinship, friendship, and co-workers. Research has recognized SNA as a promising methodology to analyze the structural properties of criminal networks [5, 22, 23, 26, 35]. SNA was originally used in sociology research to extract patterns of relationships between social actors in order to discover the underlying social structure [38, 39]. A social network is often treated as a graph in which nodes represent individual members and links represent relations among the members. The structural properties of a social network can be described and analyzed at four levels: node, link, group, and the overall network. SNA provides various measures, indexes, and approaches to capture these structural properties quantitatively.

There have been some empirical studies that use SNA methods to analyze criminal or terrorist networks. For instance, based on archival data, Baker and Faulkner analyzed the structure of an illegal network depicting a price-fixing conspiracy in the heavy electrical equipment industry. They find that individual centrality in the network, as measured by degree, betweenness, and closeness [17], is an important predictor of an individual's possible prosecution [1]. Krebs relied on open source data and studied the terrorist network centering around the 19 hijackers in 9/11 events. He found that Mohamed Atta, who piloted the first plane that crashed into the World Trade Center, had the highest degree and acted as the ring leader of the network [23]. Xu and Chen employed clustering, centrality measures, blockmodeling, and multidimensional scaling (MDS) approaches from SNA to study criminal networks based on crime incident data [41]. The system they developed can also visualize a network and its groups.

However, all these studies are static analysis in which data is collected at a single point in time and the snapshot of a criminal network is generated and studied. The dynamics in network nodes, links, groups, and the structure are ignored. How does an individual acquire a central position in a network and gain more power over time? Do relations between individuals become stronger or weaker? How does a group's membership or structure change? What do these changes imply about the future of the network? With a static point of view, many of these important questions regarding the development and evolution of criminal networks remain unanswered.

In order to address these questions we propose to use a set of methods and measures from SNA to describe and capture patterns of changes in criminal networks. In addition, visualization and animation are used to present network dynamics.

## 3 Literature Review

In this section we review related SNA research about dynamic network analysis and visualization.

### 3.1 Analyzing Social Network Dynamics

Recently, the research on social network dynamics has received increasing attention. However, there has not been a consensus on what analytical methods to use [4, 14, 27]. Research uses various methods, measures, models, and techniques to study network dynamics. Doreian and Stokman classified existing approaches into three categories: descriptive, statistical, and simulation methods [15].

**Descriptive Methods.** The purpose of descriptive analysis is often to detect structural changes in social networks and test how well a sociologic theory is supported by empirical data. With descriptive methods, structural properties of a social network are measured by various metrics and indexes and compared across time to describe the dynamics in nodes, links, or groups in the network. Little research has been found which studied the dynamics at the overall network level.

Node level measures often focus on changes in individuals' centrality, influence, and other characteristics. To study how an individual's social position relates to his or her technology adoption behavior, Burkhardt and Brass studied a communication network of 94 employees of an organization at four time points after a new computerized information system was deployed [3]. They found that the centrality (degree and closeness) and power of early adopters of new technology increased over time. Using Newcomb's classic longitudinal data [28], Nakao and Romney measured the "positional stability" of 17 new members in a fraternity during a 15-week period [27]. For each week, these individuals were mapped into a two-dimensional MDS diagram based on their relational strength. As individuals may change their positions over time, the lengths of their paths of movement were calculated with a short path indicating a high positional stability. The positional stability index was used to examine how popular and unpopular individuals differ in the speed with which they found their appropriate social groups. In the area of citation analysis where an author citation network is treated as a social network, centrality type metrics have been used to trace the dynamics of authors' influence on a scientific discipline. For example, an author citation network in information science during 1972-1995 was studied in [40]. A centrality index is calculated based on an author's mean number of co-citations with other authors. This index is used to reflect the changes in the author's influence over time.

Link stability in terms of link breaking and replacement rate was analyzed in several inter-organizational network studies. Ornstein examined the interlocking relations among the 100 largest Canadian companies between 1946-1977 [30]. He calculated the percentage of relations that were previously broken but later restored and used that to test whether the network was dominated by planned liaisons. Similarly, Fennema and Schijf used "chance of restoration" to identify a stable set of interlocking relations among companies across several countries [16].

To describe group level dynamics, research has focused on group stability and group balance processes. To analyze group balance processes, Doreian and Kapuscinski used Newcomb's fraternity data [28] to measure relation reciprocity, transitivity, and imbalance across the 15 weeks [14]. Results for each week were then plotted to study the trend of group balance over time. Group stability is defined in Nakao and Romney's study as the similarity between the two sociomatrices representing the same group at two different points of time [27]. In citation analysis, Small proposes a "Cluster Stability Index", which is defined as the number of common elements in two clusters divided by the total number of elements in the two clusters [32]. By calculating this index between two similar clusters in two successive time periods, it is possible to quantify the stability or continuity of a scientific field as represented by a group of authors [2].

**Statistical Methods.** Statistical analysis of social network dynamics aims not only at detecting and describing network changes but also at explaining why these changes occur. With statistical methods, structural changes are assumed to result from some stochastic processes of network effects such as reciprocity, transitivity, and balance [34]. In this type of analysis, links are modeled as random variables that can be in different states (e.g., positive, negative, or neutral) at different time. The purpose is to examine which network effect fits the empirical data and better accounts for the observed structural changes.

Discrete or continuous Markov models are often used in statistical analysis. The most important property of a Markov model is that the future state of a process is dependent only on the current state but not on any previous state [25, 33, 34]. The process is governed by a transition matrix, which contains the conditional probabilities of changing from the initial state to the current state, and the intensity matrix whose elements are transition rates [19, 25]. For example, Leenders used continuous time Markov models to examine three effects (gender similarity, reciprocity, and proximity) on children's choices of friendship over time [25]. By comparing the three resulting models' goodness-of-fit, he found that gender similarity was the most important criterion for children to choose a friend. Snijders applied a continuous time Markov model to Newcomb data [28] and found that both reciprocity and balance have significant effects on the structural changes in the fraternity network [33]. The advantage of Markov models is that they can be statistically tested. However, it is often difficult to estimate the parameters of the models.

**Simulation Methods.** Unlike descriptive or statistical methods, which examine social network dynamics quantitatively, simulation methods rely on multi-agent technology to analyze network dynamics. In this method, members in a social network are often modeled and implemented as computer agents who have the abilities to behave and make decisions based on certain criteria. The collective behaviors of all members in a network will determine how the network evolves from one structure to another.

Several SNA studies have employed simulation methods. For example, Hummon uses agent-based simulation to study how individuals' social choices of establishing or ceasing a relationship with others affect the structure of a network [20]. The basic assumption is that maintaining a relationship has its associated costs and benefits and individuals aim to maximize their utilities by altering their relationships with others. A social network will keep changing until the joint utility of all members is maximized. Carley et al. use multi-agent technology to simulate the evolution of covert networks such as terrorist groups [4]. Moreover, using a multi-agent system called DYNET, they can perform a "what-if" analysis to anticipate how a network adapts to environmental changes such as the removal of a central member [4, 5, 13]. A simulation model can be a powerful tool predicting a network's future. However it often oversimplifies the behavior and decision-making of humans and may not be able to model the complex reality of social networks.

Some SNA research, especially citation analysis, has employed visualization techniques to study network dynamics. This approach relies on visual presentations of social networks and is quite different from the descriptive, statistical, and simulation methods.

## 3.2 Visualizing Social Network Dynamics

With the visualization approach a social network is portrayed at different points in time and a series of network portrayals are compared across time to find the structural changes. In citation network analysis the purpose of visualization is often to detect shifts in research focus and paradigms [32, 40], track emergent research trends [6, 12], and find evolving patterns of a scientific domain [2, 7, 8, 29].

To visualize a social network, an appropriate layout algorithm must be chosen to assign locations to nodes. Traditionally, multidimensional scaling (MDS) was used to project a social network onto a two dimensional display based on the proximity between nodes [29, 32, 37, 40]. The algorithm arranges nodes so that similar nodes or strongly linked nodes are close to each other and different nodes or weakly linked nodes are far from each other. For example, to examine the dynamics of information science research between 1972-1995, White and McCain employ MDS to project 100 researchers onto three maps corresponding to three 8-year segments [40]. By comparing the locations of the same author in different maps they trace the paradigm shifts in information sciences during the 24-year period. Small [32] and Sullivan [36] propose to use MDS to generate the locations of documents based on document co-citation frequencies and use the "attitude" to represent a document's citation frequency. The result is a "contour map" in which documents on the same contour line have the same citation density. Comparing the yearly contour maps for 1970-1974, Small identified the paradigm shifts in collagen research [32]. Recently a network layout algorithm called spring embedder algorithm [18, 21] has gained increasing popularity. This algorithm treats a network as an energy system in which nodes are connected by springs containing energy. Nodes attract and repulse one another until the energy in the system is minimized. The spring embedder algorithm can be combined with the Pathfinder network scaling algorithm [9], which reduces the number of links by finding the shortest path between nodes, to generate a tree-link network representation [6-9, 11]. Some other layout algorithms including simple triangulation method [24] have also been used in citation analysis network visualization [31].

With the development of computer technology, some visualization tools have been developed to show the evolution of citation networks. For example, Chen and Carr [7] generate a series of citation networks using the spring embedder algorithm and the pathfinder algorithm. They then use animation to visually present the evolution of the hypertext research field between 1989-1998. Moreover, their visualization tool incorporates several visual cues to present the changes of other network characteristics [6-8, 10]. For example, nodes representing authors are color-coded so that authors with the same research specialty receive the same color. They also attach a citation bar to each node in a three-dimensional display to present citation rate change of an author from year to year.

Research in these dynamic SNA studies provides a good foundation for criminal network dynamics analysis. Although the purpose of analyzing criminal network dynamics is not to test theories, the methods, measures, and models from SNA can help detect and describe structural changes, extract the patterns of these changes, and even predict the future activities and structure of criminal organizations.

## 4  Research Methods

In our research a criminal network is represented as an undirected, weighted graph in which each link receives a weight based on the frequency that the two involved criminals commit crimes together [41]. The link weight then represents the relational strength between two criminals. In this paper we propose to use several descriptive measures and the animation approach to analyze and visualize criminal network dynamics over time.

### 4.1  Descriptive Approaches

As reviewed previously, a criminal network can change in its nodes, links, groups, and even the overall structure. In this paper, we focus on the detection and description of node level and group level dynamics.

**Node Level Measures.** As criminals establish new relations or break existing relations with others their social positions, roles, and power may change accordingly. These node dynamics resulting from relation changes can be captured by a set of centrality measures from SNA. Centrality is often used to indicate the importance of a member within a group or a network. Various centrality measures have been proposed and they have different interpretations and implications. Freeman defines the three most popular centrality measures: degree, betweenness, and closeness [17].

*Degree* measures how active a particular node is. It is defined as the number of direct links a node $k$ has. An individual with a high degree could be the leader or "hub" in his group or the network. However, degree is not a reliable indicator of leadership role in criminal networks [41]. We therefore use this measure to only represent an individual's activeness. Considering that a group or network may change its size over time we use a normalized degree measure [38]:

$$C_D(k)_{norm} = \frac{\sum_{i=1}^{n} a(i,k)}{n-1}, \qquad i \neq k \qquad (1)$$

where $n$ is the total number of nodes in a group or a network and $a(i, k)$ is a binary variable indicating whether a link exists between nodes $i$ and $k$.

*Betweenness* measures the extent to which a particular node lies between other nodes in a network or a group. The betweenness of a node $k$ is defined as the number of geodesics (shortest paths between two nodes) passing through it. An individual with high betweenness may act as a gatekeeper or "broker" in a network for smooth communication or flow of goods (e.g., drugs). A gatekeeper criminal should often be targeted for removal because the removal may destablize a criminal network or even cause it to fall apart [5]. Again, considering group or network size, we define normalized betweenness as:

$$C_B(k)_{norm} = \frac{\sum_{k}^{n} \sum_{j}^{n} g_{ij}(k)}{n-1} \qquad i \neq k \qquad (2)$$

where $g_{ij}(k)$ indicates whether the shortest path between two other nodes $i$ and $j$ passes through node $k$.

*Closeness* is the sum of the length of geodesics between a particular node $k$ and all the other nodes in a network. It actually measures how far away one node is from other nodes and sometimes is called "farness" [1]. It indicates how easily an individual connects to other members. The normalized closeness is defined as:

$$C_C(k)_{norm} = \frac{\sum_{i=1}^{n} l(i,k) - C_c \min}{C_c \max - C_c \min} \qquad i \neq k \qquad (3)$$

where $l(i,k)$ is the length of the shortest path connecting nodes $i$ and $k$. $C_c min$ and $C_c max$ are the minimum and maximum lengths of the shortest paths respectively. When calculating the closeness, a link weight needs to be converted to a length using logarithmic transformation [42]:

$$l = -\ln(w)$$

The values of these three normalized centrality measures range from 0 to 1. For a particular individual, each centrality measure will be calculated at different points of time to capture its change.

**Group level measures.** Criminal groups are not random sets of individuals but relatively tight units in which members have denser and stronger relations with one another. There are a variety of indexes in SNA for measuring the structural properties of social groups. We chose three measures (link density, group cohesion, and cluster stability) to detect and describe network dynamics at group level. Each measure has its specific implication to criminal network investigation.

*Link density* measures how complete a group is in terms of the relations among its members. It is defined as the proportion of the maximum possible number of links that actually exist among all group members [38]:

$$Density = \frac{2\sum_{i}^{n}\sum_{<j}^{n} a(i, j)}{n(n-1)} \tag{4}$$

where $n$ is the size of the group and $a(i, j)$ is a binary variable indicating whether a link exists between nodes $i$ and $j$. Members in a dense group have relations to a large number of other group members. When the density achieves 1, a group becomes a clique where each member connects with every other member. Communication and collaboration are easier for members in a dense group and this may imply more efficient planning and execution of offenses in criminal networks. However, a dense group may also be vulnerable because when one member is caught he or she may release critical information about many other group members [23].

A group is a *cohesive group* if, on average, its members have stronger relations with members in the same group than with individuals outside of the group [38]. A group cohesion measure is defined as the average link strength within the group divided by the average link strength with outsiders [38]:

$$Cohesion = \frac{\dfrac{\sum_{i \in G} \sum_{j \in G} w(i, j)}{n(n-1)}}{\dfrac{\sum_{i \in G} \sum_{j \notin G} w(i, j)}{N(N-n)}} \tag{5}$$

where $n$ is the group size; $N$ is the network size; $G$ represents the group's node set; $w(i,j)$ is the weight of the link between nodes $i$ and $j$. A group is considered cohesive if the cohesion value exceeds 1. Members in a cohesive criminal group tend to have higher loyalty and are less likely to be recruited to other groups.

For a specific group both density and cohesion can be calculated and compared across different points of time.

*Group stability* measures how well a group maintains its membership over time. We use the cluster stability index introduced by Small [32] because a group can be treated as a cluster of nodes. It is calculated based on the overlapping membership of a group at two different points of time. We define the stability of group $G$ from time $t_1$ to $t_2$ as:

$$Stability = \frac{|G_{t1} \bigcap G_{t2}|}{|G_{t1} \bigcup G_{t2}|} \qquad (6)$$

## 4.2 Animation Approaches

In addition to quantitative analysis of the dynamics of criminal networks, we use the animation approach to present the changes of a network visually. In our previous study we developed a prototype system that can perform structural analysis and visualization of static criminal networks. The system is able to partition a network into groups, calculate centrality for group members, and uses the blockmodeling approach [38] to capture patterns of interactions between groups [41]. The system employs MDS to visualize a network on a two-dimensional display based on the weights of links between individual criminals. Moreover, several visual cues are used to represent structural network properties. For example, the thickness of a link represents the strength of the relation; the size of a circle representing a group is proportional to the number of members in that group.

In this study we add an animation function to the system. Several new visual cues are combined with the animation.

*Node location.* With MDS, node locations on the display are determined by the link weights between nodes. As link weights change, MDS will assign different locations to the same node from time to time. Alteration in node locations will add a high cognitive load to users because they must compare different MDS layouts to track the nodes [8]. To address this problem, we calculate node locations based on link weights cumulated from all past incidents and rely on the changes of the thickness of links to represent the link weight change.

*Node size.* A criminal may commit more or fewer crimes at different times. To visualize the activeness change of a criminal, we make node size proportional to the number of crimes an offender commits in a specific year. A user can see whether a criminal becomes more or less active over time by watching the node size change.

*Link darkness.* A link exists between two criminals when they commit a crime together. In our previous system the thickness of a link indicates the relational strength between two criminals. However, relational strength cannot capture the time frame of a link. Two criminals who have not recently committed crimes together but often co committed crimes previously may appear to have a strong link. To reflect the recency of a relation, we change the darkness of the link over time. As a result, a darker link represents a more recently formed relation and a faded link represents an older relation.

In our system the animation of network evolution is controlled by a time slider. When a user adjusts the time slider, he or she can visualize the network while nodes change their sizes and links change their thickness and darkness. In addition, the system can perform network partition, blockmodeling, and centrality calculation at the specified point of time. By comparing the network at different points of time, a user can visually detect the changes in nodes, links, groups, and overall structure. Figure 1 shows an example of a narcotics network in 1994 and 2002. It can be seen that this network has changed not only in its nodes and links but also in its structure[1].

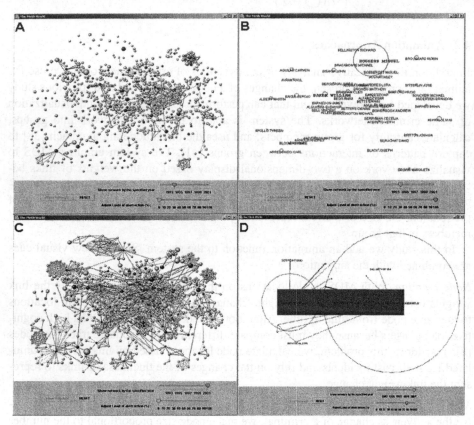

**Fig. 1.** The narcotics network and its reduced structures in 1994 and 2002. A node represents an individual. A line represents a relation. The thickness of a line represents the relational strength. A group is represented by a circle labeled with the leader's name. The size of a circle is proportional to the number of members in the group. (A) The network in 1994. (B) The reduced structure of the network in 1994. (C) The network in 2002. (D) The reduced structure of the network in 2002

## 5 Evaluation

We conducted a field study to evaluate the usefulness of our proposed methods and to answer the following research questions:

---

[1] All criminal names in this paper are scrubbed for data confidentiality.

- Can the descriptive measures for nodes capture the dynamics in network members' roles and activeness?
- Can the descriptive measures for groups capture the dynamics in criminal groups?
- Can the animation provide an intuitive and useful presentation of the dynamics of a criminal network over time?
- Will the measures and visualization be useful for crime investigation?

In our previous study we performed a static analysis on a narcotics network which was called "Meth World" because most of the network members committed crimes related to methamphetamines [41]. In this study we obtained a list of 103 major criminals in the Meth World from the Gang Unit Sergeant at the Tucson Police Department and generated a network consisting of 924 criminals surrounding these major offenders. These offenders committed 11,074 crimes ranging from theft and aggravated assault to drug offences from 1983 to 2002. Because these major offenders had long-term relationships established when they were in high schools we calculated link weights for each year based on crime incidents that had occurred up to that year. A series of yearly networks were then generated beginning from 1994, when the Sergeant started investigating this criminal network.

Several domain experts, including the Sergeant, evaluated our analytical findings and the system's visualization features. We summarize the results as follows.

- *Simple indicators of individual characteristics can reflect the changes in individual criminal's activity level.*

In this study we focused on the behavior of the leaders of the major Math World groups, William Baker and Robert White. They were correctly identified by our system in our previous study [41]. These two criminals had been involved in drug offenses since mid-1990s. Over time, they formed two groups and obtained leadership in their own groups. For each criminal, we represented his individual characteristics based on the number of crimes he committed and the number of relations in each year. These two measures are somewhat correlated. The correlations are 0.89 and 0.69 for William Baker and Robert White, respectively. This implies that William Baker tended to commit crimes more often with others than Robert White. Also notice that the number of relations is the number of people an offender commits crimes with. It is an absolute degree value based on yearly incident data and is different from the normalized degree in equation (1). Figure 2 presents the curves of the individual characteristics for the two criminals.

According to Figure 2 (a), William Baker was not a very active offender initially. He committed only a few crimes and had few relations with others in 1994. He became more active in 1995. His two curves drop to zero in 1996. According to our experts, William Baker was prosecuted and imprisoned during 1996. After he was released in 1997, he committed an increasing number of crimes from year to year until he was imprisoned again in 2000. Figure 2 (b) presents the behavioral trace of Robert White. Unlike William Baker, he was very active initially. His curves drop to zero or a very low level in 1995, 1998, and 2002, when he was put into prison.

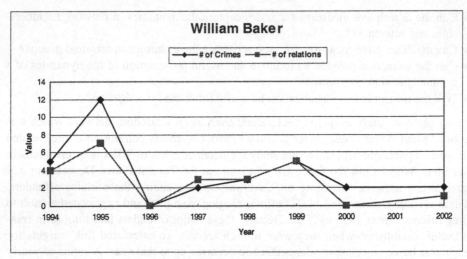

**a.**    Changes in individual characteristics of William Baker

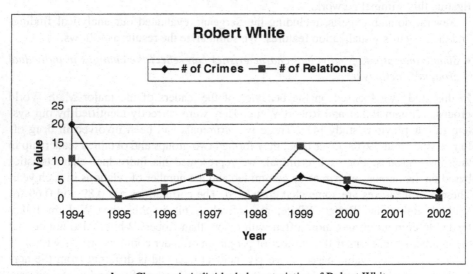

**b.**    Changes in individual characteristics of Robert White

**Fig. 2.** Changes in individual characteristics of the two group leaders in Meth World

Comparing the two figures, we found that these two leaders' activeness alternated in turn over time. As one offender was put into prison and left the network temporarily, the other became very active. For example, William Baker committed few crimes while Robert was active in 1994. However, when Robert White's curves drop to zero, William Baker committed more crimes. Based on the experts' experience, this is because they always competed for the leadership of the whole network. In addition, a similar pattern was found for the two leaders: after they were released from prison, they became increasingly active until they were caught again. (See the curves for William Baker during 1996-2000 and the curves for Robert White during 1995-1998.)

- *Descriptive measures of centrality can reflect the changes in individual criminal's roles.*

Considering the long-term relations among the members in Meth World, we did not base individual centrality on yearly incident data but calculated the accumulative centrality. For example, the degree of a criminal in 1995 actually measures the number of relations he had established by 1995 rather than the number of relations that occurred in the single year of 1995.

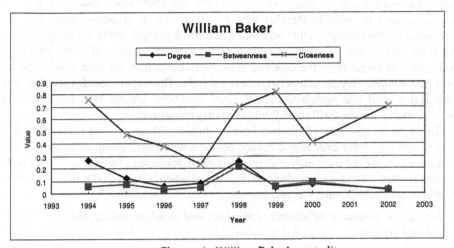

**a.** Changes in William Baker's centrality

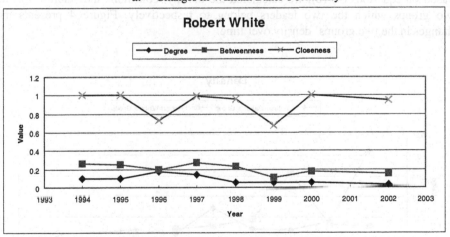

**b.** Changes in Robert White's centrality

**Fig. 3.** Changes in individual roles measured by centrality for the two group leaders

To capture the changes in individual's network roles we charted the curves of three normalized centrality measures based on equations (1)-(3) for the two group leaders. For easier interpretation and comparison among the three centrality measures, we subtracted the closeness in equation (3) from 1 so that a higher closeness indicated a higher easiness connecting to other group members.

Figure 3(a) indicates that William Baker's centrality in terms of degree and betweenness decreased from 1995-1997, quickly increased in 1998, and has slowly decreased since then. His closeness presents a similar pattern by 1998. After 1998, the closeness curve proceeded totally differently from the other two centrality curves and increased quickly while degree and betweenness decreased after 2000. This implies that it had been easier for him to connect to other members while maintaining only a few relations with another member who had high degree or betweenness [3]. The advantage of this strategy is that he could maintain leadership while avoiding connecting with many other people so that he could reduce the chance of being caught by police. It was found from the data that William Baker connected with another person who had a higher degree and betweenness recently. The experts confirmed that William Baker used that person to control other members. Unlike William Baker, the three centrality curves for Robert White are fairly consistent.

Based on the analysis of the two leaders' behavioral patterns, it seems that they tend to commit fewer crimes and reduce contacts with other group members as time progresses. However they may still maintain their leadership by connecting to other active criminals. Such a prediction was confirmed when, during 2003, the two leaders started to hide behind others in the network.

- *Descriptive measures of density, cohesion, and stability reflect the dynamics in criminal groups.*

Based on equations (4)-(6), we calculated the density, cohesion, and stability for the two groups which the two leaders belong to respectively. Figure 4 presents the changes in the two groups' density over time.

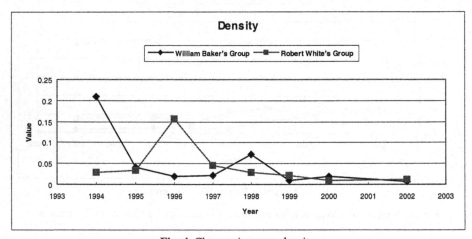

**Fig. 4.** Changes in group density

For both groups the curves show a decreasing trend in group density over time. There is one peak in William Baker's group in 1998 and one peak in Robert White's group in 1996. Such a peak implies a high density followed by a low density. As mentioned previously, a dense group may be subject to a high vulnerability because of a caught member's release of critical information to police. According to the experts, when a member from such a dense group was caught police officers could often find in his car or house a phone book which contained contact information for many other group members. The police could than take effective strategies to catch these group members. As a result the group density would drop dramatically.

Interestingly, the density curves of the two groups increase and decrease alternately. This again confirms the experts' observation that the two groups always competed for members and leadership.

The dynamics in group cohesion also present similar patterns with a decreasing trend for both groups and an alternate pattern between groups (See Figure 5). This implies that group members tend to have fewer and weaker connections with other group members and the groups become less cohesive over time. According to the experts, as more people join Meth World, people have tried to form their own groups and gain leadership.

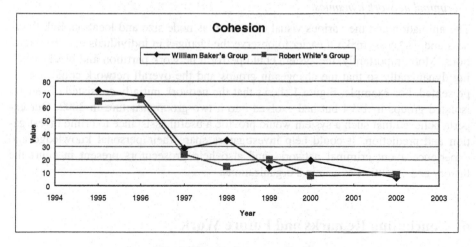

**Fig. 5.** Changes in group cohesion

We also charted the stability changes for each group over time, as shown in Figure 6. Robert White's curve dropped dramatically from 1995-1996. This corresponds to the fact that he was put into prison in 1995 and many members left this group. After he was released in 1996, the group stability increased and exceeded William Baker's group after the 1997-1998 period. This is because Robert was a quite violent person and his group members learned that they might be killed if they left the group. As a result, his group tends to be more stable over time. In contrast, William was relatively mild. His group stability increased during 1994-1997 period even though he was put into prison during 1996.

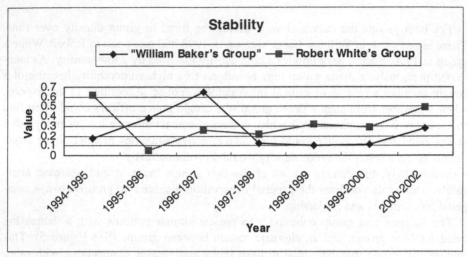

**Fig. 6.** Changes in group stability

- *Visualization and animation features provide a useful and intuitive presentation of criminal network dynamics.*

The animation and the various visual cues, such as node size and location, link thickness and darkness, make it easier to observe the changes in individuals and their relations. More importantly, the system could perform network partition and blockmodeling dynamically so that the changes in groups and the overall network could also be presented. For example, Figure 1 shows that the network initially consisted of several isolated groups in 1994 but had evolved into a two-group structure in 2002. Our experts believed that such a system would provide a useful assistance to crime investigation and prediction. It could help investigators share their personal knowledge and experience about criminal networks and also help prosecutors present in court the history and evolution of criminal organizations.

# 6  Concluding Remarks and Future Work

Dynamic criminal network analysis is important for national security but also very challenging. Little research has been done in this area. In this paper we proposed using several descriptive measures from social network analysis research to help detect and describe changes in criminal organizations. These measures include centrality for individuals, and density, cohesion, and stability for groups. We also employ visualization and animation methods to present the evolution process of criminal networks. The feedback from our domain experts in the field study showed that our approaches and the prototype system could be very helpful for capturing the dynamics of criminal organizations and assisting crime investigation and criminal prosecution.

Future work on dynamic criminal network analysis will be done in the following directions:

*Employ more advanced methods and approaches to analyzing network dynamics.* In this study, we use only descriptive measures from SNA research. These measures are relatively straightforward and simple and can only detect and describe the changes without revealing the mechanisms that lead to the changes. With statistical SNA models such as Markov models and simulation methods, it might be possible to generate some criminal network models based on criminology, psychology, cognitive, and behavioral theories that explain the dynamics.

*Incorporate data from multiple sources and perform cross-jurisdictional analysis on criminal networks.* We currently rely only on crime incident data from the local police department. It would be beneficial to include data from other sources such as courts, prisons, and customs. The combined data set will provide more complete and accurate information about criminal organizations.

# Acknowledgements

This project has primarily been funded by the National Science Foundation (NSF), Digital Government Program, "COPLINK Center: Information and Knowledge Management for Law Enforcement," #9983304, July, 2000-June, 2003 and the NSF Knowledge Discovery and Dissemination (KDD) Initiative. We would like to thank the members at the University of Arizona Artificial Intelligence Lab for their support and assistance during the entire project development and evaluation processes. We also appreciate important analytical comments and suggestions from the Tucson Police Department personel: Sergeant Mark Nisbet of the Gang Unit, Detective Tim Petersen, and others.

# References

1. Baker, W.E. & R.R. Faulkner (1993). The social organization of conspiracy: Illegal networks in the heavy electrical equipment industry. *American Sociological Review*, *58*(12), 837-860.
2. Braam, R.R., H.F. Moed, & A.F.J. van Raan (1991). Mapping of science by combined co-citation and word analysis ii: Dynamical aspects. *Journal of American Society of Information Science*, *42*(4), 252-266.
3. Burkhardt, M.E. & D.J. Brass (1990). Changing patterns or patterns of change: The effects of a change in technology on social network structure and power. *Administrative Science Quarterly*, *35*, 104-127.
4. Carley, K.M., et al. (2003). Destabilizing dynamic covert networks. In *Proceedings of the 8th International Command and Control Research and Technology Symposium*. Washington DC., VA.

5. Carley, K.M., J. Lee, & D. Krackhardt (2002). Destabilizing networks. *Connections*, *24*(3), 79-92.
6. Chen, C. & L. Carr (1999). Trailblazing the literature of hypertext: Author co-citation analysis (1989-1998). In *Proceedings of the 10th ACM Conference on Hypertext and Hypermedia*.
7. Chen, C. & L. Carr (1999). Visualizing the evolution of a subject domain: A case study. In *Proceedings of IEEE Symposium on Information Visualization (INFOVIS '99)*.
8. Chen, C., et al. (2002). Visualizing and tracking the growth of competing paradigms: Two case studies. *Journal of American Society of Information Science and Technology*, *53*(8), 678-689.
9. Chen, C., J. Kuljis, & R.J. Raul (2001). Visualizing latent domain knowledge. *IEEE Transactions on Systems, Man, and Cybernetics--Part C: Applications and Reviews*, *31*(4), 518-529.
10. Chen, C. & R.J. Paul (2001). Visualizing a knowledge domain's intellectual structure. *IEEE Computer*, *34*(3), 65-71.
11. Chen, C., R.J. Paul, & B. O'Keefe (2001). Fitting the jigsaw of citation: Information visualization in domain analysis. *Journal of American Society of Information Science and Technology*, *52*(4), 315-330.
12. Culnan, M.J. (1986). The intellectual development of management information systems, 1972-1982: A co-citation analysis. *Management Science*, *32*(2), 156-172.
13. Dombroski, M.J. & K.M. Carley (2002). Netest: Estimating a terrorist network's structure. *Computational & Mathematical Organization Theory*, *8*, 235-241.
14. Doreian, P., et al. (1997). A brief history of balance through time, in *Evolution of social networks*, P. Doreian & F.N. Stokman (eds.). Gordon and Breach: Australia. 129-147.
15. Doreian, P. & F.N. Stokman (1997). The dynamics and evolution of social networks, in *Evolution of social networks*, P. Doreian & F.N. Stokman (eds.). Gordon and Breach: Australia. 1-17.
16. Fennema, M. & H. Schijf (1978/79). Analyzing interlocking directories: Theory and methods. *Social Networks*, *1*, 297-332.
17. Freeman, L.C. (1979). Centrality in social networks: Conceptual clarification. *Social Networks*, *1*, 215-240.
18. Fruchterman, T.M.J. & E.M. Reingold (1991). Graph drawing by force-directed placement. *Software--Practice & Experience*, *21*(11), 1129-1164.
19. Hallinan, M.T. (1978/79). The process of friendship formation. *Social Networks*, *1*, 193-210.
20. Hummon, N.P. (2000). Utility and dynamic social networks. *Social Networks*, *22*, 221-249.
21. Kamada, T. & S. Kawai (1989). An algorithm for drawing general undirected graphs. *Information Processing Letters*, *31*(1), 7-15.
22. Klerks, P. (2001). The network paradigm applied to criminal organizations: Theoretical nitpicking or a relevant doctrine for investigators? Recent developments in the netherlands. *Connections*, *24*(3), 53-65.
23. Krebs, V.E. (2001). Mapping networks of terrorist cells. *Connections*, *24*(3), 43-52.
24. Lee, R.C.T., J.R. Slagle, & H. Blum (1977). A triangulation method for the sequential mapping of points from n-space to two-space. *IEEE Transactions on Computers*, *26*, 288-292.
25. Leenders, R. (1997). Evolution of friendship and best friendship choices, in *Evolution of social networks*, P. Doreian & F.N. Stokman (eds.). Gordon and Breach: Australia.

26. McAndrew, D. (1999). The structural analysis of criminal networks, in *The social psychology of crime: Groups, teams, and networks, offender profiling series, iii*, D. Canter & L. Alison (eds.). Aldershot: Dartmouth.
27. Nakao, K. & A.K. Romney (1993). Longitudinal approach to subgroup formation: Reanalysis of newcomb's fraternity data. *Social Networks, 15*, 109-131.
28. Newcomb, T.M. (1961). *The acquaintance process*, ed. Series. New York: Holt, Rinehart, & Winston.
29. Noyons, E.C.M. & A.F.J.v. Raan (1998). Monitoring scientific developments from a dynamic perspective: Self-organized structuring to map neural network research. *Journal of American Society of Information Science, 49*(1), 68-81.
30. Ornstein, M.D. (1982). Interlocking directorates in canada: Evidence from replacement patterns. *Social Networks, 4*, 3-25.
31. Small, H. (1999). Visualizing science by citation mapping. *Journal of American Society of Information Science, 50*(9), 799-813.
32. Small, H.G. (1977). A co-citation model of a scientific specialty: A longitudinal study of collagen research. *Social Studies of Science, 7*, 139-166.
33. Snijders, T.A.B. (1997). Stochastic actor-oriented models for network change, in *Evolution of social networks*, P. Doreian & F.N. Stokman (eds.). Gordon and Breach: Australia.
34. Snijders, T.A.B. (2001). The statistical evaluation of social network dynamics. *Sociological Methodology, 31*, 361-395.
35. Sparrow, M.K. (1991). The application of network analysis to criminal intelligence: An assessment of the prospects. *Social Networks, 13*, 251-274.
36. Sullivan, D., D.H. White, & E.J. Barboni (1997). Co-citation analyses of science: An evaluation. *Social Studies of Science, 7*, 223-240.
37. van den Besselaar, P. & L. Leydesdorff (1996). Mapping change in scientific specialties: A scientometric reconstruction of the development of artificial intelligence. *Journal of American Society of Information Science, 47*(6), 415-436.
38. Wasserman, S. & K. Faust (1994). *Social network analysis: Methods and applications*, ed. Series. Cambridge: Cambridge University Press.
39. Wellman, B. (1988). Structural analysis: From method and metaphor to theory and substance, in *Social structures: A network approach*, B. Wellman & S.D. Berkowitz (eds.). Cambridge University Press: Cambridge.
40. White, H.D. & K.W. McCain (1998). Visualizing a discipline: An author co-citation analysis of information science, 1972-1995. *Journal of American Society of Information Science and Technology, 49*(4), 327-355.
41. Xu, J. & H. Chen (2003). Untangling criminal networks: A case study. In *Proceedings of NSF/NIJ Symposium on Intelligence and Security Informatics (ISI'03)*. Tucson, AZ.
42. Xu, J. & H. Chen (Forthcoming). Fighting organized crime: Using shortest-path algorithms to identify associations in criminal networks. *Decision Support Systems*.

# Discovering Hidden Groups
# in Communication Networks*

Jeff Baumes, Mark Goldberg, Malik Magdon-Ismail, and William Al Wallace

Rensselaer Polytechnic Institute, 110 8th Street, Troy, NY 12180, USA
{baumej,goldberg,magdon}@cs.rpi.edu, wallaw@rpi.edu

**Abstract.** We describe models and efficient algorithms for detecting groups (communities) functioning in communication networks which attempt to hide their functionality – *hidden groups*. Our results reveal the properties of the background network activity that make detection of the hidden group easy, as well as those that make it difficult.

## 1 Introduction

The tragic events of September 11, 2001 underline the need for a tool which can be used for detecting groups that hide their existence and functionality within a large and complicated communication network, such as the Internet. In this paper, we view communication networks as random graphs. The nodes in this graph are the individuals or *actors* of the network, and an edge in the graph between two vertices represents a communication between the corresponding actors. We assume the communication infrastructure allows for any two actors communicate if they so choose. The randomness arises from the fact that two actors do not communicate in a deterministic fashion over time. Rather, at "random" times they are communicating, and at other times they are not. Thus, the graph that describes the communication dynamics of a network evolves with time according to some stochastic process. The question we ask is:

> *What properties of this evolving random communication graph will change if there is a hidden group attempting to camouflage its communications by embedding them into the background communications of the entire communication network?*

We must assume that any approach to detecting hidden groups should not rely on the semantic information contained in the communications. The reason is that communication within a hidden group on a public network is usually encrypted in some way, hence the semantic information may be either misleading or unavailable. The idea behind our approach is based upon the following observation:

> *Normal communications in the network are voluntary and "random;" however a hidden group communicates because it **has to** communicate (for planning or coordination).*

---

* This research was partially supported by NSF grants 0324947 and 0346341

Thus, the hidden group communication dynamics will display, out of necessity, certain non-random behavior. Detecting this non-random behavior will help us establish the presence of a hidden group, as well as identify its members. The property which we use to reveal non-randomness is the connectivity of certain subgraphs of the communication graph. Our analysis and simulations show that, for reasonable communication models of a society, it is possible to efficiently identify the hidden group. This forces a hidden group to face one of two outcomes, both of which are detrimental to the functioning of the hidden group: either continue with its planning or coordination (non-random communication dynamics) and risk being detected, or lower its planning or coordination activity to a level indistinguishable from the random background communication dynamics and risk not achieving its objectives. Our results indicate that there are three major factors that affect our ability to detect a hidden group.

 i. The overall density of communications in the society. A higher density makes it more difficult to detect hidden groups. More specifically, there is a phase change at which the groups become significantly more difficult to detect with a relatively small increase in communication density.
 ii. The presence of dense clusters. It is more difficult to detect a hidden group when the society communications are more structured into groups, keeping the overall communication density constant.
 iii. The type of hidden group. We differentiate between *trusting* and *non-trusting* (or paranoid) groups. Trusting groups allow messages among group members to be delivered by non-group members, whereas non-trusting groups do not. Trusting groups tend to be benign, while non-trusting groups are more likely to be malicious. The surprising result is that it is **easier** to detect non-trusting groups; such groups are undermined by their own paranoia.

The implications of our results are two-fold. First, we can identify when it is feasible to detect hidden groups. Second, our results allow us to determine how long we must collect communication data to ensure that a hidden group is discovered.

The study of identifying hidden groups was initiated in [1] using Hidden Markov models. Here, our underlying methodology is based upon the theory of random graphs [2, 3]. We also incorporate some of the prevailing social science theories, such as homophily ([4]), by incorporating group structure into our model. A more comprehensive model of societal evolution can be found in [5, 6]. Other simulation work in the field of computational analysis of social and organizational systems [7–9] primarily deals with dynamic models for social network infrastructure, rather than the dynamics of the actual communication behavior. Our work is novel because we analyze the dynamics of communication intensities in order to detect hidden groups.

The outline of the remainder of the paper is as follows. First, we describe random graph models of communication networks. Then we discuss hidden groups and algorithms for detecting them, followed by extensive simulations that justify our conclusions in Section 5.

# 2    Random Graphs as Communication Models

Social and information communication networks, such as the Internet and World Wide Web, are usually modeled by graphs (see [10, 7–9]), where the actors of the networks (people, IP-addresses, etc.) are represented by the vertices of the graph, and the connections between the actors are represented by the graph edges. Since we have no *a priori* knowledge regarding who communicates with whom, *i.e.* how the edges are distributed, it is appropriate to model the communications using a random graph. In this paper, we study hidden group detection in the context of two random graph models for the communication network. In describing these models, we will use standard graph theory terminology (see [11]), and its extension to *hypergraphs* (see [12]). In a hypergraph, the concept of an edge is generalized to a *hyperedge* which may join more than two vertices.

**Random Model.** A simple communication model is one where communications happen at random uniformly among all pairs of actors. Such a communication model can be represented by the random graph model developed and extensively studied by Erdős and Rényi, [13–15, 2]. In this model, the graph is generated by a random process in which an edge between every pair of nodes is generated independently with a given probability $p$. The class of graphs generated by such a random process is denoted $G(n, p)$.

**Group Model.** The $G(n, p)$ random graph model may not be a suitable model for large communication networks. Actors tend to communicate more often with certain actors and less frequently with others. In a more realistic model, actors will belong to one or more social groups where communication among group members is more frequent than communication among actors that do not belong to the same group. This leads us to the hypergraph model of the communication network, in which the actors associate themselves into groups. In this paper, we assume that each group is static and contains $m$ actors. While this is a simplification, it serves to illustrate all the essential ideas and results without undue complication. A group of actors is represented by a hyperedge in the graph, and an actor may belong to zero or more hyperedges. The set of all hyperedges represents the structure of the communication network. Since groups tend to be small, it is appropriate to model the communications within a group as a $G(m, p_g)$, where $p_g$ is the probability within the group. We also allow communication between two actors that do not share a group in common; we denote such communications as background. The probability of a background communication is $p_b$; we further assume that $p_b \ll p_g$ because intra-group communications are much more likely than extra-group communications.

*Connectivity of Random Graphs.* The key idea of our algorithms is based on the following observation. For any subset of actors in a random model network, it is very unlikely that this subset is connected during a "long" consecutive period of time cycles, while a hidden group must stay connected (for its operations) as long as it functions as a group. Thus, we summarize here some results from random graph theory that we will use regarding how the connectivity of a $G(n, p)$

depends on $n$ and $p$, [13–15, 2]. These results are mostly asymptotic (with respect to $n$) in nature, however, we use them as a guide that remains accurate even for moderately sized $n$.

Given a graph $G = \{V, E\}$, a subset $S \subseteq V$ of the vertices is connected if there exists a path in $G$ between every pair of vertices in $S$. $G$ can be partitioned into disjoint *connected components* such that every pair of vertices from the same connected component is connected and every pair of vertices in different connected components is not connected. The size of a component is the number of its vertices; the size of the largest connected component is denoted by $L(G)$.

The remarkable discovery by Erdős and Rényi, usually termed *The Double Jump*, deals with the size of the largest component, and essentially states that $L(G)$ goes through two phase transitions as $p$ increases beyond a critical threshold value. All the results hold asymptotically, with high probability, *i.e.*, with probability tending to 1 when $n \to \infty$:

| $p = \frac{c}{n}$ | $p = \frac{\ln n}{n} + \frac{x}{n},\ x > 0$ |
|---|---|
| $L(G(n,p)) = \begin{cases} O(\ln n) & 0 < c < 1 \\ O(n^{2/3}) & c = 1 \\ \beta(c)n & c > 1, \beta(c) < 1 \end{cases}$ | $L(G(n,p)) = n$ with prob. $e^{-e^{-x}}$ |

Note that when $x \to \infty$, the graph is connected with probability 1. Thus, for $p = $ constant or $p = d\ln n/n$ with $d > 1$, the graph is asymptotically connected. However, when $p = $ constant, connectivity is exponentially more probable, which will have implications on our algorithms.

## 3   Hidden Groups

The hidden group uses the normal society communications to camouflage communications of its members. On account of the planning activity, the hidden group members need to stay "connected" with each other during each "communication cycle." To illustrate the general idea, consider the following time evolution of a communication graph for a hypothetical society; here, communications among the hidden group are in bold, and each communication cycle graph represents the communications that took place during an entire time interval. We assume that information must be communicated among *all* hidden group members during one communication cycle.

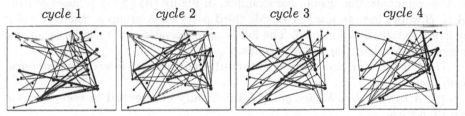

cycle 1          cycle 2          cycle 3          cycle 4

Note that the hidden group is connected in each communication cycle, *i.e.*, information can pass from any one group member to another, perhaps using other actors as intermediaries, which is a requirement of our assumption that a message is passed from some group member to every other during every communication cycle. A hidden group may try to hide its existence by changing its connectivity pattern, or by throwing in "random" communications to non-hidden group members. For example, at some times the hidden group may be connected by a tree, and at other times by a cycle. None of these disguises changes the fact that the hidden group is connected, a property we will exploit in our algorithms.

*Trusting vs. Non-trusting Hidden Groups.* Hidden group members may have to pass information to each other indirectly. Suppose that $A$ needs to communicate with $B$. They may use a number of third parties to do this: $A \to C_1 \to \cdots \to C_k \to B$. *Trusting* hidden groups are distinguished from *non-trusting* ones by who the third parties $C_i$ may be. In a trusting hidden group, the third parties used in a communication may be any actor in the society; thus, the hidden group members $(A, B)$ trust some third-party couriers to deliver a message for them. In a non-trusting hidden group, *all* the third parties used to deliver a communication *must* themselves be members of the hidden group, *i.e.*, no one else is trusted. One expects that the more malicious a hidden group is, the more likely it is to be non-trusting.

Hidden groups that are non-trusting (vs. trusting) need to maintain a higher level of connectivity. We define three notions of connectivity as illustrated by the shaded groups in the following figure.

(a) Internally Connected | (b) Externally Connected | (c) Disconnected

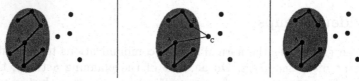

A group is *internally connected* if a message may be passed between any two group members without the use of outside third parties. In the terminology of Graph Theory, this means that the subgraph induced by the group is connected. A group is *externally connected* if a message may be passed between any two group members, perhaps with the use of outside third parties. In Graph Theory terminology, this means that the group is a subset of a connected set of vertices in the communication graph. For example, in Figure (b) above, a message from $A$ to $B$ would have to use the outside third party $C$. A group is *disconnected* if it is not externally connected. The following observations are the basis for our algorithms for detecting hidden groups.

*(i) A trusting hidden group is **externally connected** in every communication cycle.*

*(ii) A non-trusting hidden group is **internally connected** in every communication cycle.*

We can now state the idea behind our algorithm for detecting a hidden group: a group of actors is *persistent* over communication cycles $1, \ldots, T$ if it is connected in each of the communication graphs corresponding to each cycle. The two variations of the connectivity notion, internal or external, depend on whether we are looking for a non-trusting or trusting hidden group. Our algorithm is intended to identify persistent groups over a long enough time period as potential hidden groups. A hidden group can be hidden from view if, by chance, there are many other persistent subgroups in the society. In fact, it is likely that there will be many persistent subgroups in the society *during any given short time period*. However, these groups will be short-lived on on account of the randomness of the society communication graph. This is the reason our algorithm performs well over a long enough time period.

## 3.1   Detecting the Hidden Group

The task of our algorithms is to efficiently identify maximal components that are persistent over a time period $\Pi$, and to to ensure with high probability that, over this time period, no persistent component can arise by chance, due to background communications.

Select $\Delta$ to be the smallest time-interval during which it is expected that information is passed among all group members. Index the communication cycles by $t = 1, 2, \ldots, T$. Thus, $T = \Pi/\Delta$. The communication data is represented by a series of communication graphs, $G_t$ for $t = 1, 2, \ldots, T$. The vertex set for each communication graph is the set $V$ of all actors. Below, we give algorithms to find persistent components.

| (a) Externally persistent components | (b) Internally persistent components |
|---|---|
| 1: Ext_Persistent($\{G_t\}_{t=1}^T, U$) | 1: Int_Persistent($\{G_t\}_{t=1}^T, U$) |
| 2: //**Input:** Graphs $G_1, \ldots, G_T$ and $U \subseteq V$. | 2: //**Input:** Graphs $G_1, \ldots, G_T$ and $U \subseteq V$. |
| 3: //**Output:** A partition of $U$. | 3: //**Output:** A partition of $U$. |
| 4: Use DFS to get the connected components of every $G_t$; | 4: $\{U_i\}_{i=1}^K$ = Ext_Persistent($\{G_t\}_{t=1}^T, U$) |
| 5: Partition $U$ into components $\{U_i\}_{i=1}^K$ such that two vertices are in the same component *iff* they are connected in every $G_t$; | 5: **if** $K = 1$, **then** <br> 6:    **return** $\{U_1\}$; <br> 7: **else** <br> 8:    **return** <br>     $\cup_{k=1}^K$Int_Persistent($\{G_t\}_{t=1}^T, U_k$); |
| 6: **return** $\{U_i\}_{i=1}^K$; | 9: **end if** |

The efficient implementation of step 5 in algorithm (a) above and the runtime analysis of these algorithms are postponed to a later exposition, as they are not central to our results.

Let $h$ be the size of the hidden group we wish to detect. Let $X(t)$ denote the size of the largest persistent component over the communication cycles $1, \ldots, t$ that arises due to normal societal communications. $X(t)$ is a random variable with some probability distribution, since the communication graph of the society follows a random process. Given a confidence threshold, $\epsilon$, we define the detection time $\tau_\epsilon(h)$ as the time at which, with high probability governed by $\epsilon$, the largest persistent component arising by chance in the background is smaller than $h$, *i.e.*,

$$\tau_\epsilon(h) = \min\{t : P[X(t) < h] \geq 1 - \epsilon\}.$$

Then, if after $\tau_\epsilon(h)$ cycles we observe a persistent component of size $\geq h$, we can claim, with a confidence $1 - \epsilon$, that this did not arise due to the normal functioning of the society, and hence must contain a hidden group. $\tau_\epsilon(h)$ indicates how long we have to wait in order to detect hidden groups of size $h$. Another useful function is $h_\epsilon(t)$, which is an upper bound for $X(t)$, with high probability, *i.e.*,

$$h_\epsilon(t) = \min\{h : P[X(t) < h] \geq 1 - \epsilon\}.$$

If, after a given time $t$, we observe a persistent component with size $\geq h_\epsilon(t)$, then with confidence at least $1 - \epsilon$, we can claim it to contain a hidden group. $h_\epsilon(t)$ indicates what sizes hidden group we can detect with only $t$ cycles of observation. The previous approaches to detecting a hidden group assume that we know $h$ or fix a time $t$ at which to make a determination. By slightly modifying the definition of $h_\epsilon(t)$, we can get an even stronger hypothesis test for a hidden group. For any fixed $\delta > 0$, define

$$H_\epsilon(t) = \min\{h : P[X(t) < h] \geq 1 - \tfrac{\delta}{t^{1+\delta}}\epsilon\}.$$

Then one can show that if $X(t) \geq H_\epsilon(t)$ at any time, we have a hidden group with confidence $1 - \epsilon$.

Note that the computation of $\tau_\epsilon(h)$ and $h_\epsilon(t)$ constitute a pre-processing of the *society's communication* dynamics. This can be done either from a model (such as the random graph models we have described) or from the true, observed communications over some time period. More importantly, this can be done off-line. For a given realization of the society dynamics, let $T(h) = \min\{t : X(t) < h\}$. Some useful heuristics that aid in the computation of $\tau_\epsilon(h)$ and $h_\epsilon(t)$ by simulation can be obtained by assuming that $T(h)$ and $X(t)$ are approximately normally distributed, in which case,

| Confidence level | $\tau_\epsilon(h)$ | $h_\epsilon(t)$ |
|---|---|---|
| 50% | $E[T(h)]$ | $E[X(t)]$ |
| 84.13% | $E[T(h)] + \sqrt{Var[T(h)]}$ | $E[X(t)] + \sqrt{Var[X(t)]}$ |
| 97.72% | $E[T(h)] + 2\sqrt{Var[T(h)]}$ | $E[X(t)] + 2\sqrt{Var[X(t)]}$ |

## 4   Experiments

In our simulations, we fix the size $n$ of the society at $n = 1000$. The results for both communication models, the random model and group model, are presented in parallel. For each model, multiple time series of graphs are generated for communication cycles $t = 1, 2, \ldots, T$, where $T = 100$. Depending on the nature of the plot, five to thirty time series were computed to smooth the plot reasonably. In order to estimate $h_\epsilon(t)$, we estimate $E[X(t)]$ by taking the sample average of

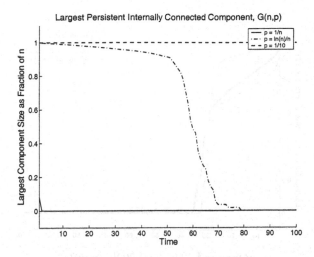

**Fig. 1.** The largest internally persistent component $E[X(t)]$ for the $G(n,p)$ model with $n = 1000$. The three lines represent $p = 1/n$, $p = \ln n/n$, and $p = 1/10$. Note the transition at $p = \log n/n$. When $p$ is a constant, the graph is almost always connected

the largest persistent component over communication cycles $1, \ldots, t$. Given $h$, the time at which the plot of $E[X(t)]$ drops below $h$ indicates the time at which we can identify a hidden group of size $\geq h$.

We first describe the experiments with the random model $(G(n,p))$. The presence of persistantly connected components depends on the connectivity of the communication graphs over periods $1, 2, \ldots, T$. When the societal communication graph is connected for almost all cycles, we expect the society to generate many large persistent components. By the results of Erdős and Rényi described in Section 2, a phase transitions from short-lived to long-lived persistent components occur at $p = 1/n$ and $p = \ln n/n$. Accordingly, we present the results of the simulations with $p = 1/n$, $p = \ln n/n$, and $p = 1/10$ for $n = 1000$. The rate of decrease of $E[X(t)]$ is shown in Figure 1. For $p = 1/n$, we expect exponential or super-exponential decay in $E[X(t)]$ because $L(G)$ is at most a fraction of $n$. An abrupt phase transition occurs at $p = \ln n/n$. At this point the detection time begins to become large and infeasible. For constant $p$, the graph is connected with probability equal to 1, and it becomes impossible to detect a hidden group using our approach without any additional information.

The parameters of the experiments with the group model are similar to that of the $G(n,p)$-model. We pick the group size $m$ to be equal to 20. Each group is selected independently and uniformly from the entire set of actors; the groups may overlap; and each actor may be a member of zero or more groups. If two members are in the same group together, the probability that they communicate during a cycle is $p_g$, otherwise the probability equals $p_b$. It is intuitive that $p_g$ is significantly bigger than $p_b$; we picked $p_b = 1/n$, so each actor has about one background communication per time cycle. The values of $p_g$ that we use for the

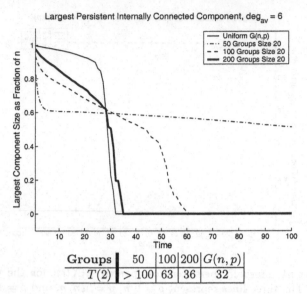

Fig. 2. Times of hidden group discovery for various amounts of group structure; each group is independently generated at random and has 20 actors. In all cases, $n = 1000$, $deg_{av} = 6$, and the group size $m = 20$. Note how, as the number of groups becomes large, the behavior tends toward the $G(n, p)$ case

experiments are chosen to achieve a certain average number of communications per actor, thus the effect of a change in the structure of the communication graph may be investigated while keeping the average density of communications constant. The average number of communications per actor (the degree of the actor in the communication graph) is set to six in the experiments. The number of groups is set to $g \in \{50, 100, 200\}$. These cases are compared to the $G(n, p)$ structure with an average of six commuications per actor. For the selected values of $g$, each actor is, on average, in 1, 2 and 4 groups, respectively. When $g$ is 50, an actor is, on average, in approximately one group, and the overlaps of groups are small. However, when $g$ is 200, each actor, on average, is in about 4 groups, so there is a significant amount of group overlap. The goal of experiments is to see the impact of $g$ on finding hidden groups. Note that as as $g$ increases, any given pair of actors tends to belong to at least one group together, so the communication graph tends toward a $G(n, p_g)$ graph.

We give a detailed comparison between the society with structure (group model) and the one without (random model) in Figure 2. The table shows $T(2)$, which is the time at which the size of the largest internally persistent component decreases to 1. This is the time at which any hidden group would be noticed, since the group would persist beyond the time expected in our model.

We have also run the simulations for trusting groups. The results are shown in Figure 3. As the table shows, for the corresponding non-trusting communication model, the trusting group is much harder to detect.

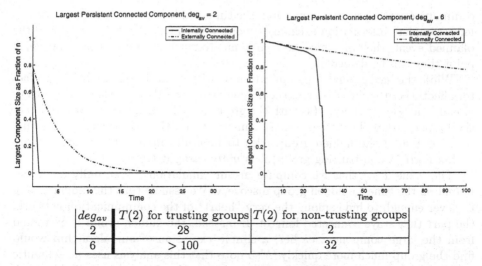

| $deg_{av}$ | $T(2)$ for trusting groups | $T(2)$ for non-trusting groups |
|:---:|:---:|:---:|
| 2 | 28 | 2 |
| 6 | > 100 | 32 |

**Fig. 3.** Times of hidden group discovery for non-trusting (internally connected) hidden groups and trusting (externally connected) hidden groups. In all cases the communication graphs are $G(n, p)$ with $n = 1000$

**Summary of Experimental Results.** If the background society communications are dense, then it is harder to detect the hidden group. In fact, a phase transition occurs when the average node degree exceeds $\ln n$, at which point hidden groups of moderate size become hard to detect. If the hidden group is trusting, or the background society communications are structured, the hidden group is also harder to detect.

## 5  Discussion

The experiments run in this study show that it is possible to discover malicious groups based upon structural properties of the communication graph, without using the contents of communications which may be misleading or difficult to decipher. Group identification done by an algorithm, such as the one proposed in this paper, could be used as the initial step in narrowing down the vast communication network to a smaller set of groups of actors. The communications among these potential hidden groups could then be scrutinized more closely.

Our results indicate a phase transition at $\ln n$ for the average number of communications that the average actor makes in one communication cycle. For moderately sized societies, from 10,000 to 100,000 actors, this phase transition occurs at about 10; *i.e.*, if the average number of communications is 10 per actor per communication cycle, then it becomes hard to detect the hidden group. Thus, depending on the type of communication, the duration of the communication cycle may have to be made shorter to ensure that one is in the regime where a hidden group could be detected. Such an adjustment of the duration of a communicationb cycle may not match the time a hidden group ordinarily spends for a complete information exchange among its members. However closer to the planned event, they may need to communicate much more frequently, at which point they can be detected.

While the background communication density seems to be the dominant factor affecting our ability to detect the hidden group, we also find that if the society already has some structure (as with the group model), then it is harder to detect the hidden group. This result seems somewhat intuitive. However, a surprising result is that if the hidden group tries to hide all important communications within itself (a non-trusting group),it is *more easily* detected!

The value $T(h)$ that we compute in our simulations, is actually an upper bound on the time to hidden group discovery. We assume that the hidden group is clever enough to hide among the very "heart" of the communication network, the part that stays connected longest. If instead, the hidden group is extracted from the large component earlier, a simple extension of our algorithm would find the group much more quickly. Also note that this analysis uses no semantic information whatsoever. If there is any additional information available, such as certain individuals who should be watched, or certain type of messages, our algorithms can be modified to yiled a more efficient procedure for identification hidden groups.

Our results are of course only as accurate as our model is valid. However, we expect that the qualitative conclusions are robust with respect to the model, The extension of this work will explore more robust and realistic models of communication networks. Such models may explore the notion of a *conversation* between two actors, where their communication tends to persist over a certain length of time instead of being random at every time period. Also the groups can be made dynamic, where actors sometimes decide to enter or leave groups depending their preference.

The properties unique to the hidden group may also be modified for better results. A hidden group may not communicate at *every* time step, but may be connected more often than legitimate background groups. Also, a property not used in this analysis is that a hidden group is likely to be sparse (i.e. very nearly to a tree) to avoid detection. If there is a often-connected group that is sparse, it could be noted as more suspicious.

# References

1. Magdon-Ismail, M., Goldberg, M., Wallace, W., Siebecker, D.: Locating hidden groups in communication networks using Hidden Markov Models. In: International Conference on Intelligence and Security Informatics (ISI 2003), Tucson, AZ (2003)
2. Bollobás, B.: Random Graphs, Second Edition. New york edn. Cambridge University Press (2001)
3. Janson, S., Luczak, T., Rucinski, A.: Random Graphs. Series in Discrete Mathematics and Optimization. Wiley, New york (2000)
4. Monge, P., Contractor, N.: Theories of Communication Networks. Oxford University Press (2002)

5. Goldberg, M., Horn, P., Magdon-Ismail, M., Riposo, J., Siebecker, D., Wallace, W., Yener, B.: Statistical modeling of social groups on communication networks. In: Inaugural conference of the North American Association for Computational Social and Organizational Science (NAACSOS 2003), Pittsburgh, PA (2003)
6. Siebecker, D.: A Hidden Markov Model for describing the statistical evolution of social groups over communication networks. Master's thesis, Rensselaer Polytechnic Institute, Troy, NY 12180 (2003) Advisor: Malik Magdon-Ismail.
7. Carley, K., Prietula, M., eds.: Computational Organization Theory. Lawrence Erlbaum associates, Hillsdale, NJ (2001)
8. Carley, K., Wallace, A.: Computational organization theory: A new perspective. In Gass, S., Harris, C., eds.: Encyclopedia of Operations Research and Management Science. Kluwer Academic Publishers, Norwell, MA (2001)
9. Sanil, A., Banks, D., Carley, K.: Models for evolving fixed node networks: Model fitting and model testing. Journal oF Mathematical Sociology **21** (1996) 173–196
10. Newman, M.E.J.: The structure and function of complex networks. SIAM Reviews **45** (2003) 167–256
11. West, D.B.: Introduction to Graph Theory. Prentice Hall, Upper Saddle River, NJ, U.S.A. (2001)
12. Berge, C.: Hypergraphs. North-Holland, New York (1978)
13. Erdős, P., Rényi, A.: On random graphs. Publ. Math. Debrecen **6** (1959) 290–297
14. Erdős, P., Rényi, A.: On the evolution of random graphs. Maguar Tud. Acad. Mat. Kutató Int. Kozël **5** (1960) 17–61
15. Erdős, P., Rényi, A.: On the strength of connectedness of a random graph. Acta Math. Acad. Sci. Hungar. **12** (1961) 261–267

# Generating Networks of Illegal Drug Users Using Large Samples of Partial Ego-Network Data

Ju-Sung Lee

Social and Decision Sciences
Carnegie Mellon University
Pittsburgh, PA 15213
jusung@andrew.cmu.edu

**Abstract.** Use of drugs, including illegal ones such as marijuana and cocaine, is primarily a socially learned behavior. Friendship relationships often serve as the means by which youths are given the opportunity to try and continue using a drug. Counter-forces against use can also include friends, but often consist of close ties to parents. Since current research into youth drug use and abuse tends to focus on localized social networks of youths, we have yet to understand general characteristics of drug networks and how they might vary across subpopulations, such as youths of different cities. In this paper, I explore a method of sampling large networks of youths using the National Household Survey on Drug Abuse (NHSDA). This method enables me to obtain population level network measures and assess risk of contact between non-users, users, and sellers and how that risk varies across different metropolitan statistical areas (MSAs).

## 1 Introduction

Use of drugs, including illegal ones such as marijuana, is primarily a socially learned behavior. Friendship relationships often serve as the means by which youths are given the opportunity to try a drug [2]. These relationships can also be the sources of influence that perpetuate use. Counter-forces against use can also include friends but also other close ties, such as those to parents [15].

Social network, or link, analysis has become an effective method for studying various kinds of covert or illegal behavior structures including drug use [19]. Prior research has shown that the instances of illegal behavior are dispersed over the larger network rather than conspicuously centralized [1, 6].

For local drug networks, key differences between user and non-user networks include a lesser participation by kin [13] and less stability [7]. Of course, the primary difference is that user networks include far more peer users constituting the "peer influence effect" on drug use [3, 5, 7, 11, 12, 14, 20]. Further differentiation of drug user networks has also been explored. Trotter et al [20] classified categories of drug networks delineated by their openness, ethnic and socioeconomic homogeneity, and intimacy.

Current research into youth drug use and abuse often focus on specific social networks of youths, either as localized ego-networks or somewhat larger networks gathered from a single community. A few studies have obtained networks of sizes larger

H. Chen et al. (Eds.): ISI 2004, LNCS 3073, pp. 390–402, 2004.

than mere ego-networks and were able to assess some global properties of user networks. Specifically, networks of drug injectors at risk of HIV appear to exhibit a rough core-periphery structure [4, 10, 18].

Clearly, we gain more explanatory power when we know the entire network, or have some estimate of it [17]. But, we have yet to understand how drug networks vary across subpopulations, say youths in different cities. So, while the exact characteristics of user networks, whole or fragmented, vary from study to study, there is consensus in the literature on the importance and usefulness of networks for informing intervention and law enforcement strategies [5, 7, 9, 16, 20]. Being able to identify youths at high risk, for either initiating use or selling, has immense value for intervention as policies can be directed at youths exhibiting risk-associated characteristics, demographics, and/or ego-networks. Furthermore, law enforcement can benefit from a network map of users, potential users, and sellers by being able to isolate crucial links and estimate the effects of eliminating them.

In this paper, I explore one method of sampling large networks of youth networks using the NHSDA (National Household Survey on Drug Abuse) enabling me to obtain population level networks measures and assess the risk for non-users across different subpopulations, primary statistical units (PSUs) which represent counties or metropolitan areas. The NHSDA has been administered by the U.S. Dept. of Health and Human Services since the 1970's and measures the prevalence and correlates drug use of household individuals in the U.S. over the age of 12; however, the survey over-samples youths.

## 2   Drug Use as a Social Network Process

In order understand how friendship structures might vary for users and non-users, we first need to know if there are differences in one of the most basic of network measures: size of the friendship circle. Since marijuana is often a social drug, youths who use would often do so at social gatherings or parties. So, we might expect users to be members of larger social groups than non-users. In the 1979 and 1982 NHSDA, and in only those survey years, respondents were asked to give a count of the number of close friends who also live in household settings. Since the distribution of friendship counts is highly skewed, I use a log transformation so the distribution is roughly normal. The following figures show that the transformation yields a roughly normal distribution:

In contrasting the log distribution for marijuana users with the one for non-users, I employ a t-test and find that the $\mu$ difference between those who have ever tried marijuana and those who have not is 0.13019, significant at $p < .001$, which retransformed gives us a difference of 1.15 friends; a youth in 1979 or 1982 who once tried marijuana is, on average, going to have 1.15 more friends than a youth who hadn't.

This significant difference is somewhat surprising given that marijuana use was at its height around this time. The difference between more recent users (within the last year) and non-users is 1.13 friends, also significant at $p < .001$. The point of this analysis is to demonstrate that real differences exist between friendship circles of users and non-users, even during the period of history when use was least stigmatized; These mean friendship counts give a starting point for generating friendship ego-networks, addressed later in this paper.

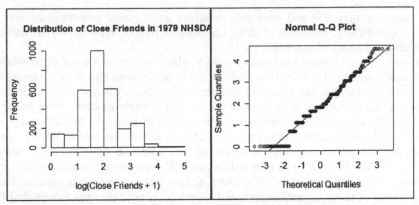

**Fig. 1.** The left shows a histogram of the log transformed friendship counts for all youths in the 1979 NHSDA. Q-Q plot demonstrates relatively normality

The 1998 and 1999 NHSDA, and only those two years, provide us with other data on the composition of friendship circles. For simplicity, I focus on the 1998 NHSDA in examining the variable that provides us with marijuana prevalence for each youth respondent's friendship circle. In the FDMJ response item, youths are asked how many of their friends use marijuana.

**Table 1.** FDMJ response item

```
How many friends use marijuana?
1 = None of them, 2 = A few of them,
3 = Most of them, 4 = All of them.
```

The 1998 NHSDA contains variables that indicate sources of anti-drug influence: communication relationship between the youth and his or her parent(s). Youths are asked if they would go their mothers and/or fathers to discuss serious problems. For the sake of simplicity, I combined the NHSDA variables into a single summary variable, TALKPAR, containing the count of parents that the youth considers a confidant. So, the range of values is $0 - 2$.

We can directly test the strength of association between the friendship level use and individual use. I use a binary logistic regression to assess the impact of significant demographic variables, age (AGE) and gender (SEX), level of use in friends (FDMJ), and the parental influence (TALKPAR) on recent year use (MRJYR), a binary indicator variable.

**Table 2.** Logistic regression for past year use marijuana

```
Dependent Variable: MRJYR
Coefficients:
            Estimate Std. Error z value Pr(>|z|)
(Intercept) -8.34286    0.45277 -18.426  < 2e-16 ***
AGE          0.31595    0.02772  11.399  < 2e-16 ***
SEX         -0.21410    0.08233  -2.600  0.00931 **
FDMJ         1.39878    0.04881  28.655  < 2e-16 ***
TALKPAR     -0.41285    0.05191  -7.954 1.81e-15 ***
---
Signif. codes:  0 '***' 0.001 '**' 0.01
R² = 0.385
```

These results strongly support prior findings on importance of network forces on use. Not surprisingly, the level of friends' use (FDMJ) has by far the strongest effect, while parental influence (TALKPAR) also has a strong and significant effect. Youths are more likely to use marijuana if a) more of their friends use and b) they have fewer parents to whom they communicate personal issues.

As to whether parental influence can have a direct effect on a youth's friendship structure, we turn to the following row-conditional cross-tabulation percentages and corresponding contour plot:

**Table 3.** Distribution of friendship drug network conditioned on parental influence

```
                 FDMJ
        TALKPAR None  Few   Most  All
              0 0.411 0.354 0.176 0.060
              1 0.554 0.299 0.112 0.035
              2 0.681 0.240 0.055 0.024
```

The proportions are row-conditioned. E.g., In the TALKPAR=0 and FDMJ= 'None' category, of the youths who do not talk to any parents about serious problems, 41.1% of them have friendship circles which contain no marijuana users. Of the youths who have two parents with whom they discuss problems, 68.1% have non-using friendship circles. We observe that as a youth who go to more parents to discuss serious matters, his or her friendship group is more likely to contain no marijuana users. The pattern is monotonic as the contour plot below depicts:

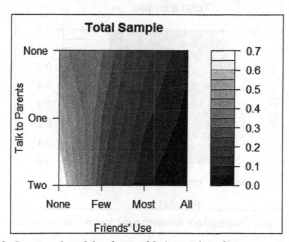

**Fig. 2.** Contour plot of the above table interpolates between categories

Both the table and plot indicate that an increase in the number of confiding ties to parents correlates with friendship circles containing more non-using friends, suggesting that a policy geared towards the strengthening of parent-to-youth relationship can influence both the youth as well as the friendship circle composition[1].

---

[1] An auxiliary regression, not included here, confirms that talking to parents has a strong, significant effect on FDMJ, independent of the youth's use (MRJYR) correlation with FDMJ.

## 3  Inferring Friendship Networks from Partial Ego-Network Data

By making some reasonable assumptions, we can use the level of friends' use (FDMJ) response item to first calculate a ratio of friendship network sizes for users to non-users and then to generate samples of entire friendship networks. First, I interpret drug "use" as "current use" and employ the past year marijuana use variable (MRJYR) as its indicator. Cross-tabulating the FDMJ with binary MRJYR gives us the following tables:

**Table 4.** Friends' use by Personal past year use: raw count and row-percents

| | FDMJ | | | |
|---|---|---|---|---|
| MRJYR | None | Few | Most | All |
| 0 | 3784 | 1475 | 273 | 108 |
| 1 | 93 | 409 | 385 | 130 |
| | FDMJ | | | |
| MRJYR | None | Few | Most | All |
| 0 | 0.671 | 0.262 | 0.048 | 0.019 |
| 1 | 0.091 | 0.402 | 0.379 | 0.128 |

The counts in each cell denote the number of youth respondents in the 1998 NHSDA who have responded accordingly about their own use and that of their friends. Most youths do not use and have no friends who use. The latter row-percent table is graphically depicted in the following contour plot:

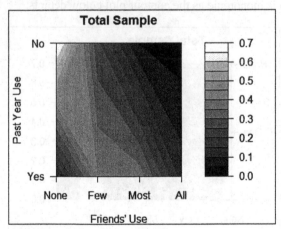

**Fig. 3.** Contour plot showing how friendship use varies with personal marijuana use

From the tables and contour plot, we observe a distinction in the levels of use between friends of users and non-users. Essentially, a current user is more likely to have some friends who use, while a recent non-user will more likely have few or no friends who use marijuana. The chi-square (df = 3) statistic for this table is 1791.9 ($p <$ 0.001).

Given that the 1998 NHSDA is a relatively unbiased sample (i.e. a respondent's use is unknown prior to survey and targeted sampling does not affect FDMJ), I consider the frequencies in these tables as representative of the youth population[2]. Hence,

---

[2]  Also, the distribution of ages 12-17 is uniform.

I can match user and non-user respondents to one another using the FDMJ variable to form the underpinnings of a complete network. For instance, a respondent in the upper-left cell (MRJYR = 0 & FDMJ = 1) is a non-user with only non-using friends. If we were to select friends for this respondent from others in the data set, we would use the pool of respondents who are also not recent users (MRJYR = 0). Another example: a respondent who does use and few of whose friends also use (MRJYR = 1 & FDMJ = 2) would select a few friends from the pool of users (MRJYR = 1) and most of his or her friends from the pool of non-users (MRJYR = 0).

To demonstrate how we can infer a ratio of the friendship ego-network sizes for non-users to users, I will use constants, $c_0$ and $c_1$, as the number of friends that a non-user and user can have, respectively; in this paper and for simplicity, I do not distinguish between subtypes of users or non-users. I quantify "few" and "most" as 1/3 and 2/3, while "none" and "all" are 0 and 1, respectively. Hence, the vector $\mathbf{p}$, for proportion friends who use, is (0, 1/3, 2/3, 1) and $\mathbf{1}$ denotes a vectors of ones: (1, 1, 1, 1). The total marginal counts of non-users and users are $n_0$ and $n_1$. $\mathbf{N_0}$ and $\mathbf{N_1}$ are vectors, which contain the counts of individuals in the FDMJ cells also for non-users and users. With these assignments and the unknown variables $c_0$ and $c_1$, I construct the equations that qualify the friendship ties in each user and non-user category:

$$n_0 c_0 = c_1 \mathbf{N_1}(1 - \mathbf{p}) + c_0 \mathbf{N_0}(1 - \mathbf{p}) . \tag{1}$$

Essentially, the friendship ties that non-users send out are divided among users and non-users accordingly. That is, each tie of the $n_0 c_0$ set must be received by someone else in the dataset. These receivers are determined by the right hand side of the equation.

(1) reduces to our "friendship ratio":

$$c_0 / c_1 = \mathbf{N_1}(1 - \mathbf{p}) / (n_0 - \mathbf{N_0}(1 - \mathbf{p})) . \tag{2}$$

Conversely, we can use the ties the users send out to obtain the same ratio:

$$n_1 c_1 = c_1 \mathbf{N_1}(\mathbf{p}) + c_0 \mathbf{N_0} \mathbf{p} . \tag{3}$$

(3) yields:

$$c_0 / c_1 = (n_1 - \mathbf{N_1} \mathbf{p}) / \mathbf{N_0} \mathbf{p} . \tag{4}$$

Equations (2) and (4) are equivalent:

$$\mathbf{N_1}(1 - \mathbf{p}) / (n_0 - \mathbf{N_0}(1 - \mathbf{p})) = (n_1 - \mathbf{N_1} \mathbf{p}) / \mathbf{N_0} \mathbf{p} . \tag{5}$$

For the population of youths in the entire 1998 NHSDA, the $c_0/c_1$ ratio is .632 implying that current marijuana users have 1.58 times more friends than non-users, a significant increase in difference over those from 1979, but this discrepancy could easily be due to a difference in cultures[3]. Marijuana back then was less stigmatic and more easily available so using it would have not have the same limiting effects on friendship networks as it would in more recent times.

---

[3] In comparing the friendship measures between 1979 and 1982, a drop in marijuana use correlates with a reduction in the $c_0/c_1$ ratio. Hence, the dropping prevalence of use in 1998 is consistent with the lower ratio.

Another assumption made is that marijuana users' definitions of "few" and "most" are the same as those of non-users. While there does not seem to be an obvious reason why these definitions would differ, there is no evidence that confirms or refutes the assumption; so again for simplicity, I will keep these definitions consistent across respondents.

## 4  Generating Network Samples

From the 1979 and 1982 NHSDA, we have some sense of the distribution of friendship counts; that is, we can use that data as the value for $c_0$ or $c_1$, mean count of friends for a non-user or user. We can now start sampling networks by matching respondents in accordance to their FDMJ responses. In generating our distribution, I draw random friendship counts for each user respondent from a normal distribution with mean of $log(5)$ friends for users and the empirically derived standard deviation s.d. of .75 and then perform the appropriate exponential transformation[4]. The friendship count mean for non-users will depend on the $c_0 / c_1$ ratio. At this point, we want to start controlling for regional or subpopulation differences. Currently, I match networks solely based on marijuana use requirements; future research will include ties also contingent on homophilous attributes such as age and gender; homophily refers to common attributes between individuals that have been shown repeatedly to promote friendship relationships.

So, for this example, I use one of the larger primary sampling units (PSU); its encoded identifier (ENCPSU) is 116, and we know that it is a metropolitan statistical area (MSA) containing 1 million or more people somewhere in the south central region of the U.S.[5]

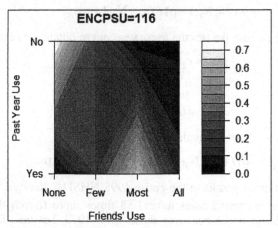

**Fig. 4.** Past year marijuana use by friends' use for PSU 116. Note, already we are seeing some variation from the same plot for the entire sample in Fig. 3. Hence, our the $c_0/c_1$ ratio will differ

---

[4]  The mean friendship count for all respondents does not significantly vary between 1979 and 1982 despite a significant decrease in marijuana prevalence between those years; hence, it is reasonable to assume that the distribution of friendship counts is roughly the same in 1998.

[5]  Due to confidentiality reasons, the public does not have information on the exact city.

I generate a sample network based on the data for PSU 116 and assign respondents to become each others' hypothetical friends according to their MRJYR and FDMJ responses. The following network depicts one such sample network containing the $n = 91$ individuals of PSU 116.

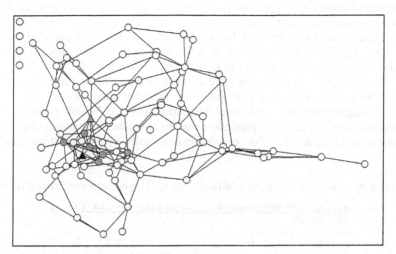

**Fig. 5.** Hypothetical friendship network of users and non-users for PSU 116. Color codes: non-user in white, current user in grey, and seller in black. Shape codes: triangle denotes a recent cocaine user. Graph is positioned using Gower principal components

Not surprisingly, the current users are relatively clustered around one another and in proximity to the seller. The counts of white to gray reflect the measure of 10% of PSU 116 sample youths having used marijuana in the past year. We are interested in exposure and risk of contact non-users to other users, including sellers (in black), so we want to assess the degree of risk of contact for non-users as well as the cohesiveness of the user friendship structures as well as potential reachability of the seller to non-users. I use two measures for reachability: the 'geodesic' network measure and 'betweenness centrality', which I discuss below. A geodesic is defined as the shortest path between two nodes. Fewer paths between a user and a non-user imply a higher probability of contact between the non-user and the user **or** between the non-user and the behavior itself, which can become adopted by those closer to the non-user. I obtain the following geodesic network measures from the above sampled network:

**Table 5.** Geodesics between different types of users and non-users of PSU 116

```
average of shortest paths (geodesics) between:
     users (u2u)                          = 1.79
     users and non-users (u2n)            = 3.99
     non-users (n2n)                      = 5.17
     seller and non-user (s2n)            = 4.32
     seller and non-user (s2np)
          w/parental influence            = 4.43
     user and cocaine user (u2c)          = 1.64
```

These numbers confirm what we observe in the graphical network. Users exist in cohesive sub-networks, as denoted by the short number of links between each of them. Sellers might be embedded in the user network or exist in the outskirts, while proximal to users; either explanation supports the greater path length for sellers to non-users. Interestingly, non-users with parental influence seem be even more distant from the seller than non-users who lack such influence, suggesting parents protect even through network position. Finally, I examine the risk to more serious drug use by assessing marijuana user links to cocaine users (i.e. past year cocaine use). On average, marijuana users are 1.64 links away from potential cocaine influence or source. This number is slightly lower than the user-to-user links suggesting that cocaine users are centrally embedded within the marijuana user group.

The "betweenness" centrality measure assesses the degree to which an individual acts as a bridge between other individuals in the population/network (i.e. between shortest paths/geodesics of other individuals); specifically it represents the number of times an individual resides on a geodesic between two other individuals. Normalizing the measure involves dividing the betweenness centrally by the maximum value possible.

**Table 6.** Normalized betweenness of different types of users and non-users of PSU 116

```
normalized betweenness centrality scores (%) of
non-users = 1.99
users     = 7.21
seller    = 5.04
```

The higher betweenness centrality score of users indicates they are more centrally located than the average non-user; hence, the user cluster happens to act as a bridge for sub-populations of non-users. As for the sellers, we learn that both hypotheses of sellers' location are supported. They are almost as integrated as users, however less so, suggesting they reside towards the periphery of the user network. We still need more rigorous statistics to support this claim. If the sellers were embedded in the user network, their betweenness scores would be similar to or higher than those of users.

## 5  Monte Carlo to Obtain Certainty of Risk Measures

However, measurements from a single sample are unreliable. In order to make proper inferences, I generate Monte Carlo samples of 100 networks for PSU 116 and obtain the following mean values for the average shortest paths:

**Table 7.** Means and s.d.'s of network measures derived from a Monte Carlo distribution of PSU 116 networks

|       | u2u  | u2n  | n2n  | s2n  | s2np | c2u  |
|-------|------|------|------|------|------|------|
| mean  | 1.86 | 4.20 | 5.19 | 4.12 | 4.19 | 1.75 |
| s.d.  | (.39)| (.57)| (.68)| (.70)| (.72)| (.48)|

betweenness measures of:

|       | non-user | user   | seller |
|-------|----------|--------|--------|
| mean  | 1.90     | 6.13   | 6.37   |
| s.d.  | (.005)   | (.02)  | (.05)  |

The Monte Carlo results reveal that the earlier measurements are roughly representative of the bootstrapped distribution with the exception of the sellers' betweenness measures. The higher scores indicate that sellers must exist within the core of the user network, which is not at all surprising. In a sense, sellers exist at the outside of 'normal' society since their primary contacts are users.

## 6   Variation in Drug Networks Across Subpopulations

I compare these network results for PSU 116 to a different SMA with similar sampling size $n = 99$ (ENCPSU = 108) located in one of the Pacific states.

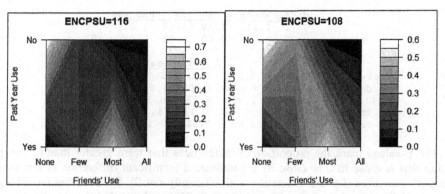

**Fig. 6.** Comparing FDMJ distributions between prior PSU 116 and PSUs 108

The above contour plots expose some notable differences in composition of friendship circles between these to subpopulations. Specifically, in PSU 108, the peaks are lower, around 0.6, meaning that personal use and friendship use categories are not as clearly distinct as they are for PSU 116. The larger light gray regions in the right plot reveal this. Performing the same matching process, I obtain the following sample network:

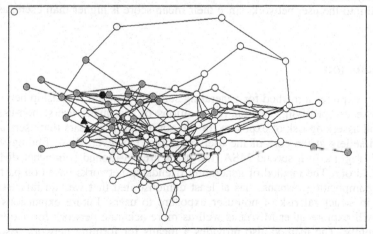

**Fig. 7.** Hypothetical friendship network of users and non-users for PSU 108. Color codes: non-user in white, current user in grey, and seller in black. Shape codes: triangle denotes a recent cocaine user. Graph is positioned using Gower principal components

We observe a denser network given the higher prevalence of recent marijuana users (i.e. 25% of PSU 108 respondents). I obtain similar network measures as I did for PSU 116 and compare these sets.

**Table 8.** Network measures for PSU 108 and differences with PSU 116 measures

|          | u2u    | u2n   | n2n   | s2n   | s2np  | u2c   |
|----------|--------|-------|-------|-------|-------|-------|
| mean =   | 2.58   | 3.09  | 2.81  | 3.12  | 3.14  | 2.50  |
| s.d. =   | (.20)  | (.12) | (.12) | (.28) | (.28) | (.28) |
| PSU 116 =| 1.86   | 4.20  | 5.19  | 4.12  | 4.19  | 1.75  |

|            | differences = PSU 116 - PSU 108 | | | | | |
|------------|--------|--------|-------|-------|-------|-------|
|            | -0.71  | **1.11** | **2.38** | 1.00  | 1.06  | -.75  |
| p-value =  | 0.08   | **0.00** | **0.00** | 0.08  | 0.09  | .92   |

|                | non    | user   | seller |
|----------------|--------|--------|--------|
| betweennesses =| 2.03   | 1.81   | 2.01   |
| s.d.=          | (.002) | (.002) | (.017) |
| PSU 116 =      | 1.90   | 6.13   | 6.37   |
| difference =   |        | -0.13  | **4.32** | 4.37 |
| p-value =      | 0.65   | **0.01** | 0.19   |

The p-values mark the proportion of differences that were greater than 0; any p-value that is close to 0 or close to 1.0 indicate a significant difference in the mean network measures (i.e. the difference is significantly not 0). So, focusing on the significant differences (p-value < .05 or p-value > .95), we learn that the structural positions of users and non-users may differ significantly between these two MSAs. The paths between just non-users and those between users and non-users are significantly shorter in PSU 108 suggesting that those users are less centrally located. The slightly increased user-to-user path lengths for ENCPSU 108 suggest this is the case. We confirm this with the betweenness scores. The relative betweenness scores of users are significantly lower for ENCPSU 108 than for 116, again suggesting that they are less centrally located. In the case of PSU 108, this is might result from a greater density of ties; further tests will confirm this. Additionally, the sellers of PSU 108 are integrated into the user network, since their mean score is higher than users, as it is in PSU 116.


# 7 Conclusion

This paper explores a method for generating samples of youth friendship networks for the purpose of specifying the relative positions of marijuana users, non-users, and sellers and assessing risk of exposure for the non-users. It appears that users are clustered and sellers at the core of the user networks. However, those findings seem to vary with region. In a second MSA, the users are positioned somewhat differently, even spread out. The method of generating friendship networks based on partial ego-network composition response has at least demonstrated that we can infer some differences in structural risk of non-user exposure to users. Future expansions on this method will explore other MSAs as well as more accurate network formation, based on homophily. The method also provides a means for forming network-based intervention and enforcement strategies as well as assessing their efficacy; I will explore these issues in subsequent writings.

# References

1. Baker, Wayne E. and Robert R. Faulkner. 1993. The social organization of conspiracy: illegal networks in the heavy electrical equipment industry. *American Sociological Review*. 58: 837-860.
2. Bauman, Karl E. and Susan T. Ennett. 1996. On the importance of peer influence for adolescent drug use: commonly neglected considerations. *Addiction*. 91(2): 185-198.
3. Curran, Geoffrey M., Helene R. White, and Stephen Hansell, 2000. Personality, environment, and problem drug use. *Journal of Drug Issues*. 30(2): 375-406.
4. Curtis, Richard, Samuel R. Friedman, Alan Neaigus, Benny Jose, Marjorie Goldstein, Gilbert Ildefonso, 1995. Street-level drug markets: Network structure and HIV risk. *Social Networks*. 17: 229-249.
5. Elliott, D.S., D. Huizinga, and S. Menard. 1989. *Multiple Problem Youth: Delinquency, Substance Use, and Mental Health Problems*. New York: Springer-Verlag.
6. Erickson, Bonnie E., 1981. Secret societies and social structure. *Social Forces*. 60(1): 188-210.
7. Fraser, Mark and David J. Hawkins. 1984. Social network analysis and drug misuse. *Social Science Review* 58: 81-97.
8. Frey, Frederick W., Elias Abrutyn, David S. Metzger, George E. Woody, Charles P. O'Brien, and Paul Trusiani. 1995. Focal networks and HIV risk among African-American male intravenous drug users. *NIDA Monograph 151: Social Networks, Drug Abuse, and HIV Transmission*. Pp 3-19. Richard H. Needle, Susan L. Coyle, Sander G. Genser, and Robert T. Trotter II, eds. Rockville, MD: U.S. Dept. of Health and Human Services.
9. Friedman, Samuel R. 1995. Promising social network research results and suggests for a research agenda. *NIDA Monograph 151: Social Networks, Drug Abuse, and HIV Transmission*. Pp 196-1993. Richard H. Needle, Susan L. Coyle, Sander G. Genser, and Robert T. Trotter II, eds. Rockville, MD: U.S. Dept. of Health and Human Services.
10. Friedman, Samuel R., Alan Neaigus, Benny Jose, Richard Curtis, Marjorie Goldstein, Gilbert Ildefonso, Richard B. Rothenberg, and Don C. Des Jarlais. 1997. Sociometric risk networks and risk for HIV infection. *American Journal of Public Health*. 87(8): 1289-1296.
11. Gainey, Randy R., Peggy L. Peterson, Elizabeth A. Wells, J. David Hawkins, and Richard F. Catalano. 1995. The social networks of cocaine users seeking treatment. *Addiction Research*. 3(1): 17-32.
12. Hawkins, J.D. and M.W. Fraser. 1985. "The social networks of street drug users: a comparison of two theories." Social Work Research and Abstracts, 4(3): 3-12.
13. Kandel, Denise and Mark Davies. 1991. Friendship networks, intimacy, and illicit drug use in young adulthood: a comparison of two competing theories. Criminology. 29: 441-469.
14. Kaplan, Howard B., Steven S. Martin, and Cynthia Robbins. 1984. Pathways to adolescent drug use: self-derogation, peer influence, weakening of social controls, and early substance use. *Journal of Health and Social Behavior*. 25: 270-289.
15. Krohn, Marvin D., James L. Massey, and Mary Zielinski. 1988. Role overlap, network multiplexity, and adolescent deviant behavior. *Social Psychology Quarterly*. 51(4):346-356.
16. Latkin, Carl A. 1995. A personal network approach to AIDS prevention: an experimental peer group intervention for street-injecting drug users: the SAFE study. *NIDA Monograph 151: Social Networks, Drug Abuse, and HIV Transmission*. Pp 181-195. Richard H. Needle, Susan L. Coyle, Sander G. Genser, and Robert T. Trotter II, eds. Rockville, MD: U.S. Dept. of Health and Human Services.
17. Morris, Martina. 1993. Epidemiology and social networks: Modeling structured diffusion. Sociological Methods and Research 22: 99-126.

18. Rothenberg, Richard R., Donald E. Woodhouse, John J. Potterat, Stephen Q. Muth, William W. Darrow, and Alden S. Klovdahl. 1995. Social networks in disease transmission: the Colorado Springs study. *NIDA Monograph 151: Social Networks, Drug Abuse, and HIV Transmission*. Pp 3-19. Richard H. Needle, Susan L. Coyle, Sander G. Genser, and Robert T. Trotter II, eds. Rockville, MD: U.S. Dept. of Health and Human Services.
19. Sparrow, Malcolm K. 1991. The application of network analysis to criminal intelligence: An assessment of the prospects. *Social Networks*. 13: 251-274.
20. Trotter, Robert T. II, Richard B. Rothenberg, Susan Coyle. 1995. Drug abuse and HIV prevention research: Expanding paradigms and network contributions to risk reduction. *Connections*. 18(1): 29-45.

# Using Speech Act Profiling
# for Deception Detection

Douglas P. Twitchell, Jay F. Nunamaker Jr., and Judee K. Burgoon

Center for the Management of Information,
114 McClelland Hall, Tucson AZ 85721, USA
{dtwitchell,jnunamaker,jburgoon}@cmi.arizona.edu

**Abstract.** The rising use of synchronous text-based computer-mediated communication (CMC) such as chat rooms and instant messaging in government agencies and the business world presents a potential risk to these organizations. There are no current methods for visualizing or analyzing these persistent conversations to detect deception. Speech act profiling is a method for analyzing and visualizing online conversations, and this paper shows its use for distinguishing online conversations that express uncertainty, an indicator of deception.

## 1 Introduction

Whether it's governments protecting their citizens from terrorists or corporations protecting their assets from fraud, many organizations are interested in finding, exposing, and ridding themselves of deception. With the increasing use of computer-mediated communication (CMC) tools such as chat, instant messaging, and e-mail, persistent conversations are becoming more common and are increasingly used as methods for transmitting deception. However, automated tools for studying human behavior in online conversations are rare. Even more rare are tools for aiding deception detection in these conversations.

The need for tools to aid in searching, analyzing, and visualizing text-based online conversations for deception is evident. The National Association of Securities Dealers (NASD) recently issued a Notice to Members that clarifies the responsibility of securities firms to store all instant messaging conversations for three years [1]. As the use of instant messaging in the finance industry becomes more commonplace, there is a need for software to filter through the large amount of resultant data. Furthermore, both management and government regulators are likely to be interested in deceptive messages that occur in these large reposito ries of conversations. Software to make the search for and the visualization of deceptive conversations easier than reading through all of the conversations or using keyword search would be useful.

### 1.1 Deception

Deception is defined as the active transmission of messages and information to create a false conclusion [2]. Messages that are unknowingly sent by a sender

H. Chen et al. (Eds.): ISI 2004, LNCS 3073, pp. 403–410, 2004.

are not considered deceptive, as there is no intention to deceive. The problem is that most people are poor at detecting deception even when presented with all of the verbal and non-verbal information conveyed in a face-to-face discussion. The problem becomes even more acute when the deception is conveyed in text such as written legal depositions, everyday email, or instant messaging, and it is nearly impossible when there are large amounts of text to sift through. Furthermore, deception strategies may change from situation to situation as the deceiver attempts to fool possible detectors.

Deception in face-to-face conversations has been studied extensively for many years. Several meta-analyses exist that attempt to summarize the large body of studies in lying and deception. Zuckerman et. al. [3] found in their meta-analysis that negative statements, verbal immediacy and discrepancies in the narrative were the most powerful indicators of deception. DePaulo's latest meta analysis [4] revealed several correlates of deception including internal consistency and logical structure of a story, how "engaged" the participant is, the number of details in the participants message, and how uncertain the participant seems.

Interpersonal Deception Theory (IDT) presents deception as a strategic interaction among participants. According to IDT, before a conversation, both the sender and receiver of deception bring to an interaction their expectations, goals, familiarity, etc. During the interaction or conversation, the sender will begin his or her deceit with certain strategies but will modify those strategies throughout the interaction based on perceived deception success. The receiver, on the other hand, begins with some level of suspicion (even if that level is zero), which is modified throughout the interaction based on credibility judgments. Both parties will likely leak nonstrategic behaviors indicating their psychological state. In the end, both sender and receiver will be able to evaluate their success at deceiving and detecting deceit, respectively. Speech acts are the vehicle by which both strategic and nonstrategic behaviors are transmitted.

## 1.2   Deception Detection

To advance toward the goal of automated deception detection in text-based CMC, Zhou et. al. [5, 6] introduce a number of automatable linguistic cues to deception. They show that some are not only significant but are also in line with theoretical constructs used in face-to-face deception theories. For example, their study of task-based email communications found that the diversity of language of deceivers was significantly less than that of truthful participants. They extend their idea further in a more recent paper [7] by feeding the automatically detected cues into several statistical and machine learning techniques to classify messages as truthful or deceptive. This method turns out to have between 60% and 70% accuracy–better than chance.

Despite its accuracy, the cues used in this method have some shortcomings. Many of the cues are best suited for asynchronous messages like email. Because of its asynchronous nature, email messages tend to be longer than synchronous CMC such as IM and chat. The average length of the messages in the Desert Survival study used by Zhou et al. [5] is 133 words. Messages, or in this case individual utterances, in the two corpora utilized by this paper rarely exceed 20 words. The lack of message length renders many of the cues found by Zhou et. al. [5] incalculable. For example, lexical diversity is calculated as the number of unique words in a message divided by the total number of words. This potential deception cue becomes useless in messages that are so short that not a single word is repeated (the Lexical Diversity is 1). Similarly, cues such as the number of sentences, ratio of passive voice verbs to total verbs, and the amount of positive affect expressed by a message become useless when the messages only have a few words. For synchronous CMC such as IM and chat another method is needed.

## 1.3 Speech Act Profiling

Speech act profiling is a method of automatically analyzing and visualizing synchronous CMC such as chat and instant messaging with an aim to make searching for deception in large amounts of conversational data easier than searching by keywords and reading through whole conversations. Also presented is a visualization scheme for conversations that emphasizes the nature of each participant's conversation as a whole and allows the analyst to get an overall view of the interaction between the participants. The method, called speech act profiling, is based on the work of Stolcke et. al [8] on dialog act modeling. Their method utilizes n-gram language modeling and hidden Markov models to classify conversational utterances into 42 dialog act categories. Speech act profiling takes the probabilities (not the classifications) created by the combination of the language model and the hidden Markov model, sums them for the entire conversation. The resulting probabilities are an estimate of the number of each of the dialog acts uttered by the participants. The probabilities for each participant can be separated and displayed on a radial graph. The graph is further organized according to Searle's [9] taxonomy of speech acts, which gives the analyst an overall view of the conversation. The resulting conversation profiles could be useful in a number of situations, including visualizing multiple simultaneous CMC conversations, testing hypotheses about the conversation's participants, and, of course, the post-hoc analysis of persistent conversations for deception. A full introduction to speech act profiling, including a guide to the speech acts and abbreviations, can be found in [10].

## 2    Methodology

The speech act profiles used in this paper come from the StrikeCom corpus, which originated in a study where subjects played a three-player military decision-making game named StrikeCom. The game required teams to search a grid-based game board for enemy camps. Each player had two assets with which to search the board. During each of five turns, the players searched the board and submitted their search. At the end of each turn, the game returned one of three results: likely nothing found, uncertain, or likely something found. After the end of the five searching turns, the teams used the information to place bombs for destroying the enemy camps. During some of the games, one of the players was given the actual locations of the enemy camps and told to deceptively steer the group away from bombing those locations. The game was designed to foster communication and allow experimenters to assign different players to various treatments such as deceptive and truthful. All communication was conducted through text-based chat, which was captured and now comprises the StrikeCom corpus. The conversations in the StrikeCom corpus are different from the telephone transcriptions used to train the speech act profiling model; however, as some of the examples will show, the profiling method is robust enough to be useful despite these differences.

Of a total of 32 games played, 16 included a player who was told that he or she was actually an agent for the enemy and that they should use deception attempt to steer the other players off course. The other 16 games were played without any mention of deception. In all instances of the deception condition, the participant playing the user "Space" was instructed to be the deceiver. All other players were unaware of the possible deception. The 16 deceptive games include 2,706 utterances containing a total of 13,243 words.

Figure 1 is a speech act profile created from all of the utterances from a single game. In this particular game the profile indicates that the participant playing Space1 is uncertain compared to the other participants, Air1 and Intel1, as indicated by the greater number of MAYBE/ACCEPT-PARTs (maybe) and OPINIONs (sv) and fewer STATEMENTs (sd). An example of this uncertain language is shown in the excerpt in Table 1. Early in the game, Space1 hedges the comment "i got a stike on c2" with the comment "but it says that it can be wrong...". Later Space1 qualifies his advocacy of grid space e3 with "i have a feeling". In reality there was no target at e3, and Space 1 was likely attempting deceive the others as instructed. In Depaulo et. al.'s meta-analysis of deception [4], vocal and verbal impressions of uncertainty by a listener were significantly correlated with deception ($d = .30$). That is, when deception is present, the receiver of the deceptive message often notices uncertainty in the speaker's voice or words. Since the voice channel isn't available in CMC, any uncertainty would have to be transmitted and detected using only the words. The uncertainty is transimitted in the words is picked up by the profile in Figure 1 in the form of a high proportion (relative to the other players) of MAYBE/ACCEPT-PARTs (maybe) and OPINIONs (sv) and a low proportion of STATEMENTs (sd).

**Table 1.** Excerpt of conversation represented by the speech act profile in Figure 1

| Speaker | Utterance |
|---------|-----------|
| Space1 | i got a stike on c2. |
| Space1 | but it says that it can be wrong... |
| ... | ... |
| Space1 | i have a feeling theres on at e3... also , on the next turn we need to check columns one and two. |

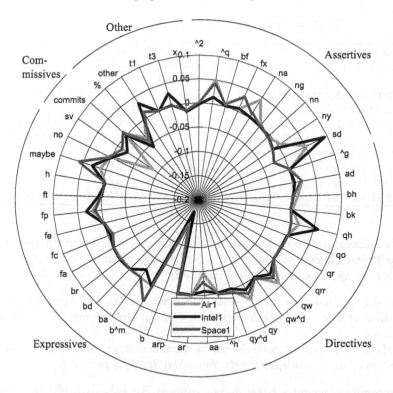

**Fig. 1.** Sample speech act profile from the StrikeCom corpus showing submissive and uncertain behavior by the deceiver

## 2.1 Preliminary Statistical Analysis

The example shown above is useful for envisioning how an investigator might use speech act profiling; however, the probabilities produced by speech act profiling can also be used for statistical comparison. More specifically, the average probabilities for each speaker obtained from the speech act profile represent the probable proportion of utterances that were of a given speech act. These probable proportions can be compared across experimental treatments when attempting to support hypotheses.

In addition to the profile shown in Figure 1, another way to detect the possible uncertainty is to obtain the proportion of all speech acts that express uncertainty. For example, HEDGE and MAYBE/ACCEPT-PART are two speech acts that express uncertainty. A HEDGE is used specifically by speakers to introduce uncertainty into their statement (for example: *I'm not quite sure, but I think we should probably do it*). MAYBE/ACCEPT-PART, also indicates uncertainty as in the phrase *It might be*. [11]. A set of speech acts that often express uncertainty are shown in Table 2. These uncertain speech acts can be combined by summing their probable proportions. The result is the probable proportion of speech acts that express uncertainty.

**Table 2.** Speech acts that often express uncertainty

| | |
|---|---|
| OPINION (sv) | TAG-QUESTION (^g) |
| HEDGE (h) | ABANDONED, TURN-EXIT OR UNINTERPRETABLE (%) |
| DISPREFERRED ANSWERS(arp) | ACKNOWLEDGE(BACKCHANNEL) (b) |
| APPRECIATION (ba) | DOWNPLAYER (bd) |
| BACKCHANNEL IN QUESTION FORM (bh) | RESPONSE ACKNOWLEDGMENT (bk) |
| SIGNAL-NON-UNDERSTANDING(br) | NEGATIVE-NON-NO ANSWERS (ng) |
| OTHER ANSWERS (no) | YES-NO-QUESTION (qy) |
| WH-QUESTION (qw) | OPEN-QUESTION (qo) |
| OR-QUESTION (qr) | OR-CLAUSE (qrr) |
| DECLARATIVE YES-NO-QUESTION (qy^d) | DECLARATIVE WH-QUESTION (qw^d) |

Given uncertainty's correlation with deception, the uncertain speech acts, and the StrikeCom corpus that contains both deceptive and truthful participants, the following hypotheses can be constructed.

Hypothesis 1: *Deceptive participants in a conversation will have a higher proportion of uncertain speech acts than truthful participants in other conversations.*

Hypothesis 2: *Deceptive participants in a conversation will have a higher proportion of uncertain speech acts than their truthful partners.*

The results of a simple t-test do not support Hypothesis 1, but the results of a paired t-test do lend support to Hypothesis 2. As expected, deceptive participants express more uncertainty in their language than do their truthful partners. The specific results are shown in Table 3.

**Table 3.** Means (and p-values)† for uncertainty

| Deceptive Participants | Partners of Deceptive Participants | Unrelated Participant |
|---|---|---|
| 0.32 | 0.27(0.03*) | 0.29(0.20) |

† p-values indicate the probability that the mean is different than the mean uncertainty of deceptive participants
* Significant at $\alpha = .05$ (one-tailed)

Hypothesis 2's significance is likely due to the tendency for participants in a conversation to sometimes compensate for their partner's behavior [12]. So, if one participant in a conversation expresses what seems to the other participants to be overly uncertain language, the other participants will likely compensate by using more certain language. Therefore, the difference in uncertainty between a deceptive participant and his or her partner's language will likely be more than the difference between a deceptive participant and another unrelated, truthful participant.

The results of this statistical test serve a two-fold purpose: (1) they lend support to previously supported hypotheses, namely that uncertain language accompanies deception; (2) they give statistical support to the validity of using speech act profiling to aid in deception detection in persistent conversations. Obviously, there are several potential hypotheses one could test on deception using the StrikeCom corpus and speech act profiling, but the focus of this paper is the use of speech act profiling with deception, not deception itself. Therefore, the statistical support of the validity of speech act profiling is of more import in this paper than replicating previous findings in the deception field.

## 3 Conclusions

Speech act profiling creates a new way to visualize and analyze online conversations for deception. The example profile and accompanying statistical analysis illustrate how insight into conversations and their participants can be gained and how that insight can be used to improve deception detection. Speech act profiling as it is presented here is in its first stages of development, but still represents a potentially valuable automated tool for detecting deception.

## References

1. NASD: Instant messaging: Clarification for members regarding supervisory obligations and recordkeeping requirements for instant messaging.
http://www.nasdr.com/pdf-text/0333ntm.pdf (2003)
2. Buller, D.B., Burgoon, J.K.: Interpersonal deception theory. Communication Theory 6 (1996) 203–242
3. Zuckerman, M., Driver, R.E.: Telling lies: Verbal and nonverbal correlates of deception. In Siegman, A.W., Feldstein, S., eds.: Multichannel Integrations of Nonverbal Behavior. Lawrence Erlbaum Associates, Hillsdale, New Jersey (1985)
4. DePaulo, B.M., Malone, B.E., Lindsay, J.J., Muhlenbruck, L., Charlton, K., Cooper, H.: Cues to deception. (under review) (2000)
5. Zhou, L., Twitchell, D.P., Qin, T., Burgoon, J.K., Nunamaker Jr., J.F.: An exploratory study into deception detection in text-based computer-mediated communication. In: Thirty-Sixth Annual Hawaii International Conference on System Sciences (CD/ROM), Big Island, Hawaii, Computer Society Press (2003)
6. Zhou, L., Burgoon, J.K., Nunamaker, J.F.J., Twitchell, D.P.: Automated linguistics based cues for detecting deception in text-based asynchronous computer-mediated communication: An emperical investigation. Group Decision and Negotiation (In press) 13 (2004)
7. Zhou, L., Twitchell, D.P., Qin, T., Burgoon, J.K., Nunamaker Jr., J.F.: Toward the automatic prediction of deception - an empirical comparison of classification methods. Journal of Management Information Systems (In Press) (2004)
8. Stolcke, A., Reis, K., Coccaro, N., Shriberg, E., Bates, R., Jurafsky, D., Taylor, P., Van Ess-Dykema, C., Martin, R., Meteer, M.: Dialogue act modeling for automatic tagging and recognition of conversational speech. Computational Linguistics 26 (2000) 339–373

9. Searle, J.R.: A taxonomy of illocutionary acts. In: Expression and Meaning: Studies in the Theory of Speech Acts. Cambridge University Press, Cambridge, UK (1979) 1–29

10. Twitchell, D.P., Nunamaker, J.F.J.: Speech act profiling: A probabilistic method for analyzing persistent conversations and their participants. In: Thirty-Seventh Annual Hawaii International Conference on System Sciences (CD/ROM), Big Island, Hawaii, IEEE Computer Society Press (2004)

11. Jurafsky, D., Shriberg, E., Biasca, D.: Switchboard SWBD-DAMSL shallow-discourse-function annotation coders manual, Draft 13 (1997)

12. Burgoon, J.K., Stern, L.A., Dillman, L.: Interpersonal Adaptation: Dyadic Interaction Patterns. Cambridge University Press, Cambridge, UK (1995)

# Testing Various Modes of Computer-Based Training for Deception Detection

Joey F. George[1], David P. Biros[2], Mark Adkins[3],
Judee K. Burgoon[3], and Jay F. Nunamaker, Jr.[3]

[1] College of Business, Florida State University, Tallahassee, FL 32306, USA
jgeorge@garnet.acns.fsu.edu
[2] USAF Chief Information Office, Washington, DC, USA
David.Biros@pentagon.af.mil
[3] Eller College of Business and Public Administration, University of Arizona
Tucson, AZ 85721, USA
{madkins,jburgoon,jnunamaker}@cmi.arizona.edu

**Abstract.** People are not very good at detecting deception in normal communication, and past efforts to train them to become better detectors have been mixed. This paper reports on a training study involving 177 military officers. In addition to developing and testing a training program to improve deception detection, this study also aimed to test different versions of a computer-based training system. Participants received training on deception generally and on specific indicators. The training program was delivered via a videotaped lecture or via one of four versions of Agent99, the computer-based training system. Participants completed pre- and post-tests on their knowledge of deception and on their ability to detect it. Detection accuracy was measured by asking participants to judge if behavior in video, audio and text examples was deceptive or honest. Agent99 users and video lecture viewers all improved their knowledge of deception and their ability to detect it.

## 1 Introduction

Deception is a part of everyday life [3]. Most of the deception we engage in is trivial and inconsequential, as when we tell someone with an awful haircut that it looks good. Sometimes, however, deception has substance and impact, as in the case of complicity in a crime, marital infidelity, or national security. Unfortunately, people are not very good at detecting deception. As Miller and Stiff ([7]) point out, in laboratory studies, detection accuracy rates peak between 40 and 60 percent. To improve people's ability to detect deception, researchers in communication have studied deception and its detection for decades. Much of what they have learned can be incorporated into a training curriculum designed to help people better recognize the indicators of deception and hence improve their ability to find deception when it is present.

Results of past training have been mixed, however [5, 6], so it is important to continue to study training for deception detection. Given the pervasiveness of the Internet and the potential it brings for lower cost delivery of training, it is also important to compare different delivery modes for deception detection training. Both of these issues frame the research questions for this study: Can we develop a training curriculum

H. Chen et al. (Eds.): ISI 2004, LNCS 3073, pp. 411–417, 2004.
© Springer-Verlag Berlin Heidelberg 2004

that helps people better detect deception? And can we deliver this training in a cost-effective web-based system that is at least as good as traditional formats?

This paper reports on a development and testing of a training program designed to teach managers about deception and its detection. The study was designed to compare the more traditional training format of a lecture, captured on video, to an interactive computer-based delivery system with web-capabilities. Four different versions of the computer-based system, each more sophisticated than the last, were tested in the study, and compared to a videotaped lecture. We found that the training program increased participant knowledge about deception and improved the ability to detect deception. Users of multiple versions of the computer-based system performed just as well, if not better, than participants exposed to a lecture only.

The next section of the paper is a review of the study's design and procedures. This is followed by a section on findings and a closing discussion of what the results mean.

## 2  Study Design and Procedures

The study was conducted at a US Air Force base in the fall of 2003. The deception detection training was added on to the training regimen for which the participants had come to the base originally. A total of 177 officers participated. They attended two separate training sessions, one covering an introduction to deception and its detection, the other covering specific cues that have been demonstrated to be effective indicators of the presence of deception (see [4], for examples). For each group, the second training session was held five days after the first. The training curriculum, consisting of a Powerpoint presentation, the text of the lecture, and a series of examples for each of the two lecture topics, was developed jointly by the authors and their respective research teams. Participants were randomly assigned to either the control group, which featured a videotaped lecture on each topic, or to one of four treatments that featured a different version of the Agent99 training system (Figure 1).

|  | Video | Linear A99 | A99 + Ask-A-Question | A99 + AAQ + content | A99 + AAQ + content + quizzes |
|---|---|---|---|---|---|
| Intro | Pre-tests | Pre-tests | Pre-tests | Pre-tests | Pre-tests |
|  | Instruction |  |  |  |  |
|  | Post-tests | Post-tests | Post-tests | Post-tests | Post-tests |
| Cues | Pre-tests | Pre-tests | Pre-tests | Pre-tests | Pre-tests |
|  | Instruction |  |  |  |  |
|  | Post-tests | Post-tests | Post-tests | Post-tests | Post-tests |

**Fig. 1.** Study design

The control group saw a professionally videotaped and edited lecture. The video was built around a taped lecture featuring an expert giving a scripted and rehearsed talk about deception. The video was intercut with Powerpoint slides and video, audio and text examples of behavior both deceptive and not deceptive. Video lectures were used instead of live instructors to standardize the presentation order and content.

The other groups used the Agent99 training system. Agent99 is a multifaceted information system. (For details on the system and its development, see [1] and [2]) Agent99 allows users to access training materials in any format, in whatever order users decide to access them in, through a web browser interface. The standard design contains four windows: 1) for video and/or audio presentation of lecture content; 2) for a Powerpoint presentation that accompanies the lecture; 3) for a transcript of the lecture, and 4) for an index that allows users to jump to and from different content (when activated) (Figure 2).

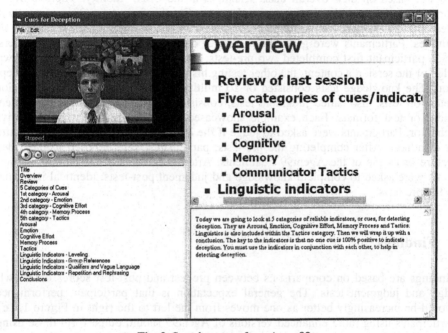

**Fig. 2.** Sample screen from Agent99

For the purposes of the experiment, four different versions of Agent99 were designed and used:

*Linear Agent99:* This version of Agent99 included the same lecture video, Powerpoint presentation, and examples as the video lecture used in the control. Users could only access the material in a linear manner, in the same order in which the lecture had been organized.

*Agent99 + Ask-A-Question:* This version added the Ask-A-Question feature. Ask-A-Question allowed users to enter a question about the content in a natural language format. The system response lists locations in the content where more information about the topic of the question can be found. This version of Agent99 also allowed users to jump to any topic listed in the index, allowing them to move though the training material at their own pace and governed by their own interests and priorities.

*Agent99 + Ask-A-Question + More Content:* This version of Agent99 is exactly like the former version except that one additional feature was added: More content about deception and its detection than was included in the prior versions or the video lecture. The additional content was in the form of more examples of deception indicators.

*Agent99 + Ask-A-Question + More Content + Quizzes:* This version adds quizzes designed to test the user's comprehension of what he or she has been exposed to thus far.

Participants were randomly assigned to different treatment groups or to the video lecture, based on their overall class schedules at the USAF facility. There were 28 participants in the video lecture control group. For the four Agent99 groups, there were 40, 29, 42, and 38 participants, respectively. Each training session lasted 90 minutes. Participants were greeted by a USAF officer working with the researchers. Each participant first completed two pre-tests, one testing his or her existing knowledge of the session's content, the other testing his or her native ability to detect deception. The knowledge tests consisted of 10 multiple choice questions. The deception detection tests, also called judgment tests, consisted of 10 examples in either video, audio or text formats. Each example showcased either deceptive or non-deceptive behavior. Participants were asked to judge if the behavior in the example was truthful or dishonest. After completing the pre-tests, participants were exposed to the video lecture or to one of the Agent99 treatments. After 45 minutes of instruction, participants were asked to complete knowledge and judgment post-tests, identical in format to the pre-tests.

## 3  Findings

Findings are based on comparisons between pre-test and post-test scores on knowledge and judgment tests. The general expectation is that participant performance should be increasingly better as one moves from the left to the right in Figure 1, i.e., participants using more enhanced versions of Agent99 should outperform those using less enhanced versions and those viewing the video lecture. Three comparisons were made, two within sessions, and one across sessions. For the within session comparisons, pre-test scores were compared to post-test scores for that session, either the introductory or cues material. For the across session comparison, pre-test scores for the introductory session were compared to post-test scores for the cues session. Descriptive statistics for the control and treatment groups for knowledge tests are presented in Table 1. Descriptive statistics for the control and treatment groups for judgment tests are presented in Table 2.

For the introductory training session, there was an overall improvement on the knowledge test ($t(176)=17.53$, $p < .001$) and on the judgment test ($t(174)=3.88$, $p < .001$) for all conditions. There were no statistically significant differences between groups for either deception knowledge or detection judgment. For the cues lecture, there was an overall improvement on the knowledge test ($t(176)=5.82$, $p < .001$). An ANOVA test revealed there were differences among the groups ($F(4,172)=4.28$, $p < .003$). Post hoc comparisons showed that users of Agent99 with Ask-A-Question outperformed users of Agent99 with Ask-A-Question and additional content (Scheffe test with p < .029). For the cues lecture, there was also an overall improvement on the judgment test (t(175)=9.95, p < .001), and there were no differences among groups.

**Table 1.** Means and standard deviations (in parentheses) for knowledge pre-tests and post-tests

|  | Con-dition | Introductory | | Cues | |
|---|---|---|---|---|---|
|  |  | Pre-test | Post-test | Pre-test | Post-test |
| Video lecture | 1 | 5.32 (1.16) | 7.61 (1.62) | 5.50 (2.06) | 5.79 (1.57) |
| Agent99 | 2 | 5.00 (1.43) | 7.52 (1.65) | 5.48 (1.91) | 6.78 (1.53) |
| Agent99+AAQ | 3 | 5.38 (1.24) | 7.90 (1.11) | 5.17 (2.05) | 6.79 (1.47) |
| Agent99 + AAQ + content | 4 | 5.05 (1.71) | 7.21 (1.80) | 5.95 (1.78) | 6.02 (1.63) |
| Agent99 + AAQ + content + quizzes | 5 | 5.21 (1.09) | 8.05 (1.79) | 5.84 (2.06) | 7.03 (1.53) |

**Table 2.** Means and standard deviations (in parentheses) for judgment pre-tests and post-tests

|  | Con-dition | Introductory | | Cues | |
|---|---|---|---|---|---|
|  |  | Pre-test | Post-test | Pre-test | Post-test |
| Video lecture | 1 | 4.68 (1.81) | 6.07 (1.46) | 4.64 (1.50) | 5.64 (1.39) |
| Agent99 | 2 | 5.60 (1.55) | 6.18 (1.55) | 4.75 (1.55) | 6.28 (1.15) |
| Agent99+AAQ | 3 | 5.55 (1.40) | 5.41 (1.35) | 4.52 (1.43) | 6.14 (1.16) |
| Agent99 + AAQ + content | 4 | 5.58 (1.45) | 6.27 (1.23) | 4.81 (1.33) | 6.24 (1.22) |
| Agent99 + AAQ + content + quizzes | 5 | 5.34 (1.40) | 5.87 (1.71) | 4.87 (1.38) | 6.47 (1.16) |

For the cross-session comparison, pre-test scores for the introductory session were compared to the post-test scores for the cues session. There was an overall improvement in knowledge about deception across both training sessions (t(176)=8.94, p < .001). There were also differences across groups (F(4,172)=2.89, p < .024). Post hoc comparisons showed that the improvement in the group using the version of Agent99 with the most features outperformed those exposed to the video lecture (Figure 3).

There was also an overall improvement in judgment from the first training session to the second one (t(174)=5.55, p < .001). There were no differences across groups (Figure 4).

## 4  Discussion

Overall, the training program developed for this study worked. Whether they viewed the videotaped lecture or used one of the four versions of the training program implemented in Agent99, participants demonstrated an increased knowledge about deception and its detection. They were also better able to detect deception in video, audio and text-based examples after the training than they were able to before.

**Knowledge Change Scores t1-t2**

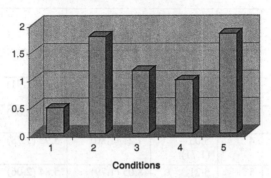

**Conditions**

**Fig. 3.** Change scores for knowledge tests from the pre-test for the Introductory session to the post-test for the Cues session

**Judgment Change Scores t1-t2**

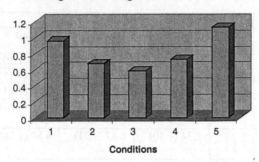

**Conditions**

**Fig. 4.** Change scores for judgment tests from the pre-test for the Introductory session to the post-test for the Cues session

Whether within sessions or across both sessions, participants improved their ability to detect deception in the scenarios they viewed, heard, or read, regardless of how the training was delivered. To enable this type of improvement is the ultimate goal of any training program for deception detection. That all groups of participants improved their performance also has implications for the remote provision of the training curriculum we designed. All implementations of our training program, as tested here, could be delivered over the web, including the video lecture. Given that all implementations lead to improved performance at detection deception, the question then becomes which implementation of the program should be used. The answer will depend on variables and conditions we did not test, such as the learning style and preferences of students, or the relative sophistication of the computing technology available to the organization desiring the training. As one moves from left to right in Figure 1 (or top to bottom in Tables 1 & 2), the complexity of the technology increases, and some organizations may not have the ability or the desire to deal with more complex configurations if simple (and cheaper) configurations produce the same results.

Similarly, participants were able to improve their knowledge of deception and its detection, within and across sessions, and regardless of delivery system used. In fact, there were only two situations where there were differences in performance across delivery systems, once for the cues session, and once across sessions. For the cues session, users of Agent99 with Ask-A-Question outperformed those who used the version of Agent99 with AAQ and more content. This difference is difficult to interpret, as the direction of the difference is opposite of what we would expect.

The across-session difference in performance was more in line with our expectations. The single difference among groups across sessions was between viewers of the video lecture and users of the most enhanced version of Agent99: The latter group outperformed the former (Figure 3).

Additional research is called for in determining why improvement was generally even across delivery modes, especially across the four different versions of the training implemented in Agent99. It may be that some of the features implemented are not as powerful as we thought, or that participants did not have enough time to fully take advantage of all the features that were made available. It should also be noted that our training program was designed for people who know little or nothing about deception. Future training efforts should be targeted to a more knowledgeable population.

# References

1. Cao, J., Crews, J., Lin, M., Burgoon, J. & Nunamaker, J.F. Jr. (2003). Designing Agent99 trainer: A learner-centered, web-based training system for deception detection. In H. Chen et al (eds.) *ISI 2003*, LNCS 2665. Berlin: Springer-Verlag, 358-365.
2. Cao, J., Lin, M., Deokar, A., Burgoon, J.K., & Crews, J. (2004) Computer-based Training for Deception Detection: What Users Want? Working paper, Center for the Management of Information, University of Arizona.
3. DePaulo, B. & Kashy, D.A. (1998). Everyday lies in close and casual relationships. *Journal of Personality and Social Psychology, 74*, 63-79.
4. DePaulo, B., Lindsay, J., Malone, B., Muhlenbruck, L., Charlton, K., & Cooper, H. (2003). Cues to deception. *Psychological Bulletin, 129*(1), 74-118.
5. Frank, M., & Feeley, T. H. (2003) To catch a liar: Challenges for research in lie detection training. *Journal of Applied Communication Research,* 31(1).
6. George, J.F., Biros, D.P., Burgoon, J.K. and Nunamaker, J.F. Jr. (2003). Training professionals to detect deception. In H. Chen et al (eds.) *ISI 2003*, LNCS 2665. Berlin: Springer-Verlag, 366-370.
7. Miller, G., & Stiff, J. (1993). *Deceptive communication.* Newbury Park, CA: Sage Publications, Inc.

# The Use of Data Mining Techniques
# in Operational Crime Fighting

Richard Adderley

A E Solutions (BI), 11 Shireland Lane, Redditch, Worcestershire, B97 6UB, UK
RickAdderley@A-ESolutions.com

**Abstract.** This paper looks at the application of data mining techniques, principally the Self Organising Map, to the recognition of burglary offences committed by an offender who, although part of a small network, appears to work on his own. The aim is to suggest a list of currently undetected crimes that may be attributed to him, improve on the time taken to complete the task manually and the relevancy of the list of crimes. The data was drawn from one year of burglary offences committed within the West Midlands Police area, encoded from text and analysed using techniques contained within the data mining workbench of SPSS/Clementine. The undetected crimes were analysed to produce a list of offences that may be attributed to the offender.

## 1 Introduction

The police force like any other business relies heavily on the use of computers not only for providing management information via monitoring statistics but also for use in investigating major serious crimes (usually crimes such as armed criminality, murder or serious sexual offences). The primary techniques used are specialised database management systems and data visualization [3]. Although policing procedures such as problem oriented policing and crime mapping techniques use stored information for the investigation and detection of volume crimes such as burglary, little use has been made of that information to link crimes through a combination of modus operandi (MO), temporal and spatial information. This is partly because major crimes can justify greater resources on grounds of public safety but also because there are relatively few major crimes making it easier to establish links between offences. With volume crime the sheer number of offences, the paucity of information, the limited resources available and the high degree of similarity between crimes renders major crime investigation techniques ineffective. This project will evaluate the merit of using data mining techniques [5] for volume crime analysis. The commercial data mining package SPSS/Clementine is being used within a Cross Industry Platform for Data Mining (CRISP-DM) methodology [8].

In this paper the author report the results from applying the Kohonen self organising map (SOM) to MO, temporal and spatial attributes of crimes attributed to an individual offender for a particular type of crime, burglary offences in licensed premises.

H. Chen et al. (Eds.): ISI 2004, LNCS 3073, pp. 418–425, 2004.

Those premises are also known as off licenses, bars, public houses, pubs etc. and will be referred to as "pubs" in this document.

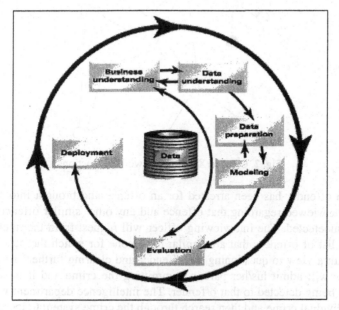

**Fig. 1.** CRISP-DM – Data modeling life cycle

A SOM [14] is an unsupervised technique that uses the many variables in the data set (multi dimensions) and recognises patterns to form a 2 dimensional grid of cells. This technique has similarities to the statistical approach of multi-dimensional scaling. The output from this technique is a cluster co-ordinate indicating that all crimes contained within the same cluster are similar in some way.

## 2  Business Understanding

A large number of crimes are committed by offenders who operate together in loosely formed co-offending groups [16], they more resemble an organic structure than a hierarchical gang structure and there is no "Mr. Big" for the entire network but there may be key persons [11]. Figure 2, illustrates a group of 13 offenders who have extensively 'worked' together. The circles represent individual offenders and the connecting lines represent co-defendant instances (people who have been arrested and charged for the same offence(s)). The black circle represents the target offender, OffenderX, and it is interesting to note that the link to the larger group of offenders is through his offending with the person represented by the grey circle.

Within the network, all of the offenders have burglary offences recorded against except the two who are represented by lined patterns. None of the offenders have a 'standard' MO, and it is only OffenderX who has pub burglary offences recorded against him which is the subject of this study.

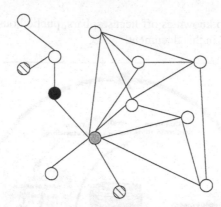

**Fig. 2.** OffenderX and his network connections

When an offender has been arrested for an offence and brought into custody, the person is interviewed regarding that offence and any other similar offences that may, as yet, be undetected. The interviewing officer will request from the intelligence department, a list of offences that are similar to the one for which the person has been arrested, with a view to questioning the offender and clearing further crimes. That is, the offender will admit his/her part in committing the crime and it is subsequently recorded as being detected to that offender. The intelligence department will examine the base individual crime and then search through the crime system to locate those that have similar spatial, temporal and MO features. This semi manual process can take between 1 and 2 hours depending on the complexity of the base crime and staff estimate that they are about 5% to 10% accurate in supplying a list for interview [1, 2, 4].

It is here that data mining can assist; the aim of this study is to present an accurate list of offences to the interviewing officers with a view to clearing more crimes.

### 2.1  Offender Behaviour

Environmental Criminology is interested in understanding the daily routines (movements) surrounding victims, offenders and places including areas that attract crime and people, where offenders live and subsequently offend [6, 7, 9, 10, 12,13,15].

Although much of the specific data is not captured in West Midlands Police recording systems, significant information can be derived from existing data fields and used in the mining process.

### 2.2  Problem Description

As a result of intelligence received, a planned Police operation took place resulting in the arrest of OffenderX during the commission of a crime, breaking into a pub. His MO was quite distinct in that he after gaining entry through the front window, he attacked the fruit/gaming machines.

When arrested, the offender was interviewed and admitted a total of six crimes. He was subsequently charged and sentenced to 6 months imprisonment. The local crime analysts were tasked with producing a list of similar crimes that could possibly be attributed to the offender with a view to the Officers visiting him in prison and re-interviewing him about similar crimes. A list of 164 crimes were initially produced that had similarities but due to the difficulties within the crime recording system, discussed later, 36 were immediately discounted by the Officers leaving 128 similar offences. It was believed that the revised list was too extensive and the Officers further reduced it to 70. It took about 3 hours for the analysts to produce the initial list and a further three days for the officers to reduce it to the list of 70 which they still believed was too large but were unable to have it further reduced. They required a highly specific list of crimes for the interview.

## 3 Data Understanding

To ensure that the widest possible range of offences were analysed, the database used in this study contained 23175 recorded burglary other building offences i.e. not domestic properties (houses, flats etc.), that occurred between 1st January 2003 and 12th December 2003, 1121 offences of which related to pubs.

The detection rate for all burglary other building offences is currently 8.1% but on examining the rate for pubs this rose to 16.4%. To examine this further, the building types for "other building" offences were categorised and the ratio of offending identified. Figure 3 illustrates that individual offenders are more likely to re-offend against financial institutions and pubs than other building types. This is possibly due to the offenders gaining relevant experience and re-using that 'specialist' knowledge as in Brantinghams *backcloth* templates [7] and Eck's attractors [12].

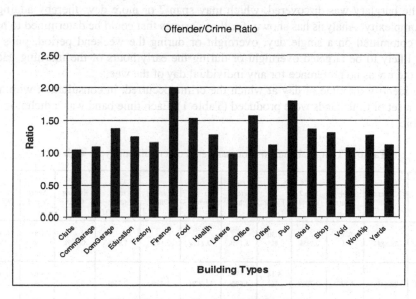

**Fig. 3.** Ratio of offender to building types

## 4 Data Preparation

With a small number of persons responsible for transcribing and entering the data it was assumed that the quality of the data would be high. However there are inconsistencies within the subsequent transcription particularly within the MO entries.

When a paper crime report is completed, the MO is classified in two ways: -

1. Check box categorisation that provides a broad overview
2. A section of unstructured free text that describes in detail the actions taken to commit the crime

Both are entered into a computerised recording system. However, with no guidelines indicating the language to be used, the variety of wording and spelling is vast and it is important that the richness of information contained within the free text is not lost to the Investigator. In this paper, the Clementine software has been used to encode certain aspects of the free text and derive new data fields. Due to the nature of the data, even after the encoding process, it was not 100% clean.

### 4.1 Data Encoding

The data was encoded in three sections to conform to the required spreadsheet type format [17] in which temporal, spatial and MO variables were identified.

### 4.2 Temporal Analysis

Temporal analysis presents problems within the field of crime pattern analysis due to the difficulty of ascertaining the exact time at which the offence occurred. There are generally 2 times that are relevant, the time that the building was secured and the time that the burglary was discovered, which may span 2 or more days thereby adding to the complexity. Analysis has shown, for those crimes that could be determined to have been committed on a single day, overnight or during the weekend period, pubs are more likely to be targeted overnight or during the early hours of the morning. However, there was no preference for any individual day of the week.

To identify the time of day at which the crime occurred, in consultation with analysts, a set of time bands were produced (Table 1). Each time band was a dichotomous variable.

**Table 1.** Temporal analysis comparing all other building types with pubs

| | Over night | Early Hours | Take 2 School | Lunch | Get From School | Evening | Morning Other | After-noon Other | Evening Other | Short Wend | Long Wend |
|---|---|---|---|---|---|---|---|---|---|---|---|
| Pubs | 72.88% | 26.67% | 0.71% | 3.30% | 3.13% | 9.11% | 2.14% | 1.96% | 0.00% | 1.88% | 0.00% |
| All BOB | 28.54% | 4.72% | 2.32% | 5.14% | 4.69% | 11.37% | 1.43% | 2.73% | 0.00% | 4.69% | 1.01% |

### 4.3  Spatial Analysis

Based on 12 months of burglary other building crime in the West Midlands Police area the average distance that an offender travels from his/her home address varies between just over a mile to just under three miles depending upon age. The type of premises targeted is also a factor in determining the distance that an offender is prepared to travel (Figure 4). Comparing travelling distance to specific building types, in most age bands it would appear that offenders who target pubs are prepared to travel further than average.

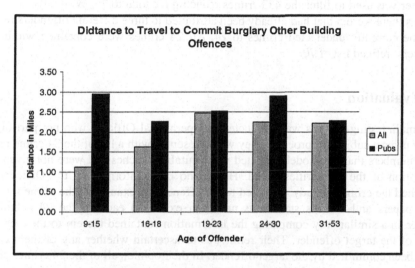

**Fig. 4.** Distance to travel by age of offender

### 4.4  MO Classification

As stated in the section above, data encoding is a critical stage in the mining process. In previous work by the author [2], a generic MO classifier was constructed creating 33 dichotomous variables for analysis. In this study, two additional nodes were created to encompass the specific MO attributes that are exhibited by offenders who target pubs.

## 5  Model Building

The database contained 1121 individual crimes that could be classed as being similar to the relevant offender in that they were all the same building type, pubs. The attributes of these crimes that have been described above were selected for modelling, the aim of which was to cluster (group) crimes having similar attributes. After clustering, those crimes that could be attributed to the offender would be overlaid on the grid thereby indicating similarity based upon the clusters in which the offender's crimes were placed.

A Kohonen self organising map algorithm was used to cluster similarities in the descriptive elements. In setting the network parameters a 10 x 10 cluster arrangement was used in all variations of the training process. Given a uniform allocation of crimes approximately 11 would be located in each cluster.

The six crimes that could be attributed to the offender were overlaid onto the SOM and were placed in clusters 0-0, 2-9, 4-2, 6-4, 9-2 and 9-6. All 433 crimes that appeared in those clusters were extracted and further analysed using the geographical aspects of Environmental Criminology. None of the crimes that could be attributed to this offender occurred more than six miles from his home address therefore this parameter was used to filter the 433 crimes reducing the total to 29. Within the set of 29 crimes there were 5 that had already been attributed to three different offenders reducing the currently undetected crimes to 24. All 24 crimes were contained within the Officers' refined list of 70.

## 6  Evaluation

The main testing process was conducted by operational Officers who not part of the study using a subjective process. They were presented with a list of the 24 crime reference numbers that the model indicated were suitable matches and were not given any indication of the similarities found. Having no other information, the Officers researched the crimes already attributed to the offender by examining the crime reports, case papers and witness statements and then examined each of the 24 submitted crimes in a similar way comparing the information contained therein to their knowledge of the target offender. Their remit was to ascertain whether any of them could have been committed by the target offender. In their opinion all of the 24 crimes could have been committed by that person.

The results are encouraging, after extracting the 12 months of burglary other building crimes into Clementine, a relevant list for interview was prepared within two days. This is in comparison to three days and three hours it had taken for the analysts to prepare the initial list and the Officers to reduce it to their list of 70.

## 7  Discussion

The limitations identified in section missing data, cannot be overstated; however, the results are not disappointing and they have practical uses in operational policing: -

1. The ability to examine a number of currently undetected crimes with a view to targeting the intelligence gathering and investigative work towards a limited number of potential offenders.
2. Having arrested an offender, there is a requirement to collate information and intelligence prior to interviewing. Using a SOM reduced the time to prepare a satisfactory list for subsequent interview.
3. Having trained a SOM, the results can be reused for similar offences. Although the initial time to complete this study took two days, to reuse the Clementine stream on new offenders would take less than one hour.

How accurate were the analysts in their opinionated research? At the time of preparing this paper it is not possible to tell. The analysts are trying to arrange for OffenderX to be released into their custody for the purpose of further interviewing.

The benefits of data mining software have been clearly demonstrated in operational Police work.

# References

1. Adderley, R. (2003), The use of data mining techniques in active crime fighting, International conference on computer, communication and control technologies and the 9th international conference on information systems analysis and synthesis, 2003, 31 July – 3 August 2003. (Orlando): CCCT.
2. Adderley, R (2004), The use of data mining techniques in operational crime fighting in Zurada, J., Kantardzic, M., (eds) New Generations of Data Mining Applications. Due to be published in April 2004.
3. Adderley, R., Musgrove, P. B., (2001), General review of police crime recording and investigation systems. A user's view. Policing: An International Journal of Police Strategies and Management, 24(1) pp100-114.
4. Adderley, R., Musgrove, P. B., (2003), Modus operandi modelling of group offending; a data mining case study, Accepted by An International Journal of Police Science and Management. 5(4) pp265-276.
5. Adriaans, P. & Zantige, D. Data Mining, pub: Addison-Wesley, 1996.
6. Brantingham, P.L., Brantingham, P.J.,. (1991), Notes on the geometry of crime, in Environmental Criminology, USA: Wavelend Press Inc.
7. Brantingham, P.J., Brantingham, P.L., (1998) Environmental criminology: From theory to urban planning practice. Studies on Crime and Crime Prevention, 7(1), pp.31-60.
8. Chapman, P., Clinton, J., Kerber, R., Khabaza, T., Reinartz, T., Shearer, C., Wirth, R., (2000) CRISP-DM 1.0 Step-by-step data mining guide, USA: SPSS Inc. CRISPWP-0800 2000.
9. Clarke, R.V., Felson M. (1993), Introduction: Criminology, Routine activity, and rational choice in Routine activity and rational choice: Advances in criminological theory, volume 5. Clarke, R.V., Felson. (eds.) New Jersey, USA: Transaction Publishers
10. Cohen, L.E., Felson, M. (1979), Social change and crime rate trends: A routine activity approach. American Sociological Review, 44 pp588-608.
11. Coles, N., (2001), It's not what you know – it's who you know that counts. Analysing serious crime groups as social networks. British Journal of Criminology, 44, pp 580-594.
12. Eck, J.E., (1995) A general model of the geography of illicit marketplaces. Crime Prevention Studies, 4 pp.67-94
13. Felson M., (1992), Routine activities and crime prevention: armchair concepts and practical action. Studies on Crime and Crime Prevention, 1 pp30-34.
14. Kohonen T. (1982), Self organising formation of topologically correct feature maps, Biological Cybernitics, 43(1), p59-69 1982.
15. Policing and Reducing Crime Unit (1998) Opportunity makes the thief: Practical theory for crime prevention. Police Research Paper 98, London; Home Office.
16. Reiss, A. J., (1988) Co-offending and criminal careers. In M. Tonry, & N. Morris (eds.), Crime and justice: A review of research 10, pp 117-170
17. Weiss, S.M., Indurkhya, N., (1998), Predictive data mining: a practical guide. San Francisco, USA: Morgan Kaufman Publishers Inc.

# Spatial Forecast Methods for Terrorist Events in Urban Environments

Donald Brown, Jason Dalton, and Heidi Hoyle

Department of Systems Engineering, University of Virginia
151 Engineer's Way, Charlottesville, VA 22906
{brown,dalton,hjh7g}@virginia.edu

**Abstract.** Terrorist events such as suicide bombings are rare yet extremely destructive events. Responses to such events are even rarer, because they require forecasting methods for effective prevention and early detection. While many forecasting methods are available, few are designed for conflict scenarios. This paper builds on previous work in forecasting criminal behavior using spatial choice models. Specifically we describe the fusion of two techniques for modeling the spatial choice of suicide bombers into a unified forecast that combines spatial likelihood modeling of environmental characteristics with logistic regression modeling of demographic features. In addition to describing the approach we also provide motivation for the fusion of the methods and contrast the results obtained with those from the more common kernel density estimation methods that do not account for variation in the event space. We give an example of successful use of this combined method and an evaluation of its performance. We conclude that the fusion method shows improvement over other methods and greater scalability for combining larger numbers of spatial forecasting methods than were previously available.

## 1 Introduction

Conflict in the modern world has seen a shift from large-scale conventional wars to asymmetrical warfare. Subsequently, recent acts of terrorism and attacks against civilians surfaced due to an imbalance in the weapon systems of warring factions. [1] Before September 11, 2001 attacks against U.S. citizens by foreign terrorists occurred primarily overseas and were typically conducted by young adult males of Middle-Eastern descent. Those trends have changed and the U.S. now realizes increased vulnerability to attacks on its own soil. In response to the events on September 11th, the Department of Homeland Security (DHS) was created with the mission of preventing and responding to future attacks.

The prevention of terrorism is a challenging mission. For example, suicide bombings are one of the most commonly reported acts of terrorism and one that presents enormous difficulties in understanding and prevention. These difficulties arise first because successful suicide bombings include the death of the bomber. Second, the equipment used is simple and easy to acquire so interdiction and tracking of devices is not easy. Third, penetration of the organizations that promote suicide bombing has not succeeded because they recruit based on an understanding of the local populace. Finally, the characteristics of the suicide bombers have adapted to thwart prevention, changing from men to women and, in some cases, children.

H. Chen et al. (Eds.): ISI 2004, LNCS 3073, pp. 426–435, 2004.

Despite these drawbacks to prevention, there are methods that can exploit the patterns in the behavior of suicide bombing organizations. A number of government agencies are looking for these patterns in their databases through the use of spreadsheets and other statistical measures. But there currently exists no method to find the key variables to explain or uncover suicide bombing patterns. The focus of this research is the use of spatial choice analysis to uncover the bombing patterns in past incident locations and to develop an empirical prediction model for future suicide bombings.

# 2  Background

This section depicts the rising threat of terrorist organizations. Next, it introduces two common techniques for analyzing this type of data; density estimation and spatial data mining. Finally, it gives basic information about the database used in our analysis.

## 2.1  Terrorist Organizations

To date, only two Middle East terrorist organizations have targeted U.S. interests. The first was the Palestinian Liberation Front (PLF) attack on the Achille Lauro cruise ship where one U.S. citizen died. The second was a series of 1983 attacks where Hezbollah bombed the U.S. Embassy, Marine Barracks, and an annex of the Embassy, all in Beirut. A third attack by a lesser known Israeli terrorist organization, the Harakat ul-Mujahidin (HUM)/Movement of the Holy Warrior, recently abducted and murdered U.S. journalist Daniel Pearl.

Regardless of where these terrorist organizations strike, operating in the U.S. or in Israel, there has been a substantial loss of innocent life. The United States recognized the terrorist threat within its borders and around the world, and subsequently initiated the Global War on Terror.

Agencies are in great need of tools to help them allocate limited resources, proactively engaging and defending against this threat. Because terrorist attacks are rare, we have few data points to make our forecast models. Because they are highly destructive, we need to enact measures that will estimate the threat before an incident occurs so that defensive measures can be taken. There is little response that can be made when a likely target for suicide bombers is found by the bomber before the security agencies.

## 2.2  Density Estimation

Multivariate density estimation fits a probability density function to empirical data. Techniques for performing density estimation include goodness of fit tests for fitting distributions and nonparametric techniques. Among these nonparametric techniques are clustering methods, e.g., k-means estimation, mixture models, and kernel methods [3]. In a very high dimensional space, it is necessary at times to reduce the dimensionality of the space in order to reduce computation and avoid redundant data elements (multicolinearity). Most current approaches to performing spatial density estimation use only the location of an event, creating a density function in the two coordinate dimensions. In this paper, we demonstrate a method for extracting environmental variables using geographic information systems. These variables more closely model an offender's preferences in target selection, and therefore produce a density of preferred target locations, rather than a density of past event locations.

### 2.3 Spatial Knowledge Mining

Spatial knowledge mining is a derivative of Knowledge Discovery in Databases (KDD). Spatial knowledge is stored in geographic information systems (GIS), which are databases with additional functionality for performing spatial manipulations and queries from the data. Spatial knowledge mining merges the techniques of data mining and GIS to form high dimensional analysis, the results of which are then projected onto the two dimensional geographical view. This synergy is important because it allows the results of sophisticated multivariate analysis to be presented in an intuitive display for the user.

### 2.4 Data Sources

The data for this analysis came from several sources. The Israeli regional maps came from the Israeli Central Bureau of Statistics. The suicide bombing event data came from the International Policy Institute for Counter-Terrorism (ICT) at the Interdisciplinary Center in Herzliya, Israel, the largest public international terrorism/terror attack database available on the internet and multiple worldwide news sources. ICT was founded in 1996 in Israel and recently opened an Arlington, Virginia office. Their goal is to "help evaluate the threat that terrorism poses to America and the rest of the world and organize strategic training and orientation activities for officials in the executive, legislative and judicial branches of government." [4] . These data include 517 attacks indexed by date, location, type of attack, organization, and a description of the event. These data were transferred to a GIS and divided into two partitions for model training and testing. Seventy-five percent of the events were used for training and the remaining twenty-five for testing and evaluation. Analysis was conducted using tools developed by the authors for S-Plus, Visual Basic, and ArcGIS.

## 3   Data Preparation

### 3.1  Data Extraction

From our raw data, we extracted over 100 candidate features from the spatial environment. From base layers such as the street network, embassy locations, and critical borders we calculated the Euclidian distance from each training event to the nearest feature using GIS. This data was stored in an attribute table for the test set. Due to the regional nature of demographic data, we applied the demographic attributes of the surrounding polygon to each test point. To serve our evaluation and visualization purposes, a reference polygon grid was created in our chosen area of interest. This polygon grid was composed of square cells 50 meters on each edge. The same data extraction steps were performed on the reference grid to derive distance and demographic features. The area of interest grid used in this paper was centered on Jerusalem and contains forty thousand 50 meter cells.

## 3.2   Feature Reduction – Correlation Structure

In cases where the dimensionality of the data is far larger than its cardinality, a given model cannot give an unbiased estimate of the variance contributed by each feature. This would lead to improper fitting of the model and little robustness. By examining the correlation structure of the data, feature pairs with high correlations can be found and stepwise removed from consideration. By using this method, we can reduce the feature space to a more manageable size, and reduce colinearity of the data set.

## 3.3   Feature Reduction – Principal Components

Another method of feature reduction is principal component analysis or PCA. PCA seeks to reproject the data onto a new coordinate space such that each successive dimension accounts for a maximal amount of variance of the original process. For a data set of p features, p principal component projections are required to fully and generally account for all of the process variance, but quite often a large portion of the variance can be accounted for by a subset k of feature projections. PCA accomplishes this by projecting each successive feature onto the vector that accounts for the maximum amount of variance remaining. PCA uses the eigenvalue of the correlation matrix to find the projection of data that captures the greatest variance among the data. That projection we call the first principal component, and subsequent orthogonal components are then found and added to the model until we achieve the desired level of cumulative variance.

# 4   Target Preference Models

## 4.1   Spatial Preference Model

Most spatial prediction methods use only the past locations to predict future locations (e.g., kriging). In addition, approaches such as density estimation are frequently applied to geography even when assumptions, such as constant variance or homogeneity are violated.

Our approach models spatial preference in a higher dimensional space formed from distances to important geographic or key features. These distances are assumed to have a Gaussian distribution with a mean of zero (i.e, the terrorist would prefer to locate the attack at specific distances from these locations). By measuring the distances of an incident from key features we build an increasingly more precise view of the terrorist preferences. These features are far more descriptive than a geographic coordinate, which is simply an index of the data vector.

We use the index $i$ to indicate a spatial location, and the random variable $D_{in}$ to indicate the measured distances to key feature $i$ for terrorist attack n. Key features in this problem are features believed to be relevant to decision making by the terrorists, such as government buildings, bus stops, or road junctions.

Next we address the problem of feature selection. The number of possible features is large, if not unbounded. Without knowing the key features we must estimate them using the techniques of principal components and correlation described earlier. These techniques provide either a subset (correlation analysis) or a weighted set (principal component analysis) that provides the basis for predicting the likelihood of an attack.

The likelihood of an attack is given by the density ρ of the location's feature vector in the multidimensional feature space $D_i$ Each event has this vector D with $D_i$ = distance from the event to the nearest key feature $i$. The resulting density function for the distance to feature $i$ is given by

$$f(D_{ik}) = \sum_{n=1}^{N} U(D_{ik} - D_{in}) \tag{1}$$

where U(•) is a kernel density operator and k indexes an arbitrary distance and assumes we have discretized over the range of distances.

To evaluate the joint density over the region of interest, assume we have converted the area into a discrete set of 2D points or a grid and let g=1...G be the grid point index. Then the joint density for a single grid point for distances from key features, 1,...,I is

$$f(D_{ig}) = c \prod_{i=1}^{I} f(D_{ig}) \tag{2}$$

$c$ is a constant of proportionality. Substituting from (1) we now have the formulation of the attack likelihood based on spatial preference as

$$\rho(D_g) = c \prod_{i=1}^{I} \frac{1}{N} \sum_{n=1}^{N} U(D_{ig} - D_{in}) \tag{3}$$

Under our assumption of Gaussian uncertainty which implies a Gaussian kernel in (1) the equation in (3) becomes

$$\rho(D_g) = c \prod_{i=1}^{I} \frac{1}{N} \sum_{n=1}^{N} \frac{1}{\sqrt{2\pi\sigma_i^2}} e^{\frac{-(D_{ig} - D_{in})^2}{2\sigma_i^2}} \tag{4}$$

where $\sigma_i$ is the bandwidth in the Gaussian kernel given by the normal reference density [5].

In this case, this model gives a likelihood for each location, the product of densities for the distances to each feature. When this density is discreetized, the resulting multivariate density can be projected onto the geographic space as a regular grid. This grid is then shaded according to percentiles for visualization. Figure 1 shows 2D and pseudo-3D representations. The points indicate suicide bombing incidents.

## 4.2  Logistic Regression

Another approach to compute the probability for an attack event is logistic regression. [6] Logistic regression provides a closed form solution to modeling the choice probabilities involved in terrorist site selection and can account for distances to key features as well as categorical variables (e.g., the presence of a holiday).

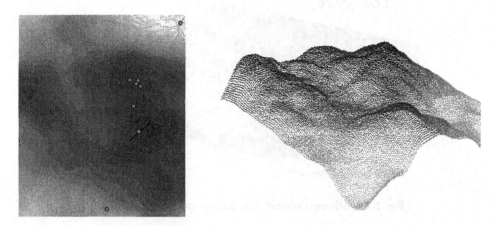

**Fig. 1.** Spatial Likelihood model

To formulate this model let $\pi_i(x)$ be the probability of a terrorist event at location i given attributes x, where x is a vector of length k.

$$\pi_i(x) = \frac{\exp[B_0 + B_1 x_{i1} + ... + B_k x_{ik}]}{1 + \exp[B_0 + B_1 x_{i1} + ... + B_k x_{ik}]} \tag{5}$$

and 1- $\pi(x)$ is the probability of a non-event:

$$1 - \pi_i(x) = \frac{1}{1 + \exp[B_0 + B_1 x_{i1} + ... + B_k x_{ik}]} \tag{6}$$

so the odds o(x) of an event are:

$$\frac{\pi_i(x)}{1 - \pi_i(x)} = o(x) = \exp[B_0 + B_1 x_{i1} + ... + B_k x_{ik}] \tag{7}$$

The probability of an event is then compared against a threshold and a classification decision is made.

As noted previously, logistic regression can incorporate variables other than distances and for the prediction of suicide bombings we used demographic attributes. As before, each reference grid cell, i, is given a score between 0 and 1 that represents a likelihood that an event occurs. This grid is then shaded according to similar means as the spatial likelihood model for display purposes. Figures 2 and 3 show the demographic model with its characteristic edge effects rising from the use of aggregate polygons such as census tracts.

**3D view of demographic forecast**:

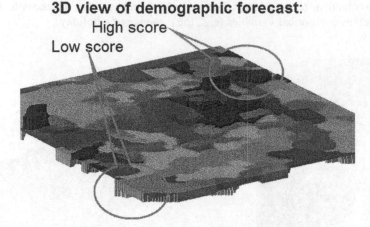

Fig. 2. Logistic regression of demographic model – Perspective

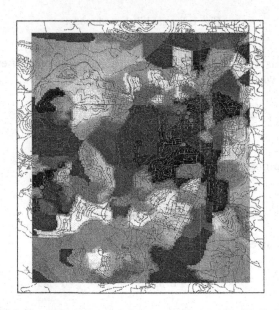

Fig. 3. Logistic regression of demographic model – Bird's Eye

## 4.3  Fusion of Spatial Models

Because the spatial models are not independent, we cannot fuse the two probabilities as we would two independent sensors. Instead we use the demographic data to augment or detract from the spatial model according to its own score. Because the demographic model is inherently disjoint due to the edges of the aggregation polygons, this merge has the effect of "jig sawing" the spatial model and shifting regions toward higher or lower scores. The areas that appear torn away in the perspective view are regions that have been shifted due to the model fusion. Figure 4 shows this effect.

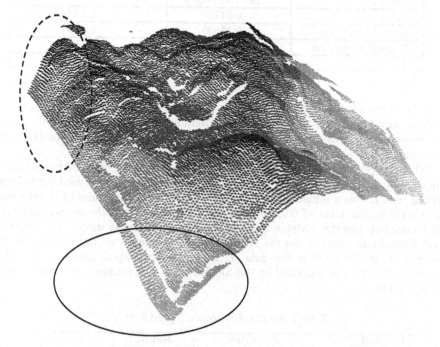

**Fig. 4.** Aggregate model. Dashed oval shows area of augmented probability. Solid lined oval shows area with reduced probability

## 5 Evaluation

For the evaluation phase we compare each method using our test set. Spatial forecast evaluation does not have a convenient analog to a simple goodness of fit test as in function estimation. So we use a concept called the percentile score, which computes the percentile given by the forecasted surface for each terrorist event in the test set. The percentile score has values from 0 to 100 and shows the percentage of the estimated distribution that is at or below the value given by the density function at that point. A large value indicates that the predicted surface showed a high likelihood at the actual attack location, while a low value shows that it incorrectly predicted the attack.

Table 1 shows the average percentile [7] scores for the methods described in this paper and also density estimate using Gaussian kernels (KDE) over just the spatial data. Table 1 also shows the sum of the absolute difference between the kernel density estimate with the test set and the estimate provided by each modeling approach. This difference or error shows how well the predictions approximated the surface representation of the actual data.

**Table 1.** Comparative results

| Method | Percentile score | Absolute difference from na-ïve model (KDE at $t_0$) |
|---|---|---|
| KDE | 0.04320 | 0.4500 |
| Spatial Preference | 0.15600 | 0.3540 |
| Logistic Regression | 0.19340 | 0.3391 |
| Fused | 0.27390 | 0.3069 |

Table 1 shows that each method in this paper performs better than spatial analysis without key features or demographic information. In addition, the fused approach combines the strengths of the distance measures with the demographic preferences in the logistic regression model to further improve performance.

While the percentile score shows the level of improvement obtained by implementing each model, we also need to formally test the comparisons. We used the Wilcoxon signed rank test as a measure of the statistical validity of our claim of improvement. At a significance level of 0.95, the test rejects the null hypothesis that there is no difference between the model in question and the naïve density model. The alternative hypothesis in all cases is that the density value is higher at all test points. The Wilcoxon tests are required in this data set as we cannot assume independence of the densities. The results generated by the SPLUS statistical package are summarized in table 2 below.

**Table 2.** Results of Wilcoxon Signed Rank Test

| Method | P value | Result |
|---|---|---|
| Geographic | 0.0002 | Alt Hypothesis True |
| Demographic | 0.0001 | Alt Hypothesis True |
| Merged | 0.0001 | Alt Hypothesis True |

## 6  Conclusion

This paper introduces two new methods for forecasting of spatial point processes. Both methods are individually better forecasters of events than the kernel density estimators commonly in use. By using the non-smooth demographic forecast to augment the spatial forecast, additional improvement is gained over the naïve model. More tests into the ability of the forecast fusion method will determine if there is a significant improvement over either of the two methods individually. While this method was created and implemented for analyzing crimes and terrorist events, there are many applications in resource management and planning that could benefit as well. Currently we are researching the use of the preference modeling techniques used herein to train a behavior engine for agent-based simulation. Further developments will attempt to use the modeling techniques to determine environmental rather than purely spatial bounds for gang activity.

# References

1. Cordesman, Anthony H. "The Lessons of Afghansitan: War fighting, Intelligence, and Force Transformation," The Center for Strategic and International Studies, Washington, D.C. 2002.
2. U.S. Department of Justice. FY 2002 Program Performance Report. "Strategic Goal One: Protect America Against the Threat of Terrorism," Downloaded from http://www.usdoj.gov/ag/annualreports/ar2002/sg1finalacctperftpt.htm on October 20, 2003.
3. Parzen, E. "On Estimation of Probability Density Function and Mode," *Annals Math. Statist,* 1962, pp 1065-1076.
4. International Policy Institutes for Counter-Terrorism, "International Terrorism/Terror Attack Database," http://www.ict.org.il/.
5. Venables, W.N.& Ripley, B.D., "Modern Applied Statistics with S," Springer-Verlag New York 2002 p.127.
6. Lattin, James & Carrol, J Douglas, "Analyzing Multivariate Data," Thomson Learning Inc, 2003 Ch 13.
7. Liu, Hua, & Brown, Donald E, "Criminal incident prediction using a point-pattern-based density model," *International Journal of Forecasting,* pp 603-622.

# Web-Based Intelligence Notification System: Architecture and Design

Alexander Dolotov and Mary Strickler

Phoenix Police Department, Computer Services Bureau
620 W Washington St., Phoenix, Arizona, USA 85003
{alex.dolotov,mary.strickler}@phoenix.gov

**Abstract.** This paper includes a concept, design and implementation of the WEB-based intelligence and monitoring Crime Free Program Notification System (CFPNS). The ultimate goal of the CFPNS is to produce automatic and customized notifications and reports, alerting multi-housing property managers and police supervisors of any historical and predicted criminal behavior. This system could be considered the second phase of a Group Detection and Activity Prediction System (GDAPS), which had been proposed by authors. As a first stage of this concept, Phoenix Police Department Reports System (PPDR) is currently in operation. CFPNS includes the most populated residential rental properties in the City, which usually have high criminal activity levels, targeted to prevent criminal activities. The system is scalable, reliable, portable and secured. Performance is supported on all system levels using statistical models, a variety of effective software designs, statistical processing and heterogeneous databases /data storage access and utilization.

## 1  System Concept

The ultimate goal of the Crime Free Program Notification System (CFPNS) is to produce automatic and customized notifications alerting multi-housing property managers of any predicted criminal behavior. CFPNS covers the most populated residential rental properties citywide, which usually have high criminal activity levels.

CFPNS is designed as the next step of the Group Detection and Activity Prediction System (GDAPS) (fig.1). The fundamental idea of this concept involves information collection and access to the information blocks reflecting the activities of an individual or groups of individuals. This data could then be used to create a system that would be capable of maintaining links and relationships for both groups and individuals in order to predict any abnormal activity [1]. The plan for the design of GDAPS was to break the system into two subsystems. The first subsystem is "Data Maintaining and Reporting Subsystem" renamed to PPDR, which is currently operational within the Phoenix Police Department and explained in detail in [1]. The PPDR subsystem supports access to heterogeneous databases using data mining search engines to perform statistical data analysis. Ultimately, the results are generated in report form.

The second phase of the GDAPS System is the Crime Free Property Notification System (CFPNS), which is implemented in the Phoenix Police Department, as well. This system is explained in detail in the remaining sections of this document.

H. Chen et al. (Eds.): ISI 2004, LNCS 3073, pp. 436–448, 2004.

Other notification systems are in existence and are implemented in a variety of industries. Below is a brief list of such systems:

- The Automated Weather Notification System (AWNS) was designed to be proactive by providing the public with timely severe weather information via Email. AWNS fetches a URL from a data source and parses the information into separate statements. It then detects for the presence of new statements. New statements are delivered to the appropriate Email address for distribution. This system has no analytical blocks and consumes information from dependent resources.
- Patient Notification System (PNS) is administered by the Notification Center. Special groups, such as Health Care Researchers and Providers, are providing input into the system regarding the pharmaceutical products. All registered participants are notified by Email, fax or phone if a product is withdrawn or recalled. PNS is not an intelligence system but rather operates more like a specific alert system.
- U.S. EPA Emergency Response Notification System (ERNS) reports oil and chemical spills. This system works as an information carrier for the registered users.

In a conclusion, it appears that the most common notification systems use a minimum of intelligence features and operates mostly for Email delivery only. Of course, CFPNS builds on the positive experience of other known notification systems. A distinctive difference between CFPNS and other notification systems is the use of imbedded analytical and predictable mechanisms relative to the initial concept. Analytical functionality allows for the consumption of comprehensive information blocks from the multiple sources (Fig. 1), using database mining mechanisms which are implemented in the PPDR System and the ability to organize this information into multiple groups of analytical reports. Some examples of these reports include; incident reports, properties statistical reports, activity prediction reports and special services reports. This kind of comprehensive information access has some commonality with the ideas of "Total Information Awareness" project that was designed as a part of an anti-terrorism technology for the Defense Department [3].

## 2  Predictable Functionality

A predictable function is designed based on a time serial analysis model and a geometric smoothing method used for forecasting. In application terms, the system predicts daily activity for each property, on a daily basis, using a two-day interval for predictions. In our case, each time series could be interpreted as the observation level of activity for each particular property per day of week, $X$ itn where i = property number, t=1 to 7 for day of week, and n for observation number. The full set of $X$ itn can be represented by a matrix M (i*t). Each element of M is represented by a smoothed moving average at observation time n as $S$ ì,t n.

Each time series is generated by a constant process, in our case, a daily number of activities for each property, plus an independent random error:

$$Xitn=b+Et .$$
(1)

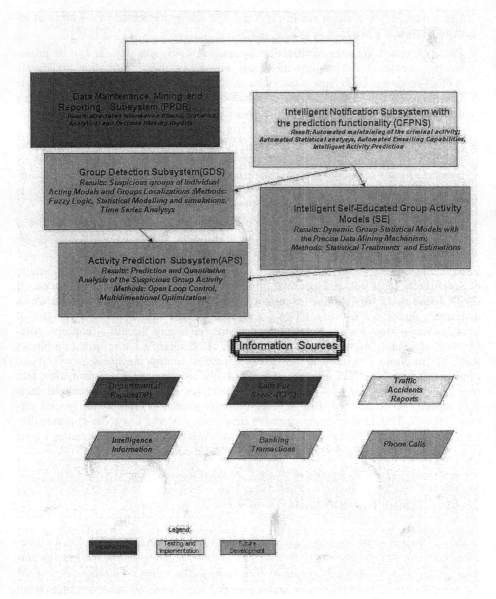

**Fig. 1.** Group Detection and Activity Prediction System (GDAPS) Concept with the Information Sources

A decomposition of the series onto the days of week will allow a "duality" between the moving average process and the autoregressive process [6] resulting in matrix $M(I*7)$. That is, the moving average equations below and their matrix structure could bring a non-stationary process to seven (number of days per week) stationary processes. This can only be done if the moving average parameters follow certain conditions, that is, a daily stationary time series. Using $S_{i,t,n-1}$ and $X_{i,t,n}$, one is able to calculate an updated estimate $S_{i,t,n}$.

The forecast error is:

$$X_{i,t,n} - S_{i,t,n-1} \qquad (2)$$

so that if $\gamma$ is the desired fraction, the new estimate of $b$ is:

$$S_{i,t,n} = S_{i,t,n-1} + \gamma(X_{i,t,n} - S_{i,t,n-1}). \qquad (3)$$

The first-order of geometric smoothing would be:

$$S_{i,t,n} = \gamma X_{i,t,n} + (1-\gamma) S_{n-1}. \qquad (4)$$

If we continue to substitute recursively for $S_{i,t,n-2}, S_{i,t,n-3}, \ldots$ the final results are shown below [4,5]:

$$S_{i,t,n} = \gamma \sum_{\mu=0}^{n-1} (1-\gamma)^{\mu} X_{i,t,n-\mu} + (1-\gamma)^{n} S_{i,t,0} \qquad (5)$$

where $S_{i,t,0}$ is the initial estimate of b used to start a geometric smoothing process.

For a complete forecasting model for CFPNS, all calculations of $S_{i,t,n}$ should be performed based on matrix $M(i*t)$ for each property i and day of week t, where $t = 1$ to 7.

$S_{i,t,n}$ can be interpreted as a weighted average, where weights decrease exponentially with the age of observation.

The weights are:

$$\gamma, \gamma(1-\gamma), \gamma(1-\gamma)^{**}2, \ldots \gamma(1-\gamma)^{**}n-1, (1-\gamma)^{**}n \qquad (6)$$

The value $S_n$ of the geometric smoothing can be used as an estimation of the unknown parameter $b$ from formula (1) so the forecast of the property crime activity at any future $n+p$ period would be:

$$X_{i,t,n+p} = S_n. \qquad (7)$$

The choice of the smoothing constant $\gamma$ is important in determining characteristics of the geometric smoothing. The larger value of $\gamma$ cause the smoothed value to react quickly to both real changes and random fluctuations. The average age of the data in an n – time moving average is [5]:

$$(n-1)/2 \qquad (8)$$

As a result, if we want to define a geometric smoothing system, which is equivalent to an n-time moving average, then we can set the smoothing average as a weighted average of the past observations. In [5] it is shown that the weights sum to unity, since:

$$\gamma = 2/(n+1). \qquad (9)$$

For CFPNS, a technique to determine $\gamma$ is used when carrying out a sequence of trials on a set of actual historical data using several different values of $\gamma$. Then selecting values of $\gamma$, would minimize the sum of squared errors. For CFPNS, the smoothing constants are between 0.1 and 0.3.

As a result of this technique, CFPNS coordinators will have the ability to obtain, on a daily basis, a two day forecast of predicted activity for each of their respective rental properties.

The remainder of this article will focus on the design and development of CFPNS, including database solutions, WEB design and other implementation issues.

# 3  Application

The CFPNS became an important application for law enforcement agencies, multi-housing associations, and residential properties management personnel. It is used to make informed decisions for crime prevention by Emailing, on a regular basis, alerts and other information relating to criminal activities occurring at multi-housing properties. The Crime Free Program (CFP) consists of complex multi-functional activities committed to reduce crime levels of multi-housing residential properties and to support citizens' safety. The City provides this program through the Police Department, the Multi-Housing Association, Law Enforcement Associations, and volunteers. CFPNS provides an excellent method to coordinate the efforts of all CFP participants and serves as a crime prevention process and a public safety tracking system for more than 1000 properties at a time. By examining historical criminal activity at multi-housing properties, it will be possible to identify criminal activity trends and to put a stop to the activity before it has a chance to occur. The ultimate benefit of this system is a reduction in crime in the multi-housing communities resulting in safer neighborhoods, the ability to attract higher quality residents and improved economic performance of the participating properties. This information would also aid in police manpower deployment for a more efficient use of police personnel.

# 4  Objectives

A WEB-based CFPNS was designed arising and interfacing from the PPDR System, which was considered the first stage of the GDASP [1]. Like the PPDR system, CFPNS could easily be ported for use by other law enforcement agencies where a Computer Aided Dispatch System is implemented.

The major entities for CFPNS are:

- property P and its parameters P(a,b,c,...) where a,b,c are the vectors of the properties characteristics (i.e., multiple addresses, multiple Emails, multiple managers or owners, etc.), and
- calls for service Ci(P) where Ci is the type of call for service relating to the
- criminal activity occurring on the property.

Within seconds, this system provides detailed, comprehensive, and informative statistical reports reflecting the crime situation for each particular property, for any date/

time period, within the City. These reports, along with other information blocks, are automatically sent via Email to the property managers, property owners and other recipients. This system simultaneously maintains more than 1000 residential rental properties along with seven years worth of calls for service history. The statistical data from these reports and notifications provide information for use in making decisions concerning property certifications, public notifications, and necessary safety improvements in each particular neighborhood. CFPNS, like PPDR, uses a powerful database mining mechanism, which might be effective for use in the next stage of the development of a GDAPS System.

In order to satisfy the needs of all users, the CFP system is designed to meet the following requirements:

- maintain accurate and precise up-to-date information regarding calls for service;
- use of a specific mathematical model for statistical analysis and optimization [2] [6} performed at a high level, with quick response times;
- have the ability to support different security levels for different categories of users;
- maintain an automatic comprehensive Emailing process;
- have a user friendly presentation that is convenient for all categories of users; and
- inherit from PPDR, security issues and database mining mechanisms.

The CFPNS is scheduled for full implementation by April 2004. The testing period demonstrated the necessity of the CFPNS System across all levels of management, the Police department, the City and the Arizona Multi-housing Association. The test period showed that the development concept concerning business logic and different controversial requirements is satisfactory. Incorporating original effective solutions, this system could aid in achieving one of the basic community goals, **improve citizens' safety.** The system could be considered the next phase of a complex Intelligence Group Detection and Activity Prediction System.

# 5 Relationships to Other Sources of Information

## 5.1 Calls for Service

There are two categories of information that are used for the CFPNS. They are calls for service data and information on crime-free properties. Calls for service are obtained from the Department's Computer Aided Dispatch and Mobil Data Terminal (CAD/MDT) System. The data is stored in a proprietary Image database for six months. Phoenix Police Department's CAD/MDT System handles over 7,000 calls for service daily from citizens of Phoenix.

Calls for Service data is collected when a citizen calls the emergency 911 number or the Department's crime stop number for service. A call entry clerk enters the initial call information into CAD. The address is validated against a street geobase which provides information required for dispatching such as the grid, the beat and the responsible precinct where the call originated. After all information is collected, the call is automatically forwarded to a dispatcher for distribution to an officer or officers in the field. Officers receive the call information on their Mobile Data Terminals (MDT). They enter the time they start on the call, arrive at the scene and the time they complete the call. Each call for service incident is given a disposition code that relates to how an officer or officers handled the incident. Calls for service data for completed incidents are transferred to a SQL database on a daily basis for use in the CFPNS/ PPDR System.

## 5.2 Properties Information

There are up to 1000 rental properties throughout the Phoenix area. In order to maintain the Crime Free Program, information related to multi-housing properties is organized in a separate database with its own infrastructure.

The major information blocks in this database are:

- general property information;
- property address/multiple addresses;
- property Emails;
- property manager's information;
- property owner's information;
- property CFP implementation data.

The WEB design allows for the maintenance of this information to be assigned to designated personnel throughout the department.

# 6  CFP System Architecture

CFPNS has been designed with three distinctive subsystems and utilizes such important PPDR features as security and database mining. These subsystems are as follows: CFPNS infrastructure maintenance, Prediction Calculation and Modeling, Notifications and Emailing, and Reports (fig 2). Each subsystem is designed to be flexible as well as scaleable. Each one has an open architecture and the capability of being easily expanded or modified to satisfy user enhancement requirements.

# 7  CFPNS Structural Design

## 7.1  CFPNS Infrastructure Maintenance

CFPNS infrastructure is grouped in a special separate database named CFP. The principle infrastructure groups could be classified as those which are related to each particular property, $G_{ij}$, and those which are generic for all properties or group of properties $E_n$ where:

- $i$ is an infrastructure information entity with one-to-one or many-to-one relationships;
- $j$ is the property's ID; and
- $n$ is the infrastructure element, which relates one-to-many properties or a group of them.

A full set of $G_{ij}$ will describe a property $j$.

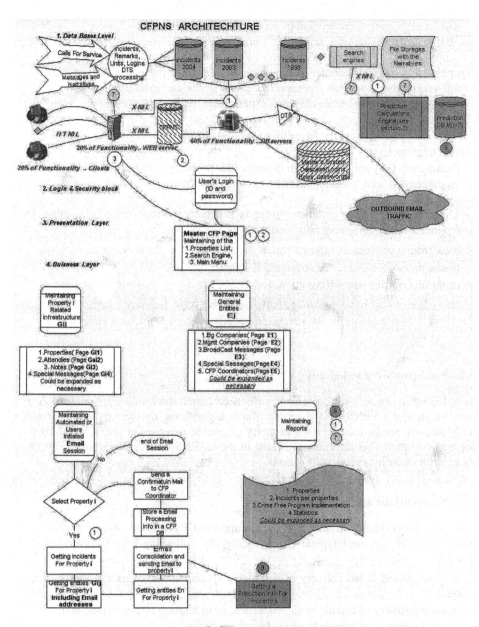

**Fig. 2.** CFP Architecture

At this point the system has four entities with the one-to-one relationships (**i=4**). To maintain each **Gij,** four special web pages are designed: Special Messages **G1j**, Notes **G2j**, Attendees **Ga3j**, and Properties **G4j**. This approach allows the ability to create a simple user-friendly procedure for maintaining entities with the one-to-one or one-to-many relationships, select a property from the list, and then to select a function from the main menu.

The critical values in properties group **G4j** are addresses and Emails. Addresses are the key parameters for database mining and Emails are used for the automated communications. All groups are subject to strict validation rules when editing or adding properties **j**. Each address is subject to validation using a city grid geobase. For Email validations, a special expression template is designed and used.

The group of parameters **Ga3j** are "Attendees", which are people who attend special seminars that are part of the certification process where: a is the number of attendees related to the property (**a >=0**) and dated information regarding each attendee related to property **j**.

Parameters **G4j** are those which describe the property certification process as well as management and owners information with one-to-one or many-to-one relationships.

The last infrastructure parameter group is **E n** with one-to-many relationships. This group includes the following information:

- background companies information, **E 1**;
- management companies information, **E 2**; and
- program coordinators' information, **E 3**.

Each **E n** group has its own specially designed page for easy maintenance of any **En** block and the ability to keep required security access level for a particular user or group of users.

## 7.2  Predictable Functionality

This functionality is fully described in Section 2 and should be implemented in the next version of CFPNS. Based on the above algorithms, the system would produce daily activity predictions for each property city-wide using eight years' worth of data for observations. This information is sent to the CFPNS Coordinators on a daily basis along with other historical verifications.

## 7.3  Notifications and Emailing

The core functionality of the CFPNS is supported by a notification subsystem. In order to cover the most typical requirements, the following notification modes are designed:

- automated scheduled delivery of Emails to all properties, or to a group of properties;
- manual delivery of Emails to all properties, or to a group of properties; and
- manual delivery of Emails to one selected property.

Each single Email (**M k**, where **k** is from 1 to the maximum number of Emails per session) has the following sections (each section is subject to querying a particular database or group of databases):

- Destination address **D k,**
- Sender address **N k,**
- Subject **S k,**

- Attention Section **T k,**
- Broadcast Message **BM k,**
- Special Message **SM k,**
- List of Incidents **L k,y where y is a current incident number for each property per Email session,**
- Summaries of the Incidents **Sum k**, and
- Disclaimer D.

The design concept provides for easy maintenance of all functionality for Email creation and for the delivery of Emails by the database server. This provides exceptional performance, even when processing thousands mails at a time and when multiple WEB users are online. Each single Email has a variable structure and may have different sections controlled by the user (fig.3). The algorithm of this process is shown in figure 2.

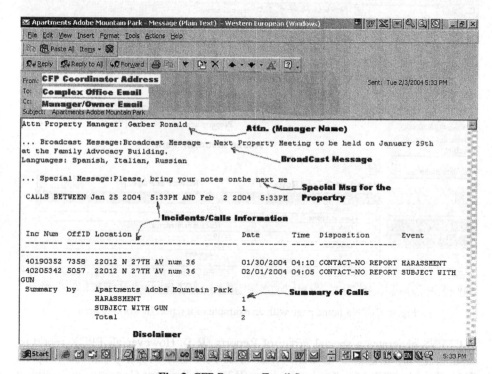

**Fig. 3.** CFP Property Email Structure

## 7.4 Reports

CFPNS generates a group of reports using the inherit capabilities of the PPDR reporting mechanism. Based on business rules, each generated report has input parameters entered by the user through the WEB page. The report generation becomes the responsibility of the database server. It performs using the following specially designed innovations:

- multiple databases which include "summary" tables [1],
- cross tables reporting functionality, which allows for the creation of a cross table record set on a database level,
- generic XML stream on output with universal XSLT performance and formatting on the client side instead of using any kind of downloaded controls for the final report formatting; and
- distinct functionality separation between the database server and the client workstation. This means that the database server should generate a final XML stream that is passed through the WEB server right to the client workstation. The client workstation is performing all kinds of formatting using XSLT performance.

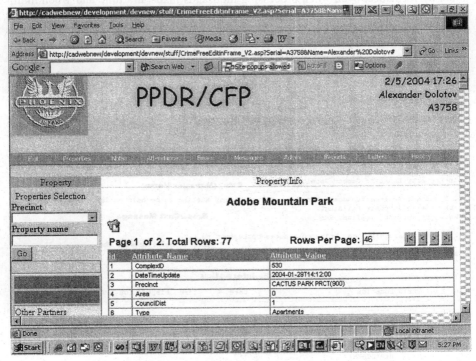

**Fig. 4.** CFPNS home page with an example of a report in working area

CFPNS generates a special group of Reports (**R i**). However all PPDR reporting capabilities are available, as well. A set of **R i** includes Property statistical reports (**R1**), Property Calls for Service Reports (**R2**), and Property Certification Group of Reports (**R3**). A variety of statistical analysis reports (**R4**) will be included in the next version of CFPNS. See example on figure 4.

## 7.5  System Security

Security begins when a user logs into the system and is continuously monitored until the user logs off. The CFPNS incorporates the PPDR security system, which is based on the assignment of roles to each user through the Administrative function. Role assignment is maintained across multiple databases including a CFP. Each database maintains a set of roles for the PPDR and CFPNS.

Each role has the possibility of being assigned to both a database object and a WEB-based functionality. This results in a user being able to perform only those WEB and database functions that are available to his/her assigned role. When a user logs onto the system, the userid and password is validated with the database security information.

Database security does not use custom tables but rather database tables that contain encrypted roles, passwords, userids and logins. After a successful login, the role assignment is maintained at the WEB level in a secure state and remains intact during the user's session.

## 8 Database Solutions

The CFPNS uses the PPDR many dimensional databases along with its own separate CFP database that uses a "star schema" The PPDR databases consist of several original solutions that are designed to improve performance, maintenance and reliability. After two years of implementation, PPDR has shown that all projected goals have been achieved. Described below is only a list of these solutions, which are described in details in [1]:

- multiple databases, w here each of them accumulate an annual volume of data;
- use of multidimensional "summary" tables with pre-calculated data, grouped by various keys such as police precinct, shift, type of call, and priority into a summary table;
- use of compressed file storage with binary long unstructured objects, equipped with an effective search engine and an easy access mechanism through the metadatabase;
- use of a full query performance on the database side with a final XML stream generation; and
- use of a "cross-table" performance for statistical calculations and a final XML cross-table stream.

## 9 Conclusion

CFPNS could be considered the second phase of the Group Detection and Activity Prediction System (GDAPS). Having an original design solution, CFPNS supports a notification process through the Email mechanism, using access to heterogeneous databases, data mining, search engines, and the ability to produce diverse statistical reports and predictable/ intelligence features. CFPNS is highly secured using database driven security. It is a system with administrative functionality and versatile log functionality. The architecture of CFPNS is easily expanded to add new features and functionality for future enhancement requests. CFPNS covers a very important sector of public safety. It collects information on all multi-housing properties throughout the City and delivers this information to all participants of the Crime-Free Program. Implementation of this system will allow for the prevention of criminal activity and improve upon citizens' safety at multi-housing properties.

## Acknowledgement

Special thanks go to the reviewers of the papers for submission for the ISI-2004 Conference who provided important analytical comments and suggestions for improvement to our paper. We also appreciate the support and assistance received from Mr. Chuck Lucking of the Phoenix Police Department in designing and implementing the database for the CFPNS project. And lastly, we would like to thank Ms. Ann Donohue for her editing and formatting skills in preparing our document for submission.

## References

1. Dolotov, Alexander; Strickler, Mary: "Web-Based Intelligence Reports System, The First Phase of a Group Detection and Activity Prediction System" Proceedings of the 2003 "Intelligence and Security Informatics" Symposium, Tucson (2003)
2. Dolotov, Alexander: "Experiments Design In a Process of a Statistical Modeling Optimization" Journal of "Systems and Machines Control of the Ukraine Academy of Science" vol. 4 (1973)
3. Burns, Robert: "Pentagon Defends Domestic Experiment" Associated Press, Nov 21 (2002)
4. Robinson and Wold: "Time Series Analysis and Applications" (1999)
5. Johnson and Gardiner :"Forecasting and Time Series Analysis" (1990)
6. Box and Jenkins: "Time Serial Analysis" (1976)

# Cross-Lingual Semantics for Crime Analysis
# Using Associate Constraint Network

Christopher C. Yang and Kar Wing Li

Department of Systems Engineering and Engineering Management
The Chinese University of Hong Kong
{yang,kwli}@se.cuhk.edu.hk

**Abstract.** In light of the Bali bombings, East Asia nations rally the international community into a broad-based coalition to support a war against terrorism. The information sharing among different countries provides a challenge for cross-lingual semantic interoperability. In this work, we model the problem as an associate constraint network and propagation by backmarking is proposed for creating the cross-lingual concept space. The approach deals with structured as well as unstructured data, addresses relevancy of information, offers the user with associative navigation through the information embedded in the database, enables conduction of multiple languages. Evidence is presented to show that a constraint programming approach performs well and has the advantage in terms of tractability, ordering and efficiency over the Hopfield network. The research output consisted of a thesaurus-like, semantic network knowledge base relied on statistical correlation analysis of the semantics embedded in the documents of English/Chinese parallel corpus.

## 1 Introduction

Since the attacks in the United States on 11 September 2001, efforts have increased to coordinate regional and international action against terrorism. The Association of Southeast Asian Nations (ASEAN) announced increased cooperation with the U.S., China, Russia on region-wide security concerns. These countries agreed to build up the strong links among their law enforcement, defense and security agencies. The agencies exchange information and intelligence on international terrorist activities and related transnational organized crime. The agencies also focus on combating the financing of terrorism and countering money laundering. The terrorist events have demonstrated that terrorist and other criminal activities are connected, in particular, terrorism, money laundering, drug smuggling, illegal arms trading, and illegal biological and chemical weapons smuggling. Criminal activity such as drugs trafficking is widespread in East Asia and can assist resource movement of terrorist groups. Since East Asia has large supplies of weapons, the potential for terrorists to use weapons of mass destruction raises the attention of national security considerably in the past few years. For example, North Korea exported ballistic missiles to the Middle East.

Successfully combating crime and sharing information depend upon countries having information systems for evaluating threats and vulnerabilities and issuing required warnings and patches. By identifying and sharing information on a threat before it causes widespread harm, an intelligent system is required to retrieve relevant information from the criminal records and suspect communications. The system should con-

H. Chen et al. (Eds.): ISI 2004, LNCS 3073, pp. 449–456, 2004.

tinuously collect information from relevant data streams and compare incoming data to the known patterns to detect the important anomalies.

The information sharing creates a challenge for *cross-lingual semantic interoperability* since numerous databases containing structured and unstructured data are available to intelligence analysts. Much of this data and information written in different languages and stored in different locations may be seemingly unconnected. It is a major challenge to generate an overview of this disparate data and information so that it can be analyzed, searched, summarized and visualized.

One of the difficulties to retrieve relevant information is the lack of explicit semantic clustering of relevant information [3]. The problem is further elevated by the language boundary. There is no single and common representation of data. This results in a requirement for translators and often leads to a reduction in accuracy as data is propagated and shared among different systems in different languages. Currently, many approaches to retrieve textual materials from databases depend on a lexical match between keywords in user queries and those in documents – controlled vocabulary approach. Because of the tremendous diversity in the words people use to describe the same document, simple lexical matching methods are incomplete and imprecise. The limits of conventional keyword-driven search techniques pose a difficulty to retrieve relevant information [3]. The creation of conceptual relationships allow the system to deduce users' information needs correctly and retrieve relevant documents, even though the documents contain different terms from the queries. In addition, the queries may be written in languages different from the languages used in the documents. Linguistic barriers caused by translation or interpretation mistakes may also cause the analysts to misunderstand the information or to miss subtle yet vital nuances.

The objective of the proposed associative constraint network is to present analysts with a comprehensive, consistent view of textual data. The approach deals with structured as well as unstructured data, addresses relevancy of information, offers the user with associative navigation through the information embedded in the database, enables conduction of multiple languages. With this data handling capability, various items of information in different languages will be linked together according to their conceptual relationships included in a parallel corpus, and presented to the analyst as the result of a single query.

In this paper, we propose the backmarking propagation technique for the associate constraint network. Experiments will be conducted and benchmarked with the previous technique, Hopfield network. The result of the associate constraint network consisted of a thesaurus-like, semantic network knowledge base relied on statistical correlation analysis of the semantics embedded in the documents of English/Chinese daily press release issued by Hong Kong Police Department. In terms of criminal analysis, the knowledge base can aid pursuing and apprehending suspects, searching evidence and allocating resources. With an adequate knowledge base, there will be a basis for collective action in response to the elusive tactics of the global terrorists.

## 2   Concept Space Construction Based on Hopfield Network

In our previous work, we have presented the concept space approach based on Hopfield network [4][5][14] to resolve the cross-lingual semantic problem. The automatic Chinese-English concept space generation consists of English and Chinese phrase extraction from parallel corpus, co-occurrence analysis, and Hopfield network. The Chinese and English phrase extraction identifies important conceptual phrases in the corpus. In the co-occurrence analysis, the association between the extracted terms is computed. After completion of the Hopfield network parallel spreading activation process, the output from the network produces a set of concepts that are strongly related to the Chinese and English important conceptual phrases as input. Since the concept space contains knowledge obtained from the entire collection, the system is able to find a set of global concepts drawn from the entire collection without restriction. These concepts are analogous to concept descriptors (i.e., keywords) of the document. The parallel corpus was dynamically collected from the Hong Kong Police website using a text-based approach.

## 2.1  Drawbacks of Hopfield Network

Along with many desirable properties of Hopfield network, it has some drawbacks. In terms of concept space construction, the Hopfield network approach does not converge efficiently toward a feasible equilibrium state. There is often a trade-off between *computational time* and *minimizing the network error*. Besides, the Hopfield network consists of a sequence of *random* variables evolving over time. The value of a particular variable at time t+1 is dependent only on the state of the variable at time t. As the number of iterations increases, the network is not tractable. In addition, Hopfield network is recurrent [6][7]; the order in which units are updated can have a significant affect on processing. However, the concept space approach based on Hopfield network does not take the order of units into consideration.

After the study of the drawbacks of the Hopfield network approach, we developed an alternative to the Hopfield network design, using a constraint programming based algorithm. The constraint programming based algorithm attempts to take the advantage in terms of time and precision over the concept space approach based on Hopfield network.

# 3  Constraint Programming – Constraint Satisfaction Problems

Constraint programming, a methodology for solving difficult combinational problems by representing them as constraint satisfaction problems (CSPs), has shown that a general purpose search algorithm based on constraint propagation combined with an emphasis on modelling can solve large, practical scheduling problems [12].

Constraint Satisfaction Problem (CSP) has been a subject of research in Artificial Intelligence (AI) for many years. The pioneering works on networks of constraints were motivated mainly by problems arising in the field of picture processing[13][9].

A **Constraint Satisfaction Problem** (CSP) is a triple (V, D, C), where:

1. V is a set of *variables* (V={$v_1$, $v_2$ ,...,$v_n$}),

2. D is a function which maps every variable in V to a set of possible values,
(D:V→ a set of possible values)
The set $D_i$ is the domain of variable $v_i$.

3. and C is a set of *constraints* on an arbitrary subset of variables in V restricting the values that the variables can simultaneously take.

A **solution to a CSP** is an assignment of a value from its domain to every variable, in such a way that every constraint is satisfied. A CSP is satisfiable if a solution tuple exists. A solution tuple of a CSP is a compound label for all those variables which satisfy all the constraints [10].

Solutions to CSPs can be found by searching systematically through the possible assignments of values to variables. Search methods divide into two broad classes, those that traverse the space of partial solutions (or partial value assignments), and those that explore the space of complete value assignments (to all variables) stochastically [8].

A CSP can be depicted by a **constraint network** [11]. A constraint network is a declarative structure that consists of nodes and arcs. Each node represents a variable, and each arc represents a constraint between variables represented by the end points of the arc.

In this work, a constraint network approach is proposed to simulate the associate memory in a human brain in order to construct an automatic thesaurus termed a Concept Space. The associate constraint network is the associate network of the extracted terms from a parallel corpus with constraints imposed on the nodes of the associate network. Given an input term in either English or Chinese, a cross-lingual concept space of the input term is generated if the associate constraint network is satisfied.

### 3.1 Formulation of the Associate Constraint Network

A constraint network is a declarative structure that consists of nodes and arcs. The nodes represent the variables and the arcs represent the relationship between the variables and the constraints.

As illustrated in Figure 1, the nodes of associate constraint network $(x_1,x_2,...,x_n)$ represent the extracted terms of the parallel corpus. The values of the nodes are binary. Binary means that the value of nodes can be either assigned 1 or 0 ( $x_j=\{0,1\}$ ), where

- $x_j =1$ if $x_j$ is a terms in the cross-lingual concept space and
- $x_j =0$ if $x_j$ is not a terms in the cross-lingual concept space.

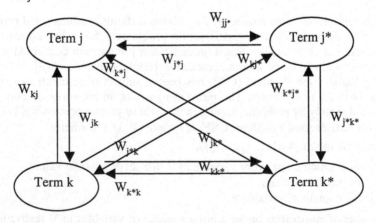

**Fig. 1.** Associate network of extracted terms from the parallel corpus

The arcs of the associate network represent the association between the extracted terms. The **constraint** on $x_j$, $c_j$, is

$$
x_j = \begin{cases} 1, & \text{if } \displaystyle\sum_{i=0}^{n-1} W_{ij} x_i \geq \text{threshold} \\[2em] 0, & \text{if } \displaystyle\sum_{i=0}^{n-1} W_{ij} x_i < \text{threshold} \end{cases}
$$

The threshold will be determined statistically based on the distribution of relevance weights $W_{ij}$. $W_{ij}$ denotes the relevance weight from node $i$ to node $j$. n is the number nodes in the network.

The generation of cross-lingual concept space can then formulated as the constraint satisfaction problem (CSP). We define the node consistency and network satisfaction as follows:

**Definition 1:** $x_j$ is consistent if and only if $c_j$ is satisfied in the associate constraint network.

**Definition 2:** The associate constraint network is satisfied if and only if all nodes in the associate constraint network are consistent and $\sum_j x_j < C$ , where C is a threshold.

## 3.2  Constraint Propagation

Most algorithms for solving CSPs search systematically through the possible assign-ments of values to variables [1][2]. The algorithms have focused on two phases: mov-ing forward (forward checking and look-ahead schemes) and look-back (backtracking schemes). By integrating systematic algorithms with consistency techniques, it is possible to get more efficient constraint satisfaction algorithms

### 3.2.1  Backmarking
In the concept space construction, a backmarking algorithm is proposed to solve the constraint satisfaction problem (CSP).

**1. Initialization:**
The values of all nodes are initialize to be 0.

$x_i(0)=u_i$, $0 \leq i \leq n-1$

$x_i(t)$ is the value of node $i$ at time t.

$x_i(t)$ is the output of node $i$ at time t. $u_i$ indicates a value of node $i$ where $u_i$ can be either 0 or 1.

$u_i=1$ if $u_i$ represents the input term;otherwise, $u_i=0$. n is the number of terms in the constraint network.

$S = \varnothing$     S is a set of indexes for input terms.

$S = S \cup \{i\}$  if the node $i$ is an input term.

$S'= \varnothing$    S' is a set of indexes for the nodes which cause the infeasible solution.

An infeasible solution is found if $\sum_{i=0}^{n-1} x_i \geq C$    where C is a threshold.

## 2. Search for potential solution(s)

$$v_j(t) = \sum_{i=0,i\neq j}^{n-1} W_{ij}\, x_i(t)$$

$x_{j*}(t)=1$ where $j*= \arg \max_{j,\, j\notin S',S} ( v_j(t) )$

$W_{ij}$ is the relevance weight from node $i$ to node $j$. n is the number nodes in the network.

## 3. Determine whether or not a solution is found
Check node consistency for *all the nodes*
IF *all nodes are consistent*

IF $\sum_{j=0}^{n-1} x_j < C$

THEN  the solution(s) is found
ELSE
// an infeasible solution is found
$x_{j*}(t) = 0$  //$x_{j*}(t)$ caused the infeasible solution
$S'= S' \cup \{ j*\}$  //j* is marked
go to Process 2 // backtracking is needed
ELSE // next iteration
$t = t+1$
$S=S \cup \{ j*\}$
go to Process 2

# 4  Experiment

An experiment has been conducted to evaluate the performance of the associate constraint network approach and benchmark with the Hopfield network. 10 subjects were invited to examine the performance of the automatically generated concept space. The concept space is generated from the Hong Kong Police parallel corpus with 9222 Chinese/English concepts. The thesaurus includes many social, political, legislative terms, abbreviations, names of government departments and agencies.

The result is presented in Table 1. It is found that the associate constraint network outperforms the Hopfield network in both precision and recall.

**Table 1.** Precision and Recall of Hopfield network and associate constraint network

|  | Hopfield network | Constraint network- backmarking |
| --- | --- | --- |
| Precision | 0.835 | 0.891 |
| Recall | 0.795 | 0.824 |

# 5  Conclusion

The information sharing among different countries to combat the terrorist attacks provides a challenge for *cross-lingual semantic interoperability* since numerous databases containing structured and unstructured data are available in different languages. In this paper, we have presented a cross-lingual concept space approach using associate constraint network. The concept space allows the user to interactively refine a search by selecting concepts which have been automatically generated and presented to the user. The research output consisted of a thesaurus-like, semantic network knowledge base relied on statistical correlation analysis of the semantics embedded in the documents of English/Chinese parallel corpus of the Hong Kong Police Department. It is found that the associate constraint outperforms the previous proposed Hopfield network in both precision and recall.

# Reference

1. Bartak, R., "Constraint Programming: In Pursuit of the Holy Grail," In *Proceedings of the Week of Doctoral Students (WDS99)*, Part IV, MatFyzPress, Prague, June 1999, pp. 555-564
2. Bartak, R., "Theory and Practice of Constraint Propagation", In Proceedings of the 3rd Workshop on Constraint Programming for Decision and Control (CPDC2001), Wydavnictvo Pracovni Komputerowej, Gliwice, Poland, June 2001, pp. 7-14.
3. Chen, H., Lynch, K. J., "Automatic construction of networks of concepts characterizing document database" *IEEE Transactions on Systems, Man and Cybernetics,* vol. 22, no. 5, pp. 885-902, Sept-Oct 1992
4. Li, K. W. and Yang, C. C. "Automatic Construction of Cross-lingual Networks of Concepts from the Hong Kong SAR Police Department," *Proceedings of the First NSF/NIJ Symposium on Intelligence and Security Informatics (ISI 2003)*, Tucson, U.S.A., June 2-3, 2003.
5. Li, K. W. and Yang, C. C. "Automatic Cross-Lingual Thesaurus Generated from the Hong Kong SAR Police Department Web Corpus for Crime Analysis," *Journal of the American Society for Information Science and Technology,* to appear
6. Hopfield, J.J.(1984) Neurons with graded response have collective computational properties like those of two-state neurons", In *Proceedings of the National Academy of Science, USA*, 81:3088-92, 1984
7. Hopfield, J. J. "Neural network and physical systems with collective computational abilities". In *Proceedings of the National Academy of Science, USA*, 79(4):2554-2558, 1982.
8. Kumar, V. "Algorithms for Constraint Satisfaction Problems: A Survey", *AI Magazine* 13(1):32-44,1992.
9. Montanary, U. "Network constraints fundamental properties and applications to picture processing", In *Information Sciences* 7:95-132,1974

10. Tsang, E. Foundations of Constraint Satisfaction, Academic Press, London,1995
11. van Beek, P. and Dechter, R. "On the Minimallity and Global Consistency of Row-Convex Constraint Networks," In Journal of the Association for Computing Machinery, Vol.42, No.3, may, 1995, pp.543-561
12. van Beek, P. and Chen, X.. "CPlan: A constraint programming approach to planning," In *Proceedings of the 16th National Conference on Artificial Intelligence*, Orlando,Florida, July, 1999.
13. Waltz, D. L. "Understanding line drawings of scenes with shadows," In *Psychology of Computer Vision*, McGraw-Hill, New York,1975.
14. Yang, C. C. and Luk, J. "Automatic Generation of English/Chinese Thesaurus Based on a Parallel Corpus in Law," *Journal of the American Society for Information Science and Technology, Special Topic Issue on Web Retrieval and Mining: A Machine Learning Perspective*, vol.54, no.7, May, 2003, pp.671-682.

# Experimental Studies Using Median Polish Procedure to Reduce Alarm Rates in Data Cubes of Intrusion Data

Jorge Levera[1], Benjamin Barán[2], and Robert Grossman[1]

[1] University of Illinois at Chicago, Chicago, IL, USA 60612
jlevera@cs.uic.edu, grossman@uic.edu
http://www.uic.edu/
[2] Centro Nacional de Computación, Universidad Nacional de Asunción
San Lorenzo, Paraguay
bbaran@cnc.una.py
http://www.cnc.una.py

**Abstract.** The overwhelming number of alarms generated by rule-based network intrusion detection systems makes the task of network security operators ineffective. Preliminary results on an approach called EXOLAP shows that false positive alarms can be avoided by detecting changes on the stream of alarms using a data cube and median polish procedure. A data cube aggregates alarms by hierarchical time frames, rule number, target port number and other feature attributes. The median polish procedure is used on materialized relational views of the data cube to detect changes on the stream of alarms. EXOLAP shows promising results on labeled and unlabeled test sets by focusing on exceptions on the normal stream of alarms, diverting the attention away from false positives.

## 1  Introduction

Given the proliferation of valuable assets on the Internet, it has become clear that network security operators are looking for robust intrusion detection systems (IDS) that are efficient, effective and easy to manage. A popular approach to network intrusion detection is rule-based intrusion detection systems (RBIDS) [5].

A great number of alarms generated by RBIDS are false positives [4, 9, 14] (i.e., attack did not actually take place). False positive alarms could be reduced by tuning the IDS or by eliminating the rules that causes the noise. Sometimes, it is difficult to apply any of those changes because either the IDS belongs to another organization (e.g., outsourcing, cooperative distributed IDS) or it is not safe to delete a specific rule. Then, the security operator is faced with the problem of detecting true positive alarms among a pile of false positives.

This paper studies an alarm reduction approach based on Exploratory Data Analysis (EDA)[18] and On-line Analytical Processing (OLAP) techniques called EXOLAP (EXploratory OLAP). EDA and OLAP techniques do not make assumptions about the data, and they are especially useful when there is no a priori information about the data [4, 5]. Experimental results show that EXOLAP can detect changes on the trend

H. Chen et al. (Eds.): ISI 2004, LNCS 3073, pp. 457–466, 2004.

of alarms by focusing on exceptional data. Generalized alarms could be generated to turn the operator's attention towards the interesting part of the data instead of a pile of false positives.

EXOLAP is based on the progressive aggregation of alarms in multiple summarized views of a time-related data cube [6]. The median polish procedure [18] is used on two-dimensional views of the data cube to detect changes on the stream of alarms. A predictable and manageable number of generalized alarms are generated to help network security operators focus on the most interesting data first.

The rest of the paper is organized as follows: Section 2 surveys related work on alarm reduction. Section 3 presents the EXOLAP approach to alarm reduction. Section 4 shows experimental results. Section 5 discusses future work and concluding remarks.

## 2 Related Work

Exploratory data visualization tools [4, 19] are similar to EXOLAP because they aid the analysis process by exploratory means. The set of tools focuses on visualizing abnormal states based on raw audit data whereas EXOLAP focuses on real-time alarm reduction using EDA techniques. Visualization improves the work of forensic analysts [4]. Vert et al. [19] propose a geometric approach to help in the analysis of large amounts of audit data.

Data mining techniques has been applied to intrusion detection in different ways [12, 14, 16, 20]. Lee and Stolfo [12] use clustering and association rule on system and network features in order to learn their normal behavior. Manganaris et al. [14] use alarm features to characterize the normal stream of alarms using association rules. Ye and Li [20] use clustering and classification on alarm features. Most of the previous approaches require a carefully selected training set. Portnoy et al. [16] tackle this problem.

Julisch and Dacier [10] use a conceptual clustering technique that reduces alarms. In a later work, Julish [11] uses clustering to find the root of most false positives. Shortcomings of their approaches include periodic tuning to adjust the model to changing network conditions, and the numerous parameters that are not trivial to determine [5].

Lately, several authors have proposed techniques to correlate alarms [3, 15]. Cuppens and Miege [3] cluster, merge and correlate alarms in a cooperative IDS environment. Ning et al. [15] build attack scenarios. They correlate alarms by partial match of prerequisites and consequences of attacks. Correlation condenses alarms to a few groups and facilitates the distinction between false and true positives. However, prerequisites and consequences conditions are trivial to find.

## 3 The EXOLAP Approach to Alarm Reduction

In EXOLAP a data cube aggregates raw alarms generated by RBIDS. A data cube is a data abstraction that allows one to view aggregated data from a number of perspectives. We refer to the dimension to be aggregated as the *measure* attribute, while the remaining dimensions are known as the *feature* attributes.

EXOLAP uses the number of alarms generated as its measure attribute. The feature attributes are based on the alarms' attributes and the network packets that triggered them. A suggested set of feature attributes is: identifier of the rule that triggered the alarm, time-to-live attribute of the packet, target port number, and at least two time related attributes.

Time related attributes (e.g., $T_0$, $T_1$, ..., $T_K$) should be hierarchical. The time attribute at the lowest level, $T_0$, should be small enough to detect recent attacks and big enough to avoid overloading the database storing alarms. For example, if $T_0=15$ minutes, alarms will be aggregated every fifteen minutes. Time attributes at intermediate levels, say $T_i$, should include the one below so that aggregated alarms at $T_{i-1}$ could be used to fill the cells of time attribute $T_i$. Following the previous example, if $T_0=15$ minutes, then the time attribute above, $T_1$, could be sixty minutes (i.e., $T_1=T_0*4$).

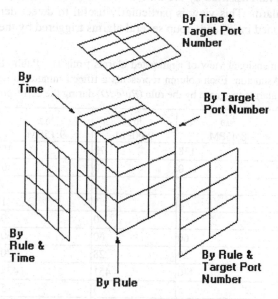

**Fig. 1.** A three dimensional data cube aggregates the number of alarms by feature attributes (*Rule*), (*Time*), and (*Target Port Number*). Besides, two dimensional tables show the aggregated alarms by (*Rule and Time*), by (*Rule and Target Port Number*) and by (*Time and Target Port Number*)

EXOLAP uses data cubes because they are useful in identifying trends [7] and offer a summary of the alarms generated by the RBIDS. Considerations regarding view materialization strategies and efficient implementation of data cubes are beyond the scope of this paper. The authors used some of the ideas found in [2, 7]. Figure 1 shows a three dimensional data cube with the corresponding feature attributes. Additional feature attributes can be easily included.

For simplicity, the following relational views are used in this paper:

- *By rule and time.* Every $T_0$ minutes, a new column $t_{0,i}$ of alarm frequencies in the database is added to a table with the trend of alarms in the last $T_1$ minutes at $T_0$ minutes intervals. This view shows the number of alarms triggered by each rule during each time interval.
Table 1 shows a *Rule and Time* view of alarms generated by a Snort system [17] installed on the Public Sector Metropolitan Area Network of Asuncion, Paraguay. In this case, a fifteen minutes interval is the smallest time attribute (i.e., $T_0=15$ minutes and $T_1=60$ minutes).

- *By target port number and time.* This view shows the number of alarms at each time interval classified by the target port number of the network packet that triggered the alarm.

- *By time-to-live and time.* This view summarizes the number of alarms triggered at each time interval classified by the time-to-live attribute of the network packet that triggered the alarm. This view is particularly useful to detect denial of service attacks as mentioned in [8] and group several alarms triggered by the same attack.

**Table 1.** A two dimensional view of aggregated alarms from The Public Sector Metropolitan Area Network of Asuncion. Each column represents a fifteen minutes time interval, and each row the number of alarms triggered by the rule (*Rule ID*) during the corresponding time interval

| Rule ID | $t_{0,0}$ 8:45PM | $t_{0,1}$ 9:00PM | $t_{0,2}$ 9:15PM | $t_{0,3}$ 9:30PM |
|---|---|---|---|---|
| 1 | 138 | 72 | 35 | 21 |
| 7 | 0 | 0 | 0 | 2 |
| 10 | 4 | 2 | 4 | 4 |
| 14 | 1 | 5 | 1 | 0 |
| 16 | 1 | 0 | 0 | 0 |
| 17 | 60 | 60 | 60 | 60 |
| 18 | 29 | 28 | 30 | 28 |
| 19 | 440 | 451 | 434 | 459 |
| 22 | 5 | 3 | 5 | 6 |
| 24 | 0 | 0 | 0 | 1 |
| 27 | 3 | 0 | 0 | 0 |
| 29 | 0 | 1 | 0 | 1 |
| 38 | 0 | 1 | 0 | 0 |
| 46 | 0 | 1 | 0 | 0 |

Once several relational views of the cube are built, an EDA technique is used to find the most interesting subset of alarms. The following section introduces this technique.

## 3.1  Median Polish Procedure

A traditional way of performing EDA is *median polish procedure* (MPP)[18]. MPP fits an additive model by operating on a data table. The algorithm works by alternately removing the row and column medians, and continues until the proportional reduction in the sum of absolute residuals is less than a specified tolerance value or until there has been a maximum of iterations specified. In principle, the process continues until all the rows in each dimension have zero medians.

MPP finds the *effect* that each row and column has on the model, given by the algebraic sum of the medians that have been subtracted in that row at every step. Besides, MPP provides the *residual* in each cell of the table, which tells how far apart that particular cell is from the value predicted by the model.

To illustrate the procedure, the values $Y=\{y_{ij}\}$ given in Table 1 are used as input to MPP. The relational view *Rule and Time* can be considered a two-way table of the number of alarms generated per time frame. An *additive model* can express the relationship between time and rule. Equation 1 shows the additive model, where $\mu$ is the overall typical value for the whole table, $\alpha_i$ is the row effect of row i, $\beta_j$ is the column effect of column j, and $\iota_{ij}$ is the deviation of $y_{ij}$ from the model (i.e., residual)

$$r_{ij} = \mu + \alpha_i + \beta_j + \iota_{ij} .\tag{1}$$

Table 2 shows the residual values for the two-way table given in Table 1. The exceptional values on Table 1 are found by locating the largest absolute values on the residual table. In Table 2, the cell on the first row and first column has the biggest absolute value.

In IDS terms, a big residual value means that there is a significant change in the trend of alarms. For example, the largest deviation value in Table 2 indicates an increase on alarms generated by the rule with id = 1 in the time window between 8:45 PM and 9:00 PM. Particularly, the largest positive value on the last column, 9:30 PM, indicates a recent increase on the normal values on the table.

Small residual values suggest that the stream of alarms of a particular type has been stable and can be considered "normal" noise. By examining the abnormal cells, the operator has reduced the searching space of alarms to the rule ID and time frame indicated. The reduction obtained depends on the frequencies of alarms generated during that time frame. This gives the operator enough flexibility to adapt to different scenarios. Since EXOLAP is exploratory, the final judgement is left to the expert. In addition, generalized alarms could be generated for the top $n$ exceptions on the last time interval of a particular view.

The median polish procedure is used on other relational views of the data cube as well. As a result, there are as many residual tables as relational views.

In the following section, relational view construction and MPP are combined and automated to reduce the number of alarms to be inspected.

**Table 2.** The residual table for the two dimensional view of aggregated alarms in Table 1. Each column represents a fifteen minute time interval, and each row the deviation of the number of alarms triggered by the rule (*Rule ID*) with respect to the model built during the corresponding time interval

| Rule ID | 8:45 PM | 9:00 PM | 9:15 PM | 9:30 PM |
|---|---|---|---|---|
| 1 | 84.5 | 18.5 | -18.5 | -32.5 |
| 7 | 0.0 | 0.0 | 0.0 | 2.0 |
| 10 | 0.0 | -2.0 | 0.0 | 0.0 |
| 14 | 0.0 | 4.0 | 0.0 | -1.0 |
| 16 | 1.0 | 0.0 | 0.0 | 0.0 |
| 17 | 0.0 | 0.0 | 0.0 | 0.0 |
| 18 | 0.5 | -0.5 | 1.5 | -0.5 |
| 19 | -5.5 | 5.5 | -11.5 | 13.5 |
| 22 | 0.0 | -2.0 | 0.0 | 1.0 |
| 24 | 0.0 | 0.0 | 0.0 | 1.0 |
| 27 | 3.0 | 0.0 | 0.0 | 0.0 |
| 29 | -0.5 | 0.5 | -0.5 | 0.5 |
| 38 | 0.0 | 1.0 | 0.0 | 0.0 |
| 46 | 0.0 | 1.0 | 0.0 | 0.0 |

## 3.2  Alarm Reduction

The processes of building relational views of the data cube presented in the previous section can be automated. First, a reasonable set of relational views should be chosen. Those views are materialized and updated at predefined time intervals as more alarms are generated by the RBIDS. For example, the *Rule and Time* view given in Table 1 can be considered a moving time window. Every $T_0=15$ minutes, a new column, say $t_{0,i}$, is added with the aggregated alarms seen in the last $T_0$ minutes. To save space, the oldest $t_{0,j}$-minute interval (where $j<i$) could be aggregated on the next time frame level (e.g., $T_1=60$ minutes).

EXOLAP generates *trend alarms* (t-alarms) at every time interval $t_{l,i}$ of a time feature attribute $T_l$. Using the Rule and Time view shown in Table 1, t-alarms could be generated every fifteen minutes for each of the top $n$ exceptions on that particular view. Similarly, t-alarms are generated for other views of the data cube. With t-alarms, operators can quickly locate potential hazards caused by a sudden increase or decrease on the number of alarms generated by a RBIDS.

The advantage of using t-alarms is that the operator receives a predictable number of alarms pointing towards an interesting subset of raw alarms. The number of t-alarms generated could be set ahead of time to a manageable number. In this way, the operator is not overwhelmed and can start analyzing RBIDS alarms from the most interesting part.

Equation 2 shows how to compute the number of t-alarms per hour. For every time related feature attribute $T_l$, we multiply the number of relational views ($RV_l$) involving $T_l$ by the number of exceptional values ($n$) retrieved from each relational view by the number of intervals $T_i$ included in sixty minutes.

$$\text{t-alarms per hour} = \sum_{i=0}^{k-1} RV_i * n * 60/T_i \qquad (2)$$

In the following section, experiments with EXOLAP show encouraging results on diverse sets of alarms, including labeled and unlabeled datasets of different sizes.

## 4  Experimental Results

EXOLAP was tested with four sets of alarms generated by Snort IDS version 1.9.1 with default set of rules. One of the systems was located on a Public Sector Metropolitan Area Network of Asuncion, Paraguay. Another set of alarms was generated by a Snort located on the Abilene network [1]. An additional set belongs to an IDS running at the University of Illinois at Chicago (UIC). The last set of alarms was generated using DARPA99 Intrusion Detection Set [13]. Table 3 gives an overview of the datasets used.

**Table 3.** Datasets used on experimental results. Some characteristics are shown to indicate their diverse nature and evaluate the results on each set

| Dataset | Network Type | Number of Alarms | Distinct Rules | Time Span (in days) | Distinct Source IP Addresses | Distinct Target IP Addresses |
|---|---|---|---|---|---|---|
| UIC Network | LAN | 592,121 | 52 | 180 | 20,161 | 2,429 |
| Pub. Sect. MAN | MAN | 430,794 | 67 | 7 | 514 | 272 |
| Abilene Network | WAN | 10,357,673 | 49,571 | 90 | 208,527 | 253,790 |
| DARPA99 | Synthetic | 23,050 | 84 | 10 | 109 | 187 |

Three relational views were used during the experiment: Rule and Time, Time-to-live and Time, and Target-port-number and Time views. The data cube used time attributes $T_0$=15 minutes and $T_1$= 60 minutes (i.e., $k=1$). MPP ran every $T_0$ minutes on all views and t-alarms were triggered for the biggest exception on each view (i.e., $n=1$). The reduction is computed as the number of RBIDS alarms to be examined on the exceptional cell pointed by t-alarms over the total number of RBIDS generated during the same time interval $T_0$. Table 4 shows the reduction obtained.

In general, datasets DARPA99 and UIC network do not have many alarms at 15 minute intervals. In order to obtain greater reduction on these datasets, a larger $T_0$ value was needed.

**Table 4.** Average reduction on four datasets divided by Rule and Time view, Time-to-live and Time view, and Target-port-number and Time view

| Dataset | Avg. Reduction on Rule-Time view | Avg. Reduction on TTL-Time view | Avg. Reduction on Port-Time view |
|---|---|---|---|
| Public Sector MAN | 77.98 % | 84.39 % | 67.72 % |
| Abilene Network | 80.52 % | 85.49 % | 78.98 % |
| UIC Network | 46.75 % | 74.07 % | 41.25 % |
| DARPA 99 | 48.69 % | 36.88 % | 54.77 % |

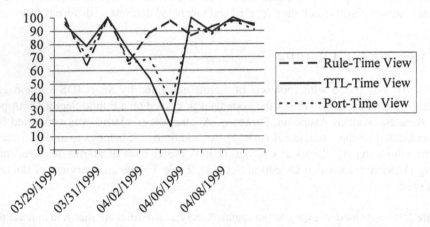

**Fig. 2.** Percentage of true positive alarms detected on the labeled dataset DARPA99 using EXOLAP. T-alarms were defined for the cell with the largest deviation value during the last time frame

Figure 2 shows the percentage of true positives detected on the labeled dataset DARPA99 using EXOLAP. Most true positives detected were in the subset of raw alarms indicated by t-alarms (i.e., the cell with the biggest residual value). A big drop observed on April 5, 1999 was caused by many attacks taking place on an eleven minute interval and network packets having many different time-to-live and target port number values. In this case, most true positives were among the top five exceptional values indicated by t-alarms. Rule-Time view was not affected and managed to detect most true positives with the top t-alarm.

## 5 Conclusion and Future Work

Experimental studies with EXOLAP aim at reducing the number of intrusion alarms to be analyzed by network security experts. A multidimensional data cube aggregates alarms by several feature attributes. MPP finds exceptional values or changes on the stream of alarms on two-dimensional views of the data cube. Tests on several datasets show promising reduction on the number of alarms to be examined. In particular, the labeled dataset DARPA99 showed that EXOLAP could improve the effectiveness of network security operators by focusing on the most interesting data first.

In the future, EXOLAP will be tested with an n-dimensional extension of MPP for data cubes proposed by Barbará and Wu [2]. This will reduce the number of t-alarms without significant computational demand, integrating several views into only one global view. Intuitively, many change detection algorithms can also be applied to the data cube. A performance comparison would be appropriate to study complexity and effectiveness of different algorithms.

Further testing needs to be done on labeled datasets like DARPA99 to verify the reduction on the number of false positives versus the percentage of true positives detected by t-alarms.

In addition, a distributed EXOLAP system is being designed to exploit the fact that views can be exchanged in a distributed IDS environment to improve the efficiency and cooperation between composing IDS.

# References

1. Advanced Network Management Lab, *The Abilene Project*, University of Indiana, Bloomington, Indiana, USA.
2. Daniel Barbara and Xintao Wu, "Using approximations to scale exploratory data analysis in datacubes," Proceedings of the ACM SIGKDD International Conference, August 1999.
3. Frederic Cuppens and Alexandre Miege, "Alert correlation in a cooperative intrusion detection framework," In Proceedings of the 2002 IEEE Symposium on Security and Privacy, May 2002.
4. Robert F. Erbacher and Karl Sobylak, "Improving Intrusion Analysis Effectiveness," Workshop on Statistical and Machine Learning Techniques in Computer Intrusion Detection, George Mason University, September 24-26, 2003.
5. Eleazar Eskin, Andrew Arnold, Michael Prerau,  Leonid Portnoy and Salvatore Stolfo, "A Geometric Framework for Unsupervised Anomaly Detection: Detecting Intrusions in Unlabeled Data," Data Mining for Security Applications. Kluwer 2002.
6. Jim Gray, Adam Bosworth, Andrew Layman, Hamid Pirahesh, "Data Cube: A Relational Aggregation Operator Generalizing Group-by, Cross-tabs and Sub-totals," In Proceedings of the 12th Int. Conf. on Data Engineering, pp 152-159, 1996.
7. Venky Harinarayan, Anand Rajaraman, and Jeffrey D. Ullman, "Implementing data cubes efficiently," In Proceedings of the ACM SIGMOD '96, pp 205-216, Montreal, June 1996.
8. Alefiya Hussain, John Heidemann and Christos Papadopoulos, "A framework for classifying denial of service attacks," In Proceedings of the 2003 conference on Applications, technologies, architectures, and protocols for computer communications, pp 99-110, Karlsruhe, Germany, August 25-29, 2003.
9. Klaus Julisch, "Mining alarm clusters to improve alarm handling efficiency," In 17th Annual Computer Security Applications Conference (ACSAC), pp 12-21, December 2001.
10. Klaus Julisch and Marc Dacier, "Mining Intrusion Alarms for Actionable Knowledge," in SIGKDD'02, Edmonton, Alberta, Canada, 2002.
11. Klaus Julisch, "Clustering Intrusion Detection Alarms to Support Root Cause Analysis", in ACM Transactions on Information and System Security 6(4), November 2003.
12. Wenke Lee and Sal Stolfo. "Data Mining Approaches for Intrusion Detection" In Proceedings of the Seventh USENIX Security Symposium (SECURITY '98), San Antonio, TX, January 1998.

13. Lincoln Laboratory, Massachussets Institute of Technology, DARPA 99 Intrusion Detection Data Set Attack Documentation. [Online] Available: http://www.ll.mit.edu/IST/ideval/docs/1999/attackDB.html.
14. Steganos Manganaris, Marvin Christensen, Dan Zerkle, and Keith Hermiz, "A Data Mining Analysis of RTID Alarms," Computer Networks, 34(4) , October 2000.
15. Peng Ning, Yun Cui and Douglas S. Reeves, "Constructing attack scenarios through correlation of intrusion alerts, "In Proceedings of the 9th ACM conference on Computer and communications security, Washington, DC, USA, 2002.
16. Leonid Portnoy, Eleazar Eskin and Salvatore J. Stolfo. "Intrusion detection with unlabeled data using clustering" In Proceedings of ACM CSS Workshop on Data Mining Applied to Security (DMSA-2001). Philadelphia, PA: November 5-8, 2001.
17. Martin Roesch, "Snort - lightweight intrusion detection for networks," In Proceedings of Thirteenth Systems Administration Conference (LISA '99), pp. 229--238, The USENIX Association, Berkeley, California, 1999.
18. John W. Tukey, *Exploratory Data Analysis*, Addison-Wesley, 1977.
19. Greg Vert, Deborah A. Frincke, and Jesse C. McConnell, "A visual mathematical model for intrusion detection" In Proceedings of the 21st National Information Systems Security Conference, Crystal City, Arlington, VA, USA, October 5-8 1998.
20. Nong Ye and Xiangyang Li, "A Scalable Clustering Technique for Intrusion Signature Recognition," In Proceedings of the 2001 IEEE, Workshop on Information Assurance and Security, United States Military Academy, West Point, NY, 5-6 June, 2001.

# Information Sharing and Collaboration Policies within Government Agencies

Homa Atabakhsh[1], Catherine Larson[1], Tim Petersen[2],
Chuck Violette[2], and Hsinchun Chen[1]

[1] Department of Management Information Systems
University of Arizona, Tucson, AZ 85721, USA
{homa,cal,hchen}@eller.arizona.edu
[2] Tucson Police Department
270 S. Stone Avenue, Tucson, AZ 85701, USA
Tim.Petersen@tucsonaz.gov, cviolet1@ci.tucson.az.us

**Abstract.** This paper describes the necessity for government agencies to share data as well as obstacles to overcome in order to achieve information sharing. We study two domains: law enforcement and disease informatics. Some of the ways in which we were able to overcome the obstacles, such as data security and privacy issues, are explained. We conclude by highlighting the lessons learned while working towards our goals.

## 1 Introduction

The need for information sharing between government agencies has been highlighted in the post-9/11 scrutiny of terrorism events. Historically information sharing between law enforcement agencies has occurred in a very limited manner: ordinarily, only by person to person or case by case basis. In our current age of high mobility and increasing availability of technology, criminals are able to take advantage of the fact that limited information sharing between law enforcement jurisdictions reduces the likelihood of getting caught.

In the public health realm, health-related data is also shared on a case by case basis, between doctors, hospitals, laboratories, insurance providers, and others involved in the provision of healthcare services. Public health data is often shared at an aggregated level. The mechanisms used for data transmission (such as fax, telephone, email and other methods) are often cumbersome and rudimentary, and do not support analysis, disease management or prediction at a regional or national level [13]. Data that is published on the Web is not necessarily interactive. Data sharing is guided and restricted by both a plethora of legal regulations as well as informal guidelines such as those in private practices. Aggregated data is reported to local and/or state and national agencies but not in real time.

There are many roadblocks to overcome in the process of sharing information between agencies, whether law enforcement or public health. Most of these roadblocks are no longer technical in nature. Political and social barriers are far and away the greater obstacles to overcome. Factors such as variations in state and federal laws, city codes and department policies affect this process greatly. We have experienced that as the size of the involved bureaucracies grows, the size of the barriers increases proportionally.

In this paper, two case studies are described, one in law enforcement and one in disease information. For each case study, the need for information sharing between government agencies is described followed by obstacles encountered and some of the ways in which we have overcome these obstacles. Data privacy and security issues are also described. Technical solutions for solving security problems present a research topic of their own and are out of the scope of this paper. We conclude with some of the lessons learned during this process.

## 2   Background and Motivation: Information Sharing between Government Agencies

### 2.1   Case Study: Law Enforcement

**2.1.1 Introduction.** In response to the September 11 terrorist attacks, major government efforts to modernize federal law enforcement authorities' intelligence collection and processing capabilities have been initiated. At the state and local levels, crime and police report data are rapidly migrating from paper records to automated records management systems in recent years, making them increasingly accessible.

However, despite the increasing availability of data, many challenges continue to hinder effective use of law enforcement data and knowledge, in turn limiting crime-fighting capabilities of related government agencies. For instance, most local police have database systems used by their own personnel, but lack an efficient manner in which to share information with other agencies [8, 10, 12]. More importantly, the tools necessary to retrieve, filter, integrate, and intelligently present relevant information have not yet been sufficiently refined.

As part of nationwide, ongoing digital government initiatives, COPLINK [3, 4, 6] is an integrated information and knowledge management environment aimed at meeting some of these challenges. Funded by the National Institute of Justice and the National Science Foundation, a prototype for COPLINK was initially developed at the University of Arizona's Artificial Intelligence Lab in collaboration with the Tucson Police Department (TPD) and Phoenix Police Department (PPD). COPLINK was developed into a product by Knowledge Computing Corporation (KCC) and deployed in approximately one hundred law enforcement agencies nationwide [1, 11].

The main goal of COPLINK is to develop information and knowledge management systems technologies and methodology appropriate for capturing, accessing, analyzing, visualizing, and sharing law enforcement related information. The COPLINK project has already bridged gaps between law enforcement agencies by allowing secure access by officers of some of the participating agencies. COPLINK has already shown its capabilities in the area of data sharing. As an example, the following is a quote from one of the Tucson Police Department (TPD) officers using COPLINK.

"COPLINK saved me tens of hours and the possible closure of a child rape case. My case involved a suspect only known as (NAME WITHHELD). We did not know how to spell his name and no address. Using COPLINK 's wildcard search I located a lost wallet report to the suspect's father and at the list location I found the suspect's vehicle. Several months later San Diego has a DNA hit on a child kidnap/rape case and I was able to provide them with suspect information. If COPLINK had been connected to Phoenix [this investigation occurred prior to TPD-PPD COPLINK connection] I would have been able to pull his photograph and fingerprints from an arrest I learned about later. This person has a warrant for his arrest. Without COPLINK I probably would have closed the case as unsolved."

### 2.1.2 Data Sharing for Law Enforcement: From Knowledge Discovery and Dissemination to Border Safe.

The Knowledge Discovery and Dissemination (KDD) project (funded by the National Science Foundation) and the BorderSafe project (funded by the Department of Homeland Security) are recent AI Lab initiatives that encompass collaborative efforts between the University of Arizona's AI Lab, law enforcement agencies in Arizona such as TPD, PPD, Pima County Sheriff's Department (PCSD) and Tucson Customs and Border Patrol (CBP) as well as San Diego ARJIS (Automated Regional Justice Systems) and San Diego Supercomputing Center (SDSC). These projects expand on existing partnerships and technologies in addition to breaking new ground in both areas.

Federal, State and local regulations require that agreements between agencies within their respective jurisdictions receive advanced approval from their governing hierarchy. This precludes informal information sharing agreements between those agencies. We found that requirements varied from agency to agency according to the statutes by which they were governed.

For instance, the ordinances governing information sharing by the city of Tucson varied somewhat from those governing the city of Phoenix. This necessitated numerous attempts and passes at proposed documents by each cities law enforcement and legal staff before a final draft could be settled upon for approval by the city councils. We found in general that similar language existed in the ordinances and statutes governing this exchange but the process varied significantly enough to require modification in almost every case. It appears as though the size of the jurisdiction is proportional to the level of bureaucracy required.

Our initial experience in developing an agreement between agencies in Arizona and agencies in California is following this premise. Negotiating a contract between University of Arizona and ARJIS (Automated Regional Justice Information System) of Southern California required two to three months of negotiation between legal staff, contract specialists and agency officials. We are hopeful that many of the solutions to barriers in that process may be applied to the formation of formal agreements for information sharing with other agencies that cross state boundaries.

In an effort to facilitate data sharing between the agencies involved in the KDD and Border Safe projects, TPD has recently written an Intergovernmental Agreement (IGA) that will be signed between different law enforcement agencies. This IGA was condensed from MOU's (memorandum of understanding), policies and agreements that previously existed in various forms between numerous agencies. The IGA was drafted in as generic a manner as possible, including language from those laws, but excluding reference to any particular chapter or section. That allowed the required verbiage to exist in the document without being specific to any jurisdiction.

Sharing of information between agencies with disparate information systems has also lead to bridging boundaries between software vendors and agencies (their customers). We took care not to violate licensing terms by insuring that non-disclosure agreements existed and that contract language assured compliance with the vendors' licensing policies.

There is now a working VPN between ARJIS and TPD over which a small group of investigators from each department have begun querying the others' dataset. One day after implementing this connection a TPD crime analyst investigating information about a suspect from California involved in a TPD incident was able to obtain mug photos and drivers license photos from the ARJIS connection. The information and photos will be used to create a bulletin warning of officers' safety issues related to this person. Also, the gang sergeant at TPD has already found information in the ARJIS dataset relevant to criminals he is currently investigating in Tucson.

The activities of many individual criminals clearly span across multiple jurisdictions. There is obvious value in the sharing of data between jurisdictional authorities. The Border Safe project has begun exploration of the integration of information across datasets provided by multiple jurisdictions in the southwest United States. Many local incidents involve vehicles registered in other jurisdictions. This analysis is even more powerful when border-crossing information can be merged with networks of incident information. The Tucson sector of the Bureau of Customs and Border Protection (CBP) has shared a list of border crosser license plates with the AI lab for analytical research. Tying together criminals, their vehicles and activity histories can produce powerful tools to create leads for criminal investigation.

**2.1.3 Access and Control Issues for Law Enforcement Data.** The information being shared in COPLINK, KDD, and the BorderSafe projects is for law enforcement use only and is compiled from documented law enforcement contacts. Data sources such as medical records, bank records, credit histories, and other non-law enforcement related information are not (and will not be) a part of these projects. The sharing of law enforcement information is vital in solving crime and not intended to provide broad access to private information.

In any data sharing initiative, it is essential to make sure that the data shared between agencies is secure and that the privacy of individuals is respected. We have taken the necessary measures to ensure data privacy and security. It is important to note that the data shared between agencies through the initiatives discussed above, contains only law enforcement data and is available only to individuals screened by these agencies using TPD Background Check, Employee Non-Disclosure Agreement (NDA) and the TOC (terminal operator certificate) test.

Currently all personnel who have access to law enforcement data fill out background forms provided by TPD and have their fingerprints taken at TPD. They also sign a non-disclosure agreement provided by TPD. In addition, they take a TOC (terminal operator certificate) test every year. The background information and fingerprints are then checked by TPD investigators to ensure the lack of involvement in criminal activity and for verification of identity.

In addition to the above forms and test, all law enforcement data in the University of Arizona's AI Lab reside behind a software firewall and in a secure room accessible only by activated cards to those who have met the above criteria (i.e., background check, NDA and TOC test approved by TPD). As soon as an employee stops working on projects related to law enforcement data, their card is de-activated. However, the NDA is perpetual and remains in effect even after an employee leaves.

## 2.2    Case Study: Developing a National Infectious Disease Information Infrastructure (NDII): An Experiment in West Nile Virus and Botulism (WNV-Bot)

**2.2.1 Introduction.** Public health agencies have long recognized the need to develop new models for partnerships and improve data and information sharing about disease outbreaks, particularly since the anthrax bioterrorism event of 2001 [2] and the recent SARS outbreak [5]. The increasing awareness of bioterrorism as a threat to the health and safety of U.S. citizens has intensified recognition of the need to develop disease surveillance and data sharing capabilities that support real time analysis, and facilitate communications about outbreaks, whether naturally occurred or human-caused [7]. As public health records migrate from paper-based to automated records management systems, it becomes even more critical to design system architectures that are flexible, scalable and inter-operative.

As part of broader national efforts to improve information sharing about disease outbreaks, the National Science Foundation awarded funding to the University of Arizona's Artificial Intelligence Lab in collaboration with its partners, the New York State Department of Health (NYDOH), and the California Department of Health Services (CADHS). The National Biological Information Infrastructure/National Wildlife Health Center of the United States Geological Survey is also participating as a data provider. The partnership, under the direction of the Disease Informatics Senior Co-ordination Committee, has developed the West Nile Virus-Botulism (WNV-Bot) portal as a prototype of a national infectious disease information infrastructure.

The prototype is intended to apply advanced informatics techniques and demonstrate that an architecture for capturing, accessing, analyzing, and visualizing disease-related data from multiple sources can be successfully created and can be extended to include real-time reporting and alerting capabilities and the ability to interoperate with other systems. The research objectives of the portal include:

- Demonstrating and assessing the technical feasibility and scalability of an infectious disease information sharing, alerting, and analysis framework
- Developing and assessing advanced data mining and visualization techniques for infectious disease data analysis and predictive modeling
- Identifying important technical and policy-related challenges to developing a national infectious disease information infrastructure

Test data belonging to participating state agencies has been integrated into the portal and includes scrubbed and abbreviated case records for humans and birds, mosquito counts, chicken sera, dead bird data, and botulism data. Additional data has been integrated into the portal to allow spatial and temporal visualization and analysis, and to support experimentation with hot-spot analysis. Such data includes, for example, vegetation, temperature, rainfall, bird migration, and unemployment. The inclusion of these datasets supports the analysis of disease outbreaks against the backdrop of their environmental or demographic factors.

When fully developed, the WNV-Bot portal prototype will be enhanced to include other diseases, and will be made available to public health officials for extensive testing. If successful, it will be expanded to the national level with a different funding and governance structure.

**2.2.2 Access and Control Issues for Disease-Related Data.** In the U.S., the states exercise the primary power for protecting citizen health, but the federal government plays an important role in gathering and disseminating public health data through a plethora of agencies; and city and county level health agencies also fulfill information gathering and other functions [9]. As with law enforcement data, state and local regulations require that agreements between agencies receive advanced approval from their governing hierarchy, precluding informal information sharing agreements between those agencies. We also found that requirements varied from agency to agency according to the statutes, regulations or policies by which they are governed. For example, CADHS, NYDOH and the University of Arizona each have different regulations regarding the treatment of confidentiality and for how long data may be kept.

Similar to the law enforcement case study, the WNV-Bot portal project is now attempting to make its agreement structure as flexible and scalable as its system architecture. A generic memorandum of understanding (MOU) has been collaboratively drafted and principles agreed to that meet the requirements of current partners. The MOU specifies that data must be returned or destroyed after five years; that the data may not be shared with anyone outside of the agreement; that collaborating partners retain data ownership, but mutually own data analysis; and that the agreement may be expanded to include diseases other than those currently specified.

In drafting this more generic MOU, we hope to meet the requirements of future collaborators as well as current partners. As a new agency, organization, or other entity joins the partnership, it will be required to agree with the terms and conditions specified in the MOU. Confidential disclosure agreements specifying the level of access privilege will be signed by individuals as their organizations join the project.

Challenges to drafting an MOU that all parties can agree on has included meeting differing state requirements, the ineffectiveness of communication methods used to resolve differences and negotiate legal compromises, and heavy workloads and shifting priorities within the various agencies and offices. Differing state requirements can sometimes be negotiated and compromises made, but emailing and faxing are not necessarily effective communication means for resolving sensitive issues. Instead, having the contracting officers from the participating offices actually talk on the telephone point by point has been more effective and we believe, more apt to result in a workable agreement. Heavy workloads and shifting priorities may not be in the control of the project team, but daily attention through phone calls has proven to be the best method for ensuring that the paperwork does not get continually placed at the bottom of the priority list.

Resolving these access and control issues through a small prototype is, of course, far more workable than trying to resolve them directly at a national level.

Disease outbreaks do not recognize political boundaries, and may not necessarily be confined by geographic boundaries. *Overt* (naturally occurring) outbreaks may be initially noticed and managed by a public health agency. *Covert* (human-caused) outbreaks may not be initially recognized as such and thus may first be managed by a public health agency followed by a law enforcement agency [2]. Overt diseases can often be tracked through a geographic spread, enabled by animal or human movement. The possibility of a covert disease outbreak triggered by large-scale bioterrorism events that are not geographically co-located makes sharing at the national and even global levels even more critical, and the negotiation of data-sharing agreements even more complex. The WNV-Bot portal project will serve as a test case for identifying legal and contractual issues around the sharing of sensitive information.

**2.2.3 Privacy Issues for Disease-related Data.** As of this writing, formal agreements that will allow the sharing of real-time data are in the process of being signed. Data currently in use in the portal is test data. The information in the WNV-Bot portal is for use by participating public health officials and research partners only. As with the law enforcement data, it is essential to protect the privacy of individuals whose data may be included in the portal. The portal is to be used only for disease tracking and analysis, across jurisdictions, and is not intended to provide broad access to private information.

The design for user data access control is modeled after the New York State Health Information Network/Health Provider Network (HIN/HPN). Data providers and users (including their institutions) need to register with the Portal, and the data providers assign access privilege level to individual users. Predefined access privilege levels include:

- Aggregated data (for example, access to weekly data at county level only)
- Detailed data (access may still be restricted to certain fields)

Access and authorization is being managed through a Java-based User Access Control API and access privilege definition. Data is loaded into the portal using Secure Sockets Layer encryption. Once formal agreements are reached, real data can be loaded into the portal for extensive user testing by project partners.

It is envisioned that, once fully implemented, a national disease information sharing infrastructure would be used by public health professionals, researchers, policy makers, law enforcement agencies and other users with a need for the information.

# 3   Lessons Learned and Conclusion

Our planned time for reaching agreements on contracts, MOUs, CDAs and IGAs and other required legal documentation was originally far too optimistic in both our law enforcement and disease informatics case studies. We found that agreement processes often took in excess of six months to complete. The upside has been the creation of a framework and templates, which will hopefully speed and smooth the process in future endeavors. We anticipate providing free access to models of the types of documentation we used and developed, which may facilitate duplication of this process by others. It is very important to keep security of information among the highest priorities to ensure confidence and trust between participants.

Throughout this process we have found it necessary and helpful to have a single person within each agency responsible for ensuring that the process does not slow down or stop. We needed daily emails, phone calls and face-to-face contact in order to follow up on commitments, check on progress and move the project forward.

Our initial research and experience has bolstered our belief that as our society becomes more mobile and criminal activity follows that trend, the need for law enforcement and public health officials to keep pace is reinforced. Law enforcement must be able to follow the activities of criminals beyond the boundaries of a city, county or state. New criminal venues such as cyber-crime, identity theft and international and domestic terrorism require that the law enforcement community respond with measures such as better information access among officers. Increased mobility also means that public health officials must be able to track the spread of microbes around the world. The hazards posed by new, naturally occurring diseases as well as the threat of bioterrorism events requires that public health agencies actively develop the means to share information and analysis more quickly and accurately than ever before. Given the possibility of covert outbreaks, partnerships between law enforcement and public health, and the ability to share information across domains and not just across jurisdictions, becomes even more critical.

## Acknowledgements

These projects have primarily been funded by the following grants:

- NSF, Digital Government Program, "COPLINK Center: Information and Knowledge Management for Law Enforcement," #9983304, July, 2000-June, 2003.
- NSF, Knowledge Discovery and Dissemination (KDD) # 9983304, June 2003-March 2004 and October 2003 – March 2004.
- NSF, ITR: "COPLINK Center for Intelligence and Security Informatics Research – "A Crime Data Mining Approach to Developing Border Safe Research." Sept. 1, 2003 – Aug. 31, 2004.
- DHS / CNRI: "Border Safe," Sept. 2003 – Nov. 2004.
- National Institute of Justice, "COPLINK: Database Integration and Access for a Law Enforcement Intranet," July 1997-January 2000.

We would also like to thank: Members at the University of Arizona Artificial Intelligence Lab and especially the COPLINK and West Nile Virus-Botulism portal teams, Tucson Police Department, Phoenix Police Department, Pima County Sheriff's Department, Tucson Customs and Border Protection, ARJIS (Automated Regional Justice Information System), SDSC (San Diego Supercomputing Center), and our partners at New York State Department of Health, California Department of Health Services, and the National Wildlife Health Center.

## References

1. *Anchorage Daily News*, November 23, 2003, "Software Joins Cops on the Beat," COPLINK program links databases, speeds police investigations in the state of Alaska.
2. Butler, J., L. Cohen Mitchell, C. R. Friedman, R. M. Scripp, C. G. Watz. "Collaboration between Public Health and Law Enforcement: New Paradigms and Partnerships for Bioterrorism Planning and Response. " *Emerging Infectious Diseases* 8(100): 1152-1156.
3. Chen H., Jenny Schroeder, R. V. Hauck, L. Ridgeway, H. Atabakhsh, H. Gupta, C. Boarman, K. Rasmussen, A. W. Clements (2002), "COPLINK Connect: Information and Knowledge Management for Law Enforcement"; *Decision Support Systems*, 34: pp. 271-285.
4. Chen H., Zeng D., Atabakhsh H., Wyzga W., Schroeder J. "COPLINK: Managing Law Enforcement Data and Knowledge." *Communication of the ACM. Special Issue on Digital Government: Technologies and Practices*. 2003

5.  Dignan, L. (2003), "Diagnosis: Disconnected." *Baseline*. http://www.baselinemag.com/ print_article/0, 3668, a=41305, 00.asp, accessed Feb. 8, 2004.
6.  Hauck R., H. Atabakhsh, P. Ongvasith, H. Gupta, and H. Chen (2002), "Using COPLINK to Analyze Criminal Justice Data," *IEEE Computer*. March 2002.
7.  Henderson, D. A. (1999), "The Looming Threat of Bioterrorism, " *Science* (283), Feb. 26: 1279-1282.
8.  Hoogeveen, M. J. & K. van der Meer (1994). "Integration of Information Retrieval and Database Management in Support of Multimedia Police Work, " *Journal of Information Science* 20(2): 79-87.
9.  Institute of Medicine (1988). *The Future of Public Health.* http://www.nap.edu/books/0309038308/html/, accessed February 8, 2004.
10. Lingerfelt, J. (1997). "Technology As A force Multiplier, " *Proceedings of the Conference in Technology Community Policing*. National Law Enforcement and Corrections Technology Center.
11. Los Angeles Daily News, December 6, 2003, "Cops Could Hit the Links Soon: New Search Engine Would Catalog, Interpret Data for Investigations,"
12. Pliant, L. (1996). "High-technology Solutions, " *The Police Chief* 5(38): 38-51.
13. Thacker, S.B., K. Choi, P.S. Brachman (1983). "The Surveillance of Infectious Diseases, " *JAMA* 249(9): 81-5.

# Intrusion-Tolerant Intrusion Detection System*

Myung-Kyu Yi and Chong-Sun Hwang

Dept. of Computer Science & Engineering Korea University,
1,5-Ga, Anam-Dong, SungBuk-Gu, Seoul 136-701, South Korea
{kainos,hwang}@disys.korea.ac.kr

**Abstract.** Recently, numerous studies have focused on multi-agent based intrusion detection systems (IDSs) in order to detect intrusion behavior more efficiently. However, since an agent is easily subverted by a process that is faulty, a multi-agent based intrusion detection system must be fault tolerant by being able to recover from system crashes, caused either accidentally or by malicious activity. Many of the existing IDSs have no means of providing such failure recovery. In this paper, we propose the novel intrusion-tolerant IDS using communication-induced checkpointing and pessimistic message logging techniques. When the failed agent is restarted, therefore, our proposed system can recover its previous state and resume its operation unaffected. In addition, agents communicate with each other by sending messages without causality violation using vector timestamps.

## 1 Introduction

As the size of the Internet grows, so do the risks to private networks attached to the Internet. Internet security has been disrupted by a steady flow of denial of service (DoS) attacks and the increase of various attacks through multiple means, such as the Web, e-mail, file sharing and instant messaging. To detect such unauthorized intrusions, proper technique is required. Intrusion detection is a key research area in the realm of Internet security [1]. It was developed to extend security visibility into the network and monitor the activity of users while they are on the network. Intrusion detection is the process of detecting and identifying unauthorized or unusual activity on the system. By using the audit trails, IDSs successfully detect any malicious or suspicious activity. Despite the great deal of substantive research for an intrusion detection method, many of the existing IDSs have no means of providing failure recovery methods that are able to recover its previous state and resume its operation unaffected [2]. It is critical that the design of a system be performed within the framework in chich IDS itself be resistant to and tolerant of attack attempts designed to obstruct its ability to correctly detect intrusions. To achieve high reliability, checkpointing and rollback recovery techniques are widely used in the parallel and distributed computing environment [3]. We believe that fault tolerant techniques can build

* This work was supported by grant No. R01-2002-000-00235-0 from the Basic Research Program of the Korea Science & Engineering Foundation

H. Chen et al. (Eds.): ISI 2004, LNCS 3073, pp. 476–483, 2004.

reliable intrusion detection systems from various intrusion patterns. In this paper, we propose a novel intrusion-tolerant IDS using communication-induced checkpointing and pessimistic message logging techniques. In addition, agents communicate with each other by sending messages without causality violation using vector timestamps. The rest of this paper is organized as follows. Section 2 illustrates the system model used in our proposal. Section 3 describes the novel fault tolerant mechanism using communication-induced checkpointing. Section 4 addresses and discusses the correctness for the proposed scheme. Finally, conclusions are presented in Section 5.

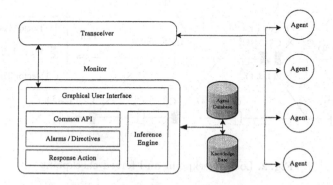

**Fig. 1.** The architecture of our proposed system

## 2   Architecture and Design

As shown in Fig. 1, our proposed system architecture is similar to that in [4], but it has an additional function compared to existing works. Each agent is an independently-running entity that performs *distributed computation* for certain aspects of a target host and reports doubtful activity to the appropriate transceiver. We define *distributed computation* as a collection of all communication events to detect intrusion behavior and agent failure of the target hosts. A distributed computation is performed by a set of $N$ agents, $\{A_1, A_2, \cdots, A_n\}$, running concurrently on target hosts in the network. Generally, a transceiver or a monitor will generate an alarm for the user based on information received from one or more agents. By combining the reports from different agents, transceivers build a picture of host status, and monitors build a picture of network status. Agents communicate directly or indirectly with each other in our proposed system. Each agent has a sequence of state transition for its execution and the atomic action. We assume that each ordered pair of agents is connected by an asynchronous, reliable, directed logical channel whose transmission delays are unpredictable but finite. Each agent runs on a different target hosts. For simplicity, we assume that agents follow fail-stop behavior [3]. Communication-induced checkpointing avoids the domino effect while allowing agents to take some of their checkpoints independently. However, agent independence is constrained to guarantee the eventual progress of the recovery line, and therefore agents may be forced to take additional checkpoints. The checkpoints that an agent takes independently are call local checkpoints, while those that an agent is forced to take are called forced checkpoints. A local checkpoint $C$ is a recorded state of an agent. $C_i^k$ represents the $k$-th local checkpoint of agent $A_i$ and $k$ is called the *sequence number* of this checkpoint.

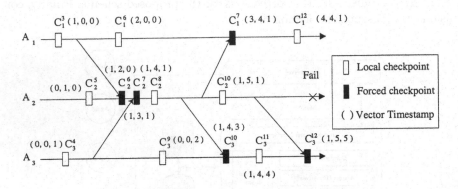

**Fig. 2.** Local checkpoint and forced checkpoint

Fig. 2 shows an example of local checkpoints and forced checkpoints in our proposed system. We assume that each agent $A_i$ takes an initial local checkpoint $C_i^0$, and after each event a checkpoint will eventually be taken. A global state is a collection of the individual states of all participating processes and of the states of the communication channel. Intuitively, a consistent global state is one that may occur during a fail-free, correct execution of a distributed computation, whereas inconsistent states occur because of failure. Causality is an important issue in the message passing system. Send and receive events signify the flow of information among agents and establish causal dependency from the sender agent to the receiver agent. Consequently, the causal precedence relation induces a partial order on the events of a distributed computation.

To avoid causality violation, each agent $A_i$ maintains a vector $vt_i[1, \cdots, n]$, where $vt_i[i]$ is the local logical clock of $A_i$ and describes the logical time progress at $A_i$. Let us consider the cases that each $A_1$ and $A_2$ sends monitoring message $m_1$ and $m_2$ to $A_3$, respectively. Upon the reception of $m_1$ and $m_2$, $A_3$ can detect whether intrusion behavior occurs on the target system. Assume that $m_1$ contains monitoring information for the "password crack" and $m_2$ contains monitoring information for the changing value in "/etc/passwd" files. In this case, $A_3$ has to receive the message $m_1$ prior to $m_2$. Using the vector timestamp, the proposed system can represent the causal precedence relation between these messages.

# 3   The Proposed Fault Tolerant Mechanism

In this section, we propose a rollback recovery algorithm for multi-agent based IDS. Each agent performs *distributed computation* to detect intrusion behavior and agent failure of the target system. It also sends monitoring message $m$ to the transceiver periodically. Sometimes multiple agents are required with each performing a single task. In that case, the transceiver receives monitoring messages from the several agents. To recover from agent failure, each agent takes local and forced checkpoints independently as follows.

---

**Algorithm 1 :**   Agent_CheckPointing Procedure

---

**I. Actions at Agent** $A_i$

```
00    Upon sending message m with C_i^{sn} to T_k :
01        sn ← sn + 1 and sflag ← 0
02        Takes a local checkpoint C_i^{sn} with its sn
03    Upon sending message m to A_j :
04        sflag ← 1
05    Upon receiving message m from A_j :
06        sn ← sn + 1
07        Takes a forced checkpoint C_i^{sn}
08    Upon receiving an ACK message from T_k :
09        if ( sn < rsn ) sn ← rsn
```

---

Each transceiver has a variable $gsn$, and each agent has the two variables $sn$ and $sflag$. We denote $sn$ as the sequence number of the latest local checkpoint taken by agent $A_i$. Also, $rsn$ denotes the received sequence number from the transceiver. Finally, we denote $gsn$ as the sequence number of the received latest local checkpoint from the agent at the transceiver and $lsn$ as the previous serial number of the last successful local checkpoint $C_i^{sn}$ in failed agent $A_i$. The initial value of $sn$ and $gsn$ are equal to 0. Whenever agent $A_i$ sends or receives message $m$ from and to other agent, it uses the following steps to update its clock.

- Step 1 : Before it takes local and forced checkpoints, $A_i$ updates its local logical time as $vt_i[i] = vt_i[i] + 1$.

- Step 2 : Each sender process piggybacks a message $m$ with its vector clock value at sending time. Upon receiving such a message $(m, vt)$, $A_i$ executes the following sequence of actions:

  1. Update its logical global time as $1 \leq k \leq n : vt_i[k] = \max(vt_i[k], vt[k])$.
  2. Execute Step 1.
  3. Deliver the message $m$.

An event's timestamp is the value of its agent's vector clock at the time the checkpointing is executed. Fig. 2 shows an example of a vector clock's progression. For example, if $A_3$ receives the message $m$ with $C_3^{12}$ prior to $C_3^{10}$, causality violation occurs (i.e., $5 > 4$). In this case, $A_3$ hold a monitoring task until reception of message $m$ with $C_3^{10}$ if there is the causal precedence relationship between $C_3^{10}$ and $C_3^{12}$ at $A_3$. Algorithm 1 shows the agent checkpointing procedure in each agent. When it is time for agent $A_i$ to take a local checkpoint, it increases the value of $sn$ and sets the value of $sflag$ to zero. Then, it takes a local checkpoint with sequence number $sn$ and sends $C_i^{sn}$ with its monitoring message $m$ to transceiver $T_k$. Finally, $A_i$ receives an acknowledge (ACK) message with $rsn$ from transceiver $T_k$. If the value of $rsn$ is larger than $sn$, $A_i$ changes the value of $sn$ to $rsn$. Whenever $A_i$ sends monitoring message $m$ to other agent $A_j$, it sets value of $sflag$ to 1. After receiving monitoring message $m$ with $C_i^{sn}$ from $A_i$, transceiver $T_k$ performs the transceiver checkpointing procedure as shown in Algorithm 2.

---

**Algorithm 2 :**  Transceiver_CheckPointing Procedure

**II. Actions at Transceiver $T_k$**
```
00   Upon receiving message m with C_i^{sn} from A_i :
01      rsn ← sn
02      Compares the received sn from C_i^{sn} with its gsn
03      if ( sn > gsn ) gsn ← sn
04      else if (sn ≤ gsn) rsn ← gsn
05      Takes local checkpoint C_k^{gsn}
06      Sends an ACK message to A_i with rsn
07      Finally, it sends monitoring message m to its monitor
```

---

Then, $T_k$ then sets the value of $rsn$ to $sn$ and compares the received $sn$ from $C_i^{sn}$ with its $gsn$. If the value of $sn$ is larger than $gsn$, it sets the value of $gsn$ to $sn$. Otherwise, it sets the value of $rsn$ to $gsn$. After setting the value of $gsn$, it takes local checkpoint $C_k^{gsn}$ and sends the monitoring message $m$ to its monitor. Finally, transceiver $T_k$ sends an ACK message to $A_i$ with $rsn$. The value of $gsn$ is used to keep the sequence number of the latest local checkpoints of the agents at the transceiver and helps in the progression of the consistent global snapshot. In Fig. 2, the initial sequence number $sn$ of $A_1$, $A_2$, and $A_3$ is 1 and the current value of $gsn$ of $T_4$ is 3. When $A_1$ takes a local checkpoint, its $sn$ changes to 2, and sends monitoring message $m$ with $C_1^2$ to $T_4$. Because $gsn$ is larger than $sn$ (i.e., $3 > 2$), $T_4$ sets the value of $rsn$ to 3 and sends an ACK message with $rsn$. Finally, $A_1$ changes $sn$ to 3 because $rsn$ is larger than its $sn$ (i.e., $3 > 2$).

---

**Algorithm 3 :**  Asynchronous_Recovery Procedure

**III. Actions at Failed Agent $A_i$**
```
00   When an agent A_i fails :
01      A_i send message m to transceiver T_k with i and sflag
02   When the failed agent is restarted :
03      Transceiver sends RollbackRecovery(C_i^{lsn}) message to A_i
04      A_i recovers its previous status
05      A_i resumes operation after latest checkpoint using C_i^{lsn}
```

**IV. Actions at Transceiver $T_k$**

```
00   When a transceiver receives message m from failed agent A_i :
01        It finds lsn from earliest local checkpoint C_i^{sn}
02        if (sflag ≠ 0) {
03           gsn ← lsn
04           It rolls back to checkpoint C_k^{gsn}
05           All checkpoints beyond gsn are deleted
06           It sends RollbackRecovery(gsn) message to all other agents
07        }
```

**V. Actions at Agent $A_j$**

```
00   When A_j receives RollbackRecovery(gsn) message from T_k :
01        if (sn from its C_j^{sn} > gsn){
02           sn ← gsn and it rolls back to checkpoint C_j^{sn}
03           All checkpoints beyond C_j^{sn} are deleted
04        }
```

Algorithm 3 shows an asynchronous recovery algorithm for a consistent global snapshot in multi-agent based IDS. When an agent $A_i$ fails, it sends a message to the transceiver with agent number $i$ and $sflag$, which then finds the previous serial number $lsn$ from the last successful local checkpoint $C_i^{sn}$ for the failed agent. Then, the transceiver examines the value of $sflag$ from the received message for $A_i$. If $sflag$ is equal to zero, it implies that $A_i$ does not send any messages to other agents after the last checkpoint $C_i^{lsn}$. Thus, transceiver $T_k$ only sends $RollbackRecovery(C_i^{lsn})$ message to failed agent $A_i$ after failed agent $A_i$ is restarted, enabling $A_i$ to recover its previous status and resume its operation after the latest checkpoint using $C_i^{lsn}$.

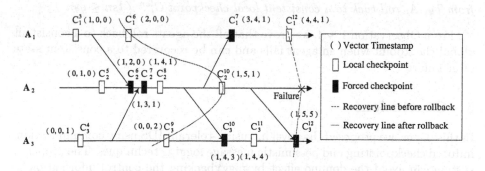

**Fig. 3.** Local checkpoint and forced checkpoint

Conversely, if $sflag$ is not equal to zero, it sets a value of $gsn$ to $lsn$ and rolls back to checkpoint $C_k^{gsn}$ and all the checkpoints beyond $C_k^{gsn}$ are deleted for all agents. Finally, it sends $RollbackRecovery(gsn)$ messages to all other agents as well as sending a $RollbackRecovery(C_i^{lsn})$ message to failed agent $A_i$ after failed agent $A_i$ is restarted. Thus, all agents roll back to their latest local checkpoint where the sequence number $sn$ is less than or equal to consistent global snapshot $gsn$. In Fig. 3, $T_4$ receives the value of 2 $(i)$ and 1 $(sflag)$ from failed agent $A_2$, and finds a value of 10 $(lsn)$ from its checkpoints. Then, $T_4$ rolls back to checkpoint $C_4^{10}$ and all the checkpoints beyond $C_4^{10}$ (i.e., $C_4^{11}$ and $C_4^{12}$) are deleted. Finally, $T_4$ changes the value of $gsn$ to 10 and sends $RollbackRecovery(10)$ message to all other agents because the value of $sflag$ is equal to 1. As a result, $A_1$ and $A_3$ roll back to checkpoint $C_1^6$ and $C_3^9$. When the failed agent $A_2$ is restarted, $T_4$ sends a message with $C_2^{10}$ to $A_2$. Fig 3 illustrates the recovery line before and after the rollback.

## 4    Discussion

In this section, we present a formal proof of correctness to the proposed system.

**Observation 1** *A rolled-back agent maintains the consistency of inter-agent collaboration and internal services state since communication channels and stable storage are assumed reliable.*

**Observation 2** *If $sent(m) \in C_i^{sn}$ then sn is less than gsn for any message m sent by $A_i$ based on the Lamport's happen-before relationship [3]. The converse is true. For any message m received by $A_i$, if $receive(m) \in C_i^{sn}$ then sn is less than gsn. Also, the converse is true.*

**Observation 3** *All the agents roll back to its local checkpoint $C_i^{sn}$ (where sn $\leq$ gsn) when they receive $RollbackRecovery(gsn)$ message from $T_k$. Thus, the value of gsn is larger than or equal to sn.*

**Observation 4** *When the failed $A_i$ receives $RollbackRecovery(C_i^{lsn})$ message from $T_k$, $A_i$ roll back to a consistent local checkpoint $C_i^{lsn}$ ( lsn $\leq$ gsn ).*

From Observation 1 $\sim$ 4, we prove that all the agents roll back to a consistent global checkpoint when an agent fails and can be recovered to a consistent state after failure.

## 5    Conclusions

In this paper, we proposed the novel intrusion-tolerant IDS using communication-induced checkpointing and pessimistic message logging techniques. The proposed system can avoid the domino effect by piggybacking the control information to the application message. In our proposal, each agent takes a local checkpoint as well as forced checkpoint when it receives a message from another agent. Using the sequence number and global sequence number, all agents roll back to a consistent global checkpoint when an agent fails. When the failed agent is restarted, it can recover to its previous state and resume its operation unaffected. In addition, agents communicate with each other by sending messages without causality violation using vector stamps. Thus, our proposed system guarantees a consistent global snapshot.

# References

1. Denning, D. E.: An intrusion-dection model. Proceeding of Symposium on Security and Privacy (1986) 118-131
2. Crosbie, E., Spafford, E. H.: Active defense of computer system using autonomous agents. Technical report, COAST Group, Purdue University (1995)
3. Elnozahy, E. N., Johnson, D. B., Wang, Y.M.: A survey of rollbalck-tecovery protocols in message passing systems. CMU Technical Report CMU-CS-99-148 (1999)
4. Balasubramaniyan, J. S., Farcia-Fernandez, J. O., Isacoff, D., Spafford, E., Zamboni, D.: An architecture for intrusion detection using autonomous agents. Technical report, COAST Laboratory, Purdue University (1998)
5. Myung-Kyu Yi., Chong-Sun Hwang.: Design of fault tolerant architecture for intrusion detection system using autonomous agents," Proceedings of the International Conference on Information Networking (2003)
6. Myung-Kyu Yi., Maeng-Soon Baik., Chong-Sun Hwang.: Design of fault tolerant mechanism for multi-agent based intrusion detection system. Proceedings of the International Conference on Security and Management (2003)
7. Ran Zhang., Depei Qian., Chongming Ba., Weiguo Wu., Xiaobing Guo.: Multi-agent based intrusion detection architecture. Proceedings of the International Conference on Computer Networks and Mobile Computing (2001) 494 -501

# Optimal Redundancy Allocation
# for Disaster Recovery Planning in the Network Economy

Benjamin B.M. Shao

W. P. Carey School of Business
Arizona State University
Tempe, AZ 85287
Ben.Shao@asu.edu

**Abstract.** In the present network economy, businesses are becoming increasingly reliant on information technology (IT) to perform their operations and exchange information with business partners. This heavy dependence on IT, however, poses a potential threat for an organization. When disasters strike and cause malfunction to its computing and communicating systems, it would be vulnerable to business discontinuity. As a result, the issue of how to strengthen IT capabilities so that a company can prevent or quickly recover from disasters becomes a serious concern. In this paper, a discrete optimization model is proposed to allocate redundancy to IT assets for disaster recovery planning. The objective is to maximize the overall survivability of an organization's critical IT functions by selecting their appropriate redundancy levels while still satisfying a budgetary resource constraint. A solution procedure based on probabilistic dynamic programming is proposed to solve the problem, and an example is used to illustrate its usage and effectiveness.

## 1 Introduction

Modern organizations have become increasingly reliant on information technology (IT) to facilitate their businesses. Large-scale databases handled by high-speed computers retrieve, analyze, and synthesize data collected from different sources. Communication networks like the Internet exchange, share, and transmit information in real time between suppliers, vendors, and buyers in an industry value chain to carry out business transactions. Computer-aided design technologies help the development team capture more customer requirements and develop better products that meet their specific needs. These few examples demonstrate that IT is being harnessed as a key enabler for an organization's operations in the present network economy [4].

This increased reliance on IT, however, poses a potential threat for an organization. When the occurrence of disasters affects its IT operations and causes failures, the organization may suffer from the interruption of business functions. As a result, the issue of how to strengthen IT capabilities so that a company can prevent or quickly recover from disasters becomes a serious concern. Clearly, an organization depending on IT to support its business processes and functions needs effective IT security measures to ensure business continuity in the event of disaster strikes [10]. Further, firms in the network economy no longer suffer alone from disasters. When a disaster occurs,

H. Chen et al. (Eds.): ISI 2004, LNCS 3073, pp. 484–491, 2004.

business partners, both upstream and downstream in the industry value chain, may too suffer from the concomitant consequences. The effects caused by a disaster can migrate to other entities over the virtual or physical network [7]. A thorough decision analysis aids in identifying, evaluating and strengthening critical IT functions that must be maintained in case of a disaster [13]. A disaster recovery plan is defined as "a system for internal control and security that focuses on quick restoration for critical organizational processes when there are operational failures due to natural or manmade disasters [3]." The objective of an IT disaster recovery plan is to ensure that an organization's computing and communication systems operate smoothly and uninterruptedly during and after the occurrence of a disaster.

Despite the unequivocal importance of IT disaster recovery planning, little research has been done so far on the formal modeling of its decision-making process. It has been suggested that many of the issues encountered in disaster recovery planning can benefit from the application of quantitative decision-making techniques [3]. In this paper, a discrete optimization model is proposed to assist IT managers in allocating redundancy level for IT assets so that the overall risks against potential disasters can be reduced. Our model takes into account the criticality and costs of IT assets as well as the limitation on resources subject to budget availability.

## 2 Redundancy for IT Disaster Recovery

The use of redundancy in preparation for disasters is of potential advantage because it can simultaneously address two aspects of disaster preparation–proactive prevention and reactive recovery. Before a disaster occurs, redundant components can mitigate the potential risks by working as backup facilities and preventing the disastrous consequences in advance [5]. After a disaster occurs, organizations can quickly restore business functions and processes back to normal by substituting redundant components for the primary but disabled parts while they are being repaired.

Clearly, IT assets differ in their potential risks and costs. As such, redundancy at different levels also has different cost and benefit implications. A redundant module in fault-tolerant software would likely cost only a little to develop but the risk mitigated by its presence is probably small as well. On the other hand, a full-scale duplicated hot site requires a large investment but can provide a much better protection against a disaster; thus, it may be a viable option for large size companies only. The objective is thus to select among these competing alternatives for redundancy level and reap the best returns subject to resource limitations. A quantitative analytical model can provide the guidelines for allocating the optimal redundancy level to valuable IT assets that need the most protection in a cost-conscious and rational way.

While the technique of integer programming has recently been applied to the selection of disaster scenarios [8], most other studies have either focused on the area of risk analysis [13] or been reactive in nature by primarily dealing with the operational post-disaster activities [11]. In answer to the call for more rigorous quantitative analyses of the pre-disaster IT recovery planning [3], we develop a discrete optimization model to help ensure that IT disaster recovery plans function as expected when put into work.

## 3  Redundancy Allocation Model

Suppose a firm is planning for disaster recovery by considering incorporating redundancy level for its IT functions, and the budget is limited. Several possible disasters have been identified with the potential to cause business discontinuity by affecting the supporting IT functions. The question is how to allocate redundancy to these IT functions such that the overall survivability of these IT functions against disasters is maximized and the cost remains under control. Below are the notations and their definitions used in the model.

$D$: number of potential disasters + 1 (the last one for no disaster occurring);

$p_d$: probability of disaster $d$ occurring, $p_d \in (0, 1)$ and $\displaystyle\sum_{d=1}^{D} p_d = 1$;

$M$: number of IT functions the organization needs to perform;

$w_m$: importance weight (or frequency of usage) of IT function $m$, $w_m \in (0, 1)$

and $\displaystyle\sum_{m=1}^{M} w_m = 1$;

$n_m$: number of solutions (assets) available for IT function $m$ to select from;

$X_{mi}$: 1 if solution $i$ (= 1, ..., $n_m$) is selected for IT function $m$, or 0 otherwise;

$C_{mi}$: cost of selecting solution $i$ for IT function $m$;

$S_{mid}$: survivability of solution $i$ for IT function $m$ against disaster $d$;

$e_{mid}$: failure probability of solution $i$ for IT function $m$ against disaster $d$, i.e.,

$e_{mid} = 1 - S_{mid}$;

$B$: available budget.

The following model is formulated to maximize the overall survivability of the $M$ independent IT functions:

$$(RAP) \quad \max S^* = \sum_{d=1}^{D} p_d \sum_{m=1}^{M} w_m \left[ 1 - \prod_{i=1}^{n_m} e_{mid}^{X_{mi}} \right]$$

subject to

$$\sum_{i=1}^{n_m} X_{mi} \geq 1, m = 1, \ldots, M \tag{1}$$

$$\sum_{m=1}^{M} \sum_{i=1}^{n_m} C_{mi} X_{mi} \leq B \tag{2}$$

$$X_{mi} = 0 \text{ or } 1, \quad \text{for } m = 1, \ldots, M \text{ and } i = 1, \ldots, n_m \tag{3}$$

# 4 Solution Procedure and Example

The proposed model of (RAP) is a 0-1 integer programming problem with a nonlinear objective function. For small problem instances, total enumeration or mathematical software packages can be used to solve (RAP). However, for relatively large problems, such approaches are likely impractical. Further, owing to the non-linearity of the objective function, Lagrangian relaxation cannot be employed to help tackle this discrete optimization problem. As such, a partial enumeration solution procedure based on probabilistic dynamic programming [14] is presented to accelerate the solution of (RAP). We first reformulate (RAP) as a minimization problem by rewriting the objective function as follows:

$$S^* = \sum_{d=1}^{D} P_d \sum_{m=1}^{M} w_m \left[ 1 - \prod_{i=1}^{n_m} e_{mid}{}^{X_{mi}} \right] = \sum_{d=1}^{D} P_d \sum_{m=1}^{M} w_m - \sum_{d=1}^{D} P_d \sum_{m=1}^{M} w_m \prod_{i=1}^{n_m} e_{mid}{}^{X_{mi}}$$

$$= \sum_{d=1}^{D} P_d - \sum_{d=1}^{D} P_d \sum_{m=1}^{M} w_m \prod_{i=1}^{n_m} e_{mid}{}^{X_{mi}} = 1 - \sum_{d=1}^{D} P_d \sum_{m=1}^{M} w_m \prod_{i=1}^{n_m} e_{mid}{}^{X_{mi}}$$

To maximize $S^*$ is equivalent to minimizing $F^* = \sum_{d=1}^{D} P_d \sum_{m=1}^{M} w_m \prod_{i=1}^{n_m} e_{mid}{}^{X_{mi}}$ , which

is the sum of failure probabilities of any IT function due to any disaster. Next, we define a state of system $T$ as the remaining budget, and stage $m$ to represent IT function $m$ for $m = 1,\ldots, M$. Let $F_m(T)$ be the failure rate of the system composed of IT functions $m, m + 1,\ldots, M$, given that $T$ is the remaining budget for IT functions $1,\ldots, m - 1$. The recursive formula for $F_m(T)$ when $m < M$ is:

$$F_m(T) = \min\left( w_m \sum_{d=1}^{D} P_d \prod_{i=1}^{n_m} e_{mid}{}^{X_{mi}} + F_{m+1}(B - \sum_{i=1}^{n_m} C_{mi} X_{mi}) \right) \qquad (4)$$

where the variables $X_{mi}$ are restricted to those that satisfy

$$\sum_{i=1}^{n_m} X_{mi} \geq 1, \quad \text{and} \quad \sum_{i=1}^{n_m} C_{mi} X_{mi} \leq T$$

For stage (IT function) $m$, state (budget) $T$ cannot exceed the total available budget $B$ minus the minimum costs to be allocated for previous stages $1,\ldots, m - 1$, and it must be at least equal to the cost of the least expensive solution in the current stage to guarantee at least one solution for IT function $m$. Thus, $F_m(T)$ should be calculated for all $T$ values in the range:

$$T = \left( \min_{i=1,\ldots,n_m} \{C_{mi}\}, \ldots, B - \sum_{r=1}^{m-1} \min_{i=1,\ldots,n_r} \{C_{ri}\} \right) \qquad (5)$$

For states not in the specified range, $F_m(T)$ can be defined as 1 so it would never be the minimum chosen by Eq. (4) for stages $1,\ldots, m - 1$.

The solution procedure is based on probabilistic dynamic programming because, unlike deterministic dynamic programming, $F_m(T)$ of Eq. (4) deals with the uncertainty of disaster occurring and involves the calculation of *expected* failure rate of IT function $m$ based on the remaining budget $T$. The solution procedure solves (RAP) by working backwards with the initial stage $m = M$ and

$$F_M(T) = \min\left( w_M \sum_{d=1}^{D} p_d \prod_{i=1}^{n_M} e_{Mid}{}^{X_{Mi}} \right) \qquad (6)$$

where again the variables $X_{Mi}$ satisfy

$$\sum_{i=1}^{n_M} X_{Mi} \geq 1, \quad \text{and} \quad \sum_{i=1}^{n_M} C_{Mi} X_{Mi} \leq T$$

The optimal objective value $F^*$ is obtained as $F_1(B)$ and represents the overall failure rate of the whole system, and the original survivability $S^*$ is equal to $1 - F_1(B)$.

## Example

To demonstrate the effectiveness of the proposed model and solution procedure, we consider a hypothetical example in which a company performs two IT functions ($M = 2$) for its business operations. IT function 1 is used 30% of the time ($w_1 = 0.30$) and IT function 2 is used 70% of the time ($w_2 = 0.70$). The company is susceptible to a flooding disaster that occurs with a likelihood of 0.05 ($p_1 = 0.05$ and $p_2 = 0.95$ for no disaster). The company is now considering incorporating redundancy for these two IT functions with a budget $B = 14$.

For IT function 1, four solutions are available ($n_1 = 4$), with associated costs of $C_{11} = 8$, $C_{12} = 3$, $C_{13} = 7$, and $C_{14} = 5$. Their survival rates against the flooding are $S_{111} = 0.10$, $S_{121} = 0.05$, $S_{131} = 0.08$, and $S_{141} = 0.12$ (i.e., $e_{111} = 0.90$, $e_{121} = 0.95$, $e_{131} = 0.92$, and $e_{141} = 0.88$). Their reliabilities when no disaster occurs are $S_{112} = 0.95$, $S_{122} = 0.88$, $S_{132} = 0.92$, and $S_{142} = 0.85$ (i.e., $e_{112} = 0.05$, $e_{122} = 0.12$, $e_{132} = 0.08$, and $e_{142} = 0.15$). For IT function 2, three solutions are available ($n_2 = 3$), with associated costs of $C_{21} = 4$, $C_{22} = 6$, and $C_{23} = 3$. Their survival rates against the flooding are $S_{211} = 0.06$, $S_{221} = 0.10$, and $S_{231} = 0.20$ (i.e., $e_{211} = 0.94$, $e_{221} = 0.90$, and $e_{231} = 0.80$). Their reliabilities when no disaster occurs are $S_{212} = 0.92$, $S_{222} = 0.78$, and $S_{232} = 0.84$ (i.e., $e_{212} = 0.08$, $e_{222} = 0.22$, and $e_{232} = 0.16$). The example problem can be formulated as:

$$\max S^* = 0.05\left[0.30\left(1 - 0.90^{X_{11}} 0.95^{X_{12}} 0.92^{X_{13}} 0.88^{X_{14}}\right) + 0.70\left(1 - 0.94^{X_{21}} 0.90^{X_{22}} 0.80^{X_{23}}\right)\right]$$
$$+ 0.95\left[0.30\left(1 - 0.05^{X_{11}} 0.12^{X_{12}} 0.08^{X_{13}} 0.15^{X_{14}}\right) + 0.70\left(1 - 0.08^{X_{21}} 0.22^{X_{22}} 0.16^{X_{23}}\right)\right]$$

subject to

$$X_{11} + X_{12} + X_{13} + X_{14} \geq 1$$
$$X_{21} + X_{22} + X_{23} \geq 1$$
$$8X_{11} + 3X_{12} + 7X_{13} + 5X_{14} + 4X_{21} + 6X_{22} + 3X_{23} \leq 14$$
$$X_{mi} = 0 \text{ or } 1, \quad \text{for all } m, i$$

To apply the solution procedure to this problem instance, we start with stage $m = 2$. Since the least expensive solution for IT function 2 has cost $C_{23} = 3$ and the least expensive solution for the only remaining IT function 1 also has cost $C_{12} = 3$, the valid range for $T$ is $3 \leq T \leq 11$ ($= 14 - 3$). Eq. (6) then calculates $F_2(T)$ for $T = 3,\ldots, 11$. For instance, $F_2(7)$ is calculated as:

$$F_2(7) = \min \left\{ (0.70)[\ (0.05)(0.94)^{X_{21}}(0.90)^{X_{22}}(0.80)^{X_{23}} + (0.95)(0.08)^{X_{21}}(0.22)^{X_{22}}(0.16)^{X_{23}}\ ] \right\}$$

where the variables $X_{2i}$ satisfy $X_{21} + X_{22} + X_{23} \geq 1$ and $4X_{21} + 6X_{22} + 3X_{23} \leq 7$. There are four sets of $X_{2i}$ qualified for $F_2(7)$, and they are $(X_{21}, X_{22}, X_{23}) = (0, 0, 1)$, $(0, 1, 0)$, $(1, 0, 0)$, and $(1, 0, 1)$. The minimum $F_2(7)$ is found associated with $(X_{21}, X_{22}, X_{23}) = (1, 0, 1)$ with $F_2(7) = 0.0348$. The complete results for $F_2(T)$ are shown in Table 1.

**Table 1.** State $T$, Solution, and $F_2(T)$ for Stage 2 with $B = 14$

| $T$ | Solution | $F_2(T)$ |
|---|---|---|
| 3 | $X_{23} = 1$, other $X_{mi} = 0$ | 0.1344 |
| 4 | $X_{21} = 1$, other $X_{mi} = 0$ | 0.0861 |
| 5 | $X_{21} = 1$, other $X_{mi} = 0$ | 0.0861 |
| 6 | $X_{21} = 1$, other $X_{mi} = 0$ | 0.0861 |
| 7 | $X_{21} = 1$, $X_{23} = 1$, other $X_{mi} = 0$ | 0.0348 |
| 8 | $X_{21} = 1$, $X_{23} = 1$, other $X_{mi} = 0$ | 0.0348 |
| 9 | $X_{21} = 1$, $X_{23} = 1$, other $X_{mi} = 0$ | 0.0348 |
| 10 | $X_{21} = 1$, $X_{23} = 1$, other $X_{mi} = 0$ | 0.0348 |
| 11 | $X_{21} = 1$, $X_{23} = 1$, other $X_{mi} = 0$ | 0.0348 |

Next, we proceed to find the optimal solution $F_1(14)$ in the next stage $m = 1$:

$$F_1(14) = \min \{ (0.30)[(0.05)(0.90)^{X_{11}}(0.95)^{X_{12}}(0.92)^{X_{13}}(0.88)^{X_{14}}$$

$$+ (0.95)(0.05)^{X_{11}}(0.12)^{X_{12}}(0.08)^{X_{13}}(0.15)^{X_{14}}] + F_2(14 - \sum_{i=1}^{4} C_{1i}X_{1i})\}$$

where the variables $X_{1i}$ satisfy $X_{11} + X_{12} + X_{13} + X_{14} \geq 1$ and $8X_{11} + 3X_{12} + 7X_{13} + 5X_{14} \leq 14$. There are seven sets of $X_{1i}$ qualified for $F_1(14)$, and they are $(X_{11}, X_{12}, X_{13}, X_{14}) = (1, 0, 0, 0)$, $(0, 1, 0, 0)$, $(0, 0, 1, 0)$, $(0, 0, 0, 1)$, $(1, 1, 0, 0)$, $(0, 1, 1, 0)$, and $(0, 1, 0, 1)$. The minimum $F_1(14)$ is found associated with $(X_{11}, X_{12}, X_{13}, X_{14}) = (0, 0, 1, 0)$ with $F^* = 0.0714$ using $F_2(7) = 0.0348$. Therefore, the maximum overall survivability $S^*$ against flooding is $1 - F^* = 1 - 0.0714 = 0.9286$ by selecting solution 3 for IT function 1 ($X_{13} = 1$) as well as solutions 1 and 3 for IT function 2 ($X_{21} = X_{23} = 1$).

490    Benjamin B.M. Shao

# 5  Conclusion

The proposed model is a generalization of the reliability optimization models for software and hardware [1]. When no disaster is considered possible (i.e., $D = 1$ in our model), (RAP) is reduced to a reliability problem dealing with fault tolerance [9]. In other words, the model proposed in the paper is able to handle such special cases of software and hardware reliability as well. In addition, (RAP) is closely related to the general discrete resource allocation problems [6][12], but it considers a variety of IT resource types for supporting specific IT functions, instead of general resources that can be allocated to every activity or agent.

Topics are suggested for future research. The IT functions considered are treated as independent. This assumption may have an effect on the granularity of IT assets being relatively large since finer-grained IT assets typically can serve multiple purposes. In future study, the proposed model can be extended to address interrelated IT functions by modifying the objective function. The approach of probabilistic dynamic programming is still applicable for this extended problem [2]. Moreover, we can categorize IT assets as hardware, software, human capitals, and other types to examine the impacts of IT asset characteristics on the redundancy allocation decisions. For example, tangible hardware cannot be duplicated without purchasing two equipments, but software with proper licenses can be easily deployed to many IT assets. Their costs implications thus are expected to be distinct. Another topic can look at redundancy allocations at the industry level and analyze disaster recovery planning across business partners in a coordinated and collaborative manner.

# References

1. Ashrafi, N., Berman, O.: Optimization Models for Selection of Programs, Considering Cost & Reliability. IEEE Trans. Reliab. 41 (1992) 281-287.
2. Berman, O., Ashrafi, N.: Optimization Models for Reliability of Modular Software Systems. IEEE Trans. Softw. Eng. 19 (1993) 1119-1123.
3. Bryson, K., Millar, H., Joseph, A., Mobolurin, A.: Using Formal MS/OR Modeling to Support Disaster Recovery Planning. Eur. J. Oper. Res. 141 (2002) 679-688.
4. Chengalur-Smith, I., Belardo, S., Pazer, H.: Adopting a Disaster-Management-Based Contingency Model to the Problem of Ad Hoc Forecasting: Toward Information Technology-Based Strategies. IEEE Trans. Eng. Manage. 46 (1999) 210-220.
5. Grabowski, M., Merrick, J.R.W., Harrald, J.R., Mazzuchi, T.A., van Dorp, J.R.: Risk Modeling in Distributed, Large-Scale Systems. IEEE Trans. Syst. Man Cybern.-Part A: Syst. Hum. 30 (2000) 651-660.
6. Ibaraki, T., Katoh, N.: Resource Allocation Problems. MIT Press, MA (1988).
7. Iyer, R.K., Sarkis, J.: Disaster Recovery Planning in an Automated Manufacturing Environment. IEEE Trans. Eng. Manag. 45 (1998) 163-175.
8. Jenkins, L.: Selecting Scenarios for Environmental Disaster Planning. Eur. J. Oper. Res. 121 (2000) 275-286.
9. Kuo, W., Prasad, V.R.: An Annotated Overview of System-Reliability Optimization. IEEE Trans. Reliab. 49 (2000) 176-187.

10. Lewis, Jr., W., Watson, R.T., Pickren, A.: An Empirical Assessment of IT Disaster Risk. Commun. ACM 49 (2003) 201-206.
11. Pidd, M., deSilva, F., Eglese, R.: A Simulation Study for Emergency Evacuation. Eur. J. Oper. Res. 90 (1996) 413-419.
12. Shao, B.B.M., Rao, H.R.: A Comparative Analysis of Information Acquisition Mechanisms for Discrete Resource Allocation. IEEE Trans. Syst. Man Cybern.-Part A: Syste. Hum. 31 (2001) 199-209.
13. Tamura, H., Yamamoto, K., Tomiyama, S., Hatono, I.: Modeling and Analysis of Decision Making Problem for Mitigating Natural Disaster Risks. Eur. J. Oper. Res. 122 (2000) 461-468.
14. Winston, W.L.: Operations Research: Application and Algorithms. PWS Publishers, Boston, MA (1987).

# Semantic Analysis for Monitoring Insider Threats

Svetlana Symonenko[1], Elizabeth D. Liddy[1], Ozgur Yilmazel[1],
Robert Del Zoppo[2], Eric Brown[2], and Matt Downey[2]

[1]Center for Natural Language Processing, School of Information Studies,
Syracuse University, Syracuse NY 13444
+1 315.443.5484
{ssymonen,liddy,oyilmaz}@mailbox.syr.edu
[2]Information Technologies Center, Syracuse Research Corporation
6225 Running Ridge Road, North Syracuse NY 13212
+1 315.452.8000
{delzoppo,brown,downey}@syrres.com

**Abstract.** Malicious insiders' difficult-to-detect activities pose serious threats to the intelligence community (IC) when these activities go undetected. A novel approach that integrates the results of social network analysis, role-based access monitoring, and semantic analysis of insiders' communications as evidence for evaluation by a risk assessor is being tested on an IC simulation. A semantic analysis, by our proven Natural Language Processing (NLP) system, of the insider's text-based communications produces conceptual representations that are clustered and compared on the expected vs. observed scope. The determined risk level produces an input to a risk analysis algorithm that is merged with outputs from the system's social network analysis and role-based monitoring modules.

## 1 Introduction

Malicious insiders' activities pose serious threats to the intelligence community (IC) when they go undetected. A malicious insider is someone who, while a valid user of IC systems, decides to perform unauthorized malicious acts, including sharing of information with groups unfriendly to the US. The research described herein is being conducted as part of ARDA's Information Assurance for the Intelligence Community Program, and therefore, it is being modeled on and tested in a simulated IC malicious insider threat scenario developed by Subject Matter Experts (SMEs) on our project with years of experience with the community. The goal of this ARDA program is to develop solutions for efficiently detecting such unwanted behaviors. While the IC is the main focus of our development efforts, the banking and securities industries have the same need to recognize potential insider threats and will be able to utilize this model for recognizing abnormal cyber behavior of their employees.

To accomplish our goal, we are developing and testing an Insider Threat Model that integrates Context, Role, and Semantics, here defined as: Context – the social network of the analyst's organizational relationships and patterns of communication; Role – the analyst's assigned job functions, and; Semantics – the content of the in-

---

[1] http://www.ic-arda.org/Advanced_IC/

H. Chen et al. (Eds.): ISI 2004, LNCS 3073, pp. 492–500, 2004.

formation produced or accessed by the analyst. Our full insider threat solution integrates evidence from social network analysis and role-based access monitoring of system usage with our semantic analysis of insiders' cyber communications as inputs to a risk analysis algorithm. Given these inputs, the model will detect levels of insider threat risk by comparing expected cyber behaviors against observed cyber behaviors. The output is an indication of the potential risk of an insider threat within the organization.

This paper reports on the Semantic Analysis approach that combines Natural Language Processing (NLP) and machine learning (clustering). NLP has proven successful in a range of applications of significance to the intelligence community (IC). Most of these applications support the IC's need for improved representation of, and access to, large amounts of textual information for tasks such as information retrieval, question-answering, cross-language information retrieval, cross-document summarization, and information extraction. In the research we are herein reporting, we adapt our proven NLP capabilities to provide fine-grained content representation and analysis of text-based communications in a novel application – detecting insider threats via semantic analysis of texts produced or accessed by IC analysts.

## 2 Operational Scenario

Intelligence analysts operate within a mission-based context, focused mainly on specific topics of interest (TOIs) and geo-political areas of interest (AOIs) that they are assigned. The role the analyst plays dictates the TOI/AOI, organizational relationships, communication patterns, intelligence products and information systems needed, and the intelligence work products created, thereby the need for monitoring Context, Role, and Semantics. The demonstration scenario we will be testing within is based on an organizational network of analysts working in various groups. Our scenario is based on a fictitious government agency with fictitious information targets. However, our SMEs will ensure that the scenario will be representative of the information assurance problem of malicious insider threats in the U.S. Intelligence Community.

## 3 Related Work

To the best of our knowledge, there is no account of the integrated social context, role, and semantics approach that we are taking. While some projects have addressed these dimensions individually, most research appears to be focused on *cyber threat* and *cyber security*. When semantics has been utilized, it is applied to describe the role-based access policy of an organization [4,16]. Research by Raskin et al. [12] aims to use a natural language-based ontology to scan texts for indicators of possible intellectual property leakage.

The 2003 NSF/NIJ Symposium on Intelligence and Security Informatics marked an increased interest in the research community in applying linguistic analysis to the problems of cyber security. Stolfo et al. [15] mined subject lines of email messages for patterns typical for particular user groups (e.g. software developers vs. the legal department). Patman & Thompson [11] reported on the implementation of a personal name disambiguation module that utilizes knowledge of cultural contexts. Burgoon et al. [6] looked for linguistic indicators of deception in interview transcripts. Zhou et al. [20] conducted a longitudinal study of linguistic cues of deception in email messages. Zheng et al. [19] compared machine-learning algorithms on the task of recognizing the authorship of email messages, and evaluated the efficiency of using different semantic, structural, and content-specific features. Sreenath et al. [13] employed latent semantic analysis to reconstruct users' original queries from their online browsing paths and applied this technique to detecting malicious (terrorist) trends.

Our work is aligned with intrusion detection (ID) research in that it addresses the problem of unauthorized access to or manipulation of information and, methodologically, is close to anomaly detection [3, 8]. The novelty of our work is in the problem and the scope. First, the insider is not equaled to an intruder, as the former may possess required system security clearance. Next, the patterns that we are seeking to detect may look legitimate but, when considering the users' assignment (topics and geopolitical focus), they indicate that the insider's activities are out of range of "expected behavior". Finally, while document access is an important characteristic of insider behavior, the content of information accessed eludes the existing ID techniques, as only so much can be detected from resource names and tags. To address this, we propose a document-driven approach that focuses not on the system- or network-related events, but on the content of information accessed or manipulated. Our task is to assess the semantic distance between the content of the documents that the insider is currently accessing and creating and the expected content, given the analyst's assigned TOI and AOI. For this purpose, concept-based semantic analysis will be applied to the wide range of textual documents that analysts use and produce while working on a task, e.g. documents provided by other organizations or from internal collections, email communication, or database or Internet query logs.

## 4 Approach

The insider threat scenario described above presents the following *problem* amenable to the semantic analysis module of our system. Given the set of textual data available electronically and ranging in genre from news articles to analyst reports, official documents, email messages, query logs, and so on, the system will identify the TOI / AOI mentioned in the documents and compare them against the expected TOI and AOI. In other words, the task is to detect an outlier, i.e. a TOI and/or AOI, which is significantly different from the expected ones.

Our approach is based on a number of assumptions developed in the course of our talks with members of the IC. First, we assume that analysts are assigned relatively long-term tasks and dedicate most of their work time to it.[2] Next, we assume, there may be more than one analyst who is assigned the same main topic and that each would then work on particular subtopics. Finally, we assume that the analysts work with documents and engage in email communication on topics related to their assigned task. We can also expect that the analysts working on subtopics of the same main topic would access different, but topically related, documents. Given the above assumptions, we can expect that clustering documents that the analysts work with

---

[2] This assumption does not cover analysts working on time-critical requests that need to be turned in within a couple of hours. Such analysts are *expected* to change topics quickly. A different TOI / AOI model would be needed for them.

would yield a larger cluster(s) containing on-topic documents, and a few smaller clusters of off-topic documents. Further, we can train a clustering model on the dataset containing mainly on-topic documents. The topical description of a cluster will be generated from the $n$ most frequent concepts in the clustered documents. Then, we can assess whether the documents accessed or created by the analyst fall within the scope of on-topic cluster(s) or whether they are significantly far from such topical cluster(s).

We will experimentally compare and select from the range of available clustering methods[3] the most appropriate one for our task of developing a model of expected TOI/AOI for the documents that the analyst accesses/generates. Then, each new document will be assessed in terms of its semantic distance from the existing cluster(s). As a result, the document will be merged with on-topic cluster(s), or existing off-topic cluster(s), or will start a new off-topic cluster. It is important to note that not every off-topic cluster should raise an alert flag. First, clustering algorithms can generate sporadic clusters. Also, realistically, analysts cannot be expected to work on their assigned topic 100% of their time. Finally, the emergent topic can be a legitimate development in the analyst's work. Therefore, the system will check the semantic distance between the off-topic cluster and the on-topic cluster(s), and also the size of the off-topic cluster. When both parameters exceed thresholds[4], the semantic analysis module emits an indicator to the risk assessor. A human (e.g. an information assurance engineer) can then review the indicators for their relevancy. Documents assessed as being on-topic will be added to the model; thus, adjusting the semantics of the expected TOI/AOI and the on-topic cluster parameters.

We will boost the efficacy of clustering methods by applying NLP techniques to extract entities (nouns and noun phrases) and named entities (proper names) from texts and, using ontologies, map individual terms and locations to appropriate categories, thus, reducing the high dimensionality of data[5] and, more importantly, contributing to the conceptual coverage of the resulting clusters.

Natural Language Processing consists of a range of computational techniques that provide a powerful approach for interpreting documents because of their ability to recognize and represent both explicit and implicit content [9]. To build content representations, our rule-based NLP system first outputs generic extractions of entities, events, and relations[6]; and then uses further linguistic clues to enhance extractions with additional semantic information specific to the domain. Extractions are represented as frames with dynamically defined slots and stored in a relational database.

# 5   Resources

## 5.1   Data

One of the challenges of this project is to develop a test collection of questions / topics and related documents for training and testing that adequately represent the spec-

---

[3] See [5, 17, 18] for details on methods.
[4] Empirically tuned and adjustable.
[5] Known to negatively affect computational effectiveness of clustering algorithms [7].
[6] Each noun phrase is extracted and indexed. Each verb is potentially extractable as an event and the appropriate noun phrases are labeled as to their roles with respect to the verb.

trum of textual data accessed / generated during the analyst's work processes. Such data collection is bound to be diverse in both, format (such as *txt, html, doc, tabular*) and genre (e.g. formal documents, analytic reports, online news stories, email messages). Being aware of the constraints on data procurement from operational settings, we gathered resources that would best fit the context of the IC. The resulting collection, discussed in greater detail below, is an example of collaboration and sharing among different research teams involved in ARDA and DARPA funded projects.

The analysts' tasks were modeled on scenarios developed by the Center for Non-Proliferation Studies (CNS)[7] experts for use in ARDA's AQUAINT (Advanced Question and Answering for Intelligence) Program. We also make use of the scenario-based questions generated at the 2003 ARDA-NRRC workshop on Scenario-Based Question-Answering [10]. A scenario consists of a question (i.e. particular task that the analyst is charged with) and a set of sub-questions, thus, modeling the analyst's decomposition of the main question into a set of contextually related sub-topics that are posed iteratively against the appropriate information resources (Table 1).

**Table 1.** Sample AQUAINT scenario

| **Main Question/Topic** |
|---|
| *Despite having complete access, to this day UN inspections have been unable to find any biological weapons, or remnants thereof, in Iraq. Why has it proven so difficult to discover hard information about Iraq's biological weapons program and what are the implications of these difficulties for the international biological arms control regime?* |

| **Question Decomposition / Subtopics** *(selected from 15)* |
|---|
| 1.  What does it take to determine/find signatures of a biological weapons program?<br>2.  What are UN capabilities and procedures for inspection?<br>3.  Where are they likely to be?<br>4.  Signature of the inspections: how predictable were they?  Did they lend themselves to deception?<br>5.  What is the Iraqi denial and deception capability?  How much effort is involved in hiding it? What evidence is available? |

| **Sources to Answer the Question(s)[8]** |
|---|
| •  *Arms control agreements*<br>•  *UN databases, guidelines, and procedures*<br>•  *UNSCOM report*<br>•  *CNS data for weapons info*<br>•  *Office of Technology Assessment reports*<br>•  *Foreign press reports*<br>•  *General search*<br>•  Talk to inspectors<br>•  Geospatial sources |

---

[7]  http://cns.miis.edu/
[8]  Italicizing indicates data amenable to semantic analysis.

From our conversations with intelligence analysts, we have learned that these scenarios fairly accurately represent actual analysts' tasks.

Another benefit of the AQUAINT scenarios is that they were developed under the premise that much of the needed information can be found in the CNS collection, in particular, in: datasets on nuclear weapons and missile proliferation; country profiles for North Korea and China; NIS Nuclear Profiles; a Nuclear Trafficking Database; the news archive on CBW / WMD. The resources are of various genres: news (including translations); analytic reports by various agencies, and; treaties. Our data set also includes a collection of online news topically related to the CNS data, compiled by the AQUAINT team at SUNY-Albany[9].

## 5.2 Ontology

In the semantic analysis approach, rather than using the literal words in texts, we develop algorithms to augment the document terms selected for clustering with appropriate concepts. Given that the focus will be on TOI and AOI, we needed an ontology for the nonproliferation domain, as well as a gazetteer.

Through collaboration with ISI / SAIC / Ontolingua, we obtained access to an ontology of CNS concepts[10], which also includes topics from non-CNS knowledge bases on terrorism. We will adjust this ontology to incorporate our currently employed taxonomy. Table 2 illustrates the current semantic mapping of the terms *sarin* and *mustard gas* to a type *cweap* (chemical weapon) and its augmentation with CNS topics (*WMD, weapons*).

**Table 2.** Example of term-mapping

| cbw092502 |
| --- |
| *the regime has accumulated substantial stockpiles of deadly liquid agents such as* **mustard gas**, *and ominous nerve agents, such as* **sarin** *and* **VX**, *the report said.* |
| entity = mustard_gas\|NN<br>type  = cweap<br>Cat = WMD<br>Top Cat = weapon<br><br>entity = sarin\|NN<br>type  = cweap<br>Cat = WMD<br>Top Cat = weapon |

For the conceptual organization of AOI, we will utilize the SPAWAR Gazetteer, also developed under the AQUAINT Program. It combines resources of four publicly available gazetteers (NGA[11]; USGS; CIA World Factbook; TIPSTER[12]), and is dynamically updated. The gazetteer uses a comprehensive categorization scheme based

---

[9]  http://www.hitiqa.albany.edu/index.html

[10] http://ontolingua.stanford.edu

[11] National Geographic Intelligence Agency; former name is NIMA.

[12] http://www.itl.nist.gov/iaui/894.02/related_projects/tipster/

on the Alexandria Digital Library thesaurus[13]. When tested on text annotation tasks, it was shown to cover 90% of geographic references in texts.

# 6 Preliminary Example

To exemplify our methods, consider the following example that we developed in order to familiarize ourselves with the data collection we were assembling. We selected a small set (five) of documents from the North Korea collection compiled by CNS. All documents were of a similar genre, namely, chronology of proliferation events. Two documents came from the *Missile* subset, and three documents came from the *Chemical* subset. We ran the documents through CNLP's text processor and analyzed the extracted entities and named entities[14]. The analysis led to a few important observations. First, selecting only entities to represent the conceptual scope of the document reduces it by about 3/4th, and further limiting to the named entities cut it to about 1/10th of its original size (Table 3), thereby addressing the dimensionality issue:

**Table 3.** Count of document terms

| Tokens | Doc92 | Doc95 | Doc47_96 | Doc97_00 | Doc01_02 |
|--------|-------|-------|----------|----------|----------|
| Words | 5356 | 4102 | 2736 | 1787 | 690 |
| Entities + Named Entities (NE) | 1399 | 1136 | 748 | 462 | 181 |
| NE only | 420 | 405 | 252 | 161 | 81 |

Second, using a gazetteer to resolve individual location names to their upper level geographic concept appears beneficial for identifying important AOIs. For instance, out of 39 *Russia*-related place names in Doc92, 23 were literally *Russia[n]*. The rest (one third) constituted city names (*Moscow* – 11, *Miass* – 4) and a region name (*Ural*). Another example: of 13 mentions of *South Korea*, 8 (two thirds) referred to *Seoul*. Assuming that locations are almost exclusively proper names, we estimated AOI frequencies against the named entities only. Table 4 shows prevalent AOIs (in %) for the two *Missile* documents.

**Table 4.** AOI frequency for *Missile* documents

| AOI | Doc92 | Doc95 |
|-----|-------|-------|
| North Korea | 29.05 | 19.01 |
| South Korea | 3.1 | 4.44 |
| United States | 4.29 | 4.94 |
| Syria | 6.19 | 0 |
| Iran | 8.57 | 4.94 |
| Russia | 9.29 | .25 |

---

[13] www.alexandria.ucsb.edu/~lhill/FeatureTypes

[14] Extracted entities include nouns (*missile*), noun phrases (*biological warhead*), and named entities (*China, Scud*).

Next, we wanted to compare the topicality of *Missile* vs. *Chemical* documents. Table 5 shows TOI frequency across all five documents. Obviously, Doc92 and Doc95 focus on the *Missile* topic, whereas the other three documents mainly discuss *Chemical/Biological Weapons*. Again, the concept-based approach seems promising. For example, out of 174 *Missile*-related terms in Doc92, 131 were literal *missile[s]*. The document also contained 40 mentions of a topically important term, *Scud* (a missile); including 23 cases where the term was used just as a proper name. Applying the TOI ontology would group these and other[15] terms under the *Missile* concept, thus, increasing its frequency by 24.7%[16].

**Table 5.** TOI frequency for *Missile* and *Chemical* documents

| TOI | Doc92 | Doc95 | Doc47_96 | Doc97_00 | Doc01_02 |
|---|---|---|---|---|---|
| Missile | 12.44 | 14.35 | 3.21 | 2.6 | 1.66 |
| Chem/Bio | .07 | .7 | 4.95 | 5.19 | 6.63 |

# 7   Conclusion

This project further extends the idea of combining NLP and machine learning (clustering) techniques to an application in the field of information security. This merging presents a few challenges, as well as potential areas of contribution, to the problem of knowledge acquisition. First, the majority of the prior research focused on a particular genre (news stories, or email messages, or query logs). Our data collection combines various genres, differing in style, syntax, and semantics[17]. We will, therefore, be enhancing our existing NLP tools to deal with genre specifics at the term extraction, term mapping, and term/concept-weighting stages[18]. Next, we will further investigate benefits and issues related to an ontology-driven approach to identifying important topical structures in large and stylistically diverse datasets.

While this is a nascent project, we believe that the application area, the approach, and the model described herein will be of interest to researchers in the area of insider threats and anomaly detection where analysis of texts plays an important role.

# Acknowledgements

This work is supported by the Advanced Research and Development Activity (ARDA).

---

[15] Such as: *launcher, gun, nuclear, Nodong* (a proper name for the nuclear missile).
[16] For Doc95, the TOI frequency would be boosted by 31.5%.
[17] Compare, for example, the style of email communication (informal, abundant in morphologic and syntactic shortcuts) and official briefing reports.
[18] For instance, in query logs, every word is assumed to be on topic, which is not true for a news story where most content-indicative terms are located in the lead sentence/paragraph.

# References

1. "Intelligence and Security Informatics: First NSF/NIJ Symposium". Proceedings of First NSF/NIJ Symposium, Tucson, AZ. H. Chen, R. Miranda, D. D. Zeng, C. Demchak, J. Schroeder, and T. Madhusudan, Eds. Heidelberg: Springer-Verlag, 2003
2. J. Allan, V. Lavrenko, D. Malin, and R. Swan, "Detections, Bounds, and Timelines: UMass and TDT-3," 2000, http://citeseer.nj.nec.com/455856.html.
3. J. Anderson, "Computer Security Threat Monitoring and Surveillance," James P. Anderson Co., Fort Washington, PA 15 April 1980.
4. R. Anderson, "Research and Development Initiatives Focused on Preventing, Detecting, and Responding to Insider Misuse of Critical Defense Information Systems: Results of a Three-Day Workshop.," 1999, http://www.rand.org/publications/CF/CF151/CF151.pdf.
5. P. Berkhin, "Survey Of Clustering Data Mining Techniques.," 2000, http://citeseer.nj.nec.com/berkhin02survey.html.
6. J. Burgoon, J. Blair, T. Qin, and J. Nunamaker, Jr., "Detecting Deception Through Linguistic Analysis," presented at First NSF/NIJ Symposium on Intelligence and Security Informatics, Tucson, AZ, 2003
7. A. Hotho, S. Staab, and G. Stumme, "Text clustering based on background knowledge," 2003, http://citeseer.nj.nec.com/hotho03text.html.
8. R. H. Lawrence and R. K. Bauer, "AINT misbehaving: A taxonomy of anti-intrusion techniques," 2000, http://www.sans.org/resources/idfaq/aint.php.
9. E. D. Liddy, "Natural Language Processing," in Encyclopedia of Library and Information Science, 2nd ed. New York: Marcel Decker, Inc., 2003
10. E. D. Liddy, "Scenario Based Question-Answer Systems," presented at AQUAINT 2003 PI Meeting, 2003, http://cnlp.org/presentations/present.asp?show=conference.
11. F. Patman and P. Thompson, "A New Frontier in Text Mining," in Intelligence and Security Informatics, vol. 2665, 2003, pp. 27-38
12. V. Raskin, C. Hempelmann, K. Triezenberg, and S. Nirenburg, "Ontology in Information Security: a Useful Theoretical Foundation and Methodological Tool," presented at 2001 Workshop on New Security Paradigms, 2001, pp. 53-59
13. D. V. Sreenath, W. I. Grosky, and F. Fotouhi, "Emergent Semantics from Users' Browsing Paths," Intelligence and Security Informatics, vol. 2665, 2003, pp. 355-357
14. M. Steinbach, G. Karypis, and V. Kumar, "A comparison of document clustering techniques," 2000, http://citeseer.nj.nec.com/steinbach00comparison.html.
15. S. Stolfo, S. Hershkop, K. Wang, O. Nimeskern, and C. Hu, "Behavior Profiling of Email," presented at First NSF/NIJ Symposium on Intelligence and Security Informatics., Tucson, AZ, USA, 2003
16. S. Upadhyaya, R. Chinchani, and K. K., "An Analytical Framework for Reasoning About Intrusions," presented at 20th IEEE Symposium on Reliable Distributed Systems, 2001, pp. 99-108
17. J. H. Ward, Jr., "Hierarchical grouping to optimize an objective function," Journal of the American Statistical Association, vol. 58, pp. 236-244, 1963
18. Y. Zhao and G. Karypis, "Evaluation of Hierarchical Clustering Algorithms for Document Datasets," 2002, http://citeseer.nj.nec.com/zhao02evaluation.html.
19. R. Zheng, O. Yi, H. Zan, and C. Hsinchun, "Authorship Analysis in Cybercrime Investigation," Intelligence and Security Informatics, vol. 2665, 2003, pp. 59-73
20. L. Zhou, J. K. Burgoon, and D. P. Twitchell, "A Longitudinal Analysis of Language Behavior of Deception in E-mail," Intelligence and Security Informatics, vol. 2665, 2003, pp. 102-110

# Towards a Social Network Approach
# for Monitoring Insider Threats to Information Security

Anand Natarajan and Liaquat Hossain

School of Information Studies, Syracuse University
4-108 Center for Science and Technology, Syracuse, New York 13244-4100
{anataraj,lhossain}@syr.edu

**Abstract.** Monitoring threats to information security is increasingly becoming important to protecting secured organizational documents. There is increasing number of threats to information security, which originates from the internal users of the system. Insider is defined as a trusted person and has access to classified documents. Our focus here is on understanding mechanisms for monitoring insiders working with the intelligence community. The analyst working with the intelligence community usually works on a TOI (Topic of Interest) and AOI (Area of Interest) so that they can develop a report about a very specific question. How do we ensure that these analysts do not perform malicious act during their course of collection, analysis and report generation for a given task? We suggest the need for social network monitoring of these analysts, which would help decreasing the threats of malicious intent of the insider. In this paper, we first provide a logical representation of analyst workflow model. Secondly, we describe the use of social network approach in general and suggest its application to monitoring insider threats. Thirdly, we provide an analysis of the properties and characteristics of social network analysis as they relate to monitoring insider threats for the intelligence community[1].

## 1 Insiders Threats to Information Security

An insider is an individual within the organization who is empowered to fulfill certain job functions. The empowerment of the individual depends on the context as well as the time duration of the job requirement. For example, a financial broker working in the stock market industry might have access to certain financial information of his or her customer as long as the customer has business transactions with the broker. An insider for this study is defined as someone who has been (explicitly or implicitly) granted privileges authorizing use of a particular system or facility [1].

It is important to acknowledge that there is an increasing abuse of responsibilities and power for malicious use by insiders. Cases of moles within the Intelligence Community (IC), insider trading in financial stock markets, bank fraud by employees are some of the common insider threats facing current organizations. Unfortunately, there are no fully developed technologies or mechanisms for detecting or preventing insider threats to occur. The subtle nature of these threats and the innumerous ways by which these threats can happen makes it extremely difficult to detect or prevent these

[1] This work was supported by Advanced Research & Development Activity (ARDA's) Information Assurance for the Intelligence Community (IAIC) program.

insider threats. Therefore, it is increasingly important for developing effective strategies and methods to detect and prevent these insider threats.

In this conceptual paper, we focus our effort on monitoring insider threats to information security for the intelligence community. First, we provide a general overview of the insider threats within the intelligence community using an analyst workflow model that focuses on social interactions. Secondly, we provide a description of background and techniques of social network analysis and suggest it application to monitoring insider threats for the intelligence community. Lastly, we suggest a social network approach as they relate to monitoring the insider threats for the IC.

## 2   Insider Threats in the Intelligence Community

Intelligence community spans across multiple organizations like the CIA, FBI, NSA, etc. The functioning of these organizations is largely dependent on highly critical information. The reliability and the security of this information are important for the operations and the success of these organizations. The NSTISSC (currently CNSS) report on insider threat [2], suggests an increasing number of insider malicious behavior, which posses threats to the national security. However, the measures proposed in these studies largely focuses on securing insider's use (or abuse) of information systems within the community. However, securing the information systems alone does not eliminate the risk of insider threats. Malicious behavior of "logical outsiders" [1], where people from outside can obtain secure information through social contacts (friendship, kinship relations), can be equally threatening. In this paper, we propose that monitoring and profiling the social behavior of insiders within the community would help us better manage the threats to the community from the insiders.

One of the critical operations of the analysts within the IC is the production of intelligence reports, which contains critical and classified information. The process of information collection for producing intelligence reports involves the collaboration of various socio-technical entities to accomplish specific tasks. The various social and technical entities involved in the intelligence reports production process are the agents, roles and the resources within the various organizations. The general logical workflow model of the process of production of intelligence report by analysts within the US Intelligence Community is shown in the figure below. This workflow model is a result of observations and discussion at the workshop to develop workflow scenarios of analysts. This validated model is a very general description of the operations of analysts. The process flow model suggests that production of report involves several steps: (i) task assignment, (ii) collection assignment, (iii) analysis and production, and (iv) dissemination of the reports.

At each stage of the process, various roles are required to accomplish specific tasks (such as SME, linguist). These roles interact with each other and with other technical resources (such as UN Database, OTA Database) for collecting information required for analysis. Figure 2 represents the social interactions of analysts with other actors and resources in the production of the intelligence reports. As mentioned above, it requires the cooperation and coordination of various social and technical entities within the community. The request for report is in the form of a "Question". Within the context of this "question", various analysts (A) are assigned (or enrolled) into various roles (R). These roles interact with each other and with resources (information systems) within and across the various organizations in the community. These interactions of insiders seeking intelligence information serve as source to model their social behavior.

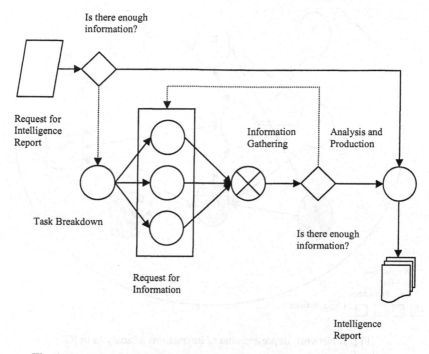

**Fig. 1.** A general Logical Representation of Intelligence Analyst Workflow

Instances of malicious behavior by insiders include collection of information about topics that are not of interest, disseminating information to unauthorized individuals, and accessing information sources that are not relevant to current task that is assigned to the analyst. Information about the activities of analysts could be collected and compared (peer comparison) with other analysts working on similar problem to identify malicious behavior. The obtained social behavior can also be compared to an expected behavior to measure deviations from normal activities. Social Network Analysis serves as a powerful tool to perform this analysis.

## 3   Social Network Analysis: Background and Techniques

Network data consists of a square array of measurements (in most cases), with both the rows and columns having the same cases (or actors, subjects). Network data focuses on the actors and their attributes. Thus the analysis is on the relationship among the actors rather than the attributes of the actors by itself. The two major emphases on network analysis include, seeing how actors are embedded within the overall network structure, and seeing how the whole pattern of individual choices gives rise to more holistic patterns. One major difference between the conventional data analysis is that the samples in network analysis are not independent. [1]

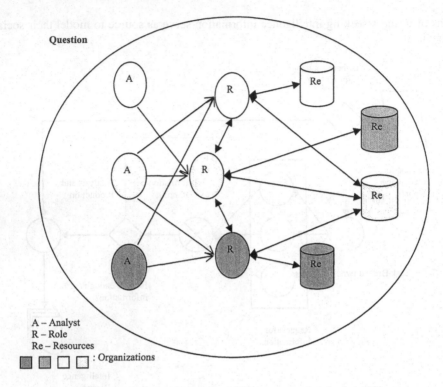

Question

A – Analyst
R – Role
Re – Resources
■ ■ □ □ : Organizations

**Fig. 2.** Network Representation of interactions of analysts in IC

The various strategies to perform social network analysis include analysis of the complete network or partial network or egocentric network. The critical element in social network analysis is to specify the type of relationship (ties) that determines the association between the actors. There maybe several relations between a given set of actors, but typically the researcher is specifies one of few types. Binary, nominal or ordinal measure could then be used for measuring the relationships. The types of analysis include descriptive analysis (median tie strength of actor, mean density of network, degree of similarity among actors, finding patterns in the network) and interpretive analysis (includes stability, reproducibility or generalizability of result in single sample).

### 3.1  Analyzing Data in Graphs and Matrix

Social scientists use mathematical concepts from "matrix algebra" and "graph theory" to create "sociograms". A dataset in the form of a matrix can be used to measure the degree of symmetry in the pattern of relations among the actors. Correlations between matrices say how similar they are and regression is used to predict the scores of a matrix using another [3]. For example, we might be able to analyze if the kinship predicts the strength of friendship. The paths between the nodes are used in calculating the number and length of pathways among actors, which is critical to notions of power, centrality, and the formation of groups and substructures. Granovetter [4] used network concepts like the "strength of weak ties" to analyze the opportunities and constraints for individuals. Burt [5] used the theory of "structural holes" to measure "social capital" of managers.

## 3.2  Properties of Networks and Actors

Difference in how the individuals are connected within the network can be very important in understanding their attributes and behaviors. It is important to go beyond the simple calculations of density of the network and the individuals. The ideas of distance between the actors and the connectedness help in understanding the "opportunities" and "constraints" faced by individuals within the social groups. One important constraint is that a single example (or representation of a relationship) of the graph cannot and usually does not capture all of the possibilities (other possible ties) [1]. Two important social attributes of actors lie in the connection (the relationship) and the number of connections between actors (path).

**3.2.1 Connections.** In a network, the number of actors, the number of possible connections and the actual connections that is present provides valuable information about the population, like the "moral density" and the "complexity" of the social organization. The number and the kinds of ties that individuals have help determining how much embedded they are within the social structure, the opportunities and constraints towards their behavior, and the influence and the power that they have. Dyadic analysis of the directed data can tell us about the stability of the social network. It is perceived that a network with predominance of null or reciprocated ties maybe more stable than asymmetric connections. Triadic analysis could be performed to analyze the transitivity of the actors within the network that contributes to their equilibrium.

a) *Size, density and degree*: The size of the network is calculated by counting the number of nodes. The density of the network is the proportion of all ties that could be present that actually are. In a binary network, the mean gives the percentage of all possible ties. The standard deviation gives an idea of how different the ties are. Calculating the *out-degree* of each row ("source") describes the role of that actor as source within the network. The variance of each row tells us how predictable the behavior of the actor is. Similarly, for *in-degree*, we can calculate the mean, SD and variance that provides information about the power of individuals or how much of information overload they manage.

b) *Reachability*: An actor is said to be reachable if he can be tracked through a set of connections regardless of the number of actors between them. Calculating reachability can identify formation of sub-groups.

c) *Reciprocity and Transitivity*: Dyadic and Triadic relationships are used to calculate reciprocity and transitivity. By identifying the number of "In ties", "Out ties", "No ties", "Reciprocated ties", and the "Neighborhood size" of each actor, we can analyze the social roles of the actors within the network.

**3.2.2 Distance.** The distance among the actors is an important macro-characteristic of the network as a whole. In a simple graph, a *walk* is a general connection between two people, a sequence of actors and relations that begins and ends with actors. *Geodesic distances* (the shortest walk between two nodes) are used to measure how accessible the actors are within the network. It helps to assess the nature of the network, like the ease of information flow. *Eccentricity* is the measure of how far an actor is from the furthest other. Row-wise and column-wise measures of the mean and standard deviation of the eccentricity would give us an idea about how "far" an actor is from each other and how far each actor is from each other who might be trying to influence them. The *diameter of a network* is the largest geodesic distance in the network. It can be used to calculate the upper bound of the lengths of connections that we want to study.

## 4  A Case for Application of SNA for Monitoring Insider Threats

Network analysis is a powerful tool for modeling and analyzing the behavior and intentions of actors within any social network. Modeling expected behavior and comparing it with the actual behavior will produce variances in the output that predicts and detects malicious intent and behavior. For example, the calculation of in-degree for an information collector is an indicator of the high information that he has requested. An analyst performing the role of information collection is "expected" to have a high density of in-degree. The density can be peer evaluated and the variance will predict the nature of the analyst's behavior or intentions. On the other hand, an analyst performing the role of "analysis" of the collected information should have a lesser density of in-degree.

Similarly, the nature of the connections between the analysts could be determined by the analysis of transitivity and reciprocity attributes present in the relationship within the social network. Analysts working in groups (informal) due to their past association (friendship) can be determined by transitive and reciprocity analysis of their interactions. The network distance between various actors within the social network is an estimation of the power wielded by these actors due to their position within the social structure [6]. Every analyst within the organization can use this to perform an impact analysis of malicious behavior. Contingency plans can be developed to mitigate and minimize the impact of such malicious activities.

As seen above, social network analysis could be used as a powerful tool for modeling and analyzing the behavior and intentions of actors, especially analysts working within the intelligence community. These examples provided represent only a small percentage of the immense potential of the use of social network analysis. There are several other properties and methods in social network analysis that help identify social characteristics or attributes of individuals and groups such as power, creation of social roles and comparing structural equivalence of network relations. Further research needs to be done to realize the complete potential of this powerful tool. Currently, the authors are involved in the experiments that involve the use of social network analysis for modeling the behavior of analysts within the intelligence community. The use of social network analysis could be the move towards the solution for monitoring and detecting the threats posed by the malicious intentions and behaviors of the insiders.

# 5  Conclusions

We provided a logical representation of analyst workflow model for developing an understanding of how intelligence analyst progress from task assignment to completion of the report. We further discussed social network approach in general and concluded that it is a useful paradigm for monitoring insider threats and in particular for the Intelligence Community.

Implications of future research will include the development of specific strategies in social network analysis to model the behavior of analysts. The authors, along with other researchers, are currently involved in research to design and develop a working model that incorporates the capabilities of social network analysis, along with other techniques, for monitoring insider threats.

The social network approach towards monitoring threats can be applied in other industries that face similar risks from insiders. We conclude by saying that social network approach is a very useful approach for modeling and analyzing the hidden behavioral characteristics of actors within social groups.

# References

1. Neumann, P. (1999). Risks of Insiders. *Communications of the ACM*, Vol. 42(12), pp. 160.
2. NSTISSC (July, 1999). The Insider Threat to US Government Information Systems. Retrieved on Feb 01, 2004.
   URL: http://www.nstissc.gov/Assets/pdf/NSTISSAM_INFOSEC1-99.pdf
3. Hanneman, R. A. (2001). *Introduction to Social Network Method*. Retrieved on Jan 28, 2004. URL: http://faculty.ucr.edu/~hanneman/SOC157/NETTEXT.PDF
4. Granovetter, M. (1973). The Strength of Weak Ties. *The American Journal of Sociology*, 78(6), 1360 – 1380.
5. Burt, R. S. (1997). The contingent value of social capital. *Administrative Science Quarterly*, 42(2), 339 – 365.
6. Wellman, B. (1983). Network Analysis: Some Basic principles. *Sociological Theory*, Vol. 1, pp. 155 – 200.

# Policy-Based Information Sharing with Semantics

Eric Hughes, Amy Kazura, and Arnie Rosenthal

MITRE Corporation, 202 Burlington Rd., Bedford, MA 01730,USA
{hughes,alk,arnie}@mitre.org

**Abstract.** Information sharing is not strictly a technical problem. But, we believe that a reasoned technical approach can address the technical concerns, and also ameliorate the non-technical issues. We have designed and prototyped key components of an information sharing system that uses semantic web standards for description of information available and needed, uses a broker that accepts profiles for information available and needed, and uses policy rules to approve any brokered information exchanges. We compare this approach to related work and discuss possible future research.

## 1 Introduction

Recently, significant attention has been paid to the difficulties government agencies have in sharing information. While much progress has been made, new approaches are needed if agencies are to share as effectively as required. We propose a flexible approach that uses available technology to enable agencies to share precisely the information they must, with the people and agencies they must, at the approved time and place. Our approach automates some of the more routine aspects of information sharing, but relies on humans to adjudicate unanticipated situations, and for appeal of automated decisions. The approach has several key attributes:

- *Flexible:* adjusts automatically to changing threat levels and new situations
- *Secure:* manages sharing according to flexible, system-independent policies and roles which (we hope) allow substantial sharing, but monitors for insider threats
- *Scalable:* can be configured in many ways to support any size community

## 2 Approach

Our approach allows a participant to *publish* information that it can provide, and *subscribe* to information that it needs. We use a *broker* to index these descriptions, and match them appropriately. A participant uses a query-like description to publish objects that match the description. The approach allows brokers that store information, but we focus on those that notify participants of matches and provide a separate means for dissemination. We recognize that other approaches are being defined for peer-to-peer (P2P) information sharing, but we focus on communities of participants that form relatively stable networks (for which policies can be more easily specified). A community is the set of participants connected by a given broker, which can span *boundaries*, such as agency affiliation or topic of interest.

H. Chen et al. (Eds.): ISI 2004, LNCS 3073, pp. 508–509, 2004.

The approach lets participants join and leave a community easily, since participants need not know about each other to share information. We treat brokers as participants so that small communities can be created without preventing scale up. This approach is comparable to the *super-peer* approach for P2P systems.

The broker uses *policy services* to determine whether a given piece of information (including a notification) can be shared. Our approach is designed to allow an agency to specify what information can be shared in pursuit of its legally-defined mission. We use policy rules to resolve routine cases, enabling validation of the rules, and enabling logging of policy decisions to ensure consistent enforcement. Our rules use descriptive attributes of the information, the participants (e.g., roles), and the context (e.g., threat level). Policy services can allow or deny sharing of a given piece of information, or can alert a human to resolve areas not covered by codified policy rules.

We use the Resource Description Framework (RDF) standard for description of information offered or desired. RDF defines constructs for *concepts*, which can be related by *properties* and can have properties with atomic data values. We are currently exploring emerging RDF query languages for publish and subscribe descriptions. We are also exploring the use of RDF for policy rules, since RDF is convenient for the descriptive attributes above. This use of RDF is also important for the (common) case where legacy data is mapped to more generic RDF concepts and properties, since it allows the creation of rules that are not specific to the current set of databases available, attribute names used by those databases, etc.

We do not assume that a global ontology can be (or should be) defined for our use. In addition to the challenge of gaining agreement among the various government agencies, we also recognize the need to use external sources, which will not generally use government ontologies. One alternative is for each brokered community to use a single ontology, which would simplify brokering. However, this approach limits a community to information described in its ontology (increasing the chances that the ontology will become too large to be manageable), and a participant that is a member of many communities must use the many corresponding ontologies even to publish or subscribe to essentially the same information across the communities. Instead, we give each participant the freedom to define their own concepts, and we expect that participants will tend to use widely-shared ontologies in most cases, and will relate their own concepts to those in other ontologies. We recognize that data integration researchers are creating technologies for mapping between ontologies, but we expect that consensus can be gained for government communities that are relatively stable.

# 3 Future Work

More work is needed to filter very complex information objects. In RDF, an information object is represented as a graph of concepts and properties. If the policy removes some concepts and properties from a graph, the graph may become disconnected and incoherent, and it may also be possible to infer the filtered information since some concepts and properties may be logically redundant.

# Determining the Gender
# of the Unseen Name through Hyphenation

Robert H. Warren[1] and Christopher Leurer[2]

[1] University of Waterloo
Waterloo, On, Canada
rhwarren@uwaterloo.ca
[2] McGill University
Montreal, PQ, Canada
leurer@math.mcgill.ca

**Abstract.** The accepted method of determining name gender is to use a probabilistic model based on observations, which fails to classify unseen names. We
attempt to solve this by utilising a hyphenation-driven method which is also more
space efficient.

The ability to cross-check several fields within a record is of value as it permits us to
validate the information provided. We concentrate here on determining the probable
gender of a name so that it can be compared with other gender-related fields. Thus, a
record of a person with the salutation "Mr.", given name "John", and whose gender is
coded as a woman may be of questionable value and require additional inspection.

A common method involves the use of a probabilistic model built from name observations [1]. This approach suffers from the inability to provide information on names
which have not been previously observed. Alternatives which have been explored are
the use of edit distance methods [2] or soundex matching to identify similar names. In
our method we use the hyphenated form of the name to infer its gender[1].

We used a trivial method to generate rules from hyphenated words by extracting the
last token and using this as the basis for a probabilistic model (e.g.: "elizabeth" would
hyphenate to "eliz-a-beth" from which we would extract the "beth" suffix.). The generated rules can be looked up without hyphenating the names themselves by matching
the right-hand-side of the word to the rules. For this experiment, we used the readily
available LATEX hyphenation files for the English and German languages along with an
open-source hyphenator [3,4]. The hyphenation method is not critical as it provides a
segmentation method; syllables could also be used, but with a high complexity cost.

A dataset of name-gender pairs generated from GEDCOM [5] genealogy files with
over 60,000 individuals and more than 5,000 unique names was used to validate the
method. To avoid cumbersome data cleaning and character set issues, we only processed
names which contained the basic US-ASCII character set.

---

[1] The authors wish to thank Dr. Brett Kessler of Washington University in St. Louis for help
with this approach.

H. Chen et al. (Eds.): ISI 2004, LNCS 3073, pp. 510–511, 2004.

Table 1 contains a breakdown of the precision and recall figures for each of the classification models. We found that the hyphenation driven classification was correcly assigning gender in 80% of applicable cases. Interestingly, only about 20,000 names were required for all models to return a consistent performance[2].

Table 1. Precision / Recall measures.

| Method | Precision | Recall | Decision table size in rows |
|---|---|---|---|
| Name lookup | 85% | 87% | 5742 |
| Hyphenation lookup | 87% | 96% | 1560 |
| Name + Hyph. fallback | 93% | 96% | 7302 |
| Hyphenation (unseen only) | 80% | 10% | 1560 |

The hyphenation model is very efficient as it requires 66% less rules than a name lookup model with a comparable performance on observed names. Hyphenation was able to classify an additional 10% of the names with a high precision. About 3% of names remained unclassifiable.

A valuable aspect of using a hyphenated model to identify gender is that the recall histogram of its rules is narrower than a basic name model. In situations where space is very limited, such as in field data-entry applications, a hyphenated model delivers a higher value than a standard name lookup model. This novel heuristic to classify unseen names is computationally inexpensive and allows us to cross check database records for proper gender identification.

## References

1. F. Patman and P. Thompson, "Names: A new frontier in text mining," in *Proceedings of the First NSF/NIJ Symposium on intelligence and security informatics* (H. C. et al., ed.), (Tucson, AZ), pp. 27–38, Springer-Verlag, June 2003.
2. M. Bilenko and R. J. Mooney, "Learning to combine trained distance metrics for duplicate detection in databases," Tech. Rep. Technical Report AI 02-296, Artificial Intelligence Laboratory, University of Texas at Austin, Austin, TX, Feb. 2002.
3. F. M. Liang, *Word Hy-phen-a-tion by Com-put-er*. PhD thesis, Department of Computer Science, Stanford University, Stanford, CA 94305, August 1983.
4. D. Tolpin, *TeX Hyphenator in Java*. 2003. http://www.davidashen.net/.
5. F. H. Department, *The GEDCOM Standard Release 5.5*. The Church of Jesus Christ of Latter-day Saints, January 1996. http://www.gendex.com/gedcom55/55gctoc.htm.

---

[2] The complete probabilistic name and hyphenated models can be found on the web at http://jill.math.uwaterloo.ca/~warren/name-gender.xml and http://jill.math.uwaterloo.ca/~warren/h-name-gender.xml respectively.

# A Framework for a Secure Federated Patient Healthcare System

Raj Sharman[1], Himabindu Challapalli[2], Raghav H. Rao[1], and Shambhu Upadhyaya[2]

[1] School of Management, Management Science and Systems Department, SUNY, Buffalo, New York 14260, USA
{rsharman,mgmtrao}@buffalo.edu

[2] Dept. of Computer Science & Engineering, SUNY, Buffalo, New York 14260, USA
{hc29,shambhu}@cse.buffalo.edu

**Abstract.** Medical records contain personal information like names, Social Security Number (SSN), Birth Date etc. The exposure of this information could cause considerable damage and lends itself to misuse in multiple ways However it is widely recognized that information from hospital information systems is needed for research and development. In this paper we propose a new framework to secure data from multiple sources.

## 1 Introduction

Privacy in healthcare has become a growing concern since the massive theft of 500,000 Pentagon medical files at TriWest in December 2002. Medical records contain personal information. The exposure of this information could cause considerable damage and lends itself to misuse in multiple ways. Yet, information from hospital information systems is needed for research and development. However, there is no acceptable unified framework that can be used to provide data to researchers from existing data residing in hospital information systems.

In this paper we propose a new framework to secure data from multiple sources for research availability. The design includes security considerations based on metadata and data classification as well as categorizing the user in to security classes.

## 2 Architecture for a Federated Patient Healthcare System

Most of the projects discussed in prior literature deal with either global information sharing or the security problem. However, in this paper, we address both the problems. By integrating heterogeneous database sources of various hospitals into a centralized database system, we enable information sharing. The proposed architecture involves building a federated system through heterogeneous database integration as shown in Figure 1.

H. Chen et al. (Eds.): ISI 2004, LNCS 3073, pp. 512–513, 2004.
© Springer-Verlag Berlin Heidelberg 2004

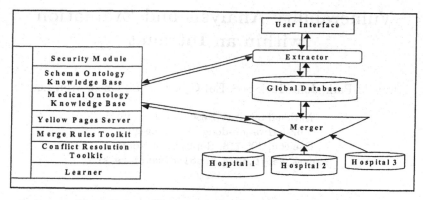

**Fig. 1.** Federated Patient Healthcare System Architecture

## 3  Experimental Results

For the purpose of testing the performance of the implementation three sets of data along with memo fields were constructed and stored in different formats such as MS Access, MS Excel and flat file. Further the three sets of data files included tables for the following entities: Administrator, Employees, Diagnosis, Patients, etc. Each Set was given a different source rating reflecting the reliability of the information from each hospital. Each piece of metadata was given a security classification. Researchers who posed queries were given security ratings.

An algorithm successfully merged the three heterogeneous databases semi-automatically. The tables (schemas objects) are identified using fuzzy logic which includes choosing the object which has maximum score (The scores are pre-assigned based on feature matching).

## 4  Conclusions

The main contribution of the paper is the framework for extracting medical data from several sources for research purposes. There is no such framework that we know of. More details including other contributions including scrub rules, merge rules and performance analyses will be presented at the conference.

**References Available on Request**

# Vulnerability Analysis and Evaluation within an Intranet

Eungki Park, Jung-Taek Seo, Eul Gyu Im, and Cheol-Won Lee

National Security Research Institute
62-1 Hwa-am-dong, Yu-seong-gu
Daejeon, 305-718, Republic of Korea
{ekpark,seojt,imeg,cheolee}@etri.re.kr

## 1   Introduction and Related Work

Recently computer incidents have increased rapidly and their ripple effects have also grown. Since computer systems become critical infrastructures in various areas, it is more and more important to protect the network and computer system assets from malicious incidents. Attackers try to search the vulnerabilities of the network and system, and penetrate to the network and system to do some malicious actions.

BS7799 is a specification for managing important informational assets [1], it is composed of two parts. The part 1 is methods for standard practical affairs including integrated security controls, and the part 2 presents how to construct ISMS(Information Security Management System).

Problems with BS7799 are 1) it is hard for system administrators to find systematic steps of analyzing vulnerabilities of systems in their domains, becuase BS7799 covers a large set of control items. In addition, system administrators must find a subset of BS7799 control items that can be applied to their domains. 2) In practical, some steps that are not included in BS7799 must be added for vulnerability analysis. For example, penetration tests must be done to prove that systems can be compromized.

In this paper, we proposed a new vulnerability analysis procedure so that more systematic and effective vulnerability assessments for the computer network can be possible.

## 2   Procedure of Vulnerability Analysis and Evaluation

Our vulnerability analysis procedure can be divided into five steps:

**Preparation Step.** In this step, levels of vulnerability assessment are decided in the aspects of physical, administrative and technical areas. To decide technical analysis levels and target systems, data flows and critical systems must be recognized. For effective vulnerability assessment, task force team should be formed. Administrators of the organization's network and system must be included in the task force team.

H. Chen et al. (Eds.): ISI 2004, LNCS 3073, pp. 514–515, 2004.

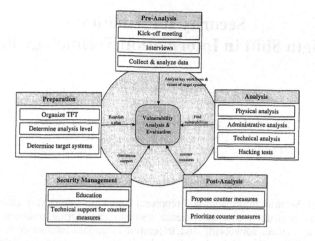

**Fig. 1.** Procedure of vulnerability analysis and evaluation

**Pre-analysis Step.** In the pre-analysis step, vulnerability assessment processes are described to the organization members, and documents are collected. System/network administrators are interviewed to gather information about current status of network/system/overall organization's security and to distinguish critical organizational assets. Using information and documents gathered so far, the current security status is observed.

**Analysis Step.** In this analysis step, an assessor tries to locate physical, administrative and technical vulnerabilities, and tests feasibilities of attacks using found vulnerabilities, and estimates their risk levels and priorities.

**Post-analysis Step.** In the post analysis step, an assessor formalizes and recommends the security countermeasures based on the results of the analysis step. Countermeasures are categorized into immediate ones, mid-term ones, and long-term ones depending on vulnerability severity and available resources.

**Security Management.** In the security management step, an assessor continues to check how the organization implemented the recommended or proposed countermeasures. Sometimes additional security educations are required to increase secuirity.

As a conclusion, this paper proposed a systematic and effective vulnerability assessment procedure. Using this procedure, an assessor can identify the vulnerabilites and their degrees of risk, and can recommend appropriate security countermeasure systematically.

# References

1. British Standard Institution. *BS7799: Guide to BS7799 Risk Assessment and Risk Management*, 1998.

# Security Informatics:
# A Paradigm Shift in Information Technology Education

Susan M. Merritt, Allen Stix, and Judith E. Sullivan

School of Computer Science and Information Systems
Pace University, New York, NY 10038
{smerritt,astix,jsullivan}@pace.edu

**Abstract.** Security informatics will represent a paradigmatic shift in college and university curricula in computer science, software engineering, information systems and science, networking and telecommunications, Internet technologies and related disciplines – the disciplines that might be assumed under the broad umbrella of "information technology" – though most programs have not yet understood the import or implemented the systemic change. Faculty have experienced much technology change over the short history of computing and are much more frequently introducing change into courses and programs than their colleagues in other disciplines. The need for security in information applications in virtually every discipline will generate robust interdisciplinary and multidisciplinary opportunities for informatics (as different from information technology) programs.

## 1 Security Across the Curriculum

The requirements for security in all information applications is generating interdisciplinary and multidisciplinary needs for security informatics programs. Security informatics is propelling a paradigm shift in college and university curricula as awarenesses, practices, products, and theory are added to address the sweeping demands of information assurance.

The National Security Agency (NSA) with its curricula certification and center of excellence designations is encouraging colleges and universities to assess where security surfaces within their course offerings and provides a guide to how and where coverage may be strengthened or augmented.

Even more important, the NSA offers a typology, created by John R. McCumber [1], for curriculum evaluation and planning. It is a conceptual model that is practical, comprehensive, and transcends particular technologies and products. This typology has the potential, if used creatively and effectively, to enable the organization of security content with elegance and pervasiveness, and thereby to approach and ultimately achieve systemic change in college curricula.

The typology is presented as the "annex" to the National Security Telecommunications and Information Systems Security (NSTISS) reference number 4011 of 20 June 1994, titled "National Training Standard for Information Systems Security (InfoSec) Professionals." (The "annex" was extracted from the Proceedings of the 14th National Computer Security Conference, October 1991). It begins with the definition of computer security offered by Charles P. Pfleeger [2]. Pfleeger identifies security with

H. Chen et al. (Eds.): ISI 2004, LNCS 3073, pp. 516–517, 2004.

respect to maintaining the confidentiality, integrity, and availability of the system's information:

- Confidentiality – information is viewable only by authorized parties (this is often characterized as privacy)
- Integrity – information is modifiable only by authorized parties and only in pre-scribed ways (information should not become corrupted)
- Availability – information is available to authorized parties when expected (the system should not be down when it is supposed to be in service)

These are the three concerns related to information security and therefore the categories of activity pertinent to securing automated information systems.

System vulnerabilities (i.e. potential weak points), the various kinds of threats, and the prospective methods of defense can be studied with greater precision by examining each principle together with the locus of information: in transmission, in storage, in processing. The cells in the resulting two-dimensional model may be approached on three levels. The levels relate to technology (T), practices including policy formulation (P), and awarenesses including education and training (A):

|                 | Transmission | Storage | Processing |
|-----------------|--------------|---------|------------|
| Confidentiality | T/P/A        | T/P/A   | T/P/A      |
| Integrity       | T/P/A        | T/P/A   | T/P/A      |
| Availability    | T/P/A        | T/P/A   | T/P/A      |

# 2  Questions for Discussion

1. Can the scope of practices and technologies associated with information assurance be accommodated by current curricula or will curricula be fundamentally changed?
2. How can the transient technology of digital security be dissociated from the transcending, enduring concepts?
3. How does security informatics presage a change of paradigmatic magnitude in technology education?

# References

1. McCumber, John R.: National Training Standard for Information Systems Security (Info-Sec) Professionals - Annex. Reference Number 4011, June 20, 1994.
2. Pfleeger, Charles P., Pflleger, Shari Lawrence: Security in Computing, Third edition. Prentice Hall, 2003, pages 10-12.

# Research of Characteristics of Worm Traffic*

Yufeng Chen, Yabo Dong, Dongming Lu, and Zhengtao Xiang

College of Computer Science, Zhejiang University, Hangzhou, China
{xztcyfnew,dongyb,ldm,xztcyf}@zju.edu.cn

Worm is becoming a more and more serious issue because worm attacks can cause huge loss in short time due to the fast-spreading character. When breaking out, worms induce abnormal traffic unlike the normal traffic, which gives us a clue of worm detecting by analyzing the abnormal characteristics of traffic involving worms, i.e. lumped traffic. Worm detection based on analyzing abnormal traffic characteristics has the advantage that it can detect novel worms without understanding the nature of the worms. And worm detection at network level is one possible detecting path, especially for Network Intrusion Detection Systems(NIDS). In this poster, we present the diversity of traffic characteristics between the normal traffic and worm traffic from the self-similarity point of view, which can be a preparation for the further investigation of the diversity of traffic characteristics between the normal traffic and lumped traffic.

Many researches have given evidences accounting for the self-similar nature of network traffic. The motivation of the researches mainly focuses on the traffic engineering. However, we try to extend the application range of self-similarity characteristic to worm detection because self-similarity is the nature of network traffic and worms induce traffic diversity, especially in the phase of worm scanning. Due to the goal of worm scanning, which is locating the victims furthest, the self-similarity characteristic of worm traffic is different from that of normal traffic. As a preliminary research of finding the anomaly characteristics of lumped traffic, we separate the lumped traffic into two parts: the normal traffic and worm traffic generated by worm scanning, and study the diversity of self-similarity of the two types of traffics. Because the traffic generated by many individual ON/OFF sources or source-destination pairs exhibits self-similarity characteristic, we first study the normal and worm traffic at individual source level, and then at aggregated traffic level, to show the diversity of self-similarity at different level of granularity. Here, traffics of individual source mean the normal and worm traffics generated by individual normal and infectious computers, respectively, and aggregated traffics mean the normal and worm traffics generated by all normal computers and all infectious computers, respectively.

The investigation is based on the datasets collected on a 100Mbps link connecting one dormitory building to our campus network from two half-hours: 10:00am~10:30am, 3:00pm~3:30pm, which involves scanning traffic generated by "Welchia" worm. Each data set contains information of source and destination IP address, timestamp, packet length. And each observation represents the number of

---

* This work is supported by a grant from Zhejiang Science and Technology Program (No.2003C31010), Ningbo Software Industry Development Program(No.R200336), and National Network and Information Security Ensurence Development Program (No.2004-Yan1-917-A-005).

H. Chen et al. (Eds.): ISI 2004, LNCS 3073, pp. 518–519, 2004.

packets sent over the Ethernet by normal or worm sources with the time unit of 100 milliseconds. Compared with other methods used to estimate self-similarity, the Abry-Veitch(AV) estimator is fast, and robust in the presence of non-stationarities. Thus, we use the AV method to estimate the values of Hurst parameters.

In the case of investigation at individual source level, we choose one worm source from each data set. The two worm sources generate worm traffic all through the two observed period. And then, we choose two normal sources that not only generate approximate traffic to the worm traffic during the two observed period, but also are corresponding to many destination addresses. We find that the degrees of self-similarity of worm traffic are significantly lower than that of normal traffic because the values of Hurst parameters of the two worm traffics are less than 0.6, while that of the two normal traffics are around 0.7. Here, we try to explain the diversity of self-similarity at source level intuitively. When "Welchia" worm breaks out, the character of the packet-train is sending ICMP echo request packets continuously, which leads the less burstiness of the wide range of time scale. And in the case of investigation at aggregated traffic level, the aggregated worm traffic exhibits less self-similarity, too, because the values of Hurst parameters of worm traffic are less than 0.7, while that of aggregated normal traffic are above 0.9. Because the individual infectious computers generate worm traffic with approximate constant rate, the aggregated worm traffic exhibits a little self-similarity characteristics when the worms breaks out in large scale, unlike the normal traffic does.

We conclude that the degrees of self-similarity of worm traffic are less than that of normal traffic, no matter at individual source level or aggregated traffic level. However, the studies is a beginning because the impact of worm traffic on the characteristics of network traffic needs to be explored to obtain the proper criterion for worm detection. And, the explanation of the impact should be proposed in a formalized manner, which may lead to other measurements for worm detection. Thus, to achieve the goals of worm detection, further investigation should be carried out: 1) analyzing the impact of worm traffic on the characteristics of lumped network traffic; 2) based on the characteristics of worm and normal traffic, exploring the reasons of the diversity of traffic characteristics.

## Acknowledgements

The authors acknowledge the continuing support from the Networking Center of Zhejiang University. We also would like to thank the reviewers for their comments.

# MIPT: Sharing Terrorism Information Resources

James O. Ellis III

Memorial Institute for the Prevention of Terrorism*
P.O. Box 889, Oklahoma City OK 73101
ellis@mipt.org

**Abstract.** The National Memorial Institute for the Prevention of Terrorism (MIPT) acts as a living memorial to the victims, survivors, rescuers, and family members of the bombing of the Alfred P. Murrah Federal Building in Oklahoma City on April 19, 1995. MIPT conducts research into the social and political causes and effects of terrorism, and its mission is to prevent terrorism or mitigate its effects on U.S. soil. Serving the needs of emergency responders, practitioners, scholars, policymakers, and the public, MIPT is addressing a dynamic terrorist threat environment by developing and sharing pioneering information resources, including its Terrorism Knowledge Base system.

## 1 Understanding Changes in Terrorism and Problems for Analysis

The ability to prevent terrorist attacks presupposes good intelligence about terrorist organizations and their activities. Though intelligence is more important than ever, changes in the nature of terrorism over the last fifteen years have made the collection of that intelligence exceedingly difficult. The United States Intelligence Community has traditionally been outward-looking and heavily oriented toward state actors, so it is still in the early stages of learning how to monitor and control non-state actors and weapons of mass destruction proliferation. Analyzing terrorism presents new and difficult challenges; terrorists typically do not control territory, wear uniforms, carry their weapons openly, function in discernable formations, or maintain permanent bases. Terrorists do not require high levels of operational sophistication and massive industrial infrastructure. The shrinking size and organizational self-sufficiency of non-state terrorist groups limit their financial traces and the size of their footprint. The plans, motivations, and preferred targets of small terrorist organizations are less transparent than those with an established reputation and constituency. Lone zealots do not offer communications to intercept nor co-conspirators to capture for information about upcoming operations. Experts across academia, business, and government sectors have indicated that terrorism is becoming more amorphous, more complex, more sporadic, more amateurish, more difficult to predict, more difficult to trace, and more difficult to observe and analyze.

---

* MIPT is supported under award number 2000-DT-CX-K002 from the Office for Domestic Preparedness, Department of Homeland Security. Points of view in this document are those of the author and do not necessarily represent the official position of MIPT or the Department of Homeland Security.

H. Chen et al. (Eds.): ISI 2004, LNCS 3073, pp. 520–525, 2004.

In the heyday of the 1970s and 1980s, terrorist organizations consisted of a core, elite vanguard that conducted the violence, a more moderate, political wing, and a wider support network of fundraisers, volunteers, front groups, and safe house suppliers. Terrorist groups learned that it is easy to disable groups formed into corporate-style organizations with discernable power structures. Many groups now depend less on formal leadership and no longer maintain traditional hierarchies. This, in turn, requires less frequent communications and makes them much more difficult to spot, track, and intercept. Though traditional terrorist organizations still commit the majority of terrorist attacks using the standard tactics of bombing, assassination, armed assault, kidnapping, hostage-taking, and hijackings, other groups and individuals are increasingly responsible for terrorist violence and innovations. The classic conceptual model of recognizable, restrained, tightly-knit, professional, political organizations with clear aims appears to be breaking down in favor of groups and individuals with more varied and hazy objectives, shorter life spans, and a greater interest in violence for its own sake. Terrorism is increasingly perpetrated by amateurs and splinter groups, de-emphasizing the organizational and ideological aspects of terrorism in favor of short-term interests and planning.

Terrorist organizations have changed in size and structure. Though the number of groups has risen sharply, the number of members per group has dropped. The cost-effective nature of free-floating cells has rendered formal state support unnecessary. Many groups have moved toward a networked organizational structure, opting for highly decentralized decision-making and more local initiative and autonomy. Networks can be much more difficult to visualize and combat, and they are hard to threaten initially because they have fluid organization and infrastructure. When fighting a terrorist network, usually only small portions of the network can be revealed and confronted at one time, presenting itself as a group of more or less autonomous, dispersed entities linked by advanced communications and perhaps nothing more than a common purpose. A network may simply absorb a number of attacks on its distributed nodes, leading counterterrorism agencies to believe it has been harmed and rendered inoperable when, in fact, it remains viable and is seeking new opportunities for tactical surprise. Analytically, it is difficult to predict and protect against the proliferation of amateur terrorists and ad hoc cells of like-minded individuals seeking to conduct do-it-yourself warfare, briefly joining forces for come-as-you-are attacks and then disbanding. Researchers, analysts, and the public require new information tools to help them make sense of such a complex threat.

## 2  MIPT as an Information Clearinghouse

Out of the rubble of the April 19, 1995 Murrah Building bombing in Oklahoma City came the vision of the Memorial and its research component – the National Memorial Institute for the Prevention of Terrorism (MIPT). The United States Congress directed MIPT to conduct "research into the social and political causes and effects of terrorism" and to "serve as a national point of contact for antiterrorism information sharing among Federal, State and local preparedness agencies, as well as private and public organizations dealing with these issues." MIPT firmly believes that the accurate dissemination of knowledge on terrorism is a critical ingredient for combating terrorism on U.S. soil. We realized early on that a high priority need for terrorism research in

522    James O Ellis III

the United States is the creation of authoritative and accessible databases. Therefore, some of the first research projects undertaken by MIPT were to create and maintain comprehensive electronic databases on terrorism-related subjects. To this end, MIPT partnered with the RAND Corporation to improve the nation's awareness of the history of and emerging trends in terrorism. In order for responders to prepare and leaders to plan, their policies must first be informed by what has gone before. By learning lessons from past incidents and grasping current trends, they can better understand the nature of future threats and how to protect against them. MIPT serves the counterterrorism community by offering access to a wealth of information resources including its terrorism databases, knowledge base initiatives, website, and library collection.

As there was no authoritative, central source of unclassified information on terrorism, MIPT has worked to develop a world class collection of unclassified resources on terrorism, antiterrorism, and counterterrorism. With information and research on terrorism developing almost daily, creating and maintaining a comprehensive repository of that knowledge and data is a difficult task, which has become more daunting following the September 11th attacks. MIPT's physical library houses thousands of books, videos, reports, articles, and pamphlets on terrorism and related subjects. It collects more than two dozen journals and bulletins, with complete sets of the two most influential journals in the terrorism field – *Terrorism and Political Violence* running since 1989 and *Studies in Conflict & Terrorism* dating back to 1977. MIPT also holds complete sets of the two most important U.S. government chronicles of international and domestic terrorism – the State Department's "Patterns of Global Terrorism" and the Justice Department's "Terrorism in the United States" – both of which date back to 1985. These have been made available electronically in their entirety for the first time through the MIPT website. The MIPT Library employs numerous electronic resources like the Foreign Broadcast Information Service, Nexis, and Jane's Terrorism Watch, and its staff monitors approximately twenty-five listserves dealing with terrorism, first responders, emergency management, and weapons of mass destruction. Ultimately, MIPT intends to acquire all available English language material on terrorism and related subjects for on-site study by researchers, response practitioners, government agencies, and the public at large. A special effort is underway to house scholarly archival collections by major terrorism experts. Employing SIRSI, Hyperion, and OCLC, MIPT will make this information electronically available, to the maximum extent possible.

Since many individuals may not be positioned to take advantage of the physical library, MIPT's website – www.mipt.org – provides a virtual resource to patrons around the world. The MIPT website contains over a thousand links to documents and other websites. It also offers an annotated terrorism bibliography with over two thousand book titles, a database of university terrorism courses and responder training, a conference calendar, and a terrorist anniversary and significant dates calendar. Hundreds of other sites link to the MIPT website. As of this writing, MIPT's website appears first, second, or third with a Google search for "terrorism databases," "terrorism prevention," "homeland security library," or "first responders library." Some of the most valuable assets located through the website are a number of unique terrorism databases.

# 3  Terrorism Databases

In 2000, MIPT began collaboration with RAND to create open, online databases that capture domestic and international acts of terrorism. This venture encompassed two databases – the RAND Terrorism Chronology and the MIPT-RAND Incident Database. The RAND Terrorism Chronology (also known as the RAND-St. Andrews Chronology) represents thirty years of research on international terrorism that RAND collected and maintained from 1968 to 1997. By working with MIPT, RAND has opened this large, proprietary database to the public for the first time through the MIPT website.  Though several excellent chronologies of terrorist events exist, other systems are limited in their ability to let users manipulate the data, drawing out, for example, only terrorism involving certain kinds of weapons, or certain groups or places, or any combination thereof. The new MIPT-RAND Incident Database covers both international and domestic terrorism incidents worldwide beyond 1998 to the present day. These incident databases contain data collected from open sources and publications, collected by RAND. This collection process has been conducted in accordance with the same definition and vetting standards established at the beginning of the RAND Terrorism Chronology. In conjunction with the databases, RAND has produced terrorism updates and a yearbook containing articles by subject matter experts, who draw heavily upon these databases. These publications offer contemporary analysis and insights, probe cross-cutting issues, and describe the terrorist threat environment. They are also intended to inspire others to take advantage of these tools in order to develop further knowledge. By keeping these databases open-source, objective, and online, we afford our users unparalleled access to a unique resource. Eventually, MIPT should be able to make the over 20,000 supporting documents from the RAND databases available for study on-site at the MIPT Library.

MIPT also hosts a robust database focused on indicted terrorists in the U.S. Headed by the University of Arkansas and the University of Oklahoma, the MIPT Indictment Database compiles records related to federal criminal cases as a result of official terrorism investigations under the Attorney General Guidelines from 1980 to the present day. The project provides a powerful quantitative dataset for researchers. The Indictment database includes information on nearly 500 terrorists from about 60 terrorist groups indicted for over 6,600 federal criminal counts over the last 20 years. Approximately 75 variables can be analyzed, including: (1) demographic descriptions of indicted and convicted persons; (2) terrorist group type, affiliation, and ideology; (3) case and count outcomes (conviction, plea, acquittal, etc.); (4) and sentencing information. Analyses can be conducted on any combination of these variables, and the source court records are also being made available as Acrobat PDF documents. This material is invaluable in looking for pre-incident indicators or discovering more historical information about specific groups and incidents within the United States. It will also aid in the development of practical recommendations regarding the investigation, prosecution, and sanctioning of persons indicted for terrorism-related crimes. MIPT continues to update these databases as more incidents of terrorism occur and more terrorists are indicted. As individuals access the data, MIPT welcomes feedback on how to improve these databases to make them more beneficial to the user community.

## 4  MIPT Terrorism Knowledge Base

Currently, there is no single, comprehensive site where policymakers, practitioners, and the public can have the facts concerning global terrorism at their fingertips. By working with DFI International, MIPT is moving to meet this need by combining its databases, web documents, library materials, and other resources into an in-depth, interactive, and inclusive Terrorism Knowledge Base system. This system represents the most advanced, web-based tool of its kind. The initial Terrorism Knowledge Base offers unprecedented access to: thirty-five years of international terrorism data; five years of worldwide domestic data; over twenty years of terrorism indictments and court case documents; GIS mapping of groups and attacks; group and leader profiles; daily news articles relating to terrorism; country-specific information; lists of additional information resources; and updates. The system includes remarkable analytical capabilities across a single, integrated knowledge base, including statistical summaries, trend graphing, and side-by-side comparisons. In essence, MIPT is building a terrorism "analyst-in-a-can" that can aid in tracking trends and developing threat assessments.

Users will be able to search the MIPT Terrorism Knowledge Base through an interactive map, through directory links, through keyword searches, or through an advanced search option. The interactive map provides the capability to drill down on a region or country and see incidents or groups in this area. Advanced future versions of this capability will offer new ways to visualize terrorist acts and actors. Profiles of terrorist groups give the name in the mothertongue language, their base of operations, founding philosophy, and current goals. The group profiles also contain Quick Facts, offering a snapshot of vital data and acting as a "baseball card" of statistics. These Quick Facts include information on related groups and key leaders, with links to a biography and photographs where available. The profiles also integrate incident statistics from the RAND databases, displaying tactic, casualty, and target statistics for all incidents attributed to the selected group and links to these incidents. Related legal cases and additional information resources are included in the profiles. As for analytical tools, the MIPT Terrorism Knowledge Base includes access to the previous individual terrorism databases, but it also includes advanced new capabilities. Analysts and researchers can create all manner of graphs and charts examining incidents by region, by target, by tactic, by weapon, by group, by court case, and more. For less experienced users, the system includes a primer, featured graphs, and graphing wizards to walk patrons through the process of creating their own specialized tables and graphs. The Terrorism Knowledge Base offers quick reports and tables as well as more sophisticated ones.

## 5  Serving the Responder and Counterterrorism Communities

The dynamic nature of terrorism and the threat posed by chemical, biological, radiological, nuclear, and high-explosive weapons translates into a constant need to supply information on a wide array of topics and subject areas. The MIPT Terrorism Knowledge Base will be key to sharing better information on terrorists and trends, which is vital to anticipating and preventing future attacks. MIPT is thus working to further understanding of terrorists' history, motives, structures, targets, weapons, and tactics. Our consolidated, encyclopedic knowledge base system will allow users to search across multiple fields and databases through an intuitive interface. It will also compliment our larger Lessons Learned and Best Practices initiative, which seeks to capture insights and innovations from previous counterterrorism exercises and terrorist incidents.

MIPT fills an important niche by providing a comprehensive collection of both electronic and print information resources and making them available on-site and via the World Wide Web. In today's ever-changing digital world, information centers must strive to form global networks to serve their patrons. MIPT prides itself on its ability to serve as a bridge linking like-minded institutions. MIPT has worked to establish a network of collections related to terrorism and to encourage cooperation among them in order to eliminate competition and duplication. By sharing unique information resources, the National Memorial Institute for the Prevention of Terrorism can help find new preventative strategies and ways to reduce risk, thereby improving homeland security and helping our nation defend itself against the scourge of terrorism.

# Post-9/11 Evolution of Al Qaeda

Rohan Gunaratna*

International Center for Political Violence and Terrorism Research
Institute of Defense and Strategic Studies (IDSS), Nanyang Technological University
Blk S4, Level B4, Nanyang Avenue, Singapore 639798
isrkgunaratna@ntu.edu.sg

**Abstract.** Before the 11 September 2001 attacks, Al-Qaeda had conducted an average of one attack every two years. Since then, Al-Qaeda and its associated groups – what could be termed the Al-Qaeda movement – have mounted an attack, on average, every three months. US successes in disrupting the Al-Qaeda network have also dispersed its operatives. Al-Qaeda organizers, operatives, financiers and other experts have moved out from Afghanistan and Pakistan to lawless zones in Asia, the Horn of Africa, the Middle East, and the Caucasus. To compensate for the loss of its training and operational infrastructure in Afghanistan, Al-Qaeda is seeking to establish new bases in Yemen, the Philippines, Indian Kashmir, Georgia and Chechnya. Whether this dispersed threat will escalate or de-escalate in the coming year depends on the USA's ability to manage the deteriorating situation in Iraq and the willingness of Muslim governments to cooperate with the West. Certainly, Washington's decision to intervene in Iraq complicated the security environment rather than reduced the threat of terrorism.

## 1 A Global Phenomenon

In contrast to the highly successful US-led global response that gravely weakened Al-Qaeda after the 11 September 2001 attacks, the US intervention in Iraq has facilitated the growth of existing Islamist political parties and terrorist groups, and the emergence of new ones.

The resurgence of the Taliban, Hizb-i-Islami and Al-Qaeda in Afghanistan, and the resistance of secular Saddam Hussein loyalists and Ansar al-Islam, an indigenous Al-Qaeda associate group, is likely to mean violence will continue in 2004. Al-Qaeda and its associate groups are aggressively harnessing resentment among Muslims living in the West and elsewhere. In Iraq's immediate region and beyond, the growing anger directed towards the USA and its partners has provided Islamist groups with the opportunity to exercise greater influence among Muslim communities.

Unprecedented security, intelligence, and law-enforcement co-operation; heightened public vigilance; and an aggressive hunt for Al-Qaeda and associated cells has so far prevented terrorists from mounting another large-scale attack on Western soil. However, although terrorist capabilities to attack the USA, Western Europe and Australasia have suffered, the intention to mount an attack on Western soil has not dimin-

---

* Rohan Gunaratna is Head of International Centre for Political Violence and Terrorism Research, Institute of Defence and Strategic Studies, Singapore, and author of Inside Al-Qaeda: Global Network of Terror (Columbia University Press).

H. Chen et al. (Eds.): ISI 2004, LNCS 3073, pp. 526–530, 2004.
© Springer-Verlag Berlin Heidelberg 2004

ished. The November 2003 double suicide attacks in Turkey were a grim reminder that terrorists can strike even amid tight security measures, and that the targets terrorists can choose from are too numerous to be protected. As terrorists who are determined to survive and succeed adapt to the post-11 September 2001 security environment, they are likely to identify loopholes and gaps in Western security architecture, enabling them to breach security and overcome countermeasures.

The frequency of attacks in the Middle East, Asia, the Horn of Africa and the Caucasus will continue, but as the terrorists aim for greater impact they are likely to kill, maim and injure more people. To achieve this, the terrorists will continue to attack economic, religious and population targets using the tactic of coordinated simultaneous suicide operations.

Sustained global action against Al-Qaeda will further force the mother group into the background: this will empower its associates who will come to the fore, making it more difficult for intelligence and enforcement agencies to monitor and respond to a numerically larger number of Islamist groups.

The US intervention in Iraq has weakened the resolve of Muslim leaders and their governments and publics to fight terrorism. The failure of the international community to provide more grants and aid to Afghanistan and Pakistan ensures the support for extremist ideologies and the survival of the Al-Qaeda leadership. Furthermore, Iran is likely to develop into a safe zone for Al-Qaeda unless the West strengthens the hand of the moderates over the hardliners in Tehran.

Islamist terrorist groups from Asia, Middle East, the Horn of Africa and the Caucasus will conduct the bulk of the terrorist attacks. Most of the attacks will be conducted in Muslim countries against symbolic targets of the USA and its partners. Due to the hardening of US targets, and as governments continue to enhance the security of military and diplomatic targets, terrorists are now shifting their attention to allies and friends of the USA and going for soft targets, such as hotels and banks; religious targets; and population centers – a prime example being the attack that focused on Australian tourists in Bali on 12 October 2002. Almost all the attacks will be suicide vehicle bombings - an Al-Qaeda hallmark - and will result in mass casualties, including the deaths of Muslims. Nonetheless, Islamist groups will find sufficient support to continue the fight against the USA and its partners.

Al-Qaeda itself will conduct fewer attacks, although it will remain in the background inspiring, instigating and coordinating attacks by groups it has trained, armed, financed and indoctrinated. In particular, six groups – Ansar al-Islam in Iraq; the Salafist Group for Preaching and Combat in Algeria; Al Ansar Mujahideen in Chechnya; Hizb-i-Islami, Islamic Movement of the Taliban; and Jemaah Islamiah in Southeast Asia are capable of conducting Al-Qaeda-style attacks.

## 2 Searching for New Weapons

Terrorist groups are increasingly expressing an interest to acquire, use and develop dual technologies. In the hands of a terrorist, certain civilian technologies can enhance terrorist performance, demonstrated spectacularly by the use of commercial airliners in the 11 September 2001 attacks.

Al-Qaeda members are now scouring agricultural farms in search of fertilizer to develop bombs; pharmacies and chemist stores to acquire material to build bombs in garages and kitchens; and hospital and industrial complexes to smuggle out radiological devices. The recovery of manufacturing apparatus that had traces of ricin – but not the ricin itself – in the UK in 2003 suggests that Al-Qaeda and its associated groups are in the process of acquiring chemical, biological and radiological (CBR) weapons in some form.

In 2002, a Tunisian Al-Qaeda member attacked a Jewish synagogue in Djerba using a Liquid Petroleum Gas (LPG) vehicle, killing 22. The recovery of 36 terrorist manuals from Afghanistan and other theatres that contained formulae to manufacture chemical and biological agents and radiological dispersal devices suggests that several hundred members may have such specialist capabilities.

As the Al-Qaeda movement continues to recruit from a cross-section of society, they will gain access to specialist technologies. Although conventional terrorist attacks (using the gun and the bomb) will be the most common, the likelihood of terrorists using dual technologies, particularly CBR agents, is increasing.

The threat of hijacking air and sea transportation to strike human and infrastructure targets remains significant. Al-Qaeda and its associated groups have tried and tested this technique several times since 11 September 2001 to hijack aircrafts with the intention of attacking ground and maritime targets. A weakness in the transportation chain in a target or a neighboring country is likely to pave the way for success.

Despite terrorist failures to destroy commercial airliners in Iraq in 2003 and Kenya in 2002, and a US fighter plane in Saudi Arabia in 2001, the attempts demonstrate the continuing threat. With the failure of operational agencies to disrupt the fleet of merchant ships linked to Al-Qaeda (in which lethal cargo can be transported relatively easily) the future threat posed by Surface to Air Missiles (SAMs) remains significant.

With the difficulty of hijacking aircraft, even a non-suicide conventional hijacking, terrorists are likely to invest in attacking aviation targets with other stand-off weapons – rocket-propelled grenade launchers and light anti-tank weapons. As aerial and ground targets harden, the vulnerability of the maritime domain to infiltration and strike has increased. A vessel could be used not only to transport lethal cargo but also as a bomb to attack a port city. Investing in vessel profiling is the key to identifying and searching high-risk ships over the horizon.

# 3  Regions of Concern

Al-Qaeda and its associated members are concentrated in four regions of the world: Iraq and its border regions; Yemen and the Horn of Africa; the Pakistan-Afghanistan border; and the Indonesian and Philippine archipelagos. Following sustained US-led Coalition action in Afghanistan, since October 2001 the threat posed by Al-Qaeda has globalized and diffused.

Like Afghanistan during the Soviet occupation, Iraq is becoming a magnet for politicised and radicalised Muslims worldwide. Islamists have declared Iraq the new land of jihad. In the short term, the scale and intensity of fighting there will increase due to the flow of mujahideen through Iran, Syria and Saudi Arabia; collaboration between foreign mujahideen and Saddam loyalists; increased support from angry Muslims worldwide; and tacit and active sanctuary, as well as covert support from Iraq's neighbors.

Unless Western and Muslim governments invest more resources and personnel, the situation in Iraq will deteriorate even further; and in the longer term it is likely to produce the next generation of mujahideen. While the bulk of the foreign mujahideen at present are from the Levant, in time youths from North Africa and the Gulf, the Horn of Africa and the Caucasus, cradle and convert European Muslims, and Asian Muslims are likely to enter Iraq.

Yemen: Al-Qaeda has developed significant infrastructure in the Horn of Africa, including Somalia, and is using the region as a base to launch operations in the Gulf and in Africa. Several hundred Al-Qaeda members in Yemen move back and forth to East Africa, developing the Horn as a sanctuary. In the coming years, East African Islamist groups influenced by Al-Qaeda will increasingly participate in international terrorism, while sub-Saharan Africa will remain the Achilles heel for Western security and intelligence agencies.

Afghanistan: In the period between the Soviet withdrawal in February 1989 and the US intervention in October 2001, Afghanistan was a terrorist haven, with Al-Qaeda, the Taliban and other Islamist groups training several tens of thousands of mujahideen. Although nearly 600 Al-Qaeda members and associates that fled to Pakistan have been arrested, the reservoir of trained mujahideen is huge, being concentrated in the Afghanistan-Pakistan border area.

Hizb-i-Islami, the Taliban and Al-Qaeda are seeking to develop Pakistan's Northwest Frontier Province as a launchpad for conducting operations into Afghanistan, making Pakistan the most pivotal state in the fight against terrorism.

As President Pervez Musharraf continues to target Al-Qaeda and Taliban members in his country, support for Islamism and opposition to his regime is growing. To prevent an Islamist government taking power, sustained Western assistance to Musharraf, improved Pakistan-Afghanistan relations, and an international resolution of the Indo-Pakistan dispute over Kashmir is essential.

Iran: Hardliners in Iran have advocated support for the anti-US insurgency in Iraq. Many Al-Qaeda leaders and members moved to two countries - Iran and Pakistan - in late 2001 and early 2002. Western intelligence sources claim that several hundred Al-Qaeda operatives, led by Saif Al Adil and Saad bin Laden, are located in Iran. Although Iranian moderates have called for tougher action against Al-Qaeda, the duality of Iran's response to Al-Qaeda is likely to continue. The USA identifying Iran as 'evil' will neither help the West nor Muslim moderates in Iran.

## 4  What Lies Ahead?

The fight against Al-Qaeda and its associated groups, as spearheaded by the USA, has met with partial success. The effectiveness of the fight against Al-Qaeda and its associated groups is strictly dependent on long-term international co-operation and co-ordination to share intelligence and conduct operations against terrorist groups and suppress their support bases.

To succeed, it is paramount that the USA maintains a robust anti-terrorism coalition, particularly with the support of Middle Eastern and Asian Muslim governments. By resolving the Israeli-Palestinian dispute and by investing in public diplomacy (as opposed to government-to-government relations), the USA must seek to change its image from that of an aggressor to that of a friend in the Muslim world.

# Appendix

To survive and remain relevant, Al-Qaeda has undergone three distinct transformations, and continues to evolve.

**Phase One:** Following the Soviet withdrawal from Afghanistan in 1989, Al-Qaeda Al Sulbah (The Solid Base) began as a group to support local jihad movements, and assisted associated groups or directly targeted opposing governments, mostly in Muslim countries. By providing finance, weapons and trainers, the group played or attempted to play critical roles in the lands of jihad – Algeria, Tajikistan, Bosnia, Chechnya, Mindanao, Kashmir and Egypt.

**Phase Two:** Al-Qaeda developed its own capability to mount operations throughout the 1990s, largely due to close co-operation with Egyptian groups – Egyptian Islamic Jihad and the Islamic Group of Egypt – culminating with the 11 September 2001 attacks on the USA.

**Phase Three:** Due to security measures in Western countries taken after the 2001 attacks, Al-Qaeda and its associated groups were no longer able to mount attacks on Western soil, and so switched their attention to targets in Muslim countries where they were still able to operate. Attacks have taken place in Chechnya, Indonesia, Kenya, Tunisia, and Morocco, and against Western targets in Saudi Arabia, Turkey, and Iraq. In this phase, most of the attacks were not staged by Al-Qaeda but by associated groups. As they lack Al-Qaeda's level of expertise, the number of Muslim casualties has climbed.

The loss of training and rehearsing bases in Afghanistan and intense networking with associated groups has forced Al-Qaeda to change from a group into a movement. Having successfully performed its vanguard operational role by attacking iconic US targets, a hunted Al-Qaeda is investing in an ideological role, mostly through the internet. While Western governments are largely investing their resources to fight Al-Qaeda, the centre of gravity has shifted into its associated groups, posing varying scales of threat in different regions.

# Utilizing the Social and Behavioral Sciences to Assess, Model, Forecast and Preemptively Respond to Terrorism

Joshua Sinai

Science & Technology Directorate
Department of Homeland Security, Washington, DC 20528
joshua.sinai@dhs.gov

## 1 Terrorism Social and Behavior Program in DHS

To stay ahead of the terrorist threat curve, we need to utilize leading edge and innovative conceptual methodologies and software-based systems that are grounded in the social and behavioral sciences. It is by means of theoretically grounded, conceptually precise, methodologically rigorous, and analytically oriented research that we can attain the capability to fully understand the underlying conditions that give rise to terrorist insurgencies and the measures required to contain such threats. Such a comprehensive and multidisciplinary approach will enable us to understand how to assess, model, forecast and preemptively respond to current and future terrorist threats. Some of these leading edge methodologies and software systems may already be available – although not yet applied to the terrorism/combating[1] terrorism discipline – while others may yet to be developed. To achieve the capability required to win the war on terrorism, we must first substantially improve and strengthen our social and behavioral scientific baseline understanding of all the root causes underlying the terrorist-based conflicts, as well as the organizational formations, nodes and linkages involved in how terrorists operate and conduct warfare.

This is the overall research objective of the Terrorism Social & Behavioral Program (TSBP) in the Science & Technology Directorate, Department of Homeland Security. Such a research approach must start by addressing the underlying conditions, also known as root causes, and primary components in the terrorist life cycle (TLC) and terrorist attack cycle (TAC) in order to understand how to anticipate and disrupt such potential attacks by formulating preemptively capable combating terrorism strategies and programs.

## 2 Research Focus and Methodology

In a social and behavioral sciences approach, such a research effort would begin with a comprehensive study of the types of warfare that adversary terrorist groups are currently conducting, or are likely to conduct in the future.

---

[1] Combating terrorism is used as an umbrella concept incorporating the defensively-based anti-terrorism and offensively-based counter-terrorism.

H. Chen et al. (Eds.): ISI 2004, LNCS 3073, pp. 531–533, 2004.

## 2.1  Terrorist Threats Analysis

To understand the magnitude of the threat posed by such warfare, the manifestations of the terrorist threat would then be 'drilled down' into their component elements, such as (1) conventional low impact (CLI), conventional high impact (CHI), or chemical, biological, radiological or nuclear (CBRN) warfare, (2) whether this warfare is politically-driven 'conventional' or religiously-based 'martyr' suicide terrorism, and (3) the frequency and intensity of such incidents. Once the magnitude of the terrorist threat is identified, one would then begin the process of trying to understand the underlying conditions, or root causes, for why such warfare is being waged against a specific adversary (or adversaries). Such an approach would then seek to determine all the underlying components associated with the terrorist insurgency,[2] not just a select few that may be perceived as most likely. It is here that the underlying root causes would be itemized and categorized (e.g., poverty, political inequality, foreign subjugation, religious extremism, nihilism, etc.) and codified (e.g., 1st order root cause, 2nd order root cause, etc.).

Once the root cause analysis driving a terrorist insurgency is completed, then the component nodes and linkages in the TLC and TAC would need to be identified and prioritized for effective counteraction. It is here, for example, where the latest advances in social science conceptual approaches, such as social network theory, would be applied to model how terrorist groups organize themselves, plan attacks, conduct recruitment, develop operational capabilities, link up with counterparts, etc. In such a way, identifying strengths and vulnerabilities in a group's leadership, ideology, recruitment patterns, support infrastructure, organizational formation and modus operandi could be exploited in a counteraction campaign. Other components of the TLC and TAC also would need to be addressed, such as the individual, group, community, and societal conditions that influence certain groups to embark on 'martyr'-driven suicide terrorism, as opposed to other forms of warfare where operatives seek to stay alive and escape from the scene of the incident, and the types of measures that would be required to effectively counteract such warfare. Finally, such a research effort would conclude by formulating appropriate combating terrorism measures that address a prioritized listing of root causes and links and nodes in the TLC and TAC that would succeed in containing and defeating the terrorist insurgency, as well as metrics for assessing the effectiveness of such measures. The metrics for assessing combating terrorism effectiveness should always take into account the spectrum of measures, whether conciliatory or coercive (or a mix of the two) that would be required to resolve an insurgency, because some insurgent movements are amenable to the give and take of a peace process, whereas others may not.

## 2.2  Forecasting Terrorist Activities

In parallel to the TLC/TAC research effort, a second research focus is also required to develop the capability to understand how to forecast future terrorist warfare. Here, again, the social and behavioral sciences can be utilized to develop a user-friendly

---

[2] The term 'terrorist insurgency' is used due to the protracted nature of most terrorist outbreaks against their state adversaries.

software-based forecasting terrorism analytic system – which heretofore has never been developed for the non-governmental terrorism analytic community. Such a forecasting system should be capable of explaining and predicting the likelihood and rationale for current and 'generic' terrorist groups to conduct general warfare along the lines of CLI, CHI, CBRN – or a combination of the three, as well as 'conventionally'-driven political terrorism versus religiously-driven 'martyr' suicide terrorism. Such an expert system for classifying current terrorist groups in terms of their potential warfare propensity would support the educational and training needs of the terrorism/counterterrorism analytic communities, whether in government or in the private sector. It would help them better understand the processes and links driving terrorist groups to decide on a spectrum of possible warfare against their adversaries, which may be more important for educational and training purposes than predicting imminent attacks, including location and identification of likely targeting, because only intelligence agencies may possess the analytical and technical capability to make tactical predictions.

It is hoped that such research efforts would upgrade our capabilities to better understand and respond with the most effective.

# Author Index

# Lecture Notes in Computer Science

For information about Vols. 1–2982

please contact your bookseller or Springer-Verlag

Vol. 3092: J. Eckstein, H. Baumeister (Eds.), Extreme Programming and Agile Processes in Software Engineering. XVI, 358 pages. 2004.

Vol. 3091: V. van Oostrom (Ed.), Rewriting Techniques and Applications. X, 313 pages. 2004.

Vol. 3084: A. Persson, J. Stirna (Eds.), Advanced Information Systems Engineering. XIV, 596 pages. 2004.

Vol. 3083: W. Emmerich, A.L. Wolf (Eds.), Component Deployment. X, 249 pages. 2004.

Vol. 3076: D. Buell (Ed.), Algorithmic Number Theory. XI, 451 pages. 2004.

Vol. 3074: B. Kuijpers, P. Revesz (Eds.), Constraint Databases and Applications. XII, 181 pages. 2004.

Vol. 3073: H. Chen, R. Moore, D.D. Zeng, J. Leavitt (Eds.), Intelligence and Security Informatics. XV, 536 pages. 2004.

Vol. 3070: L. Rutkowski, J. Siekmann, R. Tadeusiewicz, L.A. Zadeh (Eds.), Artificial Intelligence and Soft Computing - ICAISC 2004. XXV, 1208 pages. 2004. (Subseries LNAI).

Vol. 3066: S. Tsumoto, R. Słowiński, J. Komorowski, J.W. Grzymala-Busse (Eds.), Rough Sets and Current Trends in Computing. XX, 853 pages. 2004. (Subseries LNAI).

Vol. 3065: A. Lomuscio, D. Nute (Eds.), Deontic Logic in Computer Science. X, 275 pages. 2004. (Subseries LNAI).

Vol. 3064: D. Bienstock, G. Nemhauser (Eds.), Integer Programming and Combinatorial Optimization. XI, 445 pages. 2004.

Vol. 3063: A. Llamosí, A. Strohmeier (Eds.), Reliable Software Technologies - Ada-Europe 2004. XIII, 333 pages. 2004.

Vol. 3062: J.L. Pfaltz, M. Nagl, B. Böhlen (Eds.), Applications of Graph Transformations with Industrial Relevance. XV, 500 pages. 2004.

Vol. 3060: A.Y. Tawfik, S.D. Goodwin (Eds.), Advances in Artificial Intelligence. XIII, 582 pages. 2004. (Subseries LNAI).

Vol. 3059: C.C. Ribeiro, S.L. Martins (Eds.), Experimental and Efficient Algorithms. X, 586 pages. 2004.

Vol. 3058: N. Sebe, M.S. Lew, T.S. Huang (Eds.), Computer Vision in Human-Computer Interaction. X, 233 pages. 2004.

Vol. 3056: H. Dai, R. Srikant, C. Zhang (Eds.), Advances in Knowledge Discovery and Data Mining. XIX, 713 pages. 2004. (Subseries LNAI).

Vol. 3054: I. Crnkovic, J.A. Stafford, H.W. Schmidt, K. Wallnau (Eds.), Component-Based Software Engineering. XI, 311 pages. 2004.

Vol. 3053: C. Bussler, J. Davies, D. Fensel, R. Studer (Eds.), The Semantic Web: Research and Applications. XIII, 490 pages. 2004.

Vol. 3052: W. Zimmermann, B. Thalheim (Eds.), Abstract State Machines 2004. Advances in Theory and Practice. XII, 235 pages. 2004.

Vol. 3051: R. Berghammer, B. Möller, G. Struth (Eds.), Relational and Kleene-Algebraic Methods in Computer Science. X, 279 pages. 2004.

Vol. 3050: J. Domingo-Ferrer, V. Torra (Eds.), Privacy in Statistical Databases. IX, 367 pages. 2004.

Vol. 3047: F. Oquendo, B. Warboys, R. Morrison (Eds.), Software Architecture. X, 279 pages. 2004.

Vol. 3046: A. Laganà, M.L. Gavrilova, V. Kumar, Y. Mun, C.K. Tan, O. Gervasi (Eds.), Computational Science and Its Applications - ICCSA 2004. LIII, 1016 pages. 2004.

Vol. 3045: A. Laganà, M.L. Gavrilova, V. Kumar, Y. Mun, C.K. Tan, O. Gervasi (Eds.), Computational Science and Its Applications – ICCSA 2004. LIII, 1040 pages. 2004.

Vol. 3044: A. Laganà, M.L. Gavrilova, V. Kumar, Y. Mun, C.K. Tan, O. Gervasi (Eds.), Computational Science and Its Applications – ICCSA 2004. LIII, 1140 pages. 2004.

Vol. 3043: A. Laganà, M.L. Gavrilova, V. Kumar, Y. Mun, C.J.K. Tan, O. Gervasi (Eds.), Computational Science and Its Applications – ICCSA 2004. LIII, 1180 pages. 2004.

Vol. 3042: N. Mitrou, K. Kontovasilis, G.N. Rouskas, I. Iliadis, L. Merakos (Eds.), NETWORKING 2004, Networking Technologies, Services, and Protocols; Performance of Computer and Communication Networks; Mobile and Wireless Communications. XXXIII, 1519 pages. 2004.

Vol. 3039: M. Bubak, G.D.v. Albada, P.M. Sloot, J.J. Dongarra (Eds.), Computational Science - ICCS 2004. LXVI, 1271 pages. 2004.

Vol. 3038: M. Bubak, G.D.v. Albada, P.M. Sloot, J.J. Dongarra (Eds.), Computational Science - ICCS 2004. LXVI, 1311 pages. 2004.

Vol. 3037: M. Bubak, G.D.v. Albada, P.M. Sloot, J.J. Dongarra (Eds.), Computational Science - ICCS 2004. LXVI, 745 pages. 2004.

Vol. 3036: M. Bubak, G.D.v. Albada, P.M. Sloot, J.J. Dongarra (Eds.), Computational Science - ICCS 2004. LXVI, 713 pages. 2004.

Vol. 3035: M.A. Wimmer (Ed.), Knowledge Management in Electronic Government. XII, 326 pages. 2004. (Subseries LNAI).

Vol. 3034: J. Favela, E. Menasalvas, E. Chávez (Eds.), Advances in Web Intelligence. XIII, 227 pages. 2004. (Subseries LNAI).

Vol. 3033: M. Li, X.-H. Sun, Q. Deng, J. Ni (Eds.), Grid and Cooperative Computing. XXXVIII, 1076 pages. 2004.

Vol. 3032: M. Li, X.-H. Sun, Q. Deng, J. Ni (Eds.), Grid and Cooperative Computing. XXXVII, 1112 pages. 2004.

Vol. 3031: A. Butz, A. Krüger, P. Olivier (Eds.), Smart Graphics. X, 165 pages. 2004.

Vol. 3030: P. Giorgini, B. Henderson-Sellers, M. Winikoff (Eds.), Agent-Oriented Information Systems. XIV, 207 pages. 2004. (Subseries LNAI).

Vol. 3029: B. Orchard, C. Yang, M. Ali (Eds.), Innovations in Applied Artificial Intelligence. XXI, 1272 pages. 2004. (Subseries LNAI).

Vol. 3028: D. Neuenschwander, Probabilistic and Statistical Methods in Cryptology. X, 158 pages. 2004.

Vol. 3027: C. Cachin, J. Camenisch (Eds.), Advances in Cryptology - EUROCRYPT 2004. XI, 628 pages. 2004.

Vol. 3026: C. Ramamoorthy, R. Lee, K.W. Lee (Eds.), Software Engineering Research and Applications. XV, 377 pages. 2004.

Vol. 3025: G.A. Vouros, T. Panayiotopoulos (Eds.), Methods and Applications of Artificial Intelligence. XV, 546 pages. 2004. (Subseries LNAI).

Vol. 3024: T. Pajdla, J. Matas (Eds.), Computer Vision - ECCV 2004. XXVIII, 621 pages. 2004.

Vol. 3023: T. Pajdla, J. Matas (Eds.), Computer Vision - ECCV 2004. XXVIII, 611 pages. 2004.

Vol. 3022: T. Pajdla, J. Matas (Eds.), Computer Vision - ECCV 2004. XXVIII, 621 pages. 2004.

Vol. 3021: T. Pajdla, J. Matas (Eds.), Computer Vision - ECCV 2004. XXVIII, 633 pages. 2004.

Vol. 3019: R. Wyrzykowski, J.J. Dongarra, M. Paprzycki, J. Wasniewski (Eds.), Parallel Processing and Applied Mathematics. XIX, 1174 pages. 2004.

Vol. 3016: C. Lengauer, D. Batory, C. Consel, M. Odersky (Eds.), Domain-Specific Program Generation. XII, 325 pages. 2004.

Vol. 3015: C. Barakat, I. Pratt (Eds.), Passive and Active Network Measurement. XI, 300 pages. 2004.

Vol. 3014: F. van der Linden (Ed.), Software Product-Family Engineering. IX, 486 pages. 2004.

Vol. 3012: K. Kurumatani, S.-H. Chen, A. Ohuchi (Eds.), Multi-Agnets for Mass User Support. X, 217 pages. 2004. (Subseries LNAI).

Vol. 3011: J.-C. Régin, M. Rueher (Eds.), Integration of AI and OR Techniques in Constraint Programming for Combinatorial Optimization Problems. XI, 415 pages. 2004.

Vol. 3010: K.R. Apt, F. Fages, F. Rossi, P. Szeredi, J. Váncza (Eds.), Recent Advances in Constraints. VIII, 285 pages. 2004. (Subseries LNAI).

Vol. 3009: F. Bomarius, H. Iida (Eds.), Product Focused Software Process Improvement. XIV, 584 pages. 2004.

Vol. 3008: S. Heuel, Uncertain Projective Geometry. XVII, 205 pages. 2004.

Vol. 3007: J.X. Yu, X. Lin, H. Lu, Y. Zhang (Eds.), Advanced Web Technologies and Applications. XXII, 936 pages. 2004.

Vol. 3006: M. Matsui, R. Zuccherato (Eds.), Selected Areas in Cryptography. XI, 361 pages. 2004.

Vol. 3005: G.R. Raidl, S. Cagnoni, J. Branke, D.W. Corne, R. Drechsler, Y. Jin, C.G. Johnson, P. Machado, E. Marchiori, F. Rothlauf, G.D. Smith, G. Squillero (Eds.), Applications of Evolutionary Computing. XVII, 562 pages. 2004.

Vol. 3004: J. Gottlieb, G.R. Raidl (Eds.), Evolutionary Computation in Combinatorial Optimization. X, 241 pages. 2004.

Vol. 3003: M. Keijzer, U.-M. O'Reilly, S.M. Lucas, E. Costa, T. Soule (Eds.), Genetic Programming. XI, 410 pages. 2004.

Vol. 3002: D.L. Hicks (Ed.), Metainformatics. X, 213 pages. 2004.

Vol. 3001: A. Ferscha, F. Mattern (Eds.), Pervasive Computing. XVII, 358 pages. 2004.

Vol. 2999: E.A. Boiten, J. Derrick, G. Smith (Eds.), Integrated Formal Methods. XI, 541 pages. 2004.

Vol. 2998: Y. Kameyama, P.J. Stuckey (Eds.), Functional and Logic Programming. X, 307 pages. 2004.

Vol. 2997: S. McDonald, J. Tait (Eds.), Advances in Information Retrieval. XIII, 427 pages. 2004.

Vol. 2996: V. Diekert, M. Habib (Eds.), STACS 2004. XVI, 658 pages. 2004.

Vol. 2995: C. Jensen, S. Poslad, T. Dimitrakos (Eds.), Trust Management. XIII, 377 pages. 2004.

Vol. 2994: E. Rahm (Ed.), Data Integration in the Life Sciences. X, 221 pages. 2004. (Subseries LNBI).

Vol. 2993: R. Alur, G.J. Pappas (Eds.), Hybrid Systems: Computation and Control. XII, 674 pages. 2004.

Vol. 2992: E. Bertino, S. Christodoulakis, D. Plexousakis, V. Christophides, M. Koubarakis, K. Böhm, E. Ferrari (Eds.), Advances in Database Technology - EDBT 2004. XVIII, 877 pages. 2004.

Vol. 2991: R. Alt, A. Frommer, R.B. Kearfott, W. Luther (Eds.), Numerical Software with Result Verification. X, 315 pages. 2004.

Vol. 2990: J. Leite, A. Omicini, L. Sterling, P. Torroni (Eds.), Declarative Agent Languages and Technologies. XII, 281 pages. 2004. (Subseries LNAI).

Vol. 2989: S. Graf, L. Mounier (Eds.), Model Checking Software. X, 309 pages. 2004.

Vol. 2988: K. Jensen, A. Podelski (Eds.), Tools and Algorithms for the Construction and Analysis of Systems. XIV, 608 pages. 2004.

Vol. 2987: I. Walukiewicz (Ed.), Foundations of Software Science and Computation Structures. XIII, 529 pages. 2004.

Vol. 2986: D. Schmidt (Ed.), Programming Languages and Systems. XII, 417 pages. 2004.

Vol. 2985: E. Duesterwald (Ed.), Compiler Construction. X, 313 pages. 2004.

Vol. 2984: M. Wermelinger, T. Margaria-Steffen (Eds.), Fundamental Approaches to Software Engineering. XII, 389 pages. 2004.

Vol. 2983: S. Istrail, M.S. Waterman, A. Clark (Eds.), Computational Methods for SNPs and Haplotype Inference. IX, 153 pages. 2004. (Subseries LNBI).